C000083941

History as Thought and Action

The Philosophies of Croce, Gentile, de Ruggiero, and Collingwood

Rik Peters

imprint-academic.com

Published in the UK by
Imprint Academic, PO Box 200, Exeter EX5 5YX, UK

Distributed in the USA by
Ingram Book Company,
One Ingram Blvd., La Vergne, TN 37086, USA

ISBN 978-1845402440

A CIP catalogue record for this book is available from the
British Library and US Library of Congress

To the Memory of

H.S. Harris (1926–2007)

and

W.H. Dray (1921–2009)

Contents

Preface

The reason for publishing *History as Thought and Action* is that the intellectual and practical legacy of Croce, Gentile, de Ruggiero, and Collingwood was made clear to me in my work after finishing my dissertation on these thinkers in 1998. After my doctorate, and as I began my University teaching, I started a consulting practice; which I called Q&A after de Ruggiero's and Collingwood's logic of question and answer. In my consulting practice, I provided training and mentoring for politicians, civil servants, and professional managers in profit and non-profit organisations. Immediately, I discovered that many of the policy and management issues could be elucidated with the help of methods used in the study of philosophy and history and I used my lectures on the philosophy of history at various universities in the Netherlands and my dissertation to define the problems. In this way I discovered the practical importance of historical thinking in society. After some years, Croce's *La storia come pensiero e come azione* (*History as Thought and Action*) was no longer a book title for me, but one of the principles upon which I trained people to become more effective in their organisations. Likewise, de Ruggiero's ethics of historicism became a guideline for organisation development and Collingwood's notion of absolute pre-suppositions acquired a very practical significance in the many Socratic dialogues I led. On the function of dialogues in organisations I wrote a book in 2003.[1] In the same year, I received an appointment at the University of Groningen which provided the ideal milieu for further working out my ideas on the relationship between history as thought and action in the Centre of Meta-history and in the Course Learning Histories and Organisations.

This book owes a debt of thanks to many individuals. I thank Teresa Smith for permitting me to cite Collingwood's manuscripts in my dissertation; all citations reappear in this book. I thank Clementina Gily Reda, a leading authority on Italian philosophy, who never stopped asking me to write this book. I present it to her as a tribute to the long and rich, but unduly neglected, tradition of Italian philosophy. I thank David Boucher for suggesting publishing this book with Imprint Academic, and for his encouragement to finish it. I thank William H. Rieckmann, who gave me many good ideas on Collingwood's development.

In Groningen, Frank Ankersmit reminded me time and again to work on this book, inspiring me with his thought provoking criticism. Toon de Baets support helped me to continue the work and Dirk Jan Wolffram's repeated advice to 'go for it' got me through the final stages. I thank Christian Garrard for revising the

---

1   Rik Peters and Peter van der Geer, *In plaats van praten. Debat en dialoog bij veranderprocessen,* Utrecht, Het Spectrum, 2004 (*Instead of Talking. Debate and Dialogue in Change Processes*).

English in the manuscript and Christiaan Caspers for his advice on the translation of the Greek words. Above all, I thank Jaap den Hollander who read the entire manuscript and gave me an important clue to understanding Collingwood's system.

Finally, I thank Anne, Pieter-Bart, Saskia, and Clara for their unmitigated support over the years. Thanks to them, I discovered that 'amare' is more important than 'intendere'.

A note on citations, translations, abbreviations, and footnotes

All citations are made between single inverted commas. If not otherwise stated, all translations from the Italian have been made by the author. For the special scope of this book the translations are as literal as possible, even if this sometimes leads to deviations from English usage.

All works are fully annotated on the first occurrence. If necessary, the year of completion by the author will also be mentioned in the text, so that differences may occur between the date of completion and the date of publication.

The works of Croce, Gentile, de Ruggiero, and Collingwood are listed in chronological order of first publication in the bibliography of primary sources. This list gives the complete annotation of the work including the edition cited by the author. All other works are listed in alphabetical order in the bibliography of secondary sources.

Since the majority of Croce's work has not yet been published in the *Edizione Nazionale* (*National Edition*) the complete annotation of the first publication will be given.

The majority of Gentile's has been published in the *Opere Complete* (*Complete Works*) and most of them will be cited abbreviated as *OC* if not otherwise stated.

All of de Ruggiero's have been fully annotated.

Collingwood's manuscripts will all be cited with the deposit number of the Bodleian Library Oxford abbreviated as Dep. folder number/number of manuscript, page.

Introduction:
The Dead Past?

This book is an historical reconstruction of the relationship between three Italian philosophers, historians, and political leaders Benedetto Croce (1866–1952), Giovanni Gentile (1875–1944), Guido de Ruggiero (1888–1948), and British philosopher, archaeologist, and historian Robin George Collingwood (1889–1943). These four philosophers were far too independent and original to form a movement or a school of thought, but they shared the belief that the past is not dead, but living, which implies that knowledge of the past is a necessary condition for rational action in the present. It was this idea of history as thought and action that brought the four philosophers together, it was this idea that lay at the basis of their philosophies which won them international reputation, and eventually it was this idea that drove them apart.

In 1896, Giovanni Gentile, then student at the *Scuola Normale Superiore* in Pisa, wrote a postcard to Benedetto Croce, a private scholar in Naples. It was the beginning of a friendship that would last until 1924. In 1903, the two friends founded *La Critica*, the journal by which they shouldered a cultural revolution in their country which was soon to be noticed abroad. A year before, Croce had published his *Estetica come scienza dell'espressione e linguistica generale* (*Aesthetic as Science of Expression and General Linguistic*) which established his name as a philosopher. In 1909, he published *Logica come scienza del concetto puro* (*Logic as Science of the Pure Concept*) and *Filosofia della pratica* (*Philosophy of the Practical*), and in 1917 he published *Teoria e storia della storiografia* (*Theory and History of Historiography*). These four works formed Croce's *Filosofia dello spirito* (*Philosophy of the Spirit*), which made him famous both in Italy and abroad.[1]

In the first decade of the century, Gentile was involved in a campaign for educational reform and, in 1907, he was appointed as Professor of Philosophy at the University of Palermo. Four years later, he founded his own philosophy of 'actual idealism', or 'actualism', with 'L'atto del pensare come atto puro' ('The Act of Thought as Pure Act').[2] This article formed the basis of Gentile's philo-

---

1   B. Croce, *Estetica come scienza dell'espressione e linguistica generale*, Sandron, Milan, 1902, cited as *Estetica* from the 9th edn. Laterza, Bari, 1950; Id., *Logica come scienza del concetto puro*, Laterza, Bari, 1909, cited as *Logica* from the 5th edn. 1928; Id., *Filosofia della pratica, Economica ed Etica*, Laterza, Bari, 1909, cited as *Pratica* from the 6th edn. 1950; Id., *Teoria e storia della storiografia*, Laterza, 1917, cited from the 6th edn. 1948.

2   G. Gentile, 'L'atto del pensare come atto puro', in *Annuario della Biblioteca filosofica di Palermo*, I, 1912, cited from *La riforma della dialettica hegeliana*, Sansoni, Florence, 1975, 183–95.

sophical system, which became known as actual idealism, or actualism. This philosophy comprises a philosophy of mind, expounded in *Sommario di pedagogia* (*Summary of Pedagogy*) published in 1912, a moral and political philosophy in *I fondamenti della filosofia del diritto* (*The Foundations of the Philosophy of Right*) published in 1916, a metaphysics in *Teoria generale dello spirito come atto puro* (*General Theory of the Mind as Pure Act*) published in 1916, and a complete logic in *Sistema di logica* (*System of Logic*) which was published between 1918 and 1922.[3] For two decades these books, which form the core of Gentile's philosophy, were popular and influential amongst many young intellectuals who joined Gentile in his efforts to modernise Italy.

One of these intellectuals was Guido de Ruggiero, who had studied law and economics in Naples, but whose true passion was philosophy. As a friend of Croce and Gentile, with whom he studied in Palermo, he became a contributor to *La Critica* in 1911. A year later, at the age of twenty-four, he published *La filosofia contemporanea* (*Modern Philosophy*), the book which established his name as one of the most promising philosophers of the new generation.[4] At the same time de Ruggiero began his career as a journalist for several newspapers.

In England, the development of Croce, Gentile, and de Ruggiero was closely followed by a small but active group of philosophers led by the Waynflete Professor of Metaphysics at Oxford, J.A. Smith (1863–1939). His most gifted student was R.G. Collingwood, who was already an earnest student of Italian culture before he came to Oxford in 1908. His first publication after his graduation in 1912 was the translation of Croce's *La filosofia di Giambattista Vico* (*The Philosophy of Giambattista Vico*).[5] This book, published in 1913, was not only the beginning of a career as a translator and an authority on Italian thought; but also of his own

3   G. Gentile, *Sommario di pedagogia come scienza filosofica, I: Pedagogia generale*, Laterza, Bari, 1913, cited from *Sommario di pedagogia come scienza filosofica, I: Pedagogia generale*, OC I, Sansoni, Florence, 1970; Id., *Sommario di pedagogia come scienza filosofica, II: Didattica*, 1914, Laterza, Bari, 1914, cited from *Sommario di pedagogia come scienza filosofica, II: Didattica*, OC II, Sansoni, Florence, 1970; Id., 'I fondamenti della filosofia del diritto', in *Annali delle università toscane*, nuova serie 1916, I.5, cited from *I fondamenti della filosofia del diritto*, OC IV, Le Lettere, Florence, 1987; Id., *Teoria generale dello spirito come atto puro*, Mariotti, Pisa, 1916, cited from *Teoria generale dello spirito come atto puro*, OC III, Le Lettere, Florence, 1987; Id., *Sistema di Logica come teoria del conoscere*, Vol I, Spoerri, Pisa, 1917, cited as *Sistema di Logica, I* from *Sistema di Logica come teoria del conoscere*, OC V, Sansoni, Florence, 1964; Id., *Sistema di Logica come teoria del conoscere*, Vol II, Laterza, Bari, 1922, cited as *Sistema di Logica, II* from *Sistema di Logica come teoria del conoscere*, Vol II, OC VI, Le Lettere, Florence, 1987.
4   G. de Ruggiero, *La filosofia contemporanea*, Laterza, Bari, 1912, cited from 6th edn. Laterza, Bari, 1951. Translated by A.H. Hannay and R.G. Collingwood as *Modern Philosophy*, George Allen & Unwin, London, 1921.
5   B. Croce, *La filosofia di Giambattista Vico*, Laterza, Bari, 1911, cited from quarta edizione economica, Laterza, Bari, 1980; E.T. R.G. Collingwood: B. Croce, *The Philosophy of Giambattista Vico*, Macmillan, New York, 1913.

philosophical development which would establish his name as one of the most important British philosophers of the twentieth century.

The idea of history as thought and action not only brought the four philosophers together, but also caused a rift between them. During the First World War, Croce and Gentile began to differ about the course Italy was to take, and after it, the rise of Fascism estranged the former friends from each other. In 1921, Croce was asked to become Minister of Education by Prime Minister Giolitti (1842–1928), and a year later, after the March on Rome, Gentile was asked for the same post by Benito Mussolini (1883–1945). From that moment the roads of the two friends parted. Gentile, who was made a member of the Fascist Party in 1923, developed himself into the leading intellectual of Fascism, whereas Croce became an important spokesman of the liberal opposition. Because of his fame in Italy and abroad, the regime kept Croce under permanent surveillance during the 1920s and 1930s without being able to prevent him from expressing his criticisms. In 1938, he published one of his most important books, *La storia come pensiero e come azione* (*History as Thought and Action*), which comprises a severe criticism of totalitarian thought.

Another prominent critic of Fascism was Guido de Ruggiero. Early in the 1920s he was so worried about the crisis of liberalism in Italy that he travelled to England in order to study parliamentary democracy. On that trip he met Collingwood and this was the beginning of a lifelong friendship. In 1924, he published *Storia del liberalismo europeo* (*History of European Liberalism*) in which he fiercely attacked Fascism.[6] This book was translated by Collingwood in 1927, and was immediately acknowledged as an important contribution to political philosophy.[7] In his own country, de Ruggiero was silenced by Fascist repression; he had to give up his journalistic activities and live a relatively anonymous life as a Professor at the University of Rome. However, towards the end of the 1930s he became increasingly active in the resistance movement and, in 1943, when he published the second edition of *Storia del liberalismo europeo*, he was sent to prison.

By that time, the Allies had already occupied Sicily and, on 25 July 1943, Mussolini was arrested and subsequently liberated by the Nazis. With the Nazis' help Mussolini created the Italian Social Republic in the North of Italy, which was his last, weak effort to maintain power. All the time Gentile remained loyal to Mussolini. In a famous speech held on Capitoline Hill in Rome on 24 June 1943, he called upon the Italians to reunite in order to save their country.[8] Gentile paid for his actions; on 25 April 1944, he was shot by partisans. Meanwhile, Croce and de Ruggiero were regrouping liberal forces and began to

---

6   G. de Ruggiero, *Storia del liberalismo europeo*, Laterza, Bari, 1925.

7   G. de Ruggiero, *The History of European Liberalism*, Clarendon Press, Oxford, 1927.

8   Benedetto Gentile, *Giovanni Gentile, Dal discorso agli italiani alla morte, 24 giugnio-15 aprile 1944*, Sansoni, Firenze, 1954.

organise the new political structures of Italy, continuing with this effort after the war.

Far away, Collingwood followed the developments in Italy. Croce and de Ruggiero kept him *au courant* by sending him the latest philosophical publications and by writing letters on the actual situation in Italy. Meanwhile, Collingwood continued to elaborate his own philosophy. In reaction to the atrocities of the First World War, he decided to establish a 'New Science of Human Affairs' after his return to Oxford in 1918. In 1924, he published *Speculum Mentis,* which comprises a complete philosophy of the mind.[9] In 1933, Collingwood published *An Essay on Philosophical Method,* which was to become the basis of his a series of philosophical books which he began to write in 1937.[10] Collingwood's system would have consisted of *The Principles of Art, The Principles of History,* a work on moral and political philosophy, a book on folklore, and most probably also a book on cosmology.[11] Unfortunately, while working on the proofs of *The Principles of Art,* Collingwood suffered a severe stroke and was unable to work for several months. Knowing that he had not much longer to live, he unfolded the outlines of his project in *An Autobiography,* which was published in 1939.[12] After this, he began to write *The Principles of History,* which he never finished, and *An Essay on Metaphysics,* which was published in 1940.[13] When the Second World War broke out, Collingwood decided to write *The New Leviathan.*[14] It was his last book: on 13 January 1943, Collingwood died of the complications of his illness. After the war, some of his works were published. Among them were *The Idea of Nature,* which became influential in its field, and *The Idea of History,* which is arguably the most important book on the philosophy of history of the twentieth century.[15]

After the war Croce and de Ruggiero were active in rebuilding Italy, Croce as a Senator, and de Ruggiero as Rector of the University of Rome from 1943 to 1944, and as a member of the Partito d'Azione (Action Party) and as Minister of Public Education. On 29 December 1948, he died at age sixty of a heart attack. Croce remained active as a philosopher to his very last days, publishing a book on the philosophy of Hegel at age 86. On 25 November 1952 he died; his funeral was a national event.

---

[9]   R.G. Collingwood, *Speculum Mentis,* Clarendon Press, Oxford, 1924.
[10] R.G. Collingwood, *An Essay on Philosophical Method,* Clarendon Press, Oxford, 1933.
[11] R.G. Collingwood, *The Principles of Art,* Clarendon Press, Oxford, 1938; Id., *The Principles of History,* Oxford University Press, Oxford, 1999.
[12] R.G. Collingwood, *An Autobiography,* Clarendon Press, Oxford, 1939.
[13] R.G. Collingwood, *An Essay on Metaphysics,* Clarendon Press, Oxford, 1940.
[14] R.G. Collingwood, *The New Leviathan,* Clarendon Press, Oxford, 1942, cited from *The New Leviathan, Revised Edition Edited and Introduced by David Boucher,* Clarendon Press, Oxford, 1992.
[15] R.G. Collingwood, *The Idea of Nature,* Clarendon Press, Oxford, 1945; Id., *The Idea of History,* Clarendon Press, Oxford, 1946.

The Italian Connection

Owing to his work as a translator, and his reputation as an authority on Italian philosophy, Collingwood's name has always been connected to Croce's, Gentile's, and de Ruggiero's. A reviewer of Collingwood's *Speculum Mentis* remarked that the work suffered from the same deficiencies as the 'airy imaginings' of Croce.[16] And of *An Essay on Philosophical Method* it was said that it owed a lot to the 'Crocification of Hegel'.[17] Other reviewers, however, and notably Croce himself, related Collingwood's first publications to Gentile, whereas de Ruggiero saw close connections between Collingwood's philosophy and his own.[18]

Collingwood himself never failed to acknowledge the importance of the Italians. He translated their works, wrote some important papers about them, and discussed their thought in his lectures. Moreover, from 1912, Collingwood corresponded with Croce and de Ruggiero on philosophical topics, met them in person on several occasions, and at the end of his life he was involved in a doctorate *honoris causa* for de Ruggiero. Against this background of intensive contact over the years, it is most surprising that Collingwood remained almost silent on the role of the Italians in his philosophical development. In his autobiography, he does not mention Croce at all, de Ruggiero only once, and Gentile only indirectly to criticise his adherence to Fascism.

After the Second World War, Malcolm Knox (1900–1980), Collingwood's former pupil and literary executor, continued the ambiguity about Collingwood's relationship with the Italians. In his 1946 'Editor's Preface' to *The Idea of History*, Knox claimed that 'although Collingwood learnt much from Croce about aesthetics and something about history, it would be a mistake to regard him as essentially a follower of his'.[19] In this context, Knox emphasised that Collingwood reached his ideas on history independently from Croce and he mentions that the former used to say 'that Vico had influenced him more than anyone else'.[20] According to Knox, Collingwood worked out a philosophy of his own, which 'differed considerably from parts at least of Croce's philosophy of the spirit'. In Knox's view, this philosophy still formed the basis of *An Essay on Philosophical Method*. Later in his career, Knox says, Collingwood 'came to adopt a historicism not unlike Croce's' in which 'philosophy as a separate discipline is

---

16 C.D.B. Burns, 'Review of R.G. Collingwood, *Speculum Mentis*', in *International Journal of Ethics*, 35, 1925, 323.

17 L.J.Russell, Review of 'Collingwood, *An Essay on Philosphical Method*', in *Philosophy*, IX, 1934, 350.

18 B. Croce, Review of 'R.G. Collingwood, *Speculum Mentis* or the Map of Knowledge', in *La Critica*, XXIII, 1925, 58; G. de Ruggiero, *Filosofi del novecento*, Laterza, Bari, 1933, 91–102.

19 T.M. Knox, 'Editor's Preface', in R.G. Collingwood, *The Idea of History*, Clarendon Press, Oxford, 1946, viii.

20 Ibid.

liquidated by being converted into history'.[21] By this interpretation, Knox canonised the idea that Collingwood´s 'Italian connection' had induced him to historicism. For Knox, as for so many other interpreters, this conversion exemplified the saying "un inglese italianato è un diavolo incarnato" (an Italianised Englishman, is a devil incarnate).

Knox's preface gave rise to the much debated 'radical conversion thesis', according to which Collingwood changed to historicism after 1935. In this debate, both Knox's interpretation of Croce's philosophy as a form of historicism, and his claims concerning Croce's influence on Collingwood, have been taken for granted by both defenders and opponents of the radical conversion thesis. Alan Donagan, one of the first promoters of the radical conversion thesis, mentions Croce's influence on Collingwood, but he never seems to have studied the works of the Italian for himself.[22] Likewise, Nathan Rotenstreich stressed the influence of Croce on Collingwood's 'tendency to identify philosophy and history' without further exploring Croce's philosophy.[23] In the same vein, opponents of the radical conversion thesis, such as L.O. Mink, L. Rubinoff, W.H. Dray, and W.J. van der Dussen, did not explicitly differ from Knox's interpretation of Croce's philosophy, though they deny that it had significant influence on Collingwood's later development. However, these interpreters have not been able to definitely disprove Knox's radical conversion thesis due to their limited reading of Croce's works.[24]

Against this background, it is interesting to note that the few scholars who were acquainted with Italian philosophy always mitigated Knox's views. Already before Donagan's book, H.S. Harris had stressed the importance of Gentile's influence on Collingwood. This influence, which was already present in Collingwood's first book *Religion and Philosophy* of 1916, increased in the succeeding years, and was, according to Harris, 'unmistakeably dominant' in his second book *Speculum Mentis*.[25] Harris's views have never won broad support, only Rubinoff elaborated them in his study of Collingwood's reform of meta-

---

[21] Ibid., viii, x.

[22] Alan Donagan, *The Later Philosophy of R.G. Collingwood*, Clarendon Press, Oxford, 1962, 12.

[23] Nathan Rotenstreich, *Philosophy, History and Politics: Studies in Contemporary English Philosophy of History*, Martinus Nijhof, The Hague, 1976, 23.

[24] Louis O. Mink, *Mind, History, and Dialectic, The Philosophy of R.G. Collingwood*, Wesleyan University Press, Middletown, 1969, 16; Lionel Rubinoff, *Collingwood and the Reform of Metaphysics, A Study in the Philosophy of Mind*, University of Toronto Press, Toronto, 1970, v–vi; W.H. Dray and W.J. van der Dussen, 'Editor's Introduction' in R.G. Collingwood, *The Principles of History*, xv–xvi, xxii–xxiv.

[25] H.S. Harris, 'Introduction' in Giovanni Gentile, *Genesis and Structure of Society*, University of Illinois Press, Illinois, 1960, 16–18; Id., 'Croce and Gentile in Collingwood's *New Leviathan*', in David Boucher (ed.), *Philosophy, History and Civilization, Interdisciplinary Perspectives on R.G. Collingwood*, University of Wales Press, Cardiff, 1995, 115–130.

physics in 1970, but most other interpreters flatly deny Gentile's influence.[26] In his 1967 book on Collingwood's early development, William M. Johnston, for example, claims that 'if Collingwood was greatly influenced by Gentile, this influence may have been more fleeting than that of Vico or Croce', because he 'seldom mentions the Sicilian in any of his writings'.[27] Harris's view was also criticised by David Boucher in his 1989 *The Social and Political Philosophy of R.G. Collingwood*, in which he argues that 'Harris, in his enthusiasm to demonstrate Gentile's significance, posits too strong a link between the Italian and Collingwood'.[28] M.E. Brown, in his book on neo-idealistic aesthetics, mentions Gentile's influence on Collingwood in order to denounce it: 'Collingwood's Principles of Art is so overwhelmingly Gentilian that its Crocean elements must be mere fragments of some past wreckage in Collingwood's mind not yet swept away'.[29] Collingwood's relation to de Ruggiero, the only person whom he mentions in his autobiography as his 'friend', has been the subject of only one paper in English, which does not take the Italian works into account.[30] Finally, some interpreters have tried to retrace Collingwood's 'Italian Connection' to Vico, but these views have not yet met with broad response.[31]

Given this long, and undecided, discussion of Collingwood's relationship with Italian philosophy, it is only to be regretted that David Roberts, the foremost expert on Croce and Gentile writing in English, has never dealt with this subject.[32] Even more regrettable is the fact that Collingwood's first biographer

---

[26] Rubinoff, *Collingwood and the Reform of Metaphysics*, 311ff.

[27] William M. Johnston, *The Formative Years of R.G. Collingwood*, Nijhoff, The Hague, 1967, 85.

[28] David Boucher, *The Social and Political Philosophy of R.G. Collingwood*, Cambridge University Press, Cambridge, 1989, 17.

[29] Merle E. Brown, *Neo-Idealistic Aesthetics, Croce, Gentile, Collingwood*, Wayne State University Press, Detroit, 1966, 219.

[30] James Connelly, 'Art Thou the Man: Croce, Gentile or de Ruggiero?', in Boucher (ed.), *Philosophy, History and Civilization*, 92–114; Alessandra Greppi Olivetti, *Due saggi su R.G. Collingwood, con un'appendice di lettere di Collingwood a G. de Ruggiero*, Livania editrice, Padova, 1977. In spite of the title of this work the author does not deal directly with the relation between the two thinkers.

[31] Joseph M. Levine, 'Collingwood, Vico, and The Autobiography', in *Clio*, 9, 1980, 379–92; Leon Pompa, 'Collingwood's Theory of Historical Knowledge', in Boucher (ed.), *Philosophy, History and Civilization*, 168–81; Bruce A. Haddock, 'Vico, Collingwood and the Character of a Historical Philosophy', in Boucher (ed.), *Philosophy, History and Civilization*, 130–52; Nancy Struever, 'Rhetoric: Time, Memory, Memoir', in Walter Jost (ed.), *A Companion to Rhetoric and Rhetorical Criticism*, Blackwell Publishing, Oxford, 2004, 425–42.

[32] David D. Roberts, *Benedetto Croce and the Uses of Historicism*, University of California Press, Berkeley, 1987; id., *Nothing but History, Reconstruction and Extremity after Metaphysics*, University of California Press, Berkeley, 1995, id., *Historicism and Fascism in Modern Italy*, University of Toronto Press, Toronto, 2007. Myra Moss does not discuss Collingwood's thought in *Benedetto Croce Reconsidered, Truth and Error in Theories of Art, Literature, and History*, University Press of New England, Hanover and London,

mentions Croce, Gentile, and de Ruggiero as 'the most direct influences' on Collingwood after 1919, without giving substantial evidence for this claim.[33]

In Italy, the situation has not been much different. In his 1946 'In commemorazione di un amico inglese, compagno di pensiero e di fede: R.G. Collingwood' ('In remembrance of an English friend, companion in thought and faith'), Croce presents Collingwood as an actualist sinner who converted to the right Crocean faith just before his premature death.[34] Croce supports this view with a few quotes from letters which Collingwood wrote to him in 1938, but not on a thorough analysis of his works. Nonetheless, like Knox's 'Preface' in English speaking countries, Croce's 'commemorazione' set the tone for the reception of Collingwood in Italy. Croce's picture of Collingwood as a 'companion in thought and faith' had the effect of promoting a general neglect of his thought in Italy. The renowned interpreter of Italian historicism Pietro Rossi, for example, claims without further argument that *The Idea of History* is completely based on Croce's views.[35] In the same vein, Antimo Negri, one of Italy's leading interpreters of Gentile, holds that Collingwood's philosophy of history is only a weak version of Croce's theory of history, and therefore inferior to Gentile's.[36] For decades, interpretations like these have not inspired Italian historians and philosophers to study Collingwood.

The few Italian scholars who were acquainted with Collingwood's thought have flatly rejected the official view. According to the historian Arnaldo Momigliano, Collingwood had already ceased to be a disciple of Croce long before his premature death.[37] Gennaro Sasso, the leading interpreter of Italian Idealism went further: 'I do not know a period in which he was an authentic "disciple of Croce".'[38] Luciano Dondoli, translator of Collingwood's *The New*

1987, though she wrote a short article on Collingwood in Ian P. McGreal, *Great Thinkers of the Western World*, Harper Collins, New York, 1992, 507–10. For a critical account of Robert's interpretations of Italian historicism see Rik Peters 'Italian Legacies' in *History and Theory*, 49, 2010, 115–29.

[33] Fred Inglis, *History Man: The Life of R.G. Collingwood*, Princeton University Press, Princeton, 2009, 117. This otherwise interesting book is not always reliable. Concerning the Italians: Croce was not born in 1865 (p. 120), Gentile was definitely not Croce's 'acolyte' (p. 118), and there is no evidence for portraying de Ruggiero as a 'cordial, colourful, voluble Italian', nor as a 'social democrat' (p. 122).

[34] B. Croce, 'In commemorazione di un amico inglese, compagno di pensiero e di fede, R.G. Collingwood', in *Quaderni della Critica*, 4, 1946, cited from *Nuove pagine sparse I*, Laterza, Bari, 1948, 28–29.

[35] Pietro Rossi, *Storia e storicismo nella filosofia contemporanea*, Lerici editori, 1960, cited from *Nuova edizione*, Mondadori, Milan, 1991, 383.

[36] Antimo Negri, 'Il concetto attualistico della storia e lo storicismo', in *Giovanni Gentile, La Vita e il Pensiero, X*, Sansoni, Firenze, 1962, 127–36; Id., *L'Inquietudine del divenire, Giovanni Gentile*, Le Lettere, Firenze, 1992, 9–10.

[37] Cited by Gennaro Sasso, *Benedetto Croce, La ricerca della dialettica*, Morano, Napoli, 1975, 1058.

[38] Ibid.

Leviathan, related much of Collingwood's aesthetics in relation to Croce's, but also indicated some similarities between Collingwood's logic and Gentile's.[39]

By far the most interesting work on the relationship between the Italians and Collingwood has been done by a group of scholars around Clementina Gily Reda, the first scholar who wrote an intellectual biography of Guido de Ruggiero.[40] In several articles she has argued that Collingwood was influenced by de Ruggiero's idea of the development of science as dialectic of question and answer and by his aesthetics.[41] In 2006, she organised a conference on these subjects, publishing a volume on Collingwood's relationship with Italian philosophy.[42] In this volume, Massimo Iiritano discusses de Ruggiero's influence on Collingwood's theory of 'picture thinking' on which he also published an interesting book.[43]

In spite of all these important contributions, Sasso's claim that 'the peculiar feature of Collingwood's philosophy has never been studied in Italy as it should be appropriate and the limits of his "Croceanism" have not been seriously put in light' still needs to be answered since most recent books on Italian idealism still do not mention Collingwood's name, let alone discuss his thought.[44]

Against this background, both in English speaking countries and in Italy, the remark in the *Stanford Encyclopedia of Philosophy*, that 'the relationship of Collingwood's philosophy to Italian idealism has been relatively under-explored', can only be seen as an understatement.[45] Apart from a few studies, the relationship between the Italians and Collingwood is far from clear. As a result, it is still customary to mention Collingwood's name and those of the Italians in a single breath, suggesting a deeper relationship which needs no further exploration.[46] In aesthetics, this has led to the canonisation of the 'Croce-Collingwood

---

[39] Luciano Dondoli, *Genesì e svillupi della teoria linguistica di Benedetto Croce, I*, Bulzoni, Roma, 1988, 228.

[40] Clementina Gily Reda, *Guido de Ruggiero. Un ritratto filosofico*, Società Editrice Napoletana, Napoli, 1981.

[41] Clementina Gily Reda, 'De Ruggiero e Collingwood', in *Criterio*, IX, 1991, 75–83; id., 'Considerations on Collingwood and Italian Thought', in *Collingwood Studies*, II, 1995, 213–32; id., 'Specular Phenomenology: Art and Art Criticism', in *Collingwood and British Idealism Studies. Incorporating Bradley Studies*, 17.2, 2011, 247–61.

[42] Clementina Gily Reda (ed.), *Robin George Collingwood e la formazione estetica. Atti del Covegno di Napoli, Giugno 2006*, Graus editore, Napoli, 2007.

[43] Massimo Iiritano, 'Picture Thinking' in *Robin George Collingwood e la formazione estetica*, 11–141; id., *Picture Thinking. Estetica e filosofia della Religione nei primi scritti di Robin Collingwood*, Rubbetino, Soveria Mannelli, 2006.

[44] Sasso, *Benedetto Croce*, 1058.

[45] James Connelly and Giussepina d'Oro, 'Robin George Collingwood', in *Stanford Encyclopedia of Philosophy*, http://plato.stanford.edu/entries/collingwood/

[46] Many modern dictionaries mention Croce and Collingwood together, see, among others, sub 'Collingwood'; Edwards, P. (ed.) *Encyclopedia of Philosophy*, Macmillan, New York, 1967; *Enciclopedia Garzanti di Filosofia*, 1981; Audi, R. (ed.), *Cambridge Dictionary of Philosophy*, Cambridge University Press, Cambridge, 1995. *The Concise*

Theory of Art'.[47] In the philosophy of history, the alleged connection between Croce and Collingwood has also played an important role in various schools of thought. W.H. Walsh, in his influential *Philosophy of History* of 1951, mentions Croce and 'his follower' Collingwood as giving the 'standard idealist account of historical knowledge'.[48] A.C. Danto, in his seminal *Analytical Philosophy of History*, develops his theory of history partly against the idealist view of history whose 'main representatives' are Dilthey (1833–1911), Croce, and Collingwood.[49] R.F. Atkinson, another representative of the analytical school, holds that there 'are to be found many apparent echoes of Croce, to whom he [Collingwood] is manifestly deeply indebted!'[50] This view is, however, most awkwardly based on a comparison between Collingwood's *The Idea of History*, which was largely written in 1936, and Croce's *La storia come pensiero e come azione*, which was published in 1938.

Among constructivist philosophers of history, J.W. Meiland bases his theory of history on both Croce's and Collingwood's views, though he also mentions some differences between them.[51] In the same vein, L. Goldstein elaborates Collingwood's alleged constructivism in a full-blown constructivist theory of history without mentioning Croce, let alone Gentile, though the latter came much closer to a constructivist position.[52] W.B. Gallie presents his own theory of history in *Philosophy and the Historical Understanding* as an attempt 'to breathe new life into a way of philosophising' of which Rickert, Croce, and Collingwood were 'the main spokesmen'.[53]

In his seminal *Wahrheit und Methode* (*Truth and Method*), H.G. Gadamer lauds Collingwood as the only philosopher after Plato who truly understood hermeneutics. In this context he mentions that Collingwood was 'strongly influenced by

---

Routledge Encyclopedia of Philosophy, Routledge, London, 2000, however, only mentions Wittgenstein in connection to Collingwood.

[47] John Hospers, 'The Croce-Collingwood Theory of Art', in *Philosophy*, 31, 1956, 291–308; Alan Donagan, 'The Croce-Collingwood Theory of Art', in *Philosophy*, 33, 1958, 162–7; Angelo De Gennaro, 'Croce and Collingwood', in *The Personalist*, 46, 1965, 193–202; Anne Sheppard, *Aesthetics, An Introduction to the Philosophy of Art*, Oxford University Press, Oxford, 1987, 22–8; Antoon Van den Braembussche, *Denken over Kunst, Een Kennismaking met de Kunstfilosofie*, Coutinho, Bussum, 1994, 66–72.

[48] W.H. Walsh, *Philosophy of History: An Introduction*, Harper & Row, New York, 1967, 43.

[49] Arthur C. Danto, *Analytical Philosophy of History*, Cambridge University Press, Cambridge, 1965, 205. Now in *Narration and Knowledge*, Columbia University Press, New York, 1985, 205.

[50] R.F. Atkinson, *Knowledge and Explanation in History, An Introduction to the Philosophy of History*, Cornell University Press, Ithaca, New York, 1978, 25.

[51] Jack W. Meiland, *Scepticism and Historical Knowledge*, Random House, New York, 1965, 81–2.

[52] Leon J. Goldstein, *Historical Knowing*, University of Texas Press, Austin and London, 1976.

[53] W.B. Gallie, *Philosophy and the Historical Understanding*, Shocken Books, New York, 1968 (1st edn. 1964), 1.

Croce', but, strangely enough for a hermeneutician, he never explores their rela-tionship in depth.[54] This omission is continued in most of the hermeneutic litera-ture, which tends to overlook the role of the Italians in this tradition. P. Ricoeur, for example, extensively discusses Collingwood's thought in *Temps et récit* (*Time and Narrative*) but mentions Croce only twice.[55]

H. White, the dean of the narrativist school in the philosophy of history, has been an assiduous student of Croce, to whom he dedicates the last chapter of his influential *Metahistory*.[56] In none of his publications, however, has White dis-cussed the relationship between Croce and Collingwood in depth. This is sur-prising, because the subtitle of *Metahistory* contains the keywords of Collingwood's 1935 inaugural: 'The Historical Imagination.' White's relationship to Gentile became the subject of a fierce polemic which broke out when he referred to the notion of the sublime in Gentile's thought, and Mussolini's 'intuitions', as a 'perspective on history' he had 'implicitly been praising'.[57] This reference to Gentile is most remarkable, since at the beginning of his career White had related Collingwood's philosophy of history to Gentile's Fascism.[58] Finally, another leading narrativist, F.R. Ankersmit, has dedicated some articles to Collingwood, whom he primarily regards as a hermeneutician, and one to Croce, but without discussing the relationship between the two thinkers.[59]

---

[54] Hans Georg Gadamer, *Wahreit und Methode, Grundzüge einer philosophischen Hermeneutik,* Gesammelte Werke, Band 1, J.C.B.Mohr, Tübingen, 1990, 375–84; English Translation, *Truth and Method,* Sheed and Ward, London, 1979, 333–41.

[55] Paul Ricoeur, *Temps et Récit,* I, Éditions du Seuil, Paris, 1983, 209, 229.

[56] Hayden White, *Metahistory, The Historical Imagination in Nineteenth-Century Europe,* John Hopkins, Baltimore, London, 1973, 375–425.

[57] Hayden White, 'The Politics of Historical Interpretation, Discipline and De-Subli-mation', in *Critical Inquiry,* 9, 1982, cited from id., *The Content of the Form. Narrative Dis-course and Historical Representation,* The John Hopkins University Press, Baltimore and London, 74–5. David Roberts critically analyses the polemic in *Historicism and Fascism in Modern Italy,* 237–65. See also: Rik Peters, 'Nolite iudicare. Hayden White between Benedetto Croce and Giovanni Gentile,' in *Storia della storiografia,* 58, 2010, 19–35; Herman Paul, *White,* Polity Press, Cambridge, 2011, 119–24.

[58] Hayden White, 'Collingwood and Toynbee. Transitions in English Historical Thought', in *English Miscellany,* 8, 1957, 168. Since White published this article unchanged in *The Fiction of Narrative: Essays on History, Literature, and Theory, 1957–2007,* John Hopkins University Press, Baltimore, 2007, it seems he has not changed his mind on the issue of Collingwood's relationship with Gentile.

[59] F. R. Ankersmit, 'The Dilemma of Contemporary Anglo-Saxon Philosophy of History', in *History and Theory,* Beiheft 25, 1986, 1–27; id., 'Croce als spiegel van onze tijd', in *Theoretische Geschiedenis,* 16, 1989, 319–31. In general, Ankersmit has not been very pos-itive about R.G. Collingwood's philosophy of history. See f.e. his 'Danto's Philosophy in Retrospective' in Arthur C. Danto, *Narration and Knowledge,* 364–95, he says that with Collingwood we 'lose our openness to the past', and mentions the 'shallowness' and its 'absence of historical sensitivity' (p. 393). For a reaction, see Chinatsu Kobayashi and Mathieu Marion, 'Gadamer and Collingwood on Temporal Distance and Understanding', in *History and Theory,* 50.4, 2011, 81–104.

Owing to the long history of partial and incomplete interpretations of the philosophical relationship between the Italian idealists and Collingwood, contemporary philosophers, and in particular philosophers of history, ignore a large and important part of the history of their own discipline. At best, they take out bits and pieces of the legacy, attributing all kinds of -isms to them, such as 'idealism', 'constructivism', 'narrativism', 'historicism', or 'relativism'. At worst, they use their thought as foils to set up their own positions, or as an excuse to neglect the contributions of the four philosophers altogether.

Neglecting the history of their own discipline, philosophers are bound to repeat it. From this perspective, much of the debate on the value of the covering law versus the rational explanation in the 1950s and 1960s was a slightly more sophisticated repetition of Croce's and Gentile's battles with the positivists of their times. A decade later, constructivist philosophers of history unknowingly repeated Gentile's philosophy of history, and therefore they did not take the possible political implications of their own position into account. Likewise, most narrativists, with the exception of White, never realised that Croce's first essay in the philosophy of history proudly states that history is a narrative which represents the past. Against this background, it is not suprising that White's followers could not understand why he began to stress the importance of the historical sublime in the 1980s, invoking the views of Gentile. In the same vein, Ankersmit, in his *Sublime Historical Experience,* does not take into account that the concept of experience played a dominant role in Italian idealism, and that Collingwood's most famous doctrine dealt with 'the re-enactment of past experience'.[60] Finally, the latest fashion in the philosophy of history, the theory of presence as the unrepresented past, overlooks the glaring fact that a very similar theory formed the core of Gentile's Fascist interpretation of history.[61]

Aim and Method of this Study

The main aim of this book is to clear up an important part of the historical background of the contemporary discussions in the philosophy of history, by reconstructing the role of the Italians in Collingwood's development. In this context, 'role' is not to be taken as 'influence'. It is not my intention to trace all kinds of similarities and differences between the four thinkers in order to discuss how they may or may not have affected each other. Nor is it my intention to show what the four thinkers 'borrowed' from each other. In contrast, throughout the book I will follow the logic of question and answer which the four thinkers

---

[60]   F.R. Ankersmit, *Sublime Historical Experience*, Stanford University Press, Stanford, 2005.

[61]   Hans Ulrich Gumbrecht, *Production of Presence: What Meaning Cannot Convey*, Stanford University Press, Stanford, 2004; Eelco Runia, 'Presence', in *History and Theory*, 45, 1–29. For the relationship between Gentile's Fascist philosophy and presence see Rik Peters, 'Actes de présence: presence in Fascist political culture', in *History and Theory*, 45, 2006, 362–74.

applied themselves when analysing other thinkers. Collingwood concisely rendered the main principle of this hermeneutics as follows:

> An intelligent inquiry into the influence of Socrates on Plato, or Descartes on Newton, seeks to discover not the points of agreement, but the way in which the conclusions reached by one thinker give rise to problems for the next.[62]

On the basis of this principle, I will reconstruct the development of the dialogue between Croce, Gentile, de Ruggiero, and Collingwood in a chronological narrative. This narrative is based on a close scrutiny of their published and unpublished works, including letters and marginal notes. This book thus discusses the entire corpus of Italian writings available to Collingwood, and his writings as discussed by the Italians. On this basis I will reconstruct as accurately as possible how the four philosophers interpreted each other's works.

This means, firstly, that I will keep as closely as possible to their own language in order to avoid the anachronisms that have plagued the literature on the four thinkers so far. I have read the Italians in Italian, rendering their words as they them wrote them and as Collingwood read them. If this causes modern readers troubles, let them remind themselves that Collingwood had to overcome the same difficulties when he tried to make Italian thought understandable to himself and to his readers.

Secondly, I have only employed secondary literature when it throws light on the relationship between the four thinkers. With the exception of the publications on de Ruggiero, the literature on Croce, Gentile, and Collingwood is too vast to be digested in a single life, let alone to pay tribute to it in a single book.

Thirdly, and most importantly, I have tried to interpret the thought of the four philosophers in the context of their lives and times. Croce, Gentile, and de Ruggiero were not philosophers of the ivory tower, but active historians, literary critics, and political leaders who continually reflected on their practical experience. Although he was not a man of action like the Italians, the relationship between theory and practice was at the centre of Collingwood's interests. In fact, 'all thought exists for the sake of action' was the motto of his life's work.[63] Throughout the book I have paid attention to the relationship between the practical problems of the four philosophers and the way by which they sought to solve these in their philosophical systems. This includes Collingwood's unfinished system, which will be reconstructed in the last chapter by comparing it to its Italian predecessors.

All in all, this book wants to be more than a study of influences; it aims at reconstructing the story of four philosophers living in the most turbulent decades of the twentieth century. Great historical events, such as the First World War, the rise of Fascism and Nazism, and the decay of Western civilisation con-

---

[62] R.G. Collingwood, *The Idea of History*, 313.
[63] R.G. Collingwood, *Speculum Mentis*, 15; Id., *An Autobiography*, 150–153.

tinually challenged the four to raise and answer questions about the nature of history and philosophy. Like Croce, Gentile, de Ruggiero, and Collingwood we are nowadays confronted with the problems of nationalism, populism, the fragility of democracy, and the 'clash of civilisations'. The four philosophers never meant to provide solutions to our problems, but they did point out how the beginning of a solution can be found in history. The plea of this book is therefore not to go back to Croce, Gentile, de Ruggiero, and Collingwood, but to study the way in which they dealt with the problems of their times, to solve the problems of our times.

Chapter One

The Early Development of Croce and Gentile (1893–1903)

Introduction

In his autobiography of 1915, which carries the unusual title *Contributo alla critica di me stesso* (*Contribution to a Criticism of Myself*), Croce gives a lively account of the way in which he became involved in philosophy. Born in 1866 to a wealthy land-owning family of the Abruzzi, history played an important role in his youth. Croce's mother, who was fond of art, old monuments, and of reading history books, was the first to awaken her son's interest in the past. When he was just six or seven years old, she introduced him to the local bookseller thus making her son a book addict for the rest of his life. She also accompanied him to Naples where she showed him old tombstones, pictures, and monuments. By the time Croce went to school in the same city, history and literature were already his favourite studies.[1]

In 1883, Croce's happy youth suddenly ended when his parents and his sister died in the earthquake of Casamicciola on the Isle of Ischia. Croce himself was rescued the next day and underwent surgery for a fractured leg and arm. The tragedy would have a lasting effect on Croce. For many years, he confesses in his autobiography, he was so depressed that he hoped not to wake up in the morning. Only with history could he occupy his tormented mind, though he pursued it more 'out of natural vagueness and to do something in the world'.[2]

After the death of his parents, Croce was put in the care of his uncle Silvio Spaventa (1822–93), a veteran of the *Destra storica*, the right-wing liberals who governed Italy from the unification until 1876. Silvio, who lived in Rome, was the brother of Bertrando Spaventa (1817–83), the Neapolitan philosopher who became one of Gentile's main sources of inspiration. Croce, however, did not

---

[1] B. Croce, *Contributo alla critica di me stesso*, *Edizione di 100 esemplari fuori commercio*, 1918, reprinted i0n *Etica e politica*, Laterza, Bari, 1931, cited from *Etica e politica*, Laterza, Bari, terza edizione economica, 1981, 316–17.

[2] Ibid., 323.

appreciate his uncle's philosophy. 'Spaventa', Croce writes in his autobiography, 'came from the church and from theology and the highest and almost the only problem for him was always that of the relationship between Being and Knowledge, the problem of immanence and transcendence, the special problem of the philosophy of theology'.[3] Croce himself was not so interested in this kind of problem because, after rejecting Catholicism when he was still at school, he 'found rest in a sort of unconscious immanentism'.[4] In this sense, Croce felt more attracted to the philosophy of Antonio Labriola (1843–1904), a pupil of Bertrando Spaventa, who taught at *La Sapienza* in Rome. In the 1890s Labriola became one of Europe's leading Marxists, and later he was a major influence on Antonio Gramsci (1891–1937).

In his autobiography, Croce pays credit to Labriola for teaching Herbart's (1776–1841) view of philosophy as the 'elaboration of concepts' and to his idea that ethics revolves around the distinction between the real and the ideal.[5] Surprisingly, Croce does not mention Labriola's lectures on the philosophy of history which the latter held from 1887. In these lectures Labriola dealt with 'historical evidence', 'objectivity', the 'theory of civilisation', and 'progress', which were subjects Croce would study in his own philosophy of history.[6] In spite of his admiration for Labriola, Croce did not become a philosopher himself. Instead, he continued with his 'erudite studies' in the libraries and archives of the capital, returning to Naples in 1887 without having taken an academic degree.

In his autobiography Croce describes Naples as a city full of 'librarians, archivists, erudites, interested amateurs, and other honest, good and gentle people, for the most old and mature men who did not have the habit of thinking too much'.[7] In the footsteps of these men Croce began to study the history of his city, writing dozens of articles for local journals.[8] Yet this work did not entirely satisfy him and soon he sought to do 'something more intimate and serious'. Along these lines, Croce conceived the plan of writing a great history of Italy.[9] This history should not be political in the first place, but moral, it was not to be a history of 'events', Croce writes, but a history 'of the sentiments and of the spiritual life of Italy from the Renaissance onwards'.[10]

Croce's ambitious project confronted him with many methodological problems, which he tried to solve with the help of German and Italian philosophers

---

3   Ibid., 342.
4   Ibid.
5   Ibid., 322-3; Id., 'La storia ridotta sotto il concetto generale dell'arte', in *Atti della Accademia Pontaniana*, XXIII, 1893, cited from *Primi Saggi*, Laterza, Bari, 1919, 3–41.
6   Antonio Labriola, *Scritti Filosofici e Politici*, Einaudi Editore, Torino, 1976, 5.
7   B. Croce, *Contributo alla critica di me stesso*, 324.
8   Ibid., 326.
9   Ibid., 326-7.
10 Ibid.

of history. In this way Croce discovered Vico's *Scienza Nuova* (1744), which was to remain his philosophical Bible for the rest of his life. In the meantime, Croce also began to work as a literary critic, preparing himself by studying the works of the literary historian Francesco de Sanctis (1817–83) as well as some German books on aesthetics.[11] Together with Vico's *Scienza Nuova* these studies inspired him to approach the problem of history from an aesthetic point of view in his first philosophical essay 'La storia ridotta sotto il concetto generale dell'arte' ('History Subsumed under the General Concept of Art') in 1893.[12] In this 'indirect way', via history and literary criticism, Croce became involved in philosophy, as he wrote to Gentile in 1898.[13] However, after some time, he got so immersed in philosophical problems that he decided to postpone the writing of the great moral history of Italy for a while.[14] At that time, he could not foresee that it would take him more than thirty years of intense philosophical study before he could carry out his initial plan in his famous historical 'tetralogy' which was published between 1925 and 1932.[15]

Croce's Historical Project and its Problems

It is not easy to retrace Croce's autobiographical account in his early writings. Most of the articles before 1893 deal with the local history of Naples and do not give an idea of 'a great moral history of Italy' and the 'methodological problems' which were involved in it.[16] But one lecture on the German *Kulturhistoriker*, given in 1895 for the Accademia Pontaniana in Naples, gives a clue.[17] In this lecture, Croce approaches the problem of the nature of the history of culture as it had recently been discussed in Germany. The *Kulturhistoriker*, led by Eberhard Gothein (1853–1923), Ernst Bernheim (1859–1942), the author of the famous *Lehrbuch der historischen Methode*, Gustav von Schmoller (1838–1917), Georg Steinhausen (1866–1933), and Karl Lamprecht (1856–1915) had attempted to develop a form of historiography which somewhat resembles contemporary history of mentalities. Although the *Kulturhistoriker* did not agree about the exact

---

[11] Ibid., 327.

[12] Ibid.

[13] B. Croce, *Lettere a Giovanni Gentile, (1896–1924)*, Arnaldo Mondari Editore, Milan, 1981, 37.

[14] B. Croce, *Contributo alla critica di me stesso*, 327.

[15] B. Croce, 'Note autobiografiche', in *Etica e politica*, 4th edn. Laterza, Bari, 1956, cited from *Etica e politica*, Laterza, Bari, terza edizione economica, 1981, 359–60. (These notes were written in 1934.) The four works are *Storia del Regno di Napoli*, Laterza, Bari, 1925; *Storia d'Italia dal 1871 al 1915*, Laterza, Bari, 1928; *Storia del età barocca in Italia*, Laterza, Bari, 1929; *Storia d'Europa nel secolo decimonono*, Laterza, Bari, 1932.

[16] B. Croce, *I teatri di Napoli*, Pierro, Napoli, 1891, cited from *I teatri di Napoli*, Adelphi Edizioni, Milan, 1992.

[17] B. Croce, 'Intorno alla storia della cultura (Kulturgeschichte)', in *Atti della Accademia Pontaniana*, XXV, 1895, cited from *Conversazioni Critiche, serie prima*, Laterza, Bari, 1918, 201–24.

nature of the object of history, they all aimed at enlarging the scope of historical studies by exploring history from a non-political point of view. Some of them intended to include the realm of feelings in history, others wished to explore the history of the family, or the history of art and religion. The synthesis of these studies would constitute *Kulturgeschichte*, or 'history of civilisation'.[18] Against this, opponents of the *Kulturhistoriker*, led by the historians Dietrich Schäfer (1845–1929) and Heinrich von Treitschke (1834–96), objected that the history of civilisation could never constitute an autonomous form of history; in their view only politics could be the unifying factor in history, because at its heart all history is history of the state.[19]

In this debate, Croce explicitly sympathised with the *Kulturhistoriker*, whose idea of history came very close to his own project of a history of morals. But he also endorsed Schäfer's and Treitschke's contempt for the 'bric-à-brac history' into which the historians of culture tended to lapse.[20] In this context, Croce remarked that this lapse was not the result of failing to recognise the importance of politics, but of failing to establish a criterion of 'the historically interesting' which enables historians to determine which facts should be taken into account and which not.[21] This concept of 'the interesting', which Croce derived through Labriola from Herbart's pedagogy, would play an important role in Croce's early writings on art and history and reappear in the articles of 1912 and 1913, which constitute the first chapters of *Teoria e storia della storiografia*.[22]

In both his early and later works, the concept of the interesting enabled Croce to link the theoretical and practical activities of the human mind. In his early articles, he expressed this view by saying that all works of art and history should have an 'interesting content'. Though Croce does not define this idea of interesting content precisely, he describes it in 1893 as 'something which interests individuals in their daily life and which is therefore related to their psychology'.[23] According to Croce, an interesting content must carefully be distinguished as an 'antecedent' from its artistic or historical 'elaboration'. In other words, the interesting content functions as a presupposition for a work of art or historiography which is based on it. Along these lines, Croce concluded that the literary critic can judge the value of the content of poetry and prose on the basis of a criterion of 'the interesting'.[24] To establish such a criterion was in Croce's view not an artistic but a 'methodological problem' to be solved on the basis of an elaboration of the concepts of literary criticism.[25]

---

18 Ibid., 201–12.
19 Ibid.
20 Ibid., 212–15.
21 Ibid., 216.
22 B. Croce, *Teoria e storia della storiografia*, 3–40.
23 B. Croce, 'La storia ridotta', 32.
24 B. Croce, 'Intorno alla storia della cultura (Kulturgeschichte)', 216, 221.
25 B. Croce, 'La storia ridotta', 32–5, 68.

In the methodological articles of his early development Croce repeatedly tried to define a criterion of the interesting. This is not surprising when we consider that both his work as a literary critic and as an historian depended on it. Even more important in these articles is Croce's view that the criterion of 'the interesting' is closely related to history and practice. Like geography, geology, ethnography, Croce says, history is a 'descriptive science' which serves 'the practical interests of mankind', whereas the 'conceptual sciences', like the natural sciences, philosophy, and even ethics, serve theoretical interests only.[26] Although Croce later revised this distinction between the practical and theoretical sciences, he never left his original idea that history serves practical interests. By 1893 this conviction was already so strong that Croce decided to reject 'mere erudite history' to begin a query for the theoretical foundations of a form of history which would serve practical life.

'History Subsumed Under the Concept of Art' (1893)

The first step towards a theoretical foundation of a new conception of history was Croce's claim that history is a form of art. Given his overall problem of relating history to practice, this was a most remarkable thesis, since most of his contemporaries did not see art as a form of knowledge, let alone as a form of knowledge which serves practice. Moreover, Croce presented his claim with a straightforwardness and acumen that offended many of his critics. Even today, Croce's first essay is remarkable for omitting academic rituals; it raises the problems *da capo* and solves them in a straightforward way.

'Is history a form of art or a form of science?' is Croce's first question. In his view, this question arises because of all the forms of knowledge only history has been associated with both art and science.[27] Croce's answer to this question employs Herbart's method of elaborating concepts. Typically, this elaboration proceeds along a sequence of questions and answers. To the question 'What is art?' Croce answers that it is not sensuous pleasure, the expression of truths, the construction of formal relations, nor the expression of some metaphysical idea, but the 'representation of the individual'.[28] Science, on the other hand, is knowledge of the universal, or concepts. Philosophy is the highest form of science, because it only 'elaborates' concepts and has nothing to do with the individual.[29]

On this basis Croce answers the question about the nature of history. History, he says, does not 'elaborate concepts' like science and philosophy do, but it is, like art, 'knowledge of the individual'. Qua form, history is therefore identical to

---

[26] B. Croce, 'L'arte, la storia, e la classificazione generale dello scibile', in *Il concetto della storia nelle sue relazioni col concetto dell'arte. Ricerche e discussioni*, Loescher, Roma, 1896, cited as 'Sulla classificazione dello scibile', in *Primi Saggi*, Laterza, Bari, 1919, 62–3.

[27] B. Croce, 'La storia ridotta', 3.

[28] Ibid., 15.

[29] Ibid., 16–17.

art.[30] In order to distinguish history from art proper, Croce concentrates on the content of both and here he uses the concept of 'the interesting' again. The content of art, Croce says, is 'the artistically interesting', or 'the possible', whereas history is concerned with 'the historically interesting' or 'the real'.[31] Since the real is part of the possible, it follows that history should be 'subsumed' under the concept of art. On this basis Croce defines history as 'the species of artistic production that has as the object of its representation that which really happened'.[32] According to Croce the artistic aspect of history is revealed most clearly by the fact that history, like poetry, tells a story: 'la storia narra.'[33]

Croce's essay of 1893 immediately attracted attention in Italy and Germany, where it was discussed and criticised by historians like Pasquale Villari (1826–1917) and Ernst Bernheim and by philosophers like Raffaele Mariano (1840–1912) and Labriola.[34] Most of the critics found that Croce had degraded history by identifying it with art, which they did not see as a form of knowledge, but as a pleasant construction of formal relations. Croce, however, was not only convinced that art is a form of knowledge, but also that all other forms of knowledge were based on it. This is the purport of 'The Classification of the Knowable', a paper delivered in 1895 in which Croce argued that art forms the basis of all descriptive sciences such a geography, palaeontology, and others.[35]

Croce's English speaking interpreters have disputed the originality of his first essay. In his lectures of 1929, and again in 1936, Collingwood taught his students that Croce, by identifying history with art, 'cut himself at one blow loose' from the naturalism that still beset the German view of history and 'set his face towards an idea of history as something radically different from nature'.[36] Collingwood's claim for Croce's originality has been contested by various interpreters like White and Roberts who argued that Croce merely echoed the Neo-Kantian view that history is knowledge of the individual.[37] To some extent this is true, because Johann Gustav Droysen (1808–84), Georg Simmel (1858–1918), and

---

[30] Ibid., 24.

[31] Ibid., 35.

[32] Ibid., 36.

[33] Ibid., 19.

[34] B. Croce, 'Di alcuni obiezioni mosse a una mia memoria sul concetto della storia', in *Atti della Accademia Pontaniana*, XXIV, 1894, reprinted and revised as 'Noterelle polemiche' in *Il concetto della storia nelle sue relazioni col concetto dell'arte. Ricerche e discussioni*, Loescher, Roma, 1896, cited from *Primi Saggi*, Laterza, Bari, 1919, 46–60.

[35] B. Croce, 'L'arte, la storia, e la classificazione generale dello scibile', in *Il concetto della storia nelle sue relazioni col concetto dell'arte. Ricerche e discussioni*, Loescher, Roma, 1896, cited as 'Sulla classificazione dello scibile', in *Primi Saggi*, Laterza, Bari, 1919, 66.

[36] R.G. Collingwood, 'Lectures on the Philosophy of History – II Trinity Term 1929', Dep. 12/6; id.,*The Idea of History*, 193.

[37] White, *Metahistory*, 381–3; Roberts, *Benedetto Croce and the Uses of Historicism*, 39–40. Roberts is more cautious than White, but both authors claim that Croce's position did not differ in more than in terminology from Windelband's.

Wilhelm Dilthey (1833–1911) had defended this view before Croce.[38] But, unlike Croce, these Germans had never identified history with art, because they did not recognise art as a form of knowledge. Simmel, for example, in his 1892 *Die Probleme der Geschichtsphilosophie*, described history as an *a priori* synthesis on the basis of empirical data. From this viewpoint, he recognised the role of imagination in history, although he never regarded it as *a priori* of historical thought.[39] Likewise, in his inaugural lecture of 1894, Windelband (1848–1915) described the 'idiographic sciences' as knowledge of individual events, but never as art. Instead, he holds that history proceeds on the basis of 'given experience'.[40]

Most importantly, and in contrast to contemporary interpreters, the Germans themselves clearly understood that Croce's aesthetic notion of intuition was different from their Kantian idea of 'Anschauung'. Heinrich Rickert (1863–1936), in his *Grenzen der Wissenschaftlichen Begriffsbildung*, explicitly defines 'Anschauung' as 'unmittelbare sinnliche Erlebnis' (immediate sense-experience) and rejects the identification of history and art most emphatically, without mentioning Croce however.[41] Max Weber (1864–1920), who did explicitly discuss Croce's first paper, argued that it confused several meanings of the term intuition.[42] These criticisms show that these German philosophers did not endorse Croce's view of art as the basis of history. Instead, they still based history on 'Anschauung', that is, a passive non-cognitive apprehension of something given, whereas Croce, by identifying history with art, stressed history's creative aspects from the beginning. Starting from the notion of 'Anschauung', the German philosophers were not able to explain how the historian ever gets the past into his mind, whereas Croce, by identifying history with art, provides the key to this problem; the act of intuition is the first step of making the past present to the mind. From this it follows that the historian does not start from some 'given' experience, but he gives experience to himself by an act of intuition. Like the artist who can draw a line or a man's profile without using any concepts, the historian can imagine past events without using concepts. Croce had not elaborated this view in 'La storia ridotta', but in the *Estetica* of 1902 he comes closer to it when he says that history does not construct universals or concepts, but 'posits intuitions' not 'ad demonstrandum' but 'ad narrandum'.[43]

---

38 Croce cites and discusses their views in 'La storia ridotta', 25–6.
39 Georg Simmel, 'Die Probleme der Geschichtsphilosophie', in *Aufsätze 1887–1890, Über soziale Differenzierung. Die Probleme der Geschichtsphilosophie*, in Georg Simmel, *Gesamtausgabe*, Heraugegeben von Otthein Rammstedt, Band 2, Suhrkamp, Frankfurt, 1989, 303–7.
40 Wilhelm Windelband, *Präludien, Aufsätze und Reden zur Philosophie und ihrer Geschichte*, Zweiter Band, Mohr, Tübingen, 1924, 148.
41 Heinrich Rickert, *Die Grenzen der Naturwissenschaftlichen Begriffsbildung, Eine logische Einleitung in die historischen Wissenschaften*, Mohr, Tübingen, 1921 (1st edn. 1896), 268.
42 Max Weber, 'Knies und das Irrationalitätsproblem', in *Gesammelte Aufsätze zur Wissenschaftslehre*, herausgegeben von Johannes Winckelmann, Mohr, Tübingen, 1988, 109.
43 B. Croce, *Estetica*, 29.

In spite of its originality, Croce's first essay still showed some weaknesses. In 1919 Croce himself formulated them as follows:

> I did not detect the new problem raised by the conception of history as artistic representation of the real. I did not see that a representation in which the real is dialectically distinguished from the possible is something more than a merely artistic representation or intuition; it comes about by virtue of the concept; not indeed the empirical or abstract concept of science, but the concept which is philosophy and, as such, is both representation and judgement and individual in one.[44]

In this passage Croce avows that he had not sufficiently distinguished art and history, because he had not clearly understood the nature and method of philosophy. In 'La storia ridotta' Croce still saw philosophy as a form of science, which, as knowledge of the 'universal', had no connection with art and history, seen as 'knowledge of the individual'. In an autobiographical note in his *Logica* of 1909 Croce indicated that this view of philosophy had led him to a mistaken employment of the classificatory method, which is based on sharp distinctions.[45]

Classification indeed guides all distinctions of 'La storia ridotta'; the notions of form and content, the universal and the individual, the possible and the real, are all conceived as mutually exclusive species of a genus. But when these distinctions are applied to mental activities they run the risk of coinciding. From an epistemological point of view, the most important distinction in 'La storia ridotta' is the one between content and form, which reveals Croce's early realism. If content and form can be shown to 'overlap', that is, if content and form are interpreted as two complementary aspects of a single mental process, the whole argument of 'La storia ridotta' crumbles, because all other distinctions are based on it. For example, the distinction between the possible and the real can be rejected by showing that reality plays a part in poetry, or by showing that the possible appears in historical and scientific conjectures. In the autobiographical note in the *Logica* of 1909 Croce expresses his deep gratitude to the philosopher who drew his attention to the fundamental weakness of his philosophical method, his realistic position, and the metaphysics on which it was based. That philosopher was a 22-year-old student at the *Scuola Normale Superiore* in Pisa. His name was Giovanni Gentile.

Gentile's Early Development

Although Gentile never wrote an autobiography, his development can be reconstructed on the basis of his early articles and three excellent biographies.[46]

---

[44] B. Croce, *Primi Saggi*, xi. English translation by Collingwood, *The Idea of History*, 192–3.
[45] B. Croce, *Logica*, 210.
[46] Manlio Di Lalla, *Vita di Giovanni Gentile*, Sansoni, Florence, 1975; Sergio Romano, *Giovanni Gentile. La filosofia al potere*, Bompiani, Milano, 1984; Gabriele Turi, *Giovanni Gentile. Una biografia*, Torino, UTET, 2006.

Gentile was born to a middle class family on 29 May 1875, in Castelvetrano on Sicily. His father was a pharmacist and his mother was the daughter of a public notary. Sicily was one of the poorest regions of Europe; the rates of illiteracy, unemployment, and crime were high, and its culture was decaying. Later in his life, Gentile would give a picture of this decadence in *Il tramonto della cultura siciliana* (*The Sunset of Sicilian Culture*), which breathes the same atmosphere as Giuseppe Tomasi di Lampedusa's novel *Il Gattopardo*, better known through Visconti's movie *The Leopard*.[47] One should never forget Gentile's social and cultural background which partly explains his everlasting desire for reforming Italy.[48]

In 1893, Gentile won a bursary to the *Scuola Normale Superiore* in Pisa which was then, as nowadays, one of the most prestigious institutes of higher education in Italy. In Pisa, his teachers, Alessandro d'Ancona (1835–1914), professor of Italian literature, and Donato Jaja (1839–1914), professor of theoretical philosophy, had a lasting influence on Gentile's development. From d'Ancona, who was a friend and pupil of Francesco de Sanctis, Gentile learned the importance of philology, which would mark all of his many works on the history of philosophy.[49] Jaja, a pupil of Bertrando Spaventa, taught Gentile the importance of the Kantian *a priori*.[50] Moreover, both teachers inspired their pupil so much with the zeal of the Italian Risorgimento, that the latter came to see himself as a heir to this movement.[51]

The influence of both d'Ancona and Jaja appears very clearly in Gentile's thesis of 1898 about two important philosophers of the Risorgimento, Antonio Rosmini (1797–1855) and Vincenzo Gioberti (1801–1852).[52] Just five months before his assassination in April 1944, Gentile claimed that his *Rosmini e Gioberti* contained the core ideas of his later thought.[53] In hindsight, the book, written when Gentile was only twenty-three years old, does indeed contain the three pillars of his later philosophy.

Firstly, with his study of the two Risorgimento philosophers, Gentile hoped to contribute to the 'cultural awakening' of his country.[54] For Gentile, the Risorgimento represented the dawn of a new culture, Italy's first step into history, and the days of glorious and united action. In his Fascist writings, Gentile

---

47 G. Gentile, *Il tramonto della cultura siciliana*, Zanichelli, Bologna, 1919.

48 Turi, *Giovanni Gentile. Una biografia*, 9–11.

49 di Lalla, *Vita di Giovanni Gentile*, 16–22.

50 Augusto Del Noce, *Giovanni Gentile. Per una interpretazione filosofica della storia contemporanea*, Il Mulino, Bologna, 1990, 19–20.

51 Ibid. 123; Sergio Romano, *Giovanni Gentile*, 18.

52 G. Gentile, 'Rosmini e Gioberti. Saggio sulla filosofia italiana del risorgimento', in *Annali della R. Scuola Normale Superiore di Pisa, Filosofia e Filologia*, 1898, cited from *Rosmini e Gioberti*, OC XXV, Sansoni, Florence, 1958.

53 Ibid., xvii–xix.

54 Ibid., xiii.

stressed the religious devotion of the Risorgimento men; these were not ironically laughing Italians (*l'italiano chi ride*), but serious men committed to a single
cause, men with a mission, men of action.[55] From the beginning of his career,
Gentile would follow in the footsteps of his heroes, and until his death he kept
the cultural awakening of the Risorgimento alive.[56]

Secondly, Gentile firmly believed that the cultural awakening had to be
grounded on history, and in particular on the history of philosophy. In this
context, he points out that the historian of philosophy should distinguish
between the 'contingent' and the 'eternal' aspects of philosophy.[57] The contingent or historical aspect of philosophy, Gentile says, is found in its 'content',
and its eternal aspect in its 'form', which he identifies with the self-conscious
formation of thought. This distinction between content and form of philosophy
is based on Gentile's interpretation of the Kantian *a priori*, which he adopted as a
foundation of his own philosophy. In Gentile's view, Kant was not searching for
ready-made concepts to apply to experience, but for the categories, or functions,
which 'elaborate' experience.[58] The concept, Gentile explains, is only the passive
and contingent 'product' of thought; it always presupposes the category or the
act of thought which is eternal.[59] In philosophy, therefore, content and form
mutually presuppose each other; the concept must always be understood in the
light of the philosophical activity that formed it. Vice versa, this activity can only
be understood as the formation of concepts. In this way Gentile stresses the
logical and ontological priority of the act of thought, which he always identified
with its historicity; thought is primarily an activity which develops in time. In
his early works, Gentile presented this doctrine as the identity of philosophy and
the history of philosophy, which expressed his view that the formation of philosophy presupposes the history of philosophy, and, vice versa, that the history of
philosophy presupposes philosophy. From this point of view, mere 'erudite' history of philosophy is useless and so is philosophy that is not based on its own
history. True philosophy takes its own history into account.

From the thesis of the identity of philosophy with its own history, Gentile
derives his third and most basic principle, which is the doctrine of absolute
immanentism.[60] For Gentile philosophy is not a superfluous activity, but a
necessary characteristic of human life. All life, all action, all experience is
inherently philosophical and this means that all men, from the shepherds and
farmers of his native Sicily to Rosmini and Gioberti, are all philosophers, each in

---

[55] G. Gentile, *I profeti del risorgimento italiano*, Vallecchi, Florence, 1923, cited from 3rd
      edn., Sansoni, Florence, 1944.
[56] del Noce, *Giovanni Gentile*, 123.
[57] G. Gentile, *Rosmini e Gioberti*, xiv.
[58] Ibid., 175–6, 178.
[59] Ibid., 175.
[60] Ibid., xiv.

his own way.[61] This doctrine of absolute immanentism is crucial to understand Gentile's philosophical development; from the beginning of his career, he believed that all problems of human life are from the start philosophical problems. It cannot be denied that this is a most inspiring idea, especially to philosophers, but Gentile often jumped to the conclusion that all problems of mankind can be solved in a philosophical way. That this is not always the case, Gentile began to realise after twenty years of Fascism.

With the three doctrines, the young Gentile expounded a view of the relation between philosophy, history, and practice which considerably differered from Croce's. Whereas the latter still distinguished between some fixed entities, like 'the content', 'the interesting' from their further 'elaboration', Gentile viewed the mind as an activity, or act, in which content and form are merged. Along these lines, he tried to 'resolve' all fixed entities into the spiritual act of the mind, that is, he tried to interpret them as products of mental activity. Most importantly, from the view of the mind as an activity stems Gentile's tendency to soften the distinction between theory and practice. Whereas Croce sharply distinguished between theory and practice, Gentile tended to identify them. In his view, the formation of concepts must in the first place be seen as an activity, and this activity cannot be clearly distinguished from practice, because the formation of concepts is a creative activity in the first place; thought does something, it is an act which changes reality. From this viewpoint, Rosmini and Gioberti were not only good philosophers because of the quality of their conceptual analyses, but also because of their significance for the unification of Italy. Vice versa, Gentile greatly admired men of action, and saw leaders like Mazzini (1805–1872), Garibaldi (1807–1882), and later Mussolini, as great thinkers. The relationship between thought and action would always divide Croce and Gentile, and with the rise of Fascism, it would lead to their break.

Gentile's Criticism of Croce's Concept of History

One of Gentile's first contributions to philosophy was his 1897 review of Croce's 'La storia ridotta'. In this review Gentile is positive about Croce's fusion of art and history, but he also raises two major objections. Firstly, he criticises Croce's 'subordination' of the real to the possible. In this context he says that the 'concrete particular' differs in one fundamental respect from the merely possible, because it can pass from possible being to actual being, whereas the merely possible never becomes actual. From this it follows that the concrete particular can be possible or real; it is possible, or it really happens. Therefore, Gentile concludes, the real is not subordinated to the possible, as Croce held, but the real

---

61   Ibid.

and the possible form two coordinated species of a single genus.[62] Along these lines, Gentile does not distinguish as sharply as Croce between the ideal and the real. In his view the content of art, which Croce had identified with 'the possible', should be seen as an 'ideal reality', or with 'ideality' *tout court*, because the possible is 'the real which is not yet actual'.[63] This view implies the possibility of a development from the ideal into the real which is incompatible with Croce's distinction between the two.

Secondly, Gentile defends Hegel's theory of art as the expression of an idea against Croce's criticisms.[64] Whereas the latter defends the autonomy of art by keeping it free from any reference to reality through conceptual thought, Gentile tends to merge art and thought as a view of reality. For Croce, art primarily aims at beauty, for Gentile it aims at truth. This idea of art as a view of reality is clearly reflected in his paper 'Arte sociale' ('Social Art') of 1896, in which he holds that 'art in act' cannot escape 'the universal laws of life' and that it always 'conforms itself to its historical surroundings'. Most importantly, the historicity of the spirit in general and of the artist in particular implies that there is no real separation between the artist and the public; art is in the first place a social activity.[65]

Gentile's main objections to Croce's position follow directly from his idea of the unity of content and form. Unlike Gentile, Croce distinguished between content and form; the content of art and history is independent of their formal development or 'elaboration'. Along these lines, Croce identified art and history on the basis of their content, without taking their form into account. But from Gentile's viewpoint the content can only be understood in the light of the form, which he identifies with the 'elaboration of the spirit', or the mental activity, which is logically and ontologically prior to its products. The implication of this doctrine comes most clearly to the fore when Gentile points out against Croce that facts are dependent on the mental activities of the historian:

> How do we conceive history apart from historiography, the facts apart from their elaboration in the spirit? It is clear that it is impossible to speak about facts, pure or crude facts, if we do not consider them as abstract, as an ideal content, which we can grasp or which will surprise us as an external reality. The facts only exist for us in so far as we represent them in our mind.[66]

---

[62] G. Gentile, 'B. Croce, il concetto della storia nelle sue relazioni col concetto dell'arte', in *Studi Storici*, 6, 1897, cited from *Frammenti di Estetica e di teoria della storia*, II, OC XLVIII, Le Lettere, Florence, 1992, 123–4.

[63] Ibid., 127.

[64] B. Croce, 'Di alcuni obiezioni mosse a una mia memoria sul concetto della storia', 56.

[65] G. Gentile, 'Arte sociale', in *Helios*, 3, 1896, cited from *Frammenti di Estetica e di teoria della storia*, I, OC XLVII, Le Lettere, Florence, 1992, 255–6.

[66] G. Gentile, 'B. Croce, il concetto della storia nelle sue relazioni col concetto dell'arte', 131.

This passage marks the crucial difference between the two thinkers with regard to history. The early Croce still presupposed that the past exists as an 'antecedent', that is, as given fact for further historiographical elaboration. In contrast to this view, Gentile stressed that the past only exists in the activity of the mind; history as fact is only an abstraction of this activity. Art and history can therefore never be distinguished on the basis of their content because the historian creates, or constructs, his object as much as the artist does; both call reality into existence by representing it.

Gentile's 'The Concept of History' (1899)

Gentile did not confine himself to criticism, but also developed his own theory of history in 'Il concetto della storia' ('The Concept of History') published in 1899.[67] In this paper, he develops Croce's distinction between art and history, not on the basis of their content, but on the basis of their form. Following his interpretation of the Kantian *a priori*, Gentile interpreted form primarily as an activity, and content as its product. From this viewpoint, art and history must be seen as activities which have a certain 'aim' or 'goal'.[68] In Gentile's view, the aim of art is to satisfy our aesthetic demands by the production of beauty, whereas the aim of history is to 'satisfy our curiosity by the representation of facts'.[69] On this point, Gentile emphasises that a fact can never exist apart from its representation; there is not first a fact and then its representation, but there is first an unknown fact, the characteristics of which are further established by a process of research resulting in a representation of the past. Inquiry is therefore the essence of history. He illustrates this view with a passage on history as an activity which strikingly foreshadows his later dialectic of thought:

> There is no curiosity for something we know; and in curiosity itself there is indeed some ignorance but also a feeling of the truth which is the germ of knowledge. Therefore, history is already present as a germ in the very curiosity that brings itself to historical research. The germ will develop itself but this development is not an intervention of an external content but its formation, its form: it is thought and not crude and pure fact.[70]

In this passage Gentile presents a view of history as a development from some first moment of curiosity to knowledge of historical fact. Consequently, he concludes that the cognitive aim of history can only be understood as the form of a content and not as pure content. In other words, the aim of historical activity, or the knowledge which satisfies our pure curiosity, can never be a pure content,

---

[67] G. Gentile, 'Il concetto della storia', in *Studi Storici*, 8, 1899, cited from *Frammenti di Estetica e di teoria della storia, I*, OC XLVII, Le Lettere, Florence, 1992, 1–52.

[68] Ibid., 20.

[69] Ibid., 21.

[70] Ibid., 24.

or an 'antecedent' of historical thought, but it is formed within historical thought itself.[71]

This idea of the cognitive aim of history enables Gentile to work out the difference between art and history as subjective activities of the subject. Borrowing from Kant, Gentile points out that in art the constitutive goal and the regulative goal coincide; art is the beautiful representation of the individual and beauty is also its norm. History resembles art only in so far as it is the representation of the individual, but its norm is not beauty but truth. On this basis Gentile concludes that the constitutive goal and the regulative goal of history do not coincide. Most interestingly, he indicates that individual fact is never 'given' to history; history 'constructs' fact, just as art constructs its own objects.[72]

Along these lines, Gentile points out that the importance of the regulative goal of history has been stressed too much. Contrary to this view, he points out that it is necessary to establish the constitutive goal of history first, because it is logically prior to the regulative goal; we have to know what history is before we try to establish its method and its value.[73] Along these lines Gentile defines history as 'an essential function of the spirit' just as art, religion, and philosophy are.[74] Here again he differs from Croce, who focused on the content of art and history and not on their function in the life of the mind. From this viewpoint, Croce thought that one could distinguish the value of Dante's *Divina Commedia* (*Divine Comedy*) and Macchiavelli's *Storie fiorentine* (*Florentine Histories*) by comparing their content.[75] But for Gentile, who concentrated on art and history as mental activities, such a comparison is insufficient, because art and history cannot be separated on the basis of their content alone. In his view, the *Divina Commedia* cannot be exclusively classified as art, nor Macchiavelli's *Storie fiorentine* as history, because each work is both a form of art and a form of history, as well as a form of religion and philosophy. In other words, each mental activity has artistic, historical, religious, and philosophical aspects. This view of the 'universal functions' of the mind is the core of Gentile's absolute immanentism which he would develop *in extenso* in his later philosophy. In his early writings, this immanentism is not yet completely elaborated; Gentile only applies it to the relationship between art and history, but not to the relationship between history and philosophy. He still held that philosophy, as knowledge of the *a priori*, should be distinguished from the other forms of experience.

Later, Gentile pointed out the immaturity of this immanentism and stigmatised the resulting disowning of the universality of the individual, and of the identity of philosophy and history as the main shortcoming of his early writ-

---

71 Ibid., 23.
72 Ibid., 49.
73 Ibid., 51–2.
74 Ibid., 26.
75 B. Croce, 'La storia ridotta', 28.

ings.[76] But already before the turn of the century, in a debate with Croce on the status of speculative philosophy of history, he made a first step towards a further integration of philosophy and history.

The Controversy between Croce and Gentile
about Metaphysical Philosophy of History

Already in 'La storia ridotta', Croce had expressed his doubts about the possibility of a philosophy of history, though he conceded that historical facts could be treated 'scientifically' in the way that philosophers of history like Bernheim, Simmel, and Labriola did.[77] Two years later he took a more radical position against these philosophers of history. In his essay 'Intorno alla filosofia della storia' ('About the Philosophy of History') of 1895, Croce points out that the philosophy of history deals with three groups of questions. The first group of questions concerns the 'meaning of history' which had been the traditional object of the metaphysical philosophy of history. In Croce's view this group of questions had been replaced by a second set of questions involving the more modern search for 'real principles' of history, or so-called 'historical laws'. The third group of questions consisted largely of 'methodological problems' like those on the notions of 'historical interest', 'the limits of historical knowledge', and 'the presuppositions on the basis of which we relate historical facts'.[78] In Croce's view these three groups of questions can never constitute a single science, as some philosophers of history claim, because the three groups of questions concern different objects: the first two groups deal with history as the past, whereas the third deals with historiography.[79]

Croce's distinction between the groups of questions typically presupposes a realist conception of the past. As in 'La storia ridotta', Croce clearly distinguishes between the content and form of history, between the past and historiography, or history *a parte obiecti* and history *a parte subiecti*. This view was squarely opposed to Gentile's views on the matter. In his review of 'La storia ridotta', Gentile had pointed out that there is a necessary connection between the first two groups of questions and the third, that is, between the past and the thought of the historian.[80] Interestingly, Gentile's criticism seems to imply the possibility of a metaphysical philosophy of history, which is not based on historical fact, but on the categories of historical thought. But in 1897 Gentile had not yet drawn

---

76 G. Gentile, 'Intorno all'idealismo attuale', in *La Voce*, n.50, 1913, cited from *Frammenti di filosofia*, *OC* LI, Le Lettere, Florence, 1994, 48.

77 B. Croce, 'La storia ridotta', 22.

78 B. Croce, 'Intorno all'organismo della filosofia della storia', in *Il concetto della storia nelle sue relazioni col concetto dell'arte. Ricerche e discussioni*, Loescher, Roma, 1896, cited as 'Intorno alla filosofia della storia', in *Primi Saggi*, Laterza, Bari, 1919, 68.

79 Ibid., 69.

80 G. Gentile, 'B. Croce, il concetto della storia nelle sue relazioni col concetto dell'arte', 131.

this conclusion, because he still distinguished between historiography and its 'further integration' into the philosophy of history. However, in his debate with Croce about the status of historical materialism as a philosophy of history, he began to merge history with philosophy of history.

The occasion for this debate was Labriola's 'In memoria del Manifesto dei communisti' of 1895 ('In Memory of the Communist Manifesto'), which he was to publish in Sorel's (1847-1922) *Devenir social*.[81] In this essay, which was the first of the *Saggi sulla concezione materialistica della storia* (*Studies on the Marxist Conception of History*) which would establish his name as one of the leading Marxists of his time, Labriola rejected much of the metaphysical underpinnings of historical materialism, which he regarded in the first place as a new 'method' to understand history.[82] This methodological approach to history was in line with Croce's own view of the matter, and inspired him to plunge into Marxist literature and into a thorough study of political economy.

The first result of Croce studies was 'Sulla concezione materialistica della storia' ('On the Materialistic Conception of History'), which he read for the Accademia Pontaniana in Naples in May 1896. In this lecture, he argued, firstly, that historical materialism, as interpreted by Labriola, should not be seen as a philosophy of history, and secondly, that there is no necessary connection between historical materialism and socialism. Croce defended the first thesis by arguing that a philosophy of history is impossible, because 'the course of history as a whole can never be reduced to a single concept'.[83] Along the same lines, Croce argued in another paper that although historical materialism cannot be a philosophy of history, it still has value as a 'method', or as a 'canon' for the interpretation of historical facts. Croce thus supported an historical materialism completely stripped of its metaphysical aspects.[84] As such it cannot account for any determination or finality in history, and therefore it cannot form the basis of socialism or of any other practice.[85]

On reading these papers in 1896, Gentile began his correspondence with Croce which would last until 1924. In his first letters, Gentile criticised Croce's

[81] B. Croce, 'Come nacque e come morì il marxismo teorico in Italia (1895-1900). Da lettere e ricordi personali', in *La Critica*, XXXVI, 1937, cited from *Materialismo storico ed economia marxista, terza edizione economica*, Laterza, Bari, 1978, 254.

[82] Antonio Labriola, 'In memoria del Manifesto dei communisti' and 'Del materialismo storico', in id., *Scritti Filosofici e Politici*, 475-6, 559-60.

[83] B. Croce, 'Sulla concezione materialistica della storia', in *Atti della Accademia Pontaniana*, XXVI, 1896, reprinted in *Materialismo storico ed economia marxista*, Sandron, Milan, 1900, cited from *Materialismo storico ed economia marxista*, terza edizione economica, Laterza, Bari, 1978, 3-4.

[84] B. Croce, 'Per la interpretazione e la critica di alcuni concetti del marxismo', in *Atti della Accademia Pontaniana*, XXVII, 1897, reprinted in *Materialismo storico ed economia marxista*, Sandron, Milan, 1900, cited from *Materialismo storico ed economia marxista, terza edizione economica*, Laterza, Bari, 1978, 75.

[85] B. Croce, 'Sulla concezione materialistica della storia', 15-17.

interpretation of historical materialism, and in 1897 he wrote 'Una critica del materialismo storico' ('A Criticism of Historical Materialism') in which he advanced the opposite of Croce's views. According to Gentile, historical materialism should be seen as a philosophy of history because it aims at predicting the course of events. Interestingly, although Gentile rejects historical prediction as being impossible, he does defend the view that history has a necessary course.[86] Furthermore, Gentile points out against Croce that there is a necessary connection between socialism and historical materialism in the sense that the latter is the theoretical reflection of the former. In his view, Croce incorrectly held that one must first understand historical materialism in order to become a socialist, because one can be a socialist without being an historical materialist. Morality, Gentile concludes, is a presupposition of historical thought and not a product of it.[87]

In 'La filosofia della prassi' ('The Philosophy of Praxis') of 1899, Gentile further developed the unity of theory and practice by interpreting Marxism as a philosophy of 'praxis'. Along the lines of his *tesi di laurea* Gentile interprets 'praxis' as a unity of thought and action; thought is an activity which is as productive as action, and action is guided by thought. In this sense, Gentile traces the concept of praxis to the Greeks who already considered thought as creative. He also refers to Vico's principle, 'verum et factum convertuntur' ('the true and the made convert into each other'), interpreting it as 'action is the necessary condition for thought'.[88] But the *credo* of praxis was best formulated by Marx (1818–1883) in his eleventh thesis on Feuerbach; 'philosophers have only interpreted the world in various ways; the point is to change it'.[89]

In Gentile's hands praxis becomes a permanent dialectic of thought and action in which the two terms are only vaguely distinguished; like action, thought is productive, creative, and active.[90] Most significantly, in 'La filosofia della prassi' Gentile emphasises that in practice the object of the will and the object of thought coincide; what we shall do is what we know, and what we know is dependent on what we shall do. In this way, Gentile relates praxis to history; the product of man's praxis is society and history, and for this reason society and history should be studied in order to further develop praxis. From this notion of praxis it is only one step to Gentile's later theory of the self-creative act of thought in which volition and knowledge are completely identified.

---

[86] G. Gentile, 'Una critica del materialismo storico', in *Studi Storici*, 6, 1897, cited from *La filosofia di Marx*, Sansoni, Florence, 1974, 11–58; 31–2, 39–41, 56–7.

[87] Ibid., 52.

[88] G. Gentile, 'La filosofia della prassi', in *La filosofia di Marx*, Spoerri, Pisa, 1899, cited from *La filosofia di Marx*, Sansoni, Florence, 1974, 73.

[89] Ibid., 71.

[90] Ibid., 77.

The differences between Croce's and Gentile's interpretation of historical materialism show the underlying differences between their philosophies. Firstly, in conformity to his understanding of philosophy Croce interpreted historical materialism primarily as a methodology. In contrast, Gentile, for whom philosophy is always concerned with the *a priori*, understood historical materialism as a metaphysical theory of history. Secondly, on the basis of his distinction between theory and practice, Croce explicitly affirmed the theoretical value of historical materialism but also denies its practical value. In contrast, Gentile approved of the close link between theory and practice in historical materialism, and by claiming that practice is a presupposition of knowledge, he came close to denying any distinction between theory and practice. Not surprisingly, Gentile's idea of praxis was much appreciated by Vladimir Lenin (1870–1924) and inspired Antonio Gramsci.[91] Croce, however, never agreed with Gentile's metaphysical interpretation of historical materialism and kept to his own 'methodological' interpretation of it. Only when Gentile began to criticise Croce's aesthetics, did the latter begin to listen to Gentile's arguments concerning the unity of content and form. The result of this discussion can be seen in Croce's *Estetica*.

History in Croce's *Aesthetics as Science of Expression and General Linguistic* (1902)

The *Estetica* of 1902 is Croce's first attempt to systematise his conclusions about the nature of art, science, history, philosophy, and practice in the preceding decade. Furthermore, it is the first work in which Croce tried to meet Gentile's criticisms by conceiving all forms of the spirit as activities in which content and form are united.

This double aim raised a serious problem of philosophical method. On the one hand Croce kept to his distinctions between the forms of the spirit, but on the other hand he also had to take the 'unity of the spirit' into account. In the earlier essays he had relied on the distinction between content and form, which enabled him to distinguish the forms of the spirit qua content, like, for example, art and history, or qua form, like art and science. But in the *Estetica* Croce dealt with the forms of the spirit as activities in which form and content are unified. This view compelled Croce to find a new basis for distinguishing between the forms of the spirit as activities. Moreover, Croce saw the forms of the spirit as complementary activities and this compelled him to leave classificatory logic as a basis for philosophical method. In short, the new view of the spirit forced Croce to find a method which enabled him to distinguish the forms of the spirit without making a difference.

---

[91]   Vladimir I. Lenin, *The Teachings of Karl Marx*, International Publishers, New York, 1930, 45; Antonio Gramsci, *Il materialismo storico*, Torino, 1975, 91–144.

Croce solved this problem by what he called a 'theory of grades', which is in fact a reinterpretation of the concept of distinction, as employed in 'La storia ridotta'. In this essay, Croce had treated conceptual distinctions according to the rules of classificatory logic as mutually exclusive species of a genus. In the theory of grades, however, two concepts a and b are defined as distinct when the 'lower' concept a can be thought without the higher concept b, whereas b cannot be thought without a.[92] This new view of conceptual distinction enabled Croce to describe the forms of the spirit and their relationships as a coherent system of activities.

In the *Estetica* the most fundamental distinction of the spirit is between theory and practice. Theory does not presuppose practice, whereas practice always presupposes theory. Theory and practice have two 'subdistinctions' which are based on the distinction between the individual and the universal. The theoretical sphere contains two distinct forms, art and philosophy. Art is knowledge of the individual, and does not presuppose philosophy. Philosophy is knowledge of the universal and presupposes art, because it expresses itself in language. Along the same lines, the practical form of the spirit has two distinct forms: economic action or willing a useful end, which is individual, and moral action as willing a rational end, which is universal.[93]

In the *Estetica*, Croce no longer considers the content of art as an 'antecedent' of form. He defines art as a 'pure form', that is, as an activity in which intuition and expression are 'identical'; to intuit something is to express it. From this it follows that the content of a work of art cannot be separated from its form.[94] Moreover, Croce no longer regards philosophy as a mere formal 'elaboration of concepts', but as knowledge of the concepts which relate the intuitions of art to each other.[95] Finally, Croce views the forms of the practical sphere activities defining economic action as 'willing a useful end' and moral action as 'willing a rational end'.[96]

In Croce's view, these four forms, art, philosophy, economic, and moral action, exhaust the activity of the spirit. He rules out other forms by either arguing that they are identical with one of the four acknowledged forms, or by showing that they simply do not exist. In this way Croce bans religion and metaphysics from the theoretical realm of the spirit, and feeling, sentiment, and 'sociability' from its practical side.[97] Religion, for example, is nothing but a mixture of knowledge, legend, and dogma, each of which resides under one of the four

---

92 B. Croce, *Estetica*, 28–9; the full exposition of the theory of grades can be found in id., *Ciò che è vivo e ciò che è morto della filosofia di Hegel*, Laterza, Bari, 1907, cited from *Saggio sullo Hegel*, Laterza, Bari, 1927, 59–64.

93 B. Croce, *Estetica*, 3–5, 60–7.

94 Ibid., 11, 18–19.

95 Ibid., 3, 25–7.

96 Ibid., 60–7.

97 Ibid., 70.

forms of the spirit. As a form of knowledge, religion is identical with philosophy, as legend it is similar to historical narrative and therefore with art as well, and as dogma it is identical with science. Religion, Croce concludes, can therefore be completely 'subsumed' by other forms of the spirit.[98] An example of showing the non-existence of a form of the spirit is found in metaphysics, which has, in Croce's view, no object of its own and can be 'supplanted' by methodology.[99]

These examples clearly show that, in spite of Croce's intentions, the theory of grades still works like a classificatory logic; if a given form cannot be proven to have an autonomous status, it must be reduced to one of the truly universal forms of the spirit, or it must be explained away. The strength of this method is that many different concepts can be reduced to the four fundamental concepts of the spirit. It thus enabled Croce to build an enormous *catalogue raisonné* of the most diverse concepts. However, the crucial weakness of Croce's philosophical method is that it tends to blur essential distinctions between concepts.

In the *Estetica* Croce still identifies art and history qua form. But he does not repeat what is stated in 'La storia ridotta'. In that essay, he had distinguished content and form, but now he regards art as unity of content and form. This position makes the earlier distinction between art and history on the basis of their content impossible. In the *Estetica* Croce also identifies both art and history with 'perception'. In order to keep the distinction between the two forms of knowledge clear, Croce now specifies art as perception of 'the ideal' and history as perception of 'the real'. Most importantly, Croce argues that the distinction between the ideal and the real is not a problem for history itself, but for philosophy. History only 'applies' the concepts which are elaborated by philosophy.[100] Whereas history and philosophy were kept apart in 'La storia ridotta', they now begin to 'overlap'; history presupposes philosophy in order to make the distinction between the ideal and the real. Croce would himself develop this overlap in his *Lineamenti per una Logica come scienza del concetto puro* (*Outlines of a Logic as Science of the Pure Concept*) of 1905, in which he defined history as a synthesis of intuition and concept, and in his final version of the *Logica* of 1909 he completely identified history and philosophy.

Apart from history, several other interesting overlaps can be found in the *Estetica*. For example, Croce regards the philosophical concept of progress as a necessary presupposition of historical thought.[101] But feeling the danger of identifying history with the metaphysics of progress in this way, Croce warns that the concept of progress should simply be understood as the point of view from which the historian judges human activity:

---

98   Ibid., 70.
99   Ibid., 71–2.
100 Ibid., 5–6, 31–2.
101 Ibid., 147.

A historian, who is not a mere collector of unrelated facts, or a mere antiquary or inconsequent analyst, cannot put together the smallest narrative of human doings unless he has a determined point of view, that is to say, a personal conviction of his own regarding the facts whose history he has undertaken to relate.[102]

In this passage Croce states his methodological notion of progress which he later contrasted with the metaphysical notion, like Hegel's. But even with this methodological concept of progress, Croce has brought history much closer to philosophy. In 1893, Croce had rejected the concept of progress as a basis for history, but in the *Estetica* he acknowledged it as a necessary presupposition for historical thought, although he did not work out the exact relationship between history and progress.

All in all, the status of history in the *Estetica* is still insecure. On the one hand it is still identified with art, or knowledge of the individual, on the other hand history seems to be based on philosophical concepts, which relate the individual representations to each other. Furthermore, the concept of history presupposes the notion of progress, although this notion is not further elaborated.

In spite of these shortcomings Croce's *Estetica* contains some interesting sections in which he deals with concrete problems of historical work. The most important is Croce's analysis of language, which would have important implications for his theory of historical understanding. In this context, Croce gives the example of an individual, A, who seeks the expression of an impression that he feels or anticipates. He tries various words and phrases which he rejects as inadequate and ugly, and finally he finds the right expression.[103] If another individual, B, now seeks to understand A's expression he 'must from necessity place himself at A's point of view, and go through the whole process again, with the help of the physical sign supplied to him by A'.[104]

Croce's example makes it clear that he thought of understanding as an activity which is possible because one individual is able to reconstruct the intuition behind the expression of another individual. Typically, the doctrine of the identity of intuition and expression leads Croce to the puzzling claim that misunderstanding between A and B is impossible: if A has seen clearly, B will see clearly too, and if A has seen unclearly, B will do so too.[105] Equally puzzling is Croce's claim that aesthetic problems can be solved in only one way, namely the right way, and along the same lines he holds that a work of art can only be understood in the right way. By the 'right way' Croce means the way in which

---

[102] Ibid., 134–5. English translation by Douglas Ainslie and Collingwood in Croce, *Aesthetic, As Science of Expression and General Linguistics*, MacMillan, New York, 1922, 133–4.

[103] B. Croce, *Estetica*, 130. B. Croce, *Aesthetics*, 1922, 118.

[104] Ibid., 121. Ibid., 119.

[105] Ibid.

the 'faculty of taste', which is the activity which judges, is completely identical to the productive activity of the poetic genius:

> To judge Dante, we must raise ourselves to his level: let it be well understood that empirically we are not Dante, nor Dante we; but in that moment of con-templation and judgement, our spirit is one with that of the poet, and in that moment we and he are one thing.[106]

In this example, Croce resolves the problem of historical understanding into the problem of being the right kind of man; only the man with the right taste is able to judge art. The man with the right taste in art is, of course, the aesthetician who has elaborated the right concept of art. However, Croce's theory obfuscates the problem of understanding, because if the interpreter has the right taste, and he nonetheless does not understand the poet, the fault will always be found with the latter. But for Croce this is not a problem; the man with the right taste will also rightly understand a work of art. Here we find Croce's firm belief in the philosophy of spirit, which makes a theory of understanding almost redundant; one who masters the concepts of the *Filosofia dello spirit* understands. Or, as E.F. Carritt (1876–1964), Collingwood's tutor, pointed out in 1914: 'for Croce the identity of expression between the poet and the interpreter, or between two individuals, is a presupposition and not a problem.'[107] To this verdict it may be added that Croce firmly believed that two minds can become one, because both are embodiments of the same universal spirit, which mediates between them.

History at the End of Gentile's Early Development

Although Gentile praised Croce's *Estetica* as the 'most important philosophical work published in Italy from the sixties onwards', he does not refrain from expressing two severe criticisms.[108] Firstly, he points out that Croce cannot ban metaphysics, because his own system is metaphysical in character: 'if the spirit is reality, it cannot be but a metaphysical reality.'[109] The second criticism concerns Croce's distinctions between the forms of the spirit, which Gentile finds too sharp. Art and philosophy, he says, are two aspects of reality that cannot be kept apart; if intuition passes over into the concept, as Croce says it does, there must already be a 'ray' of the concept 'shining' in the intuition.[110]

---

[106] Ibid., 133. Ibid., 121.

[107] E.F. Carritt, *The Theory of Beauty*, Methuen, London, 1914, 200.

[108] G. Gentile, Review of 'B. Croce, Tesi fondamentali di un'*Estetica* come scienza della espressione e linguistica generale', in *Giornale storico della letteratura italiana*, XXXVIII, 1901, cited from *Frammenti di Estetica e di teoria della storia*, I, OC XLVII, Le Lettere, Florence, 1992, 56.

[109] Ibid.

[110] G. Gentile, 'B. Croce, Estetica come scienza dell'espressione e linguistica generale', in *Giornale storico della letteratura italiana*, XLI, 1903, cited from *Frammenti di Estetica e di teoria della storia*, I, OC XLVII, Le Lettere, Florence, 1992, 84.

This way of criticising Croce is typical for Gentile, who was already working out a more monistic theory of the spirit. From this viewpoint, he no longer distinguished between reality *a parte obiecti* and reality *a parte subiecti*, or between metaphysics and the spirit, but regarded reality as identical with the spirit. Secondly, he agreed with Croce that we can distinguish certain aspects of reality, but he also pointed out that we should not forget how these aspects pass over into each other.[111]

Gentile did not confine himself to criticism, but also sought to advance his own doctrine. While Croce was working on the *Estetica*, Gentile himself had concentrated on the history of philosophy and on educational problems. These were the fields which formed the basis for his later metaphysics of the act of thought. In 1913, Gentile claimed that he made his first important advance in *L'insegnamento della filosofia* (*The Teaching of Philosophy*), an educational pamphlet of 1900. In this paper he overcame his erroneous 'Aristotelian conception of individuality', by which he meant individuality understood as a particular being without any universal aspect.[112] In this regard, Gentile referred to a passage in 'L'insegnamento della filosofia' in which he developed his thesis that philosophy is immanent in all man's activities: all men are members of a universal 'I' to the extent that they are consciously reflecting.

> The present is man as made [by the past]; the past is man himself (the same individual) as child, little boy, youngster, who has now grown up. But the child who became a little boy, is not dead; he has widened the circle of his vitality, he has begun to live more, developing a greater activity than before… There is something substantial in any man, something indelible, a foundation that nature posits, and which has to be taken into account. This is the individuality of the child and this will be the individuality of man.[113]

In this passage, we find Gentile's first acknowledgment of the historical individual. Its main characteristic is that it develops itself by preserving its own past. From this, Gentile draws the conclusion that an historical individual can only be understood by historical thought because the present always contains the past within itself:

> It is said that the past is pregnant with the present, and that is true; but it is no less true that the present is pregnant with the past, because it contains the past completely within itself, that is, that what was really vital in the past. Therefore, if we study the present first and then the past, we can be sure that, when studying the present, the past will sooner or later emerge from it. And thus the study of the past will necessarily impose itself when we really want to unravel the present.[114]

---

[111] Ibid.

[112] G. Gentile, 'Intorno all' idealismo attuale', 48–9.

[113] G. Gentile, *L'insegnamento della filsofia ne' licei, Saggio pedagogico*, Sandron, Milan, 1900, 97–8.

[114] Ibid., 99.

This passage strikingly foreshadows three important notions of Croce's and Gentile's later philosophy. Firstly, it expresses the idea that all historical knowledge originates from the present. Secondly, it explicitly presents history as the self-knowledge of the present. Thirdly, if the notion of the historical individual of the first passage is related to the idea of the second passage that history emerges from the present, the core of Gentile's later philosophy emerges; man is a self-conscious individual who develops himself out of his own past. The basis of man's self-development is therefore historical philosophy or philosophical history, which is the highest form of human self-knowledge. Or, as Gentile himself used to say: 'La filosofia è l'essenza del uomo' ('philosophy is the essence of Man').[115]

This immanence of philosophy in life forms the basis of Gentile's philosophy of history which he worked out in 'Il problema della filosofia della storia' ('The Problem of the Philosophy of History'), a paper which, ironically enough, Croce read in his absence at the Congress of Historical Science held in Rome in 1903.[116] In this paper Gentile defends not only the possibility but even the necessity of a philosophy of history in the metaphysical sense of the word. He argues that two antinomies, a metaphysical and an epistemological one, run between history and the philosophy of history. In the first place, Gentile says, history and the philosophy of history seem to have a different object; history deals with the relative, the circumstantiated, the individual, the *omnimodo determinato*, whereas philosophy deals with the absolute, the ideal and eternal, and the universal.[117] In the second place, history claims to be *a posteriori* knowledge expressed in assertoric judgments whereas philosophy deals with *a priori* knowledge and expresses itself in apodictic judgments.[118]

Gentile offers a most ingenious solution of the metaphysical antinomy. He points out that every fact is contingent and relative only when it is considered in isolation from other facts. But when a fact is seen as a moment in a series of historical events, it appears as a 'necessary consequence of its antecedents' and therefore as an '*a priori* determinable fact'.[119] This necessity implies the possibility of a logic of history, which integrates historical facts in a single whole.[120] In Gentile's view this logic of history is both the legitimate object of the philosophy

---

[115] G. Gentile, 'Il concetto della storia della filosofia', in *Rivista filosofica*, XI, 1908, cited from *La riforma della dialettica hegeliana*, Sansoni, Florence, 1975, 102. This is Gentile's Inaugural in Palermo delivered in 1907.

[116] G. Gentile, *Lettere a Benedetto Croce, Volume secondo, dal 1901 al 1906*, Sansoni, Florence, 1974, 11.

[117] G. Gentile, 'Il problema della filosofia della storia', in *Atti del Congresso internazionale di scienze storiche, Roma 1–9 Aprile, 1903*, vol. III, Accademia dei Lincei, Roma 1906, cited from *Frammenti di Estetica e di teoria della storia*, II, OC XLVIII, Le Lettere, Florence, 1992, 141.

[118] Ibid., 142.

[119] Ibid., 145.

[120] Ibid.

of history and the basis of historiography as a form of knowledge. Surprisingly, Gentile does not fully apply the solution of the metaphysical antinomy to the solution of the epistemological antinomy because he still distinguishes between 'pure history' or 'historiography', and 'philosophy of history'. In historiography the logical necessity of historical fact is implicitly appealed to by the historian and therefore historiography forms the basis for the philosopher of history, who explains the logic on which it rests:

> Thus the philosopher of history presupposes the full knowledge of history as the material for his philosophising and he can not have another function (aim) than the discovery of the internal logic of events, as he sees them in history, as offered to him by historiography. In this logic of events resides not only the legitimacy of the philosophy of history, but also that of history.[121]

This passage shows, on the one hand, that Gentile does not yet completely identify history and philosophy; he still regards history as the 'material' for philosophy which is therefore not without presuppositions. On the other hand, Gentile indicates that both historiography and the philosophy of history find their *ratio essendi* in the 'logic of history'. From this conclusion it is only one step to a full identification of philosophy and history. Soon after this paper Gentile developed the thesis that philosophy is the *a priori* of all thought and therefore of all human activity. From this it follows that philosophy does not presuppose history as 'material', but that history presupposes philosophy because all human activity is based on *a priori* principles.

Gentile's paper of 1903 marks the point from which he would definitely depart from Croce. In the *Estetica* Croce maintained his rejection of the philosophy of history, but Gentile defended it in a convincing manner as the logical necessity of historical fact. From 1903, Croce would cling to his methodological view of philosophy and gradually resolved philosophy into history, whereas Gentile kept to his idea of philosophy as knowledge of the *a priori* and resolved history into philosophy.

---

[121] Ibid., 146.

Chapter Two

Croce's Middle Development and His System (1903–1917)

Introduction

In 1903, Croce and Gentile founded *La Critica*, which soon became the leading journal of art, history, and philosophy in Italy. A year later, starting from his position in the *Estetica*, Croce took up the problem of the relationship between art, science, history, and philosophy. In 1895, Croce had claimed that art and history belong to the 'practical sciences', although he did not exactly specify what their relationship was. In the *Estetica* he had made some progress on this point by admitting that history applies philosophical concepts. In this way, he identified history with the perception of reality, which he saw as a necessary condition for action. At the same time, Croce did not show how history yields knowledge of reality, because he still identified history with art.

About the same time, Croce realised that if history was to fulfil its practical function, it had to be more than art. In his view, this meant that he somehow had to acknowledge the conceptual basis of history. Yet, at the same time, Croce was aware that history cannot be based on concepts alone. Given the parameters of his system, Croce's main problem was therefore to steer history between art and philosophy. In *Lineamenti di una Logica come scienza del concetto puro* (*Outlines of Logic as a Science of the Pure Concept*) published in 1905, which was widely read in Italy and abroad, Croce made a first attempt to solve this problem.[1] The first reader of the *Lineamenti* was Gentile, who generally approved of Croce's logical explorations, but also had some severe criticisms. In this context, he advised his friend to read Hegel. Following this, Croce immersed himself completely in Hegel's works for more than a year.[2] In 1907, this study resulted in *Ciò che è vivo e ciò che è morto della filosofia di Hegel* (*What is Living and What is Dead in the Philosophy of Hegel*), which is still one of the most influential yet controversial

---

[1] B. Croce, *Lineamenti di una Logica come scienza del concetto puro, Memoria letta all'Accademia Pontaniana*, Giannini, Napoli, 1905.

[2] B. Croce, *Contributo alla critica di me stesso*, 345.

accounts of Hegel's philosophy. By studying Hegel, Croce reported in 1915, he was able to overcome some of the weaknesses that beset his *Estetica* and to refine his own views with regard to the relationship between history, philosophy, and action. On this basis, Croce definitely founded his system with *Logica come scienza del concetto puro* and *Filosofia della pratica* which form the second and third volume of the *Filosofia dello spirito*.[3] After this, Croce was still not entirely satisfied with the position of history in his system, which he began to revise from 1911 onwards. The final result of this revision was *Teoria e storia della storiografia*, the fourth of the *Filosofia dello spirito* published in 1917, which was to become a classic in the philosophy of history.

Looking back on these years, the 50-year-old Croce wrote in his personal notebook:

> Rethinking my youth and the anxiety I sometimes had of dying without having done anything, I think, that if I die now, I have at least done three important things. 1) in epistemology, that philosophy is methodology, and nothing else, but just because it is so, it is everything and it endows everything; 2) in historiography that all true history is always contemporary history; 3) in aesthetics that art is lyrical intuition (and the resulting individualistic or personalistic notion of history of literature and art).[4]

With the three doctrines mentioned in this passage, Croce claimed that he had solved the main problems of the philosophy of the spirit. The doctrine of philosophy as methodology of history solved the problem of the relationship between philosophy and history. The doctrine of the 'contemporaneity of the past', according to which all history originates from practical interests in the present, solved the problem of the relationship between theory and practice. Finally, with the doctrine of art as lyrical intuition Croce established his view of art as the expression of emotions.

In this chapter, the first two doctrines will be discussed in the context of Croce's philosophical development between 1903 and 1917. Special attention will be paid to Croce's conception of the relationship between art, history, and philosophy on the one hand, and the relationship between theory and practice on the other. The further implications of the doctrine of art as lyrical intuition will be discussed in chapter 6.

History in the *Outlines of Logic as Science of the Pure Concept* (1905)

Originally, Croce's *Lineamenti di una Logica come scienza del concetto puro* was a series of lectures read for the *Accademia Pontaniana* in 1904–05. The title of Croce's first 'logical investigations' shows that he saw logic as a 'science'. In his

---

3   Ibid., 346–8.
4   Cited by Giuseppe Galasso, *Croce e lo spirito del suo tempo*, Mondadori, Milano, 1990, 201.

own terms, logic is a 'speculative' account of the 'formal' aspects of thought.[5] In this view, logic is the part of 'general gnoseology', which deals with knowledge of the universal, the other part being aesthetics, which deals with art as knowledge of the individual.[6] Central to Croce's gnoseology is the idea that knowledge of the individual, which is expressed in language, forms the basis of thought which operates with 'pure concepts'.[7] In Croce's system, art forms the basis of conceptual thought, because all concepts can only be expressed in language. However, this primacy of art and language does not condition the formal aspect of the pure concepts, which 'transcend' the changeable and multifarious intuitions by the constant unity of their universality.[8] Art, or more precisely intuition-expressions, form the starting point for thought.

According to Croce, concepts are 'pure' in two senses. Firstly, concepts are pure because they 'transcend' the individuality of intuition-expressions. Secondly, concepts are 'pure' with regard to the practical activities of the spirit. Concepts with which these practical activities 'interfere', that is, concepts which are formed with a practical goal in mind, are not pure concepts, but 'pseudo-concepts', or 'conceptual fictions'.[9] In Croce's view, pseudo-concepts comprise all abstract universals of science which are not true, but useful.[10] Practical man, Croce explains, is able to 'abstract' certain common features from his perceptions in order to make 'conceptual fictions' of them. Croce illustrates this point by comparing a painter and a horse-dealer. The painter represents horses in their individuality; all horses are different to him and he tries to render these differences as true as possible. But the horse-dealer is not interested in the individuality of the horses, but only in some of their qualities, like their height, colour, resistance to diseases, and so forth. In order to choose the right horse, the horse-dealer forms an abstract concept, which more or less 'recapitulates' all these features in a conceptual fiction or 'pseudo-concept'.[11] In this sense of 'recapitulating', the 'pseudo-concept' is an abstraction, or 'summary of reality'. In this context, Croce explicitly compares pseudo-concepts with 'indexes' or 'labels' which refer to aspects of reality that are important for action.[12] Croce sharply distinguishes pseudo-concepts which are based on the perception of reality from another kind of pseudo-concepts which are found in mathematics. These pseudo-concepts do not presuppose perception, but intuitions.[13] In the second edition of the *Logica* Croce calls these concepts, like 'triangle' and 'circle',

---

5   B. Croce, *Lineamenti di una Logica*, 9.
6   Ibid., 12–13.
7   Ibid., 14.
8   Ibid., 14, 19.
9   Ibid., 18–19.
10 Ibid., 62–3.
11 Ibid., 64.
12 Ibid., 65.
13 Ibid., 80.

'abstract' or 'mathematical pseudo-concepts', in order to distinguish them from the 'empirical pseudo-concepts', like 'horse', 'house', 'rose', which are based on sense-perception.[14] Both kinds of pseudo-concepts presuppose the practical activities of the mind and this sets them off from the pure concepts.

On the basis of this theory of concepts, Croce builds his theory of judgment. In his view, judgments consisting of pseudo-concepts, as we find them in physics and mathematics, are not judgments in the strict sense of the word, since they are never true, but only useful. Accordingly, Croce only recognises three forms of true judgment. First, there is the aesthetic judgment, which is 'extraneous to' or 'independent from' logic and therefore identical to art.[15] Secondly, he recognises the 'defining judgment', which coincides with the pure concept and which is identical to philosophy.[16] Thirdly, he recognises the 'individual judgment', which is 'posterior with regard to the concept' and which is identical to history.[17]

With this definition of the individual or historical judgment, Croce distinguishes art and philosophy from history. In this connection, Croce points out that history depends on the 'results' of intuition and philosophy; the historian 'thinks out' the meaning of his intuitions on the basis of the pure concepts which are 'given' to him by philosophy.[18] History thus presupposes art and philosophy, which Croce regards as distinct cognitive activities.

After this preparatory work, Croce tries to solve the problem of the distinction of art and history as he had left it in the *Estetica*. Unlike art, Croce avers, history is concerned with the real. In this respect history is similar to philosophy which is also knowledge of the real. But history is not to be identified with philosophy, because it is knowledge of the individual and not of the universal. Croce's problem in the *Lineamenti* is therefore to describe history as knowledge of the real without turning it into philosophy.

Surprisingly enough for a philosopher who eschewed metaphysics, he solved this problem with the help of the ontological argument. According to Croce, the pure concept, which is the object of philosophy, guarantees its own reality; the maxim *essentia involvit existentiam* applies to all pure concepts.[19] For example, in the judgment 'virtue is knowledge' the existence of both concepts is presupposed. Collingwood, who took Croce's use of the ontological argument very seriously, later formulated the latter's position as: 'the concepts of philosophy are functions of thought, universal and necessary: to affirm them is simply for thought to think itself.'[20]

---

14 B. Croce, *Logica*, 15–18.
15 B. Croce, *Lineamenti di una Logica*, 21–2.
16 Ibid., 23.
17 Ibid., 22.
18 Ibid., 61.
19 Ibid., 27.
20 R.G. Collingwood, *The Idea of History*, 197.

In connection to history, Croce explains that the ontological proof cannot be applied to the individual judgment, because the subject of the individual judgment is an intuition, which does not necessarily imply its existence. The subject of the judgment 'Napoleon existed' does not exist anymore, and the subject of the judgment 'Frenchmen exist' will not necessarily exist in the future.[21] At the same time, both the past and present reality of these subjects cannot be denied. How then are we to account for this strange mixture of reality and unreality of the subjects of individual judgment? Croce answers this question by pointing out that only in the individual judgment is existence to be conceived as a predicate.[22] With this claim Croce challenged a long tradition in philosophy, and his argument shows that he was aware of that. All critics of the ontological argument from Gaunilo (?–1083) to Kant had warned that 'existence' cannot be a predicate. If the predication of existence is allowed, the danger arises that all our fantasies from the golden mountain to 100 dollars can be conceived as real. Croce acknowledges this danger and justifies his claim by a long discussion of the concept of existence, which illustrates how Croce endeavoured to tackle the problem of the relationship between historical judgment and the past.

Croce starts from the view that 'the criterion of existence is not given by the theoretical form alone, but can be given by the reflection of the theoretical form on the other forms of the spirit'.[23] This puzzling claim is illustrated by a line from a poem by Horace: 'Vides ut alta stet nive candidum Soracte' ('Seest thou how Soracte stands glistening in its mantle of snow').[24] According to Croce's division of judgments, this line must be regarded as an aesthetic judgment. It is clearly not concerned with the reality of its object; we never know whether the snow was really high on Mount Soracte or not, because Horace himself did not distinguish between imagination and reality when he wrote his poem.[25] But in spite of this, Croce explains, it is a fact that the line was formed in Horace's mind; this line must therefore have had a 'sufficient reason'.[26] In order to determine this reason Croce distinguishes between a practical and a theoretical form of experience. In his view, Mount Soracte can exist in the practical form of experience, for example, as an object of desire, without being existent for the theoretical form of the spirit.[27] However, this practical form of existence, which is completely ideal, may become real on the basis of the theoretical form which

---

21 B. Croce, *Lineamenti di una Logica*, 46.
22 Ibid.
23 Ibid., 49.
24 Ibid., 50. English translation by C.E. Bennet in Horace, *The Odes and Epodes, Liber I, Carmen IX*, in *The Loeb Classical Library*, Heinemann, Harvard University Press, London, Cambridge, Massachussets, 1960, 28–9.
25 Ibid., 50.
26 Ibid.
27 Ibid., 51.

elaborates the distinctions between the ideal and the real by a process of reflection.

By this argument, Croce took an interesting position between nominalism and realism, which he tried to fuse by describing a process of reflection which turns intuitions into historical facts. First, Croce says, there are ideal objects, and then there is an act of thought by which we determine their reality. Suppose, Croce says, that we want to determine whether there was really snow on Mount Soracte. In order to tackle this problem we must use Horace's text as evidence referring to a past reality, and ask ourselves questions like 'When did he write the poem?', and 'Could he really see Mount Soracte when he wrote it?'. Only by answering this kind of question are we able to 'predicate our intuitions' with the concepts of existence, that is, accept Horace's description of Mount Soracte in the snow as an historical fact.

Along these lines, Croce tries to justify his view of history as the 'outcome' of art and philosophy. On the one hand, history shares its imaginative character with art, but on the other hand it shares its conceptual, and *ipso facto* its existential, character with philosophy. As a result of this, history always comes after art and philosophy; its status is that of a product or construction of both the imaginative and conceptual activities of the mind. Most interestingly, this 'historical construction of past reality' is produced by a process of asking and answering questions, which start from imagination, and through the interference of philosophy ends with history.[28]

With this theory, Croce anticipates the logic of question and answer, which was central to his own logic as well as to those of de Ruggiero and Collingwood. In its early version, Croce still keeps history and philosophy separate as two distinct cognitive processes; the philosophical elaboration of concepts clearly precedes their application in history. This view of the relationship between philosophy and history suggests that historians are patiently waiting for philosophers to work out the meaning of the pure concepts before they apply them.

In practice historians do indeed use philosophical concepts, but they also think out concepts for themselves, as concepts such as 'Renaissance', 'Risorgimento', and 'Industrial Revolution' show. Though Croce did not address this important aspect of historical thought, his theory enabled him to improve his view of history as perception, as formulated in the *Estetica*. In the *Lineamenti* Croce claims that all our perceptive judgments are always historical judgments, because, when we perceive a fact, it is already a past fact. For Croce therefore 'the only present is the past'.[29] Perception is also a construction, but not of 'la realtà accaduta' (past reality), but of the 'realtà di fatto' (actual or factual reality).[30] To give Croce's own example: the individual judgment 'this is a dog'

---

[28]   Ibid., 13.
[29]   Ibid., 53.
[30]   Ibid., 13.

involves a representation, the concept of dog, and the application of the notion of existence to the representation that turns it into a perception.[31] Croce thus links his linguistic theory to a form of conceptual realism; we start with a representation, which we name 'dog'; next, we turn this representation into a concept, to be precise, an empirical pseudo-concept by our judgment 'this is a dog'. This judgment is ultimately based on pure concepts, by which we define reality as such.

Collingwood later contrasted Croce's conceptual realism with the nominalism of the Germans. For the nominalist all concepts are mere fictions, or constructions of the mind, and this implies that the word 'dog' is a mere word that we may apply or not. For Croce 'dog' is a concept, or to be precise, a pseudo-concept. This is also a construction, but one that presupposes the pure concepts. Therefore, Collingwood says, the judgment 'that is a dog' is not an arbitrary use of words, but a perception based on the total system of pseudo-concepts and pure concepts, or in short, our conception of reality as a whole.[32]

Given this theory of judgment, the notion of 'error' becomes highly problematic, because how are we to distinguish between true and false statements if arbitrariness is *a priori* ruled out? Being aware of this problem, Croce identifies error quite vaguely with 'the unreal', but at the same time he does not deny the reality of error; errors are unreal, because they are 'unthinkable', yet they do exist in the sense that they are committed in reality. This position is obviously unsatisfactory because it amounts to saying that we are both capable and incapable of thinking the unthinkable. In his *Lineamenti* Croce does not solve this paradox, but points out that error always arises from a confusion of the different activities of the mind.[33] For example, when artists claim truth for their works, or when practical men claim truth for their ideals. Along these lines, Croce concludes that errors are to some extent 'professional' since everyone tends to exaggerate the importance of his own activity.[34]

What is Living and What is Dead in the Philosophy of Hegel (1907)

Gentile immediately acknowledged the importance of Croce's *Lineamenti*, but had some difficulties with the latter's doctrine of error. In 1905, he wrote to Croce that he ought to distinguish more clearly between 'impersonal error as a moment of truth in the history of ideas' and 'personal error', which has no such place in the history of ideas.[35] Here Gentile employed his own dialectical conception of thought according to which error only exists for the act of thought which

---

31 Ibid., 53.
32 R.G. Collingwood, *The Idea of History*, 197.
33 B. Croce, *Lineamenti di una Logica*, 98–9.
34 Ibid., 100–1.
35 G. Gentile, *Lettere a Benedetto Croce, Volume secondo, dal 1901 al 1906*, 245–6, date 2 October 1905.

corrects it. According to Croce, this doctrine was wrong because it interpreted error as a 'moment of truth'. Truth and error, Croce wrote to his friend, must be distinguished more thoroughly because error is not a form of thought.

In spite of Croce's reply, Gentile still hoped to convert Croce to a more dialectical view of thought, and suggested that he translate Hegel's *Enzyklopädie der philosophischen Wissenschaften* for the *Biblioteca Filosofica* of their common editor Laterza. Gentile's hopes were more than fulfilled; Croce not only translated the *Enzyklopädie*, but also wrote *Ciò che è vivo e ciò che è morto della filosofia di Hegel* as a 'critical introduction' to it.

By criticising Hegel, Croce laid the foundations of his own philosophy. First, along the lines of the idea of philosophy as the elaboration of concepts, Croce interpreted Hegel's dialectic as a philosophical method and not as a metaphysic. Secondly, Croce did not replace Hegel's theory of opposite concepts with a theory of distinct concepts as some interpreters have suggested. Croce explicitly agreed with Hegel that philosophy proceeds by opposition, and he acknowledged dialectic as a valid philosophical method. According to Croce, Hegel's conception of dialectic was not wrong, but he 'abused' it by applying it to distinct concepts.

Of two distinct pure concepts a and b, Croce explains, the first does not presuppose b, whereas b presupposes a. Moreover, both concepts are concrete, that is, they are universals applicable to all aspects of reality. On this point, Croce's own example shows that he had the concepts of the mental activities in mind. For a and b he takes art and philosophy; philosophy without art is abstract whereas art is autonomous in the sense that it does not presuppose philosophy.[36] In contrast to distinct concepts, two opposite concepts α and β are both abstract, neither of the two is universally applicable to reality; only their synthesis γ is concrete. In other words, two abstract opposite concepts presuppose the concrete concept, whereas only one of the distinct terms presupposes the other. As an example, Croce takes the first triad of Hegel's logic 'being, nothing, and becoming'. Of these concepts 'being' and 'nothing' are abstract; because reality is in the first place becoming.[37]

Because of their different logical relationships, the two series of concepts proceed in a different way. The series of distinct concepts proceeds by dyads, in which both terms are concrete, whereas the opposites proceed in triads of which only the third term is concrete. The main difference between the two series is that the first term of the dyad is 'suppressed as independent and conserved as dependent', whereas the two abstract terms of the triad are both 'suppressed and conserved'.[38] As an example, Croce argues that philosophy builds on art, but

---

36   B. Croce, *Ciò che è vivo e ciò che è morto della filosofia di Hegel*, 59–60.

37   Ibid., 60–1.

38   Ibid., 61.

does not replace it, whereas the abstract opposite concepts being and nothing are superseded by the more concrete concept of becoming.

According to Croce, Hegel confused the two logical orders; on the one hand he treated opposite concepts as distinct concepts, and on the other hand he dealt with distinct concepts as if they were opposites.[39] This confusion of the logical orders led to an overall abuse of dialectic in his philosophical system.

Firstly, the abuse of dialectic led Hegel to the conversion of opposite concepts into distinct concepts. According to Croce, this abuse is exemplified in the *Science of Logic*, where Hegel deals with philosophical errors as if they were partial truths, or 'moments' of truth leading to higher truths. Croce most emphatically rejects this view; truth never proceeds on the basis of error, but only on the basis of truth itself.[40] Nor can error ever be considered as 'partial truth', as Hegel held. For this reason, Croce rejects the concept of being as the beginning of philosophy. For Hegel philosophy should begin with the concept of being since this concept, being completely empty, expressed the poorest truth of reality.[41] But Croce does not distinguish between 'poorer' and 'richer' truths and accordingly holds that the beginning of philosophy cannot be determined. Philosophy, Croce says, makes part of the 'circle of the spirit', keeping its place between art and action.[42]

Secondly, the abuse of dialectic led to a conversion of distinct concepts into opposite concepts. This abuse led Hegel to consider art, history, and science as erroneous forms of philosophy, which need to be corrected by philosophy itself.[43] Croce saw this doctrine as the origin of Hegel's errors in the philosophy of mind, the philosophy of history, and in the philosophy of nature. In the philosophy of mind the abuse of dialectic led Hegel to consider art and philosophy as opposite concepts. Art, being an imperfect form of philosophy, ceases to be an autonomous activity of the mind and 'passes' into real thought, or philosophy. This analysis brought Hegel to the false view that language must be regarded as an imperfect form of logic.[44]

According to Croce the conversion of distinct concepts into opposite concepts also led Hegel to his reinterpretation of history on a dialectical basis. This amounts to imposing the dialectic on historical facts. As an illustration of this abuse Croce refers to Hegel's idea of history as the progress of liberty stipulating that only one was free in the Oriental world, some were free in the Graeco-Roman world, and all were free in the Germanic world.[45] In Croce's view, this kind of 're-making' of history on a philosophical basis is completely mistaken,

---

39   Ibid., 64.
40   Ibid., 68–71.
41   Ibid., 74–6.
42   Ibid., 74.
43   Ibid., 80–4.
44   Ibid., 84.
45   Ibid., 119.

because history is already philosophical. In this connection, he refers to the passage in the *Lineamenti* where he points out that history contains the universal concepts within itself in the form of the predicates in the individual judgments.[46]

In spite of his severe criticisms, however, Croce fully understood Hegel's motives. Hegel, Croce explains, was looking for an objective measure to distinguish between important and less important facts, or necessary and contingent facts.[47] This distinction lay at the basis of the problem of 'the interesting content', which brought Croce to philosophy in the 1890s. For this reason, Croce fully agrees with Hegel's motives, but he also points out that it is impossible to establish the idea of historical importance *a priori*.[48] Only with respect to a certain theme, or point of view, can facts be seen as important or unimportant, Croce says.[49] Following his own methodological notion of progress as expounded in the *Estetica*, Croce stresses the importance of a point of view in history. Last but not least, Croce accuses Hegel of correcting natural science by his dialectic in his philosophy of nature. According to Croce, these corrections were completely unnecessary, because natural science is not a form of knowledge but a form of practice. For this reason, the concepts of science cannot be treated philosophically because they are not true, but only useful.[50]

Croce's final judgment of Hegel is highly critical: since the German had not sufficiently distinguished distinct and opposite concepts, he had falsely applied the logic of opposite concepts to distinct concepts and vice versa. This confusion led him to an all-pervading panlogism in which he tried to reconcile history and nature by imposing the laws of opposition upon them. On this feeble basis, Hegel raised the pseudo-problem of the transitions from the idea to nature and from nature to the absolute spirit. But in Croce's view, this problem could never be solved, because Hegel himself saw nature and history as distinct realms of reality, from which it follows that they cannot be reconciled by a third term. In short, Croce judges, contrary to his intentions, Hegel never overcame the old dualism of nature and spirit.[51]

On this basis, Croce formulates the new task of philosophy as the 'reconciliation' of Hegel's dialectic and the theory of distinct concepts.[52] This task comprises in the first place of the old problem of the relationship of dualism between nature and spirit, and must be solved by denying it, since the forms of the spirit are constitutive of reality. In the second place, philosophy must reinterpret the spirit as a unity of distinct forms of independent activities with their own principles and methods. From this viewpoint, the dialectic of opposites is

---

46 Ibid., 89–91.
47 Ibid., 96–7.
48 Ibid., 96.
49 Ibid., 98.
50 Ibid., 99–102.
51 Ibid., 126–33.
52 Ibid., 134.

not active between the forms but within them; art seeks beauty by overcoming ugliness, philosophy seeks truth by overcoming error, the economic form of the spirit seeks utility by overcoming inutility, and finally moral form seeks goodness by overcoming evil.[53] With these tasks, Croce set the agenda for his own *Filosofia dello spirito*.

Gentile's Criticism of Croce's Interpretation of Hegel

When Gentile read Croce's book on Hegel in 1906, he realised that his friend had gone in the wrong direction. Immediately he wrote 'La teoria dell'errore' ('The Theory of Error'), a small but highly critical review of *Ciò che è vivo e ciò che è morto della filosofia di Hegel*, though he did not send it to his friend. Only in 1921, when his friendship with Croce was already waning, did Gentile venture to publish this review in his own journal.[54] As in his criticisms of Croce's *Lineamenti*, Gentile aims his arrows on Croce's theory of error, but he adds a criticism of the theory of distinct concepts upon which it was built. According to Gentile, the theory of distinct concepts is based on a failure to sufficiently distinguish between the real and the ideal. From an empirical or historical point of view, Gentile points out, art never passes over into philosophy; art is art and does not contradict itself. But from an ideal point of view art must pass over into philosophy; the spirit cannot rest in the artistic contemplation of reality and must proceed to philosophical reflection. This reflection is not, as Croce thinks, cut loose from art, but unites with it.[55] From this it follows that there is only one true concept, namely philosophy, from which art and abstract philosophy may be distinguished.[56] On this basis, Gentile concludes that the relationship between art and philosophy is not dyadic, and claims that Croce's dyads are all resolvable in triads, because the nexus of distinct concepts presupposes the synthesis of opposites.[57] In other words, art and philosophy are not two distinct concepts where art does not presuppose philosophy, whereas philosophy presupposes art, but philosophy is immanent in art as its 'self-consciousness', and at the same time art is immanent in philosophy as the first step from which reflection begins.[58]

Gentile's criticism reveals his absolute immanentist conception of art and philosophy as universal and necessary mental activities, each having the characteristics of both. Philosophy is immanent in art, or in other words, art is a self-conscious activity. Vice versa, art is immanent in philosophy as the first step of

---

53 Ibid., 61–2.
54 G. Gentile, 'La teoria dell'errore come momento dialettico e il rapporto tra arte e filosofia', cited from *Frammenti di estetica e di teoria della storia*, I, OC XLVII, Le Lettere, Florence, 1992, 86–94.
55 Ibid., 92–3.
56 Ibid., 90–1.
57 Ibid., 89.
58 Ibid., 90.

philosophical reflection. From this point of view, Croce's concepts of art and philosophy are merely empirical in the sense that they do not apply to all mental activities. In particular, Croce emphatically refuses to apply the term philosophy to artistic activities. In his view art is autonomous; it does not need philosophy in order to express itself and consequently art does not necessarily pass over into philosophy as Gentile would have it. From the latter's point of view, however, Croce mistakenly pushes the notion of the self-conscious out of sight; in order to develop itself, art must be aware of the principles on which it rests. From Croce's point of view, Gentile, by identifying the principles of art with those like the philosophy of Hegel, simply fails to acknowledge the autonomy of art.

This controversy between Croce and Gentile perfectly illustrates their philosophical differences concerning the relationship of mental activities. In this sense, Croce's main aim is to provide a philosophical basis for judging the concrete experience of mental activities, that is, concrete works of art, historical and philosophical writing, and the deeds of men of action. From this point of view, it is important to distinguish between various activities as given in our empirical, or historical, experience of them: a work of art must be judged as art, a work of history as history, etc. Croce's main problem was to develop a philosophical method based on a system of concepts which helps to clarify the differences between the various mental activities in the first place. Given this aim, Croce rejects Hegel's dialectic as a philosophical method, because its concepts tend to blur the distinctions between the various mental activities.

Gentile's starting point is also concrete experience, but unlike Croce he always regarded it as a fusion of the real and the ideal, or the historical and the *a priori*. His main philosophical aim was to understand the ideal or *a priori* aspect of the activities of the mind. In other words, Gentile wanted to understand the principles upon which art, history, and philosophy are based. Accordingly, his problem was to formulate a theory which explains the activity of mental processes. From this point of view Hegel's dialectic describes these processes fairly well, though Gentile rejected it because it does not describe mental activities, but concepts in themselves.[59]

The Further Development of the *Philosophy of the Spirit*: *Philosophy of the Practical* (1909)

After his clash with Hegel, Croce was convinced that his theory of distinct concepts could carry the weight of his system. Interestingly, the first problem to which he applied his new method was the problem of the relationship between theory and practice. In the *Estetica*, this problem was still left unsolved. On the one hand, Croce had claimed that practice presupposes theory, although he had not elaborated this view, on the other hand, he had not shown how practice passes over into theory.

---

[59] See chapter 3, p. 77.

In *Filosofia della pratica*, the third volume of *La Filosofia dello spirito* finished in 1908, Croce tried to solve these problems by applying the thesis, developed from his criticism of Hegel, that there is no beginning in the philosophy of the spirit. According to Croce, the activity of the spirit does not 'begin', but proceeds in a 'circle', and therefore the central task of philosophy is to elucidate the forms of experience in a system of distinct concepts that form the circle.[60] Croce enters the circle at the point of the expession of intuition, which he regards as a necessary condition for philosophy. Intuitions and philosophical concepts subsequently form historical knowledge, which Croce identifies with perception which forms the necessary basis for action as he had already done in the *Estetica*. Along the same lines, he distinguishes action into two forms: economic action and moral action.[61]

To this circle of the spirit Croce applies his theory of distinct concepts; every subsequent form of the spirit presupposes a previous form, but not vice versa — philosophy presupposes art, but art does not presuppose philosophy; economic action presupposes both art and philosophy but not vice versa, and moral action presupposes economic action. Moreover, Croce stresses that each of the four distinct forms is internally structured as a synthesis of opposites; art poses beauty against ugliness, logic truth against error, economic action utility against inutility, and moral action the good against the bad. In this context, Croce is careful not to blur the distinctions. Beauty and truth must not be mingled with morality; a work of art must be judged by aesthetic standards, knowledge by philosophical standards. Similarly, theory and practice are carefully distinguished; knowledge must be judged by the standard of truth, and practice by standards of utility and morality. In Croce's view these four forms exhaust the activity of the spirit. All other forms, like feeling, religion, and metaphysics, for which a claim has been made by philosophers in the past, are 'subsumed' *secundum artem* under one of the four forms.[62]

Interestingly, Croce does not acknowledge history as a distinct form of experience, although it plays a very important double role in the circle. In the theoretical sphere, it appears as the outcome of art and philosophy as the highest form of knowledge, and in the practical sphere as the 'result' of all action as concrete history or as *res gestae*, thus showing a tacit realism by distinguishing between history as knowledge and history as past action. Following Croce's own agenda at the end of his book on Hegel, the renewed theory of the circle can therefore best be regarded as a theory of the logical and ontological status of activities of the spirit. Seen from a philosophical point of view, the circle of the spirit is a theory of mental processes which seeks to solve the problem of their unity and distinction. Seen from a logical point of view, the theory tries to des-

---

[60]   B. Croce, *Pratica*, 193–4.
[61]   Ibid., 201.
[62]   Ibid., 81, 196, 295.

cribe the presuppositions of the mental activities. Applied to history, Croce's 'circle of the spirit' can be interpreted as a theory of history as thought and action.

Though Croce indicates that we can enter the circle at any point, he first approaches it from the theoretical sphere. Here, Croce describes history along the lines of the *Lineamenti*, that is, as the result of art and philosophy. History is defined as individual judgment and identified with perception, the indispensable basis for action. As an illustration of this claim, Croce gives the example of cutting wood in order to make a fire that will warm someone in the cold of winter. According to Croce, this action is based on all kinds of perceptual judgments like 'it is cold', 'this is wood', and so forth. From a formal point of view these perceptions are identical with individual judgments, or history *tout court*. History is therefore the necessary theoretical basis of action, though it must not be confused with action itself; making judgments is a theoretical activity, cutting wood a practical one.[63]

Underneath this interpretation of the relationship between history and action lies Croce's view that the theoretical sphere of the spirit is not productive, whereas the practical always creates something new; history is contemplative, action is creative. Croce makes this clear by pointing out that a change of reality is always due to the will, and not to thought:

> Given the first factual situation and its complete elaboration in the judgment, no other judgment can be formed when the factual situation does not change, or if something new does not impose itself. This new thing is always my will, which, when the situation changes, provides material for a new judgment.[64]

By this statement, Croce expresses a version of the primacy of the practical according to which action forms the basis of all change. This includes conceptual change, because only action can create new situations that call for new judgments. Vice versa, however, judgments never change situations.

According to Croce, history is the only form of knowledge that can deal with these new situations; 'feeling', 'intuition', and 'conceptual thought' are explicitly ruled out as a basis for action.[65] Even the so-called 'practical judgments', by which the possible benefits of an action are established, are not a proper basis for action.[66] To give Croce's own example; when it is winter and cold and I have some wood near me, I do not first judge these facts, and then analyse my will leading to practical judgments like 'it is good to warm my body' and 'it is good to cut the wood and use it for that purpose', and so forth. I simply say: 'I want to cut wood', and this implies that it is good to do so. To say that something is

---

[63] Ibid., 25.
[64] Ibid., 28.
[65] Ibid., 14, 26.
[66] Ibid., 26–9.

good, Croce concludes, is synonymous with willing it.[67] With this thesis, Croce obviously seeks to vindicate the freedom of the will, which does not even presuppose any valuation. This view implies that it is not a task for history to decide between practical goals; after all, the historian is a 'contemplator', not a 'man of action'.

After distinguishing between theory and practice, Croce describes the forms of the will. Will begins as an intention following upon the judgment of the situation. In analogy to the doctrine of the identity of intuition and expression in the *Estetica*, Croce points out that it is impossible to conceive of an intention which is not also already action; to will something is similar to doing something, because no intention is possible without consequences. Croce illustrates this claim with the example that we do not first intend to move our arms or legs and then do it, but intention and movement form a unity.[68] Croce generalises this view as follows:

> Each volition, however small it may be, sets the organism in motion and produces so-called external effects: a proposal is already an execution, a beginning of fight; and even simple wishing is not without effects, because it is possible to be consumed by our wishes as it is said.[69]

This passage illustrates Croce's theory of the 'identity' of the will with action, which anticipates the identity of philosophy and history, the cornerstone of his philosophy, formulated a year later in the second edition of his *Logica*.

After dealing with the relationship between history and action, Croce distinguishes two forms of action; economic action and moral action. Economic action is that which wills and carries out that which corresponds to the factual conditions in which the individual finds himself. Moral action not only carries out the will in correspondence to factual conditions, but also refers to something which transcends them. Whereas economic action aims at individual ends, moral action aims at universal ends. The basis for economic action is a judgment concerning the greater or lesser consistency of action taken in itself, whereas moral action is based on a judgment concerning the greater or lesser consistency of the action with respect to the universal goal that transcends the individual.[70]

Economic and moral actions are distinct forms in Croce's sense of the word; moral action presupposes economic action in the sense that we cannot realise our universal ends without taking the factual conditions into account. On this point, history enters the circle: all actions can be judged by a 'practical judgment' which is identical to individual judgment, or history; to judge an action is the same as giving a history of it.[71] Having identified will with action Croce warns

---

[67] Ibid., 27–8.
[68] Ibid., 46–7.
[69] Ibid., 48.
[70] Ibid., 203.
[71] Ibid., 56–7.

that action can never be judged on the grounds of its success; practical judgment concerns the will, not its consequences. The final effect of the will depends on other actions as well. On this basis, Croce makes a fundamental distinction between *azione* and *accadimento*. It is difficult to render the exact meaning of these terms in English, but Croce explains that *azione* (action) is 'the work of the individual', whereas *accadimento* may be seen as history as a whole, or universal history. According to Croce, it is impossible to judge this universal history; practical judgment concerns action alone and never the *accadimento* which is the object of so-called 'cosmic judgment'.[72] Stripped of its metaphysical formulation, this doctrine seems to deal with the problem of unintended consequences in history; in order to judge someone's actions, we must be able to distinguish between his intentions and the final result of his actions.

Travelling round the complete circle of the spirit, Croce offers a picture of the individual who finds himself in a situation which he perceives by an individual judgment through which he prepares for action. Then action in both its forms, economic and moral, takes place and the result is the action-event. We judge action by practical judgments, whereas the *accadimento* lies outside our reach.

This theory not only raises great difficulties arising from an overtly dualist conception of historical reality, but also makes formidable claims on history. First of all, all action, whether 'economic' or 'moral', is based on perception, which Croce identifies with the individual judgment. From this it follows in the first place that history must be a stable basis for action, that is, it must provide knowledge which is certain enough to act upon. This can only be the case if history proceeds methodically on the basis of well-defined principles. Furthermore, action demands insight of the situation. In the case of economic action, it implies that history must provide the agent with a view of the means in relation to the ends in a situation. In the case of moral action, when the end is the 'progress of spirit', history must also enable the agent to form his values in relation to development of the spirit as a whole. At this point, limits on historical knowledge present themselves as problems. Can we know this whole or not? According to Croce we cannot know it, because the 'cosmic judgment' belongs to God. But this view leaves us with the question of how our ignorance of the whole affects our knowledge of the constituent parts. These demands made by action from history are aggravated by Croce's notion of reality. In his view, reality is always changing, because each new intention, which is for Croce identical with action, adds something new to reality. To history, and to history alone, falls the difficult task of keeping pace with this ever-changing reality. All these demands made by economic and moral action on history raise very serious problems concerning its nature, object, method, and value. These were the problems Croce tried to solve in his *Logica* of 1909 and in *Teoria e storia della storiografia* of 1917.

---

[72]   Ibid., 59–61.

Logic as Science of the Pure Concept (1909)

In the introductory note to the second edition of the *Logica* Croce minimises its differences with the *Lineamenti*, but in fact he wrote an entirely new work. The theory of concepts is elaborated. There is a new chapter about the relationship of distinct and opposite concepts in which he summarises the conclusions of *Ciò che è vivo e ciò che è morto della filosofia di Hegel* and the theory of error is more elaborately and systematically treated. Yet, the greatest novelty is the doctrine of the identity of philosophy and history, which forms the basis of the entire work. In the *Lineamenti*, Croce had introduced the conceptual element into history without acknowledging the autonomy of history; history presupposes art and philosophy, which in turn do not presuppose history. In his autobiography Croce describes how the analogy between the identities of intuition and expression and of will and action led him to the identity of philosophy and history:

> Finally, when I prepared my *Filosofia della pratica* and studied the relationship between intention and action, and denied the dualism between them and the conceivability of an intention without action, I remembered the duality in my first *Logica* between concept and singular judgment, or between philosophy as antecedent and history as consequent and I clearly grasped that a concept, which is not at the same time a judgment of the particular, is as unreal as an intention that is not an action.[73]

The most important words in this passage are 'antecedent' and 'consequent'. In the *Filosofia della pratica* Croce had explained that the will is not followed by a movement of the legs or the arms, but that these movements are identical with the will. From this viewpoint, it is nonsense to say that we first will to move the legs and the arms and then do it. The will is not the antecedent of action, but is one with it. Croce expresses this by saying that will and action are 'identical'. They form, he says, an *a priori* synthesis with the actual situation; practical man accepts his conditions and transforms them by his will and action, thus creating a new situation in which the old conditions are transformed.[74] In the *Filosofia della pratica* Croce indicated the analogy with the identity of intuition and expression which he defends with the argument that we cannot intuit without expressing ourselves.[75] For example, we cannot have an intuition of a geometrical figure without possessing an image of it. This view implies that the intuition is not the antecedent of the expression; we do not first intuit and then express what we have intuited, rather we always do both things at once; we intuit by expressing ourselves. Intuition and expression are identical; together with the passions of the poet they form an *a priori* synthesis in which something new is created.[76] Along the same lines, Croce says in his *Logica* that we cannot disting-

---

[73] B. Croce, *Contributo alla critica di me stesso*, 349.

[74] B. Croce, *Logica*, 142.

[75] B. Croce, *Pratica*, 46.

[76] B. Croce, *Logica*, 142.

uish between philosophy and history as antecedent and consequent; we do not first think out our philosophical concepts and then set out to apply them to our intuitions, but we always do both things at once. Intuition and concepts thus form an *a priori* synthesis which creates a new individual judgment. Philosophy and history are therefore born simultaneously in the act of thought and cannot be separated.

In the *Logica* Croce expresses this view by saying that *vérités de raison* and *vérités de fait* are identical. This means that philosophy, or the defining judgment, and history, or the individual judgment, mutually presuppose each other. Croce offers a 'double proof' of this thesis. Firstly, he shows along the lines of the *Lineamenti* that every individual, historical judgment contains the definitory, or philosophical, judgment within itself in the form of a predicate.[77] Secondly, he shows that every definitory judgment presupposes an individual judgment.

Collingwood, in his discussion in his 1936 lectures on the history of the idea of history, refers to this second proof with his example of the historicity of Mill's (1806–1873) definition of happiness, but he leaves out Croce's own argument, which is by far the most interesting part of his logic.[78]

> Every definition is an answer to a question, the solution of a problem; and there would not be a reason to pronounce one, if we did not ask questions or formulate problems... But the question, the problem, or the doubt, is always conditioned by particular circumstances, the doubt of a child is not the doubt of an adult, the doubt of an uneducated man is not the doubt of an educated man, the doubt of the novice is not the doubt of the learned, the doubt of an Italian is not that of a German, and the doubt of a German of 1800 is not that of a German of 1900; thus the doubt formulated by an individual at a certain moment is not that which the same individual formulates a moment later... In reality, every question is different from another, and each definition, no matter how constant it sounds and how circumscribed it is by certain words, is different from another definition because the words, even when they seem materially the same, are in fact different according to the spiritual diversity of those who pronounce them, and these are always individuals who find themselves always in new and particular circumstances.[79]

In this single passage Croce merges language, history, and philosophy into a dialectic of questions and answers. The basic idea is that questions arise in specific historical circumstances, which call for a revision of the meaning of the pure concepts. In Croce's terms this means that individual judgments give rise to questions to be answered by defining judgments. The meaning of the defining judgments therefore depends on individual judgments. Croce's dialectic of questions and answers can therefore be regarded as a theory of the creation of meaning. But by the application of the ontological proof to philosophical concepts, the

---

[77] Ibid., 129–30.
[78] R.G. Collingwood, *The Idea of History*, 195.
[79] B. Croce, *Logica*, 133–4.

dialectic is also a theory of reality since the universal concepts of philosophy are constitutive of reality. Finally, the dialectic of questions and answers is a theory of philosophical method, because it attempts to show how philosophy proceeds by questions and answers.

Croce's theory of the identity of history and philosophy has important consequences for his interpretation of both activities. First of all, Croce's theory puts an end to the ideal of philosophy for philosophy's sake. In his view, the *a priori* synthesis of two pure concepts, or philosophy *tout court*, is always and necessarily also an *a posteriori* synthesis which presupposes the *a priori* synthesis of intuition and expression.[80] This means that the defining judgment, or philosophical judgment, by which we express the meaning of our ideas presupposes the individual judgment by which we determine the meaning of our intuitions. In other words, the true philosopher cannot sit down and play around with some arbitrarily chosen concepts, but he must 'think out' the meaning of the concepts which are presupposed by our thought of reality, or history. On this point, Croce's philosophy is akin to analytical philosophy, which also stresses the role of language as used in practice. Furthermore, in Croce's view all questions about the meaning of our concepts arise from the problem of understanding our daily experience in an historical way. It is this or that poem, or this or that action, that calls for an historical judgment, and *ipso facto* for the revision of our concepts. Not only all our questions about the nature of art, science, history, philosophy, and action arise in this way, but also all questions about concepts such as development, progress, and so forth. Were the Middle Ages a period of decay, or not? Can we apply the notion of 'progress' to the history of Europe in the 19th century? The answers to these questions depend on the answer we give to questions of definition such as: 'What is decay, what is progress?' Philosophy answers questions like these by 'elaborating' the meaning of the concepts into a systematic whole. This is best exemplified by Croce's own philosophy of the spirit, which may be seen as a grand system which defines the pure concepts and pseudo-concepts of historical judgments. Croce's philosophy of the spirit may be seen as a *catalogue raisonné* of an historian who tries to give his concepts and judgments a philosophical basis. Croce's catalogue contains definitions of the most diverse concepts varying from 'the individual' and 'the universal', to 'truth', 'utility', 'morality', and to 'change', 'development', and 'progress'.

In his *Logica*, Croce points out that all concepts as defined by philosophy should be applicable to history, or in other words, all philosophical concepts should give us a firmer grasp on the past. In this sense, philosophy is the methodology of history, as Croce was to claim later in an appendix to *Teoria e storia della storiografia*.[81] From this methodological view of philosophy stems Croce's later scepticism about philosophical trends that invent new concepts, like exis-

---

[80] Ibid., 140.
[81] B. Croce, *Teoria e storia della storiografia*, 138–9.

tentialism, as well as his early acknowledgment of trends that further develop historical concepts like Marxism.

The identity of philosophy and history has important consequences for history as well. In the first place, it follows that philosophy is continuously present in history. In Croce's words:

> Philosophy is not beyond, nor before or after, nor in a moment or in some particular moments of history, but being achieved at every moment, it is always completely united to the course of events and conditioned by historical knowledge.[82]

In the *Lineamenti*, Croce still presented history as the 'result' of art and philosophy. In this passage, however, he expresses the view that philosophy is completely immanent in history as thought and action. Croce thus acknowledges the complete rationality and autonomy of history as a self-conscious activity of the mind in action.

On this basis Croce elaborates his solution to the problem of the relationship between historical thought and the past. As in the *Lineamenti*, he points out that only in the historical judgment can 'existence' be predicated of a representation. In the *Logica* he adds that the concept of existence implies all other possible predicates.[83] This doctrine follows from Croce's own theory of distinct concepts as in his book on Hegel. In history, this doctrine implies that every thought or action can be judged from different points of view and that all these points of view necessarily imply each other. For example, we cannot judge the truth of a philosophy without taking the language in which it expresses itself into account. Another important implication of this view is that all historical judgments are always value judgments and that the historian cannot be impartial.[84] Finally, Croce's theory has an important implication for the use of pseudo-concepts in history. For example, when we use terms like 'Greek Man', 'the Renaissance', and so forth we must never forget that these concepts are not true but useful, or in Croce's words: they do not constitute history but only support it.[85] Moreover, we should not forget that the pseudo-concepts presuppose the pure concepts and therefore history. To use Croce's own example, the concept 'Greek Man' presupposes our historical knowledge of the individual lives of Pericles and Alcibiades and many others.[86] What are the consequences of this doctrine for historical inquiry? Following the doctrine of history as individual judgment, an historian, studying his sources, intuits or imagines what possibly happened and then judges, on the basis of his concepts, what actually happened. The historian,

---

[82] B. Croce, *Logica*, 208.
[83] Ibid., 112.
[84] Ibid., 189–90.
[85] Ibid., 195.
[86] Ibid., 195–6.

Croce says, must 'feel again what is behind the words and signs, he must reproduce in himself the past fact'.[87]

This reproduction of the past is a highly critical activity. In this context, Croce explains that when we try to think out what is behind the signs and words in the evidence, that is, when we think out the meaning of our representations, we apply the pure concept in its universality, its particularity, and singularity.[88] In its universality the concept is predicated by the representation as the only concept in relation to the whole, in its particularity as related to other distinct concepts, and its singularity in itself. Croce gives the following example from Livy:

> Consules satis exploratis itineribus sequentes Poenum, ut ventum ad Cannas est, ubi in conspectu Poenum habebant, bina castra communiunt.[89]

> The consuls, after making a sufficient reconaissance of the roads, followed the Phoenicians until they came to Cannae, where, having the enemy in view, they fortified two camps.

In order to understand this phrase, Croce explains, we must know the significance of all its pseudo-concepts, like 'consul', 'road', 'enemy', and 'camp'. But since the meaning of these concepts presupposes the pure concepts, we must also know the meaning of the pure concepts. In order to understand the pure concepts, Croce says, we must know their full intension and extension and this is only possible when we consider them in their universality, their particularity, and singularity, that is, we must understand their meaning in relation to all other concepts. By applying the pure concept to the representation we make it real, universal, and necessary.[90] From this it follows that we can never say that something happened without saying what happened and why it happened.[91] If one of the concepts is unclear, we cannot tell what the passage means. And if our concepts change, the interpretation of the passage will change as well. This explains why different historians interpret history in different ways even if they are in possession of the same evidence.[92] However, history does not end up in subjectivism, because historians can always correct and perfect their concepts when their opinions differ.[93] The true historian is legitimately subjective as long as he is aware of the meaning of the universal concepts.

---

[87]   Ibid., 181.

[88]   Ibid., 185.

[89]   Ibid., 183. English translation by B.O. Forster in Livy, *Ab Urbe Condita, From the Founding of the City*, in *The Loeb Classical Library*, V, Book XXII, cap. XLIV, Heinemann, Harvard University Press, London, Cambridge Massachussets, 1982, 346–7.

[90]   B. Croce, *Logica*, 185.

[91]   Ibid.

[92]   Ibid., 186.

[93]   Ibid., 187.

In Croce's view, the true meaning of the pure concepts is established by correcting error. Error is now defined as a wrong conception of the individual judgment, following from a wrong combination of intuition and predicate.[94] This occurs when the concepts are not applied in their right, theoretical connection, but according to some arbitrary, non-theoretical rule.[95] In Croce's view, errors always have a practical origin and this explains why they are on the one hand unthinkable, and therefore unreal, and on the other hand real in the sense that they were committed in the past and are still being committed in the present.

Croce's list of errors is too long to deal with, but some examples are highly relevant to his theory of history. As an example of mistaking the empirical pseudo-concept for a pure concept, Croce gives the case of interpreting the concept 'Greek Man' as a universal concept that is applicable to all history. In committing this error we forget that these concepts were formed after knowing the lives of individuals such as Pericles or Alcibiades and that the concept of 'Greek Man' has no *a priori* status.[96] Another example is the empirical pseudo-judgment 'Raphael's Transfiguration is a religious painting'. From Croce's point of view, this judgment does not express any understanding of the work, but only classifies it. In contrast, the judgment 'Raphael's Transfiguration is a work of art' is a truly historical judgment which expresses our understanding of it because it involves all our concepts of art.[97] An example of the error of not taking the identity of history and philosophy into account is contained in Hegel's philosophy of history, which isolates pure concepts from history in order to apply them for a second time on history.[98] This philosophical 're-making' of history is found in several places in Hegel's philosophy of history. The worst of all errors, however, is mysticism, because it gives up all thought to plunge itself into the fullness of life.[99] This is important because Croce would reject Gentile's actualism as a form of mysticism in 1913.

Seen in the context of Croce's development, the *Logica*, with its doctrine of the identity of philosophy and history, is of paramount importance. With the help of this theory, Croce solved many of the problems with which he had been struggling from 1893. In the first place, the new theory enabled Croce to distinguish art and history; art remains on the level of intuition, whereas history transcends intuitions by elaborating and applying concepts to them. This process is a self-conscious process; the historian is aware of himself as thinking through the meaning of the concepts by which he relates his representations. By relating these representations to evidence Croce provides the basis of historical objectivity; history is founded on the critical interpretation of evidence.

---

94   Ibid., 257–8.
95   Ibid., 254–5.
96   Ibid., 195–6.
97   Ibid., 117.
98   Ibid., 272–3.
99   Ibid., 293.

In the *Logica* Croce also established his theory of philosophy as a progressive elaboration of concepts in a question and answer process that presupposes history. The importance of this doctrine lies in the fusion of Croce's earlier notion of philosophy as the elaboration of concepts, to his more recent notion of philosophy as a process into a coherent theory of conceptual development. From the beginning of his philosophical career Croce had mainly seen philosophy as the elaboration of concepts, but he had not shown how it proceeds, although he came to grips with it himself when he read Hegel on this point. With the help of the notion of the identity of philosophy and history, he solves this problem by acknowledging history as the source of conceptual development; it is the problem of understanding the past that posits the philosopher within the historian for dealing with the problem of revising his concepts. Croce does not elaborate the nature of this process in detail, but it seems that he had something in mind such as the development of language as described in the *Estetica*. In that work, Croce described this process as a struggle for expressing our impression.[100] This same idea seems to lie at the basis of his notion of the elaboration of concepts:

> Like every act of the spirit, the definition comes forth from a contrast, from a struggle, from a war that wants peace, from an obscurity that seeks light, or, as we said, it is a question that requires an answer.[101]

In the final analysis Croce finds this contrast in the 'intuitions' that call for 'predication'; the intuitions are multifarious and individual and must be put in order by the unity and universality of the pure concepts. From this standpoint, the main function of the concept is to elucidate the universal aspect of the intuitions. In practice, this means that the philosopher must define the meaning of the pure concepts so as to 'fit' the intuitions. Croce's paradigm case is the historian who is confronted with imaginations of individual events, which he tries to 'relate' by a universal concept. One may think here of an historian who, on the basis of his representations of Pericles, Alcibiades, and so forth, forms the concept 'Greek Man', or of the art historian who forms the pure concept of art on the basis of works of art. From this viewpoint Croce's theory of the formation of the pure concept is closely related to the theory of the formation of historical concepts. In both, he tries to find a dialectical relationship between the intension and the extension of concepts to make them fit to historical reality.

In spite of all these achievements, the theory of the identity of philosophy and history also raises some serious problems, which Croce leaves unsolved. In the first place, Croce 'proves' his thesis that philosophy always presupposes history with the argument that every definition of a concept is always made as an answer to a question that arises in particular historical circumstances. However, he also holds that history presupposes the concepts of philosophy. From

---

[100] See chapter 1, p. 35.
[101] B. Croce, *Logica*, 133.

this it follows that the concepts of philosophy are both *a posteriori*, or in time, and *a priori*, out of time. In order to solve this problem, Croce points out that the pure concept is not an antecedent of the individual judgment. By this he means that we establish the meaning of the predicate simultaneously with the formation of the individual judgment. And since the individual judgment is an *a priori* synthesis of intuition and pure concept, the pure concept is formed by predicating a representation. Or to say it differently, the meaning of the concept is formed in the act of predicating a representation. For example, in the judgment 'Napoleon was an immoral ruler', the historian gives a meaning to the pure concept of morality by applying it to 'Napoleon'. From this it follows that the pure concepts are eternal qua form, but qua content or meaning they are historical. In this way Croce makes the development of the philosophical dependent on the sequence of intuitions. This sequence is not a true process or development, because each intuition is created without any reflection on previous intuitions; at most they follow each other in some sort of staccato rhythm, with no relationship to each other. This 'uno intuito' view of thought is reflected in Croce's claim that there are no eternal questions in philosophy; each individual asks and answers his own questions according to the circumstances in which he lives. The problem with this view is that it pushes the notion of historical continuity out of sight. Croce never reaches this extreme consequence and whenever the continuity of history has to be explained Croce calls upon the 'eternity, universality, and necessity' of the pure concepts, of which he simply presupposes the temporal identity. In the end, therefore, Croce's attempt to reconcile the temporal and the eternal is not completely successful. While being an historian *pur sang*, Croce kept on dreaming of closing the 'gates of time' to 'fix' the fleeting moment in eternity.[102]

Secondly, it is important to notice that Croce, focusing on philosophy and history, keeps the sciences and their pseudo-concepts out of the logic of question and answer. In this way he left the development of the sciences in the dark. Croce tries to make this good by pointing out that the sciences 'presuppose' history because all science begins in perception, but this view avoids the question of how scientists develop their concepts autonomously. Apart from this, Croce's degradation of the pseudo-concepts causes severe friction within his own system, because he fails to explain the role of pseudo-concepts in historical thought. In this context, Croce explicitly acknowledges the use of pseudo-concepts in history; in fact most of his examples contain pseudo-concepts like 'Greek Man', 'Renaissance', and so forth. But the status of these concepts is far from clear. On the one hand, they presuppose history, on the other hand they 'support' it; the concept of 'Greek Man' can only be formed on the basis of our knowledge of many individual Greeks, on the other hand this knowledge can only be formed on the basis of other pseudo-concepts. In order to solve this problem, Croce

---

[102] B. Croce, *Contributo alla critica di me stesso*, 348.

tends to brush the pseudo-concepts aside as mere 'labels' or 'signs' by which we 'summarise' chunks of history for practical reasons, though he also seems to realise that these pseudo-concepts are absolutely necessary in order to think about the past at all. Indeed, a history written on the basis of pure concepts alone would no doubt turn out to be very poor. Most importantly, Croce often depicts the pseudo-concepts as 'convenient constructions', thus turning history into a construction. At the same time he explicitly recognises history, including these pseudo-concepts, as the only concrete reality.[103]

Finally, both the 'uno intuito' view of the judgment and the degradation of the pseudo-concept have important implications for the relationship between history and philosophy. Most importantly, they leave out one aspect of both, namely the questioning activity. Croce shows how historical and *ipso facto* philosophical questions arise in the process of predicating our intuitions. But why should this process take place? According to Croce it is not necessary to 'transcend' the level of intuitions. But if that is not necessary, why do we form individual judgments at all? In other words, why should we ask historical questions at all and why do we ask the questions that we ask? In Croce's philosophy this problem has become known as the problem of the 'passage' from the level of intuitions to concepts. This problem never arose for Gentile, who always held that art and philosophy are not distinct activities so that there is a 'ray of the concept' always shining in the intuition, that is, our intuitions are never pure, but always mingled with the self-conscious activity of the spirit, or philosophy. But this is exactly the point which Croce wanted to evade, because it implies that art somehow presupposes history and philosophy.

Most importantly, Croce's vindication of the autonomy of art barred the way to find a solution for the problem of the questions arising in the theoretical sphere. Realising this, Croce took the only way which was still open for him and tried to develop a theory of the practical origin of the growth of questions in order to account for the development of history and philosophy.

Theory and History of Historiography (1912–1917)

In his autobiography Croce is very clear about the practical motives of his *Teoria e storia della storiografia*:

> In the *Theory and History of Historiography*, in which I made sure to determine the nature of true history as being always contemporary history, that is as being born from intellectual and moral needs of the present.[104]

---

[103] Croce's notion of the pseudo-concepts comes close to Walsh's notion of the 'colligatory concept' in history as expounded in his *Philosophy of History*, 24–5, 59–63: both have the function of making a coherent whole of historical events by connecting them to each other. And although Walsh says that he borrows the idea of 'colligation' from William Whewell (1794–1866), he also seems to owe a lot to Croce.

[104] B. Croce, 'Note Autobiografiche', 1934, 357.

'Present needs' dominate every chapter of *Teoria e storia della storiografia*. Croce's highest aim is to vindicate 'humanistic history', or history that tries to understand the past 'as work of man and as a product of human intellect and will'.[105] It must establish the free activity of the individual against the 'slavery to an extramundane will, and to a blind natural necessity'.[106] Moreover, 'humanistic history' must provide certain knowledge against historical scepticism, and full knowledge of the past against agnosticism.[107]

In order to realise these aims, Croce first dismisses the distinction between contemporary history and 'already formed history', which is between historiography and the past. In this context, he defines contemporary history as:

> ...history that comes into being immediately after the act that has been done, as consciousness of that act, for example, the history that I make about myself when I undertake to write these pages and that is the history of my writing, necessarily related to my work of writing.[108]

In this passage, Croce presents history as self-conscious awareness of action by which we are not only aware of the action itself, but also of ourselves performing this action. This notion can best be seen as the ultimate development of the identity of philosophy and history, which expresses the view that the historian is conscious of his own thoughts and the concepts on which they are based. In *Teoria e storia della storiografia* Croce employs this notion of history to remove the distinction between past and present. The past, he says, is always present in the form of documents or 'chronicles'. Chronicles in themselves are not history; they are 'dead' history, or the 'corpse' of history. They consist of signs and words without any determined content or truth.[109] Chronicles are not true but useful; we preserve chronicles for their possible utility in the future, when some historian will interpret the chronicles in order to make the past live again. The past will then become present and this shows that the distinction between the past and the present is not as absolute as is often held. Here we find Croce's notion of the living past, the past that lives, or better, lives again in the present act of thought; it was dead but it is brought to life again. Croce illustrates this notion:

> Because the dead past relives and past history makes itself present as the development of life requires. The Romans and the Greeks lay in their graves until the new maturity of the spirit, in the Renaissance, woke them up. The primitive, corpulent and barbaric forms of civilisation lay forgotten or little observed until that new phase of the European spirit, which took the name of

---

[105] B. Croce, *Teoria e storia della storiografia*, 81.
[106] Ibid.
[107] Ibid., 41.
[108] Ibid., 3.
[109] Ibid., 8–9.

Romanticism or Restauration, sympathised with them, or recognized them as their present interest.[110]

Here Croce clearly stresses the priority of the present over the past; present thought constitutes the past, from which it follows that there is no past except that which is relived by the historian.

Along these lines, Croce explicitly describes the status of history as a 'construction'. Historical facts as such do not exist, but they are constructed by the mind that thinks, it follows that historical facts are therefore not the beginning but the end of historical thought.[111] These constructions are not made arbitrarily, but on the basis of the interpretation of evidence.[112] This interpretation is always critical and methodical; it proceeds on the basis of well-defined philosophical principles.

Most importantly, Croce finds the origin of historical thought in present interests and from this it follows that our knowledge of the past corresponds to our practical needs:

> And if contemporary history springs directly from life, the history that is called non-contemporary history will also spring directly from life, because it is evident that only an interest of present life can move one to study a past fact; this past fact does not respond to a past interest, but to a present interest, in so far as it is unified with present interest.[113]

Remarkably, the concept of 'the interesting', which was so important in his early works, resurfaces in this passage. But this time Croce presents it as a presupposition of all history; the reliving of the past presupposes the act of thought which is in contact with the practical interests of life. According to Croce, these interests are purely individual. Gathering books on history and asking which interests they represent is therefore not allowed:

> What present interest has the history that tells about the Peloponnesian or Mithridatic wars, the facts of Mexican art or Arabic philosophy? For me, at this moment, none; and therefore these histories are not histories for me at this moment, but at the most, simply titles of history books; they were history for those who thought them or they will be for those who will think them, and for me, when I thought them, or when I shall think them, re-elaborating them according to may spiritual need.[114]

This passage illustrates that contemporary history means history which stems from practical needs in the present. Contemporaneity is the norm for true history: all forms that fall short of this norm are rejected as 'pseudostorie'. Croce's account of the 'pseudo-histories' is based on his theory of error in the *Logica*, but

---

[110] Ibid., 15.

[111] Ibid., 63.

[112] Ibid., 4.

[113] Ibid.

[114] Ibid., 5.

here Croce stresses the failure of the pseudo-histories from a practical point of view. For example, philological history, which confuses the search and research of sources with true history, can never be a proper basis for action. Another form of pseudo-history tries to overcome this failure by appealing to sentiments. Still another form of pseudo-history is pragmatic history which aims at a practical end, but not at truth.[115] Last but not least, contemporary history sets aside 'negative history' or 'elegiac history', which tends to stress the negative aspects of history.[116] History, Croce explains, can only express positive judgments; a negative judgment is only a sign that some event has not been understood. For this reason, all development in history goes from the good to the better.[117] This is the doctrine of the positivity of history, which closely follows Croce's theory of error as pure negativity.

The notion of the contemporaneity of history also refutes historical scepticism and historical agnosticism. Historical scepticism is the belief that the past cannot be known. Croce answers the sceptic by showing that the object of history is not the past but the present. The past as such does not exist; only the past that lives in the historian's mind truly exists. 'Historical agnosticism' recognises that we can know the past, but argues that we can never know it completely; historical knowledge is necessarily biased and therefore uncertain.[118] Croce answers the 'agnostic' by showing that history is always a construction that we make in order to solve our present practical problems, the whole notion of history as it really was, or real history, simply disappears; the history we know is always the history we need to know.[119]

Finally, Croce holds that the notion of contemporary history abolishes all doubts about the usefulness or the value of the knowledge of the past. When the past is made present by historical thought on the basis of present interests how can we doubt its value? When I relive Greek life, or Platonic philosophy, both are just as present to me as my present friends, or the lady whom I love![120]

This view of the value of history makes all previous attempts to make history more useful completely redundant. One of these attempts is the old-fashioned metaphysical philosophy of history, which used to give some reinterpretation of the facts as found by the historians. Croce here gives the example of the French historian Hyppolyte Taine (1828–93) who tried to explain the history of English literature on the basis of concepts like 'l'homme du Nord', or 'le Germain'. He also mentions Vico and Hegel who tried to reduce the course of history to the development of pure concepts.[121] According to Croce, these attempts are nonsen-

---

[115] Ibid., 32.
[116] Ibid., 78.
[117] Ibid., 75.
[118] Ibid., 41.
[119] Ibid., 44–5.
[120] Ibid., 5.
[121] Ibid., 55, 67.

sical because there are no 'brute facts'; all facts are constructions and therefore
always the result of interpretation. The task of the philosopher is not to make
history more respectable, or more useful, but to elaborate the concepts which lie
at the basis of true historical thought. Finally, historians should not seek to write
'universal' history or seek for general laws of history, but to pursue their own
individual interests.

Conclusion

By friend and foe Croce's *Teoria e storia della storiografia* has been recognised as
one of the most important contributions to the philosophy of history of the 20th
century. Seen in the context of Croce's development, the book was the crown on
Croce's philosophy of the spirit. It reflected the problems concerning the nature,
the object, the method, and the value of history with which he had been struggling from 'La storia ridotta' onwards in a way that none of his other works do. In
Teoria e storia della storiografia Croce describes the nature of history as an inquiry
that proceeds by asking and answering questions on a philosophical basis. The
subject matter of this inquiry is not 'facts', but thought and actions done in the
past, which can be 'relived' or 'revived' on the basis of the interpretation of evidence. The whole process is a self-critical activity; the concepts involved in the
interpretation of the sources and the construction of history are elaborated in a
philosophical way by the historian himself. Philosophy is therefore the 'methodology' of history. Most importantly, the whole process finds its origin in 'present
interests'; we construct history in order to solve our present practical problems.

The metaphysical basis for these solutions is the doctrine of the contemporaneity of the past. This doctrine is the ultimate development of the identity of
philosophy and history. With the latter doctrine, Croce recognised the self-
conscious aspect of historical thought, with contemporaneity of the past, he
entirely identifies history with self-consciousness. As a result, he identified past
and present; there is no fundamental difference between someone who is conscious of reading this at this moment, and someone who is conscious of the
battle of Waterloo. By this identification of past and present, the notion of the
'real past' loses its significance; the only reality is the present.

As a form of self-consciousness history is present in every act of the spirit; we
are all continuously interpreting our world as 'evidence'. The scientist, the philosopher, and even the artist are all historians to the extent that they are aware of
their own activities. Reality thus becomes a 'construction' of historical thought;
reality is a product of the historical way of looking at things. In this reality there
is no transcendent God, no extramundane will, no 'providence', but only human
action as based on human thought which is completely transparent to historical
thought. Reality is history.

Not surprisingly, Gentile was very pleased with this metaphysics of self-
consciousness act of thought. When he read the thesis of the contemporaneity of

history, he thought that Croce had finally converted to actualism.[122] In order to show the similarity between actualism and Croce's doctrine Gentile cites one of Croce's own definitions of contemporary history:

> If we keep to real history, or the history that we really think in the act of thought, it will be easy to see that it is perfectly identical with the most personal and contemporary of histories.[123]

With this passage, Gentile points out, Croce 'takes the plunge' by identifying historiography and history, thought and reality, and finally thought and action by combining all these terms into the single act of thought.[124] But in a letter to Croce he expressed his doubts on the distinction between history and chronicles in terms of theory and practice, suggesting that the relationship should be interpreted dialectically.[125] By this Gentile meant that chronicles and history should not be interpreted as distinct concepts, but as opposites, that is, not as two different entities, but as two aspects of a single process. On this basis, Gentile would elaborate his dialectic of thought which proceeds on the opposition between present and past thought. As we will see in chapter 3, this dialectic developed the constructivist aspects of history to the extreme.

De Ruggiero was the first to criticise the presentist aspects of both Croce and Gentile's constructivism.[126] In his view both Croce's theory of the contemporaneity of histority and Gentile's actualist theory of history lead to a dangerous form of 'monochronism' by which the past is entirely reduced to the present. De Ruggiero himself suggested a theory of history that would do justice to the past by 'distancing' it from the present. Collingwood shared de Ruggiero's criticism of Croce and Gentile, but he would go deeper. Dissatisfied with both Croce's notion of the contemporaneity of history and Gentile's actualism he raised the problem of the possibility of knowledge of the past. This problem finally led him to a theory of history which is no longer dependent on a pre-established philosophy of mind.

---

[122] G. Gentile, 'Intorno all'idealismo attuale', 45.

[123] B. Croce, *Teoria e storia della storiografia*, 5. Cited by Gentile, 'Intorno all'idealismo attuale', 45.

[124] G. Gentile, 'Intorno all'idealismo attuale', 45.

[125] G. Gentile, *Lettere a Benedetto Croce, Volume quarto, dal 1910 al 1914*, Sansoni, Florence, 1980, 199, 28 October 1912.

[126] See chapter 4, pp. 98–100.

Chapter Three

Gentile's Middle Development and His System (1903–1923)

Introduction

In the first decade of the twentieth century, Gentile was active as a teacher at various universities, as an educational reformer, and as a contributor to the history of Italian philosophy for *La Critica*.[1] In this context, he elaborated the core ideas of his philosophy. Before the turn of the century, Gentile had already developed his own views on the basis of the Marxist notion of 'praxis', according to which the distinction between theory and practice almost vanished. But a full identity of theory and practice also required a close identification of philosophy and history since only a philosophy that creates itself on the basis of history in the broadest sense of the word can be considered as fully autonomous. In his early works, Gentile had held that philosophy develops itself on the basis of its own history, and in 1903 he had defended the possibility and necessity of a metaphysical philosophy of history. However, Gentile had not yet come to a complete identity of philosophy and history, that is, the notion of the mutual implication of philosophy and history.

In the years 1903–11, Gentile elaborated this idea in a large number of papers on the history of Italian philosophy and on educational theory. In this context, he also produced some papers of a more theoretical nature that formed the basis of his system. Most of these deal with the reform of the Hegelian dialectic and its consequences for the relationship between philosophy and history. The first and most important result of this reform was his inaugural lecture, 'Il concetto della *Storia della filosofia*' ('The Concept of the *History of Philosophy*'), delivered at the University of Palermo in 1907, to be followed by several other papers, like 'Le forme assolute dello spirito' ('The Absolute Forms of the Spirit'), in which he

---

[1]   di Lalla, *Vita di Giovanni Gentile*, 103–7, 142–56.

attempted to give his ideas a more systematic form.[2] These papers prepared the series of lectures 'L'atto del *pensare* come atto puro' ('The Act of Thought as Pure Act') held in 1911 in which Gentile founded actualism or actual idealism.[3] On this basis, Gentile began to work out his own philosophical system. The first publication was *Sommario di pedagogia* (*Summary of Pedagogy*) which comprised the first two volumes of the system. The *Sommario* led Croce to criticise actualism publicly in 1913. In a fierce debate in the journal *La Voce* the two philosophers crossed swords and came no closer to each other's way of thinking. In 1916, Gentile published *Teoria generale dello spirito come atto puro* (*General Theory of the Mind as Pure Act*), which can be regarded as the metaphysics of actualism, and *I fondamenti della filosofia del diritto* (*The Foundations of the Philosophy of Right*), the first version of his moral and political philosophy. He crowned his system with the monumental *Sistema di logica* (*System of Logic*) of which the first part appeared in 1917, and the second in 1922. During the war Gentile established himself as a prominent thinker capable of setting intellectual trends in his country and, being an eminent teacher, he attracted many students, first to Pisa, where he taught from 1914 until 1917, and after that year, to Rome. By that year actualism had already become the philosophy of a new generation which intended to build Italy up after the war. In 1920, Gentile founded the *Giornale critico della filosofia italiana* (*Critical Journal of Italian Philosophy*) as a forum for actualist philosophy. Meanwhile, he became increasingly involved in politics. After the March on Rome in October 1922, Mussolini made him Minister of Education and a year later a member of the Fascist Party.[4]

In this chapter, I will analyse Gentile's major works in the context of his development, focusing on the relationship between philosophy, history, and action.

The Birth of Actualism: 'The Act of Thought as Pure Act' (1912)

'L'atto del *pensare* come atto puro' was the title of a series of lectures, held in the winter of 1911 at the Biblioteca filosofica at Palermo, and published a year later in a very short summary. This summary is of great importance, because it expounds Gentile's philosophy in a nutshell and it is the seed of all its subsequent influence. For his immediate pupils, 'L'atto del pensare come atto puro' contained the articles of the actualist faith, and for other philosophers, like de Ruggiero and Collingwood, it was one of the bases from which they developed their own positions.

---

2   G. Gentile, 'Le forme assolute dello spirito', in *Il modernismo e i rapporti tra religione e filosofia*, Laterza, Bari, 1909, cited from *Il Modernismo e i rapporti fra religione e filosofia*, *OC* XXXV, Sansoni, Florence, 1962, 259–75.
3   G. Gentile, 'L'atto del pensare come atto puro', 183–95.
4   di Lalla, *Vita di Giovanni Gentile*, 211–14.

'L'atto del *pensare* come atto puro' is typical of Gentile's bold way of think-ing, which has often deterred the non-initiated. Readers who are not acquainted with Gentile's thought should keep in mind that Gentile developed his philos-ophy of the pure act as a theory of the history of philosophy in the first place. Keeping this background in mind, a lot of Gentile's otherwise obscure theses become much clearer since they all describe how thought develops itself.

As the title of the lectures indicates, Gentile's principal aim is to establish the notion of the act of thought as a pure act, that is, as an activity which is not dependent on other activities of the mind, or put into logical terms, thought without presuppositions. Following Spaventa, Gentile himself refers to pure thought as *autoctisi*. 'Ktisis' was the word used by the Greek Fathers to denote the creation of the world *ex nihilo*. *Autoctisi* can therefore best be translated as self-constitutive, or self-positing, thought as long as its creative aspect is kept in sight.[5]

Gentile establishes this concept of thought as *autoctisi* at the end of a sorites of 19 briefly substantiated theses.[6] The burden of the whole argument rests therefore on the first thesis which carries the title 'the belief of thought in itself'.[7] In this thesis Gentile argues that the only thought of which we can affirm truth is concrete thought, or actual thought. This is nothing but a further elaboration of Gentile's notion of the 'immanence of philosophy in life', stated in his first book, *Rosmini e Gioberti*. In that work, Gentile had related the notion of immanence to the logical and ontological priority of the act of thought and to the idea of the identity between philosophy and its own history.[8] In his inaugural lecture in Palermo of 1907 Gentile had generalised this thesis to the identity of philosophy and history in the broad sense of the word; philosophy proceeds by reflecting on itself as immanent in all forms of experience. In 'L'atto del *pensare* come atto puro' Gentile raises this view of the relationship between philosophy and his-tory to a metaphysical principle according to which reality is a product of self-conscious thought. Self-conscious thought is essentially historical because all reflection regards the past. Actualism can therefore be seen as a metaphysics which tries to interpret reality as history, or more precisely, as a philosophy which regards reality as a product of historical thought.

Gentile expresses this view of an historical reality with the dialectic of truth and error. Its foundation is the logical and ontological primacy of actual thought, or *pensiero pensante*. The notion 'actual' must in this context be taken both in the sense of thought that we are thinking now, and in the sense of thought as an act or process. Only with respect to this present act of thought, and not to a past act

---

5   H.S. Harris, *The Social Philosophy of Giovanni Gentile*, University of Illinois Press, Illinois, 1960, 35n21.

6   G. Gentile, 'L'atto del pensare come atto puro', 195.

7   Ibid., 183.

8   See chapter 1, p. 24.

of thought, can truth be affirmed; we can only know what we actually think, not what we thought. From this it follows that error is seen as not actual, or past thought, or *pensiero pensato*. Again, this must be taken in the sense that error is a thought that we cannot actually think. Common sense expresses the same view by saying that we cannot 'follow' someone who is erring. Against this background Gentile's identification of error with past thought becomes clear; it is simply an application of his own experience as an historian of philosophy.

According to Gentile's doctrine we cannot follow a past thought because it is 'abstracted' from a process of thought that is no longer actual. In order to understand a past thought we must therefore 'rethink', 'revive', or 'realise' the process from which it is abstracted.[9] From this it follows that a present act of thought constitutes or 'creates' the past for itself and the past is only 'living' or 'real' as 'revived' by present thought. Here we find Gentile's notion of the living past which is based on the logical and ontological primacy of the present act of thought. For Gentile, the only reality is the present act of thought; the past can therefore only be real as a function of present thought.

Gentile's theory of the living past comes close to Croce's notion of the contemporaneity of history, but must not be identified with it. Croce never took the 'creative' aspect of thought as radically as Gentile. Firstly, Croce still acknowledged that evidence of the past is not a product of present thought; evidence is not created by but given for thought. Gentile, however, stressed that present thought creates its own evidence. Secondly, Croce takes the contemporaneity of the past for granted, whereas Gentile explicitly affirms it as a metaphysical doctrine which explains the nature of reality as a whole. If Croce's doctrine is interpreted as a moderate form of constructivism, Gentile's must be seen as a more radical form of constructivism, because he holds that thought creates both present and past reality.[10]

Gentile's constructivism comes to the fore in his identification of 'past thought' with 'nature'. *Prima facie* this is the most obscure identity of actualism, but interpreted in terms of the dialectic of the act of thought, it becomes clear. Seen from this dialectic, there is no fundamental difference between the way in which the scientist and the historian constitute their objects. This does not mean that thought literally creates the universe from the galaxies to the atoms, but only that these things are what they are because of our way of understanding them. Galaxies and atoms are not manmade; but the concepts by which humanity sought to understand the galaxies and the atoms are definitely so. Human understanding is therefore intrinsically historical; by reflecting on itself thought creates the concept of 'star' or 'atom' in order to understand reality. Likewise, an

---

9   G. Gentile, 'L'atto del pensare come atto puro', 184.

10   It is for this reason that I would not describe Croce's theory of history as contructivism, or constructivism *tout court* as Meiland does in his *Scepticism and Historical Knowledge*, 37–8.

historian constructs concepts like 'Renaissance' or 'Enlightenment' in order to understand the past. By this, Gentile does not mean that thought creates these concepts from nothing; thought has some 'matter' or 'object' about which it thinks, but this is never 'brute' matter, or the 'pure object' as given in sense-perception, but concepts, or in his language, *pensieri pensati*. From this point of view a physicist like Newton was not giving order to his immediate sense-perceptions, but he was thinking about his own thought which was to some extent a product of the thought of his predecessors such as Kepler and Galileo. In reflecting on his own thought, Newton was therefore also an historian of their thoughts, correcting their errors in view of his own thought.

From this notion of error, Gentile derives the notion of the 'necessity' of actual thought. If error is that which we cannot think, truth is that which we must think. Since all thought is determination and *omnis determinatio est negatio* we think by negating error or past thought. Past thought is posited by present thought which is therefore absolutely free. Again, Gentile has nothing mysterious in mind; he only means that we are free to think whatever we want to think. Nothing impedes us from thinking about atoms while looking at the galaxies, or about the Renaissance while we are watching a game of soccer. Thought is not dependent on reality, or, in Gentile's own terms; past thought does not condition present thought. It is rather the other way around; present thought conditions past thought. Finally, from the freedom of present thought stems its morality; we must have faith in our thought and therefore we are morally responsible to think the truth.

On this basis Gentile establishes the three criteria of truth; all thought must be *norma sui*, necessary, and universal. Firstly, thought must be *norma sui*, it does not derive its truth-value from some transcendent entity but from itself; thought posits itself and its own norms in a single self-conscious act. From this principle it follows that we can never affirm another's thought as true as long as we have not affirmed it by our own free act of thought, that is, as long as we have not thought it for ourselves.[11]

Secondly, thought must be necessary; when thought affirms itself as true it cannot think another thought as true. The necessity of any assertion is therefore immanent in the assertion itself; we think what we think because we cannot think anything else.[12]

Finally, all thought must affirm itself as universal or it would not be asserted. This does not mean that truth is universal for all men because, for Gentile, reality does not contain other men, but other thoughts, and these thoughts are only real

---

[11] G. Gentile, 'L'atto del pensare come atto puro', 185; Cf. Roger W. Holmes, *The Idealism of Giovanni Gentile*, MacMillan, New York, 1937, 127.

[12] G. Gentile, 'L'atto del pensare come atto puro', 187; Cf. Roger W. Holmes, *The Idealism of Giovanni Gentile*, 151.

in so far as they are entertained by my present act of thought.[13] For Gentile, thought is not universal in the sense that it is true for all times and places, but rather because it is bound to a certain time and place. Kepler's and Galileo's thoughts have been superseded in the course of history, yet if we really try to understand their thoughts we will understand why they necessarily thought as they did and be able to share their thoughts. Gentile's notion of universality is completely historical.

By affirming the necessity and universality of thought, Gentile continues, we affirm it as the thought of a transcendental ego and reject it as thought of an empirical ego. This transcendental ego is not limited by space and time since time and space are both concepts that are 'posited' by the act of thought.[14] Transcendental ego is therefore necessarily one and self-conscious; all distinctions within it are products of thought.[15] From this it follows that both the distinction between philosophy and history and the distinction between will and thought vanish.[16] Philosophy develops itself on the basis of history, history develops itself on the basis of philosophy. In 'L'atto del pensare come atto puro' Gentile did not elaborate an argument for the identity of will and thought. Basically he holds that the will is only real in so far as it is thought. In his later works, he would develop a more cogent version of this identity by proposing that thought which is creative of its own reality must be equated with action.

In Gentile's view all thought obeys these rules; all thought must affirm itself as true, necessary, and universal if it is to be thought at all. One might say that when we really think, we are aware of the fact that we think, what we think, and why we think what we think in the given circumstances. In Gentile's system this amounts to saying that when we really know something, we know that it is, what it is, and why it is as it is. But it is important to realise that the criteria only apply to the act of thought and not to its content; they do not compel anyone to think this or that, but if he really thinks, his thought must meet the three criteria. In 1937 Roger Holmes aptly summarised this view by saying that Gentile accepts many truths, but only one metaphysics, namely the metaphysics of the act of thought, whereas all other philosophers recognise only one truth, but many metaphysics.[17]

The metaphysics of the act of thought is one of the major strengths of actualism. Its greatest appeal is its belief in human thought, and its denial of all transcendence, to begin with the transcendence of a 'given' reality. This view encourages mankind to continue to create its own reality. Not surprisingly, therefore, actualism became increasingly popular in Italy after 1912, when young

---

[13]   G. Gentile, 'L'atto del pensare come atto puro', 189; Cf. Roger, W. Holmes, *The Iealism of Giovanni Gentile*, 153.

[14]   G. Gentile, 'L'atto del *pensare* come atto puro', 190.

[15]   Ibid., 191–2.

[16]   Ibid., 192–3.

[17]   Holmes, *The Idealism of Giovanni Gentile*, 182–3.

Italians tried to create a new society. By 1917, when Gentile was appointed to the University of Rome, he had firmly established his own actualist school, and won international acclaim as a philosopher.

But the very strength of actualism also exposes its weakness. Actualism derives its strength from the notion of self-consciousness as expressed in the first thesis; 'la fede del pensiero in se stesso' ('the belief of thought in itself'). This principle cannot be denied without self-contradiction. However, the problem is that it is not entirely clear how it should be affirmed. This becomes clear in Gentile's statement of the first principle itself. Gentile says that thought must affirm itself as true and claims that even the sceptic must believe his own denial of the principle:

> The fact of thought, and therefore of philosophy whatever the solution may be to which it directs itself, presupposes this affirmation of the truth of the thought which is actually being thought.[18]

Gentile's formulation of the sceptic's position leaves room for the implicitness of principles; the sceptic explicitly denies the *norma sui* character of thought, but at the same time he presupposes its truth. But this recognition of implicit principles, or presuppositions, stands squarely opposed to his view of thought being *norma sui*. Often Gentile takes the *norma sui* character of thought in the explicit sense, that is, as thought which posits itself and its own principles simultaneously in one self-conscious act. But the recognition of implicit thought entails that there is a form of thought which is not self-consciously constituted by actual thought itself, and this means that there is thought which is somehow not present to actual thought.[19]

Gentile's theory thus calls for a distinction between the implicit and the explicit thought. This distinction is of great importance because history and science are partly based on implicit principles, whereas philosophical thought tries to explicate its principles. The exact relationship between implicit and explicit principles would haunt Gentile for the rest of his life; until his last work he struggled with the exact status of the *pensato*, identifying it with most diverse notions as 'presupposition', 'error', 'the unknown', 'the limit of thought', and 'nature'. For this reason Gentile's actualism always had two faces. Ideally, actualism takes all thought as free, self-constitutive, *norma sui*, and teaches us to be tolerant and to take others' thought seriously. This tolerant side of actualism is best exemplified in Gentile's educational theory and practice in which he stressed the importance of dialogue between master and pupil as a form of mutual understanding. But it can also be found in most of Gentile's histories of philosophy in which he shows great patience with positions that are radically different from his own. The other, less tolerant side of actualism emerged when

---

[18]   G. Gentile, 'L'atto del *pensare* come atto puro', 183.
[19]   Holmes, *The Idealism of Giovanni Gentile*, 142.

Gentile began to stress the primacy of the self-conscious act of thought at the cost of thought which is not explicitly *norma sui*. Along these lines he first reduced art, religion, and science to philosophy. Then he reduced history to philosophy and came to see the history of philosophy as the most important form of history. But the real shipwreck of actualism came when Gentile began to confound the ideal of the self-constitutive act of thought with the reality of Fascist politics, with the result that he saw Fascism as the necessary, universal, and self-justifying outcome of history.

'The Method of Immanence'

On the basis of the theory of mind as pure act, Gentile developed his philosophical method which he presented in 'Il metodo dell'immanenza' ('The Method of Immanence') of 1913. In this paper Gentile argued that all philosophies until actualism had been based on a method of transcendence, that is, a philosophical method which is based on a norm which is not immanent to the act of thought.[20] According to Gentile, Plato's Idea, Aristotle's 'pure being', Bacon's (1561–1626) concept of nature, Descartes' *cogito*, up to Hegel's Idea functioned as a transcendent norm for thought.[21] Typically, these concepts formed the basis of an 'organon', or a set of fixed rules for philosophical method, which would bring the philosopher closer to a pre-established truth. In contrast to these views, actual idealism is the first philosophy which recognises reality as actual thought. Accordingly, it does not establish a new organon but tries to free philosophy from presuppositions.[22] In 'Il metodo dell'immanenza' Gentile does not describe how this goal is to be achieved, but some of his other works show how he applied the method himself.

In Gentile's language presuppositions are *pensati*, that is, products of *pensiero pensante*. The method of immanence therefore amounts to showing how the *pensiero pensato*, or abstract thought, may be 'resolved' into *pensiero pensante*, or concrete thought. In other words, the philosopher must show for which *pensiero pensante* the *pensati* were thought as true. In plain English this means in the first place that we must re-think the past thought in the context of its presuppositions in order to think it as true. In the second place it means that we must indicate the false presuppositions of the past thought in order to reject it. False presuppositions are to be interpreted as products of the act of thought. This is the case when processes are interpreted as 'things', or in Gentile's technical language, as 'nature' which is immutable. Since things are what they are and cannot change into each other, they can be described on the basis of a classificatory logic in which each class is clearly distinguished from the other. Conceptual distinctions

---

[20] G. Gentile, 'Il metodo dell'immanenza', in *La riforma della dialettica hegeliana*, 1913, cited from *La riforma della dialettica hegeliana*, Sansoni, Florence, 1975, 196.

[21] Ibid., 198–206, 211–16, 226–9.

[22] Ibid., 230–2.

are therefore Gentile's special target. Along these lines Gentile rejected the distinctions between content and form in *Rosmini e Gioberti*, between philosophy and history in his inaugural lecture of 1907, and finally he would reject the distinction between theory and practice.

To highlight the outstanding features of Gentile's philosophical method, it can best be contrasted with Croce's. Both methods are thoroughly historical, but whereas Croce's is mainly concerned with the elaboration of the meaning of pure concepts, Gentile's focuses on the presuppositions of thought. Croce leaves the pure concepts and their distinctions intact in so far as they fit in his system; Gentile takes a distinction always as a sign of an underlying antinomy. For Croce a philosophical error always reveals a category mistake in the sense of misunderstanding the meaning of a pure concept. For Gentile a philosophical error is always a metaphysical error, that is, the error of presupposing a reality that transcends the act of thought. Croce tended to criticise other philosophers for using the wrong concepts, and 'corrects' them by showing which concept should be used instead, or by showing the true meaning of a concept. For Gentile a 'category mistake' is impossible; there is only one category, the act of thought, and all errors stem from not having clearly understood the nature of thought. Croce's list of errors is very long and subdivided into parts. For Gentile there is only one error and that is presupposing a reality outside the act of thought. Accordingly, Gentile therefore tries to correct other philosophers by resolving their antinomous distinctions into the act of thought, that is, by showing that these distinctions are nothing but the product of the process of thought. Croce's philosophical method leads to a history of philosophy as the development of an infinite number of distinct meanings of the pure concept. Gentile's history of philosophy is the incarnation of the development of the self-conscious spirit which proceeds by rejecting wrong distinctions made in the past.

The System: Theory and Practice (1912–23)

Although Gentile's identity of thought and action forbids any distinction between the two realms of the spirit, I shall discuss his social and political philosophy first. It is not my intention to give a complete picture of it, since others, such as Harris, Lo Schiavo, Bellamy, and Gregor, have done that already.[23] In this section I will follow their account of Gentile's social and political philosophy in order to understand what Gentile meant by the identity of thought and action and the *etica del sapere* (ethics of knowledge) which is based on it. Both concepts are important in order to understand Gentile's view of the value of history.

---

[23] Harris, *The Social Philosophy of Giovanni Gentile*, 84–91; Aldo Lo Schiavo, *La filosofia politica di Giovanni Gentile*, Armando, Rome, 1971; Richard Bellamy, *Modern Italian Social Theory, Ideology and Politics from Pareto to the Present*, Polity Press, Cambridge, 1987; A. James Gregor, *Giovanni Gentile: Philosopher of Fascism*, Transaction Publishers, New Brunswick, 2001.

Harris indicated the fundamental importance of Gentile's theory of discipline in the school for his social and political theory. The problem of discipline arises from what Gentile calls 'the antinomy of education', by which he refers to the difference between the aim and the process of education. In Gentile's view, the aim of all education is the moral liberty of the pupil; yet, on the other hand the educational process presupposes the authority of the master.[24]

Applying his method of immanence Gentile points out that the distinction between teacher and pupil is only empirical and arbitrary. From the philosophical point of view there is no distinction between them; the educational process is one act of thought in which both the pupil and the master partake. In this educational process the master represents the universal values of truth, beauty, and goodness to a greater extent than the pupil, who must therefore recognise the master's authority. However, the problem of all education is that the pupil may not be willing to follow the master. In that case, Gentile points out, the master is allowed to coerce the pupil, even by physical punishment. As Harris points out, this theory of punishment reveals the intolerant side of Gentile's actualism which was the seed of his later philosophy of Fascism.[25]

The method of immanence also lies at the basis of Gentile's solution of the problem of the relationship between the individual and the state. The main antinomy to be resolved here is the one between the subjective will and objective will, or morality and law. Along the lines of his method, Gentile solves the objective will into the 'willing will' of the moral individual such that the self-conscious individual synthesises the objective will with his own will. Another way of stating this is that the individual makes the law his own will by obeying it. From this synthesis it follows that the distinction between the state and the individual vanishes within the individual. Accordingly, the distinction between the self and society, or other selves, disappears; society is immanent in man. This is Gentile's doctrine of the *societas in interiore homine*. According to this doctrine the highest good for the individual is to obey the law and the lowest evil is egotism. This explains why Gentile acknowledges moral conscience and yet always despises conscientious objectors as egotists. Again, this impatience with protesters shows the intolerant side of Gentile's actualism.[26]

The regulative idea of the state is culture; its highest aim is to transmit culture from the past to the present. At this point, we are able to understand Gentile's *etica del sapere*; the highest duty of the man of letters, that is, the philosopher-historian, is to serve the universal interests of his society by preserving its cultural values. He does this by studying its history and teaching it to future generations. In this *etica del sapere* theory and practice completely coincide. From Gentile's point of view, there is no difference between building a bridge and

---

[24] Harris, *The Social Philosophy of Giovanni Gentile*, 84–91.

[25] Ibid., 92–3.

[26] Ibid., 98–111.

studying Dante; the latter is as much a contribution to culture and society as the former. Moreover, the *etica del sapere* presupposes the *societas in interiore homine*; the philosopher-historian must understand the needs of his society in order to know which universal interests he should serve by his research.[27]

This theory, which formed the core of Gentile's later Fascist writings, has been severely criticised. But the *etica del sapere* is not necessarily intolerant, as some of Gentile's articles written during the First World War show. For example, in a short paper 'Nazione e nazionalismo' ('Nation and Nationalism') Gentile attacks extreme nationalism by pointing out that a 'nation' is an historical reality which is continuously changing. Gentile gives the example of language and religion, which are not 'given' elements of nationality, but concepts which are constructed and reconstructed by the present act of thought.[28] On the same basis Gentile defends German philosophy and poetry against anti-German attacks by pointing out that they belong to the realm of a 'universal patrimony' which transcends the nations.[29] However, in other papers of the same year Gentile does show the intolerant face of actualism. In 'La filosofia della guerra' ('The Philosophy of War'), a paper of October 1914, Gentile defines the modern concept of war as an 'absolute act' in which 'all forces of the world are involved'.[30] After this he defines 'duty' as an absolute act, that is, 'an act which is not conditioned by the circumstances, but which is done categorically'.[31] On this basis he draws the conclusion that war is the duty of all Italians who must be prepared to sacrifice themselves for the holy cause. Along these lines, Gentile puts off all other opinions as sheer egotism. It was this intolerant side of actualism that Gentile began to develop after 1923 into the philosophy of Fascism.

The System: Philosophy and History (1916–23)

We will now turn once more to the relationship between philosophy and history in order to see how it can be interpreted in the light of the *etica del sapere*. Both in the *Teoria generale dello spirito come atto puro* (*General Theory of the Mind as Pure Act*) written in 1915 and in the *Sistema di logica* (*System of Logic*) which he published in instalments from 1917 until 1922, Gentile elaborated the identity of philosophy and history on the basis of his method of immanence. In the *Teoria generale dello spirito* he begins this identification with a discussion of 'the historical antinomy' to which he dedicates an entire chapter.

Gentile presents the historical antinomy as follows:

Thesis: the spirit is history, because it is dialectical development.

---

[27] Ibid., 125–30.
[28] G. Gentile, *Guerra e fede*, Riccardo Ricciardi Editore, Napoli, 1919, 51–2.
[29] Ibid., 164.
[30] Ibid., 12–13.
[31] Ibid., 17.

Antithesis: the spirit is not history, because it is eternal act.[32]

On the one hand, Gentile explains, man is history because his essence is to be free; nature is, mind becomes. Mind realises its ends, its life is value; it knows truth, creates beauty, does good, and worships God. On the other hand, when we study the history of man these values are withdrawn from history and stand for us in their eternal reality. The difficulty is therefore to conceive a reality that is both eternal and historical.[33]

This historical antinomy is not only one of the most fundamental theses in Gentile's entire system, but also in all philosophical systems which are based on the heritage of Vico's *Scienza Nuova*, to which the problem of the relationship between *storia ideale eterna* and *storia in tempo* is central. In this context, Gentile points out that the problem is inescapable because it presents itself as soon as we study history. Gentile illustrates this thesis with the example of Ariosto (1474–1533), the famous poet of *Orlando Furioso*. When we read *Orlando Furioso*, says Gentile, two Ariosto's present themselves. One Ariosto is spirit, 'unconditioned conditioner of all conditions', 'act of thought that posits its own reality'.[34] The 'other' Ariosto appears as a finite being conditioned by antecedent facts.[35] The first Ariosto is the object of literary criticism, which judges in Ariosto the eternal beauty of his poetry, the second is the object of historical criticism which is concerned with Ariosto as an historical fact, conditioned by space and time, and only understandable in relation to other facts. The first Ariosto is eternal, the second is historical.

Gentile solves the antinomy with his method of immanence, that is, by resolving the antithesis into 'concrete thought'. The only Ariosto I know, Gentile says, is the Ariosto of the poem, which is for me a concrete individual; I can affirm as much of Ariosto's reality as I can 'realise' for myself. But, in order to 'realise' this Ariosto I must read the poem and this means that I must know the language in which it is written. This language, in turn, can never be found in dictionaries, so I have to read what Ariosto himself read. And to know the language of any writer means taking the history in which Ariosto lived his life into account. 'In short,' Gentile says, 'I relive Ariosto's life in order to understand his poem'.[36] In other words, we have to understand Ariosto's historical reality in order to understand the eternal value of his poem because eternal values are realised in history.

On this point, Gentile tactfully employs his dialectic of *pensante* and *pensato* in order to resolve the antinomy between philosophy and history, or the eternal and the historical, with which he had already dealt in his Inaugural of 1907. The

---

[32] G. Gentile, *Teoria generale dello spirito come atto puro*, 192.

[33] Ibid., 192–3.

[34] Ibid., 194.

[35] Ibid.

[36] Ibid., 196–7.

main idea here is that *pensiero pensato* can be re-thought by *pensiero pensante* in the function of our present thoughts:

> The only Ariosto we know, author of Orlando Furioso, is not one thing and his poem another. And the poem which we know is known when it is read, understood, enjoyed; and we can only understand by reason of our education and that is by reason of our concrete individuality.[37]

In this passage Gentile's theory comes close to the presentist subjectivism for which it has been so often criticised. At face value this criticism is correct, because it is indeed difficult to see how subjectivism can be avoided when the historian re-thinks past thoughts according to his own norms on the basis of sources which he finds himself. But Gentile himself always insisted that he was not talking about this or that historian, but about the *pensiero pensante* of the transcendental ego which is presupposed by all thought. The present act of thought is therefore not a subjective thought, but it is a moment of eternal thought, as Gentile says:

> So true is this, that there is a history not only of Ariosto, but of the criticism of Ariosto, criticism which concerns not only the reality which the poem was in the poet's own spiritual life, but what it continues to be after his death, through the succeeding ages, in the minds of his readers, true continuators of his poetry.[38]

In other words, Ariosto's poem is eternal in the sense that it exists in the minds of thousands of readers who continue its life. All these readers together form, or embody, the transcendental ego, which pre-exists their thoughts both logically and ontologically. Gentile thus turns the whole problem of intersubjectivity upside down. Usually we think of different people with different interpretations of *Orlando Furioso* who try to come to an agreement. But in Gentile's view different people exist only empirically; the prime reality is the eternal spirit, the 'One who thinks for all'.[39] The problem of intersubjectivity can be solved by re-thinking all the different interpretations of *Orlando Furioso* as incarnations of the eternal spirit, that is, they must be re-thought as being based on different principles. These principles are made explicit in the history of philosophy. In this way the tradition of interpretations of *Orlando Furioso* runs parallel to the history of philosophy.

On the basis of his solution of the historical antinomy, Gentile solves some other antinomies that beset historical thought. In the *Teoria generale dello spirito come atto puro* he deals with antinomy between the universal and particular history, between *res gestae* and *historia rerum gestarum,* and with the problem of progress. In Gentile's view philosophy is the most universal form of the spirit, and therefore the history of philosophy is the only possible form of universal

---

37 Ibid., 196.
38 Ibid., 196.
39 Ibid., 198.

history. But he also recognises other forms of experience like art, religion, science, and practice. Accordingly, Gentile acknowledges the possibility of their particular history on the condition that they are conceived as aspects of the universal history of philosophy. Thus art, taken as an abstract form of self-consciousness, and not regarded as consciousness of reality, can never be the object of history. Conceived in this way, every work of art appears to us as an 'individuality which is closed in itself'.[40] But we can reconstruct the history in which the particular work of art was created. We are able to think Ariosto's thoughts for ourselves and to re-actualise or reconstruct his world. After this reconstruction we must 'forget the world of the poet, we must lose ourselves in his poetical world and dream with him'.[41] In other words, in order to understand the poetry of Ariosto we must know the historical reality in which he lived. In this particular example in the *Teoria generale dello spirito* Gentile does not elaborate the identity between art and history, although he concludes that art as a self-conscious activity is identical with philosophy. From this it follows that the history of art can only be understood on the basis of the history of philosophy.[42] Along the same lines Gentile shows that the history of religion, science, and action are only possible on condition that these forms of the spirit are interpreted as forms of philosophy and hence as proceeding within in the dialectic of *pensiero pensante* and *pensato*. The history of these particular forms of the spirit should be 'resolved' into the universal history of philosophy.[43]

In all his historical works, and especially in those that do not deal with the history of philosophy, Gentile follows this line. Sometimes this leads to exaggerations, for example in *I Profeti del Risorgimento Italiano* (*The Prophets of the Italian Risorgimento*) of 1923, in which he presents leaders like Cavour (1810–1861), King Vittorio Emmanuele (1820–1878), and even Garibaldi (1807–1882) as great philosophers. However, sometimes the same doctrine leads him to modern insights, when, for example, he shows us children as small philosophers in his *Preliminari allo studio dello fanciullo* (*Preliminaries to the Study of the Child*) of 1924. For Gentile history is identical with the history of philosophy, because philosophy is the essence of man.[44]

On the basis of his solution of the historical antinomy Gentile also shows that history is always progressive. In order to conceive history as progress, Gentile says, we must first reject the distinction between *res gestae* and *historia rerum gestarum*. According to Gentile, progress implies process and process is not thinkable as long as *res gestae* is understood as a necessary presupposition for

---

[40] Ibid., 214.
[41] Ibid., 215.
[42] Ibid., 218.
[43] Ibid., 223.
[44] G. Gentile, *Preliminari allo studio del fanciullo*, de Alberti, Roma, 1924, cited from *Preliminari allo studio del fanciullo*, OC XLII, Sansoni, Florence, 1969, 72–4.

historical thought.[45] History deals with facts, but the understanding of them is based on the unity of reality, in which both these facts and the historian participate. For example, between the persons in the past and ourselves in the present there must be a common language, a common spirituality, and so forth. At this point Gentile makes a typical immanentist move, arguing that this world, this common process, is only 'realised' when we study history. In other words, history presupposes the concept of the process that it creates itself; history creates its own presuppositions.

Finally, we come to the problem of the value of history. What is the function of history in the light of our practical activities? Or to formulate it in Gentile's language; how can history realise the ideal of the *etica del sapere*? The task of the philosopher-historian is to contribute to the universal values of his community by studying their history. We are now able to see how Gentile's interpretation of the identity of philosophy and history realises this ideal. History finds its origin in the thinking of the individual historian who reconstructs past thoughts on the basis of sources. His history will have value on the condition that it is interpreted in the light of the universal history of philosophy; all particular histories ranging from the history of art, religion, science, and even biographies must be interpreted in the light of the history of philosophy. Last but not least, history must be interpreted as progress. In Gentile's system this means that all particular histories must be interpreted as an aspect of the history of philosophy, because only philosophy can truly progress.

Croce's Criticism of Gentile's Identity of Philosophy and History

Gentile dedicated *Teoria generale dello spirit come atto puro* to Croce in gratitude for the *concordia discors* that had led to it. But the latter immediately realised that the book contributed more to the *discordia* than to the *concordia*. In a letter to his friend, Croce explicitly referred to the identity of philosophy and history, and urged that he should stress more that every history deals with a particular problem, instead of resolving all particular problems in the one universal problem of philosophy. Referring to Gentile's Ariosto example, Croce says that the history of literature should concentrate on 'the dialectic of a single artist'. This is not different in the history of philosophy which is in his view a history of particular problems, not of a single 'fundamental problem'.[46] In response to this letter Gentile answered that he agreed with Croce about the 'particularity of universal history and the universality of particular history', but it seems that he was only trying to placate his friend as his own views differed significantly from Croce's.[47] As we have seen, Croce made the development of the pure concepts of philos-

---

[45] G. Gentile, *Teoria generale dello spirito come atto puro*, 51.
[46] B. Croce, *Lettere a Giovanni Gentile*, 517–8, 1 June 1916.
[47] G. Gentile, *Lettere a Benedetto Croce, Volume V*, Le Lettere, Florence, 1990, 82–3, 8 June 1916.

ophy dependent on the sequence of intuitions, with the consequence that all philosophical problems are considered as particular problems. For Gentile it is the other way around; he makes the development of philosophy constitutive of all other mental activities, including art, with the consequence that all particular problems are seen as instantiations of the universal problem of philosophy.

These differences between Croce and Gentile on the relationship between the various mental activities explain their different interpretations of the identity of philosophy and history. Croce's identity of philosophy and history leaves the distinctions between universal concepts intact. Croce's historian-philosopher elaborates the meaning of the universal concepts by predicating a representation, but leaves the philosophical distinctions intact. Gentile's philosopher-historian seems to wipe out all distinctions; all distinctions are *pensati*, concepts, or presuppositions which need to be interpreted in the light of the act of thought which is the only category of philosophy.

From 1913 onwards, Croce rejected Gentile's actualism as a form of subjectivist mysticism. In Croce's view, Gentile's pure act wiped out all necessary distinctions and even the notion of distinction itself. The pure act itself is an indeterminate mystic entity which may also be called 'life', 'sentiment', 'will', and so forth, because all determination involves a distinction which is impossible in actualism.[48] According to Croce, mysticism makes the passage from actuality to history impossible, because the opposition between *pensiero pensante* and *pensiero pensato* involves a distinction which is not allowed by actualism.[49] Furthermore, Croce points out that actualism tends to liquidate philosophy, which is in his view always a discussion about distinctions.[50]

Gentile always defended himself against Croce's charge of subjectivism and mysticism. Against the charge of subjectivism Gentile responded that he distinguished between the empirical ego and the transcendental ego. The first is every natural person singly; the second is the subject of ideal eternal history. From this distinction it follows that historical beauty, truth, and goodness should not be confused with eternal beauty, truth, and goodness, just as the individual will should not be confused with the universal will of the state.[51] Against Croce's charge of mysticism, Gentile pointed out that actualism does not wipe away the distinctions, but that it tries to understand how they are formed by the act of thought. He even claimed that actualism makes an infinite number of distinctions intelligible, to begin with all distinctions made in the past.[52]

Both arguments do not fully counter Croce's criticisms because Gentile never explained what entitles the philosopher to claim that he has understood the ideal

---

[48] B. Croce, 'Intorno all'idealismo attuale', in *La Voce*, V, n.46, 1913, cited from *Conversazioni Critiche, serie seconda*, Laterza, Bari, 1918, 68–9.

[49] Ibid., 69–70.

[50] Ibid., 68.

[51] Ibid., 6, 17–18, 253.

[52] G. Gentile, *Teoria generale dello spirito come atto puro*, 263.

eternal history of the transcendental ego. Gentile had an answer to this question: we elaborate our concept of the transcendental ego by studying the history of philosophy and this means that the historian of philosophy is best equipped to say how beauty, truth, and goodness should be understood. But this highly intellectualistic argument is not satisfying, because history of philosophy does not prevail over other histories. Moreover, the historian of philosophy, being an empirical ego, like all other human beings, does not have a more 'objective' view of history than they have. Gentile himself was certainly aware of this issue in his system and tried to overcome it in his monumental *Sistema di logica*.

The Ethics of Knowing: *System of Logic* (1917–23)

Gentile's *Sistema di logica* is not a treatise on logic in the traditional sense of the word. It does not only deal with the formal aspects of thought, but also with metaphysics, because in Gentile's metaphysics of the thinking act of logic is of necessity also the theory of reality. Gentile's logic is therefore an example of 'noetic' logic, and it can be seen as metaphysics with a particular stress on the logical aspects. But Gentile also viewed his logic as ethics since the ultimate consequence of the identity between theory and practice is that truth becomes a duty, and error a sin. All this is rather bewildering to common sense and even Collingwood was baffled by the boldness and abstract generality of Gentile's identities; he always found Gentile's *Sistema di logica* less 'inspiring' than the *Sommario di pedagogia*.[53] Holmes, one of the most competent interpreters of Gentile's logic, dedicated an entire chapter to 'restating' Gentile's argument and another chapter to rendering his terminology into plain English. Leaving many neologisms aside, he still found more than ten cases of abuse of words.[54] Despite these shortcomings, the *Sistema di logica* is still of the highest importance to understanding Gentile's development, as well as the development of his critics, Croce, de Ruggiero, and Collingwood.

For Gentile the key to the solution of the problem of the *etica del sapere* lies in a new synthesis of *pensiero pensato* and *pensiero pensante*. If thought is to be ethical, it must be based on an objective norm. In this context, Gentile uses the word objective in the Kantian sense, namely as validity for different observers. Objectivity thus means intersubjectivity, and Gentile tries to base this on the logical structure of the *pensiero pensato*. At the same time Gentile wants to do justice to the purity, universality, and necessity of the *pensiero pensante*. Stated in Italian Gentile's problem is to show how *pensiero pensato* can be incorporated in *pensiero pensante* without damaging the objectivity of *pensiero pensato* or the purity of *pensiero pensante*. In plain English this problem can be rendered as: how can thought freely develop itself, while being bound by a norm?

---

[53] R.G. Collingwood, 'Letters to Guido de Ruggiero', 1920–38, Dep. 27, 2 September 1926.
[54] Holmes, *The Idealism of Giovanni Gentile*, 32–54.

In the *Sistema di logica* Gentile's tries to solve this problem by showing how thought provides itself with a truth-norm in the form of a concept. In order to illustrate this doctrine, Gentile gives an illustration from history. In this context, he claims that the consciousness of the 'circularity' of the notion of the historian's object is the condition without which he would lose his fundamental norm of judgment, or 'historical sense'. In Gentile's view, it is this conception of circularity which distinguishes an historian from a poet.

> ...if we want to know Dante's poetry (and this is the task of criticism), then we must begin to adopt (and continue this after that in all moments of our study) a spiritual attitude, in which that reality, to which we direct ourselves, is considered as a concept, and therefore as a circular thought: as something that is thinkable as a closed system and functions as norm of our thought.[55]

In other words, if we study Dante we must think of him as a concept, that is, as a 'circular' or self-identical entity in which all determinations are fixed and which functions as a presupposition of our act of thought. Gentile points out, however, that in fact we do not think of the concept of Dante as pre-existent to our thought:

> But this norm does not really exist before our thought. This ambiguity should now be eliminated definitely after all that has been said in order to show the absurdity of such a presupposition. This norm arises in our present thought as if it is pre-existent to our thinking, pre-existent because we generate it as a concept and this concept is only a concept because of its circularity.[56]

In the last line of this passage, Gentile stresses the fact that we should never forget that it is present thought which generates Dante as a concept in order to think about him. In another passage Gentile calls this norm 'idealità' ('ideality') which put itself in opposition to reality; the concept of Dante, which *pensiero pensante* generates for itself, functions as a regulative idea. Accordingly, *pensiero pensato* has two functions for *pensiero pensante*; the concept is both the presupposition and the regulative idea for the act of thought. We start from a concept of Dante aiming at a new concept of the poet. In the context of history this means that the historian must posit past thought of Dante as a presupposition to his own thought in order to develop his own concept of Dante. In this context, the historian takes the historiography of Dante as the starting point for his own investigations, which will result in a new view of Dante's poetry. This new concept of Dante, however, does not necessarily cohere with the historiography on Dante. Absolute coherence would infringe on the freedom of the act of thought; the new Dante must be in accordance with the norms of truth to which the historian submits himself.

Typically, Gentile does not interpret the subject of an individual judgment as an intuition, as Croce does, but as a concept. When we start our historical inves-

---

[55] G. Gentile, *Sistema di logica*, II, 30.

[56] Ibid., 30–1.

tigations, Dante is not a product of the imagination for us, but *pensiero pensato*, or concept, learned in education. This Dante is what he is, he is a mere A = A, a mere 'that', or a 'circular concept'. When someone asks us 'why do you think that Dante was a great poet?', we cannot answer the question, because we have not re-thought Dante's thought according to our own truth-norms. In Gentilian terms; we have not thought of Dante on the basis of concrete logos.

Pensiero pensante cannot rest in this position; Dante as concept is not my own concept, it is abstract thought and not *norma sui*. The Dante I know from the manuals and historiography is still not my Dante; it is not the Dante whom I can think according to my norms. To the question 'why?', Gentile says, I can only respond 'because he is as he is'. In order to overcome this position I must read the *Divina Commedia* for myself, that is, re-think Dante's thoughts as my own. For this reason Gentile says that all re-thinking requires the identity of the past thought with present thought. At the same time, since I am living in the present, I cannot not become Dante, though I can judge Dante's thoughts. This judging implies an objectification of Dante's thoughts which amounts to making a difference between his thoughts and mine.[57]

Judging Dante involves a development of the truth-norm or concrete logos; by reading his poetry a new 'I think' comes into being. To expand Gentile's example; yesterday I thought that Dante's *Inferno* was an ugly description of an ugly place, but today, after reading his *Divina Commedia,* I see the beauty of the poem. This means not only that my judgment about Dante's *Inferno* has changed, but also that I have changed; by reading Dante I have changed the principles of my criticism. This is the kernel of the auto-synthesis which expresses the development of the principles on which the judgment rests. According to Gentile, the A = A, the Dante as I knew him, has now become the content of my present judgment A = B in which I judge 'what' he is by re-thinking his thoughts on the basis of my principles thought by the ego which develops into a new ego. So the development from the A = A to the A = B presupposes a development from an old ego to a new ego. In other words, the development of my judgment implies a development of the grounds or principles on which it is based.[58]

What Gentile describes here is in fact a learning process in which both thought and its principles are involved. By re-thinking Dante's thoughts, I learn about myself; yesterday I thought he was a mediocre poet, today I understand the beauty of his poetry. At the same time, by confronting myself with his poetry, I have taught myself new aesthetic principles. Or to put it differently: by reading Dante not only does my judgment of his poetry develop, but also the grounds or presuppositions on which it is based develop. By reading Dante's poetry my whole notion of poetry develops.

---

57   Ibid., 40.
58   Ibid., 62.

By the doctrine of the auto-synthesis, Gentile tries to solve the problem of how philosophy changes by historical thought, that is, how our principles change by re-thinking the thought of others.[59] Along these lines, Gentile describes the learning process of philosophy in history as the development of the transcendental ego. This ego develops by continuously re-thinking past thoughts for itself as we have seen above. The result of this development of the ego, or 'auto-synthesis', is *autoconcetto* or 'auto-concept', which forms the history of 'auto-syntheses'. This can be seen as the history of an idea, or the history of the principles or norms of the development of thought. In the auto-concept the concepts from which we start our auto-synthesis find their norm. In historical terms this is the history of the principles upon which all the historiography about Dante has been based. It is 'the history of the idea of Dante', that is, the history of the principles upon which the historiography of Dante has been based.

On the basis of the notion of the *autoconcetto* Gentile tried to solve the problem of historical objectivity which is central to his *Sistema di logica*. Gentile starts from the principle that the historian is free; his thought is pure act and *norma sui*. For this reason, the historian's thought is true to himself and to all questions beginning with 'why' he answers 'because I think it so'. But behind this 'I think it so' hides the auto-synthesis, or the development of truth-norms. This auto-synthesis provides itself with truth on the basis of the auto-concept, the product of the auto-synthesis.[60] According to the doctrine of the auto-concept, the historian thinks that Dante is a great poet not only because he has re-thought Dante's thoughts and the entire historiography of Dante, but also because he has studied the principles on which this whole historiography rests. To paraphrase Gentile, we can say that when the historian says 'Dante is a great poet because I think him that he is so' he means: 'I know that Dante is a grerat poet, because I have studied his thought and the thoughts of my former and present colleagues and the philosophical principles on which his thought and their thoughts rested, and now I have come to the conclusion that Dante must be thought as a great poet, because I know where my principles differ from the principles of my colleagues'.

As an illustration of this doctrine Gentile cites Mommsen, who claimed that he knew more than Livy about Rome's earliest history:

> He (Mommsen) has thought more, that is, the human spirit, who is not only Theodor Mommsen, but that spirit that in nineteen centuries developed its historical categories, its penetration in the material evidence, that spirit that always searches and thinks, that is always dissatisfied and reflects and writes

---

59 This is the same problem Collingwood had to deal with in *An Essay on Metaphysics*, 1940, for this reason it is particularly interesting to follow the rest of Gentile's argument on this matter, see chapter 10, pp. 391–392.

60 G. Gentile, *Sistema di Logica*, II, 153.

the History of Rome as an act of a thought that renders all past thoughts inactual. [61]

With the notion of the auto-concept Gentile claimed that he had found the solution to the problem of subjectivism; the norm for historical judgment is found in the auto-concept, or in the history of philosophy considered as the self-development of synthetic *a priori* judgments. The category in which all historical categories resolve themselves is the auto-concept, or philosophy. History is therefore identical to philosophy.[62]

Conclusion

Gentile's *Sistema di logica* is an heroic attempt to elaborate the implications of the notion of history for philosophy. Its major aim is to model a philosophical logic after the logic of historical thought in order to understand philosophy that develops itself on the basis of its own past. In this sense, it is one of the greatest tributes to the belief in the creative power of human thought and rationality. On every page of his logic Gentile stresses the creative aspects of thought: man makes his world by thinking it. Accordingly, the vital problem that Gentile had to solve concerned the objectivity of present thought; somehow creative thought had to be anchored in reality. Gentile himself claimed that he had solved this problem with his notion of the *autoconcetto*. But interpreters have always differed in opinion about this solution. After reading the *Sistema di logica*, Croce kept to his verdict of mysticism, and in actualist circles philosophers such as Carlini and Scaravelli found that Gentile had sacrificed the purity and the spontaneity of the act of thought in order to show its objectivity.[63] Gentile, they said, had not shown how the abstract logic passes over into the concrete logic, or to put it differently; Gentile had not shown why we develop our thoughts instead of always thinking the same.

The English speaking critics found that Gentile had not overcome subjectivism. In the 'Libellus de Generatione' of 1920, Collingwood rejected Gentile's philosophy as a 'myth of process' because it obscured the importance of the past.[64] In 1937 Holmes was of the opinion that Gentile's *Sistema di logica* was subjectivist and even solipsist, because he still presupposed the ego in his system. Accordingly, he suggested that the ego should be banned. The result would then be something like a 'metaphysics without a thinking subject'.[65] Harris

---

[61] Ibid., 286.

[62] Ibid., 285–90.

[63] Armando Carlini, *Studi gentiliani*, Sansoni, Florence, 1958; Luigi Scaravelli, *Critica del capire*, La Nuova Italia, Florence, 1968, 143.

[64] See chapter 7, pp. 229–236.

[65] Holmes, *The Idealism of Giovanni Gentile*, 158–60.

defended Gentile from Holmes in 1960 and stressed that the concept of ego forms the indispensable basis of the *etica del sapere*.[66]

Interestingly, both the Italian and the English speaking commentators point in the direction of the problematic relationship between the abstract logic and the concrete logic in Gentile's *Sistema di logica*. The Italians criticise Gentile for not having showed the passage from the logic of the abstract to the logic of the concrete, the English criticise Gentile for having resolved abstract logic completely into concrete logic so that it can never be the norm for present thought.

In my view both problems in Gentile's system stem from his overvaluation of the *pensante* to the *pensato*. As in his previous work Gentile continues to identify the *pensante* with the pure act of thought, which is the logical and ontological source of all reality, and the *pensato* with 'error', 'nature', 'multiplicity'. This overvaluation of the *pensante* results in a sharp distinction between philosophical thought and empirical thought. According to Gentile, only philosophical thought is wholly *norma sui*, its principles are completely explicit, because it posits itself and its object in a self-conscious act. Empirical thought is not *norma sui*, its principles are implicit, and it is therefore identical with abstract thought which has no real truth-value. In 'L'atto del *pensare* come atto puro' Gentile recognised the implicitness of principles but he never explained their relationship with the *norma sui* character of thought. Already in *Teoria generale dello spirito come atto puro* Gentile began to overvalue the importance of philosophical thought above empirical thought with the result that he resolved the particular histories of art, religion, and science into the universal history of philosophy. The *Sistema di logica* forms the culmination of this development; the sole reality Gentile recognises is the self-conscious act of thought. This is seen most clearly in Gentile's analysis of the *autoconcetto*. The *autoconcetto* is the product or result of the norms that thought has posited for itself, or the history of the idea that a mental activity has of itself, for example, the history of the idea of art, or the history of *The Idea of History*, or within history, the history of the idea of Dante. The *autoconcetto* is developed in the process of thought which continually posits its own concepts; the historian must posit this concept as a starting point for his own investigations. The result of these investigations will form the conceptual basis for new acts of thought so that the process goes on for eternity. Gentile presents this positing of the concept as a self-conscious act; the historian is continuously aware of the norms to which he submits himself.

But what is the status of this concept that the historian posits for himself? In the first place it is clear that it does not come out of the blue; the concept of Dante I posit for myself as a starting point for my investigations is the result of a process of thought, involving, for example, my education, previous researches, and historiography. Moreover, the act of thought posits this concept freely. In this context, Gentile sometimes describes the positing of the concept as the mak-

---

[66] Harris, *The Social Philosophy of Giovanni Gentile*, 292–9.

ing of a choice between two alternatives, which shows that he views the concept
as an assumption and not as a presupposition. Although Gentile does not clarify
it, the distinction is important. As Holmes pointed out, both assumptions and
presuppositions are suppositions, but assumptions are made consciously,
whereas presuppositions are made unconsciously.[67] Gentile interprets history
and *ipso facto* philosophy as a thought process that proceeds on the basis of
assumptions. His view therefore does not differ much from Vaihinger's (1852–
1933) *Philosophie als Ob,* that de Ruggiero rejected as early as 1912.[68] By viewing
history as being based on assumptions, history will turn into a useful illusion;
we may think that there is some history, but in the end it turns out to be at best
one of the possible constructions that one can make or, at worst, sheer fancy.

Like no other before him Gentile described history as self-knowledge of the
human mind; all history, all re-enactment of past thought is done in order to
understand the development of the transcendental ego. But as pointed out
earlier, Gentile takes it for granted that this transcendental ego can be known as
the history of philosophy. From this he jumps to the conclusion that the historian
of philosophy can understand the whole of history; only his thoughts are *norma
sui,* necessary, and universal. History is thus turned into the justification of the
present.

All this is not so dangerous as long as it remains theory, but in practice it can
lead, and it did lead, to the philosophy of Fascism which regards the history of
the state as the self-positing act of the transcendental ego incarnated in the
Italian people and their leader. Moreover, since this act is necessary and universal, everybody in the same situation must see it as the only outcome of Italian
history.

---

[67] R.G. Collingwood, *An Essay on Metaphysics,* 27.
[68] G. de Ruggiero, *La filosofia contemporanea,* 64.

Chapter Four

Guido de Ruggiero's Early Development (1911–1918)

Introduction

Guido de Ruggiero was born in Naples in 1888. After graduating in jurisprud-ence in 1911, he worked for some time as an official in the Ministry of Education in Rome.[1] This job enabled him to continue the philosophical studies that were his true passion. Around 1906, an uncle introduced him to Croce, and in 1911 de Ruggiero met Gentile at Palermo.[2] He became friendly with both philosophers. In 1911, de Ruggiero made his debut at the International Congress of Philosophy in Bologna with a critical examination of Kant's deduction of categories.[3] In the same year he published the first chapters of *Saggio di una gnoseologia della scienza economica* (*Essay on the Gnoseology of Economic Science*) in the *Giornale degli economisti* (*Journal of Economists*) and a paper on the philosophy of religion, 'La redenzione come svolgimento dello spirito' ('Redemption as Development of the Spirit'). In 1911, Croce asked him to contribute to *La Critica* for which he pub-lished reviews of foreign contemporary philosophical works such as Cassirer's *Substanzbegriff und Funktionsbegriff* of 1910, Russell's *The Problems of Philosophy* of 1912, Royce's *The Philosophy of Loyalty* of 1908, and many others.

In 1912, de Ruggiero began a career as a journalist for *La Voce* and *Il resto del carlino*, and the work he did there would have a lasting effect on his philosophy. In the same year, he published *La filosofia contemporanea*, which established his name as an historian of philosophy in Italy and abroad. In 1912, he also pub-lished 'La scienza come esperienza assoluta' ('Science as Absolute Experience'), a theoretical essay on the relationship between science, history, and philosophy. In 1914, he published *Problemi della vita morale* (*Problems of Moral Life*), in which he applies the dialectic of question and answer in what he called 'the ethics of historicism'. In the same year, de Ruggiero wrote *Critica del concetto di cultura* (*Criticism of the Concept of Culture*), which contains a severe criticism of the

---

[1] Renzo de Felice, 'De Ruggiero, Guido', in *Dizionario Biografico degli Italiani*, Istituto della Enciclopedia Italiana, Roma, 1991, 249.

[2] Ibid., 249. Gentile, *Lettere a Benedetto Croce, Volume quarto*, 185–6.

[3] G. de Ruggiero, 'Il problema della deduzione delle categorie', in *Atti del IV Congresso internazionale di filosofia*, Bologna 1911, Kraus, Nendeln, Lichtenstein, 1968, 331–6.

German *Kulturgeschichte*. Meanwhile, de Ruggiero published dozens of articles and reviews in several philosophical journals and newspapers and translated works by Descartes, Leibniz, and Kant.

This awe-inspiring productivity—de Ruggiero was in his early twenties—was suddenly interrupted when Italy threw itself into the war in May 1915. De Ruggiero was stationed in Naples to be sent to the front in 1917.[4] During the war he published 'La pensée italienne et la guerre' in *Revue de Métaphysique et de Morale* in 1916. This important article contains the essence of de Ruggiero's philosophy of history. Back from the front, he published *La filosofia greca* (*Greek Philosophy*), the first of the multi-volume *Storia della filosofia* that he would leave unfinished upon his death in 1948, having just published the volume on Hegel.

La filosofia contemporanea (Modern Philosophy) (1912)

The best introduction to de Ruggiero's thought is *La filosofia contemporanea*, which he published in 1912. In the 'Translators' Preface' Collingwood recommends the book as 'a work which no student of modern thought can afford to ignore'.[5] Collingwood describes the book as the first comprehensive history of philosophy in the second half of the nineteenth and the beginning of the twentieth century and praises it as a product of the historical view of philosophy, which he regards as typical for the Italian idealists. His only doubt concerns de Ruggiero's 'trenchant and outspoken criticism'.[6]

Even if we do not take de Ruggiero's age into account, the book is an amazing achievement. It critically discusses dozens of philosophers in Germany, France, the Anglo-Saxon countries, and Italy, ranging from the well-known ones, like Marx, Nietzsche, Comte, Spencer, and Croce, to the relatively unknown Alois Riehl (1844–1924), Louis Weber, and the Italian neo-Kantians.[7] De Ruggiero brings order to this jumble by judging them from a most outspoken point of view, which is also the basis of his 'trenchant criticism', mentioned by Collingwood. In the preface to the third edition of the book of 1928, de Ruggiero himself did not deplore his critical attitude which expressed 'the fervour of my twenties' and his 'joy of a first conquest of a new philosophical horizon'.[8] This 'new horizon' was 'absolute empiricism', a position that de Ruggiero traces back to Bertrando Spaventa, and which he presents as the outcome of striving for 'absolute immanence', which marked the history of philosophy in the second half of the nineteenth century.[9] In his early work, de Ruggiero associates 'abso-

---

4   De Felice, 'De Ruggiero, Guido', 249.
5   R.G. Collingwood and A.H. Hannay, 'Translators' Preface' to de Ruggiero, *Modern Philosophy*, 6.
6   Ibid.
7   I have not been able to trace the dates of Louis Weber, who published *Vers le Positivisme absolu par l'Idéalisme* in 1903.
8   G. de Ruggiero, *La filosofia contemporanea*, 7.
9   Ibid., 406. E.T., 337.

lute immanence' with many of its other connotations with the unity or identity of science and consciousness (*scienza e coscienza*) on the theoretical side and with the *etica dello storicismo* (ethics of historicism) on the practical side.

The identity of science and consciousness goes back to Vico and Spaventa. Like most Italian philosophers, de Ruggiero uses the term 'science' in the first place in the broad sense of 'knowledge', and only in the second place in the sense of 'natural science'. He often expresses this difference of meaning by distinguishing between 'science' and 'the sciences', the latter referring to the natural sciences.[10] Furthermore, de Ruggiero distinguishes his own, dialectical view of science *in fieri*, from the static interpretation of it as *scienza fatta*. The first notion grasps science in its actuality, or as a process, in the sense of *pensiero pensante*, the second presents it in its ideality, or as concept in the sense of *pensiero pensato*.

Coscienza literally means consciousness, but taken in the broad sense of the word it can best be translated to 'experience'. In this sense it comes close to the German idealist use of '*Bewusstsein*' (consciousness), but it has some typical Vichian and Spaventian overtones stressing the 'creative' and mediate character of consciousness, whereas the Germans saw '*Bewusstsein*' primarily as immediate experience.

Employing his own view of absolute immanentism, de Ruggiero interprets the identity of science and consciousness as a synthesis of opposites, which develops as a dialectic of question and answer. Conscious experience, or *scienza in fieri*, reconciles itself with its own opposite, namely *scienza fatta*, by taking its answers as the basis for its own questions. This dialectic of question and answer lies at the heart of de Ruggiero's absolute empiricism, as he called his own philosophy.

In *La filosofia contemporanea*, de Ruggiero writes the history of modern philosophy from the standpoint of absolute empiricism. In his view, positivism was the first philosophical movement after Hegel, which claimed a more immanentist view of reality. Against Hegel's dialectical abstractions, positivism held that thought should be based on facts in the first place. De Ruggiero fully agrees with this demand, but he also criticises positivism for hypostatising facts. For positivism, de Ruggiero says, reality is made *ab aeterno* and consequently thought is an 'eternal answer without a problem'.[11] On this basis, positivism is stranded in a *coincidentia oppositorum*, claiming immanence, but resulting in transcendence.

The failure of positivism led to the rise of new movements, which sought a more radical form of immanentism in 'immediate consciousness'. De Ruggiero gathers these movements, like Mill's empiricism, neo-Kantian phenomenalism, and Bergson's (1859–1941) intuitionism, under 'the philosophies of immediate

---

10 G. de Ruggiero, *La filosofia contemporanea*, 457. E.T., 378.
11 G. de Ruggiero, *La filosofia contemporanea*, 452.

consciousness and under 'the philosophies of sense'.[12] He acknowledges these philosophies' claim for a more thorough immanence, but he points out that this position can never be realised on the basis of immediate experience alone. For de Ruggiero, experience separated from thought is nothing but an eternal question without an answer; without concepts experience cannot develop.[13] Like positivism, the philosophies of immediate experience destroy themselves in a radical *coincidentia oppositorum* of immanence and transcendence; from the standpoint of immediate experience the whole realm of thought is transcendent.[14]

In de Ruggiero's view, the philosophies of immediate experience have deteriorated into 'sensationalism' which infects the culture of his own times with 'arrivism' and 'opportunism':

> And just as in philosophy sensationalism finds its crowning expression in the working success of the concept, and by a kind of logical opportunism which makes thought simply play its own hand against a reality it can never conquer, so sensationalism in everyday life is expressed in a similar opportunism which induces the spirit, in face of a real world of events over which it has no control, to abandon itself to caprice and swim with the tide. The individual labours under the illusion that in this abandonment he is living in complete harmony with the whole, he is making himself the mouthpiece and in fact the master of the universe, while actually this life of dilettantism means the most complete dissipation of spiritual strength, the surrender of the individual to the caprice of events, not their master but their slave.[15]

De Ruggiero detects this opportunism in the art, science, and religion of his times. In his view, art tends to become 'hysteric' because 'it tries to create a fictitious spiritual intimacy by subtle elaborations of meaning and lives on its own disease'.[16] Along the same lines, 'the modern scientist combines the most niggardly specialism with the grossest form of empiricism which denies everything that does not enter into its narrow purview'.[17] And finally, the apparent religion of his times 'consists of a false sensual intimacy and of subjective revelations, which are not celebrations of humility but of pride'.[18]

In spite of this harsh criticism of the culture of his own times de Ruggiero is full of hope for the future. In all countries of Europe new philosophical movements find the way to immanentism. Against the false objectivism of positivism and the subjectivism of the philosophies of immediate experience, they pose Kant's *a priori* synthesis as a unity of science and consciousness.[19] Furthermore,

---

12   Ibid., 446.
13   Ibid., 452.
14   Ibid., 446-9.
15   Ibid., 447-8. E.T., 370.
16   Ibid., 448. E.T., 371.
17   Ibid.
18   Ibid.
19   Ibid., 66, 452.

with Hegel these movements refute all forms of dualism and strive for an absolute immanence. For such thinkers as Jules Lachelier (1832–1918), Louis Weber,
Maurice Blondel (1861–1949), Josiah Royce (1855–1916), Croce, and Gentile,
reality is thought and therefore the product of human activity:

> The world of thought is actuality, concreteness, search and achievement,
> aspiration and attainment; this new conception of the world as the world of
> our struggle and labour must supplant the old conception of the world as a
> natural whole which is simply the creation of our imagination, arising from
> the accumulation of our past experiences and the expectation of new experi-
> ences.[20]

In other words, reality is not a 'given entity' separate from us, but it is definitely
'human made', that is, made in the process of human thought, which is history.
In de Ruggiero's view these new movements thus announce a new, historical
culture:

> And history is held in honour by the new culture; for history forms its whole
> substance. Naturalism made history a purposeless play of the unconscious
> masses of mankind; we were the playthings of history, not its masters. But
> idealism has endowed it with an entirely new significance; we are beginning
> to understand the true meaning of human continuity throughout the course of
> history, and in possessing our past we are learning to possess ourselves.[21]

In de Ruggiero's view this new culture is expressed in numerous new forms of
historical studies, the most important being the history of the sciences and the
history of philosophy; civil and political history are in de Ruggiero's eyes still in
their infancy.[22] Moreover, in his view there are many methodological studies of
history, mostly written by Germans, but not a theory of history as a science.[23]
According to de Ruggiero this is a great shortcoming, because only on the basis
of a strong historical culture we can give our lives a direction and free ourselves
from all forms of fatalism:

> This recognition of history is doubly conducive to effort; in the first place,
> because we can only become acquainted with the history of the past through
> laborious study and not through spontaneous revelations, and secondly,
> because history teaches us that the conception of the human reality of the
> world removes all justification for laziness and fatalism and comfortable
> reliance upon a kindly providence, and that we must depend upon ourselves
> for strength, because we are what we make ourselves, and our reality is our
> own work.[24]

---

20 Ibid., 454. E.T., 375.
21 Ibid., 454. E.T., 376.
22 Ibid., 454–5.
23 Ibid., 455.
24 Ibid., 456. E.T., 377.

Two years later de Ruggiero saw this passage as the first expression of his *etica dello storicismo*. Indeed it reveals de Ruggiero's highest personal and philosophical ideals; in his struggle for freedom, he connects history to and practice against fatalism. This theme can also be found in Croce's and Gentile's works, but they never expressed it with so much fervour. Moreover, both Croce and Gentile still clung to a 'kind providence', as de Ruggiero pointed out in his criticism of their philosophies.

De Ruggiero's Criticism of Croce and Gentile

De Ruggiero's discussion of Croce's philosophy is still one of the most thorough ever written. It has been imitated, if not copied, by many later commentators, like Bernard Bosanquet (1848–1923) and H. Wildon Carr (1857–1931) in England.[25] Furthermore, Collingwood's 'Croce's Philosophy of History' of 1921 heavily relies on de Ruggiero's *La filosofia contemporanea*, as the former explicitly admitted in a letter.[26]

According to de Ruggiero, Croce's philosophy is dominated by 'two different cultures'; one is dialectical, historical, and Hegelian, the other is static, non-historical, and Herbartian.[27] These two cultures are continuously in conflict. This comes most clearly to the fore in his *Ciò che è vivo e ciò che morto della filosofia di Hegel* of 1907. Though de Ruggiero fully agrees with Croce's criticism of Hegel's 'abuse' of dialects, he points out that Croce did not succeed in synthesising the dialectic of opposites with his own theory of distinct concepts. In de Ruggiero's view Croce's theory of distinct concepts is a combination of implication and classification which is incompatible with Hegel's dialectic of opposites.[28]

Seen from an historical point of view, de Ruggiero explains, Croce's theory of grades turns the clock back to Kant. For the latter, the *a priori* synthesis was a synthesis of distinct activities, namely sensation and understanding, whereas for Hegel this relationship was a synthesis of opposites. For Hegel, de Ruggiero points out, the opposition between sensation and understanding inevitably leads to the antinomies which can only be solved by reason.[29] Croce, however, follows Kant in so far as he interprets the *a priori* synthesis as a synthesis of distincts, namely art and philosophy, or intuition and concept. For this reason, a 'reciprocal conversion' of the two terms is impossible. The *a priori* synthesis is in Croce's hand nothing more than a 'unity of static determinations', which makes all understanding of development and history impossible. In the end, de

---

[25] Bernard Bosanquet, *The Meeting of Extremes in Contemporary Philosophy*, MacMillan, London, 1921; H. Wildon Carr, *The Philosophy of Benedetto Croce: The Problem of Art and History*, MacMillan, Londonm 1917.

[26] R.G. Collingwood, 'Letters to Guido de Ruggiero', 20 March 1921.

[27] G. de Ruggiero, *La filosofia contemporanea*, 419.

[28] Ibid., 421–4.

[29] Ibid., 424–5.

Ruggiero says, Croce's 'two cultures' end up in a most fundamental dilemma which de Ruggiero renders as follows:

> ...on the one hand, in so far as he affirms development, he implicitly denies the static determinations of the forms of the spirit; on the other hand, in so far as he affirms these forms, he denies development.[30]

According to de Ruggiero, this dilemma 'paralyses' Croce's entire philosophy. In aesthetics, it prevents Croce from explaining the relationship between art and history, because the distinction of art from the other forms of experience gives it a monadic character, which prevents him from understanding its historicity.[31] In logic, it leads Croce to an interpretation of the *a priori* judgment as 'a unity of static determinations', which hinders a true understanding of error. Finally, in the *Filosofia della pratica* the theory of distinct concepts 'suffocates' Croce's dialectic of good and bad, by distinguishing between utility and morality in order to understand the positivity of badness.[32]

De Ruggiero ends his discussion of Croce's philosophy with a task for future philosophy:

> Since Croce—or rather, since the Philosophy of the Spirit; for Croce is an indefatigable thinker, and in the development of his thought may yet surpass that position—the task before philosophy is in our view, to fuse into a fresh unity the distinctions of the Crocean system, without, however, ignoring the just demands which these distinction are designed to satisfy.[33]

De Ruggiero does not work out this task in more detail, but on the basis of the foregoing we are able to reconstruct the full meaning of this passage. The starting point of the new philosophy is Croce's theory of the distinct forms of the spirit. Croce designed his theory in order to vindicate the autonomy of the different forms of experience. De Ruggiero endorses this claim for autonomy, but he points out that the forms must be fused into a new unity. From the foregoing it is clear that de Ruggiero thought that new unity should be founded on the Hegelian interpretation of Kant's *a priori* synthesis, in which sensation and understanding are understood as opposites in order to enable their mutual conversion. Only on this basis can the 'dialectical motive' be brought back into forms of the spirit, thus vindicating their historicity. Moreover, de Ruggiero's new interpretation of the *a priori* synthesis must also lead to a new theory of error, or negativity, which will be the heart of the new philosophy.

According to de Ruggiero, he and Gentile were already elaborating these ideas; although he criticises Gentile's 'Le forme assolute dello spirito' of 1909. In this sketch Gentile had still distinguished art, science, and religion as lower

---

30 Ibid., 425. E.T., 352.
31 Ibid., 426.
32 Ibid., 430.
33 Ibid., 431. E.T., 357.

forms of experience that are reconciled by philosophy, the highest form. De Ruggiero criticises this view as follows:

> Thus the process from subjectivity to objectivity is not something initiated in art and completed elsewhere, for this would imply a transcendence; it is completed in art itself, in so far as the moment of subjectivity is the mere abstract over against the concrete concept of art: hence art is not resolved into philosophy, but it is itself philosophy in so far as it is reality and concreteness.[34]

This passage clearly reveals the differences between Gentile's and de Ruggiero's interpretation of the relationship between the different forms of experience. Along actualist lines, both philosophers consider these forms of experience primarily as activities, but for Gentile the lower forms of the spirit overcome their abstractness only in the highest form, that is, philosophy, whereas de Ruggiero finds philosophy in the forms of experience themselves. In other words, in Gentile's view philosophy is the highest form of experience in which the lower forms find their rationality. In de Ruggiero's view, however, philosophy is to be found in the forms of experience themselves. For Gentile, the only true transcendental experience of the mind is self-consciousness, for de Ruggiero all forms of experience are transcendental activities of the mind. These fundamentally different views of the relationship between the various forms of experience lie at the basis of Gentile's monistic interpretation of actualism and de Ruggiero's pluralistic interpretation of it.

According to de Ruggiero, Gentile overcame the shortcomings of 'Le forme assolute' with 'L'atto del *pensare* come atto puro' by which he moved towards a form of absolute empiricism. However, de Ruggiero's formulation is extremely cautious: 'this is the goal towards which, if I am not mistaken, Gentile seems to be moving.'[35] But he would soon discover that this was not the case. In his later works, Gentile interpreted 'L'atto del *pensare* come atto puro' in the opposite way; instead of resolving philosophy into the various forms of experience, he resolved these into the pure act of thought which he identified with philosophy. From de Ruggiero's point of view, Gentile did not realise the ideal of absolute empiricism, but stuck to his transcendentism of 1909. This explains why de Ruggiero and Collingwood not only saw themselves as philosophers 'after' Croce but also 'after' Gentile. De Ruggiero's took a first step to this position when he began to elaborate his absolute empiricism in 1912.

'Science as Absolute Experience' (1912)

De Ruggiero's first realisation of the task he had assigned to modern philosophy in *La filosofia contemporanea* was to vindicate the autonomy of science.[36] In his view, this vindication was needed because idealists had not yet taken science

---

[34]   Ibid., 434. E.T., 359.

[35]   Ibid., 435. E.T. 360.

[36]   In this section, 'science' means the natural sciences.

seriously enough. Croce had degraded science to the production of useful pseudo-concepts, thus refuting its status as knowledge. Likewise, Gentile had relegated science to the sphere of abstract logos. De Ruggiero, who was well acquainted with both the natural and social sciences, was convinced that the nineteenth century had shown that 'the sciences are wholly justified in vindicating their complete autonomy'.[37] From this viewpoint, the distinction between philosophy and science was based on 'an optical illusion'. Only as a finished product does science appear to the philosopher as a system of abstract concepts but *in fieri* science is a concrete experience, that is, it is a self-consciously developing form of experience. For the scientist 'in action' scientific concepts are not abstract at all, they form part of his actual experience and are based on the questions and answers with which he develops his science. For the scientist, de Ruggiero argues, a 'pre-scientific' form of experience or 'hyper-scientific' form of experience does not exist.[38]

Given this starting point, de Ruggiero's problem considerably differs from Croce's and Gentile's. These philosophers had not acknowledged the sciences as true knowledge. Consequently, their problem was to show how the sciences become more rational via history and philosophy. In contrast, de Ruggiero recognised science as a form of knowledge. His main problem was therefore to show the philosophical and historical foundations upon which it is based, or, in his own terminology, he had to prove the identity of science and philosophy.

In de Ruggiero's view, the greatest obstacle for proving this identity is the distinction between consciousness and science which creates a barrier between the spontaneous, immediate, and subjective play of imagination on the one hand, and the necessary objective principles of science on the other. De Ruggiero tries to remove this obstacle by showing that science is 'absolute experience', that is, a form of experience which has reconciled its own opposite (universal and necessary principles) by including them into itself.[39] Interestingly, de Ruggiero solves this problem by interpreting the development of scientific consciousness as a dialectic of question and answer. In 'La scienza come esperienza assoluta' de Ruggiero discusses this dialectic from three different perspectives: he deals firstly with 'science as a question', then with 'science as an answer', and he ends with an analysis of 'science as a question and answer'.

De Ruggiero first focuses on the 'moment' of the question in consciousness. He begins by rejecting the common sense view according to which questions arise from the clash between our consciousness and a given object.[40] Following the basic principle of actualism, de Ruggiero argues the object is not 'given' to consciousness, because it is nothing but a 'condensation of past experience' to be

---

[37] Ibid., 458. E.T., 379.

[38] Ibid., 457.

[39] G. de Ruggiero, 'La scienza come esperienza assoluta', 231–2.

[40] Ibid., 248–9.

'acknowledged' by the scientist. The object is therefore completely ideal, that is, it is only real for the thought that thinks it. On this basis, de Ruggiero argues in an actualist vein that thought does not presuppose the object, but that the object presupposes thought. The subject is therefore always prior to the object; it is the scientist who raises the question and not the object.[41]

Questions begin with sensation. Sensation is always in flux, it is immediate, actual, and subjective. Using Bradley's (1846–1924) and Royce's terminology, de Ruggiero says that in sensation we experience the 'that' of reality, without its 'what', its actual existence without its essence.[42] Sensation, being immediate, can never explain itself. Explanation is the task of thought; sensation thus raises a question, which subsequently calls for an answer.[43]

The task of thought is to give an answer to the question which has arisen. It must explain sensation, by determining the 'what' of the 'that' or the essence of existence. In this way, thought transforms the endless variations of sensation into an identity which persists in time. The main effect of thought is 'neutralisation' of time, space, and difference. The result of neutralisation is an ideal object in which experience and concept coincide.[44]

Up to this point, de Ruggiero has analysed the moment of the question and the moment of the answer separately. In reality, however, questions and answers form a continuous process. This continuity is the subject of the last and most important section of 'La scienza come esperienza assoluta'. De Ruggiero begins by applying the most important principle of actualism to the dialectic of question and answer. This is the principle that the *pensato* only exists for the *pensante*. In the dialectic of question and answer the answer stands for the concept, or a *pensato*, but the *pensato* exists only in the present act of thought, that is, in the dialectic of the thinking mind itself. The present act of thought overcomes the abstractness of the concept by a process which de Ruggiero calls 'idealisation'. Idealisation overcomes the ideality of thought by transforming it into an 'ideal actuality'.[45] De Ruggiero describes this notion of idealisation, which he considers as the apex of his investigations, as follows:

> Ideality belongs to the *pensato*, to the object that is fixed in thought, but since the *pensato* does not exist but for the actuality of thought, ideality is nothing but a transcendental and abstract moment of the idealisation which is in fact the process of thought as the overcoming of the ideality of the object.[46]

Unfortunately, de Ruggiero does not explain this very important notion of idealisation, nor does he give any examples that enable the reader to understand

---

[41] Ibid., 249.
[42] Ibid., 256.
[43] Ibid., 260.
[44] Ibid., 266–8.
[45] Ibid., 302.
[46] Ibid., 303.

what he means. But on the basis of the foregoing it is possible to give an interpretation of his text. In order to understand what de Ruggiero means by 'idealisation', it is important to keep the identity of science and consciousness in mind. On this basis, sensation and thought form an inseparable unity, that is, every thought or concept is a transformation of a specific moment in experience. From this it follows that every *pensato*, or concept, 'belongs' to a specific 'sensation', or to put it into de Ruggiero's terms, every ideality belongs to its own actuality. But this ideality is only present in *pensiero pensante*, or actual thought, which is also a unity of sensation and thought. The task of present thought can therefore be described as 'matching' the past unity of sensation and thought to the present, and this process of matching is what de Ruggiero calls idealisation. Present thought is able to match the two moments, because it knows that the concept belongs to a past experience. This past experience is the sufficient condition for the establishment of the concept, de Ruggiero says. Present thought matches past thought by relating it to present experience, which is the sufficient condition for a new concept. As we have seen above, thought transforms the actuality of sensation by 'neutralising' all its distinguishing features, such as time, space, and so forth, into an ideal object, which is an identity that is not in time or in space. This ideality is now 'deneutralised' by actualising it, that is, present thought 'updates' past thought by fusing it with actual time, space, and so forth, thus giving it distinguishing features.

Translated into the terms of dialectic of question and answer, de Ruggiero's theory becomes a little clearer. If we want to answer our present scientific questions we must study their history in order to understand how they have arisen from past answers. Given the unity of science and consciousness we can only understand past answers in the context of the questions which they answered. By taking this context into account, the history of questions and answers becomes actual again. From this viewpoint 'idealisation' can best be described as the question and answer process which actualises its own past in order to continue itself. Collingwood describes this idealisation process in a way with which de Ruggiero would certainly have agreed:

> If Einstein makes an advance on Newton, he does it by knowing Newton's thought and retaining it within his own, in the sense that he knows what Newton's problems were, and how he solved them, and, disentangling the truth in those solutions from whatever errors prevented Newton from going further, embodying these solutions as thus disentangled in his own theory.[47]

In 'Scienza come esperienza assoluta' this is all hinted at, but it is not worked out. De Ruggiero was certainly aware of this. In a footnote he warns that 'La scienza come esperienza assoluta' is only a sketch, and in a letter to Collingwood he points out that he had concentrated on the metaphysical aspects of science at

---

47   R.G. Collingwood, *The Idea of History*, 333.

the cost of its empirical aspects.[48] What de Ruggiero means by this is not entirely clear, but he probably hints at the elaborate analysis of the various moments of the dialectic of question and answer which sometimes leaves the role of observation in science in the dark. Following the task he had set for philosophy after Croce, de Ruggiero explicitly interprets sensation and thought as opposites, but he fails to show how these opposites are to be reconciled within science. De Ruggiero tries to find this reconciliation in the process of idealisation, or the question and answer process by which science actualises its own past in order to continue itself. But focusing on reconciliation, this theory of idealisation fails to explain the clash between sensation and thought, thus suffocating the dialectic of question and answer at its most vital moment, namely the moment of the arising of questions. For this reason, de Ruggiero fails to explain the most puzzling aspect of the dialectic of question and answer, which is the problem of how questions arise from answers and how answers arise from questions.

However, in spite of these shortcomings 'La scienza come esperienza assoluta' is a great achievement and one can only regret that de Ruggiero never explained it in more detail. Seen in the context of Italian idealism, it certainly is one of the first attempts to do justice to science, as de Ruggiero claims. In contrast to both Croce and Gentile, he shows that science is both true *sui generis* and capable of rational development; science develops itself on the basis of its own history. Seen within the context of the history of actualism, it is even more important, because it shows the possibility of a pluralistic actualism, that is, an actualism that takes the presuppositions of all other forms of experience into account. In the two years after 'La scienza come esperienza assoluta' de Ruggiero elaborated this pluralistic actualism in a series of articles on the relationship between morality and history.

Morality and History (1912–14)

It is typical for de Ruggiero to discuss the problem of history in connection with moral problems. Already in *La filosofia contemporanea* he had made this connection in his discussion of the *etica dello storicismo* in 'La redenzione come svolgimento dello spirito', one of his more detailed essays on moral philosophy written in 1912, morality and history come together again. The starting point of this essay is the contrast between the concept of the fall of man in the Old Testament with the Christian concept of the redemption of sin. According to de Ruggiero, the first notion of morality presupposes a static view of reality, whereas the second one expresses a dynamic view of reality. The notion of the 'fall of man' implies something 'given' from eternity, a fate that man has to

---

48   G. de Ruggiero, 'Letter to R.G. Collingwood', 28 June 1920. In possession of Ms Smith.

undergo, whereas the Christian view of sin is only present in the act of overcoming it; only for my present remorse are my past actions a sin.[49]

This notion of the redemption of sin as a development of the human mind leads de Ruggiero to the problem of the possibility of redemption:

> Man has committed a fault; that constitutes a fact, a past, which is irrevocable and which no force on the world can remove. How is it then possible to redeem the fault?[50]

In de Ruggiero's view this notion of the redemption of sin seems to imply the concept of the 'resolution' (*risoluzione*) of the past in the sense that the past can be made undone. In his view, this is absurd; nothing can change the past. But on the other hand, if the past is absolutely unchangeable, we can never redeem our sins.

This dilemma leads de Ruggiero to a closer scrutiny of the notion of the past. The past is not, but was, de Ruggiero says, the past is therefore not actual, but wholly ideal. On this point he offers the following description of 'ideality':

> Ideality is not affection by some entity, but it is a creation by some activity. Recollection (the ideality of a representation) implies some activity in the past, some mental activity, or judgment. Likewise, the ideality of a past experience (which is its reality) is constituted by the actual experience. The act, the eternal present of our life, founds the reality of the past. The act is a light that illuminates itself and the dark. The past has therefore an ideal value: as such it is only real in so far as it is really idealised, in so far as it is included and understood by actual consciousness.[51]

The main contention here is that present thought is constitutive of the past; both memory and past experience become 'real' through the present act of thought. This thesis foreshadows Gentile's thesis of the priority of the *historia rerum gestarum* over the *res gestae* in *Teoria generale dello spirito* of 1916 in a most striking way. Interestingly, de Ruggiero uses the notion of idealisation again, and, as in 'La scienza come esperienza assoluta', he uses it in the sense of making the ideal actual by including it in our present consciousness. What makes this notion of idealisation particularly interesting is its moral context; all forms of redemption are based on it! Only by idealising the past, de Ruggiero argues, can the past cease to 'press' on man's present consciousness as something irrevocable, but it is resolved in the present act of thought. On this point de Ruggiero gives one of his very few illustrations of this act of idealisation:

> I think of the fault that I committed, and I think that I did wrong. In this thinking, the past is already overcome, and the past fault stands in front of me

---

[49] G. de Ruggiero, 'La redenzione come svolgimento dello spirito, Saggio di una dialettica della coscienza morale', in *Rassegna di Pedagogia*, VI, Sandron, Palermo, 1912, 5–6.

[50] Ibid., 19.

[51] Ibid., 20.

as present, since it has been idealised by my act of thought. I can therefore redeem my fault, and I can redeem it because I need not transport myself by some incomprehensible mystery to a past moment of my life. But in the act of the will that tends to create goodness, I anticipate my past in the future, so to speak, as the goal of my struggle, as a moment and factor of the new life that I want to create. In so far as I want the good, I dominate the past.[52]

In a moral context, idealisation appears as an act of the good will by which we create ourselves by making the past present. But the past is only real in so far as it is included into the present of the self-creating present mind. From this it follows that the act of self-creation, or self-affirmation, in which theory and practice are fully united, is constitutive of the past. This conclusion implies that historical truth and morality cannot be distinguished within the self-creating process. To put it bluntly; history as self-knowledge of the mind is a moral form of knowledge and its truth implies goodness. If this thesis is combined with the notion of idealisation as a question and answer dialectic, the conclusion is that we can only redeem our faults by questioning our past. The striking implication of this view is that the past must be viewed as a result of moral thought. This is the step which de Ruggiero would make in his *Problemi della vita morale* of 1914.

Problems of Moral Life (1914)

De Ruggiero further developed his views concerning the relationship between morality and history in his *Problemi della vita morale* of 1914. In this work de Ruggiero uses his dialectic of question and answer in order to bridge the gap between theory and practice, or in de Ruggiero's own terminology; to prove the identity between 'science' (in the broad sense of the word) and morality. The plan of the book reveals de Ruggiero's approach. In the first chapter he tries to show that science is moral because it develops itself along the lines of a dialectic of question and answer. In the second chapter, he goes the other way around, showing that all morality is a form of thought proceeding as a dialectic of question and answer. Thus having proved the identity between thought and morality, de Ruggiero finally shows that historicism, being a form of thought, is identical to ethics.

De Ruggiero begins from the view that all science begins as a questioning activity. One of the sciences is moral science or ethics. By asking questions, moral science disputes the status of its 'data' and more specifically their logical priority and their 'modifiability'. The logical priority of the data is rejected in the act of questioning which establishes the priority of the questioning subject over the 'data'; when the subject begins to express his doubt about the data, he implicitly acknowledges the priority of the question over the answer.[53] De

---

[52] Ibid., 20–1.
[53] G. de Ruggiero, *Problemi della vita morale*, Battiato, Catania, 1914, 5–6.

Ruggiero points out that one is morally active when one begins to have doubts about one's 'character' as determining his actions:

> The appearance of the problem, as a simple problem, as doubt or as present-ment of a moral life, is already the beginning of moral life.[54]

In de Ruggiero's view this problem is subjective; only 'philosophical hacks' study problems for the sake of studying them. Real problems are only those 'which express the peculiarity of a spiritual attitude, and I would almost say, as a new reaction of the individual to his environment'.[55]

By questioning the data, the subject also discovers their modifiability. For example, when one questions whether his character is given or not, he also assumes that he can change his character. Subject and object thus coincide in the questioning activity, which is therefore fundamentally creative:

> With the investigation of my object (that is me, as object), I create a deeper knowledge of myself, and creating this, I re-create my object (that is, me as object), and resolve my character into a new life.[56]

In this passage de Ruggiero indicates that the questioning activity is always a moral act; by questioning we expand our self-knowledge and thereby transform ourselves as well as our past. In this context, he firmly believes that the past must be seen as a 'creation', or 'construction', which we constitute in the func-tion of our self-knowledge, thus forming the basis of our 'self-creation'. In this respect, de Ruggiero's philosophy of history is as constructivist as Croce's and Gentile's.

In the second chapter of *Problemi della vita morale* de Ruggiero approaches the identity of science and morality from the other side in order to show that moral-ity is always a form of thought:

> ...morality is knowledge, that is, it is knowledge of ourselves which is always at the same time also realisation of ourselves.[57]

This moral self-knowledge, or self-realisation, organises itself in the same way as every form of thought; it organises its object by 'a process of coordination and unification'. Coordination is an act of the subject which is also the object of this act:

> We are the subject of our knowledge, we are organising an activity, but we are also the closest object, as content of the life which is to be organised.[58]

According to de Ruggiero, the aim of our action is 'unification' and 'individu-ation' of ourselves; by unifying our activities we become true individuals and

---

54 Ibid., 7.
55 Ibid., 11.
56 Ibid., 15–16.
57 Ibid., 30.
58 Ibid., 34.

this enhances the force of our actions. From this premise it follows that the wider the range of our organisation of the object, the more intensive is our act of individuation, that is, the more we expand our relationship to others, the more we become individuals and the more powerful our action becomes.[59] In principle, therefore, our individuality becomes richer the more we enter into relationships with other individuals. But this is only true on the condition that we resolve all objectivity within ourselves, that is, that we recognise that all knowledge of the object leads to a fuller actualisation (*attuazione*) of the subject. De Ruggiero clarifies this point as follows:

> If I, during my action, come to know that I am not isolated in the world, but that I am connected by a thousand relationships to the surrounding reality, to the environment, to society, and going back to the past, to my past life, and to those of my ancestors and to all the history of which I am a product; and if the knowledge, which is a recognition of so many bonds, were not to be at the same time a liberation from them, I would irredeemably be a slave of these bonds; my action would fatally be conditioned by space and time and all liberty and spontaneity would vanish forever from the spiritual horizon.[60]

In contrast to Croce and Gentile, de Ruggiero here implicitly admits that the past lives in the present, in the sense that it is still active; if we do not study the past we become enslaved by it. But if we study the past we make ourselves aware of its force and this forms the basis of our 'liberation' from the past. The meaning of this 'liberation' must be seen in the context of moral problems; a fault exists only as a past act for the present good will that redeems it. De Ruggiero's notion of the liberation from the past raises the main problem: how is this liberation of the past possible? On this point de Ruggiero uses the key notion of idealisation again:

> The object is not known simply as an object but also as subjectivity; in so far as this object only exists and lives in the idealisation of it that the subject performs it. Its realisation only represents an evolution of the content of the subject.[61]

In order to understand this notion of idealisation we must keep in mind that the subjectivity of the object becomes manifest in the act of questioning. This questioning activity, by which the subject develops itself, idealises the past, that is, the past is constituted or formed in the function of our own self-determining activity. In this act, it is identical with science, which is idealisation, or 'rational memory of ourselves, conservation of ourselves when we act and create new life'.[62] On this basis de Ruggiero concludes that morality and science are identical.

---

59   Ibid., 36–7.
60   Ibid., 38–9.
61   Ibid., 33.
62   Ibid.

After this 'double proof' of the identity of science and morality de Ruggiero radicalises his *etica dello storicismo* in the third chapter. If science is morality and morality is science, if the questioning activity of all our thought is basically a moral activity and if all morality organises itself as a dialectic of question and answer, then we cannot escape the conclusion that 'historicism is theory in so far as it is praxis'.[63]

Before de Ruggiero reaches this conclusion he first frees the notion of history from all traces of fatalism by the concept of self-development. The first obstacle to be removed here is the whole idea of an objective history, or 'history as it really was'.

> If we let a ready-made, objective history exist in the field of historical studies, a history that is seen as existing before its construction by thought, all history ends as a mere epiphenomenon, and all liberation from fatalism and causal mechanism that history seems to give us, will become illusory.[64]

By rejecting the notion of a 'ready-made' history de Ruggiero clears the way for the constructive work of the historian by rejecting the whole idea of the objective past. In his view *'la storia fatta'* must be seen as a product of our present thought:

> The historicity of our present is conditioned by the realisation of our consciousness of the whole development that culminates in ourselves.[65]

On first sight, de Ruggiero seems to adhere to the primacy of present consciousness just as Gentile. But as we have seen, de Ruggiero also recognised that the past conditions the present. In the following passage he tries to elucidate this double relationship between the past and present:

> By everything that is said up to this point it is revealed how the action of the past on the present is conditioned by the consciousness that we acquire of that past; however, according to what we already know about the deciding and renewing efficiency of consciousness, we must conclude that the action of the past comes forth from the spontaneity and the freedom of our labour.[66]

Again de Ruggiero recognises 'the action of the past on the present', arguing that the only way to get to know the way in which the past conditions the present is history. History is a free activity, so that our knowledge of the past and its effects on the present depend on our own initiative. In other words; we are all conditioned by the past, but the past does not determine what questions we ask about it. We are free to ask the questions which liberate us from the burden of history.

According to de Ruggiero, this recognition of the freedom of the historian leads to the opposite of fatalism, that is, subjective and arbitrary will. And this

---

[63] Ibid., 58–9.
[64] Ibid., 46.
[65] Ibid., 47.
[66] Ibid., 48.

arbitrariness must be removed in order to come to a rational rejection of fatalism. De Ruggiero's solution for this problem is based on the notion of auto-determination. This reconciles determination and freedom by showing that determination is only possible for a spirit that imposes necessity on itself.

> The historicity of our thought and action is not something that is imposed, but it is something that we posit ourselves with the spontaneity of our labour.[67]

From this follows the fundamental principle that we are only conditioned by history in so far as we are conscious of being conditioned by it.[68] De Ruggiero gives the following example to illustrate this notion:

> When it is said that our mentality is the daughter of the French revolution and of the Restoration that followed from it, such affiliation only exists for consciousness and for our consciousness that we acquire of the Revolution and the Restoration.[69]

In other words, we are not 'blindly' conditioned by the French Revolution, but its sense depends on our act of self-determination by which we become aware of it. Again, de Ruggiero only recognises the past as being active in the present in so far as we are aware of it in the function of our present self-determination. In this concept of auto-determination, freedom and necessity perfectly coincide, de Ruggiero avers, in the concept of duty:

> It is my duty to determine myself in history, and this duty, in so far as it also expresses my activity of self-formation, creates being, or the reality of the formation, which is consequently free from the old fatalism, because it is no more than a moment of my freedom.[70]

De Ruggiero here explicitly relates the constitution of the past to the moral self-determination of the individual. At the same time de Ruggiero acknowledges that history conditions my self-determination as well:

> The consciousness that I have of myself as historical reality is at the same time the activity of making the history of my spiritual content present, and it is the norm of this activity, as the duty to affirm the historicity of my life and to put it into practice.[71]

Essential in this passage is that de Ruggiero recognises that the past functions as the 'norm' for present activities. But since this past is only called into being by the present it does not differ from Gentile's notion of the *pensato* and it is therefore subject to the same ambiguities.

On the basis of the notion of the present which constitutes a past for its own moral self-determination de Ruggiero draws an entire programme for the *etica*

---

67 Ibid., 50.
68 Ibid., 49.
69 Ibid., 47.
70 Ibid., 52.
71 Ibid., 51.

dello storicismo of which the most important aspects are the notions of historical determination, of individuality, and 'historical labour'.

De Ruggiero first points out that if our reality is historical, our freedom cannot but consist of determining our reality in an historical way.

> If our reality is history and if it becomes more coherent when we deepen our consciousness of the relations which tie us to our past, then our freedom can only consist of determining more historically our action.[72]

On the basis of this notion of history de Ruggiero intends to found an entire 'phenomenology of historical determination, which must demonstrate that the realisation of liberty proceeds by determining our actions more comprehensively'.[73] The basic idea behind this phenomenology is that freedom consists in self-determination, or 'individuation'. Our freedom is therefore dependent on the scope of our historical thought; the more universal its scope, the more we can individualise ourselves:

> ...we are then more ourselves when we determine ourselves more in the history that produced us, and when we accept the bonds which history has made, and the more we unify ourselves with the whole, the more we individuate our lives.[74]

De Ruggiero summarises this important passage into 'man lives his own life in the lives of others'. From this principle it follows that historical thought is an endless 'labour' (*lavoro*) which is one of the central concepts of the *etica dello storicismo*. De Ruggiero presents his notion of labour as an extension of Marx's. But whereas the latter restricted the term to its economic sense, de Ruggiero considers all social, moral, and intellectual activity as labour. De Ruggiero stresses the task of history in this labour:

> Only our labour has moral value, not only as creation of new activity, but also as conservation of the whole wealth that has been produced in history.[75]

At the end of *Problemi della vita morale* de Ruggiero calls this form of labour 'historical labour', which he contrasts with mere erudite history, thus foreshadowing Gentile's notion of 'humanism of labour'.[76] Historical labour does not consist of 'digging up the past, visiting the archives and consulting manuscripts':

> But historical labour is in the broadest sense every activity, every effort directed to actualising the reality in which we live, and this reality which lives by historical labour in us, unfolds all the richness of its historical content for our benefit.[77]

---

[72] Ibid., 50.

[73] Ibid., 52.

[74] Ibid., 53.

[75] Ibid., 56.

[76] See chapter 8, p. 309.

[77] G. de Ruggiero, *Problemi della vita morale*, 59–60.

On this point de Ruggiero goes so far that he finds the work of the peasant as much an example of historical labour as the work of the philosopher.

The root of our historical labour is practical, all our knowledge stems from our present interest to 'actualise ourselves'.

> It is not so that we first know our present and then occupy our place in the world, but our taking place in the world is nothing else than our becoming conscious of ourselves through the past.[78]

On this basis de Ruggiero concludes that ethics and historicism coincide: the 'ethics of historicism' is also 'historicism as ethics': 'It is ethics in so far as it is the revelation of our own intimacy to ourselves, it is the consciousness of the freedom and the autonomy of our labour, and of the creation of the dignity and height of our spiritual lives.'[79]

With this lyrical passage de Ruggiero ends *Problemi della vita morale*, which may be seen as his most important contribution to the ethics of historicism. The kernel of de Ruggiero's moral philosophy is his theory of the self-determination of man. Being a spontaneous process, self-determination is always also a moral process; my choice to develop myself in a certain way is essentially a moral choice. From this it follows that the dialectic of question and answer, by which self-determination proceeds, must also be viewed as a moral activity. Along these lines de Ruggiero views the highest form of self-determination as 'historical labour', that is, the labour by which the individual individuates himself by asking questions concerning the past. Crucial to de Ruggiero's theory is the connection between the degree of individuation and the scope of the questioning activity; the more of the past we study, the stronger our act of individuation becomes. Only by understanding the past, can man understand himself.

Most of this is similar to Gentile's actualism. De Ruggiero's notion of self-determination and its relationship to present and past consciousness is essentially the same as Gentile's *autoctisi* in relation to *pensante* and *pensato*. The most important difference between Gentile and de Ruggiero is that the latter tries to describe the activities of individuals by these notions and not the transcendental ego. In contrast to Gentile's monistic actualism, de Ruggiero advocates a pluralistic actualism from the outset. It is this pluralism that mitigates de Ruggiero's adherence to the primacy of the present. Unlike Gentile, de Ruggiero is only interested in the value of history for the self-determination of the individual in relation to other individuals both in the past and the present. It is on this basis that he comes very close to admitting that the past conditions the present but, as we have seen, he undoes this insight by claiming that it is only on behalf of our present consciousness that we come to know how we are related to the past.

---

[78]   Ibid., 39.
[79]   Ibid., 60.

De Ruggiero's notion of the ethics of historicism contains a programme for a new philosophy of history. It was certainly de Ruggiero's intention to develop this. In *La filosofia contemporanea* he had already indicated the importance of history for moral life and the lack of a true philosophy of history. Unfortunately, the war prevented de Ruggiero from carrying out his plans. What he left, apart from the passages in *La filosofia contemporanea* and the methodological considerations in his *Storia della filosofia*, are a long series of reviews on the German philosophy of history in *La Critica* of 1911–12 and *Critica del concetto della cultura* (1914), a trenchant criticism of the phenomenon of culture and its cultivators. But de Ruggiero's most important contribution to the philosophy of history is his 'La pensée italienne et la guerre', which was published in *Revue de Métaphysique et de Morale* in September 1916.

De Ruggiero's Philosophy of History

In *La Critica* of 1911–12 de Ruggiero published a long series of reviews on the philosophy of the so-called Badian school of neo-Kantians. This school had its origins in the philosophy of Herbart and Lotze (1817–81), and flourished with figures such as Windelband, Rickert, and Lask (1875–1915), and it came to an end with Max Weber whose thought is not discussed by de Ruggiero. The motto of the neo-Kantians was '*keine Metaphysik mehr*'. But de Ruggiero argues that their philosophy is in fact based on a dualism between nature and spirit, in which the former is identified with being or the object, and the latter with value or the subject.[80] Consequently, the neo-Kantians distinguish two modes of knowing reality; one is science, which is theoretical and constitutes the real by predicating existence on it. The other is history, which values the given object from the point of view of the subject.[81] The two forms of knowledge are therefore complementary; science studies the natural laws that underlie natural phenomena, and history studies the individual. Likewise, the logic of science and history are complementary. Formal logic studies the mechanism of concepts by which the objects are predicated, whereas philosophical logic studies the eternal values by which the individual should be understood. The task of the historian, then, is to show how these values are embodied in history, and this is the idea that underlies the German idea of *Kulturgeschichte*.

In de Ruggiero's view the main shortcoming of the German philosophers is their confusion of natural and historical facts. Seeing both as disconnected events, forming a 'series of rigid points', they try to connect these by a law or value that transcends them. Accordingly, the task of the philosopher is almost similar to that of the scientist; whereas the latter elaborates the concepts that connect the natural events, the former tries to formulate the eternal values that connect historical events.

---

80   G. de Ruggiero, 'La filosofia dei valori in Germania', in *La Critica*, IX, 1911, 371.
81   Ibid.

But in de Ruggiero's view historical fact is not at all identical with natural fact, as Vico had already pointed out:

> Historical fact is fact as Vico conceived it. In order to understand it, it is necessary to overcome the intellectualistic position of the natural sciences; it is necessary to understand reality as spirit, as mind and therefore as a process, auto-genesis, and development. Only in this way reality, mentality and history coincide, and the truth of historical fact will be discovered. This truth is not outside the process, but it is in the process, from which it is isolated by the transcendental abstraction, which considers the process (mentality) as an a priori condition for the occurence of the fact and of the individual.[82]

This passage contains the core of de Ruggiero's resistance against the German philosophers of history. In his view, they abstracted some 'eternal values' from history by considering them as logically and ontologically prior to the individual. This individual is therefore not a true individual, but only an incarnation of some values that lie outside its development. For de Ruggiero, values are only real in the development of the individual and cannot be understood separately from this development. In contrast with this, the Germans still have a naturalistic concept of the individual and this reveals itself in their *Kulturwissenschaften*, in which they try to establish a so-called realm of 'universal human values', or some kind of 'normal consciousness'.[83] Such a concept of culture pushes all subjectivity out of sight; it 'dementalises' all knowing and replaces 'living thought' with 'dead thought'. The Germans thus turn spirit into matter and history into natural science.[84] They also concentrate too much on the 'results' of history at the cost of history itself; they are only interested in the 'solutions' at the cost of the 'intimacy of the problems'.[85] But for de Ruggiero history springs from an intense subjective experience of problems that we share with the past. In this context, he denounces both the specialists, who pile up all kinds of petty knowledge by simply repeating each other, and the 'universalists', who never come to any precise knowledge of their object. According to de Ruggiero both the specialists and the universalists lack the necessary 'intimate understanding of study and life' by which knowledge and its object are created by ourselves as individuals.[86]

De Ruggiero's criticism of the Germans is of special interest because, by stressing the difference between nature and history in this way, it foreshadows Collingwood's later philosophy. In this context it is important to note that de Ruggiero stresses that any attenuation of the distinction between nature and spirit involves a perversion of the latter.[87] Furthermore, de Ruggiero's criticism of the German philosophy of history is related to his and Collingwood's later

---

[82]   Ibid., 47.
[83]   G. de Ruggiero, 'La filosofia dei valori in Germania', in *La Critica*, X, 1912, 51.
[84]   G. de Ruggiero, *Critica del concetto di cultura*, Battiato, Catania, 1914, 64.
[85]   Ibid., 56–8.
[86]   Ibid., 75–9.
[87]   Ibid., 56.

criticism of Croce. In his early development de Ruggiero was rather positive about Croce's articles which would be fused into *Teoria e storia della storiografia*.[88] Just like Gentile, he welcomed Croce's distinction between chronicles and history, because 'in this conception history finally merges with life'.[89] However, at the end of his review he makes it clear that this concept implies a revision of the whole *Filosofia dello spirito*. How correct he was in this is shown by the fact that it took Croce almost twenty years before he was able to present this revision in *La storia come pensiero e come azione* of 1938.

However, de Ruggiero's fiercest battle with Croce lay in the field of morality. In December 1914 he clashed for the first time with Croce on the question of neutrality towards German intellectuals. Responding to an appeal for tolerance, made by the German Professor Delbrück, who was living in Rome, Croce had pleaded for a 'suspension of judgment' on the war, arguing that historians should wait until an impartial history could be written. De Ruggiero reacted furiously; Croce's plea revealed a 'depreciation of the history of today and by making a utopia of the history of tomorrow'.[90] Against this view, de Ruggiero pointed out that 'the chronicles of today are true and living history in spite of their shortcomings and their partialities' and that 'history is and will always be passionate, because passion is the colouring of human mentality'.[91] To the question 'is everything history?' de Ruggiero consequently answers with a wholehearted 'yes'! Using Croce's own definition of contemporary history as the 'immanent consciousness of action' he points out that 'even the germanophobic hubbub that fills the newspapers of the province' should be seen as history.[92] But de Ruggiero warns that it does not follow that all histories have the same value; everybody thinks history to the best of his abilities, and the value of history is accordingly dependent on the intellectual force of the minds that create it. For this reason 'the judgment of people and events reflects the sense of responsibility of those who make it'.[93] Therefore, de Ruggiero concludes, the intellectuals, who have a great responsibility for thought, must not keep aloof from the war of thoughts, but actively participate in it.[94]

This conflict between Croce and de Ruggiero shows their profound differences of opinion on the relationship between history and action. Both define history as the consciousness of action, but Croce holds that this consciousness must always be distinguished from the action itself, whereas de Ruggiero saw con-

---

[88] G. de Ruggiero, 'La storia vivente', in *Il resto del Carlino*, 14 February 1913, cited from id., *Scritti Politici*, 85.

[89] Ibid., 89.

[90] G. de Ruggiero, 'Storia di oggi e storia di domani' in *L'Idea Nazionale*, 5 December 1914, cited from id., *Scritti politici*, 120.

[91] Ibid., 121.

[92] Ibid.

[93] Ibid., 122.

[94] Ibid., 123.

sciousness and action as united. For the Olympian Croce, true history is primarily a contemplative activity and can only be written some time after the events, whereas for a *filosofo combattente* like de Ruggiero all history is combating history, that must be written when the smoke of battle still lingers. This difference on the relationship between thought and action, and in particular between history and action, would divide the two thinkers until the end of their lives.

Although de Ruggiero shared his convictions about the unity of thought and action with Gentile, he did certainly not endorse the latter's theory of history. This is made clear by de Ruggiero's reaction to Gentile's 'Il concetto del progresso' of 1911, in which the latter held that mechanistic, naturalistic, or mathematical philosophies, such as that of Descartes, cannot have a concept of progress.[95] According to de Ruggiero, however, this view is based on a 'closed concept of progress', which reserves this concept for some philosophies and denies it to others. De Ruggiero reminded his former teacher that reality is basically spirit, thought, and consequently development and progress. Each philosophy therefore finds its place in history; each philosophy has an idea of its own contribution to it and therefore each philosophy must have its own notion of progress. The concept of progress is therefore 'open' in the sense that it is presupposed by all philosophies and therefore by all thought. De Ruggiero illustrated his thesis by citing another paper by Gentile, thus showing that the 'pupil' can remind the teacher of his true doctrines.[96] This is characteristic of the relationship between the two thinkers. On the one hand, it cannot be denied that de Ruggiero's philosophy had much in common with Gentile's, for both regard the mind as an activity that constitutes reality and both see reality as a unity of history and action. As we have seen, however, Gentile only acknowledged the pure act of thought as a transcendental activity of the mind. On this basis Gentile reserves the concept of progress for dialectical philosophies, that is philosophies which proceed as pure act, and denies it to other philosophies which are based on transcendence. But for de Ruggiero, all activities have an empirical and a transcendental aspect in their own way; all activities proceed as a pure act in their own way, even past philosophies which were based on transcendence. Consequently, de Ruggiero regarded progress as an 'open' or truly transcendental concept; each mental activity has the characteristics of progress and therefore all reality can be seen in the light of progress. All his life de Ruggiero fought against Gentile's tendency to 'close' his philosophy. Finally, and when the 'master' converted to Fascism, the 'pupil' broke with him.

---

[95]   G. Gentile, Review of 'J. Delvaille, Essai sur l'histoire de l'idée de progrès jusqu'à la fin du XVIIIe siècle', cited as 'Il concetto del progresso' from *La riforma della dialettica hegeliana*, Sansoni, Florence, 1975, 178.

[96]   G. de Ruggiero, 'Per una storia dell'idea di progresso', in *La* Cultura, 1, 1912, 11n1.

'La pensée italienne et la guerre' (1916)

De Ruggiero's philosophy of history, which expresses his pluralistic actualism, comes most clearly to the fore in 'La pensée italienne et la guerre'. The aim of this article is to sketch the contribution of Italian thought to the war effort. The 'openness' of de Ruggiero's approach is revealed by the fact that he takes all forms of thought into account; from the man at the front, to that of politicians, statesmen, and thinkers. De Ruggiero describes the 'idealities' that lie at the basis of all these thoughts and tries to trace their historical root. The result is a striking, philosophical-historical analysis of the ideals for which the Italians and their allies were fighting at that time.

In de Ruggiero's view economic factors are certainly of importance in war, but he warns against underestimating the role of ideas and ideals. Civilisation has been described as a beautiful plant growing up in dung, de Ruggiero says, but that does not take away the fact that the plant transforms the dung within itself.[97] Ideals are formed in history, for this reason they are always to a certain degree inadequate for understanding new events and must accordingly be revised.[98] All ideas are thus formed in history and their effectiveness depends accordingly on their historicity.

In this sense de Ruggiero criticises both the 'misunderstood national egoism' and the 'misunderstood internationalism' as 'anti-historical abstractions'; the first only recognises the historical particularity of one's own nation, whereas the second lowers all peoples to the level of atoms, thus annulling their particular histories. Typical of de Ruggiero's unity of thought and action is his remark that a theoretical synthesis of the two views does not work; only a synthesis *in re*, or an αληθές (truth) that is at the same time πραγμα (action) really matters!

Finally, as a true journalist de Ruggiero points out that the historians of today must write the *historia rerum gestarum* today, because they possess already all materials of today's *res gestae*.[99]

The most striking section of the article is the one in which he compares the ideals of the Germans and the Allies. Taking up his analysis of the neo-Kantians and their idea of *Kulturgeschichte*, de Ruggiero points out that the Germans tend to cling to 'transcendent values'. From this stems their tendency to 'transform each of their own acts into a duty, and each moment of their own realisation in history into a moment of the realisation of the universe', as well as their striving for 'civilising' the whole world.[100] But the allies also tend to make their ideals too absolute; in particular the French and the Italians have clung to their illusions of a 'unity of Latin civilisation'. Because of these abstractions all people paid their

---

[97] G. de Ruggiero, 'La pensée italienne et la guerre', in *Revue de Métaphysique et de Morale*, 1916. Cited from Italian translation by de Felice in *Scritti Politici*, 146.

[98] Ibid., 130.

[99] Ibid., 128.

[100] Ibid., 142–3.

toll in the 'hard experience of the war that has revealed the vanity of a right that has no power to be effective and of a justice that is not truly righteous and of a civilisation that only defeats some alleged barbarism'.[101] According to de Ruggiero, these abstractions can be overcome if they are transformed into 'immanent and pragmatic values'. By doing this, he places all his hope in the 'philosophy of the humble people', who, while fighting, carry the 'ideality of action' within themselves. These people have a sense of the 'seriousness of action', the 'love for their country', the 'concord between men', and of true 'unselfishness'. In action the individual will rise not as the result of his egoism but as an expression of his universality.[102]

In spite of this rhetoric 'La pensée italienne et la guerre' exemplifies de Ruggiero's philosophy of history very well. De Ruggiero's vindication of the individual, even of the most humble, is the final outcome of his pluralistic actualism. In 'La scienza come esperienza assoluta' and in *Problemi della vita morale* he recognised the autonomy of science and morality by showing how each activity is truly philosophical in itself. In 'La pensée italienne et la guerre' he recognises the autonomy of the 'philosophy of the humble'; each man, from the man in the trenches to the one in the government, is a philosopher and has to be taken seriously as a philosopher. Philosophy has always fixed its eyes on the eternal and had a disdain for the contingent problems of life itself. Since modern thought realised that the eternal is present in the contingent act itself, philosophers have been attracted to life itself and to its 'absolute empiricism'; 'they do not fear spoiling the purity of thought with the impurity of life; without the contamination of the flesh the Logos of the hellenico-judaic speculation would not have become the Spirit of christian consciousness.'[103]

Here we find de Ruggiero's philosophical credo; the task of the philosopher-historian is to understand all human activity, from the 'lowest' to the 'highest'. This ideal distinguishes his philosophy from that of Croce and Gentile. All of them regard the spirit as an activity that constitutes reality, but unlike de Ruggiero, Croce and Gentile made a distinction between the empirical and the transcendental aspect of activities, favouring the latter. For Croce the pure concepts are more 'real' than the pseudo-concepts, the s*toria ideale eterna* is somehow more real than the *storia in tempo*. Likewise Gentile finds the *pensiero pensante* and the *logo concreto* more 'real' than *pensiero pensato* and the *logo astratto*. Moreover, he tends to identify *pensiero pensante* with philosophy *tout court*, thus placing it on a pedestal at the cost of the other forms of experience. Although de Ruggiero does not underestimate the transcendental aspect of activities, he recognises, in contrast to his "masters", that each activity is always both empirical and transcendental, and that philosophy must take both aspects into account. For an

---

[101] Ibid., 145.
[102] Ibid., 149.
[103] Ibid., 128.

absolute empiricist there are no pseudo-concepts or *pensieri pensati* that are not also *pensieri pensanti*; all concepts have value and all have their own rationality. Nor can abstract and concrete logos be distinguished; all thought has its own principles, presuppositions on which its truth-value is based. Nor can any philosophical concept, such as truth, beauty, goodness, or process and progress, be denied to any mental activity. Last but not least, the 'transcendental level' cannot be an ultimate court of appeal as it was for Gentile; there is no transcendental ego apart from the empirical ego, but the empirical ego is transcendental as well. And if this is so, no individual can claim that he knows the transcendental ego better than anyone else. For this reason there is no absolute certainty in absolute empiricism. Like Croce and Gentile, de Ruggiero holds that reality is history, but for him history remains fundamentally problematic. All solutions given in the past lead to new problems in the present. We can never find rest in some kind of privileged knowledge of the pure concept of the spirit or the transcendental ego; we must always go on with our Sisyphean task. The only certainty we have is that other individuals solved their problems in the past and that other individuals are solving new problems in the present. All these individuals are both empirical and transcendental egos. The only way of solving our problems is to understand the problems of others, so that their efforts may contribute to ours. Absolute empiricism vindicates the individual and accepts that it can be approached from a plurality of perspectives; '*l'uomo vive nella vita altrui la propria vita*' ('man lives his life in the lives of others') truly is the motto of de Ruggiero's open actualism.

Conclusion

This moral metaphysics would have important consequences for de Ruggiero's philosophy of history. *A parte subiecti* de Ruggiero explicitly describes history as an inquiry with the ultimate aim of solving moral problems. The object of history is thought, but for de Ruggiero thought is a dialectic of question and answer. History must therefore understand the questions and answers of the past and the present. Since de Ruggiero takes all men seriously, history should deal with all problems of men in the past and in the present. De Ruggiero never worked out the methodological principles of his theory of history, but in his *Storia della filosofia* he always discusses the historiography of his subjects, which shows that he was well aware of the problem of intersubjective validity of the interpretation of sources. Most importantly, the value of history is that it provides the individual with the self-knowledge which forms the basis for his self-development. This self-knowledge is obtained by studying the problems and the solutions of other individuals and not on the history of some transcendental ego and enables the individual to understand himself amidst other free individuals.

Croce always found this much too popular and vulgar.[104] Although he considered de Ruggiero as Gentile's most intelligent pupil, he despised his 'journalistic tendencies'. For him both philosophy and history should deal with the higher forms of experience, and Croce himself spent all his life studying poets, philosophers, and statesmen. As we have seen, de Ruggiero was opposed to this view; history should deal with the past in order to understand the *hic et nunc*. However, Croce was not altogether wrong in his criticism; sometimes de Ruggiero exaggerates when recognising the value of all forms of thought, thereby putting them on a par. His philosophy thus calls for differences of both degree and kind. Moreover, the phenomenology of error was never worked out by de Ruggiero; so his logic calls for a new theory of distinction and opposition as well. Gentile never criticised de Ruggiero's views of history openly, probably because they reminded him too much of the true ideal of actualism. However, it cannot be denied that de Ruggiero's idea of the priority of the *historia rerum gestarum* over the *res gestae* makes the present constitutive of the past. Like Gentile, de Ruggiero stressed the creative aspects of the present subject too much. But this stress never leads to Gentile's morally radical subjectivism because de Ruggiero's absolute empiricism was fundamentally 'pluriperspectival'. Nonetheless, de Ruggiero's philosophy raises the problem of the relationship between the activity of the historian and the past as that of Croce and Gentile. Like them, de Ruggiero did not deal with the problem of how the past, and especially the remote past, with which Collingwood was concerned, can be understood without becoming stranded in some kind of presentism. However, de Ruggiero's philosophy contains a most promising suggestion for a solution of this problem in the form of the dialectic of question and answer, which reflects the problematic character of reality. This was the element that Collingwood took up before the war and to develop it into the basis of his own position in the 1920s.

---

[104] B. Croce, *Lettere a Giovanni Gentile*, 533, 10 January 1917.

Chapter Five

Collingwood's Early Development (1889–1917)

Introduction

The major theme of Collingwood's early development, as he described it in his autobiography, is the confrontation of his education at home with the teaching at Oxford. In his autobiography, Collingwood gives a detailed chronology of his struggle with his realist teachers. His initial 'feelings of dissatisfaction' began shortly after his arrival at Oxford in 1908, and developed into 'doubts' before the beginning of the war and ended in a 'rejection' of the realist doctrine around 1916.[1] Collingwood indicates that his clash with realism had practical as well as theoretical grounds. Collingwood's initial feelings of 'vague dissatisfaction' began when the realists tried to teach him that moral philosophy should do 'no more than study in a purely theoretical spirit a subject-matter which it leaves wholly unaffected by that investigation'.[2] In contrast, Collingwood's father had educated his son in the tradition which firmly stood for the idea that 'moral philosophy is taught with a view to making the pupils better men'.[3] Moreover, W.G. Collingwood had given his son some 'ideals to live for and principles to live by'.[4] These ideals were Christian with a strong Ruskinian flavour, stressing tolerance and social life.[5]

This education was not without effect. In 1905, Collingwood had himself baptised and in the following year he was confirmed.[6] All this may explain why the young Collingwood was so shocked when he heard from philosophers like H.A. Prichard (1871–1947) that all moral philosophy rests on a mistake or that

---

[1] R.G. Collingwood, *An Autobiography*, 22, 28, 42.

[2] Ibid., 147.

[3] Ibid., 51.

[4] Ibid., 48.

[5] Johnston, *The Formative Years of R.G. Collingwood*, 27–30; Teresa Smith, 'R.G. Collingwood: "This Ring of Thought": Notes on Early Influences', in *Collingwood Studies*, 1, 1994, 38–9.

[6] James Patrick, *The Magdalen Metaphysicals. Idealism and Orthodoxy at Oxford, 1901–1945*, Mercer Univeristy Press, 1985, 85.

there is no common good, or that all goodness is private.[7] Perhaps, he found
G.E. Moore's (1873–1951) attempts to define goodness less shocking, but he
certainly did not agree with the latter's claim that goodness is a simple notion.
All his life, Collingwood believed that the notion of goodness could only be
based on a living experience of it.[8]

Apart from these difficulties with the moral philosophy of the realists,
Collingwood was never without reservations to their epistemological doctrines
and critical methods.[9] In this context, he explicitly mentions Prichard's (1871–
1941) *Kant's Theory of Knowledge* of 1909 and H.W.B. Joseph's (1867–1943) *Introduction to Logic* of 1906.[10] According to Passmore, Prichard's was the first book
with which Cook Wilson's (1849–1915) realist philosophy reached an audience
outside Oxford.[11] Its basic thesis was that all knowledge 'unconditionally presupposes that the reality known exists independently of the knowledge of it' and
that all theories which reject this must be seen as 'subjective idealism'.[12] In
Collingwood's view, this thesis was the basis of the typical British misunderstanding of history, which was also reflected in Joseph's *Introduction to Logic*,
which simply glosses over the special problems of historical thinking.[13] 'The
Oxford realists', Collingwood argues in his autobiography, 'talked as if knowing
were a simple "intuiting" or a simple "apprehending" of some "reality".'[14] For
him, however, knowing was not that simple. From both Ruskin and his father he
had learned that thought forms a unity with the other activities of the mind, like
feeling, imagination, and the practical activities.[15] Collingwood's father, who
was an accomplished painter, archaeologist, and historian, put this doctrine into
practice by preparing his historical studies with historical fiction, thus teaching
his son the importance of imagination for historical thought.[16] Moreover,
Collingwood's father also took his son to archaeological expeditions. Here the
young Collingwood learned that knowledge consists of two halves; a question-

---

7   R.G. Collingwood, *An Autobiography*, 47, 49.
8   R.G. Collingwood, 'Goodness, Rightness, Utility, Lectures delivered in Hilary Term
    1940 and written as delivered', cited from *The New Leviathan, Revised Edition Edited and
    Introduced by David Boucher*, Oxford University Press, Oxford, 1992, 407.
9   R.G. Collingwood, *An Autobiography*, 22.
10 Ibid., 20, 36.
11 John Passmore, *A Hundred Years of Philosophy*, Penguin Books, Harmondsworth, 1984,
    248.
12 H.A. Prichard, *Kant's Theory of Knowledge*, Clarendon Press, Oxford, 1909, 115.
13 R.G. Collingwood, *The Idea of History*, 142–3.
14 R.G. Collingwood, *An Autobiography*, 25.
15 R.G. Collingwood, 'Ruskin's Philosophy, An Address delivered at the Ruskin Centen-
    ary Conference, Coniston, August 8th', 1919, Titus Wilson, Kendal, 1922, cited from
    Donagan, A. (ed.), *Essays in the Philosophy of Art by R.G. Collingwood*, Indiana
    University Press, Bloomington, 1964, 17–19.
16 D.H. Johnson, 'W.G. Collingwood and the Beginnings of *The Idea of History*', in
    Collingwood Studies, 1, 1994, 4–12.

ing and an answering activity.[17] Back at home, W.G. Collingwood taught his son to approach philosophy in an historical way. This meant in the first place that one should always try 'to get inside other people's heads' in order to understand them.[18] The realists, however, did not really appreciate the history of philosophy. And to the extent that they did venture into it, they considered the history of philosophy as a series of answers to 'eternal problems'.[19] They thought, for example, that Plato and Aristotle were discussing the same problems that were discussed in modern ethical theory. In Collingwood's view this was like having a nightmare about a man who had got it into his head that *trières* was the Greek word for 'steamer'.[20]

Collingwood's vague feelings of dissatisfaction turned into serious doubts around 1912, when he began directing excavations of his own and teaching history of philosophy at Pembroke College.[21] Meanwhile, the archaeological sites had become Collingwood's 'laboratory for testing epistemological doctrines' and for developing his logic of question and answer.[22] Having become a tutor at Pembroke College in 1912, he taught his pupils to approach philosophy in an historical way; they should always use the original sources and not criticise an author before they had found out what he meant.[23] However, these two 'flank attacks' on realism, as Collingwood calls them, could not take away his 'diffidence of youth'; by 1914 he still did not feel strong enough to reject the realist doctrines. The main reason for this was that he had not yet convinced himself that there was a necessary connection between realist epistemology on the one hand and its critical methods on the other. Until he had understood this connection, Collingwood felt bound to remain a realist.[24]

It took Collingwood two more years to trace the most basic error of realism. The turning point took place around 1916, when Collingwood tried to come to terms with the ugliness of the Albert Memorial on his daily walk to the Admiralty, to work in the Geographical Section of Naval Intelligence.[25] In his autobiography, Collingwood indicates that his struggle with the Albert Memorial led to a further development of a thought with which he was already familiar, namely the 'principle that a body of knowledge consists not of "propositions", "statements", "judgements", etc., but always of these together with the questions they are meant to answer'.[26] The development of this principle enabled him to reject

---

[17] R.G. Collingwood, *An Autobiography*, 26.

[18] Ibid., 58.

[19] Ibid., 59.

[20] Ibid., 63–4.

[21] Ibid., 23–4.

[22] Ibid., 28.

[23] Ibid., 27.

[24] Ibid., 23.

[25] Johnston, *The Formative Years of R.G. Collingwood*, 10.

[26] R.G. Collingwood, *An Autobiography*, 30–1.

all current theories of truth, from the theory which holds that a proposition is true or false in itself, to the realist correspondence theory of truth and the idealist coherence theory of truth, to the pragmatic theory of truth.[27] Moreover, Collingwood's discovery led to a rejection of the notion of 'eternal problems' on which the realist critical methods were based.[28] All this he wrote down in 1917 in a book called *Truth and Contradiction* which was not published in spite of Sir Henry Jones' (1852–1922) positive report.[29]

In his autobiography, Collingwood does not mention the role of Italian philosophy in his early development. This is surprising because, having read the Italian philosophers for himself since 1909, he must have known that they had made great progress in developing a theory of history and a dialectic of question and answer. To these subjects I will turn after reconstructing Collingwood's early relationship to the Italians.

Oxford and Italian Philosophy

In order to understand the role of the Italians in Collingwood's early development we first need to know how they came into his life. In this context, it is important to note that Collingwood already had a keen knowledge of the history of Italian culture before he went to Oxford in 1908. Collingwood's first interests in Italian culture were doubtlessly aroused by his father and Ruskin. The latter had frequently travelled to Italy, knew Italian, and had written many books about Italian art and history. As Ruskin's secretary and biographer, W.G. Collingwood shared Ruskin's admiration for Italy, and in 1882 he accompanied him on a Grand Tour.[30] The young Collingwood followed in their footsteps; at Rugby he read Ruskin's *Stones of Venice*, taught himself to read Dante and studied Italian medieval history.[31] Without doubt, therefore, Collingwood was an enthusiastic Italianist before he went to Oxford.

Collingwood's arrival at Oxford coincided with the rising of Croce's fame in England. Philosophers like H. Rashdall (1858–1924), F.C.S Schiller (1864–1937), and J.B. Baillie (1872–1940), returning in 1908 from the International Conference of Philosophy at Heidelberg, had been impressed by Croce's paper on the lyrical character of art.[32] In 1909, Douglas Ainslie (1865–1948) published the English translation of Croce's *Estetica*. This was probably the book Collingwood was discussing with his friend Arthur Ransome (1884–1967) in a boat on Lake Coniston

---

[27] Ibid., 36.
[28] Ibid., 41–2.
[29] R.G. Collingwood, *Essays in Political Philosophy*, 230–1.
[30] Johnston, *The Formative Years of R.G. Collingwood*, 4.
[31] Smith, 'R.G. Collingwood: "This Ring of Thought"', 36; R.G. Collingwood, *An Autobiography*, 7, 9.
[32] T. Elsenhans (ed.), *Bericht Über den III. internationalen Kongress für Philosophie zu Heidelberg*, 1–5 September 1908, Nendeln, Lichtenstein, 1974, 22–32.

in the summer of that year.[33] After 1909, Ainslie continued the series with translations of *Filosofia della pratica* in 1913, of *Ciò che è vivo e ciò che è morto della filosofia di Hegel* in 1915, and of the second edition of the *Logica* in 1917. Meanwhile, *Materialismo storico* was translated and published by C.M. Meredith in 1914 with an introduction by A.D. Lindsay. From 1908 onwards, Croce's works were often discussed in the philosophical journals by British philosophers such as Paton, Bosanquet, and others.[34] Collingwood's own tutor, E.F. Carritt (1876–1964) was one of the first to write a long chapter on Croce's aesthetics in *The Theory of Beauty* of 1914.[35] After 1909, interest for other Italian philosophers was also growing. Gentile's works were increasingly reviewed by prominent philosophers such as Bosanquet, as was de Ruggiero's *La filosofia contemporanea*.[36] Works by other Italian philosophers like Antiono Aliotta (1881–1964) and Varisco (1850–1933), were also translated before the war.

The centre of this small but very active group of translators, commentators, and reviewers was J.A. Smith (1863–1939). He personally knew Ainslie, Baillie, Hannay, Bosanquet, and many other philosophers who were interested in Italian philosophy. In 1909, he travelled to Italy where he visited the *Scuola Normale* in Pisa, where Gentile had studied from 1893 until 1898.[37] In Naples, he 'was struck by the fact that the booksellers' shops displayed a widespread local interest in philosophy, and purchased two or three volumes by Benedetto Croce'.[38] Smith was immediately impressed with the 'freshness and independence of the views expressed, and by the scholarly manner of their presentation'.[39] Back in England, he began to read 'around and behind' Croce, and from 1910 he lectured on and wrote about Italian philosophy. Smith's inaugural lecture 'Knowing and Acting', delivered in October 1910, shows Croce's influence, and his paper 'On Feeling', delivered on 1 December 1913 for the Aristotelian Society, is the first paper by an English thinker showing the influence of Gentile.[40]

What J.A. Smith meant by reading 'around and behind' Croce becomes clear from the bibliography to his lectures on Gentile's philosophy of 1916–17 which go back to earlier versions. This shows that he had read almost every book and article that Croce and Gentile had published! Moreover, it shows that Smith was an assiduous reader of *La Critica* who was well acquainted with other writers in

---

33 Levine, 'Collingwood, Vico, and The Autobiography', 390n16.
34 S. Blackburn (ed.), *Index to Mind, Vol. 1–100*, (1892–1991).
35 Carritt, *The Theory of Beauty*, 179–219.
36 Harris, 'Introduction', 62–3.
37 J.A. Smith, 'Lectures on Gentile', Manuscript of about 1916 or 1917 based on earlier lectures, Magdalen Ms 1026/XI/13, no page numbers.
38 J.A. Smith, 'Philosophy as the Development of the Notion and Reality of Self-Consciousness', in *Contemporary British Philosophy, Second Series*, Allen and Unwin, London, 1925, 230–1.
39 Ibid., 231.
40 Harris, 'Introduction', 8–9.

Croce's and Gentile's journal. In this context, he describes de Ruggiero as 'another independent ally of Croce's and a collaborator with him and Gentile in the journal *La Critica*'.[41] Finally, Smith was well acquainted with the more remote history of Italian philosophy. The 1916–17 lectures begin with a long introduction on the history of Italian philosophy, mentioning and often discussing the thoughts of Dante, Bruno (1548–1600), Telesio, Campanella (1568–1639), Vico, Spaventa, Mazzini, Carducci (1835–1907), Villari, and Gentile's tutors at Pisa d'Ancona, and Jaja. In most of his discussions, Smith follows Gentile's history of Italian philosophy, but his comments clearly show that he had developed his own point of view.

In general, Smith's view of Italian philosophy was very positive. He taught his students that 'any philosophical good was to be expected from Italy and especially from southern Italy'.[42] He also told his audience that Italian thought had been 'strangely and wrongly neglected'.[43] In this context, Smith points out that Croce and Gentile worked in the long tradition of Italian thought, which had always been 'markedly idealistic, non-materialistic, scarcely even naturalistic and not in conflict with religion'.[44] According to Smith, the originality of Croce and Gentile lay in their 'historical preparation' which constituted 'a large part of their modernity'. In this sense, Smith stresses that both thinkers consider 'the study of history as the only sound basis for speculation'.[45]

Smith's own historical preparation on the topic was outstanding. He compares the Italians' identity of philosophy and history with Hegel's and Windelband's views on this issue, and he also discusses Croce's development from the *Lineamenti di una logica* of 1905 to the second edition of the *Logica*. This is most remarkable, because Croce's *Lineamenti* was and still is a rarity, which has never been discussed in English. According to Smith, the Germans took the identity in the sense of mutual presupposition, whereas Croce and Gentile interpreted it as 'a thorough going unity or identity, not data and principle or matter and form, or content and continent but to sunolon [complete whole]'. In this context, Smith observes that this identity was not yet complete in Croce's *Lineamenti di una logica*, and that it was under the influence of Gentile that Croce arrived at a fuller identity in the *Logica* of 1909 thus reaching a 'complete agreement' with his friend.

Smith's detailed comments and thorough interpretations show that he was completely up to date with regard to the relationship between Croce and Gentile. Most importantly, unlike so many other interpreters, he did not see Gentile as a follower of Croce but, on the contrary, as one of Croce's sources of

41   Smith, 'Lectures on Gentile', no page numbers.
42   Ibid.
43   Ibid.
44   Ibid.
45   Ibid.

inspiration. However, Smith's view that the two Italians completely agreed on the identity of philosophy and history is disputable, because the two philosophers differed on this issue.[46] Smith was certainly not blind to the differences underlying Croce's and Gentile's general agreement which he describes as follows:

> Croce is an historian and a critic and approaches philosophy from that side: his philosophy is the result of a reflection on what is implied in a certain spiritual activity or experience in which he finds the greatest though still incomplete satisfaction (a dissatisfied satisfaction) viz. the contemplation of the individual personalities, structures etc. which constitute themselves in history: the apprehension and appreciation of these and he speculates on what underlies and supports such experience. Here he feels himself freest and best rewarded, and the work of himself and others at once purified and elevated. Gentile on the other hand is fundamentally a teacher, it is in the antagonism and confrontation of teacher with pupil that he in the almost slang phrase, 'finds himself'. Even when he is alone he is still teacher and pupil in one, though that really means that he is never alone solus cum solo he is still in and at school. Life, the life of the mind – presents itself always to him as a history of the corporative self-formation of minds. Here lies all its worth, its joy, its sacredness: in this is the fullness of life. And it is of this that he seeks to philosophise – the intelligible meaning is meaning not beyond or outside it but within it.[47]

The wording of this passage shows that Smith had delved deeply into the thought of both Italian philosophers. Interestingly, Smith bases his interpretation of Gentile's philosophy on his educational theory, thus stressing the 'open' or dialogical character of actualism. This is correct since Gentile had not yet published his *Teoria dello spirito come atto puro*, in which he defended a more monistic view of actualism. But already in 1916 Smith had some difficulties with Gentile's philosophy because it 'overemphasises the character of one-ness and makes its necessary articulation a pressing problem', a criticism that he would repeat in an article of 1920.[48]

It goes without saying that Smith's lectures on Croce and Gentile aroused the interest of his students, and without doubt they fascinated the young Collingwood who had already read the Italians for himself. Smith's comments on Croce's philosophy provided Collingwood with a guide through the *Filosofia dello spirito*, and Smith's positive appraisal of actualism certainly made the young Collingwood curious about Gentile and his followers. Interestingly, Smith cites 'L'atto del pensare come atto puro' from its original version in the *Annuario della Biblioteca filosofica di Palermo* of 1912, which also contains de Ruggiero's 'La

---

[46] See chapter 2, pp. 50–51, and 3, pp. 84–86.
[47] Smith, 'Lectures on Gentile', no page number.
[48] Smith, 'The Philosophy of Giovanni Gentile' in *Proceedings of the Aristotelian Society*, XX, 1919–20, 74.

scienza come esperienza assoluta'. It is probable, therefore, that Collingwood took notice of both works before the war.

Thanks to Smith, therefore, Collingwood came to know quite early in his career that, far from Oxford, there were some philosophers in the world who, unlike his own realist teachers, took all the activities in which he had been interested in since childhood very seriously. In Smith's portrait of Croce, Collingwood could recognise his own need for a philosophy, which would explain his own experience as an artist, archaeologist, and historian. Smith's description of Gentile probably inspired Collingwood's own reflections on the teaching of the history of philosophy from 1912 onwards. Finally, Smith certainly drew Collingwood's attention to the new generation of Italian philosophers like de Ruggiero. In this way Collingwood discovered that the Italians were providing answers to his questions on art, history, and philosophy, which the realists left unanswered. Moreover, both Croce's and Gentile's practical philosophy stood squarely opposed to the realist tendency to regard moral philosophy as a mistake. Smith's legendary gift for teaching and his friendliness towards his pupils did the rest; Collingwood's already great interest for Italian philosophy became a passion for the rest of his life.

This passion is most clearly illustrated by the fact that he read and annotated the three published volumes of Croce's *Filosofia dello spirito* in Italian in 1912, the year of his graduation. The annotations in these books show that Collingwood read Gentile's works as early as 1912. Furthermore, he most probably read de Ruggiero's *Filosofia contemporanea*, which his friend A.H. Hannay was translating at the time.[49] Collingwood finished this translation in 1919–20 from Hannay's first draft.[50] It seems a safe conclusion, therefore, that around 1912 Collingwood spent much of his time reading and translating Italian philosophy. This development of his own interest shows that he began to free himself from his realist teachers. Towards the end of 1912 these explorations in Italian philosophy became more serious when he sent Croce a translated specimen chapter of *La filosofia di Giambattista Vico*.[51] The Italian readily approved of the translation and this would lead to Collingwood's first publication: *The Philosophy of Giambattista Vico*.[52]

The Philosophy of Giambattista Vico (1913)

Collingwood's correspondence with Croce in the years 1912–13 does not indicate whether Collingwood himself proposed to translate the book, or whether he was

49 R.G. Collingwood, *Essays in Political Philosophy*, 8n24.
50 R.G. Collingwood, 'List of Work Done', Dep. 22/2, 61.
51 Amadeo Vigorelli (ed.), 'Lettere di Robin George Collingwood a Benedetto Croce (1912–1939)', in *Rivista di storia della filosofia*, 3, 1991, 549.
52 B. Croce, 'Letter to Collingwood' about 1912 in Collingwood's copy of *La filosofia di Giambattista Vico*, 1911. In possession of Ms Smith.

asked to do it. Both Ainslie and Collingwood's friend Hannay were involved in the enterprise and J.A. Smith certainly knew about it. The fact that Douglas Ainslie gave some advice to Collingwood shows that the latter had not 'unwittingly transgressed on Ainslie's exclusive right to translate Croce', as Knox thought.[53] A.H. Hannay was wuarking with Dent&Co publishers and it seems that he had arranged the translation; the first letters between Croce and Collingwood all passed through his hands.[54]

It is not clear whether Collingwood had particular philosophical reasons for translating Croce's book on Vico. On the one hand Collingwood certainly had heard Smith talking about the Neapolitan philosopher and possibly began to read *La Scienza Nuova* as an undergraduate. On the other hand, Collingwood had no other choice; the book on Vico was the most recent monograph by Croce and Ainslie was already translating Croce's *Filosofia dello spirito* and had probably also claimed the translation of *Ciò che è vivo e ciò che è morto della filosofia di Hegel*, which he would publish in 1915. Moreover, financial and professional reasons played a role as well; the translation would pay him £60 and would establish his name as a translator.[55]

Whatever Collingwood's reasons for translating Croce's book were, the choice was a very happy one. Croce had written the book in 1910, in full maturity, right after completing philosophy of the spirit. Since its publication in 1911, it has been one of the most influential introductions to Vico's thought, and though Croce's interpretation of Vico has become outdated, it is still recognised as a masterpiece in the history of philosophy.

The translation of the book on Vico had a great effect on Collingwood's development. According to Knox, he used to say 'that Vico had influenced him more then anyone else'.[56] The historical part of *The Idea of History* shows that Collingwood's interpretation of Vico was in many respects similar to Croce's. Right at the start of the book Croce contrasts Descartes' doctrine of the clear and distinct ideas with Vico's *verum et factum convertuntur* principle. Collingwood follows this interpretation in *The Idea of History*.[57] Croce dedicates a whole chapter to Vico's contributions to historical method as being a) the use of linguistics in historical studies, b) the use of mythology, c) the use of tradition, and d) the comparative method.[58] In *The Idea of History* Collingwood gives the same examples of Vico's contributions to historical method and even in the same order as Croce does.[59]

---

53 T.M. Knox, Review of 'The Formative Years of R.G. Collingwood by William M. Johnston', in *The Philosophical Quarterly*, 19, 1969, 165.
54 Vigorelli (ed.), 'Lettere di Robin George Collingwood a Benedetto Croce', 549.
55 R.g. Collingwood, 'List of Work Done', 83.
56 Knox, 'Editor's Preface', viii.
57 R.G. Collingwood, *The Idea of History*, 63.
58 B. Croce, *La filosofia di Giambattista Vico*, 144–54.
59 R.G. Collingwood, *The Idea of History*, 69–70.

These and other similarities have led some other interpreters of Vico's thought, like Berlin, Badaloni, and Miller, to put Croce's and Collingwood's interpretations in the same box.[60] However, there are some interesting differences between Croce's and Collingwood's views on Vico's speculative philosophy of history, which probably go back to 1912. Firstly, in *La filosofia di Giambattista Vico*, Croce severely criticised Vico's theory of the divine providence that determines the course of the historical cycles. In his view, this theory led Vico into too close an identity of philosophy and history. For this reason, Croce found Vico's history too philosophical, which is shown by his chronic contempt for historical fact, and his philosophy too historical, which is shown by his tendency to generalise historical facts into universal truths. Following his own theory of the practical source of error, Croce could only explain Vico's speculative philosophy of history as a misplaced allegiance to the Catholic Church.[61]

Unlike Croce, Collingwood was always much more positive about Vico's speculative philosophy of history. In *The Idea of History* he holds that Vico, with his idea of history as a divine plan, was the first who reached 'a completely modern idea of what the subject-matter of history is'.[62] In this context, Collingwood points to the necessity of the concept of providence for overcoming the antithesis between isolated actions of men and the divine plan that holds them together. This interpretation probably goes back to 1912, because Collingwood contrasted history as 'a succession of detached events temporally distinct' with history as 'the discovery of absolute truth and the development of God's purposes' in his first book, *Religion and Philosophy*, though without mentioning Vico.[63]

Secondly, in an article of 1927, Collingwood spent a whole page arguing the superiority of Vico's theory of historical cycles over Spengler's (1880–1936).[64] Along the same lines, in *The Idea of History* Collingwood points out, in contrast to Croce, that Vico never understood his cycles as 'fixed phases'. In Collingwood's view the cycle 'is a not a circle but a spiral, for history never repeats itself, but comes round to each new phase in a form differentiating by what has gone before'.[65]

Thirdly, and most remarkably, Collingwood stresses that the theory of historical cycles originates in the methodological problems which confronted Vico

[60] Isaiah Berlin, *Vico and Herder, Two Studies in the History of Ideas*, Chatto and Windus, London, 1980, 27n; Nicola Badaloni, *Introduzione a Vico*, Laterza, Bari, 1988, 174; Cecilia Miller, *Giambattista Vico, Imagination and Thought*, MacMillan, New York, 1993, 30.
[61] B. Croce, *La filosofia di Giambattista Vico*, 43–4.
[62] R.G. Collingwood, *The Idea of History*, 65.
[63] R.G. Collingwood, *Religion and Philosophy*, MacMillan, London, 1916, 156.
[64] R.G. Collingwood, 'Oswald Spengler and the Theory of Historical Cycles', in *Antiquity*, 1, 311–25, cited from id., *Essays in the Philosophy of History*, University of Texas Press, Austin, 1966, 72.
[65] R.G. Collingwood, *The Idea of History*, 68.

as an historian of the remote past. In the first chapter of *The Principles of History* he remarks that 'anyone who had read Vico, or even a second-hand version of his ideas, must have known that the important question about any statement contained in a source is not whether it is true or false, but what it means'.[66] In *The Idea of History* he stresses that the meaning of language, mythology, and tradition can only be solved on a metaphysical basis, in particular on the basis of a metaphysics of the mind: 'in order to find the key to this re-interpretation we must remember that minds at a given stage of development will tend to create the same kind of products.'[67] Collingwood thus acknowledged that the interpretation of sources is dependent on Vico's metaphysical doctrine that *verum et factum convertuntur* and the theory of cycles which is based on it. This was definitely not Croce's view. As a self-declared anti-metaphysician Croce always tried to separate Vico's methodology from his metaphysics. By unifying Vico's method and metaphysics, Collingwood therefore comes closer to Gentile's interpretation of Vico. Like Collingwood, Gentile also acknowledged the importance of Vico's metaphysical doctrines, although he did not stress their connection to the problem of the interpretation of sources in the way Collingwood did.[68] It is probable therefore that Collingwood developed his interpretation of Vico's thought independently of Gentile.

The roots of Collingwood's own interpretation probably lay in his archaeological and religious experience. At the time of translating Croce's book on Vico, Collingwood was directing his first excavation at Papcastle.[69] Working in archaeological sites, which he used to liken to a 'laboratory for testing epistemological theories', Collingwood probably discovered that Vico's principal problem was, like his own, a problem of method. This view of the relationship beween Vico and Collingwood is corroborated by the following interpretation of *La Scienza Nuova* in an article of 1930:

> Vico's chosen field, as an historian, was the history of remote antiquity. He studied distant and obscure periods precisely because they were distant and obscure; for his real interest was in historical method, and, according as the sources are scanty and dubious and the subject-matter hard to understand, the importance of sound method becomes plain.[70]

In Vico's problems of method Collingwood must have recognised his own, as his self-portrait in his autobiography shows in a most remarkable way:

---

[66] R.G. Collingwood, *The Principles of History*, 15.

[67] R.G. Collingwood, *The Idea of History*, 70.

[68] G. Gentile, *Studi Vichiani*, Le Monnier, Firenze, 1927.

[69] Jan van der Dussen, *History as a Science, The Philosophy of R.G. Collingwood*, Nijhoff, The Hague, 1981, 209.

[70] R.G. Collingwood, *The Philosophy of History*, Historical Association Leaflet, 79, 1930, cited from id., *Essays in the Philosophy of History*, 127.

Obscure provinces like Roman Britain, always rather appeal to me. Their
obscurity is a challenge; you have to invent new methods for studying them,
and then you will probably find that the cause of their obscurity is some
defect in the methods hitherto used.[71]

Besides their common interest in remote history, it was religion that joined the
two philosophers. In *The Idea of History* Collingwood stresses that Vico's *verum et
factum convertuntur* principle expresses the identity between God and man; both
are creators who can understand their own creations. From this principle it
follows that nature, which is the creation of God, cannot be understood by man,
whose proper object is history.[72] In Vico's acknowledgment of the transcendence
of God and nature to mankind, Collingwood could recognise his own religious
convictions better than in Croce's rejection of transcendence, and his bold 'sub-
sumption' of religion to the other forms of experience. These differences between
Croce and Collingwood went back to his first acquaintance with the works of the
Italian.

Collingwood's Commentaries on Croce's *Philosophy of the Spirit* (1912)

In 1912, Collingwood read the first three volumes of Croce's *Filosofia dello spirito*
in Italian and wrote detailed and highly critical comments in the margins, which
enable us to reconstruct his earliest opinions on Italian philosophy. Unfortunately, apart from some remarks in the *Estetica* and in the *Filosofia della pratica*,
most of Collingwood's first commentaries on Croce's philosophy of history are
lost, because Collingwood's copy of Croce's *Logica* is missing. In order to understand these few remarks on history, I will first reconstruct Collingwood's
general opinion on Croce. This reconstruction also provides a basis for a conjecture of Collingwood's view of Gentile's thought in 1912, and for his first criticism
of Croce's *Teoria e storia della storiografia*, which he bought in 1917.[73]

In a letter to Samuel Alexander (1859–1938) of 24 May 1925, Collingwood
wrote that he rejected Croce's aesthetics 'on first reading'.[74] The fact that Collingwood was not boasting is shown by the following marginal comment which
pierces right through the identity of intuition and expression, which is the heart
of Croce's aesthetics:

> …is not this identification merely verbal? it leaves all the same problems in its
> relation to a) sensation b) externalisation.[75]

---

71 R.G. Collingwood, *An Autobiography*, 86.
72 R.G. Collingwood, *The Idea of History*, 64–5.
73 The first chapters of *Teoria e storia della storiografia* appeared in 1912 and 1913 in *La
    Critica*.
74 Cited by Donald S. Taylor, *R.G. Collingwood, A Bibliography*, Garland Publishing, New
    York & London, 1988, 55.
75 R.G. Collingwood, 'Marginal Comments in Croce, *Estetica*', 1912, 14, in possession of
    Ms Smith.

This comment anticipates Collingwood's later criticism in *Speculum Mentis*, where he points out that the identification of intuition and expression is based on Croce's method of 'pricking the concept'.[76] According to Collingwood, Croce, by failing to acknowledge the opposition between intuition and expression, simply identifies meaning with its sensuous vehicle, or the truth of art with truth of its own imaginative world.[77] In this way, Collingwood explains, art is reduced to a thing, and the relationship between sensation, feeling, and expression in the work of art cannot be understood.[78] But if intuition and expression are conceived as opposites, a dynamic view of its life becomes possible, and this shows how the artist 'toils' at expressing his feelings in his work. Raised in a family of painters, Collingwood understood art from the 'inside' and from this experience stems his keen understanding of art as an activity.

This insider's knowledge of art stood squarely opposed to Croce's, who was not an artist himself, but a critic of art. In 1912, Collingwood was well aware of the difference between these approaches. In the margin of a passage in which Croce argues that an artist never makes a stroke with his brush without having previously seen it with his imagination, Collingwood writes:

> Very weak: and shows a curious lack (quite characteristic of Croce) of under-standing the process of artistic work. He thinks of an artist as working by flashes of genius and then going round to pick up the bits – seeing a picture in his head and then just painting it out. He sees art quaintly from the outside – his aesthetic is a dilettante's aesthetic, not an artist's.[79]

Interestingly, Collingwood connects Croce's doctrine that imagination precedes expression to his approaching art from the outside. This "splitting" of the artistic activity is the basis of Croce's 'naturalism':

> With his usual naturalism he makes the two phases of the process hetero-geneous: 1) impression 2) expression whereas the phases are 1) rudimentary expression (that's a pretty view) 2) fuller expression (paint it).[80]

This passage clearly shows the difference between Croce and Collingwood. For Croce, looking from the outside at the artistic process there are two processes; whatever is expressed must first be 'impressed'. For Collingwood, looking from the artist's point of view at art, there is only one process consisting of expression, growing upon itself. This is the theory which Collingwood defended all his life. In *Speculum Mentis* and *The Principles of Art* of 1938 we find its full elaboration of this view in almost the same terminology.[81]

---

[76] R.G. Collingwood, *Speculum Mentis*, 87.

[77] Ibid., 87–8.

[78] Ibid., 91.

[79] R.G. Collingwood, 'Marginal Comments in Croce, *Estetica*', 121.

[80] Ibid., 59.

[81] R.G. Collingwood, *Speculum Mentis*, 98; Id., *The Principles of Art*, 144–51.

Collingwood's comments in his copy of Croce's *Estetica* also show that he had already developed the epistemological and logical corollaries of the concept of the mind as an activity. On the first page of the *Estetica*, where Croce points out that all knowledge has only two forms, intuitive and logical, Collingwood writes: 'examine this distinction!' From that page he criticises the typical Crocean 'distinctions in unity' like intuition and expression, intuition and sensetion, form and content, and so forth.

Collingwood's criticisms show that he had already detected the weakness of Croce's philosophical method, which was based on distinctions. As we have seen in chapter 3, distinctions, and in particular Croce's distinctions, were also the special target of Gentile's 'method of immanence'. The common ground for both Gentile's and Collingwood's criticisms of Croce's distinctions is that they both see the mind as an act, or as an activity which must be understood from the inside. Along similar lines Collingwood criticises Croce's *Filosofia della pratica*. He calls the 'distinction between man of thought and man of action' a 'fallacy' and on an inserted page he lists all 'loci' in the book where this distinction leads to identities which contradict it. Since the distinction between theory and practice is central, both to Croce's theory of error and to his doctrine of the pseudoconcept, Collingwood could not but reject both theories. At the end of chapter XII of *La Filosofia della pratica*, in which Croce rejects all kinds of pseudo-concepts in art-criticism like the 'tragic', the 'comic', the 'sublime', and many others, Collingwood writes:

> This preceding chapter (XII) is an excellent locus for C's logic (or rather alogic) of the pseudoconcept, and it is an excellent example of its weakness. He is simply too impatient to extract the meaning of an 'empirical concept' and to follow the dialectic of its changing determinations: the fact that it does change condemns it out of hand as wholly irrational. He naively assumes all the time that his own concepts, four in number, cannot change. Thus his logic is a rigid and static formal logic working very stiffly in a very narrow channel and leaving entirely outside itself the whole world of empirical concepts which are frankly abandoned to the mercy of individual caprice.[82]

Again, as in his criticism of the *Estetica*, Collingwood approaches experience from the inside, stressing its dialectic, change, and rationality. From this viewpoint, 'pseudo-concepts' are not mere practical 'fictions', as Croce held, but true concepts, which are developed in a rational way. Collingwood's criticism of Croce's theory of the pseudo-concepts is also reflected in his critical reaction to Croce's identification of bad aesthetics with astrology:

> Yes of course, and you haven't the curiosity to trace the germs of truth in astrology or to see how it develops into astronomy. This way of writing a

---

[82] R.G. Collingwood, 'Marginal Comments in Croce, *Estetica*', 111.

book as a rag-bag of miscellaneous errors, all grinned at and dismissed is jolly bad philosophy. Isn't it the work of a man at the mercy of his card-index?[83]

Again Collingwood's criticism seems to be based on his insider's knowledge of the history of science which he had cultivated since childhood. And again this insider's perspective leads to a criticism of distinctions. In the above passage Collingwood's target is the distinction between truth and error. In his view all forms of knowledge are true to a certain degree; even astrology, flatly rejected by Croce, is acknowledged by Collingwood as a form of knowledge, which eventually provided the basis for astronomy. This view of knowledge reveals Collingwood's notion of mental activities around 1912. If two phases of an activity 'overlap' each other, truth and error cannot be separated. From this viewpoint, astrology is not an error that must be eradicated before astronomy can develop, but a lower form of knowledge from which astronomy could grow.

Given the fact that Collingwood's 'insiders view' of art led him to reject Croce's identity of intuition and expression, it may be conjectured that he also rejected its counterparts in *La Filosofia dello spirito*: the identity of will and action, and the identity of philosophy and history. This hypothesis is corroborated by the following comment on Croce's theory of the origin of language:

> The doctrine is an interesting feature of Croce's naturalism. Unable to understand the concept of self-creation, or creation of the spirit by itself out of itself by a dialectical process of self-transformation, and having committed himself to the view that a spiritual activity must stand upon a heterogeneous basis (expression upon impression) he then has to explain the dial[ectical] process by saying that expression A becomes impression before expression B can arise out of it. The first phase has to die in order that, when it is dead, the second phase may grow out to be there: just as he never tackles the problem of where impressions come from, how his precious series of grades ever starts working — which is the same thing. This failure to make the circle meet itself (with the resulting profound misunderstanding of history) is very characteristic of Croce. It is in fact the problem of his philosophy.[84]

This passage strikes us because of its overtly actualist language of 'self-creation' and 'dialectical self-transformation'. On this basis, Collingwood attacks Croce's theory of the circle of art, philosophy, economic and moral action, which forms the backbone of *La Filosofia dello spirito*.[85] Ideally, this circle closes when history *a parte obiecti*, or action, is 'intuited' by the first grade of history *a parte subiecti*, which is art. In the above passage, Collingwood points out that Croce does not really explain how this circle starts working, because he assumes that the past action is connected to historical thought by some causal impression–expression process in its first 'moment' which is art. In this process, the first phase (impression) must 'die' before the second (expression) comes from of it.

---

83   Ibid., at the end of 'Capitolo XIV'.

84   Ibid., last page.

85   See chapter 2, pp. 51–55.

This naturalistic view of the mind stands squarely opposed to Collingwood's own dialectical view of the mind, according to which each mental activity is self-creative. As a result of this, the whole notion of impression–expression is redundant; the mind creates expressions all the time and develops these into fuller expressions. These fuller expressions do not arise when the earlier 'die', but they build on them, so that the new phase of activity includes the previous phases and thus keeps them 'alive'. This idea of the relationship between past and present phases in mental activities forms the core of Collingwood's later ideas of the 'living past' according to which the past does not die in the present. In 1912, Collingwood had not yet elaborated the notion of the living past, but the above passage reveals that he had understood its implications for the philosophy of mind in general, and for the philosophy of history in particular.

On the basis of the previous chapters on the Italians and Collingwood's comments on the *Filosofia dello spirito*, Collingwood's criticism of Croce's philosophy of history in 1912 can be partially reconstructed. As we saw in chapter 2, Croce held that philosophy must not be seen as an 'antecedent' of history; just as we do not intuit and then express our intuitions, and just as we do not first will our leg to move and then do it, we do not first conceive the meaning of a pure concept and then apply it, but we conceive its meaning by applying it to our intuitions. However, already in 1912 Collingwood rejected the identity of intuition and expression by pointing out that an artist begins with an expression, which he gradually develops into a fuller expression. Given Croce's own analogy between the identity of intuition and expression with the identity of philosophy and history, it may therefore be assumed that Collingwood also rejected Croce's theory of the individual judgment in which the pure concepts are developed as answers to questions simultaneously with the arising of the intuition-expressions. In analogy of his own understanding of the dialectic of art, Collingwood must have defended a theory which accounts for the gradual development of the concepts in a self-creative questions and answers process in which the meaning of the concept is adjusted to each new and fuller expression of the foregoing. Similarly to his analysis of the growth of aesthetic expression he must have held that an historian first comes to a provisional judgment, which he gradually develops into a fuller judgment by asking questions and answering them.

That Collingwood probably held such a view around 1912 is corroborated by his description of his 'archaeological laboratory' in his autobiography:

> At the same time I found myself experimenting in a laboratory of knowledge; at first asking myself a quite vague question, such as: 'was there a Flavian occupation on this site?' Then dividing that question into various heads and putting the first in some such form as this: 'are these Flavian sherds and coins mere strays, or were they deposited in the period to which they belong?' and then considering all the possible ways in which light could be thrown on this new question, and putting them into practice one by one, until at last I could

say, 'There was a Flavian occupation; an earth and timber fort of such and such plan was built here in the year a±b and abandoned for such and such reasons in the year x±y'. Experience soon taught me that under these laboratory conditions one found out nothing at all except in answer to a question; and not a vague question either, but a definite one.[86]

Without doubt Collingwood tested Croce's doctrine of history in his archeological laboratory with great interest, because, unlike the realist doctrines, it does take the question and answer process into account. But given Collingwood's general criticism of Croce's philosophy of the spirit in 1912, we can safely assume that the latter's theory did not pass Collingwood's test, because it did not take the gradual development of the question and answer process into account.

Another issue on which Croce failed to pass the test was his theory of the pseudo-concept, which stood squarely opposed to Collingwood's defence of empirical concepts. This defence was not only central to Collingwood's view of science, illustrated above with the example of astrology and astronomy, but also to his archaeological practice. In his autobiography Collingwood says that the first question an archaeologist always asks about an artefact is: 'what is it for?'[87] The first question thus always concerns the meaning of an object, 'meaning' being understood in strictly teleological terms. According to Collingwood this first question is never answered immediately, that is, in Crocean terms, we cannot immediately apply concepts to our intuitions, but only mediately, that is on the basis of evidence. In archaeology, this evidence is interpreted by scientific methods; on the basis of induction, classification, statistical research, and so forth, the archaeologist reaches some preliminary interpretations. For example, many potsherds may lead to the conclusion that not one, but two camps were built on a certain site and this in turn may say something about Roman tactics in Britain.[88] For scientific methods like these, Croce's *Logica* does not provide a proper epistemological basis. Croce always rejected induction as an historical method. In his view, real history never proceeds by induction but by reliving the past. In this context, it is highly significant that Collingwood comments on Croce's criticism of the use of induction in history with: 'but surely history is always inductive!'[89] Furthermore, Croce used to point out that pseudo-concepts are not true, but only useful in order to memorise or communicate some individual judgments. For example, 'Greek Man' summarises all individual judgments on individual Greeks like Pericles, Alcibiades, and so on. It is clear that this theory was of great help in Collingwood's archeological practice, which extensively used 'pseudo-concepts' like 'La Tène civilisation', the 'Belgae, Celts, and Romans', and so forth. These concepts are very seldom based on knowledge of

---

[86] R.G. Collingwood, *An Autobiography*, 24.

[87] Ibid., 128.

[88] Van der Dussen, *History as a Science*, 210.

[89] R.G. Collingwood, 'Marginal Comments in Croce, *Estetica*', 35.

individuals, as Croce claims, though they do provide the background for explaining an individual action, for example, in the case of Caesar's invasion of Britain. In Collingwood's archeological practice, pseudo-concepts played an important role and this is why he defended them against Croce with the remark that he is just too impatient to find out their meaning. For Collingwood, true history is not obtained at the beginning of the thought process but at the end, and only after a long and laborious process of asking questions which can be put in terms of pseudo-concepts and answered on the basis of inductive methods.

Finally, outside his archeological laboratory, Collingwood had another axe to grind with Croce, and this was religion. As we have seen in chapter 2, Croce had banned 'religion' from the realm of the spirit, by showing that it was a mixture of experiences which can all be reduced to one of the 'true' forms of spirit.[90] At the same time Croce described the spirit as being 'eternal', 'necessary', and 'universal', terms which are usually applied to God. From the beginning Collingwood had a very keen eye for this discrepancy between the *storia in tempo* and the *storia ideale eterna* in Croce's philosophy. This is reflected in his criticism of Croce's distinction between will and event (*volizione e accadimento*) in his copy of the *Filosofia della pratica*:

> The distinction between volizione and accadimento is a good example of C's abstractness. He abstracts the individual contribution from the whole which it goes to make up, as if there were 2 different things. Thus reintroducing the Dio personale e trascendente at whom he is always scoffing, in his most vicious form.[91]

In the previous chapters we have referred to the difficulties concerning Croce's distinction between *volizione* and *accadimento*. For Croce *volizione* is the will of a single man, whereas *accadimento* is the sum of these wills or the whole of the historical process. Croce presented this distinction as a parallel to the distinction between the intuition-expression and the concept. The intuition is knowledge of the individual as expressed by the human mind; only an expressed intuition is effective knowledge of the individual. Analogously to this notion, Croce points out that will and action cannot be distinguished; a will is always 'expressed' in action and if not, it is not a true will. But this does not mean that the will should be identified with the result of an action because the result of the action always depends on all the actions, the whole process.[92] On this basis, Croce held that the historian can never judge the *accadimento*, or collective action, but only individual action.

Collingwood brought up the difficulties of this dualism by interpreting it as the reintroduction of the transcendent God into history. Croce had rejected

---

[90] See chapter 2, p. 43.
[91] R.G. Collingwood, 'Marginal Comments in Croce, *Filosofia della pratica*', 1912, last page, in possession of Ms Smith.
[92] B. Croce, *Pratica*, 46–50.

Vico's speculative philosophy of history which is based on the notion of the divine providence. But his notion of *accadimento* reintroduces this concept under another name. Collingwood's process-view of reality blows all of Croce's subtle distinctions between the individual and collective action to pieces. From Collingwood's viewpoint, individual action and collective action are one and the same process which can never be separated. For this reason he sympathised with Vico's speculative philosophy of history, and repudiated Croce's degradation of philosophy to methodology.

Taken together, the 1912 criticisms of Croce's *Filosofia dello spirito* call for a thorough reinterpretation of Collingwood's early development. Contrary to all interpreters who hold that Collingwood still clung to a form of realism in his early development, it must be pointed out that Collingwood criticised a renowned idealist like Croce for being a 'realist' and a 'naturalist'. The comments show that Collingwood 'tested' Croce's concepts on his own experience as an artist, historian, and philosopher. In this context, he criticised Croce for having an 'outsider's' view of experience. This view manifests itself in all kinds of identities and distinctions which Collingwood attacks one by one. Croce's conclusions thus formed the starting point of Collingwood's own philosophical problems, of which the most important is to describe the forms of experience from the inside. This means in the first place that these should not be understood as a 'finished product' but as an activity or process. In this context, the marginal comments show that Gentile's method of immanence must have been of great use to him, even though Collingwood had already developed his own method to analyse the activities of the mind. In contrast to Croce and to a certain extent Gentile, Collingwood applied these notions of activity and process to some other forms of experience as well, most notably religion and science, which are not taken into account by the Italians, with the exception of de Ruggiero. Finally, Croce had banned 'religion' from the mind and degraded science to the formation of 'pseudo-concepts', which are not true but only useful. Gentile, in his '*Le forme assolute dello spirito*' of 1909 had described religion and science as 'abstract forms' of the mind, that is, as forms of experience which are not *norma sui*. These were the conclusions that led Collingwood to his most urging questions after 1912, to which he found a first solution in *Religion and Philosophy*.

Religion and Philosophy (1912–14)

Written between 1912 and 1914, *Religion and Philosophy* is Collingwood's first 'interim report' of his own development. Its main argument is that the Christian creed is not just feeling, intuition, or conduct, but a 'critical solution to a philosophical problem'.[93] Accordingly, Collingwood's main aim is to show that it is a right solution. In order to realise this aim, Collingwood approaches religion as 'a

---

93 R.G. Collingwood, *Religion and Philosophy*, xiii.

function of the mind', just like philosophy and history. All functions of the mind aim for truth about an object and this object is the universe.

On this basis, Collingwood first attacks all theorists who deny that religion is a function of the mind without an object at all. These are theorist like William James (1842–1910), who considered religion as pure feeling, or Albert Schweitzer (1875–1965), who interpreted religion as 'conduct'.[94] Secondly, Collingwood attacks theorists who admit the thought-character of religion, but who tend to consider thought apart from its object, and action apart from its purpose. These are 'psychologists' and modernist historians of religion.[95] In this context, Collingwood probably also aimed at the realist doctrine of practice, as expounded by Prichard and his followers. Finally, since he also attacks all doctrines that separate action from its purpose. For this reason *Religion and Philosophy* can be safely considered as Collingwood's first effort in the rapprochement of theory and practice.[96]

In his autobiography Collingwood indicates that the core of his attack on the psychological treatment is to be found in the following passage:

> The mind, regarded in this external way, really ceases to be a mind at all. To study a man's consciousness without studying the thing of which he is conscious is not knowledge of anything, but barren and trifling abstraction. It cannot answer ultimate questions, because it refuses to look with it eye to eye; and it is left with the cold unreality of thought which is the thought of nothing, action with no purpose, and fact with no meaning.[97]

For Collingwood, these 'ultimate questions' are metaphysical questions; the questions about the ultimate essence of the mind and its relationship to the world.[98] Collingwood himself gives an answer to these questions by holding that: 'the esse of mind is not cogitare simply, but de hac re cogitare.'[99] From this principle it follows that the relationship between a 'mental event' and the 'something known' or the 'reality beyond the act' must always be determined.

These remarks appear as a mixture of idealism and realism. On the one hand, Collingwood's principle that the *esse* of mind is *de hac re cogitare* echoes the idealist principle that the thought is always about an object, or in Italian terms, that thought is *pensiero pensante un pensato*. On the other hand, Collingwood seeks this object 'beyond the act' and this is what Gentile would call realism. Some interpreters have found the same mixture of realism and idealism in Collingwood's concept of history. On the one hand, they found Collingwood's realism expressed by his view that history is to be regarded as 'objectivity' and

---

94 Patrick, *The Magdalen Metaphysicals*, 90.
95 R.G. Collingwood, *Religion and Philosophy*, 38–43.
96 R.G. Collingwood, *An Autobiography*, 147.
97 R.G. Collingwood, *An Autobiography*, 93; Id., *Religion and Philosophy*, 42.
98 Ibid., 147.
99 Ibid., 100.

fact, as something independent of 'my own or your knowledge of it'.[100] On the other hand, they found the origin of the more 'idealist' re-enactment doctrine in Collingwood's view that two minds are identical if they think the same thing.[101] Moreover, Collingwood's interpreters found the strange mixture of realism and idealism explicitly justified by Collingwood's own remark that he has tried to express a doctrine that 'contains little if anything which contradicts the principles of either Realism or Idealism in their more satisfactory forms'.[102]

Seen in the context of Collingwood's development, this remark must be seen as a clear indication that Collingwood did not think of his own philosophy as being realist or idealist, or as a mixture of the two, but as a third position which is compatible with both. In *Religion and Philosophy* Collingwood established the metaphysical basis of this position in the chapter on the relation between matter and mind where he argues that the distinction between the two is not very useful because reality is always a combination of the two: 'If matter exists, mind must exist too.'[103] In the next chapter, Collingwood elaborates the epistemological consequences of this view in a general doctrine of the mind and its object. According to Collingwood, the mind is specifically that which knows the object although thought and object cannot be separated. From this it follows that the mind is not a self-identical thing; there is not thought in general, Collingwood says, but only particular thoughts about particular things. This view does not lead to an extreme form of solipsism, Collingwood remarks, because two thoughts can be the same from which it follows that two minds, thinking the same thought, actually form one mind.[104]

This 'identity-theory' has been hailed by some interpreters as the basis for Collingwood's allegedly idealist view that thoughts are public, and by other interpreters as the basis for his later re-enactment doctrine.[105] Seen in the context of Collingwood's development, however, his position was neither idealist nor realist. In *Religion and Philosophy* Collingwood does not distinguish between matter and mind, nor between object and subject, as given entities, but he regards both as aspects of a process of experience. Seen from this angle, Collingwood's position comes close to the philosophy which de Ruggiero had described as 'absolute immanentism', though it is not identical with it. If we read *Religion and Philosophy* to the end, we find that Collingwood places his theory of mind in a context which differs considerably from that of the Italians. In the chapter on God's self-expression in man, Collingwood most typically uses his

---

[100] Ibid., 49; van der Dussen, *History as a Science*, 12–13.

[101] R.G. Collingwood, *Religion and Philosophy*, 102; Rubinoff, *Collingwood and the Reform of Metaphysics*, 39–40; van der Dussen, *History as a Science*, 12–13, 261–2.

[102] R.G. Collingwood, *Religion and Philosophy*, 101n1.

[103] Ibid., 94.

[104] Ibid., 100–1.

[105] Peter Skagestad, *Making Sense of History, The Philosophies of Popper and Collingwood*, Universitetsforlaget, Oslo, 1975, 65–6; van der Dussen, *History as a Science*, 316.

'identity-theory' in order to explain the relationship between the historical Jesus and the 'countless numbers who know nothing of his life as a historic fact':

> The spirit of truth is not circumscribed by the limits of space and time. If a real community of life is possible between two men who share each other's outward presence and inward thoughts, it is possible no less between two who have never met; between the ancient poet and his modern reader, or the dead scientist and the living man who continues his work. The earlier in point of time lives on in the life of the later; each deriving the benefit from such intercourse.[106]

In this passage we find the theory of the identity of thought as the basis of the notion of the living past in the Italian sense of it; the past is living because the present thought can share thoughts with the past by reliving them. This is the position Croce expressed with his doctrine of the contemporaneity of history, and which Gentile and de Ruggiero expressed with the dialectic *pensante* and *pensato*. But right after this passage Collingwood makes the much bolder claim that the past also lives on even if we are not aware of it:

> Again, there is a union of mind between persons who are in the order of history unaware of each other's existence; between Hebrew prophet and Greek philosopher; between two scientists who cannot read each other's language. This union consists in the fact that both are dealing with the same problems; for in so far as any two minds are conscious of the same reality, they are the same mind. Thus there is a certain spiritual intercourse between men who have no outward point of contact whatever; and even if it is true, as Aristotle says, that bodily presence is the fulfillment of friendship, men may still be friends when neither knows the other's name.[107]

This passage stands squarely opposed to the Italian view of the living past. As we have seen in the previous chapters, the Italians never acknowledged a past outside, or apart from, the self-conscious act of thought. In contrast to them Collingwood acknowledges a past outside the act of thought: persons are united in history, even if they are unaware of each other's existence. Notably, this past is not an objective past in the realistic sense of the word, because history is not real in the sense in which our empirical objects are real. Its status is therefore 'ideal' or better, 'implicit'; the past is 'living' or 'active' in the present, even if we are not aware of it.

This sense of Collingwood's notion of the past is crucial in the history of religion, where an eternal truth of Christ and God lives:

> The life of the Christ then is shared not only by his professed disciples but by all who know truth and lead a good life; all such participate in the life of God and in that of his human incarnation.[108]

---

[106] R.G. Collingwood, *Religion and Philosophy*, 160.
[107] Ibid., 161.
[108] Ibid., 161.

This religious context reveals the deeper motive for Collingwood's notion of the living past; in his first book he wants to show that the identity of two minds is in the first place based on God's reality and not on the conscious rethinking of past thoughts. Along the same lines Collingwood describes God's presence in the world and his relation to man's history as follows:

> God is the reality of the world conceived as a whole which in its self-realisation and impulse towards unity purges out of itself all evil and error. History regarded in that way — not as a mere bundle of events but as a process of the solution of problems and the overcoming of difficulties — is altogether summed up in the infinite personality of God; and we can now see that it is equally summed up in the infinite personality of God-Man.[109]

In this passage Collingwood typically describes the universal and necessary aspects of history as a process of problems and solutions which move towards salvation, or redemption. This process lives on in history, and this is the key to immortality:

> The workman in a cathedral sets his own mark upon the whole and leaves his monument in the work of his hands. He passes away, but his work — his expressed thought, his testimony to the glory of God — remains enshrined in stone. Even that is liable to decay, and in time such earthly immortality is as if it had never been. But if a man has won his union with the mind of God, has known God's thought and served God's purpose in any of the countless ways in which it can be served, his monument is not something that stands for an age when he is dead. It is his own new and perfected life; something that in its very nature cannot pass away, except by desertion of the achieved ideal. This is the statue of the perfect man, more perennial than bronze; the life in a house not made with hands, eternal in the heavens.[110]

In this passage Collingwood relates the notion of the living past to his conception of God; a truth about God is a perennial, immortal truth; it lives on, even when its material embodiment has decayed. This notion of the past is not compatible to Croce's and Gentile's idea of history. As we have seen, both Croce and Gentile found the past living in the present act of thought, whereas Collingwood finds it living in the process of history. For Croce and Gentile the past only lives in so far as it is relived, or rethought, for Collingwood it lives even if it is not rethought. For Croce and Gentile eternity is found in the 'spirit', which remains self-identical through time by constructing its own past. For Collingwood eternity is only found in God's presence in history and attained by man whenever he rightly attains real truth about God's nature. Consequently, for Croce and Gentile there is no history apart from the history that is created by ourselves, whereas for Collingwood there are two aspects of history. On the one hand, there is history *a parte obiecti*, or history as a process of problems and solutions,

---

[109] Ibid., 166–7.
[110] Ibid., 167–8.

which is the universal and necessary character of all history. On the other hand, there is history *a parte subiecti*, or the thought processes that go on in the historian's mind. This distinction between the objective and subjective aspects of history is unthinkable for the Italians, who regard history as a construction of present thought.

Collingwood's idea of the living past throws more light on the passages about history which have normally been interpreted as realist. When Collingwood says that history is to be regarded as 'objectivity' or 'fact as something independent of my own or your knowledge of it', he simply recognises the existence of history *a parte obiecti* not in the sense of 'history as it really was', but in the sense that history has a universal and necessary aspect. Along the same lines, Collingwood's view sheds more light on his alleged 'idealism' in *Religion and Philosophy*. When he says that two minds are identical when they think the same thought, we must keep in mind that this identity is realised even when the two minds are not aware of each other.

On this basis it is clear why Collingwood thought that he had formulated a theory that does not conflict with realism or idealism. On the one hand, Collingwood's position is to a certain extent compatible with the realist maxim that knowledge 'unconditionally presupposes that the reality known exists independently of the knowledge of it', because Collingwood would not deny that a table exists even if we are unaware of it. On the other hand, Collingwood's position is compatible with the idealist maxim that the object must be seen as a product of our minds; 'my thought of the table is the table as I know it.'[111] Yet, at the same time, Collingwood seems to avoid a thorough actualism according to which all reality must be seen as a construction of the self-conscious human mind. Although Collingwood explicitly defends that the objective world can be seen as a creation of the mind, he seems to reserve this aspect for the practical activity of the mind excluding it from its theoretical activity. Moreover, Collingwood refrains from identifying reality with '*autoctisi*', or 'self-creation', as Gentile had done in 'L'atto del *pensare* come atto puro' of 1912. Here moral and religious reasons seem to have played the most important role. This becomes clear in his discussion of the subjective theory of atonement which he explicitly repudiates. According to Collingwood, this theory 'insists on the reality and inviolability of the individual', which 'brings us to the exclusive or individualistic theory of personality for which every person is a law to himself, supplies himself with his own standards of right and wrong and draws upon its own resources in order to live up to them'.[112] Collingwood not only stuck to the idea of the negation of atonement in the sense of redemption of man whether by man, Christ, or God, but also of social life as a whole!

---

[111] Ibid., 101.
[112] Ibid., 183.

In spite of his reservations about both realism and idealism he unites their positive doctrines in a philosophy which still has no name of its own. For the rest of his life Collingwood rejected attempts to call it either realism or idealism *tout court*. Only once, after reading de Ruggiero's 'La scienza come esperienza assoluta' in 1920, would he liken it to the latter's 'absolute empiricism', but the above discussion makes it clear that Collingwood's position is not entirely compatible with de Ruggiero's. Although both philosophers do not distinguish between subject and object in experience, and although both liken the activity of the mind to a question and answer process, de Ruggiero did not acknowledge a living past in Collingwood's sense of this notion. In my view, neither 'actualism' nor 'absolute empiricism' are adequate descriptions of Collingwood's position in *Religion and Philosophy*. The concept of the living past is more in line with 'object-ive idealism', the term by which Collingwood sometimes described his own position after 1933. But after all, what is in a name? What counts in philosophy are problems and solutions, not names. As we have seen, around 1912 Colling-wood's most pressing problem was to harmonise the lessons of his father and the Italians about history with his own religious beliefs in a system that unites God, nature, and humanity. It is to this problem that he found a preliminary solution by establishing the metaphysical basis of his own notion of the living past. But this notion still needed to be worked out. Especially the relationship between history *a parte obiecti* and history *a parte subiecti* needed elaboration in order to show how mankind develops itself in the light of the living past. In particular the 'dialectic' of this process had to be made clear. As we have seen, the Italians had already established their own view of the dialectic of mind, and Collingwood would follow soon, as we will see in the next sections.

'The Devil' and Evil: Two Steps Forward

In 1915, Collingwood took two further steps towards his own philosophy. The first step was the essay 'The Devil', written in 1915, and the second was the chapter on 'Evil' in *Religion and Philosophy*. About 'The Devil', a lecture delivered for the 'Streeter-group', Collingwood later said that it represented 'the breaking point' of his earlier philosophical beliefs, although he thought that it still tended towards realism.[113] The paper's argument does not differ much from *Religion and Philosophy*. Its most interesting passage is found at the end where Collingwood describes the relationship between God and man in terms of self-creation:

> Man's life is a becoming; and not only becoming, but self-creation. He does not grow under the direction and control of irresistible forces. The force that shapes him is his own will. All his life is an effort to attain to real nature. But 'human nature', since man is at bottom spirit, is only exemplified in the abso-lute spirit of God. Hence man must shape himself in God's image, or he ceases to be even human and becomes diabolical. This self-creation must also

---

[113] Cited by Taylor, *R.G. Collingwood, A Bibliography*, 90.

be self-knowledge; not the self-knowledge of introspection, the examination of the self that is, but the knowledge of God, the self that is to be. Knowledge of God is the beginning, the centre, and end, of human life.[114]

This passage marks the breaking point of Collingwood's early thought. In *Religion and Philosophy* only action is interpreted in terms of self-creation. But in that book, Collingwood still declined to understand knowledge in terms of self-creation, because he still identified this notion with subjectivism. In this passage, however, Collingwood not only uses the term self-creation but he even identifies it with the essence of man's life, including his thought. Collingwood thus seems to come close to Gentile's notion of self-constitution, but the above passage also reveals Vico's influence; on the one hand, there is nature that God has made, and which man cannot know, and on the other, there is the human world that man makes himself in history, which is therefore perfectly knowable for him. The idea of human nature as human history would become one of the basic concepts of Collingwood's later thought and here we find its origins in the actualist concept of self-creation in the context of Vico's metaphysics.

In 1915, Collingwood also elaborated his own theory of truth which he later added as Chapter IV to the second part of *Religion and Philosophy*. About this chapter Collingwood later wrote that it 'points forward to a much more mature point of view'.[115] Collingwood begins by formulating the problem of error and evil in theological terms: 'Why does God, being good, allow the existence of evil in his world?' Then he separates this problem into the subjects of pain, error, and evil. On the problem of pain Collingwood concludes that pain is always present in the real world, so that the problem is not to avoid it, but to raise it to an 'heroic level'.[116] Interestingly, Collingwood differs from Gentile's doctrine that pain is not real. This is important when we consider that Gentile's denial of the reality of pain would eventually lead him to legitimising the use of brute force by the Fascists.[117]

Moving to the problem of error and evil, Collingwood first rejects all theories which deny the existence of error in one way or another. Among these theories we find Croce's interpretation of error as an act of the will.[118] In contrast to these theories, Collingwood points out that error really exists as thought, and that evil is a real action. This affirmation of the existence of error and evil brings him to his real problem: 'how can evil and error co-exist in the same universe side by side with truth and goodness, and how can a universe so composed be des-

---

[114] R.G. Collingwood, 'The Devil', in Streeter, B.H. and Dougall, L., *Concerning Prayer: Its Nature, its Difficulties and its Value*, Macmillan, London, cited from Rubinoff (ed.), *Faith and Reason*, 232.*

[115] Cited by Taylor, *R.G. Collingwood, A Bibliography*, 90.

[116] R.G. Collingwood, *Religion and Philosophy*, 126.

[117] Harris, *The Social Philosophy of Giovanni Gentile*, 113–4.

[118] R.G. Collingwood, *Religion and Philosophy*, 128.

cribed?'[119] Collingwood answers that 'every truth takes its form by correcting some error'.[120] On this basis he points out that truth and error cannot co-exist in relation to one another, because if they are brought into contact, the error is abolished by truth. But, Collingwood avers, this process of correction is never completed, because 'the life of the world, like the life of man, consists in perpetual activity'.[121] On this basis Collingwood reaches his view of error as an 'unfinished thought-process'.[122] As we will see, this theory of error is central in Collingwood's early philosophy, which is thus set apart from both Croce's theory of error as action, and Gentile's theory of the error as *pensato,* which he used to identify with 'nature' and 'the unthinkable'.

Along the same lines Collingwood interprets the problem of evil; the good expels the bad and the bad always exists because the universe is always in *posse* and not in *esse.* In this way the new theory of truth and error, good and evil, expresses Collingwood's process-view of reality:

> The world we see around us is not a stationary, already-existing, "given" totality, but a totality in the making: its unity consists only the striving towards unity on the part of the minds which constitute it.[123]

As we have seen in *Religion and Philosophy,* the unity of which Collingwood speaks is God. On this basis, Collingwood develops the view that all error and evil is driven out by the human striving to reach the truth about God in order to do good.

Collingwood's theory of truth and error, goodness and badness, is compatible with the actualist dialectic of *pensante* and *pensato* to the extent that it presents truth as the correction of error, and goodness as the correction of badness. But unlike the actualists, Collingwood does not oppose truth and error, goodness and badness, categorically as *pensato* and *pensante,* but as an unfinished process to a relatively more finished process. This view of truth and error, goodness and badness, follows from Collingwood's view that the unity to which the whole process strives is God. This unity can never be fully attained, however, so that all of man's activities must be seen as 'attempts'.

In *Religion and Philosophy,* Collingwood's theory is still in its infancy; it leaves many questions open such as; how do we discover that we are in error? And if thought is no longer tied to a 'given reality' how do we secure the objectivity of thought? And if our thought is considered as a self-creating process how do we prevent it from 'drifting away'? In other words: how can we interpret mind as self-creative without falling into a bad kind of subjective idealism? In 1915, when he wrote the chapter on truth, Collingwood was certainly aware of this danger.

---

[119] Ibid., 137.
[120] Ibid., 138.
[121] Ibid., 141.
[122] Ibid., 140.
[123] Ibid., 140–1.

This is revealed by his anxious questions: 'why should it be assumed that truth must drive out error? Why should not error drive out truth?' And 'Is it not possible for all good to disappear and for the universe to become entirely bad?'[124] Collingwood admits that these things might happen; man can 'lapse into a quagmire of wickedness and idiocy from which it is progressively harder to escape'.[125] In *Religion and Philosophy* Collingwood does not tell us how this chaos is to be escaped. He only points out that absolute error and evil do not exist; they can only exist in an environment of truth and good. The universe is *a fortiori* not bad and coherence and totality can therefore always be attained.[126] This denial of the existence of absolute error and evil reveals something of Collingwood's fundamental optimism; truth and goodness really exist and man may always attain them. Only on this basis could Collingwood continue with his search for truth and goodness, while the world was lapsing into the greatest quagmire of wickedness seen in history so far.

The Moment of Kairos: The Albert Memorial Meditations (1915–16)

In 1915, Collingwood moved into the service of the Admiralty Intelligence in London.[127] Relatively isolated from Oxford, he could definitely turn away from his realist teachers; 1916 was the year of 'negative criticism' as he wrote later.[128] In his autobiography, Collingwood writes that this criticism began with his disgust provoked by the Albert Memorial, which he passed on his daily walks to the Admiralty:

> Everything about it was visibly misshapen, corrupt, crawling, verminous, for a time I could not bear to look at it, and passed with averted eyes; recovering from this weakness, I forced myself to look, and to face day by day the question: a thing so obviously, so incontrovertibly, so indefensibly bad, why had Scott done it?[129]

In his autobiography, Collingwood does not tell how he solved the problem of the ugliness of the Albert Memorial. Instead, he says that the solution led to a further development of a thought already familiar to him, namely the questioning activity of knowledge. Collingwood describes the sequence of this development in great detail. He begins by observing that you cannot discover the meaning of something unless you discover the question to which the thing said or written was meant to answer.[130] This observation was based on the 'principle of correlativity' by which Collingwood meant that a particular answer inseparably

---

124 Ibid., 139–40, 143.
125 Ibid., 143.
126 Ibid., 144.
127 Johnston, *The Formative Years of R.G. Collingwood*, 10.
128 Cited by Taylor, *R.G. Collingwood, A Bibliography*, 90.
129 R.G. Collingwood, *An Autobiography*, 29.
130 Ibid., 31.

belongs to a particular question.[131] The second step was to apply this principle of correlativity to the idea of contradiction, showing that two propositions cannot contradict each other unless they are answers to the same question.[132] The third and last step was to apply the principle of correlativity to the idea of truth by pointing out that 'if the meaning of a proposition is relative to the question it answers, its truth must be relative to the same thing'.[133]

Along these lines, Collingwood began to see that there was a necessary connection between positive doctrines of the realists and their critical methods. In his autobiography, Collingwood epitomises the positive doctrine of the realists into the maxim that 'nothing is affected by being known independently of the knowledge of it', and he argues that their critical methods were based on formal logic and the notion of 'eternal problems'.[134] In his autobiography, Collingwood claims that his meditations on the Albert Memorial helped him to see why both were false and for what reasons, although he does not explain exactly how. On this basis, Collingwood not only rejected the realist doctrines, but also the coherence theory of truth and the pragmatic theory of truth in a book, *Truth and Contradiction*, of 1917.[135]

In spite of all these details, it is far from clear exactly what Collingwood discovered during his musings on the Albert Memorial. Most interpreters mention the passage in the autobiography, but do not discuss its role in Collingwood's development. According to Donagan, Collingwood, not being able to understand the monument as art, took it as a prototype of magic.[136] Mink views Collingwood's meditations as an example of second-order thinking.[137] Russell mentions the Albert Memorial but does not discuss its relationship to Collingwood's logic of question and answer.[138] Only Peter Johnson discusses the role of the Albert Memorial in Collingwood's development at greater length. In his view, the Albert Memorial was 'the catalyst' for many of Collingwood's best known ideas in history and aesthetics.[139] Among these he mentions Collingwood's view that an author's intention is not needed in order to reconstruct his questions, because these can be reconstructed from the evidence only. Even if the answer completely failed, as was the case with the Albert Memorial, this

---

[131] Ibid., 31–2.
[132] Ibid., 33.
[133] Ibid., 33.
[134] Ibid., 48, 60.
[135] Ibid., 36, 42–3.
[136] Donagan, *The Later Philosophy of R.G. Collingwood*, 102.
[137] Mink, *Mind, History and Dialectic*, 251–2.
[138] Anthony F. Russell, *Logic, Philosophy and History*, University of America Press, Lanham, London, 1984.
[139] Peter Johnson, 'R.G. Collingwood and the Albert Memorial', in *Collingwood and British Idealism Studies incorporating Bradley Studies*, 15, 2009, 38.

reconstruction can be carried out.[140] But it is hard to see this reconstruction as a discovery, because Collingwood himself says that 'everybody who has learnt to think historically knows it already'.[141] Moreover, Johnson bases his interpretation on the premise that Collingwood saw the Albert Memorial as a total artistic failure comparable to 'corrupt art' as defined in his *Principles of Art*.[142] The problem with Johnson's interpretation is that it is at odds with Collingwood's early theory of the mind according to which absolute error, evil, and ugliness do not exist. In addition, this interpretation is also incompatible with the fact that Collingwood still defended this theory in his 1925 *Outlines of a Philosophy of Art* where he explicitly states 'that it is impossible to imagine anything that is not beautiful; that, in fact, nothing ugly exists, or that, if it does exist, it can never appear to any one'.[143] In order to understand the role of the Albert Memorial in Collingwood's early development, we should not read his later philosophy into it, but keep, as closely as possible, to the views he expounded before 1930. Moreover, granting Collingwood the benefit of doubt, we should consult his own interpretation of his development before we reach for other evidence.

In this respect, it is very fortunate that Collingwood gave a very detailed account of his own early development in *Speculum Mentis*. In a long footnote in the chapter on religion he writes that he is still in agreement with much of *Religion and Philosophy*, though he 'overlooked' and 'denied' certain principles. The most important of these was the distinction between the implicit and explicit. As a result of this omission, he did not see that theology makes explicit what is implicit in religion. This led to a 'too intellectualistic' attitude towards religion, which revealed itself in many 'errors', among which Collingwood mentions the 'all-important question of the relationship between religion and art'.[144]

In this connection it is of the highest importance that Collingwood introduces the distinction between the implicit and the explicit in a long footnote in the chapter on art. 'The distinction between explicit and implicit is so important that it seems desirable to call attention to it', Collingwood begins.[145] After this, he explains that in every experience there are principles of which a person cannot but be aware. Collingwood contrasts these 'explicit principles' to the 'implicit principles' which an observer needs in order to give an account of an experience he is studying. Collingwood illustrates the distinction with an example from art:

---

140 Ibid., 33–4.
141 R.G. Collingwood, *An Autobiography*, 70.
142 Johnson, 'R.G. Collingwood and the Albert Memorial', 17–19.
143 R.G. Collingwood, *Outlines of a Philosophy of Art*, Oxford University Press, Oxford, 1925, 19.
144 R.G. Collingwood, *Speculum Mentis*, 108n.
145 Ibid., 85n.

> Thus an artist constructs his work on principles and distinctions which are really operative in the construction, but are not explicitly recognized by himself: in art they are implicit, to become explicit only in the criticism of art.[146]

Applied to art itself, the distinction between the implicit and the explicit is of paramount importance, because it corrects the error of the belief of the 'separateness and independence of imagination' by the view of 'an aesthetic element present in all experience but exclusively or predominantly present in none'.[147]

On the basis of these two footnotes it is possible to reconstruct the role of the Albert Memorial in Collingwood's early development. The crucial question to be answered in this context is how the ugliness of the Albert Memorial induced Collingwood to make a distinction between the explicit and the implicit on the basis of which he could correct the error of the separateness of art. This question can best be answered by starting from Collingwood's position before the First World War.

Just before Collingwood was stationed in London, he had expounded the view that absolute error, evil, and ugliness cannot exist, which was based on the doctrine of the mind as a self-creative activity. From this viewpoint, the ugliness of the monument must have struck him like lightning; the Albert Memorial seemed to refute his entire philosophy! This experience was very acute; after more than twenty years, Collingwood described his feelings in the strongest terms. Curiously, the autobiography remains silent on what the Albert Memorial meant to Collingwood; but we may speculate that the Albert Memorial somehow reminded him of the Victorian age which was now irretrievably lost because of the war. Confronted with the seemingly absolute ugliness of the monument, Collingwood had two options: to reject his own doctrines, or to find a place for the ugly in his aesthetics. Given his later theory of the ugly in *Speculum Mentis* and in *Outlines of a Philosophy of Art*, it is clear that he chose the latter. He probably started from his 'insider's' view of art, which had already formed the basis of his rejection of Croce's aesthetics in 1912. From the insider's point of view the artist begins with an initial expression to be developed into a fuller expression. In this way, the question arose of what Scott had tried to do and to what extent he succeeded in this, or in terms of the autobiography: 'What relation was there, between what he had done and what he had tried to do?'[148] Given his knowledge of John Ruskin's work, one of the most important advocates of the Neo-Gothic style and a friend of Gilbert Scott, and, above all, his knowledge of art history and aesthetics, Collingwood was well equipped to answer this question. Moreover, he could probably acquire first-hand knowledge of Scott's work, because he met his son around 1915.[149] On this basis

---

[146] Ibid.

[147] Ibid.

[148] Ibid.

[149] R.G. Collingwood, *Religion and Philosophy*, vi; Patrick, *The Magdalen Metaphysicals*, 89.

Collingwood probably tried to reconstruct Scott's artistic problem in its historical context.[150] But this reconstruction did not entirely satisfy Collingwood,
because he next raised the question of whether Scott had tried to produce something different from a work of art.[151] Interestingly, this question implies a distinction between art and non-art, which is at odds with his later theories as
expounded in *Speculum Mentis*. Finally, Collingwood asked whether it was his
own fault that he found the monument merely loathsome, because he was looking for qualities it did not possess or either ignoring or despising those it did.[152]
In my view, this question was crucial because, by asking it, Collingwood involves himself in the problem of the ugliness of the monument. From this viewpoint there is not one problem, but two: first, there is Scott's problem, and
second, there is Collingwood's problem which consists of reconstructing Scott's
problem. As Mink rightly observed, this raises the problem of the Albert
Memorial into a philosophical problem because it forced Collingwood to think
about his own thought.[153] Seen in Collingwood's development, this way of philosophising is an application of the distinction between the insider's and
outsider's approach to art. But in the extreme case of the Albert Memorial not
only the question of beauty and ugliness was at stake, but the very principles
upon which this question was to be answered. The Albert Memorial had boom-
eranged Collingwood's questions about Scott back to himself.

On this point, Collingwood's dilemma becomes clear: either Scott was wrong
because he had failed to solve his artistic problem, or Collingwood was wrong
because he failed to understand Scott's solution. But as more often in his life,
Collingwood saw an escape between the horns of the dilemma by making a
distinction between Scott's principles of art and his own. Seen from Scott's perspective, the Albert Memorial was a successful solution for his artistic problem,
but seen from Collingwood's perspective it was not. This position was only a
small extension of Collingwood's own distinction between the outsider's and the
insider's view of experience, but it raised a new problem of explaining the relationship between the two points of view. Here, we come to the heart of the problem: Collingwood, like the philosophers who had inspired him, such as Vico and
Croce, and like the philosophers who had taught him, such as Cook Wilson,
Pritchard, and Carritt, believed in the universality and necessity of philosophical
principles. For these philosophers, there were no different kinds of principles of
art, but only the principles of art. On this basis, Collingwood had stated in
Religion and Philosophy that if two minds have 'real knowledge' of an object, their
thoughts must be the same, not merely similar.[154] Applied to Scott's and Colling-

---

[150] I agree with Peter Johnson that Scott's intentions were not relevant for this reconstruction.

[151] R.G. Collingwood, *An Autobiography,* 29.

[152] Ibid., 30.

[153] Mink, *Mind, History and Dialectic,* 252.

[154] R.G. Collingwood, *Religion and Philosophy,* 101.

wood's completely different views of the Albert Memorial this implied that either Scott or Collingwood was wrong. How could this view of thought be reconciled with Collingwood's attempt to show that he and Scott could both be right? To this question, Collingwood gave the answer of the historian: the relationship between the different points of view can only be explained in time. Scott's principles of art differed from Collingwood's because he lived in the Victorian age, whereas Collingwood was living during the First World War. This does not look like a startling conclusion, but Collingwood drew a radical implication from it, when he realised that the most important difference between Scott and himself concerned the status of the principles of art. In designing the Albert Memorial Scott had worked on the basis of certain principles of art without being conscious of them. From Collingwood's point of view these principles were therefore implicit in Scott's work. Yet, at the same time, Collingwood made them explicit by reconstructing Scott's problem. From this it follows that the principles of art have a double status. To the artist in the aesthetic act they are simply not present as principles; only to the art critic, who observes the work of art with a time difference, are they present as both implicit and explicit. When an art critic does not take this difference of time into account, he will fail to distinguish between implicit and explicit principles, and either identify himself with the position of the artist or commit the fallacy of wrongly assuming that his own idea of art coincides with artist's. In short, Collingwood, while trying to understand the ugliness of the Albert Memorial, discovered that art can only be understood in an historical way; the artist is not lifted above history, but lives in it, working on both implicit and explicit principles to be discovered by the historian.

This insight provided him with the solution to his problem. He states it emphatically in *Speculum Mentis*: imagination does not exist *in vacuo*![155] This means, firstly, that imagination must 'spring from a soil of concrete fact; the artist must really exist in a real world'.[156] Secondly, it means that the artist and his works of art are 'necessarily a kind of sublimated version of his experience as a real person, however unconscious of this fact he may be'.[157] Thirdly, the aesthetic element is present in all forms of experience, because 'imagination is a factor in every single cognitive act'.[158]

On this basis Collingwood could solve his problems concerning the Albert Memorial. Firstly, he could reject the question 'is it art or not-art?' This is a typical outsider's question that cannot arise from the viewpoint that art is present in all forms of experience. Along the same lines, the question whether Scott had tried to produce something different from a work of art must be rejected because

---

[155] R.G. Collingwood, *Speculum Mentis*, 77.
[156] Ibid., 79.
[157] Ibid.
[158] Ibid., 83.

it implies an invalid distinction between art and non-art. Accordingly, Collingwood moved to the question of what Scott had tried to do, which he answered by reconstructing how Scott's problem, as embodied in the Albert Memorial, arose from 'the real world of fact' around him. Finally, the question of whether Collingwood was looking for the wrong qualities in the Albert Memorial could be answered by distinguishing between the principles governing Scott's art and his own principles as an art critic. Whereas the artist tries to solve a particular artistic problem, Collingwood says in *Speculum Mentis*, the chief task of the art critic is to describe the 'abstract principles of the genesis of art'. On this point, Collingwood warns that the principles of art are never really abstract, because they always govern the origin of a particular work of art. On this basis Collingwood reaches the most important conclusion that the principles of art are 'historical concrete facts'.[159]

In his autobiography, Collingwood spends a lot of pages on his musings on the Albert Memorial. This is not surprising, when we realise that the Albert Memorial had forced Collingwood to radicalise his earlier distinction between the insider's and outsider's experience of art. This led him to the view that art and history cannot be separated; aesthetical questions are always also historical questions, from which it follows that all philosophical questions are always also historical questions.

From this radical conclusion it was only a small step to 'a further development' of Collingwood's notion of the questioning activity. Crediting Croce with the identification of the questioning activity with art he also criticises him and 'his followers' for isolating this activity as a self-contained phase from which the other phases, notably assertion, must be reached by 'some kind of transition'.[160] Already in 1912 Collingwood had criticised Croce on this point, but now, after his own self-criticism, he could provide an alternative with the theory of the correlativity of supposal and assertion:

> Supposal and assertion are not two independent chapters in the history of the mind; they are two opposite and correlative activities which form as it were the systole and diastole of knowledge itself.[161]

Seen from this viewpoint, the whole problem of the 'transition' from questions to answers and vice versa, which had troubled Croce and his 'followers', becomes irrelevant:

> The process of knowledge is therefore, strictly speaking, not so much an alternation of question and answer as a perpetual restatement of the question, which is identical with a perpetual revision of the answer.[162]

---

159 Ibid., 100.
160 Ibid., 76.
161 Ibid., 77.
162 Ibid., 80.

On the basis of this view of knowledge as an ongoing process of correlative questions and answers, Collingwood parted company with all current logical theories. In his autobiography he says that they all wrongly assumed 'the propositional principle', or the view that truth is a quality of one proposition, regardless of its context.[163] But, in Collingwood's view, truth does not belong to a single proposition as the realists held, or even to a complex of propositions as the coherence theorists of truth maintained, but only to a complex of questions and answers.

On this basis Collingwood could finally answer the question about the necessary connection between the realist positive doctrines and their critical methods. In an early stage of his career he had already understood that the realist critical methods did not take the historical meaning of thought into account. This was reflected by their habit of dealing with the history of philosophy as a series of answers to some 'eternal problems', with the result that they compared Plato's *polis* to the modern State as the similar answers to an identical question.[164] After his discovery of the principle of the correlativity of question and answer, Collingwood could dismiss this doctrine as 'claptrap'; if imagination does not exist *in vacuo*, but in a world of concrete fact, all problems are historically conditioned. But the correlativity principle also showed why the realist theory of knowledge was wrong. To equate knowing with 'intuiting' or 'apprehending' an object amounts to denying the questioning activity, and given the correlativity of question and answer, the whole complex of questions and answers as well. In short, both the realist doctrine of the apprehension of reality and the realist belief in 'eternal problems' were based on the separation of questions and answers. This separation of questions and answers had much deeper roots. It meant a separation between imagination and thought, which in turn was based on a denial of the distinction between the implicit and the explicit; only by distinguishing the explicit principles from the implicit principles in art can one see that 'imagination does not exist *in vacuo*', that is, that the imagination is conditioned by history. Collingwood himself had overlooked this distinction and it took many walks to the Albert Memorial to see it. After all these walks he understood where he and his teachers had gone wrong; they had not taken the historicity of questioning into account.

Collingwood's First Criticism of Croce's *Theory and History of Historiography* (1917)

Collingwood bought his copy of Croce's fourth volume of the *Filosofia della spirito* in 1917, the year of its appearance, and this shows that in spite of the war he was still *au courant* of Italian philosophy. On the first page he wrote in 1936:

---

[163] R.G. Collingwood, *An Autobiography*, 36.
[164] R.G. Collingwood, *An Autobiography*, 61–4.

> When I first read this book in 1917, I annotated it freely with the exuberance
> of youth. Although I am a good deal ashamed of my annotations, I have
> denied myself the pleasure of taking india-rubber to them, because I find it
> salutary to re-read them and ask myself where and why I was wrong.

For us, too, it is informative to read Collingwood's annotations because they
give us a very good insight of his first confrontation with the book, which he
used to regard as 'by far the most important work on the subject'.[165]

As we have seen in chapter 2, the guiding principle of *Teoria e storia della
storiografia* is the idea of the contemporaneity of history which forms the basis
for the distinction between chronicle and history and for Croce's notion of the
living past as 'reliving'. As we have seen, Croce identifies contemporary history
with the self-conscious awareness of an activity. From this point of view,
chronicle or evidence is not a product of thought but of action appearing as
'dead history' to be 'relived' by the present act of thought. In his marginal
comments Collingwood begins with a comment on the distinction between will
and thought:

> …the distinction between thought and volition as two independent and sep-
> arate realities. So to conceive them is definitely contrary to C's explicit theory
> of them as 'necessary abstractions': but he never lives up to that theory and
> his whole philosophy in practice is based on ignoring it.[166]

As we have seen, Collingwood did not distinguish between 'matter' and 'mind',
or 'will' and 'thought', because he regarded them as aspects of a single process.
On the endpaper of his copy Collingwood describes this process as the *a priori*
synthesis of subject and object;

> I am not sure that C. has got hold of the one root-idea of idealism, viz. the
> synthesis a priori of subject and object in the concrete act of knowing. He
> seems to vagheggiare [sic! to yearn] the silly old idea that the relation of
> subject-object is similarity (like knows like) which is pure Realism and indi-
> cates the substitution of similarity for identity.[167]

This passage clearly resembles the influence of Gentile's dialectic of *pensante* and
pensato with the synthesis of subject and object. Yet, we must not jump to the
conclusion that Collingwood had converted to the actualist faith, because he
criticises Croce's realism for substituting similarity for identity. In *Religion and
Philosophy* Collingwood had already discussed this 'substitution', pointing out
that 'my thought of the table is certainly not something "like" the table; it is the
table as I know it'.[168] As we have seen, this theory of identity is based on Collingwood's metaphysics according to which there is no real distinction between

---

[165] R.G. Collingwood, *The Philosophy of History*, 135.
[166] R.G. Collingwood, 'Marginal Comments in Croce, *Teoria e storia della storiografia*', 1917,
9, in possession of Ms Smith.
[167] Ibid., end paper.
[168] R.G. Collingwood, *Religion and Philosophy*, 101.

matter and mind. This view is definitely not actualist, for it does not sharply distinguish, let alone oppose, matter to mind as *pensato* and *pensante*. Behind Collingwood's criticism of Croce lies not the dialectic of *pensante* and *pensato*, but his own idea of the past which is still living in the present. This idea is at the back of his mind when he writes 'How do these notions cohere?' at the point where Croce draws his distinction between '*storia morta*' and '*storia viva*'.[169] Collingwood's notion of the living past is also the basis for the following criticism of Croce's distinction between 'chronicle' and 'history' as 'will' and 'thought' or as 'matter':

> Spirit is thought, which renders its object present; if you thought of the past qua past it would become history and present: therefore there is no thought in 'cronaca'. Therefore there is, by exhaustion, non-thought = will. Will thus = the unconscious, matter.[170]

Above we have seen that Collingwood did not distinguish between 'matter' and 'spirit', 'will' and 'thought'. In this passage he overtly rejects the distinction between 'chronicles' and 'history' which is based on it. For Collingwood, chronicle and history cannot be identified with 'matter' and 'spirit', 'will' and 'thought', or 'dead past' and 'living past'. For Collingwood, the past is not living on condition that it is relived 'qua past' by present thought; but it is living even if we are not aware of it.

The notion of the living past also underlies his criticism of Croce's attack on the history of science. According to Croce all science presupposes a 'thing in itself' which is unintelligible, and he warns that the one who meddles with it will lose his way through 'infinite, vain and disconnected questions'.[171] Against this view Collingwood protests:

> The conclusion is lame. It throws cold water on the difficulty instead of grasping it and saying 'of course there are infinite problems': if there weren't there couldn't be a progress of knowledge. C. seems to suggest that the infinity of problems is a reason for not solving them.[172]

Finally Collingwood criticises Croce's doctrine of philosophy as the methodology of history:

> The definition of phil. as meth. seems to imply an inconsistent 'realistic' position. These are two grades of consciousness A) History, knowledge of the historical: B) philosophy, the knowledge of the procedure of historical thought. i.e. B = the consciousness of A. while A = the consciousness of something else. Here we are moving in the circle of realism which distinguishes the object

---

169 R.G. Collingwood, 'Marginal Comments in Croce, *Teoria e storia della storiografia*', 10.
170 Ibid.
171 B. Croce, *Teoria e storia della storiografia*, 45.
172 R.G. Collingwood, 'Marginal Comments in Croce, *Teoria e storia della storiografia*', 45.

from the thought, and seeks to determine 1) what thought is 2) what different thing, not itself, it is about.[173]

This passage shows that Collingwood does not acknowledge two grades of consciousness, but only one, which is also a form of self-consciousness. On the one hand, philosophy can never be the mere methodology of history, because history is not something different from philosophy, but it is philosophical in itself, that is, it is a self-conscious form of thought. On the other hand, philosophy is historical because it always proceeds on the basis of its own history. This view of the relationship between philosophy and history comes close to the actualist view of it. Like Gentile and de Ruggiero, Collingwood interprets the immanence of philosophy in history in terms of self-consciousness, and like them he holds that the object of thought is not a 'thing' but thought itself. This description still leaves enough room to differ from the actualists about the exact status of thought as object; for the actualists its status is that of a construction of present thought, whereas for Collingwood it can also be independent from thought.

Collingwood's comments on Croce's *Teoria e storia della storiografia* read like a trial of strength between two conceptions of history. These two conceptions go back to their different understanding of processes in general and mental processes in particular. Against Croce's distinction between matter and mind, Collingwood posits his unity of matter and mind as aspects of a single activity. Against Croce's distinction between will and thought Collingwood posits the unity of both. And finally against Croce's distinction between dead past and living past Collingwood posits his own notion of the living past. This notion of the living past enables Collingwood to posit his conception of error as a form of thought against Croce's notion of error as a product of the will. It also enables Collingwood to do justice to science and its history in contrast to Croce's degradation of the pseudo-concept. Finally, it forms the basis of Collingwood's notion of the relationship between philosophy and history. The trial of strength shows that Collingwood had developed a great deal since *Religion and Philosophy*. Not surprisingly, therefore, he found himself ready to write *Truth and Contradiction*, the book in which he would establish his own theory of knowledge as based on the logic of question and answer against all other current theories.

Truth and Contradiction (1917)

Collingwood wrote *Truth and Contradiction* during his spare time in 1917 and offered it to MacMillan at the end of that year. Unfortunately, the book was not published in spite of Henry Jones's positive report to the editor. In 1938–9, while writing his autobiography, Collingwood burned the book.[174] For some unknown

---

[173] Ibid., 136.
[174] R.G. Collingwood, *An Autobiography*, 99.

reason, however, the second chapter escaped the flames and this enables us to form a picture of its contents.

In his autobiography, Collingwood says that the book contained a criticism of all current theories of truth written out 'at considerable length, with a great many applications and illustrations'.[175] Jones's report confirms this; the book contained some 60,000 to 70,000 words. Moreover, the report also reveals that the book was meant as a rapprochement between theory and practice. The last part of the book contained a dialectical view of morality dealing with the problems of politics, war, and the relationship between classes. This part was preceded by a theoretical part contrasting a dialectical theory of truth with all current theories of truth. As we have seen, Collingwood described his position in *Truth and Contradiction* as 'a new dialectical idealism'. This description is corroborated by Jones: 'All the time he is showing the true nature of philosophy, and finding that movement, activity, process is the living soul of all thinking and of all objects of thought.'[176]

Jones's opinion is confirmed by the only surviving chapter of *Truth and Contradiction* in which Collingwood shows that the coherence theory of truth is not able to describe the process of thought, because it is based on the three Aristotelian laws of thought, which leads to the mutual exclusion of truth and error. Collingwood therefore proposes to revise the laws of thought in order to interpret error as a form of truth. This doctrine, which Collingwood developed during his meditations on the Albert Memorial, forms the central thesis of the chapter and of the book as a whole.

Typically, Collingwood bases his argument on the example of a debate, in which truth is gradually developed out of error. In *Religion and Philosophy* Collingwood had also stressed the importance of dialogue and communication for the development of truth. Probably, he saw his musings with the Albert Memorial as a debate between Scott and himself. In any case, we may assume that debates formed his paradigm case for the development of knowledge.

Collingwood's debate takes the following form. At the beginning A holds the theory that $x = \gamma$, and B holds the opposite theory that $x = \xi$, at the end both agree that $x = \gamma\xi$.[177] According to Collingwood, the coherence theory of truth cannot understand the true nature of a debate, because it mutually excludes truth and error. This leads to an eristical view of debates. Facing the disagreement at the beginning of the debate, the coherence theorist holds that only one of the two theories can be right, not both. In order to find out who is right, A and B should try to bring each other to a self-contradiction, or to a contradiction with a well established truth.[178]

---

[175] R.G. Collingwood, *Essays in Political Philosophy*, 229.
[176] Ibid.
[177] R.G. Collingwood, 'Truth and Contradiction, Chapter II', 1917, Dep. 16/1, 8.
[178] Ibid., 7.

When the two parties reach agreement at the end of the debate the coherence theory cannot explain the previous disagreement nor the difference between the final view and the two views at the beginning. The coherence theory tries to solve this problem by explaining the initial disagreement as an apparent contradiction.[179] Against this view Collingwood points out: 'Two judgments are either contradictory or they are not; and the decision must rest with the people who make them, not with a transcendent spectator.'[180] To this he adds that even when people involved in a discussion are expecting a solution at the end, the spectator is not entitled to call their disagreement apparent. On this point Collingwood acidly remarks: 'We do not call a war merely apparent when we mean to express a hope that it will end some day.'[181] But even if the coherence theorist of truth admits the reality of the disagreement at the beginning of the debate, he will not be able to explain the agreement at the end of it. In that case, Collingwood remarks, he will try to describe the event by saying that the theory fell into two parts, one of which has been preserved intact, while the other has been bodily discarded and replaced with a new structure. Against this 'dissection' of theories in true and false elements Collingwood holds that:

> Truth and falsehood are attributes not of single isolated judgments but of systems of thought, systems in which every judgment is coloured by all the others.[182]

In this passage we recognise Collingwood's general description of the 'propositional principle' and the rejoinder that judgments should be interpreted in their own context. If the coherence theorist objects to this view that there are perfectly simple judgments which are absolutely true, Collingwood illustrates his point by an interesting example which shows how his theory of judgment is linked with his theory of history:

> Let us take any perfectly simple judgment, as that William the Conqueror won the battle of Hastings. Here we have a fragment of European history detached absolutely from its context; and yet surely, a critic may reply, it is still absolutely true. Yes, doubtless it is still true, but only because it has refused to be severed entirely from its context. To separate it successfully, we must forget all we know of William and of the battle of Hastings; we must force out of our mind everything about William except that he won the battle of Hastings, and everything about the battle of Hastings except that it was won by William. And so treated, it is surely clear that all meaning and therefore all truth has been removed from the judgment. If a person were absolutely ignorant of English history, and, wishing to instruct him, you began by saying William the Conqueror won the battle of Hastings, the statement would be mere noise to him until you had sketched the general situation of

---

[179] Ibid., 8.
[180] Ibid., 9.
[181] Ibid.
[182] Ibid., 11.

the time, and the significance of the battle; till, that is, you had expanded your unitary judgment into a system of judgments which for the first time gave it significance — and therefore the possibility of truth or falsehood — by defining the meaning of its terms. But for the future your pupil may carry the whole system — the whole history-lesson — in his head (so far as he remembers it at all, of course) in the form of meaning attached to the one judgment 'William won the battle of Hastings'. And so that one judgment may, to a person who knows, summarize and express in itself a whole period of English history. It is in this sense that a single judgment may be true; true not by being isolated from others, but by absorbing other into itself and acquiring in the process its significance; by becoming the concentrated vehicle of a whole system of thought.[183]

The above passage shows the true reason for Collingwood's rejection of the 'propositional principle'; every judgment, even the simplest, is the result of a long process of history which gives it significance. Collingwood accordingly describes the judgment as a 'concentrated vehicle of a whole system of thought'.[184] If the judgment is not the true unit of thought, it follows that theories cannot be dissected into true and false parts, and Collingwood concludes that 'we have no choice but to admit that one and the same judgment, theory, system of thought, may be throughout its whole fabric both true and false'.[185] This view leads to the doctrine of the degrees of truth which Collingwood formulates as follows:

…every theory (is) true in so far as it includes and embraces its rivals, false in so far as it fails to do so; true so far as it has overcome contradiction, false so far as it leaves outside itself contradictories yet unreconciled. Truth is thus a matter degree, and so is falsehood; every statement must posses both, but the aim of every statement is to become as much true, as little false, as possible.[186]

Against this view, Collingwood holds that the difference of truths is not a difference of just degree, but also a difference of kind. Truth is not a measurable quantity, because it is not separable from the judgment; truth, according to Collingwood 'is that which the judgment asserts; the content, the meaning of the judgment; the judgment itself'.[187] However, Collingwood avers, the view that differences between truths are to be considered as being only differences in kind leads to a subjectivism for which each truth is as true as it is contradictory.

At this point Collingwood realises that he has come to an impasse. He has rejected the coherence theory of truth as leading to transcendence, the doctrine of the degrees of truth as being impossible, and the doctrine of the difference of truth as being subjective. The only solution then is to reject the underlying prin-

---

[183] Ibid., 10 verso.
[184] Ibid.
[185] Ibid., 12.
[186] Ibid.
[187] Ibid., 13.

ciple of all these doctrines, namely the assumption that truth and error are two different species of a single genus:

> There is in fact—and herein lies the crux of the situation—no common genus of which true and false judgments can respectively be species. If we so define judgment as to admit the possibility of truth, we exclude the possibility of error; if we define it so as to admit the possibility of error we exclude the possibility of truth: for a verbal form apart from its meaning cannot be true. Nor indeed, can it be false: so this alternative defeats its own end.[188]

The gist of this passage is that as long as we interpret truth and error as mutually exclusive species of a common genus we will never know where to draw the line, so that all judgments may be subsumed under truth or under error. According to Collingwood the only escape from this nightmare is to accept the ultimate consequence that 'all judgments are true and that therefore error is one species of truth'.[189] In order to illustrate what this means, Collingwood again turns to the role of two antagonists in a true debate:

> We do not simply aim at showing him that he is wrong, and thereby drive him to adopt our view as the only alternative. We aim rather at understanding with his view and sympathising with it: we admit freely that within limits it is true and sound; and only when that is accomplished do we go on to show that it falls short of being as satisfactory as it might be, and that it is capable of certain more or less definable improvements.[190]

The example of the debate is helpful to explain error as a form of truth. On the one hand, error is incomplete truth, truth that has not yet resolved all contradiction. On the other hand, truth is never complete. From this it follows that every error is a partial truth, and that every truth is a partial error. All judgments are therefore capable of improvement; we can always make them more comprehensive. This, however, depends on our willingness to take up the right attitude in debates with others and ourselves.

In a later insertion Collingwood formulates the nature of truth as follows:

> We seem forced to the conclusion that the truth of a judgment is shown not by its power of resisting contradiction and of preserving itself unchanged in the face of opposition, but precisely by the ease with which it accepts contradiction and undergoes modification in order to include points of view which once it had excluded. Not self-preservation but self-criticism is the mark of a truth.[191]

With this last remark Collingwood expresses his deepest conviction on the nature of truth, and the whole chapter is meant as an explanation of this truth. In *Truth and Contradiction* Collingwood made an attempt to answer all questions

---

188 Ibid., 18.
189 Ibid.
190 Ibid., 19.
191 Ibid., 12 inserted page.

which had beset his mind from 1908 onwards. We saw how, in *Religion and Philosophy*, he tried to defend the view of religion as being a critical and criticisable form of mind. In the added chapter to *Religion and Philosophy* of 1915, he developed a theory of truth that did justice to the development of the mind. While meditating on the ugliness of the Albert Memorial he discovered the correlativity of questions and answers. On this basis he rejected all current truth theories which all assumed the 'propositional principle'. In chapter II of *Truth and Contradiction* we see how he rejected the coherence theory of truth. He opposes his dialectical view of thought to the eristical view of the coherence theory. He points out that the coherence theory cannot explain the development of thought in debates because it mutually excludes truth and error. Collingwood therefore accepts the view that all error is a species of truth. On the same basis he also rejects Croce's views of truth and error in a long note. Citing both from the *Logica* and the *Filosofia della pratica*, Collingwood finally points out that the implication of Croce's view is that:

> ...error cannot even be affirmation, it is 'something else which is improperly called affirmation'; it is simply communication but the communication of no thought at all. I have dealt in the text here and there, with various implications of this theory, and have expressed my view that the attempt to explain error by means of the distinction between thinking and acting must be unsuccessful.[192]

Given Collingwood's thesis that error must be seen as a species of truth in order to understand thought as an activity, it is clear why he rejects Croce's theory, which makes truth and error two species of the common genus or 'spirit'. As we have seen, Croce developed this theory in order to defend his view that truth always develops itself from other truths but not from error. For Croce error is pure 'negativity', it is completely unintelligible. At the same time Croce had to explain the existence of error and he did this by interpreting it as action. Collingwood now rejects this view because it presupposes a heterogeneous basis of mental activities. For him the mind is one self-conscious activity which aims at beauty, truth, and goodness and consequently he tries to understand ugliness, error, and evil as species of the single activity of the mind. We may call this actualism and perhaps this is what Collingwood meant by 'dialectical idealism'. In this context Collingwood's example of the true debate in *Truth and Contradiction* may be seen as an analysis of what happens when two thinkers whose thought is completely *norma sui* try to reach agreement in a dialogue. At the same time this kind of detailed and empirical example cannot be found in any of Gentile's works. So, even if Collingwood uses some actualist ideas in *Truth and Contradiction*, he remains true to himself all the time.

---

[192] Ibid., 21–2.

Conclusion

Looking back on Collingwood's early development we can establish which of the Italians' ideas helped Collingwood to formulate his own questions and answers. In the first place, it is clear that the Italians provided him with many ideas that his realist teachers failed to give him. Collingwood came from a family of painters, his father also wrote novels, history, and was an active amateur archaeologist. Moreover, his father had studied philosophy in Oxford and educated his son in the idealist tradition. Accordingly, most of Collingwood's questions were about the relationship between the different forms of experience and its implication for theory and practice, in particular historical knowledge and moral action.

When he came to Oxford he found that the realists had primitive critical methods in the study of the history of philosophy. They believed in eternal problems and talked about Plato's polis as if it were part of the British Empire under Edward VII. In comparison with this absolute neglect of the historical aspect of philosophy, Croce's, Gentile's, and de Ruggiero's histories of philosophy must have appeared to Collingwood as the summum of historical interpretation. Moreover, both Croce and Gentile provided a firm theoretical underground of their views of history in the form of their philosophies of mind in which the identity of philosophy and history has a central place.

The realist positive doctrines were based on the belief that knowing is a simple 'intuiting' or 'apprehending' of some 'reality'. This view of knowledge clashed with Collingwood's archaeological experience in which he learned that knowledge always consists of a questioning and an answering activity.[193] Moreover, this activity was closely linked to other activities of the mind, in particular, imagination. On this particular problem Croce provided the beginning of a solution with his 'theory of grades' which connects intuitions and concepts, or art and philosophy, and with his identity of philosophy and history according to which each pure concept must be interpreted as an answer to a question. Gentile completed Croce's account with his metaphysics of the mind as self-creation in which Collingwood certainly recognised Ruskin's ideal of life.

Finally, when we address Collingwood's moral questions in his early development it is clear that he could recognise his ideals more in the Italian philosophers than in the realists. The realists taught that moral philosophy should be a purely theoretical study which should not affect practice itself. The Italians always stressed the unity of theory and practice in their philosophies. As we have seen, Croce held that historical knowledge is a necessary condition for action and Gentile even identified thought and action. Both thinkers regarded historical knowledge as the highest form of self-knowledge.

But even if the Italians gave many answers to Collingwood's questions he was not completely satisfied with their views from the beginning. Firstly, he

---

[193] R.G. Collingwood, *An Autobiography*, 23–4.

could not completely agree with Croce's theory of history, for it did not correspond to his own historical and archaeological experience. In particular, Croce's idea of the dialectic of question and answer does not explain the continuity of the process of thought which was central to Collingwood's view of the logic of question and answer. Secondly, Croce did not assign a proper place to the empirical pseudo-concept which was fundamental to Collingwood's archeological practice. Thirdly, Croce's moral and political philosophy could not satisfy Collingwood, as we saw in his comments on Croce's *Filosofia della pratica* of 1912. In particular, the latter's exclusion of religion and metaphysics from the realm of the spirit could not be affirmed by the religious young Collingwood.

For the first problem Collingwood probably found some inspiration in Gentile's dialectic of the act of thought, and for the second in de Ruggiero's view of science as a dialectic of question and answer. These views probably also helped him to reject and overcome the unhistorical epistemology of the realists. For the third problem, however, actualism did not offer an acceptable solution to Collingwood. In the end, Collingwood could not bring the metaphysics of the pure act into accordance with his own metaphysical and religious convictions. With Gentile Collingwood believed in the self-creative power of human thought, but in his view man's self-creation could not be separated from nature and God. From this point view, Gentile at least acknowledged the importance of religion as the 'objective moment' of the spirit. But the young Collingwood could not support this view because in his first book he sees religion as the highest form of the spirit. At this point Collingwood's most important problem arose, namely that of reconciling Italian *storicismo* with his own metaphysics. In this context, Collingwood's notion of the living past as a past which lives on, even if we are not aware of it, surfaces as the most fundamental difference between him and the Italians; it was to be the difference that marked his philosophy off from theirs.

Chapter Six

Croce, Gentile, and de Ruggiero in the 1920s

Introduction

With the armistice of 1918, a new period began in the lives of Croce, Gentile, and de Ruggiero. After completing his system with *Teoria e storia della storiografia* in 1917, Croce devoted himself for several years to literary criticism. In 1919, he published *Goethe, con una scelta delle liriche nuovamente tradotte* (*Goethe, with a choice of Newly Translated Poetry*), followed by *Ariosto, Shakespeare e Corneille* in 1920, *La poesia di Dante* (*The Poetry of Dante*) in 1921, and *Poesia e non poesia* (*Poetry and Non-Poetry*) in 1923. These works were accompanied by several essays on aesthetics collected in the *Nuovi saggi di Estetica* (*New Essays of Aesthetics*) in 1920.

Gentile, who was finishing the second volume of his *Sistema di logica*, criticised these essays and contributed to aesthetics with two articles: 'Il torto e il diritto delle traduzioni' ('The Wrong and the Right of Translations') in 1920 and 'Arte e religione' in 1921. Meanwhile, he published many articles with a very nationalistic character, by which he sought to encourage his compatriots to rebuild Italy after the war.[1]

De Ruggiero, while continuing his activities as a journalist, published three new volumes of his *Storia della filosofia*: *La filosofia del cristianesimo* (*The Philosophy of Christianity*) in 1920. At the same he went to England in order to study the practice of liberal politics. It was on this trip that he became friends with Collingwood. Back in Italy, he contributed to the debate between Croce and Gentile on aesthetics with two important articles: 'Arte e critica' ('Art and Criticism') in 1921 and 'Dall'arte alla filosofia' ('From Art to Philosophy') in 1922. In the meantime, he wrote several articles and two books on British politics: *L'impero brittanico dopo la guerra* in 1921 (*The British Empire after the War*) and *La formazione dell'impero brittanico in Europa* in 1925 (*The Formation of the British Empire in Europe*). These studies formed the prelude to his masterpiece *Storia del liberalismo europeo* published in 1925, which was translated by Collingwood and published as *The History of European Liberalism* in 1927.

---

[1] G. Gentile, *Dopo la vittoria*, Società Editrice La Voce, Roma, 1920, cited from *Dopo la vittoria*, OC XLIV, Le Lettere, Florence, 1989.

In the debate on aesthetics of the early 1920s the three Italians formulated some important additions to their earlier views on history. Discussing the relationship between imagination and thought, they took different positions on the interpretation of language, with many implications for historical method. This is important because the problem of historical method had not yet been at the focus of their interest. Croce understood methodology primarily as the elaboration of concepts, and not as the interpretation of evidence, though he indicated some important relationships between the elaboration of concepts and evidence in *Teoria e storia della storiografia*. Likewise, Gentile and de Ruggiero had concentrated on the metaphysical aspects of historical thought, and not on historical methodology.

Despite its importance, the debate on aesthetics between the three Italians was soon to be silenced by the growing social and political chaos in Italy. The rise of Fascism divided the country and presented the three philosophers with new challenges. In 1921, Croce left the tranquility of his study when Prime Minister Giolitti asked him to become Minister of Education. Gentile followed Croce when he was asked to take the same post by Mussolini in 1922. A year later, Gentile decided to support Fascism, whereas Croce and de Ruggiero chose to fight it. Gentile's decision rapidly led to a schism between him and Croce and de Ruggiero which is symbolic of the crisis in Italy.

The rise of Fascism confronted the three thinkers with new problems, in particular in the field of moral and political philosophy. Their solutions for the problems had important implications for their views on the relationship between history and action. Gentile, identifying his *etica del sapere* with the Fascist creed, found that all history should contribute to the progress of Fascist culture. In contrast to this position, Croce and de Ruggiero held that history should be practised in the service of liberty. As always, the three philosophers did not confine themselves to theoretical issues, but sought to elaborate on them in their historical works as well.

Croce's New Essays on Aesthetics (1918–20)

In 1918, Croce published two important articles, 'Il carattere di totalità della espressione artistica' ('The Character of Totality of the Artistic Expression') and 'L'arte come creazione, e la creazione come fare' ('Art as Creation and Creation as Making'). In both articles he dealt with the problem of how the artistic expression of emotion can produce knowledge. This problem naturally arose from Croce's earlier aesthetics. From 1893, Croce had held that art is knowledge of the individual. In 1907, he had introduced the notion of art as the expression of emotions. In the *Logica* of 1909, he had established the identity of philosophy and history, which implies that knowledge of the universal and knowledge of the specific cannot be separated. Following from this, Croce came to understand that the unity of the universal and the individual should also apply to art. However, Croce did not give up his distinctions between art and philosophy and between theory and practice. The two central problems of the new essays on aesthetics were therefore: how can art be knowledge of the universal without identifying art and philosophy, and how can art be an expression of emotions without identifying it with emotions themselves?

In 'The Character of Totality of the Artistic Expression' Croce approaches these problems from the point of view of literary criticism. In his view 'profound art' somehow reflects something universal, or 'cosmic' as he calls it, whereas 'superficial art' does not.[2] In the paper Croce tries to establish a criterion for this distinction. He begins by showing that emotions are never purely individual, because the individual to whom they belong is part of the universal. Yet, individuals reflect on the universe within themselves and therefore their emotions must have both an individual and universal aspect.[3] The true artist becomes conscious of the universal aspect of his emotions by transforming them into a pure intuition in which their universality is reflected, whereas the bad artist does not succeed in this attempt at universality. His intuitions are not pure, because he still lingers in his immediate emotions expressing himself in 'cries and howls of lust'.[4] Every true artistic expression thus contains the universe within itself:

> In every utterance, every fanciful creation, of the poet lies the whole of human destiny, all human hopes, illusions, griefs, joys, human grandeurs and miseries, the whole drama of reality perpetually evolving and growing out of itself in suffering and joy.[5]

According to Croce, good art creates its own 'cosmos' by expressing emotions in a pure intuition. On this basis Croce elaborates his earlier view that art is cognitive or a form of cognition. Art says something about a world, not about the real world but about an imaginary world. However, this imaginary world is permeated by elements from the real world, such as hope, joy, ideals, and so forth. In this way Croce brings the world of art and the world of thought and action closer together than in any of his previous works.[6]

In the second article, 'Art as Creation and Creation as Making' the rapprochement between intuition, thought, and action is even closer. Starting from Vico's principle that *verum et factum convertuntur*, Croce claims that all knowledge is a form of making: *'verità come fare'* (truth as making).[7] From this it follows that if art is to be recognised as a form of knowledge, it must be des-

---

2   B.Croce, 'Il carattere di totalità della espressione artistica', in *La Critica*, XVI, 1918, cited from *Nuovi Saggi di Estetica*, Laterza, Bari, 1926, 119.
3   Ibid., 122–3.
4   Ibid., 123.
5   Ibid., 122.
6   Ibid., 124.
7   B. Croce, 'L'arte come creazione, e la creazione come fare', in *Atti della Accademia Pontaniana*, XLVIII, cited from *Nuovi Saggi di Estetica*, Laterza, Bari, 1926, 154–5.

cribed as a form of making, or creation.[8] In this context, Croce explains that art does not 'presuppose' other forms of mental activity since true art does not 'imitate' an empirical reality or some kind of ideality which belongs to the theoretical sphere of the spirit. Furthermore, art does not presuppose any 'emotions' which belong to the practical sphere of the spirit. On this point Croce raises the question: how can the intuition-expression be described as a creative form of the spirit without identifying it with conceptual knowledge or with action?

Croce solves this problem by identifying the intuition-expression with a process of problems and solutions:

> Expression and word are not yet a manifestation or a reflection of feeling... nor a remodelling of feeling on the basis of a concept (which is false idealisation), but they are the positing and resolving of a problem.[9]

According to Croce, this activity of positing and solving problems distinguishes art from feeling and emotions, because these never posit any problems, nor solve them, with the consequence that they cannot be true or false. Emotions 'acquire' truth only to the extent that they become problems of artistic vision, which are solved by mental constructions, or 'artistic fantasies'.[10] In more general terms, therefore, art distinguishes itself from emotions by being creative:

> As positing and solving of problems (fantastical or aesthetical), art does not reproduce something which already exists, but it always produces something new, it forms a new spiritual situation, therefore, it is not imitation but creation.[11]

This creativity distinguishes art from emotion, but not from thought, because, on the basis of the principle *verità come fare*, thought must also be seen as a creative process of positing and solving problems:

> In the same way, thought is creation, because it also consists in nothing else but positing and solving problems (called logical or philosophical or speculative); and it never consists of reproducing objects or ideas.[12]

On this basis, Croce concludes that art and philosophy are identical, in the sense that both are processes of positing and solving problems. But art and philosophy are also different, because they raise different kinds of problems. Croce describes the problem of art as follows:

> That which is life and feeling must make itself true, on the basis of the artistic expression. And truth means overcoming the immediacy of life in the medi-

---

8   Ibid., 153.
9   Ibid., 150.
10   Ibid., 151.
11   Ibid., 152.
12   Ibid.

ation of fantasy, it is creation of a fantasy which is feeling set up in its relations.[13]

From this viewpoint, the special problem of art is to relate emotions by expressing them in a fantasy or pure intuition. This fantasy is the object of art which it
constructs or creates for itself. This distinguishes art from philosophy which constructs its own objects in the form of individual and universal judgments.[14]
Croce concludes that both art and philosophy are forms of knowledge that proceed in a process of questions and answers and that both are creative because
they posit their own objects. The difference is that the object of art is fantasy,
whereas that of philosophy is thought.[15]

Though this theory may be regarded as complementing Croce's aesthetics,
the introduction of this distinction raises some difficulties. Throughout the *Nuovi
saggi* Croce stresses that art is 'mediation', 'transformation', 'suffering and toil',
and in this sense he identifies the artistic process with a process of positing and
solving problems. However, he does not clearly explain what makes this process
possible. According to Croce, the problem of art is to 'relate' emotions in a 'fantasy', but he does not clarify on what condition emotions can be related.

Nontheless, Croce elaborated the relationship between intuition and thought
more clearly than in his earlier works. In the *Logica*, Croce had claimed that the
pure concepts of philosophy take their form by predicating intuition-expressions. Given the autonomy of art, the intuition-expressions in the predicative act
are complete by themselves, that is, they do not depend on the pure concepts for
their coming into being. But in the *Nuovi saggi* Croce describes the intuition-
expression as a development, and more specifically as a development of questions and answers, with the result that they come into being gradually. This
view raises the problem of how this development of intuition-expressions, or
language, relates to the development of the pure concepts. In this sense, Croce
stresses that the two processes are distinct, but this raises the problem of how
the question and answer process of thought should be related to the formation of
language.

In his famous lecture 'Sulla filosofia teologizzante e le sue sopravvivenze'
('On Theologising Philosophy and its Survivals') of 1919, Croce addresses some
of these problems. Again, Croce's starts from *verità come fare*, which expresses
the view that knowledge is a creative process of questions and answers. But in
this lecture, his aim is to distinguish philosophy from art and action, whereas his
aim in the previous articles was to distinguish art from philosophy and action.

According to Croce all true philosophers ask 'sound' or 'precise' questions. In
his view philosophical questions are problems of definition and from this it
follows that we cannot formulate a problem if the terms are not clearly defined:

---

13   Ibid., 150.
14   Ibid., 153.
15   Ibid., 156.

To formulate a problem is to define its terms, and this implies also defining the relation of the terms to each other and to the whole. Without this, the terms would be left vague and uncertain, and so would the problem which would not, accordingly, be formulated. But to define the terms and their relation amounts to solving the problem: for after this what more would remain to be done? What was the problem set for if not to get these made clear?[16]

From this passage it follows that questions always form a unity with their answers; solving a philosophical problem is identical with formulating it. Accordingly, 'unsound' or 'imprecise questions' can never be answered because they apply vague terms, which are not really thought but only imagined. Unsound questions, Croce concludes, always rest on a 'hybridism of imagination and concept'; they rest on the belief that words are concepts.[17] The imaginative character of unsound questions is most clearly revealed by the fact that they always begin with an 'if'.[18] Based on imagination, unsound questions can only be solved by the imagination, that is, in a 'mythical' or 'religious' way. Bad philosophy is therefore always 'theologising philosophy'.[19]

As an example of a philosophical nonsense problem Croce takes 'is the soul mortal or immortal?' According to Croce the concepts 'soul', 'mortal', and 'immortal' in this question are not yet thought as pure concepts, but imagined as really existing things. The meaning of the concepts in the problem is unclear and therefore the problem will never be solved.[20] From history Croce gives the following example: 'Was Gemma Donati a good wife for Dante?'[21] According to Croce this question is meaningless, because we do not have any document that provides the answer. All answers to this question will remain as hypothetical as the question itself, as long as we do not have the necessary documents.[22]

After these two examples Croce applies his criterion to two other problems which had beset actual idealism from Spaventa onwards: firstly, the problem of the relationship between being and thought, and secondly, the problem of the unity of the spirit.[23] In Croce's view the problem of the relationship between being and thought is not well posed because the concepts 'being' and 'thought' remain vague. The two terms are treated as two 'entities' or two 'things', Croce says, but as such they are only imagined and not really thought. For this reason the solution for the problem is always found by imagining a third, transcendent entity such as God, matter, logos, absolute thought, and so forth.[24] The true

---

[16] B. Croce, 'Sulla filosofia teologizzante e le sue sopravvivenze', in *Atti della Accademia Pontaniana*, XLIX, 1919, cited from *Nuovi Saggi di Estetica*, Laterza, Bari, 1926, 341.
[17] Ibid., 343, 347.
[18] Ibid., 343.
[19] Ibid., 345.
[20] Ibid., 343-4.
[21] Ibid., 344.
[22] Ibid.
[23] Ibid., 348, 353.
[24] Ibid., 349.

philosopher, Croce says, never deals with imagined 'things', 'entities', or 'ready-made objects', but with forms of making, and one of these is knowing.[25] If knowing is considered as an activity, the question of its relationship with being does not arise: 'for a making that only mirrors, copies, and imitates would be a "non-making", which is, as such, inconceivable.'[26] Therefore, Croce argues, the other problem, that of the unity of the spirit, does not arise for the true philosopher, who takes the spirit as a circular unity of distinct activities that implicate each other. But theologising philosophers do not accept these distinctions.[27] They try to find a new unity in their 'insatiable unifying avidity'.[28] Some find this principle beyond the spirit and end with a form of 'mythologism', others find the unity in the spirit itself and end with mysticism. According to Croce, mythologism is constructive in the sense that it solves the problem of the unity of the spirit by inventing a higher principle, for example logical thought, or the will or fantasy, to which all distinctions of the spirit are reduced.[29] But mysticism is 'destructive' because it rejects all problems involving distinction as 'arbitrary' and 'empirical' in order to concentrate on the identity of all forms of the spirit.[30]

This rejection of mysticism was, of course, an attack on Gentile's actual idealism. In this respect, Croce was not altogether wrong when he claimed, contrary to actual idealism, that philosophical problems must be meaningful. Only a careful elaboration of our concepts enables us to formulate good questions, though this elaboration does not necessarily involve the distinctions of the philosophy of the spirit as Croce seemed to hold.

Gentile's Criticism of Croce's New Essays and His Own Contribution to Aesthetics

Gentile immediately recognised the novelty of Croce's *Nuovi saggi*, which he primarily saw as a move in the direction of actualism.[31] In his review, he interprets Croce's thesis of the cosmic aspect of art as a support of his own position that the history of art must be freed from monadism, and as plea for reconsidering the problem of the unity of the spirit.[32] However, this problem had already been ruled out as a nonsense-question by Croce in 'Sulla filosofia teologizzante'. Not surprisingly, therefore, Gentile aims his arrows at this lecture.

---

25 Ibid., 351.
26 Ibid., 352.
27 Ibid., 354.
28 Ibid., 356.
29 Ibid.
30 Ibid., 357.
31 G. Gentile, 'Nuove idee estetiche di B. Croce', in *Il resto del Carlino*, 27 July 1918, cited from *Frammenti di Estetica e di teoria della storia*, I, OC XLVII, Le Lettere, Florence, 1992, 103–08.
32 Ibid., 107.

Against Croce's thesis that philosophical problems can only be formulated when the solution is found, Gentile points out that problems are never clearly formulated at once. Problems 'grow' and 'develop', Gentile says, and he rightly remarks that Croce himself implicitly acknowledges this by criticising the way in which problems are formulated.[33] Indeed, as Gentile remarks, Croce's own criticisms of nonsensical questions are good examples of the way in which problems actually develop. In spite of this rebuttal, Gentile explicitly agrees with Croce that true philosophers never deal with things in themselves and that he must show that all objects are posited by the subject. This agreement need not surprise us. As we have seen, the idea that thought creates its own objects is the Alpha and Omega of actual idealism. Gentile therefore focuses on Croce's rejection of the problem of the unity of the spirit as a nonsense problem. In contrast to Croce, Gentile holds that this problem is not only meaningful, but also necessary to understand how the spirit distinguishes itself:

> The problem is precisely this: unity that distinguishes itself. Only by coming up to the unity distinguishing itself, mythology, mysticism and theologising really end.[34]

With this cryptic formulation Gentile turns Croce's thesis upside down. For Croce, the problem of the unity of spirit does not arise, because the spirit is a unity of distinct forms. Accordingly, Croce interprets *verità è fare* in the plural; the forms of the spirit are activities that mutually presuppose each other and therefore the problem of the unity of the spirit does not arise. Gentile takes *verità è fare* in the singular; for him there is only one truth and one form of 'making' and that is the pure act of thought. Gentile thus gives the problem of the unity of the spirit another meaning. His problem is not to understand how the forms of the spirit are to be differentiated, but to see how the self-conscious act of thought operates in the different forms. As always, Gentile does not aim at distinction, but at unity.

Gentile finds this unity in the pure act of thought, which is the starting point for his own contributions to aesthetics. In 'Il torto e il diritto delle traduzioni' ('The Right and Wrong of Translations') of 1920 Gentile points out that speaking is just a form of the pure act of thought; *parlare è pensare* (speaking is thinking). In an analogy to the dialectic of the *pensante* and *pensato*, Gentile points out that concrete speech (or language) is the actual spoken language that forms or creates its own content in the form of abstract speech or language. In this context, Gentile gives the example that we only know the content of a book by creating its content for ourselves in our own language, that is, by reading it. Concrete language is therefore a continuous translation; when we speak or read we

---

33 G. Gentile, 'B. Croce, "Sulla filosofia teologizzante e le sue sopravvivenze"', in *Giornale critico della filosofia italiana*, I, 1920, cited as 'La filosofia teologizzante e B. Croce', from *Frammenti di filosofia*, OC LI, Le Lettere, Florence, 1994, 141.

34 Ibid., 142.

always translate 'because the true language that sounds in human souls is never the same, not even in two consecutive moments; and exists only by transforming itself'.[35] Speaking and reading, even within one language, is therefore a continuous process of translation, even if we are not aware of it. From this viewpoint, translation is just another name for the dialectic of thought; translation is thought and thought is translation. In this sense translation is the basis of all thought, including historical thought.

> ...translation is really the condition of all thought and of all learning. And we do not only translate from a foreign language into our own, as it is said empirically, that is, presupposing different languages, but we always translate within our own language, and not only from our language of remote centuries and from authors whose readers we are, but also from our recent language as it is used by ourselves when we read and speak.[36]

This identity of speaking or reading with translating is the ultimate consequence of Gentile's identification of speech with the self-conscious act of thought and has far-reaching consequences for the interpretation of texts. According to Gentile, we cannot read without interpreting the text; we read because all reading is translation, or a 'reconstruction' of language. Reading is therefore not the repetition of a given content, but the creation of something new. From this view of reading it follows, firstly, that all texts are read by translating them, and secondly, that all thought begins with translation of other thoughts.

This conclusion is a valuable complement to Gentile's *Sistema di logica* in which he had not explicitly dealt with the problem of the interpretation of sources. In 'Il torto e il diritto delle traduzioni' he shows that all interpretation must be seen as a process of translation based on the principles of thought. The most important corollary of this theory is that the understanding of language does not presuppose a community of languages. In Gentile's view there is not some 'given' language which we 'use' in our communications, but we create our language every time that we try to communicate. The only language that really exists is therefore spoken language, or 'concrete speech'. From this it follows that two individuals do not understand each other because they speak the same language, but because they know how to translate the expressions of the other. In other words: understanding is not based on the community of language, but on translating.

Not surprisingly Croce criticised Gentile's theory of translation as a form of subjectivism. In Croce's view the identification of reading with translating inevitably leads to a clash between 'my Dante' and 'your Dante' which are incompatible with each other. Croce is not completely wrong on this point, as Gentile's argument certainly contains subjectivist elements:

---

[35]   G. Gentile, 'Il torto e il diritto delle traduzioni', in *Rivista di cultura*, I, 1920, cited from *Frammenti di Estetica e di teoria della storia*, I, *OC* XLVII, Le Lettere, Florence, 1992, 111.

[36]   Ibid., 112.

Whoever translates begins to think in some way from which he does not cease, but which he transforms, continues to develop, to clarify and to render always more intimate and more subjective to himself that which he began to think.[37]

In the same vein, Gentile defends the view and maintains that:

Our reading, if it is understanding, must rather be a development and therefore a reconstruction and a creation of something new, of which it can be said that it is the same as it was written, but not in so far as it was thought in the act of writing, but in so far it is thought in the act of reading it.[38]

In other words: when we read we reconstruct the thought that was written down and this reading is a new creation which is constitutive of the meaning of the text. Passages like these certainly justify Croce's complaints about subject-ivism because, on the basis of Gentile's theory, it is impossible to draw the line between creating and recreating the meaning of a text. Though Gentile is right that the meaning of the text can only be established by reading it, it is also evident that reading the text is not enough to establish its meaning. Establishing the meaning of the text requires a dialectic between the text and its reader, and following Croce's new essays on aesthetics, this dialectic might be described as a process of questions and answers.

Against Croce's objections Gentile retorted in 'Tradurre e leggere' ('Trans-lating and Reading') that translation does not take place between two empirical egos, but within transcendental ego, or the concrete universal. The translation Gentile refers to is 'history itself' that has produced both Dante, 'you', and 'me'; it is the process of thought of which 'Dante', 'you', and 'me' are only 'mom-ents'.[39] Gentile here applies his notion of the *autoconcetto* to the reading of texts; two interpretations of Dante can both be true depending upon the point of view on which they are based. This point of view is based on the history of the prin-ciples that thought has posited for itself, that is, the *autoconcetto*. The history of principles is the history of philosophy which can be known by rethinking past principles for ourselves. By reading 'your' comment on Dante I learn the prin-ciples on which your criticism is based, just as I come to know Dante's aesthetics by reading his *Divina Commedia*. Dante, 'you', and 'me' all embody the eternal act of thought.

In spite of their differences, both Croce and Gentile start from the presuppos-ition that it is the reader or the critic who establishes the meaning of a text or a work of art. Both views are therefore tainted with subjectivism. In the end Croce advocates the subjectivism of 'taste', whereas Gentile ends up with the subject-ivism of the present act of thought. This was the core of de Ruggiero's 'Arte e critica', in which he criticised both Croce and Gentile.

---

37 Ibid.
38 Ibid.
39 Ibid., 115.

De Ruggiero's Criticism of Croce and Gentile
and His Own Contribution to Aesthetics

De Ruggiero published 'Arte e critica' in November 1921. The article was conceived during de Ruggiero's stay in England in the second half of 1920, as the dedication shows: 'To my friends R.G. Collingwood and A.H. Hannay, in memory of our Oxford conversations.'[40] Croce severely criticised the article in *La Critica* and de Ruggiero reacted with 'Dall'arte alla filosofia' which contains a criticism of both Croce's and Gentile's philosophy of mind as well as a programme for a revision of their philosophies.

In de Ruggiero's elaborate criticism of Croce's aesthetics, we recognise many points which strongly resemble Collingwood's earlier views. Like Collingwood in 1912, de Ruggiero holds that it is impossible to understand the genesis of a work of art on the basis of Croce's notion of the identity of intuition and expression. This notion is still based on an 'illusory process of introjection and expression', implying that art 'presupposes a pre- or extra artistical material, for example, the brute matter of sensations, or something given which is not in itself art'.[41] Not surprisingly, like Collingwood, de Ruggiero concludes that Croce is not able to understand art as a self-creative and self-critical process.

In 'Arte e critica' de Ruggiero tries to provide a theory of this process by describing art as a form of self-conscious activity. This is completely in line with de Ruggiero's earlier essays where he had described science, action, and religion as self-conscious activities. Moreover, like the pre-war essays 'Arte e critica' consists of two parts. In the first part, de Ruggiero describes the genesis and development of art as a self-critical process. This forms the basis of the second part in which he describes the genesis and development of criticism by which we come to understand art. The two parts are reciprocal; all characteristics of art have implications for criticism, and all aspects of criticism are based on the theory of art.

In many respects, de Ruggiero's description of the genesis of art is similar to Collingwood's early aesthetics. All art, de Ruggiero says, begins with an 'act of appreciation'; when we say 'This is beautiful, I like this' we have already *'il quadro in fieri'* ('the picture in the making').[42] This initial act of appreciation is *a priori*, spontaneous, and autonomous; it does not presuppose any emotions, impressions, or ideas. In the initial act the artist is completely unaware of any distinctions between subject and object, or between imagination and reality. For him there is only one reality, constituted by his 'artistic seeing' in which subject and object, imagination and reality are one.[43] Distinctions between these terms

---

[40] G. de Ruggiero, 'Arte e critica', in *L'Arduo, Rivista di Scienza, Filosofia e Storia*, 2, 1921, 397.

[41] Ibid.

[42] Ibid., 399.

[43] Ibid.

are not explicit in the initial stage of art, but developed in a self-conscious 'analytic-synthetic process' which is guided by an 'ideal'. According to de Ruggiero, this process consists of asking and answering questions. After the first appreciation, that is, after we say something like 'I like this', we start asking 'what is this?' and 'why is it beautiful?' By asking and answering these questions, the artist realises his work of art by criticising it. At the same time, he becomes more conscious of the distinction between the object and himself, between the real and his imagination, between the work of art and his ideal of it. The work of art thus grows by self-conscious criticism. According to de Ruggiero, this process never stops because the ideal to which the artist strives continuously changes during the process.[44]

In 'Dall'arte alla filosofia' de Ruggiero continues this line of thought by describing self-consciousness as the 'third dimension', the other two being the object itself and consciousness of the object. In this context, de Ruggiero stresses that self-consciousness aims at an ideal in whose light the artist starts positing his problems; the raising of problems therefore presupposes a self-conscious awareness of a conflict between the real and the ideal, in the case the work of art and the artist's goals.[45]

According to de Ruggiero, this self-conscious activity is not just typical of art; all forms of the spirit are self-conscious activities. From this follows de Ruggiero's conclusion that there is no formal distinction between the forms of the spirit; art, religion, science, history, philosophy, and action are all forms of self-conscious activity, or in his own terminology; all forms of the spirit are philosophical.[46] According to de Ruggiero, the distinction between the various activities of the spirit can only be obtained by abstracting them from spiritual life. In reality the artist, the scientist, and the philosopher are one. Mental activity cannot be distinguished by 'abstract categories' but only by the individuals themselves:

> Dante does not distinguish himself from Thomas of Aquinas as a poet from a philosopher, because, at bottom, in both, the same historical mentality is living. But Dante distinguishes himself from Thomas as person from another person in the unmistakable individuality of his life.[47]

In none of his pre-war writings had de Ruggiero placed the individual person so much at the centre of his philosophy. Here he holds that it is not the categories of art and thought that form the basis of distinction, but the persons themselves. As a critic of his poetry, Dante is a philosopher, and Thomas is as much a poet as Dante; art and philosophy are therefore one and the same. The aim of the artist is therefore not pure beauty but truth, which he obtains by self-realisation:

---

44 Ibid., 400-01.
45 Ibid., 406.
46 Ibid., 405.
47 Ibid.

The merit of an artist does not lie in the effort which he makes in order to express himself as clear as possible, but in the effort which he makes in order to make himself more truly man.[48]

In order to realise this aim, the artist must deny his own 'limited egoism' and 'respire a greater and fuller humanity'. Conversely, 'the highest critical canon is given by the valuation of his universal or philosophical intuition'.[49]

In the second part of his article, de Ruggiero bases his theory of art criticism on his account of the genesis and development of art. His aim is to show that every 'moment' of the artistic process has a parallel in the critical process. According to de Ruggiero, criticism, like art, develops in 'three dimensions'; it is a self-conscious process which develops the criticism of the poem in the light of an ideal of art. The genesis of criticism is an appreciative act based on taste. In this first moment, subject and object, our comment and the poem, are not yet distinguished. But this does not alter the fact that taste is already 'criticism in embryo'; we always read 'with the comment in our eyes' even if we are unaware of it.[50] Furthermore, just like art, criticism strives towards an ideal, which lies in the future. From this it follows that criticism 'inverts time'; the true Dante is never in the past but in the future.[51]

According to de Ruggiero, this 'inversion of time' is not typical of criticism, but it is characteristic of all forms of the spirit.[52] On this point de Ruggiero reaches the fundament of his philosophy of history. All history, de Ruggiero says, begins in the present, because it is impossible to conceive a past in itself. But to say that all history is contemporary history, as Croce maintains, does not go to the heart of the matter; it only amounts to recognising the 'neutral presence of all times' in the present, which entails that the present cancels the notion of 'becoming'.[53] The becoming of time can only be made clear if present thought is regarded as 'distributing and regulating time'. De Ruggiero clarifies this important thesis as follows:

> It is to be repeated for time, what has been said about spatial experience (with the famous example of the born blind, who, after re-acquiring sight, sees all external objects as sticking to himself and who is not capable of distributing them in space, but acquires this habit slowly); in the same way, to the ignorant, or the ignorant of history, the events of the past appear outside any perspective, almost, as if stuck or joined to his present experience, in an ingenuous and infantile neutralisation of time. But the development of spiritual experience consists of the creation of this perspective, of distributing the events in their time, or, to speak with greater rigour, the series of acts with which a

---

[48] Ibid., 406.
[49] Ibid., 407.
[50] Ibid., 408–09.
[51] Ibid., 410.
[52] Ibid.
[53] Ibid.

plurality of events is acquired, is the same the one with which their temporal-isation is determined.[54]

With this illustration of 'distributing and regulating time', de Ruggiero develops his pluralistic form of actualism on the thesis that the observation of events in time depends on the perspective of the observer. The most interesting corollary of his thesis is the notion of the 'inversion of time', which stands squarely opposed to Croce's notion of the contemporaneity of history. For Croce, the most important function of history is to relive the past. For de Ruggiero, the most important function of history is to place the past in a perspective. For Croce, reliving the past takes place in the present; the present is therefore constitutive of the past. In de Ruggiero's view, the present is only one of the perspectives in the entire process which ends in the future. For Croce, the reliving of the past is self-sufficient, but for de Ruggiero, putting the past into perspective necessarily entails placing our present into perspective. By putting past and present in a wider perspective, both are enriched; by coming to know the past we come to know ourselves. This leads to the seemingly paradoxical conclusion that the more we identify ourselves with the past the more we distinguish it from ourselves.

After this excursion into the philosophy of history, de Ruggiero applies his views to art criticism. He begins by distinguishing two forms: erudite and aesthetic criticism. The object of erudite criticism is to understand the work of art in the light of the biography, the history, and other circumstances surrounding the artist. By erudite history we 'distance' the artist and the work from ourselves, that is, we see them as fundamentally different from ourselves.[55] However, we must also try to understand the 'intimacy', or the 'lyrical emotions', of the work of art. This is the object of aesthetic criticism, which 'neutralises time': 'it sees in art an eternal ray of beauty above all historicity which expresses it.'[56]

From this viewpoint, erudite criticism and aesthetic criticism stand squarely opposed to each other. The first concentrates on the historicity of the work of art, whereas the second concentrates on its non-historical aspects. But in the history of art criticism the two forms of criticism have come closer to each other; both forms have become more historical. Erudite criticism has moved to a position that compensates the process of 'distancing' by a process of 'approaching'. De Ruggiero gives the following example of this process:

> For example, only if I distance Pre-Raphaelite art from myself, that is, if I put it in its own times, I draw it nearer to myself, that is, only then I am able to feel it as alive, in so far as I create in myself those most elementary conditions of life, those mythical aspiration etc. that produced it. I cannot adhere to it if I

---

54 Ibid., 411.
55 Ibid.
56 Ibid., 412.

see it as contemporary, I adhere to it by historising it, that and myself at the same time.[57]

This passage illustrates how de Ruggiero's view differs from both Croce's notion of contemporary history and from Gentile's actualism which express the logical and ontological priority of present thought so that historisation is seen as being directed to the present. In contrast to this view, de Ruggiero stresses that historisation must go in two directions. Not only must the past be seen in its historical context in order to understand it, but the critic must see his own point of view in an historical perspective. Aesthetical criticism has also become more historical by realising that we can only understand the artist's emotions by 'historising and individuating them'.[58]

By becoming more historical two antithetical forms of criticism come together in the historical criticism. The object of historical criticism is nothing less than understanding the self-realising individual who is both 'the nude historical man and the pure poet'.[59] Along these lines, historical criticism does not conceive of a beauty without truth, or an expression abstracted from its context, or of a fantasy without the reflection in which it is concretised. Historical criticism explains the work of art in the light of the artist's biography 'by elevating the empirical experience of life in a process of ideal poetic significance and by concretising the ideality of aesthetic values in a historical human signification'.[60] Historical criticism thus places the self-realising individual at its centre and is therefore, in the first place, a 'humanistic criticism'. As such, it is a 'higher form of historicism' that proceeds by 'adapting itself to all other histories'.[61] This historicism throws all 'limited and particularistic principles of aesthetics' overboard in order to understand the 'human significance of art'.[62]

This is, in brief, de Ruggiero's 'Arte e critica'. It is a most ambitious rapprochement of art, philosophy, and history culminating in a complete historicism in which all particular histories find a place, thus unifying art and philosophy more completely than Croce and Gentile had done. Croce kept art and philosophy apart by insisting that the problem of the first is to express emotions whereas the problem of the second is to relate concepts. Gentile used to identify art and philosophy, but stressing the importance of self-consciousness in art he tended to neglect its autonomy. For Gentile art is a rational activity only in so far as it is based on philosophical principles. Along these lines he identified language and thought but again on the condition that language is formed on a rational basis or philosophy. In contrast to both Croce and Gentile, de Ruggiero

---

[57] Ibid., 413.
[58] Ibid., 414.
[59] Ibid.
[60] Ibid.
[61] Ibid., 415.
[62] Ibid.

acknowledges that art is rational *sui generis*; like all other forms of the spirit, art is an autonomous, self-conscious activity. The artist knows what he does, and why he does it, as does the art critic.

The most important contribution of de Ruggiero's 'Arte e critica' is his criticism of Croce's contemporaneity of history as a form of 'neutralisation of time' which cancels the notion of history as becoming. In contrast to this, de Ruggiero posits his own notion of the 'inversion of time' according to which present thought 'distributes' time by identifying and distinguishing itself from the past. This notion of the 'inversion of time' is a first attempt to go beyond the presentism that lurks behind Croce's notion of the contemporaneity of the past. This was also Gentile's aim in *Sistema di logica*, and not surprisingly both he and de Ruggiero claim that historical thought must both identify and distinguish itself from past thought. But for Gentile the main distinction between past and present thought is that the former does not appear as *norma sui* to the latter, which opens the door to the 'theologising' interpretation of the *autoconcetto* which flattens all distinctions between past and present by making the past thought compatible with present norms. De Ruggiero's absolute empiricism is far from this tendency to 'theologise'; he begins from the actual experience of the artist and the historian trying to develop a theory that does justice both to the past and present thought. This thesis has important consequences for the theory of language and for the theory of the individual. Language is not formed as an immediate intuition-expression but in a self-conscious process which is fully embedded in history. This means that language (ranging from works of art, gestures, to spoken language) cannot to be understood by some sort of 'intuitive' act, but only by historical thinking. Historical interpretation of language is a self-critical activity and proceeds necessarily as a process of questions and answers because the formation of language is also a process of questions and answers. The centre of the formation of language and its interpretation is not some abstract category but the historical individual. The highest aim of historical interpretation is to understand art and language as form in the history of individuals. As we have seen above, this aim can be realised on the basis of de Ruggiero's notion of the 'inversion of time', according to which both the work of art and the work of the critic must be interpreted from an historical point of view. The work of art, or language, is therefore not interpreted from a point of view outside history, but within history itself, and the relationship between the artist and the critic is a relationship between two different perspectives in history and not between some sort of 'eternal' perspective and its object. It is with this multi-perspectival view of history that de Ruggiero completes his earlier writings into a fully developed historicism.

Croce's Criticism of de Ruggiero's Aesthetics

The centrality of the individual was the main target of Croce's review of 'Arte e critica'. In this review he presents de Ruggiero as a 'hater of distinctions' whose last resort is the individual:

> For de Ruggiero the true and real categories are not art, philosophy, science and such, but persons, and, without incommodating Dante and Thomas Aquinas, those of our daily acquaintance, Peppino, Giovannino, Gaetanino, Michelino, and so forth. It is serious, but it is thus. Reality is to be individuals, physically and empirically distinct. I have believed until now that none of those names were real in truth, but rather the acts and series of acts, which the unique spirit accomplishes and which are only empirically and naturalistically grouped under those names.[63]

This criticism reveals the fundamental difference between Croce and de Ruggiero. The former held that the universal spirit is the sole reality and that persons are only incarnations of it, the latter held that only the person, or individual, holding the categories of the spirit as ideals is real. According to Croce, this stress on the importance of the individual is not antiquated, or modern, but 'modernistic' and it is reducible to the 'decadent tendencies of our days, in which the empirical I, the bad individuality, is placed on the altars'.[64] Croce was not altogether wrong, because de Ruggiero does indeed tend to take all activities of mind equally seriously. This tendency stems from his ideal to understand everything and everybody, which sometimes results in blurring necessary distinctions between the various activities of the mind. In this context, de Ruggiero himself explicitly claims that from a formal point of view there are no distinctions between the various forms of the spirit since all mental activities proceed as a question and answer process. The problem, however, is to see in what respects these processes differ from each other. After all, writing a sonnet is not the same as conducting scientific research, even though both activities proceed as a dialectic of question and answer.

In 'Dall'arte alla filosofia' de Ruggiero did not reply directly to Croce's criticism because he thought that Croce had completely misunderstood his thesis. Instead, he expounded his philosophy of the mind in a nutshell in order to distinguish it more clearly from Croce's and Gentile's theories. In this context, de Ruggiero stresses that his own philosophy is based on the notion of self-consciousness, which he again calls the 'third dimension'.[65] According to de Ruggiero, this notion of self-consciousness is lacking altogether in Croce's philosophy, because his main aim is to characterise the forms of the spirit by definitions on the basis of mental facts. In this way, Croce places himself in the situ-

---

63 B. Croce, 'Arte e critica', in *La Critica*, XX, 1922, 57.
64 Ibid.
65 G. de Ruggiero, 'Dall'arte alla filosofia', in *L'Arduo, Rivista di Scienza, Filosofia e Storia*, 3, 1922, 31-2.

ation of a mere spectator of mental activities in order to describe them. By doing so Croce assumes that all forms of the spirit are 'given' in the sense that each of them performs a standard activity to some 'given' experience. Consciousness thus remains a 'recipient'; it is not an activity that creates its own experience. From this it follows that the distinctions between the forms are 'given' before the work of consciousness begins. Moreover there is no 'communication' between the forms, each form being transcendent to the other.[66]

In de Ruggiero's view, Gentile's theory of the pure act is a great advance on Croce towards a theory of self-consciousness. But, he says, Gentile 'stopped half-way', because he failed to understand the autonomy of art.[67] In this context, de Ruggiero cites from Gentile's article 'Arte e religione', in which the latter presents art as pure intuition which only becomes real in the act of thought. According to Gentile this means that 'the poet is deaf to his own words' until he thinks what his intuitions mean. But in de Ruggiero's view this thesis only proves that Gentile did not understand that the identity of art and philosophy implies that the artist knows what he means all the time. Gentile thus commits the same error as Croce; both overlook the self-conscious aspect of intuition.[68]

According to de Ruggiero, both Croce's and Gentile's theories lead to the view that art has no history, from which it follows that art criticism cannot be based on an historical point of view. Moreover, Gentile's distinction between art, history, and philosophy shows that Gentile is a victim of the theory of 'mental faculties' like Croce. Both distinguish between art and philosophy interpreting 'transcendentals as existential data'.[69] According to de Ruggiero, 'the doctrine of the forms of the spirit must be radically revised'.[70] No longer should it interpret the spiritual activities as given forms and no longer should spiritual activity as a whole be identified with 'moments' of its development. Instead, aesthetics must take the whole spiritual process into account and not abstract some moments of it as 'art', 'religion', and so forth.[71] Moreover, we must recognise the function of self-consciousness in each form. In this sense, de Ruggiero says that 'philosophy and the forms of the spirit must mutually penetrate and reveal in themselves the higher mental forms of experience'.[72] In particular we must understand that we 'seek how experiences present themselves; consciousness is not a recipient which passively contains every content, but it is an activity that determines its own object by determining and individuating itself'.[73] Of this individuating

---

66 Ibid., 32–4.
67 Ibid., 37.
68 Ibid., 38.
69 Ibid.
70 Ibid.
71 Ibid., 39.
72 Ibid.
73 Ibid., 33.

process, which forms the basis of the revision of the philosophy of the mind, de Ruggiero gives the following example:

> It is perfectly clear that the consciousness of one who writes a sonnet is different from the consciousness of one who does research with the microscope, because he is aware of that which he is doing and not of some doing in general. It is also possible to speak elliptically in the two cases of artistic consciousness and scientific consciousness but this does not mean that there are two forms of consciousness, a fantastical and a logical consciousness; it means that there are only different specifications of spiritual objectifications.[74]

In other words, the artistic and scientific consciousness form two aspects of one and the same mind which self-consciously forms its own objects: in its artistic form it creates a sonnet, in its scientific form, research. The two forms of consciousness can therefore not be separated. 'All forms of the spirit are philosophical and each is its own philosophy', de Ruggiero says. In other words, all problems of art, science, history, and philosophy are always problems of consciousness and therefore of self-consciousness.[75] Self-consciousness develops itself by positing problems and solving them. Each form of experience is self-conscious in its own way; that is, each form of experience posits its own problems and solves them on the basis of its own principles in order to realise its own goals or ideals by its own methods. According to de Ruggiero, this concept has very important corollaries for the interpretation of language. Art is identical to language and both are formed in a process of questions and answers. In order to understand language, therefore, this process must be recreated in an historical way.

As we have seen, this view was also held by Croce and Gentile. But unlike his 'masters', de Ruggiero holds that the intuitive moment of art is also self-conscious, which implies that all language is self-consciously formed. From this it follows that all language must be understood historically. In this context de Ruggiero aims at establishing a '*storica significazione umana*' ('historical theory of meaning') and he even maintains that 'feeling' must be understood historically. Historical understanding, in de Ruggiero's view, always implies the reconstruction of self-conscious activity of philosophy and this is identical to the question and answer process. Concretely this means that we have to understand the problems of the Pre-Raphaelite artists in order to understand their art, that is, we have to understand which ideals and principles were operative in their artistic activity which consists of transforming emotions into works of art. This view can also be found in Croce's and Gentile's writings, but for de Ruggiero this is not the end of the story because he insists that the critic or the historian must also historicise his own point of view, that is, he must relate his own problems, solutions, ideals, and principles to those of the Pre-Raphaelite artist. De

---

[74] Ibid.
[75] Ibid., 40.

Ruggiero does not describe how this should be done, but it is clear from the fore-going that this process of understanding involves some form of communication between two self-conscious individuals in time.

It is not surprising that Collingwood endorsed de Ruggiero's conclusions because they come very close to the theories that he developed before and dur-ing the war. He only criticised de Ruggiero for not elaborating the differences between the forms of experience. De Ruggiero's main conclusion of 'Arte e critica' and 'Dall'arte alla filosofia', namely that all forms of experience must be seen as a dialectic of question and answer as he had established in 'La scienza come esperienza assoluta' gave rise to one of Collingwood's problems of differ-entiating the dialectic in each of the forms of experience in *Speculum Mentis* of 1924.[76]

The Rise of Fascism

After the war, Italy sank into an enormous social and economic chaos. The country had lost over 600,000 men without realising its war-aims. Like all other countries it suffered from wartime debt and post-war depression. There was massive unemployment in both agriculture and industry. Men returning from the front could not find work and social unrest began to spread rapidly. The countryside was ravaged by strikes, burning of crops, and land seizures. Indus-try in the cities was also faced with unemployment and forceful demands were raised for workers' control of the factories. This chaos was a hotbed for Fascism. Its origins lay in the *fasci di combattimento*, the first Fascist assault groups, which attempted to preserve the political heritage of the *fasci di azione rivoluzionaria* (bundles of revolutionary action), the major organisational network of the extreme interventionists remaining from the war. In the years from 1919 to 1921, called the 'red biennium', Fascism was numerically and politically irrelevant and the Fascist and nationalist squads were only sporadically active.[77] The political scene was dominated by socialists on the left and the nationalists on the right. Within two years, however, Fascism gained strength and became an important political factor after 1921.[78] Fascist *squadristi* conducted a systematic campaign of terror against socialists and communists and their local institutions.[79] In this they were supported by the army and the civil authorities, who eagerly used the Fascist squads in order to break the power of the socialists.[80]

The successive cabinets in the early 1920s failed to stop the terror, and the authority of the government quickly began to crumble. Eventually it became so

---

[76] See Chapter 7, p. 241.

[77] Adrian Lyttelton, *The Seizure of Power, Fascism in Italy 1919–1929*, Princeton University Press, Princeton, New Jersey, 1987, 37.

[78] Ibid. 1; De Felice, Renzo, 'Fascism', in Cannistraro, Philip, V. (ed.), *Historical Dictionary of Fascist Italy*, 1982, Westport, London, 207.

[79] Lyttelton, *The Seizure of Power*, 38.

[80] Ibid., 39.

weak that a *coup de grace* was not needed. On 28 October 1922, the Fascists mobi-
lised around Rome, and Mussolini, who remained safely at a distance, threatened to take over power. This event became known as the 'March on Rome'.
From a military point of view it was pure bluff. In fact there was no march at all
but only some improvised gatherings of the *fasci* which could never defeat the
Roman garrison. Mussolini himself did not take part in this event and two days
later he safely arrived in Rome by train. Politically, however, the March on Rome
was a great success; the Cabinet resigned and Mussolini was asked to form a
new one, which he did on 30 October 1922. Mussolini's first Cabinet consisted of
men who had been active in politics for a long time. The only outsider was the
Minister of Education: Giovanni Gentile.

On 25 November 1922, the King and the parliament granted Mussolini dicta-
torial powers until December 1923. In the beginning, the Fascist government still
managed to increase its popularity. On 6 April 1924 the Fascists won 65 percent
of the votes. This success was dimmed by the brutal murder of the socialist
parliamentarian Giacomo Matteotti (1885–1924) on 10 June 1924. The Fascists
were held responsible and Mussolini was asked to clear up the case. The
parliament went into the so-called 'Aventine Secession' and some members of
the Cabinet, among them Gentile, resigned in order to press Mussolini to clear
up the case. Meanwhile, the conservatives in Italy feared a swing to communism. Their feelings were reflected in the Senate's vote of confidence in the
Government on 26 June; only 21 senators voted against Mussolini, 6 abstentions
and 225 voted for him, one of them was Benedetto Croce.[81] Mussolini felt
reassured and introduced press censorship and forbade meetings of opposition
groups. By bluffing and with a lot of luck Mussolini managed to survive the
crisis. On 3 January 1925 he felt strong enough to give a defiant speech in which
he threatened to use force in order to restore law and order. According to most
historians, this speech marked the beginning of Mussolini's dictatorship.[82] The
parliament did not protest and so Mussolini was free to do as he pleased. Parties
were forbidden, leaders of the opposition were arrested, the freedom of the press
was restricted. In June 1925, the repression was further extended with the *Legge
Fascistissime,* which tightened the control of the press and gave control of local
government to the Fascists. By the end of 1926 all political opposition was out-
lawed and Fascist tyranny was firmly established.

The Involvement of Croce, Gentile, and de Ruggiero in the Rise of Fascism

In the early 1920s Croce's attitude to Fascism was ambivalent. In theory he advocated an *indifferentismo olimpico,* but in practice he gave Fascism the benefit of the
doubt. Typical of his attitude was his reaction to Mussolini's speech in Naples,

---

81   Ibid., 243.
82   Ibid., 267.

four days before the March on Rome. In this speech, which Croce attended with de Ruggiero, Mussolini threatened to use power against the government that did not have the 'historical view of Italy's problem'.[83] When Mussolini had finished his speech Croce applauded. De Ruggiero was surprised and asked Croce: 'Doesn't he seem a bit histrionic to you?' Croce answered, 'Yes, but all politicians are a bit histrionic'.[84] This answer is typical of Croce's indulgence that would last for some time. After the Matteotti crisis, when Croce voted for Mussolini, he said that Fascism just needed some time to transform itself.[85] This position induced Gentile to say that 'Croce is a Fascist without a black shirt'.[86] Even Mussolini himself did not consider Croce as an anti-Fascist; he even offered him the job of Minister of Education in 1924 when Gentile offered to resign his post after the murder of Matteotti.[87] Croce refused because, as he said in private, he did not want to sit with Mussolini at the same table.[88] This reaction reveals Croce's true opinion about Fascism; he found it vulgar and beneath his dignity. This attitude also explains why he could not forgive Gentile for becoming involved with Fascism; a true philosopher should keep to the maxim '*odi profanum vulgus*'. On the 24 October 1924 Croce wrote his last letter to his former friend:

> For many years now we have been in a mental disagreement, which was how-ever not reflected in our personal relations. But now another disagreement of a practical and political nature has been added and therefore the first dis-agreement has changed into the second and this is more bitter. But there is nothing that can be done about it. The logic of situations develops itself through the individuals and even in spite of the individuals. But I never thought of breaking away from you.[89]

The letter is a dramatic example of Croce's view of what he called '*accadimento*', that is, the way in which individuals are caught in the logic of history which transcends them. Only by distinguishing theory and practice, he accepts the *concordia discors* in theoretical matters but not in practical affairs. Gentile under-stood this message and never responded to the letter, in spite of Croce's reassur-ance that he had never thought of breaking away from him. Obviously both philosophers understood that the gap, which had always divided them, had become too wide. From their first letters onwards they had always collaborated in a *concordia discors* as they both used to call it. Gentile's adherence to Fascism

---

[83] Benito Mussolini, *Scritti e Discorsi di Benito Mussolini, Volume II, La Rivoluzione Fascista*, Edizioni Librarie Siciliane, S. Cristina Gela, s.d, 339–48.

[84] Jader Jacobelli, *Croce e Gentile, Dal sodalizio al dramma*, Rizzoli, Milano, 1989, 136.

[85] Ibid., 152; Lyttelton, *The Seizure of Power*, 243.

[86] G. Gentile, *Che cosa è il Fascismo?*, Vallecchi, Florence, 1925, cited from *Politica e Cultura*, I, *OC* XLV, Le Lettere, Florence, 1990, 28.

[87] Jacobelli, *Croce e Gentile*, 153; Romano, *Giovanni Gentile*, 188.

[88] Jacobelli, *Croce e Gentile*, 153.

[89] B. Croce, *Lettere a Giovanni Gentile*, 670.

was the straw that broke the camel's back. After his break from Gentile, Croce's opposition to Fascism quickly grew stronger.

Until 1923 Gentile's attitude to Fascism did not differ much from Croce's. Like the latter, he saw himself as a good liberal of the old style. Even when he was granted honorary membership of the Fascist party at the end of May 1923, he still thought of himself as liberal, as is shown by the letter that he wrote to Mussolini on the occasion:

> As I am today making my formal act of adherence to the Fascist party, I beg you to allow me a brief declaration, in order that I may tell you that in this adherence I believe I am fulfilling a moral obligation of sincerity and political honesty. As a liberal whose convictions are deep-rooted and firm, during these months in which I have had the honour of collaborating in your great task of government and sharing closely in the development of the principles that inform your political action, I have become absolutely convinced that liberalism, as I understand it and as the men of the glorious right that guided Italy in the Risorgimento understood it, the Liberalism of liberty within the law and therefore within a state that is strong, and a state that is conceived as an ethical reality, is not represented in Italy today by the liberals who are more or less openly opposed to you, but in actual fact by yourself. And therefore I am likewise convinced that between the liberals of today and the Fascists who understand the thought behind your Fascism, a genuine liberal who disdains equivocations and desires to stand at his rightful post must range himself at your side.[90]

This letter is not only an act of friendliness and politeness to Mussolini, but also an expression of Gentile's view that Fascism was the ultimate stage of liberalism. This identity of liberalism and Fascism is also reflected by the fact that Mussolini called Gentile's reform of education, mentioned in the letter, the 'most Fascist of all reforms', whereas Gentile himself and even Croce and de Ruggiero saw it as a liberal measure.[91] This is not so surprising because the educational reforms realised the ideals for which they had fought side by side since the beginning of the century. It brought history and philosophy to the centre of the curriculum of the secondary school and the university. In Fascist circles the reform was not welcomed with enthusiasm and this was one of the reasons for securing Gentile's adherence to Fascism by offering him the party-membership.

After May 1923, Gentile dedicated himself completely to Fascism. Symbolic of his complete loyalty to the movement was his speech held in Palermo on the 31 March 1924, in which he defended the use of the *manganello* (cudgel) against the opponents of state. After this speech Gentile was called the 'philosopher of the *manganello*' by his opponents. But Gentile's loyalty to Fascism did not make him completely blind and dependent. As mentioned above, Gentile opposed Mussolini by offering to resign his post as Minister of Education after the mur-

---

[90]   Cited and translated by Harris, *The Social Philosophy of Giovanni Gentile*, 167–8.

[91]   B. Croce, *Lettere a Giovanni Gentile*, 629; de Ruggiero, *Scritti Politici*, 605.

der of Matteotti. On this occasion he wrote a letter to the Duce in which he insists that he should solve the crisis with 'a more reconciliating collaboration'.[92] However, the Matteotti crisis did not shake Gentile's belief in Fascism as the inevitable outcome of the history of Italy, and he remained a loyal Fascist even when the repression became more severe towards the end of 1924.[93] In August 1924, the *Partito Nazionale Fascista* asked Gentile to preside a commission for constitutional reforms, and at the beginning of 1925, when Mussolini began to tighten his grip on the country, Gentile was assigned the task of organising Fascist culture. In this context, Gentile organised a conference for Italian intellectuals at Bologna. After this congress he published the famous and notorious 'Manifesto degli intellettuali italiani Fascisti agli intelletuali di tutte le nazioni' ('Manifesto of Italian Fascist Intellectuals to Intellectuals of All Nations') on the 21 April 1925, which symbolised the new year of ancient Rome.[94]

The manifesto was addressed to intellectuals of all countries. It seeks to explain the origin of Fascism, and the relationship between Fascism and the state. A special section is dedicated to explaining the necessity of the violence of the Fascist *squadri* against its opponents.[95] The manifesto does not contain profound philosophical doctrines; it mainly consists of old nationalist slogans in a new, Fascist phrasing. Croce, who had broken with Gentile in October 1924, immediately reacted and presented his 'Una risposta di scrittori, professori e pubblicisti italiani al manifesto degli intellettuali Fascisti' ('An Answer of Italian Writers, Professors and Publicists to the Manifesto of Fascist Intellectuals') on an another symbolic date: 1 May 1925. In this response, Gentile's 'Manifesto' is ridiculed as a 'schoolboy's exercise' and put off as 'an incoherent and bizarre mixture of incoherent ideas'.[96] Most significantly, Croce accuses the Fascists of an abuse of history by identifying liberalism with 'materialistic atomism' in order to justify the 'subjection of the individual to the whole'.[97] Moreover, he accuses the Fascists of abusing the term religion against which he poses his own ideas, which foreshadows his notion of the 'religion of liberty':

> The faith which for two and a half centuries has been the spirit of the resurrecting Italy, of modern Italy: that faith which consists of the love of truth and the aspiration to justice which has generous human and civil sense, zeal for

---

92 Romano, *Giovanni Gentile*, 180.
93 Ibid., 189.
94 G. Gentile, 'Manifesto degli intelletuali italiani Fascisti agli intelletuali di tutte le nazioni', in *L'Educazione politica*, 3, 1925, cited from *Politica e Cultura*, II, OC XLVI, Le Lettere, Florence, 1991, 5–13.
95 Ibid., 9.
96 B. Croce, 'La protesta contro il "Manifesto degli intelletuali Fascisti"', in *La Critica*, XXIII, 1925, 310.
97 Ibid., 310–11.

intellectual education and morality, of a readiness for freedom which is the force and the guarantee of any progress.[98]

The 'Anti-Manifesto' was signed by more than 100 prominent intellectuals, a number that astonished the Fascists. As such it was an important moment of resistance, but it came too late.

Among the signatories of the 'Anti-Manifesto' was Guido de Ruggiero. He had rung the alarm bell long before Croce had begun to worry about the decline of liberalism. In 1920, he had gone to England to learn something from the British, 'who in political matters and in matters of political science can give healthy lessons'.[99] After his return to Italy, he published *L'impero britannico dopo la guerra* in 1921 and *La formazione dell'Impero brittanico in Europa* in 1925. Already in the preface to his first book, he gives one of his first analyses of Fascism. He finds fault for the rise of Fascism with the bourgeoisie being preoccupied with 'la propria borsa' ('its own wallet'). In his view it had refused to 'elevate the proletariat' and had applauded the *fasci*, which helped to keep the poor under their thumb. Unlike Croce and Gentile, de Ruggiero complains about the violence of the Fascists. In particular, he worries about the many young people who 'train themselves in a school of violence that inevitably corrupts the soul'.[100] In 1921 De Ruggiero saw through the outer characteristics of Fascism and he recognised that it was based on violence:

> At this moment the fundamental characteristic of Fascism is not found in those sundries in which the pavid mentality of the conservatives takes so much delight. Patriotism, institutionalism, the three-coloured banner are nothing but pretexts and signs of fight. But the only real substantial thing is nothing but the conviction, which is completely suited to the young forces which have solid war experiences, that power belongs to the brave minorities, and that political force drags along the whole conquest of the economical and social structure of the country.[101]

In de Ruggiero's view this tendency to violence and tyranny distinguishes Fascism from communism since the latter acknowledges the priority of the social-economic basis, thus adopting a basically democratic and gradualist point of view. Fundamentally, however, the Fascist and communist movements are 'twins':

> Fascist action presents the greatest affinity with that of the communists. Communism is not more or less than Fascism the fruit of a revolutionary impatience, which posits the conquest of political power before all economical and social vindications.[102]

---

[98]   B. Croce, 'Protesta', 311–2.

[99]   G. de Ruggiero, *L'Impero britannico dopo la guerra*, Valecchi, Florence, 1921, 14.

[100]   Ibid., 10.

[101]   G. de Ruggiero, *Scritti Politici*, 390–1, article of 13 September 1921.

[102]   Ibid., 391.

In the course of time de Ruggiero's tone about Fascism grew more bitter. In 1922, he called the Fascist movement 'a sturdy and bloodthirsty minority which plays on all ambiguities'.[103] He saw the *squadri* as 'a praetorian guard of the bourgeoisie' and he called Mussolini 'a little Napoleon'.[104]

It goes without saying that de Ruggiero's view of Fascism stood squarely opposed to Gentile's. The latter's view that Fascism constituted the highest form of liberalism was severely criticised by de Ruggiero and, the day after Gentile published the 'Manifesto', his former pupil immediately broke with him in the following dramatic letter:

> You complain about my criticisms but you do not take the crisis which you have brought about into account, thus breaking the unity of a world which was just being formed and creating a profound disagreement in the mind of those who, like me, thought that many things could be and should be rescued from this disorder. With your programme of Fascistisation of culture and of education you were ready to sacrifice without remorse; by opposing you, we defend ourselves and perhaps we also defend something of you.[105]

The last lines of this letter reveal de Ruggiero's view that Gentile had become untrue to his own principles and that he himself defended the true Gentile. This is in line with de Ruggiero's philosophical position; it is not actualism that is wrong, but Gentile's interpretation of it. This implies that the true actualism must be defended against its perversions. This attitude throws much light on both de Ruggiero's and Collingwood's later development. De Ruggiero's most important defence of actualism is his *Storia del liberalismo europeo* of 1925.

Gentile's Moral and Political Philosophy in the 1920s

In Gentile's moral and political philosophy of the early 1920s there is no radical break with his earlier views. The speeches and articles written during and just after the war and collected in *Guerra e fede* (*War and Faith*) of 1919, and *Dopo la Vittoria* (*After the Victory*) of 1920 are in general anti-democratic, anti-socialist, and very nationalistic but not Fascist *per se*. After May 1923, it was only the form of Gentile's writings that began to change: the same themes reappear but now they are presented in straightforward Fascist language. In 1925, Gentile published *Che cosa è il Fascismo* (*What is Fascism?*) which was followed by *Fascismo e cultura* (*Fascism and Culture*) in 1928, and *Origini e dottrina del Fascismo* (*Origins and Doctrine of Fascism*) in 1929. These books contain various articles, speeches, discourses, and reviews, but not an elaborated doctrine of Fascism, let alone a 'philosophy of Fascism'. Based on simple contrasts between the blessings of Fascism and the shortcomings of opposing new movements, most of these papers do not get beyond mere propaganda. One of Gentile's hobby horses is

---

[103] Ibid., 544, 10 August 1922.
[104] Ibid., 628.
[105] Cited by De Felice, in 'De Ruggiero, Guido', 250.

the contrast between the bad individualism of classical liberalism and the Fascist notion of sacrifice or traditional Italian scepticism with the new faith. Sometimes his rhetoric becomes almost ridiculous, for example, when he contrasts 'the Italian who laughs about everything' to 'the Italian who never laughs'. The latter is exemplified by Vico who is thus presented as a precursor of Fascism.[106] But apart from this rhetoric most of the themes of Gentile's Fascist writings can also be found in his pre-Fascist writings.

In some of the more serious articles we find a startling example of what Gentile himself would call a 'self-translation' when he uses his method of imamnence as expounded in his *Sistema di logica* in order to propagate his philosophy of Fascism. For example, he uses his doctrine of the concrete logos, according to which there are as many truths as points of views, for explaining the possibility of different interpretations of Fascism.[107] Along the same lines, he justifies the anti-intellectualism of Fascism on the basis of the identity of theory and practice, saying that Fascism is will and thought that combats the 'illness of intellectualism', and he calls on the Fascist intellectuals not to be intellectual at all![108] In the same way he justifies his refusal to define the Fascist doctrine on the basis of the mysticism of which Croce often accused him.[109]

The most startling 'self-translation' in Gentile's Fascist writings is the identification of the ethical state with the Fascist state and the parallel thesis that Fascism is the highest form of liberalism. Both theses are explained in 'Il mio liberalismo', which is typical of Gentile's Fascist writings. At its beginning Gentile points out that there are two forms of liberalism. The first is the classical, English form and the other is the modern, Continental form.[110] The first considers liberty as a 'presupposition' of the state from which it follows that the state must restrict itself out of respect for individual liberty. In contrast with the classical view, the 'modern conception of liberalism' recognises that liberty is only possible within the state. The new liberalism is therefore identical with the doctrine of the ethical state. In this view the state and the individual are not opposed to each other because the state is within the individual. From this it follows that the individual 'realises his proper nature in so far as he identifies himself with the state'.[111] Obviously, this thesis is a translation of his earlier doctrine of the *societas in interiore homine*. It is important to keep this in mind, because Gentile's Fascist ideas should not blind us to the fact that he himself sin-

---

[106] G. Gentile, *Che cosa è il Fascismo?*, 18.

[107] Ibid., 8.

[108] G. Gentile, 'Il Fascismo nella cultura, Discorso di chiusura tenuto il 30 marzo 1925 al Congresso di cultura Fascista a Bologna', cited from *Politica e Cultura*, I, OC XLV, Le Lettere, Florence, 1990, 93.

[109] Ibid., 91.

[110] G. Gentile, 'Il mio liberalismo', in *Nuova politica liberale*, I, 1925, cited from *Politica e Cultura*, I, OC XLV, Le Lettere, Florence, 1990, 113.

[111] Ibid., 115.

cerely claimed that he was only repeating what he had been saying all the time. This claim was not completely unjustified, given the fact that he employed his own philosophy to interpret Italy's disorder as the result of the action of subjectivist empirical egos. In his view this *bellum omnium contra omnes* could only be stopped by the *stato forte* (strong state). The strong state was also advocated by the Fascists so that it was inevitable that Gentile regarded Fascism as the inevitable outcome of Italy's history; he interpreted Fascism as the last incarnation of the development of transcendental ego and the Fascist state as the ethical state and the only force which could stop the civil war. From Gentile's own point of view, therefore, his adherence to Fascism was a step of logical necessity and moral duty. In his view, these two always coincided, so that the *etica del sapere* morally obliged him to support Fascism. But in his support for Fascism Gentile forgot that an important part of his philosophy also advocated a tolerance which was not compatible with Fascist politics. This is a warning against all too facile judgments on the relationship between Gentile's actualism and his philosophy of Fascism. The problem is not to judge the man Gentile, but to understand why he chose to compromise the best of his thought. However, *tout comprendre ce n'est pas tout pardonner.*

Philosophy of History in Gentile's Fascist Works

From Gentile's notion of the *societas in interiore homine* follows a reinterpretation of the *etica del sapere* which has important consequences for the value of history. As we have seen in chapter 3, the *etica del sapere* prescribes that the highest duty of the man of letters, or philosopher-historian, is to serve the universal ideals of his community by studying their history and teaching them to future generations. This notion reappears in Gentile's Fascist works, but in contrast with his earlier views, it now has a definite Fascist meaning; universal cultural values are now Fascist values, history is now history from a Fascist point of view, and teaching now means Fascist education. From a purely formal point of view, however, nothing changed in his philosophy; we find the same concepts in the same connections, having the same meaning as in his pre-Fascist writings.

Against this background, it is not surprising that Gentile himself did not feel any need to change his theory of history. This is clearly illustrated by 'La storia', a paper on the philosophy of history, written in 1925. Not surprisingly under the circumstances, the theme of Gentile's article is liberty. His starting point is Vico's thesis that history is made by man, from which it follows that man is free.[112] According to Gentile this thesis had been accepted by all historians who have eliminated all forms of 'naturalism', that is, the theories of race, environment,

---

[112] G. Gentile, 'La storia', in *Scritti filosofici, per le onoranze nazionali a B. Varisco, nel suo LXXV anno di età*, cited from *Introduzione alla filosofia*, OC XXXVI, Sansoni, Florence, 1958, 104.

heredity, economic factors, and so forth in history.[113] However, Vico's thesis is no longer true for modern times, because the concept of man has changed under the influence of positivist sciences such as sociology and psychology. These sciences have raised questions like: 'Is man represented by the individual or by the masses?', or 'Is history biography or is it "sociology in movement"?' In these studies man appears to be limited in space and in time; are we then still allowed to say that he makes his own history?[114] Furthermore, the past is seen as absolutely necessary process, because in hindsight every event happened because it had to happen as it did. How is this view compatible with the thesis that man makes his own history? The real problem of today, Gentile concludes, is to establish a more precise concept of the humanity of history.

According to Gentile, Vico himself provided the key to the solution of this problem by showing that the *storia ideale eterna* makes the *storia in tempo* intelligible. That is, the metaphysics of the mind makes the relationship between historical events intelligible. At the same time, Gentile points out, it makes the past present, because 'all time contracts itself to the instant that has no part or possibility of succession'.[115] All history is thus seen from the present self-knowledge of the mind. From this it follows that the individual who seems to act on the basis of his particular emotions turns out to be the universal agent of the historical process.

From this angle, man has two aspects. From the outside, or seen as an object, he is part of the natural world and has no freedom at all and he is seen as a thing between things and other men. But when man is seen from the inside, or as subject, he is free, creative, and truly human.[116] Referring to his *Sistema di logica*, Gentile points out that the dualism between these two concepts of man can only be solved on the basis of the distinction between abstract logos and concrete logos. Seen from the outside, man's thought is abstract thought, it is finite, particular, and not intelligible. It needs to be corrected by 'an intervention of an ulterior thinking activity'. This thinking activity objectifies the abstract thought in an act of 'auto-distinction' which negates it.[117] In other words, the present thought thinks the past thought and then distinguishes it from itself by criticising it. Therefore, Gentile says, multiplicity exists only in the abstract, but in the concrete there is only a unity that makes multiplicity one. In the abstract there are many men, and among them, barbarians and civilised people. However, in the concrete there is only Man, or mankind, who is both everybody and nobody. From this idea follows that man will never be intelligible on the basis of concepts which are derived from the study of nature. Only on the basis of the concept of

---

[113] Ibid., 109.

[114] Ibid., 111.

[115] Ibid., 112.

[116] Ibid., 115–6.

[117] Ibid., 118.

freedom will man will be understandable. By this he does not mean the freedom of a particular individual but the freedom of a 'profound man' or 'that humanity that speaks the same language to all minds and to all hearts, infinite individuality, eternal and absolute'.[118]

'La storia' of 1925, which is Gentile's main contribution to the philosophy of history after *Sistema di logica*, shows that his adherence to Fascism did not lead him to revise his philosophy of history in any fundamental way. Like all his earlier work, it reflects the ambiguity of Gentile's actualism; on the one hand we find tolerance and understanding of all human beings, civilised and uncivilised, on the other hand, we find a more profound human being which transcends them all.

Gentile's Fascist Historiography

Gentile's Fascist interpretation of the *etica del sapere* involves a reinterpretation of history. But again, his historiography does not change in any fundamental way. Basically, we find the same kind of history of philosophy that he wrote in his pre-Fascist days; it is the same kind of history about the same philosophers with the same goal of making the Italians conscious of the tradition in order to continue it. From this stems Gentile's preoccupation with all kinds of alleged precursors of Fascism which is dominant in his writings.

For example, Gentile presents Vico as a 'spiritual master of Fascism' whose notion of the *morale eroica* foreshadows Fascist morality and whose analysis of barbarism correctly shows that man eternally turns to 'violent force to reorder and resurrect the degenerate states which are corrupted by liberty'.[119] In the same vein, Gentile presents Mazzini and Cavour as precursors of Fascism. Last but not least, he even tries to offer a Fascist interpretation of the Gospel by arguing that even Jesus did not detest force.[120]

It is this 'Fascistisation' of history, more than Gentile's philosophy of Fascism, that made Croce's and de Ruggiero's hair stand on end. They reacted furiously when Gentile presented Vico and Cavour as precursors of Fascism. It was certainly this kind of presentist history of philosophy which proved to Collingwood that Gentile was no longer capable of thinking clearly.[121] Nonetheless, anger is not the best guide in philosophy and the three philosophers were conscientious enough to consider Gentile's philosophy of history as a challenge to their own. This was not an easy task because from a purely formal point of view Gentile's philosophy of history and his historiography were in full accordance with the constructivism that he had always advocated. His Fascist historio-

---

[118] Ibid., 119.

[119] G. Gentile, *Che cosa è il Fascismo?*, 30.

[120] G. Gentile, 'Caratteri religiosi della presente lotta politica', in *L'Educazione politica*, 3, 1925, cited from *Politica e Cultura*, I, *OC* XLV, Le Lettere, Florence, 1990, 140–3.

[121] R.G. Collingwood, *An Autobiography*, 158.

graphy embodied the dialectic of the act of thought almost perfectly; present thought, which is now Fascist thought, posits or constructs a past, which is now a Fascist past, for itself.

With regard to Gentile's 'Fascistisation' of history Croce was in a better position than de Ruggiero, for he had already been criticising Gentile for many years. For him, Gentile's adherence to Fascism did not come as a surprise, but as a logical and inevitable outcome of the mysticism of which he had accused him in 1913. The rise of Fascism and Gentile's adherence to it did not pursuade Croce to revise his philosophy or his historiography as we shall see in the next section; he could stay on his own way. Compared to Croce, de Ruggiero was in a much more difficult position. Surely, Gentile's turn to Fascism did not surprise him, but he felt that Gentile had not only betrayed himself, but that he had also jeopardised their common cause of actualism. At the end of the 1920s de Ruggiero therefore began to plea for a 'revision of idealism'.

Croce's Moral and Political Philosophy

Croce's response to Fascism came late and in the beginning it was certainly not in the form of a revision of democratic liberalism, as some of his biographers hold. Croce was not much of a liberal before 1923 and his development to a truly liberal point of view was rather slow. Only in the late 1920s he began to develop his well-known notion of the 'religion of liberty'. But in the early twenties Croce still cultivated an 'olympic indifferentism' to all forms of politics. Although he had been a senator from 1910 onwards, he kept as far from politics as possible, and disdained all forms of political philosophy. This is shown by articles such as *'Troppo filosofia'* ('Too Much Philosophy') and *'Contro la troppa filosofia'* ('Against Too Much Philosophy') both of 1923, in which he held that Italy suffered from too much political philosophy. Croce disdained political philosophy, believing it to be an 'unjustified mixture of theory and practice, the reciprocal corruption of the philosophical and the political sense'.[122]

In spite of his disdain for political philosophy Croce himself produced *Elements of Politics* in 1924. This work can scarcely be called 'liberal'. In fact, the term liberalism does not appear in the work. The main target is Gentile's conception of the *stato etico*, which Croce tries to reject with the thesis that all political action is utilitarian:

> ...political action is nothing but action guided by the sense of the useful, it is directed at useful goals, and for this reason it cannot be qualified as moral or as immoral.[123]

---

[122] B. Croce, *Cultura e vita morale*, Laterza, Bari, 2nd. edn., 1926, 244.

[123] B. Croce, 'Politica in nuce', in *La Critica*, XXII, 1924, 129–54, cited from *Etica e politica*, Laterza, Bari, terza edizione economica, 1981, 171.

Apart from this utilitarian view of the state, Croce did not differ so much from Gentile. Like his former friend he had strong anti-democratic tendencies. In his view 'political parties are offered to various persons in order to make instruments of action for themselves and to affirm themselves and with themselves their own ethical ideals'.[124] And like Gentile he does not detest force in politics: 'force and consensus are in politics correlative terms and where there is one, the other cannot lack.'[125] Croce's concept of liberty is not much more than '*naturalis facultas eius quod cuique facere libet*' ('a natural faculty to do what one wants'), which is rather shallow.[126] Finally, Croce understands individual action and associations between individuals in merely economical terms.[127] Given these views, it was no coincidence that *Elementi di politica* was well received by the Fascist press.[128] Croce's description of political action as being utilitarian applies to a certain extent to the Fascists' reckless terror in the early twenties. Moreover, the Fascists understood that Mussolini's dictatorship came much closer to Croce's new 'Prince' then to Gentile's 'Monarch' of the ethical state.

After 1925 Croce's view of politics slowly began to change into a more substantial view of liberty and liberalism. In 'La concezione liberale, come concezione storica della vita' ('The Liberal Idea as the Historical Idea of Life') of 1928 Croce presents liberalism as a 'metapolitical' concept; it is 'a total conception of the world and reality'.[129] It originated from the 'historical intuition' of the modern age, and is therefore fundamentally an immanentist view of reality and opposed to all forms of transcendence on which all forms of authoritarianism are based. However, a more substantial theory of liberalism cannot be found in Croce's articles of the late 1920s; he does not develop a theory of the relationship between the individual and the state, nor a theory of 'liberal method' which governs the actions between individuals. On the whole, Croce's liberalism is 'formalistic', or, as he says himself:

> The liberal idea, as historical idea of life, is formal, empty, sceptic and agnostic, just as modern ethics, which refutes the primacy of laws and casuistry and tables of duties and virtues, but posits moral consciousness at its centre.[130]

Croce's notion of liberalism as formalistic is in line with his strong dislike of metaphysics. Just as philosophy should be the methodology of history, liberalism should be the method of politics. The problem with this methodological

---

124 Ibid., 192.
125 Ibid., 178.
126 Ibid., 179.
127 Ibid., 190.
128 B. Croce, *Cultura e vita morale*, 289.
129 B. Croce, 'Il presupposto filosofico della concezione liberale', in *Atti dell'Accademia di Scienza morali e politiche della Società reale di Napoli*, L, 1927, cited from 'La concezione liberale come concezione della vita', in *Etica e politica*, Laterza, Bari, terza edizione economica, 1981, 242.
130 Ibid.

view of politics is that it does not have any positive content. In particular, it lacks an elaborated theory of the function of democratic representation in the liberal state.

The Value of History in Croce's Moral and Political Philosophy

Against the background of the continuity of Croce's moral and political views, it is not surprising that he did not significantly modify his idea of the value of history. This is illustrated by his paper 'Storia economico-politica e storia etico-politica' ('Economic-Political History and Ethico-Political History') of 1924 in which he returns to the questions and answers that he set himself in the early 1890s, by presenting moral history, or *storia etico-politica*, as a synthesis of the *histoire des civilisations* and *Staatsgeschichte*.[131] In Croce's view, the former form of history is too moralistic and the latter reduces morality and ethics to politics. Ethico-political history overcomes both shortcomings because it brings the political and the moral aspects of history together in a single, meaningful whole in which the moral aspects of history are based on the economic and political aspects.[132]

In its study of the ethico-political aspects of history it does not limit itself to the history of the state:

> ...conceiving as its object not only the State and the government of the State and the expansion of the State, but also that which is outside the State, whether this cooperates with it, or whether it forces itself to modify it, destroy it and substitute it: the formation of moral institutions in the largest sense of the words, including the religious institutions and the revolutionary sects, including the feelings and customs and fantasies and myths of tendencies and practical content.[133]

Ethical history studies the ideals of history which presuppose the economic and political level. As such, it is the history of the faith in the universal ethical ideal:

> Now this faith, this force, this enthusiasm, that qualifies the epochs and the highly historical people, what is this if not the faith in the ethical universal, the work in the ideal and for the ideal, in whatever way it is conceived or theorized, because it is always theorized in some way, with a metaphysical or invisible background, that is, in the world of thought.[134]

With its study of politics and the study of the ideals that underlie moral action, ethico-political history exhausts all forms of action that Croce acknowledges within his system. From this it follows that all forms of history lose something of their autonomy to find a place in ethico-political history; the history of agricult-

---

[131] B. Croce, 'Storia economico-politica e storia etico-politica', in *La Critica*, XXII, 1924, cited from *Etica e politica*, Laterza, Bari, terza edizione economica, 1981, 229–30.

[132] Ibid., 231–2.

[133] Ibid., 230.

[134] Ibid., 233.

ure, of technical inventions, industry, war, commerce, and culture must all be dealt with from an ethico-political point of view.

Although this is a huge claim for the scope of ethico-political history, Croce is not clear about its value. In fact, he wanted to keep history as far away from politics as possible. In his view, history should be kept aloof from all forms of action, leaving the task of determining what is concretely needed for action to the science of politics. In contrast, ethico-political history should focus on the highest moral ideals of political action, not with the petty things of everyday life. Along these lines, Croce claims, for example, that ethico-political history is realised by the 'political geniuses' who created the political institutions of nations. In another context, he claims that the ethico-political historian is not so much interested in the War of the Spanish Succession, or in the Napoleonic hegemony, but in 'men of consciousness, who are aiming at their moral perfection'. Croce's heroes are Jesus and Paul, more than August and Tiberius, Luther more than Shakespeare.[135] These names are puzzling, because Croce himself had never invoked Paul and Jesus, and though he had never studied Luther, he had in fact published a book on Shakespeare. In one thing, though, Croce had been relatively coherent; he had only been interested in the highest forms of poetry, philosophy, and moral action, and not in politics.

Croce's Historiography: The Tetralogy (1925–32)

Croce's idea of ethico-political history is illustrated by his famous tetralogy: *Storia del Regno di Napoli* (1925), *Storia d'Italia* (1928), *Storia dell'éta barocca in Italia* (1929), and *Storia d'Europa nel secolo decimonono* (1932). In these histories Croce does not deal with individuals as such, but with 'ideals', 'hopes', 'spiritual forces', as they are realised by individuals. The protagonists of Croce's histories are therefore not the individuals themselves, but individuals in so far as they embody a higher ideal. For example, in Croce's *Storia d'Europa* the real protagonist is the ideal of liberty, and the individuals are presented as its humble incarnations. Liberty, in Croce's view, is to be free from all forms of transcendence. Accordingly, his hero is the practical Cavour and not the religious Mazzini. However, sometimes Croce's prejudices cause him difficulties when, for example, he portrays Pius IX as 'a liberal pope' admitting that this 'is impossible both in logic and in reality'.[136]

With its stress on supra-individual ideals Croce's *Storia d'Europa* reads almost like a sequel to Hegel's *Lectures on the Philosophy of History* to which Croce explicitly refers in the preface to the book. As would be expected, the main theme of both philosophers is the history of liberty as realised by individual men. But in Croce's history there is no 'cunning of reason'; the individuals act self-consciously for the realisation of reason. Liberty thus serves as a moral ideal

---

[135] B. Croce, *Teoria e storia della storiografia*, 312.
[136] B. Croce, *Storia d'Europa nel secolo decimonono*, 118.

in action.[137] In this context Croce develops his idea of the 'religion of liberty', which, like all religions, is 'a conception of reality and the ethics that conform to it'. However, the conception of reality and the ethics of liberalism are dialectical and historical and do not need the myths, rituals, and dogmas of other religions.[138]

This conception of the religion of liberty is in line with Croce's earlier views. In his *Filosofia della pratica* he distinguished between the history of events and cosmic history, or history as *accadimento*, which is the totality of events on which individuals do not have any grip. Croce's view of the value of history had therefore not really changed since his *Filosofia della pratica*. In that book he had defined moral action as action aiming at a goal that transcends the individual, that is, progress of the universal spirit.[139] In the later works this goal is specified as 'liberty'. But as in the earlier works this ideal lies outside the individuals who try to realise it, because it is more universal than they are.

At the end of the 1920s, when Mussolini was at the height of his power, this concept of the 'religion of liberty' was certainly most inspiring. Moreover, Croce was one of the very few intellectuals who could keep up the ideal of liberty against Mussolini's tyranny, because he was so famous that the latter did not think of putting him in jail. But, critically considered, Croce's *Storia d'Europa nel secolo decimonono* is a bit antiquated. The idea of liberty is presented as a static ideal, or as a 'pure concept', which is 'given' to individual men who 'elaborate' it by their actions. Each action is thus presented as the embodiment of a new meaning of the eternal concept of liberty. For this reason, there is no real historical development in Croce's histories. Croce does not show how the idea of liberty is gradually developed by individuals who interpret each other's theories and actions. Croce's histories are are mono-perspectival and this gives them a religious, and one would say almost theological, dimension.

De Ruggiero's Moral and Political Philosophy

De Ruggiero's moral and political philosophy was to a large extent based on his study of British political theorists and his experience of British politics. Already convinced of the centrality of the individual, British politics showed him the practice of a type of liberal method, which is based on the interaction between individuals. De Ruggiero describes this 'liberal method' as follows:

> Liberalism presents itself not as a closed system, stiffened in old individual-istic formulas, but as a method, as a spiritual energy. It has its source in the indelible and insuppressible affirmation of the spirit — of liberty — and it can become incarnate in different historical forms or take a different historical content on itself. Freedom and anarchical individualism are not necessarily

---

[137] Ibid., 13.

[138] Ibid., 20.

[139] See chapter 2, p. 55.

coextensive; the latter is nothing but the lowest manifestation of freedom, which is not an atomic opposition between individuals, but full and organic unfolding of a higher spiritual individuality through singular persons. The principle of the state, of how organic life is does not repulse liberalism so much, but is its most developed expression.[140]

De Ruggiero's starting point is the freedom of the individual, which is not necessarily identical to anarchy. This was what he had learned in England which was guided by the maxim 'trust the people'. This first germ of freedom is further developed by 'liberal method', which finds its highest realisation in the liberal state.

De Ruggiero further elaborated these views in his masterpiece *Storia del liberalismo europeo*. Written in 1924 in order to respond to the crisis of liberalism, the book incorporates theory, history, and practice in a most interesting way. In the first part de Ruggiero deals with the history of the different forms of liberalism in England, France, Germany, and Italy. In the second part de Ruggiero tries to elaborate a 'European concept of liberalism' by reconciling the differences as developed in the various countries. This European liberalism is the point of departure for a reinterpretation of the liberal state, and of the relationships between liberalism, on the one hand, and democracy, socialism, the church, and the nation on the other.

The book ends with an analysis of the crisis of liberalism and with a suggestion for avoiding it. In de Ruggiero's view the history of liberalism in Europe shows two antithetical conceptions of liberty. On the one side, we find the French concept of liberty, which deals with 'liberty as an abstraction, a concept intended to express the essence of human personality, exalted above all historical and empirical contingency'.[141] On the other side, there is the English concept of 'liberties', which 'treat liberties as a complex series of specific rights and immunities acquired one by one as circumstances dictate, independently of any conceptual formulation which might unite them and deduce one from another'.[142] According to de Ruggiero, these two opposite conceptions of liberty call for a synthesis which de Ruggiero establishes by showing that they mutually presuppose each other.

> Liberty in the singular, as a formal concept, is necessary for liberties, to prevent their degeneration into privileges and monopolies. But liberties, in their empirical particularism, are in their turn, necessary to liberty, if it is not to evaporate into an abstract formula.[143]

Along the same lines, de Ruggiero solves two other antithetical notions of liberty; negative and positive liberty. By negative liberty de Ruggiero means to be

---

[140] G. de Ruggiero, *L'Impero brittanico dopo la guerra*, 57–8.
[141] G. de Ruggiero, *Storia del liberalismo europeo*, 368.
[142] Ibid.
[143] Ibid.

free from something; it is 'the ability to do what one likes, a liberty of choice implying the individual's right not to be hampered by others in the development of his own activity'.[144] This concept forms the basis of a positive concept of liberty, that is, the liberty of the individual to do something; 'freedom is not indeterminate caprice but man's ability to "determine" himself, and thus by the spontaneous act of his own consciousness to rise above the necessities and bonds which in practical life imprison him.'[145]

This notion of positive liberty, or the liberty of individuals to determine their own lives, forms the basis of liberalism. De Ruggiero gives four definitions of liberalism in a progressive order. A closer look shows that he follows the same strategy as in his previous essays. Starting from a preliminary concept he develops the subsequent concepts in a dialectical way. The beginning of liberal experience is the acknowledgment of the 'fact of liberty'.[146] This recognition of one's own freedom is the presupposition of all other activities of the spirit like art, method, and so forth, and therefore also for the recognition of the freedom of others. This beginning is developed on the basis of liberal method.[147] Liberal method is found in the first place in the interaction between individuals, and further developed in the relationship between parties and in the state. It starts from the idea that every individual is free to choose and realise his own ethical ideals. The political parties are social groups which function as the 'upholders' of the liberal method. Their task is, in the first place, polemical and critical, and consists of removing any impediment to the expansion of the individual, in particular all 'sophisms of degrading authoritarianism'.[148] Finally, liberal method is the art of government in the state. The liberal state is a creation of free individuals on the basis of free cooperation.[149] From this it follows that the state must be considered as the creation of individuals:

> By the mere fact that the State has become a creation of the individual, it has become conscious of its duty to contribute positively to the individual's education, and to broaden and strengthen the energies of individuals and of their free and voluntary associations. By nourishing the cells of its body it nourishes itself.[150]

On this point, de Ruggiero introduces the concept of 'liberal method' which governs the relationship between the state and the individuals. All government has a synthetic character; it must operate in the interest of all individuals and its most liberal task is to protect the minorities.[151] 'Trust the people' is the maxim of

---

[144] Ibid., 371.
[145] Ibid.
[146] Ibid., 378.
[147] Ibid., 379.
[148] Ibid., 380.
[149] Ibid., 383.
[150] Ibid., 391.
[151] Ibid., 383.

the liberal state which tries to find an equilibrium between progress and conservation.

De Ruggiero's conception of the state and the individual stands squarely opposed to Gentile's. For the latter the liberty of the state is primary and the liberty of the individuals is deduced and circumscribed by it, whereas for de Ruggiero the liberty of the individuals is primary and this liberty conditions the liberty of the state. This difference between Gentile and de Ruggiero is not incidental, it is not the result of some momentary polemic, but it goes back to their different interpretations of actualism. Gentile always stressed the priority of the transcendental ego over the empirical ego, of the state over the individual. Even his notion of the *societas in interiore homine* is open to a Fascist interpretation when the freedom of man is wholly sacrificed to that of the society. De Ruggiero, however, stressed that the empirical and the transcendental form a unity, with the consequence that each individual is taken seriously as a free and moral being. The free association between individuals forms the basis of the state and not vice versa. This notion of the state as association also differs from that of Croce, who interpreted the notion of association in purely economic terms as we have seen above. In contrast to Croce, de Ruggiero acknowledges the moral basis of associations, among which include political parties which form the core of political representation in the liberal state.

The Value of History in the Liberal State

Liberal method is the basis of all interaction in the liberal state. According to de Ruggiero, this involves the idea that individuals must recognise each other as free and rational beings in order to cooperate. Mutual understanding is therefore the basis of liberal method. In de Ruggiero's own words it is based on 'a capacity to reconstruct within oneself the spiritual process of another, and to estimate their intentions and results'.[152]

Although de Ruggiero does not explicitly say, it is clear that this form of mutual understanding must be identified with historical thinking. This is most clearly reflected in the following passage in which de Ruggiero describes liberty as both an 'expansive force' that is the basis of all human activity and as an activity that 'returns upon itself' in order to control itself:

> All free action involves the ideal assumption of something opposed to itself, which trains the mind in reflection and criticism, and rouses it to a sense of its own responsibility. Only one who is free is able to render an account of his own acts either to himself or to another; only one who is free can distinguish good and evil, deserve reward and punishment, know sin and repentance, raise the contingency of his own being to the universality of the moral law.

---

152 Ibid., 379.

> Liberty is at the same time both a spur and a check, an advance and a return; the whole life of the spirit issues from it and flows back into it.[153]

In the above passage de Ruggiero contrasts the function of 'reflection', 'returning to the source', or history, with the expansive, creative force of liberty. Only on the basis of history we can judge our deeds in the light of our moral ideals, and only on the basis of history can we distinguish between good and bad. The expansive and creative aspect and the 'restrictive' or controlling aspect of freedom mutually presuppose each other.

Along the same lines de Ruggiero began to understand that a further development of liberal method implied a total revision of actualism, because Gentile's actualism was so abstract that it simplified all difficulties of political life. In this context de Ruggiero points out that Gentile's idea that true liberty can only be realised within the state and not by the individual obliterates the three meanings of the concept liberty of the state. The first meaning is that of the freedom between states. The second meaning is the Hegelian one for which the state is the highest incarnation of liberty. The third meaning refers to the freedom of the state to dispose of its citizens as it wishes.[154] According to de Ruggiero, Gentile interprets the second meaning in the terms of the third. Gentile's sacrifice of the individual to the state, de Ruggiero concludes, is therefore based on the obliteration of the various meanings of the notion 'liberty of the state'.[155]

In order to overcome this kind of simplification, actualism had to be revised completely. No longer should it degrade itself to juggling with great concepts such as the ethical state, transcendental ego, and so forth, but instead it should try to understand the concrete problems of individuals in their daily life. Already in *L'impero brittanico dopo la guerra* of 1921 de Ruggiero was convinced of this need:

> I feel that my appeal will be heard, by few but the best. It is not a question of formulating and petrifying programmes, but of living and making the liberal spirit live again, not with abstract proclamations, but in short terms, belonging to the most common things and the most banal experience. It is a question of explaining that there are problems where nothing but ready-made solutions, to be accepted passively, are seen.[156]

This knowledge of the concrete problems of daily life form the basis of a liberal education of all individuals. But de Ruggiero stresses that 'we must not pretend to educate others, if we do not first' educate ourselves.[157] De Ruggiero's political self-education began during the war, was continued in England, and culminated

---

[153] Ibid., 463.

[154] G. Gentile, 'Cavour giornalista e pensatore politico', cited from *Politica e Cultura*, II, *OC* XLVI, Le Lettere, Florence, 1991, 95–110.

[155] G. de Ruggiero, *Scritti politici*, 666–7.

[156] G. de Ruggiero, *L'Impero brittanico dopo la guerra*, 13.

[157] Ibid.

in *Storia del liberalismo europeo*. In this book he deals with the actual problems of daily life, for example, with the problems of agriculture as caused by industrialisation, the problems of administration, of the relationship between the church and the state, and so forth. These problems called for a stronger connection between moral and political philosophy, which for de Ruggiero meant a stronger connection between life and philosophy.

De Ruggiero's Revision of Idealism: *La via più ardua*

Eventually de Ruggiero's demand for understanding the concrete problems of individuals led him to a complete revision of idealism. This revision was first announced in December 1928 in a 'Nota' to the third edition of *La filosofia contemporanea*.[158] In this note de Ruggiero criticises his conclusion of the first edition of this book as being an example of 'panphilosophism', which tended to resolve all activities of the spirit, art, religion, science, and history into the activity of pure thought, that is, into philosophy which interprets these activities. But unlike Gentile, de Ruggiero refused to let philosophy 'annul' or 'absorb' these activities within itself. Instead, he tried to show how each of these mental activities is philosophical by itself.[159] In this context de Ruggiero refers to 'La scienza come esperienza assoluta', *Problemi della vita morale*, and 'Arte e critica', where he claims to have clarified his own position with regard to Gentile's.

Looking back, de Ruggiero finds that his opposition to Gentile was not sufficiently elaborated. Whereas Gentile 'fell in a sort of acosmic nirvana, I, in order to save myself, fell into the opposite error of admitting a disintegrated plurality of experiences which were only united by an apparent common philosophy which circulates in them'.[160] But in both cases, de Ruggiero points out, the basic error was the same, and consisted of 'reducing the whole life of the spirit to an abstract logical scheme (subject, object, synthesis) which was elevated to a metaphysical principle'.[161] And by believing that by resolving every content of thought into the act that thinks it the whole reality spiritualises itself; whereas in fact it did nothing but affirm a mystic indifference to that content'.[162] In other words, de Ruggiero points out that Gentile and he both believed that all reality could be understood by showing that it was an act of thought without taking the content of thought into account.

De Ruggiero then claims that since 1921 he has convinced himself of three things. Firstly, he claims that the immediate transformation of Kant's criticism from a gnoseology into a metaphysics leaves the problem of the thing in itself and the problem of nature intact. Secondly, he is convinced that the 'object' of

---

[158] G. de Ruggiero, 'Nota' , in *La filosofia contemporanea*, terza edizione, 1928, 521–3.
[159] Ibid., 521.
[160] Ibid., 522.
[161] Ibid.
[162] Ibid.

thought only identifies itself with the act of thought on the condition that it is stripped of all its content, from which it follows that the doctrine of the pure act is more rigorous the emptier it is. Thirdly, de Ruggiero is convinced that the process by which mental experience organises itself cannot 'mingle' with the activity from which reality is constituted.[163] From this it follows that the metaphysics of the mind must follow a much more 'tiring' and 'arduous' way in order to establish the spirituality of the real; idealism should go *la via più ardua* (the more arduous way).[164]

These three points indicate in which direction *la via più ardua* goes. By his appreciation of the content of thought de Ruggiero acknowledges that this content makes a difference to the form of the act of thought; what we think makes a difference to how we think.[165] To take one of de Ruggiero's own examples; writing a sonnet and doing research through the microscope involves thinking, that is, questions and answers, but the questions of the poet are not those of the scientist because their objects are different. In order to find out this difference de Ruggiero indicates that being and thought should not be immediately identified by some simple formula, but that diverse activities of the mind by which being is known should be taken into account. According to de Ruggiero this *via ardua* has been followed by such thinkers as Bergson, Hamelin, Boutroux (1845-1921), Alexander, and Whitehead (1861-1947), who do not identify being and thought by a simple 'fiat', which does not expand our knowledge of reality. In this context de Ruggiero refers to his studies of these thinkers in *La Critica* which he published in *Filosofi del novecento* (*Philosophers of the Twentieth Century*) in 1933.

In this context, he records that none of the idealists whom he described in *La filosofia contemporanea* are still alive and that they have given way to the realists.[166] However, idealism is not dead in England, as the interest in Bergson and Croce shows, and in de Ruggiero's view the torch of British Idealism is carried further by Collingwood whom he describes as the first of a new generation of English idealists.[167] About Alexander and Whitehead he is mildly positive, and he is generally negative about the epigoni of realism, such as Russell, Moore, Broad, and others. More surprising is his admiration for Dewey, whose *Reconstruction in Philosophy* he translated in 1931, because in *La filosofia contemporanea* he had described pragmatism as 'the most disquieting symptom of the present

---

[163] Ibid.

[164] Ibid., 523.

[165] Here de Ruggiero makes the same objection as Holmes made in *The Idealism of Giovanni Gentile* that Gentile had proved the necessity of the dialectic but not that of its material: he could only describe the necessity of the form of the act of thought but not its content.

[166] G. de Ruggiero, *Filosofi del novecento*, Laterza, Bari, cited from quarta edizione, Laterza, Bari, 1950, 3.

[167] Ibid., 91.

state of philosophical thought'.[168] Other philosophers of *la via più ardua* are found in France with philosophers such as Hamelin (1856–1907) and Meyerson (1859–1933), but not in Germany. De Ruggiero is negative about 'pseudo-historicists' like Spengler and Dilthey, and he found Husserl's philosophy so boring that he only managed to get through it on the third attempt.

The fruit of de Ruggiero's confrontation with all these thinkers can best be illustrated by 'Science, History and Philosophy' of 1930.[169] The influence of British philosophy is very clear in this article. At the very beginning de Ruggiero points out that 'contacts between Italian and English thought of late years have been both frequent and effective'.[170] But in spite of these contacts the British have tended to concentrate on the problems of science, whereas the Italians have concentrated on history. This parting of the ways 'whose importance for the future of European speculation is very great' confronts contemporary philosophers with the question of whether science and history are really irreconcilably opposed to each other.[171] In this context de Ruggiero observes that several 'cross-references' between the two kinds of thought have taken place. In particular, philosophers in both countries have acknowledged Bergson's maxim that science should take 'time seriously'. He also approves of Alexander who had emphasised the importance of historical elements in science.[172] However, de Ruggiero warns that science and history should not be confused by comparing them as 'finished products'.[173] Only by comparing the mental categories that preside over scientific and historical thought will their distinctions be explained methodically. De Ruggiero thus explicitly proposes dealing with science and history as activities, or 'mental categories' as he says. De Ruggiero begins with the metaphysical underpinnings of both mental activities. Following Kant he points out that 'being in space' is the basis of natural science. Kant's analysis, however, 'must be revised and broadened if it is to do justice to the wider horizon of a theoretic spirit including historical as well as scientific knowledge'.[174] Dilthey and Croce had already given illuminating contributions towards a 'Critique of Historical Reason'.[175] In particular they had shown that history is not inferior to natural science by pointing out that 'its distinguishing characteristic is not fact as something merely recorded, but fact as something thought, something brought within the universal relations of thought'. But the question about the exact relationship between history and science is still left open because the two points of view have been examined separately with the result that there is no 'reciprocal

---

[168] G. de Ruggiero, *La filosofia contemporanea*, 302.

[169] G. de Ruggiero, 'Science, History and Philosophy', in *Philosophy*, 6, 1931, 166–79.

[170] Ibid., 166.

[171] Ibid., 167.

[172] Ibid.

[173] Ibid., 168.

[174] Ibid.

[175] Ibid.

understanding' between the *Critique of Pure Reason* and a 'Critique of Historical Reason'. De Ruggiero proposes to make a first step towards this understanding by establishing the differences between science and history.

As usual, he explicitly makes his analysis in terms of the logic of question and answer. About anything which is presented to us, in us, or experienced in time we can ask ourselves four questions; 1) whether it exists, 2) what it is, 3) why it exists, and 4) what it is worth. These questions correspond to the categories of modality, substance, causality, and value.[176] The categories are used by both science and history, that is, both science and history ask one of the four questions but they answer them in different ways. In the order of modality, scientific judgments are expressed in hypothetical form whereas historical judgments are always categorical. The category of substance is interpreted by science in terms of things, whereas in history it is in terms of activity. In science we find a deterministic causality and in history an intentional or teleological form of causality. Finally, the entities studied by science have no intrinsic value and acquire it only in so far as they are included in the entire system of entities; only the system has value and 'neutralises' the value of the parts which make it up. In contrast, in history only individual action, which differentiates itself from all other actions, counts.[177]

According to de Ruggiero, the opposition between science and history is not ultimate and should be overcome by philosophy. The most important task that confronts philosophy is therefore 'to follow the rhythm of these two mental forms in their development, to grasp their necessity and constructive value for the life of the spirit, and to arrive through this process at a view of the world at the same time single and articulated'. But if this is to be done, de Ruggiero says, the 'philosophers must first of all make up their minds to abandon their present fin de non recevoir with regard to dialectic'.[178]

Collingwood, who translated 'Science, History and Philosophy' for *Philosophy*, found it 'perhaps the best compte rendu that anyone has yet produced on the progress hitherto made towards a Critique of Historical Reason'.[179] Collingwood was better equipped than anyone else to judge its value because by 1930 he had been working on the theory of history himself for more than a decade and he knew de Ruggiero's philosophical development very well. Collingwood was therefore perfectly able to read between the lines of de Ruggiero's paper. When de Ruggiero pleads for a more dialectical point of view he knew of course that dialectic meant 'dialectic of question and answer'. Collingwood also understood that 'the rhythm of these two mental forms in their development' should also be interpreted in these terms, thus forming the basis of the 'single and

---

[176] Ibid., 171.

[177] Ibid., 171–6.

[178] Ibid., 178.

[179] R.G. Collingwood, 'Letters to Guido de Ruggiero', Dep. 27, 9 January 1931.

articulated view of the world'. Most importantly, Collingwood knew that this view of the world had very strong moral and political implications which formed the basis of de Ruggiero's liberalism. This liberalism is most clearly expressed in the following description of the individual:

> What counts is the individual, not of course the atomic individual, but the individualised action which differentiates itself from all other actions. And general ideas count just so far as they are fused with this individual and help to differentiate it. Individuals do not all stand on the same plane as historical agents; the more the individual can absorb into himself of the world in which he lives, the more his action asserts itself as an individual expression of collective desires and demands and aspirations and the greater is its historical importance. In consequence, what is historically true is not general ideas but their individual embodiments.[180]

In this description of the individual action we recognise de Ruggiero's notion of 'liberal method'; the latter was based on 'mutual understanding', the former on the 'absorption' of 'collective desires, demands and aspiration'. According to de Ruggiero, this 'absorption' is based on historical thought which is 'individuating thought' whereas science is 'abstracting thought'. This connection between individual action and historical thought confirms my contention that the method of liberalism is ultimately based on history.

In 'Science, History and Philosophy' de Ruggiero laid the metaphysical basis for history as a question and answer activity by describing the categories that differentiate it from science. Collingwood did not completely agree with de Ruggiero's approach, because he found that de Ruggiero equated science and history too much. This shows that he certainly understood that the next step in the theory of history was to establish a logic of historical thought. Collingwood knew that de Ruggiero had elaborated this logic for art, science, and morality, but not yet for history. However, de Ruggiero had described parts of this logic and its implications in the volumes of his *Storia della filosofia* which Collingwood found a most brilliant synthesis of philology and philosophy, taking it as an example for his own later philosophy.[181]

De Ruggiero's Historiography

De Ruggiero's theory of history is embodied in his in *Storia del liberalismo europeo*, his history of philosophy, and in particular in his newspaper articles, in which he tries to understand daily life and the 'lower' forms of thought and action. Croce always disdained de Ruggiero's journalistic activities as 'vulgar' and 'unphilosophical'. However, de Ruggiero's journalism is completely consistent with his general philosophy; the vindication of the individual involves the notion that every individual must be understood in its own terms. The artist and

---

[180] G. de Ruggiero, 'Science, History and Philosophy', 175–6.
[181] R.G. Collingwood, 'Letters to Guido de Ruggiero', Dep. 27, 12 June 1937.

the philosopher, the scientist and the historian, the child and the adult, the soldier on the front and the politician in the parliament, they all have their place under the sun as self-realising individuals. They are all self-conscious beings and have a right to be understood. This means that history must adopt many perspectives, to understand every individual from his own perspective.

This view of the value of history explains the differences between Gentile's and Croce's histories on the one hand, and de Ruggiero's on the other. Gentile's histories deal, for the most part, with philosophers and men of culture as the embodiments of the concrete universal, the transcendental ego. The majority of the heroes of Croce's ethico-political history are for the most part political geniuses and conscientious men who realise the ethical universal. De Ruggiero's histories are much more diverse. For example, in *L'impero britannico dopo la guerra* he deals with the opinion of the man in the street, the newspapers, the problems of agriculture, the Irish problem, and so forth.

When he deals with the 'higher' forms of thought in his *Storia della filosofia*, de Ruggiero's approach has many perspectives. Unlike Gentile, who tends to present the history of philosophy as one big development towards actualism, de Ruggiero presents all philosophers as individuals who raise their problems on the basis of solutions given by previous philosophers in order to hand over their own solutions to next generations. De Ruggiero's history thus forms a perfect illustration of his dialectic of questions and answers. When discussing a philosopher, de Ruggiero always begins with his life and times in order to determine the central problems of his work. For example, in his *Filosofia del cristianesimo* de Ruggiero gives a very intricate analysis of the ways in which the problems of Albert the Great and Thomas of Aquinas were linked to those of Augustine.[182] The same pluriperspectivism led de Ruggiero to realms of thought which had never been discussed at length by other historians of philosophy. His discussion of Roman philosophy on the basis of their jurisprudence is an example of the case, just as is his discussion of Jesus's teachings.[183] More striking are his discussions of alchemy, astrology, and medicine and their relation to Renaissance philosophy. On the basis of the same principle he dedicated a separate volume to Vico and Kant whose problems are thus differentiated from those of other philosophers in the eighteenth century.[184]

De Ruggiero also applies the dialectic of questions and answers in the interpretation of texts. He keeps very close to the language of the philosophers he is dealing with and does not use of all kinds of anachronistic terms. Despite this, he is well aware that the historian must use modern language in order to explain

---

[182] G. de Ruggiero, *La filosofia del cristianesimo*, vol. I, Laterza, Bari, 1920, cited from terza edizione, Laterza, Bari, 1941, 121–2.

[183] Ibid., 16–39, 96–122.

[184] G. de Ruggiero, *Da Vico a Kant*, Laterza, Bari, 1937, cited from quarta edizione, Laterza, Bari, 1952.

the texts to the public. For this reason he rejects the approach that says 'let the sources speak for themselves'. According to de Ruggiero, the dilemma can only be solved by studying the historiography of a period:

> Each history is always, in one way or another, a history of histories. It is an illusion that it is possible to approach, with a virgin eye and mind, the study of the sources. The sources themselves are, on their turn, visions and perspectives of others; and we, when we examine them, rethink them along the whole tradition which has transmitted them to us.[185]

For de Ruggiero, true history is not the product of a 'clash' between the source and the historian, but it is the product of a tradition in which the historian relates his own perspective to that of the source and that of historiographical tradition. In *Rinascimento, Riforma e Controriforma* (*Renaissance, Reform and Counter Reform*) he remarks that the political and ecclesiastical problems of the fourteenth century are found 'encapsulated in the sources', so that an 'historical narration' which tries to group them around the conflicts between Philip IV and Boniface VIII, and between John XXII and Benedict XII, will certainly be dramatic, but only at the risk of 'confounding many distinct things'.[186]

De Ruggiero also applies the dialectic of question and answer when he discusses the epistemological and metaphysical problems of historical thought. On the first page of the first volume of *La filosofia greca*, de Ruggiero begins with 'the problem of the origin of philosophy', which de Ruggiero solves by disentangling all kinds of sub-problems about the nature of philosophy, the relationship of Greece with the Orient, its historiography, and the concepts on which it has been based. The most striking example of a discussion of historiographic principles is found in *Rinascimento, Riforma e Controriforma* which was published in 1930, two years after the note in which de Ruggiero called for the revision of idealism. In the introduction to the book de Ruggiero begins with a criticism of the view that the Middle Ages declined very rapidly in order to make way for the Renaissance. In de Ruggiero's opinion this erroneous view of the passage from the Middle Ages to the Renaissance is due to our tendency to 'accentuate the importance of that which is nearer to our life'.[187] This same tendency leads to all kinds of histories filled with 'anticipations and deifications as if an entire era only lived for preparing another'.[188] According to de Ruggiero, it is inconceivable that a whole civilisation is outstretching in one great attempt to realise progress; conservative forces are also necessary. In this context, he rejects Burckhardt's (1818–1897) interpretation of the Renaissance as the age of the individual, by pointing

---

[185] G. de Ruggiero, *La filosofia greca*, Laterza, Bari, 1918, cited from quinta edizione, Laterza, Bari, 1943, 52.

[186] G. de Ruggiero, *Rinascimento, Riforma e Controriforma*, Laterza, Bari, 1930, cited from ottava edizione, Laterza, Bari, 1966, 41.

[187] Ibid., 8.

[188] Ibid.

out that the modern concept of the individual was unknown in that era in which medieval scholasticism remained stable for a long time.[189] With his emphasis on the permanency of historical processes de Ruggiero not only rejected Burckhardt's anachronisms but also those of Gentile whose Fascist histories have even more 'anticipations and deifications' than that of the Swiss historian.

Conclusion

Croce's, Gentile's, and de Ruggiero's discussion of aesthetics in the early years of the decade led to some new solutions for the problem of the relationship between art and philosophy, imagination and thought. These solutions had important implications for the interpretation of language in general and of historical sources in particular. In this context Croce's identification of art with a process of positing and solving problems must be mentioned, as well as Gentile's interesting theory of interpretation as 'self-translation'. De Ruggiero's notion of an historical understanding of the significance of language was especially important, as well as his theory of the 'inversion of time' which called for a reconsideration of the priority of the act of thought.

The rise of Fascism did not lead the three thinkers to far-reaching revisions of their moral and political philosophy. As we have seen, Gentile and Croce did not radically change their views on these matters nor did their views on the value of history differ much from their pre-war opinions. Gentile's philosophy of history must be seen as a continuation of his *Sistema di logica* of 1923, and his Fascist historiography is completely in accordance with his views of the value of history in the ethical state. In the same way, Croce's ethico-political histories fell entirely within the principles of his *Filosofia dello spirito*. Only de Ruggiero explicitly revised his philosophy by vindicating the importance of the individual even more than he had ever done before. This revision had very strong practical motives and eventually led to his appeal for a revision of idealism as a whole. But even de Ruggiero continued what he had begun in 1912. His *Storia del liberalismo europeo* must be seen as a vindication of the individual against the assaults from totalitarianism, and his 'Science, History and Philosophy' is the theoretical counterpart to it. In conjunction with Croce's 'religion of liberty' de Ruggiero's works still form a very strong defence of liberalism.

On the more fundamental theoretical level none of the three philosophers really changed much. In his *Nuovi saggi* Croce still advocated a modest anti-metaphysical constructivism based on Vico's *verum et factum convertuntur*. Gentile, in his philosophy of history and in his moral and political writings, still expressed the same more radical constructivism which he had elaborated before his adherence to Fascism. This constructivism was the theoretical basis of Gentile's Fascist historiography which is characterised by its focus on 'anticipations' and 'precursors'.

---

[189] Ibid., 8–11.

Finally, de Ruggiero, who with his theory of the 'inversion of time' came close to abandoning the logical and ontological priority of the act of thought, still clung onto it in his histories; only at the end of the 1920s to leave the priority of the act of thought to embark on *la via più ardua*. From then, he then explicitly rejected the kind of 'anticipation' history Gentile practised and sought to understand the permanency of historical processes. Far away, Collingwood had already discovered this idea of the living past for himself and in the next chapter we will see how he elaborated this idea in the 1920s.

Chapter Seven

Collingwood's Middle Development (1918–1930)

Introduction

'The War ended, I came back to Oxford an opponent of the "realists".'[1] Thus Collingwood began a new chapter in his life which he called 'The Decay of Realism' in his autobiography. Around 1912, Collingwood had already developed serious doubts about the realists' 'positive doctrines' and 'critical methods'. During the war, he discovered the necessary connection between these doctrines and methods while meditating on the ugliness of the Albert Memorial. The first result of this was *Truth and Contradiction* of 1917 in which he criticised all existent theories of truth.[2]

Collingwood's concerns were not merely epistemological. Already before the war he realised that there was also a connection between the realist epistemology and its moral and political philosophy. According to their principle that nothing is affected by being known, realists taught their pupils that moral philosophy cannot affect action.[3] Confronted with the atrocities of the First World War, this doctrine had become completely indigestible for Collingwood. In his view, the war was a triumph for natural science, but a disgrace to the human intellect, exemplifying the contrast between the success of the modern mind in controlling nature and its inability to control human affairs.[4] The war thus showed the necessity for a 'new science of human affairs' that would give men 'insight' in human situations.[5] This 'new science' could not be the old 'scissors-and-paste history', but had to be a new kind of history.[6]

The main task of this new history was to discover the 'living past', or the presence of the past in the present. According to Collingwood, the historian should inform people how the past, 'its ostensible subject-matter, was encapsulated in the present and constituted a part of it not at once obvious to the

---

1   R.G. Collingwood, *An Autobiography*, 44.
2   See chapter 5, pp. 158–163.
3   R.G. Collingwood, *An Autobiography*, 48–9.
4   Ibid., 90–1.
5   Ibid., 92, 101–06, 115.
6   Ibid., 99–100.

untrained eye', just as the trained woodsman can discern a tiger in the grass.[7] The new history would be closest to practical life, for it could bring 'a trained eye for the situation in which one has to act' in moral and political life.[8] Driven by this ideal, Collingwood threw off his 'diffidence of youth', and fighting the realists openly, he laid down the 'foundations of the future'.[9]

In his autobiography, Collingwood precisely describes the steps of this development. In 1920, he formulated in the 'Libellus de generatione' his first principle of the philosophy of history, according to which history is to be seen as a process which is still living in the present.[10] Collingwood took the next step in 1928, when he formulated two propositions upon which he founded his philosophy of history. The first proposition is: 'All history is the history of thought'; and the second: 'historical knowledge is the re-enactment in the historian's mind of the thought whose history he is studying.'[11] Finally, around 1930, he formulated a third proposition: 'Historical knowledge is the re-enactment of a past thought encapsulated in a context of present thoughts which, by contradicting it, confine it to a plane different from theirs.'[12] With this third proposition, which has become known as the 'encapsulation theory', Collingwood solved the problem that had bothered him most, namely, the problem of the identity and difference between past and present thought. In his autobiography, Collingwood claims that with the encapsulation theory he completed the foundation for the new science of human affairs. Shortly after 1930 he conceived the plan to write a philosophical series on the basis of his concept of history.[13]

On the basis of Collingwood's manuscripts, held in the Bodleain Library since 1978, Collingwood's account of his own development has largely been corroborated. Analysing the lectures on the philosophy of history of 1926 and 1928, van der Dussen reconstructed the genesis of Collingwood's philosophy of history of the 1920s.[14] Along the same lines, Dray dedicated a whole chapter of his book on re-enactment to Collingwood's development in the same period.[15] Boucher, Helgeby, Connelly, and others reconstructed the development of Collingwood's moral and political thought in the same period, and showed that it had close connections with his philosophy of history.[16]

---

[7]   Ibid., 100, 106.
[8]   Ibid., 100.
[9]   Ibid., 89.
[10] Ibid., 97–8.
[11] Ibid., 110, 112.
[12] Ibid., 114.
[13] Ibid., 115–9.
[14] Van der Dussen, *History as a Science*, 25–41.
[15] William H. Dray, *History as Re-enactment, R.G. Collingwood's Idea of History*, Clarendon Press, Oxford, 1995, 229–70.
[16] Boucher, *The Social and Political Philosophy of R.G. Collingwood*, 80–93; Stein Helgeby, *Action as History: The Historical Thought of R.G. Collingwood*, Imprint Academic, Exeter,

In spite of these contributions to a better understanding of Collingwood's development, some problems are still unresolved. In the first place, the relationship between Collingwood's notion of the living past, the re-enactment doctrine, and the encapsulation theory remains puzzling. Collingwood's terminology suggests that there is a relationship, because he uses the term 'encapsulation' both in connection with the notion of the living past and in connection to the encapsulation theory. In his definition of the living past, Collingwood says that the 'traces' of a process P_1 in the present are not the 'corpse of a dead P_1 but rather the real P_1 itself, living and active though encapsulated within the other form of itself P_2'.[17] However, Collingwood's 'third proposition' does not seem to be related to this notion of the living past but to the re-enactment doctrine, since it expresses the idea that past thought lives 'encapsulated' in present thought.[18] However, the connection between the two uses of 'encapsulation' is far from clear. Van der Dussen, who pays attention to both the first principle and to the encapsulation theory, gives no indication of a possible connection between the two, and Dray finds most of Collingwood's talk about the 'living past' barely intelligible.[19]

In the second place, it is not clear how the notion of the living past and the three propositions should be related to practice. Collingwood's own remarks about the relationship between the 'new history' and practice are vague, but it is clear that he thought that the most important task of the new science of human affairs was to discover how the past is encapsulated in the present. But again, how this insight in the 'encapsulated past' may help men in dealing with human situations is far from clear.

In the third place, it is not clear how the notion of the living past and the three propositions of his philosophy of history should be related to the rest of Collingwood's development. In his autobiography, Collingwood suggests that he had developed the principle of the living past before 1920, and we have seen that an early form of the idea appears in *Religion and Philosophy* of 1916.[20] Moreover, that book also contains an embryonic form of the re-enactment theory. However, Collingwood does not indicate how these earlier views were related to his later views.

Last but not least, in his autobiography Collingwood remains silent about the role of the Italians in his development in the 1920s. This is most surprising, because the Italians are present both in his published and unpublished works. Notably, Collingwood's first article on the philosophy of history is a review of

---

2004; James Connelly, *Metaphysics, Method and Politics: The Political Philosophy of R.G. Colingwood*, Imprint Academic, Exeter, 2003.

[17]   R.G. Collingwood, *An Autobiography*, 98.

[18]   Ibid., 113.

[19]   Van der Dussen, *History as a Science*, 53, 72, 77–8; 269. Dray, *History as Re-enactment*, 252.

[20]   R.G. Collingwood, *An Autobiography*, 97–8; See chapter 5, pp. 143–144.

the English translation of Croce's *Teoria e storia della storiografia*.[21] Moreover, contacts with the Italians both by letter and in person were frequent and inspiring. Yet of all his contacts, Collingwood only mentions de Ruggiero and Gentile in his autobiography.[22] Even more surprising is the fact that Collingwood does not discuss Gentile´s thought, because the three basic propositions of his philosophy of history have a definite actualist ring to them. The two propositions that 'all history is the history of thought' and that 'historical knowledge is the re-enactment in the historian's mind of the thought he is studying' come very close to the doctrines which Gentile had been expounding since 1912. Moreover, Gentile had also dealt with the problem of the identity and difference between past and present thought and formulated a solution in his *Sistema di logica*. The fact that Gentile had already elaborated these ideas raises some important questions concerning his role in Collingwood's development. Did Collingwood really develop a position of his own, or was he only discovering that Gentile had been right all the time so that the only thing he had to do was to properly translate his works? However, if the latter were the case, why did it take more than eight years to formulate the three propositions of his own philosophy of history?

In this chapter, I will answer these questions by describing the three stages of Collingwood's middle development. Firstly, I will deal with Collingwood's criticism of the Italians in 'Libellus de generatione', the essay in which he formulated the principle of the 'living past'. Secondly, I will discuss *Speculum Mentis*, which contains the first form of his philosophy of the spirit. Finally, I will discuss Collingwood's elaboration of his philosophy of history in the second half of the decade.

Collingwood's Settlement with Croce (1920)

In the beginning of the 1920s, there was a lot of work in progress on Italian philosophy in England. Croce's *Ariosto, Shakespeare e Corneille*, and *Teoria e storia della storiografia* were translated in 1920. At the same time, J.A. Smith gave lectures on Croce and Gentile in Oxford and at the Aristotelian Society. Wildon Carr was translating Gentile's *Teoria generale dello spirito come atto puro*, and Dino Bigongiari *La riforma dell´ educazione*.[23] Bosanquet reviewed several works by Gentile and in 1921 he finished his last work, *The Meeting of Extremes*, which deals extensively with both Croce and Gentile.

Collingwood concentrated on the translation of de Ruggiero's *La filosofia contemporanea* and 'La scienza come esperienza assoluta', which indicates that he was more interested in the latest developments of Italian idealism. This interest

---

[21] R.G. Collingwood, 'Croce's Philosophy of History', in *The Hibbert Journal*, 19, 1921, 263–78, cited from id., *Essays in the Philosophy of History*, 5–22.

[22] R.G. Collingwood, *An Autobiography*, 99; id., 'Libellus de Generatione', 1920, Dep. 28.

[23] Harris, 'Introduction', 53.

is illustrated by the letter he wrote to de Ruggiero in July 1920, who was to visit Oxford in two months:

> My translation of your Scienza, just finished, was undertaken only to help myself to a fuller understanding of the thesis: I would most willingly publish it, for I have seen nothing that seems to me so good or so useful on this problem, which is, I think the central problem in philosophy today… To me your book has been a new inspiration; it has confirmed and defined ideas towards which I have long been travelling, and if I dared be so bold I should say that in you I for the first time find and possess myself.[24]

Collingwood was sincere when he wrote this. Like de Ruggiero, he had been working on the empirical and *a priori* principles of the question and answer activity in both archeology and philosophy. Seen in this context, de Ruggiero's 'La scienza come esperienza assoluta', based on the principle of the identity of *scienza* and *coscienza* and its focus on a dialectic of questions and answers, did indeed 'confirm' and 'define' Collingwood's own ideas.

Just two days after this letter Collingwood wrote 'Notes on Croce's Philosophy', a manuscript in which he settled his accounts with Croce on the basis of these newly confirmed ideas. In this manuscript Collingwood tried to get to grips with the metaphysical underpinnings of Croce's explicitly anti-metaphysical philosophy. As in 1912, Collingwood holds that Croce's 'attitude to philosophy and the spirit is anti-idealistic', and he repeats his earlier view that his philosophy 'is all realism'.[25] According to Collingwood, Croce's realism is best revealed by the full title of his system which is *Filosofia come scienza dello spirito*. This title, Collingwood says, indicates that philosophy is the only true science of the spirit because in Croce's system proper science is never true, but only useful.[26] Croce's view of philosophy as a science implies that science and philosophy can be set side by side and compared on the basis of some 'third principle'.[27] According to Collingwood, this principle must be something like thought, which is identified by Croce with philosophy *tout court*. In the end, Collingwood says, this position amounts to 'realism' and 'naturalism' because it reduces the mind to an object to be 'described' and 'inspected' by the philosopher from the outside.[28] Collingwood concludes that this view of philosophy is self-contradictory, because by reducing the mind to an object, philosophy reduces itself to the status of science, as the title of Croce's system reveals.

This criticism of Croce's philosophy reveals that Collingwood had come closer to the actualist method of immanence. Like the actualists, he acknowledged that reality is a process. Accordingly, he rejected all Croce's sharp distinc-

---

24 R.G. Collingwood, 'Letters to Guido de Ruggiero', 1 July 1920.
25 R.G. Collingwood, 'Notes on Croce's Philosophy', 1920, Dep. 19/1, 1, 4.
26 See chapter 2, p. 42.
27 R.G. Collingwood, 'Notes on Croce's Philosophy', 1.
28 Ibid., 2.

tions by showing that they inevitably end up in a *coincidentia oppositorum*. In the above-mentioned case he shows that Croce begins by distinguishing science and philosophy and ends by merging them completely. That it is the method of immanence behind this kind of analysis is revealed at the end of the manuscript in which Collingwood raises the question of which direction philosophy should take after Croce:

> What is the lesson of all this? That philosophy which regards itself as the description ab extra of an object called the spirit is self-condemned. But is not all philosophy this? For surely there must be a theory of the spirit, if the spirit exists: or are we to take refuge in materialism or the Realists' fantastic denial of a theory of knowledge — for that is the same thing as denying the existence of a philosophy of the spirit? How can there be any philosophy which does not claim to be the study of an object known as mind? The answer to this is that, whereas for a dualistic realist 'the mind' exists in a world consisting partly of things which are not mind, for an idealist there is nowhere a distinction between the mind and its other. For a dualistic realist there are only various empirical sciences, including psychology or the science of mind: but idealism just exists to deny that the world is divisible into minds and other things. The mind is the world, or if you like, the world is the mind: the mind is the act of thought in which the object exists and nowhere else.[29]

In the last lines of this passage, Collingwood formulates the metaphysical principle on the basis of which he rejects all other philosophies, including Croce's, as being realist. According to this principle there is no distinction between 'things' and 'mind', or between object and subject, since reality is a process in which mind and its object form an inseparable unity. From this it follows that philosophy can never study mind as an object; being immanent in mind, philosophy is the self-conscious aspect of all mental activity. This view entails that philosophy cannot be distinguished from other mental activities; philosophy is immanent in the activities themselves. On this basis, Collingwood concludes that the mental activities cannot be 'contemplated from without' but they must be 'understood from within'; the philosopher must 'live himself into' the activities which he tries to understand.[30]

Collingwood wrote his 'Notes on Croce's Philosophy' most probably in order to prepare 'Croce's Philosophy of History', a review of the English translation of *Teoria e storia della storiografia*. The most interesting aspect of this review is how Collingwood presents his criticism of Croce to an English speaking public. As in the manuscript, he criticises Croce's philosophy of the spirit as a form of naturalism and realism but, having his readers in mind, he does not discuss the metaphysics of Croce's position.[31] Nor does Collingwood expound the metaphysics of the mind as pure act on which his own criticism is based, although his

---

[29] Ibid., 3–4.
[30] Ibid., 3.
[31] R.G. Collingwood, 'Croce's Philosophy of History', 7.

analysis of Croce's philosophy of history implicitly builds on those of Gentile and de Ruggiero, as he explicitly admitted in a letter to the latter.[32] Like the actualists, Collingwood directs most of his criticism to Croce's distinction between annals and history in order to discover the basic fallacy of the thought that underlies his other doctrines, in particular the doctrines of the positivity of history, progress, and the relationship between science, history, and philosophy.

The main target of Collingwood's criticism is Croce's distinction between annals and history as 'dead past' and 'living past'. Croce himself used these terms in order to indicate the difference between annals or chronicles and history; annals are the dead past, they are not thought but will, history is the 'living past', or actual thought that brings the dead past to life.[33] Despite the fact that Croce's position comes very close to the actualist view of history, Collingwood criticises and revises it as follows:

> The distinction between history and annals is now not a distinction between what history is (thought) and what history is not (will), but between one act of thought (history) and another act of thought of the same kind, now super-seded and laid aside (annals), between the half-truth of an earlier stage in the process of thought and the fuller truth that succeeds it. This is no dualism, no relation between A and not-A, and therefore it cannot be symbolized by the naturalistic terminology of thought and will: it is the dialectical relation between two phases of one and the same development, which is throughout a process of both thinking and willing.[34]

Again, this criticism is based on the metaphysics of the mind as expounded in Collingwood's preparatory manuscript. It is in accordance with the actualist view that if reality is thought that develops itself by reflecting upon itself, no part of reality may be identified with dead matter, will, nature, or error. From this it follows that annals cannot be seen as a useful abstraction from history made for practical ends, or as 'error' as Croce holds, because they contain thoughts that can be understood and criticised by present thoughts. Collingwood expresses the same criticism in linguistic terms; annals are not 'empty symbols' to which history gives a meaning, but they have a meaning in themselves, which must be understood by the historian.[35] In other words, the past is not 'dead', but it is 'living' in the evidence; 'annals are only history whose words mean less indeed than the same words as used by history proper, but still have meaning, are still essentially vehicles of thought.'[36] From this view it follows that the past is not contemporary, because it goes on in the mind of the historian, as Croce holds, but it is contemporary because it is embodied in the evidence which must be interpreted by the historian.

---

[32] R.G. Collingwood, 'Letters to Guido de Ruggiero', 20 March 1921.
[33] See chapter 2, p. 65.
[34] R.G. Collingwood, 'Croce's Philosophy of History', 10.
[35] Ibid., 7.
[36] Ibid.

At first glance, this criticism seems to express a minor difference between Croce and Collingwood's positions, but it is in fact based on a profound metaphysical difference. The most fundamental of these is that Croce distinguishes between the mind as a process of thought (the historian) and its object. The object is therefore not thought but something 'given' to the historian. In contrast, Collingwood identifies reality with the act of thought, from which it follows that mind and its object can only be seen as two aspects of a single process of thought. For this reason Collingwood cannot interpret annals, or evidence, as a 'given' object, as Croce implicitly does by identifying them with the 'dead past'. In Collingwood's view, evidence must be seen as an expression of genuine thought which enables the historian to understand the past. The past is not dead, but it lives on in the evidence.

This idea of the 'living past' is the first principle of Collingwood's philosophy of history. Here we find it in its empirical form, that is, the past living on in the evidence. However, this empirical notion of the living past is based on Collingwood's interpretation of the metaphysics of the pure act of thought according to which mind and object form two aspects of a single process, from which it follows that not only the subject but also the object must be seen as a living process. This metaphysics gave Collingwood a key to reject and modify the whole series of doctrines which make up Croce's *Teoria e storia della storiografia*. Collingwood's strategy in this is clear: whenever Croce makes a distinction between two concepts, Collingwood stands up to stress their unity. For example, when Croce distinguishes between truth and error, or true and pseudo-history, Collingwood repeats the main conclusion of his own *Truth and Contradiction*, that 'truth and falsehood are inextricably united in every judgement, in so far as it creates itself by criticising another, and becomes itself in turn the object of further criticism'.[37] When Croce holds that history never condemns because the historian can only explain what he understands, Collingwood points out that when we rethink Caesar's thoughts, we become his contemporaries and judge him positively or negatively.[38] Along the same lines, he condemns Croce's view of progress as the change from the good to the better when seen from the right point of view by pointing out that there are many points of view and that there is no real distinction between the right and the wrong point of view.[39] Finally, Collingwood applies the metaphysics of the pure act of thought to the relation between philosophy and history. According to Croce, philosophy must be seen as the methodology of history, or the elaboration of concepts. In Collingwood's view this position implies a distinction between philosophy and history or philology, between ideas and facts. Referring to Gentile, Collingwood points out that

---

[37]　Ibid., 12.
[38]　Ibid., 14–5.
[39]　Ibid., 16.

ideas are never separated from facts; philosophy and philology are two identical forms of activity, each piece of thinking is always both at once.[40]

Some interpreters have pointed out that we find the beginnings of Collingwood's mature philosophy of history in his criticism of Croce, most notably the idea of the living past and the beginning of the re-enactment doctrine.[41] To this I wish to add that Collingwood's relationship with Croce shows a great continuity with his own early development. As we have seen in chapter 5, Collingwood criticised Croce for his misunderstanding of the concept of process as early as 1912, and he rejected Croce's doctrine of the contemporaneity of the past on first reading it in 1917. In the same year he also criticised Croce's theory of error in *Truth and Contradiction*, in which he developed his notion of error as being a form of truth which forms the basis of his rejection of the distinction between annals and history.

Moreover, Collingwood's earliest criticism of Croce was based on a metaphysics of process, which was not completely identical with the metaphysics of mind as pure act of thought. For the rest of his life, beginning with the 'Libellus', written in the same month as the review of *Teoria e storia della storiografia*, this metaphysics of process would form the basis of his philosophy of history. For this reason, Croce's view that Collingwood was an actualist in the 1920s must be rejected.[42] Though Collingwood mentions Gentile and de Ruggiero at the end of his review as Croce's successors, his notion of the past as 'living on' in present evidence does not fit in the actualist dialectic of the *pensante* and *pensato*.[43] Stated in actualist terms, Collingwood claims that annals contain a *pensante* within themselves, that is, evidence expresses concrete thought or a meaning that must be interpreted by the historian. From this viewpoint, Collingwood could only recognise a part of his own position in Gentile's and de Ruggiero's actualism, but at the same time he could not completely identify with it. How much his position actually differed from theirs will be made clear in the next section where we will deal with Collingwood's 'Libellus de generatione', where he came to terms with actualism on the basis of his interpretation of the living past.

The Sketch: 'Libellus de Generatione' (1920)

Collingwood wrote the 'Libellus de Generatione' from the 20–23 July 1920 for Guido de Ruggiero, who would visit Oxford in September. In a letter to the Italian Collingwood wrote that 'it is a little philosophical essay, it is very rough and incomplete, a mere sketch written in a few days, but I should be very much honoured if you would accept it from me in gratitude for all that your work has

---

40 Ibid., 20.

41 Van der Dussen, *History as a Science*, 25. Dray, *History as Re-enactment*, 33.

42 B. Croce, 'In commemorazione di un amico inglese, compagno di pensiero e di fede, R.G. Collingwood', 28–9.

43 R.G. Collingwood, 'Croce's Philosophy of History', 20–2.

done for me'.[44] Collingwood's gratitude is reflected in the subtitle of the 'Libellus' which reads 'An Essay in Absolute Empiricism', which was the name de Ruggiero had given to his own philosophy. Right at the beginning of the essay Collingwood traces his position back to Hume:

> In giving it this title I intend to emphasize its connexion with the Empiricism of Hume; a connexion consisting in the absolute denial of any such concept as substance and the resolution of all reality into the actuality of experience.[45]

Collingwood here explicitly agrees with de Ruggiero's thesis in *La filosofia contemporanea* that the empiricism of Hume and his followers was not 'absolute' because 'it failed entirely to achieve a clear statement of its own principles'.[46] From this verdict it appears that Collingwood saw absolute empiricism as a philosophy which tries to understand the principles on which experience is based. De Ruggiero had described this aim as the 'identity of *coscienza* and *scienza*', or consciousness and knowledge, or actual experience and the principles on which it rests.[47] Referring to de Ruggiero, Collingwood holds that 'the true successors of Hume are to be found not in England but in Germany, not in Mill and his school but in Kant and his'.[48] Collingwood describes his attitude to Mill's followers as follows:

> My relation to the new realism may be worth a word or two. I was brought up in it, in the first flush of its success at Oxford, and as the pupil of that brilliant and stimulating teacher John Cook Wilson I think I entered rather deeply into its spirit. I wrote a book working out some of its principles; and found it totally incapable of dealing with some fundamental difficulties. This led me to a close criticism of its methods and results, and finally to a complete abandonment of, at least, the latter. At the same time I look back on my apprenticeship to it with gratitude, as setting me free from the crude empiricisms of the nineteenth century and from a great deal of loose thought which presents an empiricism of this kind under the label of Idealism.[49]

Collingwood's description of the development of his relationship with the realists corroborates his own account in his autobiography. Interestingly, he does not say that he was a realist himself, but that he 'entered deeply into its spirit' only to discover that it was not consistent. Moreover, the passage strikingly suggests that Collingwood used the term realism not only for criticising the crude empiricism of the nineteenth century, but also some forms of idealism. That Collingwood did not uncritically accept the doctrine's of Kant's followers is most clearly illustrated by the following passage:

---

[44] R.G. Collingwood, 'Letters to Guido de Ruggiero', 1 July 1920.
[45] R.G. Collingwood, 'Libellus de Generatione', 1.
[46] Ibid.
[47] See chapter 4, p. 95.
[48] R.G. Collingwood, 'Libellus de Generatione', 1.
[49] Ibid., 2.

> And yet the title of absolute idealism contains a suggestion of what I have
> called 'subjectivism', which I would willingly avoid. I find even the modern
> Italian idealists, who to my mind represent the greatest and most lively con-
> structive effort of modern philosophy, tinged with this subjectivism, which I
> regard as belonging to realism rather than to what I should like idealism to
> be.[50]

Seen in the context of Collingwood's development, his claim that Italian idealism is a form of realism is not surprising as long as it concerns Croce because he
had held that his philosophy is realist in essence since 1912. But Collingwood
speaks about modern idealism in general and this obviously includes Gentile
and de Ruggiero. These two philosophers saw themselves as the champions of
absolute immanentism as Collingwood himself had acknowledged at the end of
his review of the English translation of Croce's *Teoria e storia della storiografia*.
Collingwood's suggestion that even the actualists are at heart realists is therefore
most surprising. In order to throw some light on these puzzles, I shall first discuss what Collingwood meant by 'realism' in the 'Libellus', then I shall deal with
the ways in which Collingwood applied his criticism of realism to the Italian
idealists. Finally I shall discuss how Collingwood established his own position
with regards to the Italian idealism.

The Dissolution of Realism

In his autobiography, Collingwood describes the 'Libellus' both as a 'study of
the nature and implications of process or becoming' and as an 'attack on realism'.[51] The 'Libellus' itself corroborates Collingwood's description. It consists of
two parts. The first is called the 'world of being' which contains a chapter on 'the
dissolution of realism'. The second part is called 'world of becoming' which
contains an analysis of the categories of becoming and discussion of the relationship between the new world of becoming and the old world of being.

On the first page of the 'Libellus' Collingwood describes the world of becoming as follows:

> My fundamental doctrine is that reality is becoming, that is to say, reality not
> so much is as happens; which implies that the reality of mind is the process of
> its experience, its life, and nothing else. Nor do I admit any dualism between
> mind and its object such that while mind is wholly process its object can be
> conceived as a static whole outside it. The object is process too, and these are
> not two processes but one process.[52]

In the 'Libellus', Collingwood presents realism as the opposite of absolute empiricism. In his view realism is the philosophy of 'the world of being' which has
dominated civilisation from Plato to the present where it still is the philosophy

---

[50]　Ibid., 1–2.
[51]　R.G. Collingwood, *An Autobiography*, 99.
[52]　R.G. Collingwood, 'Libellus de Generatione', 1.

of the 'man in the street and the man behind the plough'.[53] The world of being is fundamentally a world of things, not of processes; whatever exists, exists as a thing. Logically, Collingwood points out, this view leads to the eradication of opposites and the establishment of distinctions.[54] According to Collingwood, the logic of distinctions infects the epistemology of the world of being with realism, which interprets subject and object as two independent things connected by a knowledge-relation. This is the position Collingwood calls realism. It has two forms, objectivism and subjectivism, according to the way in which reality is interpreted. Collingwood illustrates both positions on the basis of an argument which typically proceeds in the form of questions and answers.

For the objectivist only the object is real and the subject is fundamentally unreal. For this reason the objectivist faces difficulties when we ask him: 'what is the subject?' The objectivist can answer this question only in terms of the object. Collingwood illustrates the objectivist's answer as follows:

> For if there is a mind which is wholly contemplative of (say) the circle & its properties, then the nature or character of that mind at that time is wholly to be that which is conscious of circularity; all its predicates are, so to speak, the subjective correlates of the predicates of the circle, & it has no properties save these.[55]

For the objectivist the subject is nothing but the object over again; the terms in which the subject is described are 'correlative' to the qualities of the object. It is, Collingwood says, a 'that' without 'what' and therefore it is identical with the object.[56] The 'formula' of objectivism runs, therefore: 'The mind is its own thought: the thought is that which is thought, i.e. the object: therefore the mind is the object.'[57] This identity of subject and object is in flagrant contradiction with the objectivist's premise, that is, the distinction between subject and object. Collingwood's conclusion is therefore that the distinction made by objectivism, as a form of realism, inevitably leads to a *coincidentia oppositorum*.[58]

Collingwood's analysis of the objectivist form of realism is only understandable when we contrast it with his own interpretation of absolute empiricism. In this view, reality is the process of its experience. Taking his own example, this means that we are conscious of the circle for a certain amount of time. Subject and object are one during this experience, that is, they form two aspects of a single process. It is only in the functioning of our self-consciousness that is a reflection of our experience that we are able to distinguish subject and object.

---

[53] Ibid., 4.
[54] Ibid., 17, 75.
[55] Ibid., 5.
[56] Ibid.
[57] Ibid., 7.
[58] Ibid., 6, 12.

According to Collingwood, the objectivist 'existentialises' this distinction between subject and object, that is, he finds himself aware of the circle and of himself and wrongly draws the conclusion that there are two things, the circle and a mind, of which the former is more real than the second.[59] This view leads to the false conclusion that the object makes conscious experience possible, or in other words, the object pre-exists thought and therefore that mind presupposes the existence of the object. For the objectivist, the circle is what it is, and the mind is only a passive copy of the circle. From an absolute empiricist point of view the basic fault of the objectivist is that he separates subject and object, with the result that he interprets the subject as a thing, and not as a process. When asked what the subject really is, he is bound to answer the question in terms of the object thus contradicting his own premise.

Along the same lines, Collingwood shows that subjectivism ends up in a *coincidentia oppositorum*. Subjectivism, like objectivism, presupposes that subject and object exist independently of each other. For the subjectivist, however, it is not the object but the subject that is real. When we ask: 'what is the object?', the subjectivist can only reply that he cannot say what the object is in itself, but that he can describe it as it appears to him, that is, he can describe the object in terms of the subject.[60] To take Collingwood's own example; the subjectivist calls the object hot, red, square, meaning by these predicates that the object is something which gives rise to the subjective feeling of hotness, redness, and squareness.[61]

For the subjectivist the object is nothing but the subject again; the terms in which the object is described are 'correlative' to the experiences of the subject.[62] The object is a 'that' without 'what' and therefore it is identical with the subject.[63] The 'formula' of subjectivism of the object 'is that which is correlative to such and such subjective states'.[64] Again, this identity of subject and object is in contradiction with the subjectivist's starting point; the distinction between subject and object because the two opposites coincide.

Again, Collingwood's account of subjectivism must be contrasted with his interpretation of absolute empiricism. The basic fault of the subjectivist is that he only regards the subject as real; the object in itself is nothing, its existence presupposes that of the subject. From the absolute empiricist point of view the subjectivist forgets that the object is a real process which is inseparable from the subject. The subjectivist separates what cannot be separated and is therefore bound to contradict this separation as soon as he is questioned about the nature of the object.

---

[59] Ibid., 71.
[60] Ibid., 7.
[61] Ibid.
[62] Ibid., 8.
[63] Ibid., 9.
[64] Ibid., 8.

It is important to note that Collingwood considers both subjectivism and objectivism as forms of realism, because the term 'realism' is usually reserved for the philosophy which Collingwood presents as 'objectivism'. In the 'Libellus', however, Collingwood stresses that subjectivism is as much a form of realism as objectivism; like objectivism, it begins with the 'existentialisation' of subjectivity and objectivity and ends with a *coincidentia oppositorum*.[65] We should keep this interpretation of realism in mind; whenever Collingwood uses the term in the early 1920s he may mean both subjectivism and objectivism. Even when he criticises only one of the two forms of realism, which is usually objectivism, he would claim that his criticism is also valid for the subjectivism which, in his view, coincides with objectivism.

Along these lines, Collingwood concludes that both objectivism and subjectivism end up in a *coincidentia oppositorum*, which is the mark of all thought in the world of being, where 'of any pair of opposites each is the undifferentiated or indistinguishable, identical of the other, so that it does not matter which of two opposite terms is used of a given reality'.[66]

Seen from a logical point of view, Collingwood says the *coincidentia oppositorum* characterises all distinctions within the world of being. Most importantly, it infects the metaphysical notions of space, time, and change.[67] Objectivism appears to admit the reality of these concepts, but in fact it does not, because 'it has no central point of view from which time or space may be envisaged: all times and spaces are equally real and real in the same way and therefore time & space as such are negated'.[68] Collingwood calls this denial of time 'monochronism'. Conversely, subjectivism ends in 'monochronism' by holding that:

> The entire universe is not only myself, but it is myself at this moment. Just as there is no other world than my world which is myself, because any other world to exist must exist as my idea & thereby become an element in my world, an element in the content of my own subjectivity, so there is no other world than that which exists at this moment.[69]

Collingwood goes on by pointing out that monochronism devastates the fundamental distinction between 'earlier' and 'later', between 'here' and 'there', and therefore denies all change.[70]

In the same way, both forms of realism wipe out all other fundamental philosophical distinctions like true and false, good and bad, 'and all those which involve valuation'. In this context, Collingwood comes to the ethical aspects of the world of being. The objectivist thesis, based on the non-existence of the sub-

---

65 Ibid., 12–3, 72.
66 Ibid., 17.
67 Ibid., 15.
68 Ibid., 16.
69 Ibid., 14.
70 Ibid.

ject and on the sole reality of the object, leads to 'a rigid moral law, objective in the sense that my judgments make no difference to it: the rightness or wrongness of actions is written down in heaven, and ignorance of the law is no plea'.[71] According to Collingwood, this view 'readily lends itself either to authoritarianism (some person or institution being in possession of the facts)', or 'scepticism (nobody possessing the facts any more than anybody else)'.[72] Collingwood renders the subjective thesis in ethics as 'the supremacy or authority of the individual conscience' according to which 'right means right for me, and what I think right is thereby right for me and therefore right absolutely'.[73]

Again, the two extremes in the ethical field, objectivism and subjectivism, will coincide. According to Collingwood, both views deny the plurality of subjects; for the objectivist only the 'objective law' exists and he denies the existence of the subject. For the subjectivist only the individual subject exists and all kinds of 'otherness' are denied. The glaring consequence of this denial of otherness is the 'denial of εὐθῦναι (euthunai = setting straight). Collingwood gives the following portrait of the subject in the world of being:

> The subject is wholly irresponsible; there is nothing with which it has to settle its accounts. It stands in awe of nothing, it has no duties; it is complete at every moment, can have no defect of anything since it possesses the entire universe already; it has nothing to aim at, because any goal is already within itself; nothing to regret, because it has achieved everything that is thinkable. There is no such thing as error or evil: there is only that which is.[74]

This is the 'final nightmare' to which realism in both its forms leads, as Collingwood indicates at various places in the 'Libellus'.[75] Obviously, Collingwood in the above passage also alludes to the nightmare that had ended in 1918, and he implicitly holds realism responsible for it, as he would do explicitly in his autobiography nineteen years later. Then he recognised that the nightmare had not stopped in 1918, but had continued in Fascism and Nazism.

The 'Libellus', however, has a happy end. At the end of the essay, Collingwood is convinced that the world of being is drawing to an end. From of the ashes of realism a new world will arise, which is the world of becoming. The first task of the philosophy of becoming is to show that change really exists. Collingwood summarises the result of the inquiry on the nature of the world of being as follows:

> While we followed the cycle of realism from its rise to its final collapse in the discovery that everything is indifferently its own opposite, something was all the time going on which was not its own opposite — namely the march of the

---

71 Ibid., 28.
72 Ibid.
73 Ibid., 29.
74 Ibid., 15.
75 Ibid., 28, 38–9, 42.

argument, the development of the position, the logical chain, the process of thought. This process is not indifferently identical with its own opposite. We began by holding a certain belief A. A process of thought took place, at the end of which we held no longer the belief A but its opposite B.[76]

In other words, the realist has to acknowledge the world of becoming as soon as he admits that his thesis has developed from a pure distinction into an abstract identity. The realist also has to acknowledge the reality of change and to give up his monochronism. If change really exists, thought will never end in a *coincidentia oppositorum* because 'where there is change, there is difference'.[77]

The Myth of Process

After his analysis of the world of being, Collingwood raises the question of the nature of the world of becoming, warning that 'it is necessary to be very cautious in answering this question'.[78] In his view 'one is tempted to see the world of becoming as the world of thought or subjectivity'.[79] Collingwood describes this position as follows:

> ...the world, matter, 'reality', objectivity is self-contradictory, makes nonsense, does not exist; the mind the self, subjectivity or consciousness, being a process, is real and makes sense. And further, since nonsense can only exist as correlative to sense and in this condition really can exist as a subordinate moment in subjectivity: the 'world' is a fiction constructed by the mind.[80]

In this passage, Collingwood implicitly refers to the actualist dialectic that identifies subjectivity, or the *pensante,* with truth and reality, and objectivity, and the *pensato,* with error, appearance, or fiction. According to Collingwood, this view contains a great deal of truth and even 'comes very near to being satisfactory'.[81] Yet he is not completely satisfied with it and claims that 'the failure of present idealism up to the present time is perhaps due to the adaption of this formula'.[82] According to Collingwood, the modern idealist view implies a return to the distinction and opposition of subject and object which belongs to the world of being. The idealist doctrine depends on a distinction or opposition between subjectivity and objectivity. Collingwood claims that his analysis of realism has shown that distinction will always end in a *coincidentia oppositorum*. Against this position Collingwood posits his own most fundamental doctrine, that if subjectivity is seen as a real process, objectivity must also be seen as such. According to

---

[76] Ibid., 41.
[77] Ibid., 42.
[78] Ibid.
[79] Ibid.
[80] Ibid., 42–3.
[81] Ibid., 43.
[82] Ibid.

Collingwood, the modern idealist does not draw this conclusion, because he sticks to a sharp distinction between the self and the world.

In Collingwood's view there are two ideas behind the position of the modern idealist. The first is that the mind 'needs something stationary to push against' or some 'static background against which the movement takes place'.[83] In Collingwood's view this idea is erroneous for two reasons. In the first place, the world of being, on which the world of becoming is built, will once again fall victim to the *coincidentia oppositorum* with the result that the world of becoming would also turn into a world of being. Collingwood thus expresses his view that the present thought should not construct an ideal stationary world for itself in order to reflect upon it, because this will make both worlds nonsensical.

The second idea of the modern idealist is that a changing thing must be identical to itself throughout the change. Collingwood rejects this view as follows:

> In the same way, if that which moves is conceived as purely identical with itself throughout the movement, then no change is happening to it, which is as much as to say it is a world of being embedded in a world of becoming, a nonentity or thing in itself to which the attributes of reality are incomprehensibly attached. Hence the world of becoming must be absolutely free from all dependence on the world of being.[84]

In this passage, Collingwood expresses the view that no 'static entity' of whatever sort is needed in the world of becoming; if A and B are two different phases in a process then the movement from A to B is real. In other words, only the process is real and not some static entity. From this basic principle it follows that none of the concepts by which we describe the world of becoming have any ontological priority.

Seen from the context of Collingwood's development, this passage is a formidable rejection of both Croce's notion of the spirit as being identical to itself through time, and an even more formidable rejection of the eternity of Gentile's transcendental ego. This becomes clear in the following passage where Collingwood overtly crosses swords with the Italian idealists:

> A modern idealist will reply to this, if he has any grasp of his own doctrine, 'When I say subjectivity I am not opposing it to objectivity at all. I am operating with a new concept of subjectivity, a concept due in the main to Kant and Hegel, according to which a subject is not the subject of an object, but the subject of itself: the concept expressed in the well-known formula that the other of apperception is itself apperception — that is to say, not an object of apperception.' This is perfectly true: but it has further consequences which are not drawn. The new concept of subjectivity is also a new concept of objectivity: why is the latter term not used? Because, we shall be told, the identity of subject and object is such that the object is resolved into the subject but not the subject into the object. The subject has turned out to be its own object, & the

---

[83] Ibid., 45, 46.

[84] Ibid., 46.

object to be its own subject: but the word 'be' is used in a different sense in the two cases. The object ἦν ἄρα the subject—what we have called object we ought to have called subject—and the subject γίγνεται ἑαυτῷ object—the subject objectifies itself to itself while remaining subject all the time. Hence, for modern idealism, the concept of subjectivity is fundamental.[85]

Here we arrive at the crux of Collingwood's objection to the Italian idealists, and in particular to the actualist view that the subject is more fundamental than the object. According to Collingwood, this view is based on the principle that the subject is not opposed to the object because the subject is always the subject of itself. This is Collingwood's way of rendering Gentile's dialectic of the *pensante* and *pensato*. As we have seen in chapter three, Gentile identifies this dialectic with reality, so that all thought is never about an object but about the thought of an object. In *Religion and Philosophy* Collingwood expressed the same view by saying that 'my thought of the table is the table as I know it'.[86] But in the 'Libellus' Collingwood's point is that this position does not justify the priority of the subject over the object because this amounts to confounding two senses of the terms 'to be an object for'. In the first sense, we mean thought as object (ἦν ἄρα = as it were) of a subject, in the second sense, we mean thought as object for a self-becoming subject γίγνεται ἑαυτῷ (becoming of itself). In other words, in the first sense we mean our awareness of an object, in the second sense we mean our awareness of that awareness, or our self-consciousness. 'Modern idealists', that is, Italian idealists, confound the first sense with the second sense so that all thought becomes self-conscious thought, or subjectivity, which they therefore regard as the basis of reality. In Collingwood's view this priority of the self-conscious subject is not justified because the thesis that the object is always a thought entails that it has the same characteristics as the subject, that is, the object is also a self-conscious act of thought. Modern idealism, Collingwood concludes, is not a theory of subjectivity as a real process, but at best a 'myth of process', because it simply opposes subjectivity qua process to subjectivity qua being. According to Collingwood, there is nothing wrong with this view as long as subjectivity is taken in both cases as 'process', but even if this is so, he proposes calling both things by their own name, that is, 'process'.[87]

In Italian terms this amounts to saying that the *pensato* must be seen as a *pensante*, that is, as an activity that is completely *norma sui*. On the basis of this view, the *pensato* or object should not be opposed to the *pensante* or subject as nonsense to sense, or as being a subordinate construction by more fundamental activity. In this context, Collingwood explicitly agrees with the 'new realism', that the theory of an object created by thought to reflect upon risks stranding in

---

85 Ibid., 44.
86 R.G. Collingwood, *Religion and Philosophy*, 101.
87 R.G. Collingwood, 'Libellus de Generatione', 47.

subjective idealism, although he rejects the realist objectivism as a philosophical absurdity.[88]

On the basis of this criticism Collingwood introduces a principle which he regards as of the highest importance. He calls it 'the principle of the pureness of the world of becoming'. This principle expresses the idea that the world of becoming does not contain, nor rests upon, nor presupposes the world of being.[89] In this sense, Collingwood explains that the world of becoming is not based on some static notion of objectivity, whether it be an 'external nature' or a *pensato*, or some kind of ideal world which is 'subordinate' to the world of subjectivity, nor some kind of static notion of subjectivity, whether it be some kind of eternal spirit or a transcendental ego. In the world of becoming, subjectivity and objectivity must be seen as two aspects of a single reality which is the world of becoming. In order to understand the world of becoming Collingwood even suggests giving up the whole terminology of subject and object and to talk about processes instead.[90]

At this point, all threads of Collingwood's development come together. Already before the war he had criticised Croce for his misunderstanding of processes, and he repeated this criticism in 1917, calling the Italian a 'realist'. Here, in the 'Libellus', we find the concept of process as the basis on which he also criticises Gentile for being a realist because he makes too sharp a distinction between subject and object. As we have seen, the dialectic of subject and object, or *pensante* and *pensato*, and the resulting 'reduction' of reality to the pure act of thought forms the Alpha and Omega of actualism. Collingwood's proposal to abolish the concepts of subject and object and to talk about processes instead amounts to an entire revision of actualist metaphysics on the basis of the concept of process. And since Gentile's dialectic of *pensante* and *pensato* formed the basis of all of his views concerning mind and its object, philosophy and history, and theory and practice, all these concepts will need to be revised as well.

Collingwood presents this revision as a 'reinterpretation of the categories of the world of being' in the last part of the 'Libellus'. The basic principle of the world of becoming is that there is change, and where there is change there is difference. But the concept of differences needs to be interpreted in a new way; not as distinction but as a 'synthesis of opposites'. Collingwood describes the procedure of this reinterpretation as follows:

> The formula of reinterpretation is easily stated. In the world of being, every determination took the form of a coincidence of opposites. Everything was identical with its own opposite, and this was the fundamental nature of the world of being. In the world of becoming, distinctions are real just because they are not pure: A is A, not by rejecting Bness, but by admitting it, by being

---

[88] Ibid., 44.

[89] Ibid., 45.

[90] Ibid., 47.

B it achieves identity just by undergoing diversity, asserts itself as itself by negating itself and becoming something else. This means that if we take any pair of opposites we shall never find either in a 'pure' state, excluding its other: we shall invariably find both together in a synthesis where the presence of each depends upon the presence of the other.[91]

Collingwood admits that this may sound like nonsense and he needs many pages to make it intelligible. The fundamental character of the world of becoming is the synthesis of opposites, which follows from the above 'reinterpretation' of the concepts of identity and difference:

Identity and difference are thus different categories, logically opposed to one another and no longer indifferently identical: but each exists in the other and only so. A is the A of not-A, and not-A is the not-A of A. Here we arrive at the fundamental principle of the world of becoming, namely the synthesis of opposites.[92]

According to this formula, the distinctions of the world of being should be reinterpreted as 'positivity' and 'negativity', which he also describes as 'affirmation' and 'negation'. With a phrasing, which foreshadows *An Essay on Philosophical Method*, Collingwood points out that affirmation implies negation and vice versa. Every determination in the world of being thus becomes a synthesis of both. At this crucial point Collingwood introduces the concept of the living past:

Take two phases of a process, A and B. At a given moment the phase in existence is A and is not B. But to leave it at this would be to deny the reality of the process, that is, continuity, as, to assert I am my present self, and not my past self. Such an assertion cuts the thread of continuity in the process, denies the world of becoming and reasserts the world of being, with the result that *coincidentia oppositorum* is set up and my present self becomes indistinguishable from my past. To reassert the process it is necessary to assert that my past self lives on in my present self, that the present phase is B as well as A, though it is definitely premised that A is not B and B not A — that they are different phases of the process. A truth in the world of becoming can only be expressed by a contradiction, a synthesis of opposites.[93]

In the above passage Collingwood for the first time explicitly states that the world of becoming is only possible if the past lives on in the present. This is the passage he explicitly refers to in his autobiography as his 'first principle in the philosophy of history: that the past which an historian studies is not a dead past, but a past which in some sense is still living in the present'.[94] In his autobiography he formulates this principle as follows.

---

[91] Ibid.
[92] Ibid., 48.
[93] Ibid., 50–1.
[94] R.G. Collingwood, *An Autobiography*, 97.

> ...if a process P_1 turns into a process P_2, there is no dividing line at which P_1 stops and P_2 begins, P_1 never stops, it goes on in the changed form P_2 and P_2 never begins, it has previously going on in the earlier form P_1.[95]

The main difference between the two passages is merely terminological: Collingwood translated the terms 'past' and 'present self' of the 'Libellus' into 'process' of his autobiography and he replaced the notion of the 'synthesis of opposites' by the notion of overlapping phases of a process. But the meaning of both passages is the same; a phase in a process is never itself pure and simple, but it always contains the 'contradictory' characteristics of an earlier phase 'encapsulated' within itself, or, in the language of the 'Libellus'; each phase in a process is a synthesis of opposites. Both in the 'Libellus' and in the autobiography the function of the living past is the same; it is necessary to assert the world of becoming, or process. This is the most basic idea of Collingwood's metaphysics of process; in order to acknowledge that the present is a 'moment' within a process, it is necessary that the past be present. In other words, in order to understand that P_2 is a phase in a process we must be able to recognise it as a sequel to P_1. But it is not enough for the past to simply be present, it must be present as an opposite from the present; the present is a synthesis of opposites, or an overlap of past and present.

By claiming that the past is living in the present Collingwood stands the Italian view on its head. As we have seen, Croce used to oppose the notion of the 'dead past' to that of 'contemporary history'. Gentile claimed that the development of the *pensante* cannot be understood without an opposition between *pensato* and *pensante*. Both Croce and Gentile claimed that this opposition could be made undone by reliving or rethinking the past by which the past becomes the present. In contrast, Collingwood does not maintain that the present overcomes the opposition between past and present by reliving or rethinking it, but that the present must assert the past within itself in order to understand itself as a synthesis of opposites. But the most fundamental difference between the Italians and Collingwood is that the former do not acknowledge that there is a past in the present, whereas the latter definitely holds that the past survives in the present. Accordingly, the past does not need to be 'constructed' by present thought, as Croce and Gentile held, but it must be 'reconstructed', or in more actualist terms, it is not 'enacted', but 're-enacted'. Most importantly, this reconstruction does not presuppose an identity between present and past, whether embodied in the pure concepts or in the transcendental ego, but it establishes this identity by reconstructing it as a process. In other words, the identity between past and present is not given, but discovered.

On this basis, Collingwood reinterprets all distinctions as syntheses of opposites, that is, syntheses of affirmations and negation, which are all constituted in an historical world. Subjectivity and objectivity, for example, are not two distinct

---

95 Ibid., 98.

things, but they are 'synthetically present in every determination of reality'.[96] In other words, the reality of experience has both a subjective and an objective aspect; subjectivity is the element of selfness in experience, objectivity that of other-than-selfness. Likewise, truth and error should not be interpreted as concrete things but as phases of a process. Even the question 'what is error?' betrays the 'realist' tendency to 'existentialise' the concept into a thing.[97]

Along the same lines, Collingwood reinterprets the categories of ethics:

> The good and bad are not two selves, but moments in one self: I am each, and am each just by being the other. It is just my laziness that makes my energy virtuous instead of priggish: just my energy that makes my laziness disgraceful instead of merely natural.[98]

The world of becoming is to be seen as one great process in which each determination only exists as a synthesis of opposites. Truth only exists in correcting error, the good only exists in correcting evil. In this context Collingwood aptly compares the world of becoming to Penelope's web.[99]

These examples show how Collingwood intended to revise both the metaphysics of realism and its logical categories. His aim is not to throw all distinction overboard and to end in a night in which all cows are black, but to revise the notion of distinction. In the world of being, distinction is conceived as the distinction between things, but this way of distinguishing cannot be applied to processes in which all 'things' are 'moments' or 'phases', or 'aspects' of a single process which can only be explained on the logical category of opposition. All this fits well in the Hegelian tradition and the theory had been applied by Croce and Gentile in their philosophies of mind, both of which use the category of opposition in order to explain the development of the spirit. Collingwood's novelty is that he shows that this opposition is only possible if there is something real to be opposed to, and this something real should not be seen as a mere abstraction, or construction made by present thought, but as something that has an existence of its own. From this viewpoint, error and evil are not abstractions or 'idealities' of present thought which aims at truth and goodness, as Gentile and de Ruggiero hold, but error and evil are a real aspect of my present experience just as truth and goodness are. Nor does error and evil need to be 'relived', 'rethought', or 'idealised' in order to reach truth and goodness, but error and evil are always real aspects of experience which is a synthesis of negativity and positivity.

---

[96]   R.G. Collingwood, 'Libellus de Generatione', 72.
[97]   Ibid., 65–6.
[98]   Ibid., 53.
[99]   Ibid., 54.

Philosophy and History in the World of Becoming

The notion of the 'pureness' of the world of becoming has important implications for the conception of history. That Collingwood was aware of this becomes clear in the section 'The Genesis of the World of Being', in which he explicitly deals with the problem of the reality of the world of being in the history of philosophy. Collingwood formulates this problem as follows. The world of being really existed for the great philosophers who inhabited it and studied it, although it was a 'fraudulent' one, because the real world was the world of becoming. How are we to account for this puzzling fact, that is, what kind of reality is attached to an erroneous conception? Collingwood first deals with the answer of the 'subjective idealist'.[100]

> An idealism which is still touched with subjectivism will reply that the world of being is the world of the object considered as distinct from the subject. The real world is the world of thought, of subjectivity: the unreal world is that of the object of thought or objectivity. And because the object apart from thought is a false abstraction, the world of being is a world of abstractions, of unstable ghosts that pass over into their own opposites, of illusions. We have already suggested that this type of theory is a myth rather than a philosophy: it means the truth, but it is not the truth. The idealistic concept of subjectivity is the concept of becoming under another name, not another concept. If this interpretation is applied to the present formula, its emptiness is at once seen. The world of being is described as the world of the abstract object: but this only means the world of abstract being. The world of becoming is the world of subjectivity; but that only means the world of becoming. The formula takes us no further than this tautology.[101]

Here Collingwood reproaches the subjective idealist for explaining the reality of the world of being by saying that it is an abstraction of the world of becoming. To say that an inhabitant of the world of being, for example Plato, abstracted his world from the world of becoming is tautologous with saying that he committed an error, but this does not explain why this error was a truth for Plato. That Collingwood here rejects Gentile's identification of *pensato*, or past thought, with error is revealed by the fact that the error committed is the one of distinguishing between subjectivity and objectivity, which is the fallacy of transcendence in Gentile's philosophy. Stated in the actualist terms, the philosophy of the world of being must be erroneous because it is not *norma sui*, that is, it presupposes a norm pre-existing to the act of thought, whereas we, inhabitants of the world of becoming, think of thought as *norma sui*, that is, we do not presuppose any norm prior to thought. Consequently, we cannot think the world of being anymore, it is a past stage of our thought and therefore we must reject it as error. According to Collingwood, this interpretation of the philosophy of the world of being amounts to reaffirming the world of being:

[100] Ibid., 62–3.
[101] Ibid., 63–4.

...if the world of the object is an abstract of the world of the subject, as we are told it is, than the world of being, the earlier phase of the process of thought, is an abstract of the world of becoming, the later phase: the later in time is prior to the earlier, and must have existed in full actuality before the earlier could arise. This contradiction conceals an important truth; but on the face of it, it is meaningless. The truth which it conceals is that only in the light of the later phase can we fully realise the character, namely the erroneousness, of the mistake we had made in the earlier. But the earlier phase existed before the later, and was not derived from it. In fact, to derive the earlier from the later is to deny the concept of process (assuming the process to be complete before it can begin) and to reassert the world of being.[102]

In this passage Collingwood points out that the claim that the world of being is an abstraction of the world of becoming implies that the world of becoming had to be present all the time in order to make the abstraction possible. In other words, if we claim that Plato really was living in a world of becoming though he did not recognise it, we claim that the world of becoming was already existent in his times but that he distorted it. According to Collingwood, this view conceals the important truth that we only realise the error of an earlier phase in the light of a later phase; only now, in the world of becoming we are able to see that Plato erred. But this does not explain why Plato erred, that is, it does not explain why he took the world of being for the real world; Plato did not see his world as the world of becoming and consequently we cannot say that his world was an abstraction from the world of becoming, that is, we cannot 'derive' his world of being from the world of becoming. If we claim that he did, Collingwood says, we claim that the world of becoming was 'complete' before the world of being, that is, we claim that our world of becoming has always been the same and this amounts to reasserting the world of being.[103] In other words, the notion of completeness is in flagrant contradiction with the principle that reality is a process.

It is interesting to note how much this criticism of the modern idealism resembles Collingwood's discussion in *Truth and Contradiction*. In that work he shows that the coherence theorist denies the reality of the development of a debate by interpreting the original disagreement in terms of the latter agreement. Here Collingwood shows that the same logic is at work when the earlier phases of a process are interpreted in the light of the latter. His position in the 'Libellus' also resembles that of *Truth and Contradiction*, because in the latter work he finally confirmed the view that all error is a partial truth, and all truth partial error. In the 'Libellus' he expresses the same view by pointing out that in the world of becoming there is no error but only truth and falsity correspondent to the moment of truth in this or that concrete phase of thought. Consequently to the question 'what kind of reality has the world of being?', Collingwood replied as follows:

---

102 Ibid.
103 Ibid.

For Plato (or any other realist) it was an explanation, the best he could com-
pass, of the world of becoming. As conditioned by the way in which he stated
his problem, it was the only sound way of meeting that problem; and it was
therefore the right answer to his questions. But it raised new problems with
which it was not competent to deal: it therefore destroyed itself by its own
logic in grappling with these problems, showing its own vitality in fighting to
the death rather than lasting on as a body of dead and decomposing dogmas:
and for us at the present phase of our thought it is simply nothing at all. It is
thus neither solid truth nor solid falsehood. In so far as we regard it as completely erroneous, it is a belief we do not believe and therefore nothing; in so
far as we regard it as the right answer to the problems of philosophy as raised
in Plato's day, we regard it as true and as permanently valuable; though its
value is only shown in its having cleared those problems (and with them
itself) out of our way and prepared the ground for further advance. Thus,
looking at it from the point of view of the mere abstract present, it is just false
but also just non-existent; this being the point of view from which Huckle-
berry Finn, who took no stock in dead men, regarded Moses. But from the
point of view of the historian, Moses being dead yet speaketh, and Platonism
is a philosophy whose truth and value we can appreciate none the less
because they belong to the past.[104]

In this passage, Collingwood explicitly applies the logic of question and answer
for the first time in full length and, interestingly, he uses it to illustrate the living
past in the history of philosophy. For Collingwood, Plato's thought is not mere
error, even though it asserts the false world of being, but his thought must be
regarded as an answer to a question that arose in particular historical circumstances. From this it follows that Plato's thought cannot be seen as 'solid' truth
or error. We see it as an error to the extent that Plato's answer does not answer
our questions, and we see it as a truth to the extent that it answers Plato's own
questions. From this it follows that the more we differentiate Plato's problems
from our own, the more we understand their value. Moreover, the value of
Plato's thought is permanent in so far as it has led to a further advance of knowledge, that is, to the extent that it has cleared obstacles from our way. If we
understand this, we will recognise that there is a continuity between Plato's
thought and ours; he solved some problems which we do not have to solve anymore. But if we do not recognise this, that is, if we look at Plato from an 'abstract
present', that is, a present which is not related to its own past, we see his thought
as having no value, as an error, as non-existent. Only if we recognise Plato's
thought as a solution to his problems, and therefore as a presupposition for all
the problems which followed in the process of thought up to our own times, we
shall see his thought as a permanent addition to thought. To sum up: only if we
see Plato's thought as an answer to his questions are we able to see how his
thought, in what sense his thought, is still living in the present.

---

[104] Ibid., 67–8.

This is a most striking example of the idea of the living past in Collingwood's sense of this idea. For the Italians the past as such does not live, it is a dead past that lives on condition that it is relived or rethought by present thought. The past thus always remains 'ideal', that is, a constructed object for present thought, which changes whenever present thought changes. For Collingwood, however, the past is alive, it has an existence of its own in the present, namely as the solution to a problem that forms the starting point of our own problems. Therefore, the past does not need to be relived, or constructed, but it must be understood in its proper context, that is, as a past solution to a past problem. The task of the historian is therefore not in the first place to identify the past with the present but to distance it from the present. This position comes very close to de Ruggiero's notion of approaching and distancing the past from ourselves which we discussed in chapter six. However, the main difference between Collingwood and de Ruggiero is that the latter still kept to the metaphysics of the pure act of thought, whereas the former tries to give the pure act of thought a place in the world of becoming.

Collingwood himself found the 'Libellus' 'quite unintelligible to the general public'.[105] This is not surprising, because he did not write the little book for the public, but for Guido de Ruggiero, to 'amuse him as a historian of philosophy'.[106] This was certainly the case, because the Italian expressed his admiration for the work in a letter to Collingwood.[107] It is not so difficult to see why, because by any standard the 'Libellus de Generatione' is a great achievement. Firstly, it is Collingwood's first mature expression of the metaphysics of becoming, or process, which had played an important role in his early development. Secondly, it is Collingwood's first attempt to go beyond the 'the most constructive effort of modern philosophy' which is clearly Italian idealism. His criticism of modern idealism as a form of realism is most challenging and his criticism of actualism hits its very core, namely the dialectic of the *pensante* and *pensato*. Thirdly, Collingwood's own principle of the pureness of the world of becoming makes short work of the view that there must be an entity that underlies becoming. On this basis, Collingwood rejects both Croce's notion of the spirit and Gentile's transcendental ego which remain self-identical in time. In Collingwood's view, the claim that we have understood the true nature of the spirit or transcendental ego amounts to affirming the eternity of the present and denying the reality of the world of becoming. In the end, idealist subjectivism leads to a denial of other subjects and a rejection of any form of moral responsibility.

By acknowledging the pureness of the world of becoming, Collingwood definitely went beyond the Italians; he presented an historical world in which

---

[105] R.G. Collingwood, *An Autobiography*, 99.
[106] Ibid.
[107] R.G. Collingwood, 'Letters to Guido de Ruggiero', 16 September 1920.

there is no room for any static entities and for sharp distinctions. In this historical world, subject and object, truth and error, good and evil, must not be seen as distinct concepts, but as a synthesis of opposites in which both terms are equally real. From this it follows that there are no eternal valid distinctions between truth and error, or good and evil; all distinctions are dependent on the time in which they were made. For the same reason, there are no sharp boundaries between pseudo-concepts and pure concepts, between the *logo astratto* and the *logo concreto*, the empirical ego and the transcendental ego.

All this is based on the metaphysics of the 'living past' which is indeed Collingwood's major contribution, as he was later to claim in his autobiography. By acknowledging the reality of the past in the present, he is able to present the opposite terms as equally real aspects of a single experience which is developing in time. By acknowledging this fundamental opposition in all experience Collingwood gets to grips with the fundamental problematic character of man's historical existence. If any of Collingwood's works is to be called historicist, it is the 'Libellus' in which he comes to the view that 'reality is history'.

The 'Libellus' may be seen as the outcome of Collingwood's early development and as the basis of his later development. On the one hand, we find his earlier ideas about process, the living past, his notions of truth and error, good and evil expressed in a coherent system. On the other hand, we find in the 'Libellus' beginnings of Collingwood's later ideas. For example, his rejection of any self-identical or eternal entity foreshadows his later criticism of the notion of 'human nature'.[108] His acknowledgment of the importance of actual experience and his criticism of abstractions are forerunners of his 'plain historical method'.[109]

Collingwood's interpretation of absolute empiricism as a form of empiricism that tries to take its own presuppositions into account explains, firstly, why he always refused to be called an idealist, because in the world of the absolute empiricist the only reality is the process of experience in which there is no priority of the subject or object. Secondly, it explains his later interest in other philosophers of the British tradition such as Alexander and Whitehead, who tried to take the presuppositions of actual experience into account. Finally, it shows Collingwood's later interest in the logic of question and answer and the doctrine of presuppositions that is related to it.

But before Collingwood could work out all these ideas he had to solve some very important problems that were not addressed in the 'Libellus'. The first problem concerns the notion of self-consciousness, which is central in the 'Libellus'. As we have seen above, Collingwood had criticised Gentile for resolving all consciousness into self-consciousness and the resulting tendency to overvaluate the self-conscious act of thought. But at the same time Collingwood

[108] See chapter 9, pp. 342–344.
[109] See chapter 10, p. 395.

himself had based the world of becoming on the notion of self-consciousness. As we have seen the 'necessity' of the world of becoming is based on the fact that even the philosopher of the world of becoming must recognise the 'march of his own argument'. Collingwood's problem after the 'Libellus' was therefore to work out a theory of the mind in which consciousness and self-consciousness are clearly distinguished.[110]

The second problem may be called the 'articulation problem'. It was raised by de Ruggiero after reading the 'Libellus'.[111] The problem concerns the 'identity' and 'difference' between the diverse forms of experience. In the 'Libellus' Collingwood had shown that all becoming implies the synthesis of opposites and he had found in the dialectic of question and answer an apt way of describing such a process in the field of philosophy. But in the 'Libellus' Collingwood did not answer the question of how this dialectic should be articulated in the other forms of experience.

The third problem concerns the status of history. As we have seen, Collingwood had established his own notion of the living past which forms the basis of the entire world of becoming. However, he had not indicated how this past presents itself in actual experience and how it can be known. It took Collingwood almost ten years to work out a philosophy of history based on his view of the living past. In the next sections we will see how he struggled with the three problems.

Painting Out the Sketch 1920–1924

In September 1920 Collingwood and de Ruggiero had long conversations about the 'Libellus' which de Ruggiero certainly approved of. Collingwood was so much inspired by these conversations that he dedicated a series of lectures to de Ruggiero's philosophy in Michelmas term 1920. In November of that year Collingwood enthusiastically wrote to de Ruggiero that he was preparing a paper in which he would announce the 'collapse of modern realism'.[112] This paper has not yet been found, which is unfortunate as Collingwood considered it important enough to mention in his autobiography.[113] In the paper, Collingwood tries to show that the realist doctrine that the knowing does not make a difference to what is known is meaningless, and he states its main argument as follows:

> For if you know that no difference is made to a thing θ by the presence or absence of a certain condition c, you know what θ is like with c, and also what θ is like without c, and on comparing the two find no difference. This involves

---

[110] R.G. Collingwood, 'Letters to Guido de Ruggiero', 29 May 1921.
[111] Ibid., 16 September 1920.
[112] Ibid., 4 November 1920.
[113] R.G. Collingwood, *An Autobiography*, 44.

knowing what θ is like without c; in the present case, knowing what you
defined as the unknown.[114]

This argument has led to much controversy among Collingwood's interpreters.
Donagan called it a 'blunder', for the whole thesis implies that knowing is assim-
ilated into 'looking', which reveals its idealistic basis.[115] J.F. Post criticised
Donagan for not remarking that the argument does not refute the realist claim
that knowing makes no difference to what is known, but it refutes the claim to
know that it does so; realism may be true, but we can never know that it is. On
this basis, Post convincingly shows that the whole argument is just as effective
against idealism as against realism by replacing 'no difference' in the above
passage with 'a difference'. From this, Post draws the conclusion that the whole
argument does not represent a return to Collingwood's early idealism because
the opposition between realism and idealism is meaningless on the basis of the
above passage.[116]

With this analysis, Post very aptly, but unknowingly, defends Collingwood's
position in the 'Libellus'. To say that the knowing makes no difference to the
known amounts to claiming that the subject is nothing and that all reality is
found in the object. According to Collingwood this analysis must be false
because the comparison between θ as known and unknown implies that the subject knows the unknown. Collingwood's dispute with the realist is obviously not
that of the experience of θ but about the way in which this experience must be
analysed. In terms of the 'Libellus' one might say that for the realist the distinction between subject and object is primary and makes the experience possible, whereas for Collingwood the experience is primary, or concrete, and makes
the analysis of it in subject and object possible. But taken by themselves subject
and object are only abstractions and therefore meaningless.

Not surprisingly, Collingwood's realist colleagues were not very interested
in his paper, as he sadly reported to de Ruggiero.[117] This reaction did not
demoralise Collingwood, however. After November 1920 he continued to elaborate his own philosophy. He pondered a 'possible work on Logic' and he tried
to 'articulate' the principle of becoming for the diverse forms of experience, first
in his lectures on moral philosophy of 1920 and then in some papers about art,
science, and history.[118] I shall not discuss all these manuscripts and papers at
length, but concentrate on the problems they deal with.

In the sketches for the work on logic, Collingwood tries to establish a logic of
the world of becoming by some fusion of 'psychology' and 'logic', which

---

[114] Ibid., 44.

[115] Donagan, *The Later Philosophy of R.G. Collingwood*, 287.

[116] John Frederic Post, 'Does Knowing Make a Difference to What is Known?', in *Philosophical Quarterly*, 15, 1965, 221–5.

[117] R.G. Collingwood, 'Letters to Guido de Ruggiero', 20 March 1921.

[118] Ibid., 22 November 1921.

reminds us of de Ruggiero's identity of *coscienza* and *scienza*.[119] The same relationship between feeling and thought also appears in 'An Illustration of Historical Thought', where Collingwood tries to show that the distinction between 'feeling' and thought leads to a 'realist' view of history which will get stranded in a *coincidentia oppositorum*.[120] Here Collingwood follows the main argument of the 'Libellus'; he starts from the actual dispute between two historians, Grote (1813–1866) and Mommsen, in order to see which principles underlie it. According to Collingwood, the difference between Grote and Mommsen is found in their 'ideals' which made them sympathise with a different side. This means that they would not only give a different account of the values of history, but also that their account of the facts would conflict:

> ...each would present a picture differing not merely in its colours but also in its forms from that of the other. Their sympathies or ideals are not super-imposed on their knowledge,... but the sympathies and ideals act upon the knowledge and distort it.[121]

According to Collingwood, the objectivist may take two roads now. Firstly he may say 'yes, feeling does act on knowing, but it can only act on one principle viz. that of selection' because 'two people with different sympathies may be led by these sympathies to concentrate their attention on different facts'.[122] Secondly, he may say 'yes, sympathies act on knowledge, and in so far as they do, it becomes not knowledge but error'.[123] According to Collingwood, the first answer presupposes 'reality as infinitely big and various', it is seen as 'a kind of stuff out of which the practical or willing mind sculpts its objects'.[124] But this view is untenable and it breaks down because the different selections contradict each other. The second view of history is also untenable; it sees the accounts of Grote and Mommsen as equally defective. On this point, Collingwood applies the notion of the *coincidentia oppositorum* as developed in the 'Libellus':

> The result is a *coincidentia oppositorum*. In 1) everything is true: in 2) nothing is true. In 1) Reality includes all subjective views, which are mere selections from its own infinite bulk: in 2) it excludes them all, and they are aberrations from it. In 1) it is a goal always attained, in 2) never attained at all. Now these opposites coincide. For the truth at which thought aims is the whole truth, the truth which includes all reality in its view and excludes all alternatives.[125]

---

[119] R.G. Collingwood, 'Notes on Hegel's Logic', 1920, Dep. 16/2; Id., 'Sketch of A Logic of Becoming', 1920, Dep. 16/3; Id., 'Notes on Formal Logic', 1920, Dep. 16/4; Id., 'Draft of Openening Chapters of a "Prolegomena to Logic" or the like', 1920–21, Dep. 16/5.
[120] R.G. Collingwood, 'An Illustration from Historical Thought', 1920, Dep. 16/6, 1–6.
[121] Ibid., 1–2.
[122] Ibid., 2.
[123] Ibid., 3.
[124] Ibid.
[125] Ibid., 6.

In Collingwood's view this *coincidentia oppositorum* is based on the false distinction between thought and action according to which 'knowledge excludes all practical or sentimental falsification'.[126] Along the lines of the 'Libellus' Collingwood then proposes giving up this distinction in order to understand thought and action as a synthesis of opposites.

This synthesis is not elaborated by Collingwood in 'An Illustration from Historical Thought'. But in a 'Draft of Opening Chapters of a "Prolegomena to Logic" or the like', to which the 'Illustration' was attached, he does try to establish this unity of thought and action. However, even this attempt seems to be abortive. After the conclusion that 'psychology' and logic should be fused in order to explain the process of thought Collingwood ends his analysis.[127] The pages that he completed show many similarities with *Truth and Contradiction*, but there is no sign that Collingwood intended to work out a logic of question and answer in which thought and action would be unified.

More successful were Collingwood's attempts to solve the problem of self-consciousness. In a letter to de Ruggiero written on 29 May 1921, Collingwood reports:

> Meanwhile I am going on with the working-out of the concept which I outlined in the paper I sent you last year; at present I am trying to construct a systematic philosophy of conduct on the same basis, showing how all the cycle of ethical concepts derive from the concept of becoming. But at the same time I find the concept of becoming is more and more closely identified in my mind with that of self-consciousness. In my last year's essay I did not demonstrate that nothing except a self-consciousness can become; but that demonstration would now take a central position if I rewrote the essay.[128]

When we turn to the 'Lectures on Moral Philosophy' of 1921, mentioned in the letter we see that Collingwood begins with the distinction between objectivism and subjectivism in ethics, just as he had done in the 'Libellus'. Upon this follows a very large section on the relationships between choice, will, and self-consciousness, which is new compared with the 'Libellus'. The kernel of Collingwood's thesis is that will and choice presuppose self-consciousness:

> Thus the act of reflection, the act of becoming self-conscious, conscious of one's own existence and (which is the same thing) able to express the general character of one's action in a formula, is the birth of morality. One might say that the use of the first person, 'I', 'we', is an infallible mark of a moral being.[129]

---

126 Ibid.

127 R.G. Collingwood, 'Draft of Openening Chapters of a "Prolegomena to Logic" or the like', 58–60.

128 R.G. Collingwood, 'Letters to Guido de Ruggiero', 29 May 1921.

129 R.G. Collingwood, 'Lectures on Moral Philosophy', 1921, Dep. 4, 84–5.

This concept of self-consciousness brings Collingwood to the problem of the relationship between memory and history on the one side and practice on the other. All agents, Collingwood says, when choosing, reflect on their thought, that is, their past thought; the past is a necessary condition for choice. Furthermore, all moral judgments presuppose 'the imaginative reproduction of the surroundings and the imaginative setting of oneself in the place of the agent'.[130] Collingwood distinguishes this imaginative reproduction from historical thought *in fieri* on the ground that the latter 'knows nothing of moral judgments'; only when the historian has finished his work can he pass a moral judgment, but then an act of imagination is needed in order to place himself in the position of the historical actors.[131]

Apparently, this view of moral judgment in history stands squarely opposed to the one he advocated in 'An Illustration from Historical Thought'. However, in the latter Collingwood is describing the principles which underlie the historian's experience *ab extra* and here he is describing the view of the historian *ab intra*. The most interesting aspects of Collingwood's analysis are his identification of self-consciousness with history, and that he recognises the importance of imagination in historical thought. The first is the beginnings of Collingwood's later notion of history as self-knowledge and the second is the start of his views on historical imagination.

Regarding imagination, Collingwood had more to say in a paper on Croce's aesthetics which he wrote in the summer of 1921. Unfortunately, this paper seems to be lost, but in a letter to de Ruggiero Collingwood mentions that it expressed the same views as de Ruggiero's 'Arte e critica' about which he was very delighted: 'it exactly says what I wanted someone to say on the subject, and says it with a most admirable clearness and convincingness'.[132] Concerning his own paper Collingwood says that it dealt with 'the resolution of the impression' into the early stage of the expression itself, the immanence of criticism within art as the self-control of the process of art, and the necessity for historical construction as the scientific aspect of the 'judgement of taste'.[133] These terms are familiar; already in his 1912 comments in his copy of Croce's *Estetica* Collingwood had pointed out that impression and expression are not to be separated because there is no heterogeneous basis of art because the 'impression' is nothing but a 'rudimentary expression'. The letter to de Ruggiero shows that in 1921 he incorporated this view of the artistic process into his newly found concept of self-consciousness before he had read 'Arte e critica'. And again, history, as history of art, played an important role in this conception of art as a form of self-consciousness. Step by step Collingwood began to focus on history.

---

[130] Ibid., 111.
[131] Ibid., 112.
[132] R.G. Collingwood, 'Letters to Guido de Ruggiero', 22 November 1921.
[133] Ibid.

This interest in history is even more clearly revealed in the article 'Are History and Science Different Kinds of Knowledge?' of 1922. Collingwood's answer to the question of the title is 'no', because in epistemological terms science and history are identical. The argument for this conclusion follows the argument of the 'Libellus', showing that the distinction between science and history implies a distinction between the universal and the particular, which leads to a *coincidentia oppositorum*.[134] Both forms of knowledge individualise and generalise, Collingwood says, and they are both concerned with the past and future. When we compare historical thought in process with science in process, Collingwood says, 'the difference of method and of logic wholly disappears'.[135] From the rest of the article it becomes clear that this "unified method" is induction. In Collingwood's view the scientist does not start with sense-data but with individual facts, and just like the historian he seeks to understand it in the light of the universal. Both the scientist and the historian therefore generalise from individual facts.

This identification of science and history suggests that Collingwood still believed in some objectivity of fact, and some interpreters have pointed out that this 'realist' interpretation of history is incompatible with the view expressed in 'An Illustration from Historical Thought', in which any past as pre-existent to the present is denied. However, from Collingwood's point of view there is no contradiction at all. In 'Are Science and History Different Kinds of Knowledge?' Collingwood describes science and history *ab intra*, and he finds that there is no real difference between the two forms of knowledge. This conclusion need not surprise us; already in 1912 Collingwood had defended that history is inductive against Croce's view that it is not.[136]

The real surprise of 'Are Science and History Different Kinds of Knowledge?' is that Collingwood did not recognise that history is more than induction. The article thus reveals that Collingwood had not yet 'articulated' the difference between science and history. In particular he was not able to indicate the difference between the ways in which empirical aspects of science and history were 'idealised' through imagination.

At the same time, Collingwood was certainly aware of some differences between science and history. This is clearly illustrated by the 1922 essay 'Science and History', which shows that Collingwood already knew where to find the differences between the two forms of knowledge:

> There is a real difference between the scientific and historical points of view, I thought, if only one could grasp it: and I felt sure that is was the clue to a right understanding of human life. The average scientist thinks of man as a complex machine, evolved by degrees out of other machines as the universe

---

134 R.G. Collingwood, 'Are History and Science Different Kinds of Knowledge?', in *Mind*, 3, 1922, 443–51, cited from Id., *Essays in the Philosophy of History*, University of Texas Press, Austin, 1966, 24–5.

135 Ibid., 33.

136 See chapter 5, p. 147.

dances its unceasing and unmeaning dance... History, I thought, valued man differently. Its concern is with seeing man as he is, in the full flush of his momentary existence; conscious of the universe and of himself, acting and reacting in a world that is not dust at all but mind, a world of moral ideals, political systems, scientific discoveries, hopes and fears.[137]

This passage reveals that the difference between science and history must be thought of in the study of man. Collingwood's description of man reveals the influence of the Italians, and in particular Vico; man is a unity of *coscienza* (momentary existence) and *scienza* (conscious of the universe and of himself). At the same time the passage reveals that Collingwood did not see science but history as the true knowledge of man. From this viewpoint, the real problem was to grasp the historical point of view from within. This is revealed by Collingwood's reaction to de Ruggiero's 'Dall'arte alla filosofia'.

> But your new paper touches things which I want you to go on explaining. Somehow there is a real identity and a real distinction between things like art, history, religion, action, science, philosophy etc. How to formulate the identity and the differences? Croce analyses the differences between his four 'elements', but misses their identity—he gives them the wrong kind of identity, the identity (merely generic) of four sails of a windmill. Your Scienza, and this paper of mine on history, seize the identity but say nothing about the differences.[138]

This letter shows that Collingwood himself recognised that he and de Ruggiero had not yet solved the 'articulation problem'. They had both shown how each form of experience proceeds in a dialectic of question and answer but they had not indicated the differences between the embodiments of this dialectic for each of the forms. Collingwood's reference to 'Are Science and History Different Kinds of Knowledge' shows that he was particularly bothered by the relationship between science and history. This distinction was crucial to his interpretation of absolute empiricism which he tried to base on history and not on science as de Ruggiero had done. However, on the basis of the foregoing it is clear he was well under way. In his 'Lectures on Moral Philosophy' of 1921 he had explicitly identified history with self-consciousness and he had recognised both the empirical and the imaginative aspects of history. Collingwood's problem now was to fuse all these aspects of history into a dialectic of question and answer that would distinguish it from science. In order to solve this problem Collingwood had to find a way in which he could differentiate between all these aspects without obliterating the differences.

Collingwood found the beginning of a solution somewhere in 1922 and most probably by revising Gentile's actualism. This is shown by 'Can the New Idealism Dispense with Mysticism?' which Collingwood read in July 1923 shortly

---

[137] R.G. Collingwood, 'Science and History', in *The Vasculum*, IX, 1923, 55–6.
[138] R.G. Collingwood, 'Letters to Guido de Ruggiero', 21 September 1922.

after completing *Speculum Mentis*.[139] In this paper Collingwood defends the
Italian idealists, and in particular Gentile, against Bosanquet's charge that the
neo-idealist tends to repudiate religion.[140] At the end of the paper Collingwood
unfolds a 'programme' for modern idealism which certainly lay at the basis of
Speculum Mentis, so that it seems that he developed his revision of Italian idealism before writing this book.

In the meeting of the Aristotelian Society Bosanquet's charge was taken up
by Evelyn Underhill (1875–1941), the author of a book on mysticism. Underhill
argued that Italian neo-idealism, being a 'philosophy of change', tends to under-
value the importance of religion, and she ends her paper by raising the question
of whether the neo-idealists can dispense with mysticism. Collingwood, making
no secret of his contempt for the vagueness of Underhill's question, takes mysticism as 'intuitive or immediate consciousness of the supreme reality as one,
eternal and spiritual'.[141] He then distinguishes between two senses of dispensing
with mysticism. In the first sense it means to deny that mysticism is a necessary
element in human life, whereas in the second sense it means that the proper
method of philosophy is different from the method of mysticism.[142] Collingwood
argues that neither Croce nor Gentile 'dispense with mysticism' in the first sense,
because both acknowledge the importance of religion for life. With regard to
Croce this is an interesting thesis, because he had explicitly banned religion from
his system. But Collingwood bases his view on Croce's *Cultura e vita morale* of
1914, which was not available to the English speaking public, thus demonstrat-
ing his superior knowledge of Italian philosophy. Gentile had always been more
lenient towards religion by recognising it as the 'objective moment of the spirit',
which Collingwood illustrates on the basis of 'Le forme assolute dello spirito' of
1909, another relatively unknown work.[143]

Then Collingwood criticises Underhill's identification of actualism with
Bergson's 'philosophy of change'.[144] In Collingwood's view this identification is
based on a confusion of change and history. This amounts to misunderstanding
Gentile's philosophy which is, 'whatever its shortcomings, one of the most
remarkable of the present-day'.[145] Collingwood gives the following account of
Gentile's philosophy:

---

[139] R.G. Collingwood, 'List of Work Done', 38.

[140] Bernard Bosanquet, *The Meeting of Extremes in Contemporary Philosophy*, MacMillan,
London, 1921, 70.

[141] R.G. Collingwood, 'Can the New Idealism Dispense with Mysticism?' in *Proceedings of
the Aristotelian Society*, Supplement, III, 1923, 161–75, cited from Rubinoff, L. (ed.), *Faith
and Reason: Essays in the Philosophy of Religion by R.G. Collingwood*, Quadrangle Books,
Chicago, 1968, 270.

[142] Ibid.

[143] Ibid., 272.

[144] Ibid., 273, 277–8.

[145] Ibid., 274.

Reality, for Gentile, is history. Now history is not, as Miss Underhill assumes, a synonym for change. Change is, if I may put it this way, a realistic concept, history an idealistic. That which changes is a mere object, which need not know that it is changing, and indeed which no one need know to be changing... That which has a history, on the other hand, is a mind, for matter may change but it cannot be said to have a history. And this mind knows its own history. It is simply by knowing its own history that, in Gentile's view, it comes to have a history at all. Hence Gentile's philosophy is a 'metaphysics of knowledge', that is to say, a philosophy which never loses sight of the question how do we come to know what we know?[146]

Some interpreters have taken this passage as evidence for Collingwood's adherence to actualism, but this is mistaken.[147] As we have seen above, Collingwood had already adequately criticised Gentile's philosophy in the 'Libellus' and likened his own position to de Ruggiero's absolute empiricism. What we read in the above passage is not a simple defence of actualism, but an absolute empiricist account of actualism. Already the opening sentence, 'Reality, for Gentile, is history', is the result of a highly developed interpretation of his philosophy, for as we have seen Gentile himself used to identify reality with the pure act of thought. It is true that Gentile also identified the pure act with history and that he gave history a very important place in his system, but this does not alter the fact that he identified the pure act of thought with philosophy in the first place, and that he used to reduce history to the history of philosophy. In Collingwood's comparison of 'the philosophy of change' as a metaphysics of being with actualism as a 'metaphysics of knowledge' for which mind knows its own history. This must be seen as a highly important indication that Collingwood began to interpret becoming in terms of history, and history in terms of self-knowledge of the mind. This identification is clearly illustrated in the following passage:

History is thus by definition something known. It is not merely a process, it is a known process. But the mind which knows a process can only do so by somehow detaching itself from and rising above this process. If it were wholly immersed in the process, it would, perhaps, be changing, but it could never know that it was changing. And this unknowable process would therefore not really be a process at all; it would not be a change in the mind, for the mind would no longer possess that continuity without which no change can take place. One mind would perish at every instant and another would come into being; and that is no change in a mind. Hence change in a mind must be change for that mind, a change of which that mind is conscious; and to be conscious of it, the mind must somehow be raised above it. How is this apparent contradiction to be realized? How is the mind to be at once in change and out of change? Only if the mind originates change in itself. For then, as the source and ground of change, it will no be subject to change; while on the

146 Ibid.
147 Rubinoff, *Collingwood and the Reform of Metaphysics*, 320.

other hand, as undergoing change through its own free act, it will exhibit change.[148]

This passage has also been interpreted as a clear indication of Collingwood's actualism, but in my view it is just another vivid illustration of Collingwood's ability to explain Gentile's theories to a British audience.[149] As we have seen, Collingwood had criticised Gentile's notion of the eternal present, the dialectic of act and fact, and the view of the self-identical transcendental ego in the 'Libellus' by pointing out that these views lead to a belief in the 'completeness' of the present which creates a past for itself as a static background for its own development. Moreover, he had shown that the basis of Gentile's overvaluation of the pure act of thought was based on a confusion of consciousness and self-consciousness. Against these views Collingwood had posited his own notion of the pureness of the world of becoming and proposed to use the concept of process in order to describe this world. But he had not yet elaborated the distinction between consciousness and self-consciousness. We have already seen how Collingwood began to identify self-consciousness with history in the 'Lectures on Moral Philosophy' of 1921. The passages cited above indicate that he developed this identity by reinterpreting Gentile. Indeed, Collingwood was so confident of his position that he unfolded a programme for 'modern idealism' at the end of his paper. After showing that all experience, such as art and religion, is never intuitive, or 'immediate', but based on principles, or 'mediate', Collingwood sketches how the philosopher should deal with such an experience as 'mysticism'. The philosopher cannot dispense with mysticism since it is a form of experience and as experience it must be a mediate experience. Despite this it should not take the place of scientific or philosophical thought, but it should have a place of its own. Collingwood tries to define this place as follows:

> Its peculiarity is perhaps to be sought in the fact that in it the mediation which is actually present is not wholly explicit: the mind reaches truths, but does not know how it has reached them. It may even think that it has not reached them by any path, that is by any describable process of thinking; but this, if it is believed, is wrongly believed. The truths in question are reached somehow, and it is the business of scientific or philosophical thought to lay bare this concealed process, to render explicit the mediation which in the mystical experience itself was only implicit. 'Substantial truth', said Hegel, and every idealist will agree, 'is not dependent for its first revelation upon philosophy'.[150]

This passage, which echoes Collingwood's meditations on the Albert Memorial, is of the greatest importance for understanding his development in the 1920s. Making the crucial distinction between consciousness and self-consciousness, he views the first as an experience for which the principles of its 'mediation' are

---

R.G. Collingwood, 'Can the New Idealism Dispense with Mysticism?', 274–5.

Rubinoff, *Collingwood and the Reform of Metaphysics*, 320–1.

R.G. Collingwood, 'Can the New Idealism Dispense with Mysticism?', 281.

implicit, and the second as an experience for which these principles are explicit. It is this distinction that Gentile sometimes failed to draw; its consequence being that he believed that the 'mediation' is always a conscious activity. Moreover, Gentile saw this mediation as an embodiment of the transcendental ego which is logically and ontologically prior to it. From this it follows that the 'implicit' principles are always perfect embodiments of the 'explicit' principles. For example, Ariosto's poetry embodies the development of the transcendental ego so that the reader of his poems can gain access to the principles which underlie it. By distinguishing implicit and explicit principles, Collingwood acknowledges that the 'mediation' may take place unconsciously. From this it follows that the relationship between implicit and explicit principles is not a conscious embodiment of the transcendental ego. Collingwood thus recognises the independence of the formation of implicit principles with regard to the explicit principles. From this it follows that the contemporary reader of Ariosto's poetry can no longer assume that his poems embody the principles of art of present times, so that he will have to reconstruct Ariosto's own principles first. Stated in actualist terms, the prime task of the interpreter is therefore not to show how the implicit principles, or *pensati*, embody the development of the explicit principles, or *autoconcetto*, but to understand the implicit principles in their own context. This view is clearly expressed by Collingwood at the end of his paper where he points out that it is of the highest importance to distinguish between 'the real mystic experience' and 'the account of that experience which the mystic himself gives', or between 'mystical experiences and descriptive theories of them'. This distinction has important implications for the history of mystic experience.[151] In Collingwood's view, the task of the historian of religion is not to show that some past mystical experience is wrong, because it is still based on the intuitive theory of knowledge. Instead, the historian should try to understand the relationship between the mystic's experience and his own self-understanding and see where the latter is wrong in order to correct his description of that past experience. It is on the basis of this distinction between explicit and implicit principles that Collingwood was able to solve the articulation problem in *Speculum Mentis*.

The First Painting: *Speculum Mentis* (1924)

After finishing *Speculum Mentis* Collingwood enthusiastically reported to de Ruggiero how he solved the 'articulation problem':

> I have just finished the book which I call *Speculum Mentis*, which is my Philosophy of the Spirit, and I must write and tell you about it. It began from two ends at once — (i) elaborate empirical studies of art, religion, science, history and philosophy and their various modifications and forms: these being my empirically chosen 'forms of the spirit'. (ii) the principle that all these must be identical (in the sense in which you proved the identity of science and philos-

---

[151] Ibid., 280.

ophy in your Scienza). The problem was to find a principle which would serve to articulate without destroying the unity of the spirit. I found this by reflecting that the spirit was not an infinite given whole but a process of self-discovery and self-creation, and therefore the principle required must be simply self-knowledge with its negative self-ignorance. I actually reached this from the empirical side, by discovering (a) that all religion is metaphor, but cannot admit that it is metaphor without ceasing to be religion; (b) that all science is hypothesis but similarly cannot admit it; and so on: thus each form contains in its definition a negative element, viz. 'in this form, the mind is an *sich* such and such, but not *für sich*'. Thus, in each form there is a contradiction between its own view of itself and an outside observer's view of it.[152]

Collingwood's account of his development seems to be adequate. By the 'elaborate empirical studies' of the forms of experience, he refers to the lectures on art, religion, and the manuscripts and papers on science and history from 1918 to 1923. These forms of experience are 'identical' to each other in the sense of de Ruggiero's 'Scienza come esperienza assoluta' of 1912; each of the forms is conceived of as a unity of *coscienza* and *scienza*; each is a form experience developing itself in a dialectic of question and answer activities on the basis of certain principles. Finally, he solved the 'articulation problem' by rejecting the view of the spirit as 'an infinite given whole'. On this point, Collingwood seems to have his criticism of Gentile's transcendental ego in mind because he claims that his rejection of the spirit as an infinite given whole provided him with the distinction between self-knowledge and self-ignorance, or the between explicit and implicit principles as we have seen above.

It is most interesting that Collingwood avows that he reached this point from the empirical side, which reveals that he still 'tested' philosophical theories on actual experience, as he had done before the war. Collingwood's distinction between self-knowledge and self-ignorance finally yielded the principle of implicit and explicit principles, which Collingwood states in Kantian and Hegelian language of 'an sich' and 'für sich'. In *Speculum Mentis* he stated the same principle in plain English; in all forms of experience there are principles of which the person who has the experience is necessarily aware and other principles 'which are not actually recognised'.[153] Worried that his British audience would miss this distinction, which he had discovered during his meditations on the Albert Memorial, Collingwood stressed that it is 'of fundamental importance'. Obviously, de Ruggiero did not need this explanation. Having the 'Libellus' on his desk, he immediately understood that this essay attacked the priority of self-consciousness, which had been the foundation of Italian idealism.

After this criticism, Collingwood applied his newly found insights to the forms of experience, and the result was *Speculum Mentis*. In this book, Collingwood distinguishes five forms of experience: art, religion, science, history, and

---

[152] R.G. Collingwood, 'Letters to Guido de Ruggiero', 24 August 1923.
[153] R.G. Collingwood, *Speculum Mentis*, 85n.

philosophy. All these forms are identical because they all proceed as a dialectic of question and answer. On the basis of the distinction between explicit and implicit principles, Collingwood arranges the five forms in an order in which each form explicates the implicit principles of the foregoing form. The highest form of experience is philosophy, which explicates all the principles of all the foregoing forms, art, religion, science, and history.

Speculum Mentis contains Collingwood's first published account of the logic of question and answer. Typically, he deals with it not first in the chapter on science, as we might expect on the basis of de Ruggiero's 'La scienza come esperienza assoluta', but in the chapter on art.[154] Seen from the viewpoint of Collingwood's development this is not surprising since he refined his logic while meditating on the ugliness of the Albert Memorial.

In *Speculum Mentis* Collingwood presents art as the 'attitude that makes no assertions' because it is 'indifferent to reality'.[155] In Collingwood's view art is identical to intuition, imagination, and with the expression of emotions. The opposite of art is thought, which is identical to the categorical and the real. In *Speculum Mentis* Collingwood translates this view of art and thought into linguistic terms; art as expression of emotions is also language or a symbol, thought is the meaning of the symbol. Collingwood 'translates' the dialectic of the ideal and the real into epistemological terms; art does not question the reality of its experience and therefore it is epistemologically equivalent with hypothesis and with the questioning activity of the mind, whereas thought is its answer to the question.

Collingwood explicitly attributes the identification of art with supposal to Croce, although he does not agree with Croce's elaboration of it.[156] According to Collingwood, Croce falls into the error of regarding art as a self-contained phase.[157] The reason for this is found in Croce's identity of intuition and expression, by which he reduces the claim to reveal something about the ultimate nature of the real world to pure imagination. Collingwood holds that this is a false reduction. In his view, art makes contradictory claims; first that it is the activity of pure imagination, and secondly that it reveals something about the ultimate nature of the world. In Collingwood's view Croce 'pricks' the contradiction between the two claims 'so that the opposition vanishes and the terms collapse into an undifferentiated or immediate identity'.[158] But in this way Croce really ignores 'expression in the true sense' which Collingwood describes as follows:

> That which is expressed is necessarily a meaning, something distinct from the intuitive vehicle of meaning. This meaning is asserted as a truth. We do not

---

154 Ibid., 76–80.
155 Ibid., 76.
156 Ibid., 76.
157 Ibid., 91.
158 Ibid., 87.

assert what we say, for what we say is simply words, but what we mean; the act of meaning something is thus identical with the act of asserting something and it is this meaning which our words express.[159]

This passage is a further elaboration of Collingwood's earliest criticism of Croce's aesthetics. For Croce, intuition and expression are identical in the sense that we can only intuit by expressing ourselves. As in 1912, Collingwood does not deny this; for him too, art is an activity that is both intuitive and expressive. But, unlike Croce, he holds that art expresses something different from itself. Croce holds that if we say something, we know what we mean, that is, we know what we express when we say something. Interpreting intuition and expression as a process, Collingwood holds that we may say something, but not yet know what we mean. What we mean is developed in a self-reflective process in which we clarify what we say. The intuition is therefore not a self-contained phase in the life of the spirit, but it continuously passes over into its opposite, the expression, assertion, knowledge. But this is a continuous process that goes through several stages.

The first stage is religion which is presented as the opposite of art; it is basically the assertion of intuitions of art as real, that is, it takes the symbols as real. However, it is unconscious of the distinction between language and thought, between symbol and meaning. The specific problem with art is that the direct objects of religious consciousness are symbolic; they point to meanings which they do no contain.[160] When this distinction between language and thought is understood we enter the realm of thought which shapes its own language. Within thought Collingwood distinguishes between science, history, and philosophy. Collingwood presents science as basically supposal, as a questioning activity, and history as assertion, or as an answering activity. Science is the cutting edge of knowledge; history is its dead weight.[161] But this relationship between science and history is hidden from the scientist himself; he thinks that he is working in the world of concepts, but in fact he is working in the world of historical fact.[162] This world of fact is established by history and history is therefore the basis of all science. However, history itself is not a stable form of knowledge, for it fails to understand the principles on which it is based. Its aim is to establish the infinite world of fact, but it fails to give an account of how it comes to know these facts. The highest form in mind then is philosophy which explicates the principles on which history is based.

Seen in the light of Collingwood's development, *Speculum Mentis* summarises the studies of the foregoing years in one comprehensive 'interim report'. The book systematises almost everything he had done from 1912 onwards, from his

---

159 Ibid., 87–8.
160 Ibid., 133.
161 Ibid., 78, 186.
162 Ibid., 187.

early criticism of Croce, *Religion and Philosophy*, and the dialectic of question and answer which he developed during his Albert Memorial meditations and in *Truth and Contradiction*, to the process metaphysics of the 'Libellus' and the results of his logical investigations and his 'elaborate empirical studies' of the forms of the experience. Experience is the Alpha and Omega of *Speculum Mentis* and in this sense the book may be seen as Collingwood's tribute to absolute empiricism. Indeed, it may be seen as the perfect realisation of de Ruggiero's ideal of absolute empiricism which he described as 'a complete fusion of phenomenology, logic, philosophy of nature and philosophy of the spirit in a single science of psychology or phenomenology, whichever term is preferred, which is at the same time an ideal eternal history of the spirit in its development'.[163]

Of all the doctrines expounded in *Speculum Mentis*, those on art and history have been criticised most of all. Brown, who compares it to Croce's and Gentile's aesthetics, finds it 'almost incredible' and he dismisses Collingwood's theory of art as being intrinsically self-contradictory as a 'contribution to the air of folly which hovers about so odd and antiquated a theory'.[164] According to Brown, this folly stems from Collingwood's attempt to reconcile Croce's aesthetics with Gentile's dialectic, but he fails in this because he is 'weakest at that very point where the actualists distinguish themselves from Croce, that is, the point of self-consciousness'.[165] In my view this criticism completely misses Collingwood's point, which was in fact to reduce the importance of self-consciousness by distinguishing between the implicit and explicit levels of experience. Furthermore, this distinction is not as 'perverse' as Brown thinks it is. When taken as Collingwood meant it, namely not as a disjunction but as a synthesis of opposites, there is a sliding scale from the implicit to the explicit. For Collingwood, the artist is not a kind of Mr. Hyde who suddenly turns into a Dr. Jekyll, but he turns from his work of art to reflection by very gradual steps. In the heat of his artistic performance the artist need not have principles of beauty before him, but after the performance he will certainly try to discover whether these principles were well embodied. Art, like all experience, is mediation but not all the time conscious mediation. This is all that Collingwood wants to say.

More ice is cut by interpreters who criticised Collingwood's view of history in *Speculum Mentis*. On the basis of such passages as 'the historical consciousness asserts concrete fact' and 'the object of history is fact as such', van der Dussen holds that Collingwood's view of history is plainly realist.[166] Boucher challenges his interpretation by emphasising that Collingwood's method is idealist and that he applies this to what he considers to be history's self-image, that is, its realist

---

[163] G. de Ruggiero, *La filosofia contemporanea*, 406. E.T. 337.
[164] Brown, *Neo-Idealistic Aesthetics*, 185.
[165] Ibid., 190.
[166] Van der Dussen, *History as a Science*, 25.

conception of itself.[167] Yet, Collingwood himself always emphatically refused to be called an idealist. In my view he was perfectly right about this. From the standpoint expounded in the 'Libellus' the whole distinction between subject and object and therefore between realism and idealism is meaningless. In *Speculum Mentis*, Collingwood expounds the same doctrine in the last section on history in which he makes it clear that the transition from history to philosophy consists in giving up the distinction between subject and object.[168] Accordingly, he rejects idealism as a form as realism, just as he had done in the 'Libellus': 'idealism in this sense leaves the opposition between subject and object unreconciled, and therefore sets the object outside the subject.'[169] And as in the 'Libellus' he shows how idealism coincides with its own alleged opposite 'realism':

> Idealism, in the sense in which it leads to theism, is the doctrine that the world is made, so to speak, of mind; and is regarded as the opposite of materialism or the doctrine that the world is made of matter. Both these theories begin by abstracting the object of knowledge from the subject, and both go on by inquiring into the nature of the object in this abstraction, regarded as a thing in itself.[170]

At the end of the book, where Collingwood gives an overview of the whole argument, he even seems to tease the reader like a magician who lifts a corner of the veil but not all of it:

> We shall not blame the reader if he sees a picture, first of a mind contemplating an entire universe, rich in detail of every kind—the picture being entitled 'Realism'; secondly, the universe blotted ruthlessly out and the mind reflecting on its own forlorn condition, this picture bearing the title 'Idealism'.[171]

In this passage Collingwood asks the reader to note that the difference between realism and idealism is not important. In *Speculum Mentis* Collingwood presents philosophy as both 'studying the process by which it [thought] comes to be aware of such an object' and 'the self-liberation of thought from uncriticised assumptions, the determined attempt to believe nothing except on good grounds'.[172] This description of the task of philosophy is completely in line with Collingwood's position in 1924.[173] Regarding the becoming of experience as the Alpha and Omega of this philosophy he saw the distinction between subject and object as a meaningless abstraction.

---

[167] Boucher, *The Social and Political Philosophy of R.G. Collingwood*, 42.

[168] R.G. Collingwood, *Speculum Mentis*, 243-4.

[169] Ibid., 266.

[170] Ibid.

[171] Ibid., 291.

[172] Ibid., 247.

[173] Ibid., 246.

On this basis it seems plausible that Collingwood's notion of history in *Speculum Mentis* still resembles that of the 'Libellus', that is, the concept of the past which lives independently of the present act of thought. Collingwood explicitly expresses this view as follows:

> In the absolute process of thought the past lives in the present, not a mere 'trace' or effect of itself in the physical or psychical organism, but as the object of the minds' historical knowledge of itself in an eternal present.[174]

Collingwood's formulation of the 'living past' as an 'object' is remarkable, for it is this notion that sets it apart from the Italian view according to which the past is living as a construction of the present act of thought of the subject. According to Collingwood, it is this notion of the living past that solves all those problems concerning finitude and infinity which have so vexed abstract thought; 'the self-knowledge of mind as finite is already his assertion of himself as infinite.'[175] In other words: man's knowledge of the past teaches him at once that he is finite and infinite; he is finite because the living past presents itself as an infinite world of facts, and he is infinite because he can overcome the infinite world of facts by his thought.[176]

As we have seen above, it was this rejection of the spirit as an infinite given whole that led Collingwood to his distinction between self-knowledge and self-ignorance. Here we find that it is the 'living past' that teaches man about his finiteness and infiniteness and *ipso facto* of his self-knowledge and self-ignorance. It is this metaphysics that lies at the basis of his alleged realist passages in the chapter on history. In all of them he wishes to stress man's finitude with regard to the 'objective' past, which presents itself as an infinity of facts. Surrendering to this objectivity, Collingwood avers, amounts to confessing 'that our histories are nothing but an expression of personal points of view, this is the very cynicism of history, the conscious acquiescence in what has now become a deliberate fraud'.[177] It is against this subjectivism, where we may recognise the bad form of actualism, that Collingwood posits his notion of the objective past, just as he had done in the 'Libellus', his first essay in absolute empiricism.

However, seen from an absolute empiricist point of view, the section on history is the weakest of all. In a fully-fledged absolute empiricist account of history, we would expect a detailed analysis of its question and answer activity. But in the chapter on history Collingwood seems to have concentrated on history as an answer, that is, as the establishment of fact, as the product of historical research. In comparison with de Ruggiero's analysis of science, Collingwood has little to say about the questioning activity of history.

---

[174] Ibid., 301–2.
[175] Ibid., 302.
[176] Ibid.
[177] Ibid., 237–8.

Instead, Collingwood focuses on perception, which he regards as the simplest form of history. Perception is a unity of sensation and thought which develops itself through intermediate stages such as annals and memoirs to the highest forms of history.[178] This reminds us of de Ruggiero's analysis of sensation and thought in 'La scienza come esperienza assoluta', but unlike de Ruggiero Collingwood does not indicate how perception leads to questions, nor does he indicate how these questions are answered in the diverse stages. Only in a few places does Collingwood remark on the questioning activity in the higher stages of history, for example when he says that its questions are distorted by misconceptions of facts.[179] He does not, however, deal with the genesis of history, or with the problem of the raising of its first questions. For this reason Collingwood fails to explain how the 'living past' can be and should be known and this is explicitly admitted when he says that 'if history exists, its object is an infinite whole which is unknowable'.[180] In short, in *Speculum Mentis* Collingwood presented his solutions to the problem of self-consciousness and the articulation problem, but he was not yet able to formulate a solution to the third problem of the status of history.

The first to see this were de Ruggiero and Croce. In November 1924, immediately after receiving *Speculum Mentis*, de Ruggiero wrote a letter to Collingwood. This letter is lost, but from Collingwood's reply it becomes clear that his friend had expressed some criticisms.[181] We may assume that de Ruggiero's criticism was related to Collingwood's view of history in *Speculum Mentis*, because this was also the main target of his review of 1928:

> ...in particular the doctrine of history, which, with its reduction of historical knowledge to objective fact, separated from the subjectivity of the spirit, seems to be the least elaborated part of the whole system.[182]

As we have seen, de Ruggiero identified the subjective aspect of the spirit, or *coscienza*, with the questioning activity, and its objective aspect, or *scienza*, with the answering activity. His criticism thus amounts to the claim that Collingwood had not sufficiently taken the questioning activity of history into account. Like no other, de Ruggiero was aware of the difficulties of working out a theory of historical questioning. In his 'Scienza come esperienza assoluta' he had shown how scientific questions arise from a sensation that cannot explain itself and how these questions are answered in the process of idealisation.[183] But in history, we do not start from sensation, nor can we 'match' our new answers to empirical data. In history, we start from evidence which we try to interpret. History and

---

[178] Ibid., 203–5.

[179] Ibid., 232.

[180] Ibid., 234.

[181] R.G. Collingwood, 'Letters to Guido de Ruggiero', 16 November 1924.

[182] G. de Ruggiero, *Filosofi del novecento*, 102.

[183] See chapter 4, pp. 102–103.

science both start from actual experience, but the crucial difference is that in science this actual experience is enough, whereas in history it refers to something which does not exist anymore. Collingwood's problem was therefore to develop a notion of historical 'idealisation' in an historical logic of question and answer.

This interpretation is corroborated by Collingwood's reply to Croce's criticism of *Speculum Mentis* which he published in *La Critica* of January 1925. Croce certainly approved of the general thesis of the book, but he rejected Collingwood's view of art and more specifically the passage from art as imagination to art as expression of meaning.[184] This criticism pierces the heart of *Speculum Mentis*, because, as we have seen, the whole logic of question and answer is based on identifying imagination with questioning and expression with answering. In his reply to Croce of 29 January 1925 Collingwood admits that this problem of the dialectic from imagination to conceptual thought needs more elaboration:

> ...my problem is to give a precise account of this dialectic: for I am not content with the abstract statement there must be such a dialectic without showing why it must exist. I want to find, in art as such, the germ of this dialectic the 'addentelation' of the passage to philosophy.[185]

In other words, Collingwood admits that his dialectic of the ideal and the real, of imagination and conceptual thought is not yet complete; it fails to explain how the ideal, or imaginations, become real, or thought. Translated in terms of the logic of question and answer this means that it is not clear how the questions become answers or, more precisely, on what grounds do we accept an answer as the right one to a certain question? After *Speculum Mentis*, Collingwood dealt both with the problem of the raising of questions and with the problem of the answering of questions as an account of history *a parte subiecti*. But it took him more than six years to relate this account of history *a parte subiecti*, or the logic of question and answer to his earlier view of history *a parte obiecti*, or the living past.

'The Nature and Aims of a Philosophy of History' (1924)

Collingwood began his investigations of history with 'The Nature and Aims of a Philosophy of History' of 1924. This article may be read as an outline of a philosophy of history on absolute empiricist principles, that is, as an account of *The Principles of History* as an autonomous form of experience, or in Italian terms, history as an identity of *coscienza* and *scienza*. This becomes clear at the end of the article where he presents the historian as a 'monad' and the philosopher as a 'monadologist'. The historian, Collingwood says, is only concerned with his object, but not with his own awareness of his object. In Italian terms this

---

184 B. Croce, 'R.G. Collingwood, *Speculum Mentis* or the Map of Knowledge', 58.
185 Amadeo Vigorelli (ed.), 'Lettere di Robin George Collingwood a Benedetto Croce (1912–1939)', in *Rivista di storia della filosofia*, 3, 552.

amounts to saying that the historian moves within his *coscienza*, whereas the
philosopher faces the question of the relationship between thought and its
object, or *scienza*. Philosophy is basically a critical attitude:

> ...which undertakes the task of inquiring not only into the results of a certain
> type of thought but into the nature and value, the presuppositions and imp-
> lications, of that type of thought itself.[186]

The explicit distinction made here between the 'results' and the 'nature', 'value',
and 'presuppositions' of that type of thought itself reveals that philosophy deals
with history primarily as an activity. Collingwood analyses this activity on an
absolute empiricist basis; following de Ruggiero's example, he describes the
genesis of history, its method, and the principles which underlie them.

As in *Speculum Mentis,* Collingwood describes the genesis of historical consciousness as perception but now he adds that in all perception 'reflection'
shows two elements: sensation and thought. Sensation and thought can never be
separated and from this it follows that perception must be seen as implicit
thought. Collingwood stresses the fact that the procedure of history cannot be
complete without an analysis of 'the ideal which it set before itself'. Collingwood
describes this ideal as follows:

> The ideal of history, then, is to be a single categorical judgement, articulated
> into an infinity of coherent categorical judgements, asserting the reality and
> expounding the nature of an infinite world individual world of fact articu-
> lated into an infinity of individual facts.[187]

Interestingly, here Collingwood still regards history as the assertion of 'reality'
and the 'world of fact', just as in *Speculum Mentis.* Guided by this ideal, history
develops itself dialectically from the simplest form, perception, to its most developed form. Collingwood does not indicate each step of this process, but it is
clear that history develops itself in a question and answer process: 'In all perception', Collingwood claims, 'we are making a judgement, trying to answer the
question what it is that we perceive, and all history is simply a more intense and
sustained answer to the same question'.[188] Perception grows more intense and
sustained by comparing past experience with present experience, first implicitly
and then in the form of memory which is the basis of a memoir, the simplest
form of history. According to Collingwood the use of memoirs opens the possibility of using everybody's memories, and this involves 'the question of supple-
menting one person's experience by another's'.[189] This question involves other

---

[186] R.G. Collingwood, 'The Nature and Aims of a Philosophy of History', in *Proceedings of
the Aristotelian Society,* 25, 1924-25, 151-74, cited from id., *Essays in the Philosophy of
History,* 45.

[187] Ibid., 46.

[188] Ibid., 50.

[189] Ibid., 51.

questions as well such as that of checking the reliability of the source.[190] The process of questions and answers is never finished, because in the first place each historian asks his questions from his own point of view and, in the second place, his point of view is continuously changing.[191] The final step in the question and answer process occurs when the historian starts asking questions about his own point of view. Doing this he discovers that he is in 'the egocentric predicament', and discovering this involves transcending it.[192] The historian thus overcomes his monadism and becomes a monadologist who does not merely see a perspective but a space of perspectives. This 'world of worlds' is infinite, it 'has no centre; its centre is everywhere and its circumference is nowhere; and in it there is no such thing as a presupposition for thought except in the sense that thought itself is its own presupposition'.[193]

On this point Collingwood states the first principle of a new programme for a philosophy of history. The most significant difference with *Speculum Mentis* is that Collingwood tries to do justice to the subjective aspect of history, that is, to its questioning aspect, without losing its objective aspect from of sight; history must be based on evidence and aims at asserting the reality of the world of fact. The question and answer activity culminates in the infinite 'world of worlds', which has the clearly Gentilian aspect of being without presuppositions except that thought itself is its own presupposition, that is, in a world in which the questioning activity proceeds on the basis of the presupposition which it posits for itself in absolute freedom. But even in this ultimate stage 'historical fact in its reality' remains unknowable, so that history never completes its task.

Collingwood's analysis of the historical questioning activity is only in its infancy because it fails to explain why perception should develop itself into history, whereas on Collingwood's account in *Speculum Mentis* it can also develop itself into other forms of experience such as art or science. In other words, Collingwood says that history is a more sustained attempt to answer to the questions that arise in perception, but he does not explain what leads us to historical questions. The reason for this omission is not far to seek. Collingwood himself had pointed out in *Speculum Mentis* that the minimum condition for all questioning is that there is something to question about, an 'object' of some sort. If historical questioning is possible there must be some historical object present in actual experience. But at the same time Collingwood holds that 'fact in its reality is unknowable'. It is also clear that the past is not present in actual experience in the same way as our sensations. For this reason Collingwood could not just adopt de Ruggiero's analysis of the genesis of scientific questions for his analysis of historical questions. It was on this point that Collingwood's problem

---

[190] Ibid.

[191] Ibid., 54–5.

[192] Ibid., 55.

[193] Ibid., 56.

concerning the ontological status of history began to arise. As we have seen, Croce tried to solve this problem by his distinction between the 'annals' or 'the dead past' and 'history' or the 'relived past', whereas Gentile and de Ruggiero tried to solve it with their doctrine of the 'ideality' of history. As we will see, Collingwood recognised the difficulty and he first attempted to combine both the notions of evidence and ideality.

The Ideality of History (1926)

Collingwood introduced the notion of 'ideality of history' in the preparatory manuscript for 'Some Perplexities about Time', a lecture which he was to read for the Aristotelian Society in February 1926.[194] In the manuscript Collingwood explains that both the past and the future are 'ideal' in the sense of being remembered or expected. On this point, Collingwood moves into the deep waters of actualism in which the object of thought is seen as a product of the act of thought. Gentile and de Ruggiero had defined history as a *pensato* for a *pensante*, that is, as an 'ideal' concept for the present act of thought. Collingwood echoes this view when he says that 'since history is not memory its *esse* is to be contemplated by a process of historical thinking'.[195] But in spite of this ideal status of history, Collingwood keeps to his claim that history must have an objective status too. Giving the examples of facts, like the one that the earth existed before there was life on it, and that there were men alive before I was born, he points out that we 'believe that they exist, because their consequences exist... but they themselves are as unreal as anything can possibly be'.[196] Collingwood's formulation gives an important indication of how he proposes to combine the ideality and the reality of the past; the past as such is completely ideal, but we believe in its reality because it has consequences in the present. This formulation comes close to Collingwood's notion of the 'living past' and must be taken as an important indication of how this notion should be understood. In the conclusion of the published version of 'Some Perplexities about Time' we find the same idea at the end of the paper. There, Collingwood distinguishes being from existing and within being the ideal from the actual.[197] The ideal is the non-existent, it is 'that which is thought, but not thought as real or existing' which is therefore 'for a mind and has no other being except to be an object of mind'.[198] The past and the future are completely ideal; they have only being for a mind. The past thus lives in the present as an object for the mind. All this is completely in accordance with

---

[194] Van der Dussen, *History as a Science*, 132; R.G. Collingwood, 'Some Perplexities about Time', 1925, Dep. 18/1.

[195] R.G. Collingwood, 'Some Perplexities about Time', Dep. 18/1, cited in van der Dussen, *History as a Science*, 133.

[196] Ibid., 132.

[197] R.G. Collingwood, 'Some Perplexities about Time: With and Attempted Solution', in *Proceedings of the Aristotelian Society*, 26, 1926, 149.

[198] Ibid., 150.

the actualist notion of ideality. However, at the end of the paper Collingwood presents us with the following surprise:

> From this it follows that we do call the past as such into being by recollecting and by thinking historically, but we do this by disentangling it out of the present in which it actually exists, transformed, and re-transforming it in thought into what it was.[199]

The first half-sentence in this passage is still compatible with actualism, but the second half is not. Firstly, Collingwood's image of 'disentangling' a past out of the present suggests that the past still exists in the present. Secondly, Colling-wood still seems to acknowledge that we can transform this 'disentangled' past into what it really was. This passage has rightly been interpreted as the fore-runner of the re-enactment doctrine which was fully elaborated in 1928.[200] At the same time it shows us that from the beginning Collingwood did not think of re-enactment in terms of the dialectic of *pensante* and *pensato*. 'Some Perplexities about Time' rather suggests that Collingwood tried to find a synthesis between the doctrine of the pure act of thought on the one hand, and his own doctrine of the living past on the other. His first attempt to bring the two views together is found in his first series of lectures on the philosophy of history of 1926.

'Lectures on the Philosophy of History' (1926)

That the notion of the ideality of the past gave Collingwood a key to under-standing the questioning activity of the historian is reflected in the lectures of 1926, in which he uses it in order to explain the genesis and the development of history. The structure of the lectures expresses the procedure which historians usually follow in their work. After a general introduction on the notions of his-tory and time, Collingwood deals with the sources of history, their interpreta-tion, and finally with the finished product which is a narrative. Collingwood introduces the notion of the ideality of the past in the discussion about time. Like the Italians, Collingwood opposes ideality to actuality; the present alone is actual, it consists of things happening now, the past and the future are 'ideal', the former consists of events that have happened, the latter of events that will happen. Collingwood also identifies actuality with reality and existence, and ideality with the not real or the not existent.[201]

The thesis of the ideality of the past leads to the question how it can be known, and the answer to this is that it is based on sources.[202] History comes into

---

[199] Ibid.

[200] Van der Dussen, *History as a Science*, 36.

[201] R.G. Collingwood, 'Lectures on the Philosophy of History', written in 1926, cited from *The Idea of History, Revised Edition with Lectures 1926–28, edited with an Introduction by Jan van der Dussen*, Clarendon Press, Oxford, 1993, 367.

[202] Ibid., 364.

existence as the finding and interpreting of sources.[203] It develops itself in the light of its ideal of being a narrative about the past. But since the past is ideal, complete knowledge of it is impossible. This leads Collingwood to the question of why we should pursue it at all. Surprisingly, he uses the notion of the ideality again in order to explain that we need not know it as it actually happened. 'The past', Collingwood says, 'is an ideal element in the present, and can therefore be studied in the same general way and to the same extent to which any abstraction may be studied'.[204] Only the present is actual, Collingwood maintains, but within it we can make ideal distinctions, or abstractions such as the past and the future. Our knowledge of the past, Collingwood concludes, 'is therefore not knowledge of the past as of an actual object, and therefore not true knowledge; it is only the reconstruction of an ideal object in the interests of knowing the present'.[205]

With these formulations Collingwood seems to come side by side with actualism. Like the actualists he regards history as an abstraction from the present, as ideality, a construction of the past by present thought. Present thought thus becomes wholly constitutive of the past. The only dissonance with actualism is his remark that history, as knowledge of an ideal object, does not yield true knowledge. On this point Gentile and de Ruggiero would have pointed out that history as knowledge of an ideal object is the only form of true knowledge. But Collingwood still keeps to his view that true knowledge is always knowledge of an existent object. Again, this view leads him to very peculiar remarks at the end of his lectures: 'whereas the past exists actually in the present, it exists ideally as the past' and 'we should study the past as we study all abstractions, namely by making ideal distinctions within it'.[206] These remarks clearly indicate that by 1926 Collingwood had not yet found the proper synthesis between history *a parte subiecti* and history *a parte obiecti*, or more particularly between the activities of the historian as they were elaborated by the Italians and his own conception of the living past. Collingwood's uncertainty is clearly illustrated by the following letter to de Ruggiero:

> For myself, I am trying to clear up my conception of History, helped greatly, but not wholly satisfied, by both Croce and Gentile, and developing further the view expressed in *Speculum Mentis*. And always pursuing the study of history itself.[207]

Yet, despite Collingwood's uncertainty about the status of history, he claims that it is 'one of the necessary and transcendental modes of mind's activity, and the

---

[203] Ibid., 368–70.

[204] Ibid., 404–5.

[205] Ibid., 406.

[206] Ibid., 404–5.

[207] R.G. Collingwood, 'Letters to Guido de Ruggiero', 18 August 1926.

common property of all minds'. It is this conception that he would elaborate during a trip to Italy on which he would meet Croce, Gentile, and de Ruggiero.

'Preliminary Discussion' (1927)

In 1927 Collingwood travelled to Italy and met Gentile and de Ruggiero in Rome. Without doubt they had long conversations about philosophy, history, and the political situation in Italy.[208] These discussions inspired Collingwood to write the 'Preliminary Discussion' for his lectures of 1926. The 'Preliminary Discussion' has the peculiar subtitle 'The Idea of a Philosophy of Something, and, in Particular, a Philosophy of History', which reveals that its central problem concerns the nature of philosophy.[209] Philosophy, Collingwood maintains, must be universal and necessary thought. A philosophical concept is universal in the sense that it inevitably arises whenever anybody thinks about a subject.[210] They are called 'transcendentals' or 'universal concepts' which are applicable to everything that exists, in contradistinction to 'non-transcendental' or empirical concepts which are only applicable to a limited sphere.[211] Art, religion, and science, for example, are transcendental concepts, because everything that exists can be a legitimate object of aesthetic or religious contemplation or of scientific thought. 'Tea-cup' and 'bald-headed station master' are empirical concepts, because there are other things than these in the world.[212] History is also a transcendental concept, because, like art and science, it is a pure form of activity.[213]

Up to this point Collingwood has said nothing that would surprise the Italians; all this is perfectly compatible with Croce's notion of the pure concepts, or with Gentile's theory of the pure act of thought. But when Collingwood begins to explain the relationship between the empirical and universal concepts, he has original things to say. Collingwood starts his analysis with an example taken from art. For the artist, he says, art is an empirical concept which is present in some works and absent in others. The artist makes clear-cut distinctions between art and non-art. From this it follows that a work of art is always good art and that a bad work of art is simply not art. The empirical concept of art can there-

---

[208] Collingwood stayed in de Ruggiero's house, and was invited to a party by Gentile, whom he describes as 'very cordial'. Gentile offered a copy of the new edition of his *Studi Vichiani* and asked Collingwood about his opinion of the political situation in Italy, remarking, after Collingwood's reply, that 'a foreigner staying three weeks in a country could not hope to form a just opinion of its political situation', see: R.G. Collingwood, 'Letters to Guido de Ruggiero', 1920–38, Dep. 27, 16 April 1927.

[209] R.G. Collingwood, 'Preliminary Discussion, The Idea of a Philosophy of Something, and, in Particular, A Philosophy of History', written in 1927, cited from *The Idea of History, Revised Edition*, 335.

[210] Ibid.

[211] Ibid., 352.

[212] Ibid., 351.

[213] Ibid., 357.

fore not be applied to all objects.[214] For the philosopher, art is a philosophical concept, this means that art is universally and inevitably present in every act of the human mind. The philosopher tries to explain how every act of the mind at least tries to be a work of art which means that he must explain to what degree the universal art is present and to what degree it is absent in a work of art. The philosopher tries to understand the process which leads to the work of art. For him, both beauty and ugliness are to a certain degree present in any object of art.[215] Empirical thought is based on the three laws of formal logic; a work of art is beautiful or ugly, *tertium non datur*. For the artist the universal is not differentiated; art is of one kind. Philosophical thought, however, transcends the three laws and allows for the coexistence of contradictory universals in one object; to a certain degree every work of art is beautiful and ugly at the same time. For the philosopher the universal is set apart differently in different works of art; every work of art tries to be beautiful in its own way.[216]

The most interesting aspect of Collingwood's example is that he shows that the dialectic interpretation of the universal involves the need for the philosopher to explain what the artist tried to do. The use of the verb 'try', which also appeared in his Albert Memorial meditations, reveals that Collingwood thinks again of the artistic activity in terms of aesthetic problems and solutions, a view he had fully expounded in *Speculum Mentis*. But even more interesting is his recognition of the autonomy of the artist; the philosopher recognises that every work of art tries to be beautiful in its own way and each work of art differentiates the universal in a different way.

Collingwood describes this 'differentiation' in terms of 'embodiment' and 'expression'; any work of art 'embodies' or realises an 'idea' of its own. This 'idea', or 'form of beauty', is deliberately chosen by the artist as the central motive of his work of art.[217] This new form of beauty, Collingwood points out, must have been present as an element in previous works of art, indeed in all previous works of art. Collingwood therefore concludes that the individual work of art may be defined as a particular subject raised to the level of beauty, or beauty expressing itself in the form of the particular subject.[218]

The most interesting aspect of Collingwood's analysis is the idea that the work of art is not explicitly conditioned by the universal concept of beauty; the artist chooses his subject self-consciously with an eye on other works of art and not on the universal concept of art; the artist need not think about aesthetics before he begins his own work of art. Yet his work of art has some characteristics in common with all art, because as art it has some universal and necessary

---

[214] Ibid., 353.
[215] Ibid., 354.
[216] Ibid., 354–5.
[217] Ibid.
[218] Ibid., 355.

characteristics. The universal and necessary characteristics of art are therefore only implicit in artistic activity, not explicit.

On the basis of this analysis of empirical and transcendental aspects of the mind Collingwood elaborates on the relationship between history, philosophy of history, and philosophy in general.

Firstly, Collingwood 'disentangles' three aspects in the philosophy of history:

First as a complex of particular methodological problems growing immediately out of historical thinking. Secondly, as an attempt to answer the question, what is history? Thirdly, as identical with philosophy in general.[219]

According to Collingwood, the methodological questions are 'in themselves chaotic, shapeless, capable of enumeration into infinity'. These questions can begin with 'ought' or with 'can', for example: 'ought history to pay special attention to any one side of human life, such as economics or politics' or 'can history exist in the absence of written records'.[220]

These methodological questions constitute the 'matter' of the philosophy of history. Its form consists of the 'elaboration of the transcendental concept of history which is the answer to the general question: "what is history?"'.[221] Collingwood indicates that the question 'what is history' has several aspects concerning the 'fundamental nature, meaning, purpose and value of history'.[222] All these questions are at their heart one because 'any answer to any one of the many involves an answer to all the others, and any alteration in the answer given to one involves an alteration in the answers given to all others'.[223] Finally, all these questions bring us face to face with problems from every department of philosophy.[224]

This analysis of the empirical and transcendental aspects of history must be seen as an emendation of the analysis given in *Speculum Mentis*. In that work, Collingwood had not clearly distinguished between the empirical and transcendental aspects of history. In 1927, he presents four levels of historical consciousness; history proper, methodology of history, philosophy of history, and philosophy proper. Moreover, all these levels are arranged as a series of questions, answers, and presuppositions; historians posit and solve their problems on the basis of certain methodological presuppositions, which in turn presuppose a transcendental concept of history, and this finally presupposes a concept of philosophy in general. Finally, philosophy itself is seen as the systematisation of all the transcendental concepts of the mind.

---

[219] Ibid., 349.
[220] Ibid., 347–8.
[221] Ibid., 348.
[222] Ibid.
[223] Ibid.
[224] Ibid., 348–9.

Again, this notion of the empirical and transcendental concepts must be seen as a clearer expression of the views Collingwood had held from the beginning of his career. A 'philosophy of something' is truly philosophy if the 'something' can be proven to be a universal and necessary activity on the basis of which the transcendental concept of that 'something' can be developed. Philosophy is therefore not some kind of intellectual intuition, but a form of experience that starts from transcendental concepts which it enriches by reflecting on the activities of the mind. All these activities are fundamentally 'problematic' in the sense that they self-consciously posit some ideal for themselves which they try to realise on the basis of certain methods and principles. The ideals, methods, and principles are based on empirical concepts which are seen as the implicit 'application' of the transcendental concepts. The task of philosophy is to show how the empirical concepts embody or apply the transcendental concepts. The philosopher must start from the concrete activities and try to understand what the artist, scientist, or historian is trying to do, that is, how their particular activities embody the universal concepts. In this way, Collingwood brought philosophical understanding closer to historical understanding, as he came to see at the end of the decade.

'Outlines of a Philosophy of History' (1928)

The lectures of 1928 are Collingwood's first attempt to elaborate a transcendental analytics of historical reason as announced in 'The Nature and Aims of a Philosophy of History'. In honour of Kant, Collingwood divided his lectures into four parts, under the headings 'Quality', 'Quantity', 'Relation', and 'Modality'. Under the heading of 'Quality', Collingwood deals with ideality of the past at a much greater length than in the lectures of 1926. The notion of the ideality of the pasts forms the basis of the rest of the lectures. Under the heading of 'Quantity', Collingwood discusses the limits of historical knowledge by opposing particular history, which deals with 'small questions', and universal history, which deals with 'larger questions'.[225] Under 'Relation', Collingwood deals with the nature of historical sequence and progress, which he conceives as the 'realisation of ideals'.[226] Finally, under 'Modality', Collingwood discusses the problem of the certainty of history and the principles on which it rests.[227]

Collingwood had already dealt with all these problems in his lectures of 1926, but now he solves them all in a much more systematical way guided by the notion of the ideality of the past. Most importantly, on the basis of this notion Collingwood tries to find a solution for the problem of the relationship between history *a parte obiecti* and history *a parte subiecti*, which he had left unsolved in

---

[225] R.G. Collingwood, 'Outlines of a Philosophy of History', written 1928, cited from *The Idea of History, Revised Edition*, 450.

[226] Ibid., 479.

[227] Ibid., 482.

the lectures of 1926. In the introduction to the lectures Collingwood describes history *a parte subiecti* as 'the thinking that goes on in the historian's mind and is reported upon in his writings', and history *a parte obiecti* as 'the facts or events about which he thinks'.[228] In Collingwood's view, philosophy of history is concerned with history *a parte subiecti* and it is primarily a logic of historical method; it deals with the universal and necessary aspects of historical thought. But it is misleading to simply call the philosophy of history the methodology of history, for if historical method is adequate for the study of its proper objects, it follows that in studying the necessary and universal features of historical method we also study the necessary and universal features of historical fact; that logic and metaphysics are the same, because a law of thought must be a metaphysical law too.[229]

On this point, Collingwood clearly applies the first rule of his 'Libellus'; there is no dualism between mind and its object, the mind is a process and some of its objects. From this principle it follows that whatever is said about the process of the mind must also apply to its object. In the particular case of history it means that whatever we say about history *a parte subiecti*, or the thought activities of the historian, must *ipso facto* also apply to history *a parte obiecti*. This basic identity between history *a parte subiecti* and *obiecti* lies at the basis of Collingwood's re-enactment doctrine which he formulated for the first time in these lectures of 1928.

Collingwood begins his discussion of this doctrine with the following remark:

> History *a parte obiecti*, the object of historical thought, is of course in some sense real, for if it were not, there would be no sense in which historical judgements could be true, or indeed false.[230]

After this opening, Collingwood discusses the notions of reality, existence, actuality, and ideality, which are all based on the difference between 'things' and 'events'. Realistic philosophies, Collingwood says in the vein of the 'Libellus', identify reality with 'existence', or the 'reality of a thing'. But history does not consist of things, but of 'events'. Events do not exist as 'things' but they 'occur'.[231] Apart from this, historical events have the peculiarity that they do not occur when the historian thinks about them. Historical events are therefore not actual, but wholly ideal. Collingwood gives a formal definition of ideality as 'the quality of being an object of thought without having actuality', and he points out that actuality implies simultaneousness with the thought in question.[232] According to Collingwood, 'things' can be both ideal and actual: 'the Matterhorn as I

---

[228] Ibid., 434.
[229] Ibid., 429–30.
[230] Ibid., 439.
[231] Ibid.
[232] Ibid., 440.

remember it ten years ago is ideal, the Matterhorn as I see it now is actual.'[233] The past can never have this double reality: 'it must be wholly and only ideal.'[234]

Up to this point Collingwood has only given a more detailed account of the notion of ideality than in the lectures of 1926, but after this he makes a crucial step, by holding that the distinction between the ideal and the actual is not absolute, because the ideal can be made actual again, that is, the present act of thought can make the ideal past actual again by 're-enacting' it. Giving an example from the history of music, Collingwood points out that the *conditio sine qua non* of the writing about past music is to have it re-enacted in the present.[235] In the same way, Collingwood says, historians rethink the thoughts which determined the tactics in a battle.

Collingwood stresses that re-enactment does not make the past thought completely actual or present. Past thought remains ideal: 'the only sense in which the object of historical thought is actual, is that it is actually thought about'.[236] For example, the historian who listens to sixteenth-century madrigals and masses is well aware that their place is in the sixteenth century and not in the twentieth.[237] To the question of how the historian can re-enact the past, Collingwood answers that the historian may re-enact a past event if that event is a thought. But Collingwood immediately points that the word 'thought' should be understood in its widest sense which includes 'all the conscious activities of the human spirit'.[238] Concluding his analysis, Collingwood says: 'All history, then, is the history of thought.'[239]

Ten years later, when Collingwood wrote his autobiography, he was still proud of his achievement in his 'Outlines of a Philosophy of History'. In these lectures he formulated his first and second propositions of the philosophy of history — 'all history is the history of thought' and 'all history is the re-enactment of past thought' — for the first time.[240] Collingwood's interpreters, however, do not agree about the value of these lectures. According to van der Dussen, the 're-enactment doctrine provides a solution for the problem how we can have knowledge of the past, though it is obviously now an object in the present, for in the re-enactment of past thought the past is actualised in re-thinking it'.[241] The re-enactment doctrine is in his view not a proposal for historical methodology, but a description of a universal and necessary characteristic of history. In Nielsen's view, the ideality doctrine must be seen as the basis of Collingwood's construc-

---

233 Ibid.
234 Ibid.
235 Ibid., 441.
236 Ibid., 444.
237 Ibid., 443.
238 Ibid., 445.
239 Ibid.
240 R.G. Collingwood, *An Autobiography*, 110, 112.
241 Van der Dussen, *History as a Science*, 147.

tivist theory of history, according to which 'the historian constructs or re-constructs history, and does not discover it ready-made'.[242] Dray challenged this constructivist interpretation by drawing attention to some explicitly 'anti-constructivist' passages in the lectures. According to Dray, Collingwood's frequent use of the prefix 're' indicates that 'the object of historical thinking is past happenings, not present constructions'.[243] Another indication of Collingwood's anti-constructivism is his claim that that the past and present thought should and can be identical.[244] Dray finds these anti-constructivist passages in the 'Outlines' next to passages which are only ambiguously anti-constructivist and even overtly constructivist. As an example of 'ambiguous anti-constructivism', Dray gives Collingwood's doctrine of the 'living past' which he finds 'barely intelligible'.[245] In the lectures of 1928 this doctrine is exemplified by Collingwood saying that the historian's inquiry is 'the study of the present and not of the past at all' because it is concerned with 'those elements of the past whose traces in the present he can perceive and decipher'.[246] Finally, Dray finds most of Collingwood's lapses into constructivism in the passages in which he deals with the ideality of the past and in his claims that only the actual can be known. Since these passages cannot be found in Collingwood's writings of the 1930s Dray concludes that the ideality doctrine must be seen as a passing stage in his development.

It is interesting to note that Collingwood himself provides some evidence for Dray's conclusion. In the 'Preface' to the 'Outlines' he makes it clear that 'the various points made in the course of the argument are in fact observations made in the course of historical studies pursued while paying special attention a special eye to problems of method', and that the idea of considering these in the light of the conception of the ideality of history 'only occurred to the writer very late in the day, after most of them had been long familiar to him as the fruits of experience in historical research'.[247] For this reason, Collingwood points out, the 'whole essay... in its present form is certain to mislead the reader, because its argument appears to rest on a single point – the ideality of history...'[248] Collingwood therefore appeals to the reader to remember that each link in the argument is not guaranteed simply by its relation to the conception of the ideality of history, but to experience of historical inquiry.

These remarks accurately describe Collingwood's development. So far, Collingwood had elaborated his philosophy of history as an archaeologist and

---

[242] Margrit Hurup Nielsen, 'Re-enactment and Reconstruction in Collingwood's Philosophy of History', in *History and Theory*, 20, 1981, 26.

[243] Dray, *History as Re-enactment*, 244.

[244] Ibid., 244–5.

[245] Ibid., 252.

[246] Ibid., 253; Collingwood, 'Outlines', 485.

[247] R.G. Collingwood, 'Outlines', 427.

[248] Ibid.

historian working in his 'laboratory'. The concept of ideality came later, to be precise, in 1925. But before that date, the concept of ideality played an important role in the Italian philosophies, especially in those of Gentile and de Ruggiero. In his first criticism of Croce, Gentile identified '*idealità*' with 'the possible' opposing it to the 'actual' and the 'real'.[249] Later, Gentile identified '*idealità*' with the *pensato*, or concept, opposing it to the *pensante* or present thought, and de Ruggiero followed him in this. At first glance Collingwood seems to use the concept of ideality in the same sense as the Italians; he defines the ideality as 'the quality of being an object of thought without having actuality', which comes close to the Italian notion of the *pensato* for a *pensante*. However, the context of Collingwood's definition also differs from that of the Italians. This is most clearly shown by Collingwood's distinction between history *a parte subiecti* and history *a parte obiecti* at the beginning of the lectures. The Italians would certainly have recognised something of their own identification of *historia rerum gestarum* with *res gestae* in this. However, unlike the Italians, Collingwood does not identify the two; throughout the lectures he keeps to the distinction. Moreover, he claims at the beginning of 'Quality' that history is in some sense real, because if it were not, history could not be true or false. The Italians would have read this claim as a clarion call for a new philosophy of history, because they never saw the past as 'real', but only as 'ideal'. Whereas the Italians only acknowledged the ideality of history, Collingwood tries to run the concept of the 'ideality' of history, which according to his own saying 'came later in the day' together with his earlier notion of the 'reality' of history, that is, the idea of the living past. The real problem behind the lectures of 1928 is to find a synthesis between the two notions of the past. Seen in this light, many otherwise puzzling passages in Collingwood's lectures become clearer, though not crystal clear.

In the first place, the synthesis explains Collingwood's frequent use of the prefix 're' mentioned by Dray. The Italians also used this prefix, but not with the subsidiary claim that the historian is doing or thinking the same thing as was done or thought in the past. In the second place, it explains Collingwood's repeated warning that the re-enactment does not cancel the 'ideality' of the past, by making it completely present. Gentile had always defended this position and Collingwood had attacked it in the 'Libellus' as monochronism, followed by de Ruggiero in 'Arte e critica' of 1921. In the third place, it explains Collingwood's concerns about identity and difference between the past and its re-enactment. He formulates this problem as a 'serious' objection against re-enactment as follows:

> Why if the historian really re-enacts the past, is this re-enactment unaccompanied by the emotional heat, the vividness and liveliness of impression, which accompanied its original enactment: and conversely, how, if this re-enactment is devoid of so important an element of the original enactment, can

---

[249] See chapter 1, pp. 25–27.

it be called the same thing over again and not a mere pale copy of it or something radically different.[250]

Gentile would certainly have recognised the above passage as a clear statement of what he had been saying since 1912. In Collingwood's opposition of the 'vividness and the emotional heat of the original enactment' to the re-enactment which is devoid of all this, he would have recognised his own 'hard and rigid opposition' between the *pensato* and the *pensante* as formulated in his *Sistema di logica*.[251] Against this background it is not surprising that Collingwood tries to solve it with the same example Gentile had used:

> I thus genuinely re-enact Dante's medievalism – if I do not, I simply fail to understand or appreciate his poetry – but I re-enact it in a context (namely the rest of my mental outfit and equipment) which gives it a new quality, the quality of being one element within a whole of thought that goes beyond it, instead of being a whole of thought outside which there is nothing. This quality of being an element within my experience, an element checked and balanced by others and as contributing to the equilibrium of the whole, is the ideality of history.[252]

Though Collingwood uses Gentile's example of the *Sistema di logica*, his phrasing comes much closer to Gentile's 'L'atto del *pensare* come atto puro' of 1912, in which the latter explains that the rethinking of past thought has two moments. In the first we think the past thought as it was thought in the past, in the second we 'objectify' the past thought in order to give it a new function in present thought. Gentile describes this second moment as follows.

> Here it is enough to realize that this second moment, which is made possible by the first moment, annuls the actuality of the thought of the other, or our past thought that is not our thought now. It annuls this (past thought) in a new act of thought, and for this new thought, the new objectivity, the true or effective objectivity that is conferred on the thought that our thought expels from itself and considers it as object, is realized in function of the new thought, which is ours and actual, it is a an organic limb of the immanent unity of the present thought.[253]

The similarities between Collingwood's and Gentile's analyses are most striking. Both start from the problem of the relationship between the present and past thought and both describe the process by which the present thought rethinks the past thought as a present thought, pointing out that this rethinking process ends by assigning a new status to the past thought within present thought. For Collingwood the past thought becomes 'an element' in present experience, which he identifies with 'ideality', and for Gentile its status is that of 'an organic

---

[250] R.G. Collingwood, 'Outlines', 447.

[251] See chapter 3, pp. 86–90.

[252] R.G. Collingwood, 'Outlines', 447–8.

[253] G. Gentile, 'L'atto del *pensare* come atto puro', 185.

limb of the immanent unity of present thought', which he also identifies with
'ideality' in several places. But these similarities should not blind us from one
important difference between Collingwood and Gentile's views of 'ideality'.
According to Gentile, it is present thought that makes the past thought. In other
places, Gentile also says that present thought constructs or creates the past.
Collingwood, in the lectures of 1926, still saw the ideal past as 'an abstraction',
because it is a part of a whole. In the lectures of 1928, he indicates that ideality is
the 'quality of being an object of thought', though he does not give an explanation of how 'ideality' comes into being. Interestingly, though he still sees ideality
as a part of a whole, he no longer describes it as an abstraction. Finally, in the
lectures of 1926 he did not make a distinction between terms with and without
the prefix 're', whereas in 1928 he reserves the prefix for his re-enactment doctrine. All this is a clear indication that by 1928 Collingwood was not heading
towards a constructivist interpretation of the ideality doctrine, but that he was
trying to run it together with his earlier view of the living past. In 1928, Collingwood only used the notion of an ideality catalyst in the development of his own
thought, but not as substitute for it. This explains the remarkable appearance of
'constructivist' Italian passages, next to 'anti-constructivist' ones as mentioned
by Dray. These passages show that Collingwood failed to solve the problem
from which he started, that is, the problem of the relationship between history *a
parte obiecti* and history *a parte subiecti*. To solve this problem Collingwood
needed two more years. By then, he completed the foundations of his 'new
science' of human affairs.

The Final Step: The Encapsulation Theory

That Collingwood was not yet completely satisfied with his lectures of 1928 is
illustrated by the fact that he continued to work on the problem of the relationship between past and present. In his autobiography, he mentions that he solved
this problem around 1930 but he does not mention any manuscript in which he
did so. So far no scholar has found a manuscript in which Collingwood explicitly discusses the encapsulation doctrine. It seems best to start from what he
says in his autobiography and then go back to his published and unpublished
works in order to reconstruct the last two years of his middle period.

In his autobiography, Collingwood starts from the same problem as in the
'Outlines' of 1928, namely the problem of the identity and difference between
the past thought and the present thought. Giving the example of Nelson's dic-
tum 'in honour I won them, in honour I will die with them', he goes on to
explain the difference between that thought and its re-enactment as follows:

> The difference is one of context. To Nelson, that thought was present thought;
> to me, it is a past thought living in the present but (as I have elsewhere put it),
> incapsulated, not free. What is an incapsulated thought? It is a thought which,
> though perfectly alive, forms no part of the question-answer complex which

constitutes what people call the 'real' life, the superficial or obvious present, of the mind in question.[254]

The similarity between this formulation and that of 1928 is as striking as the difference. The main similarity between the two formations is that they are both meant as an answer to the question of how the historian can distinguish between the past and present thoughts. Both in 1928 and in 1938 Collingwood points to the notion of 'context' as the basis for their difference. But whereas he states the earlier version in terms of identity and difference between thoughts, he reformulates the later version in terms of identity and difference between thoughts making up parts of different question and answer complexes. Obviously, the later formulation is more sophisticated than the earlier, because it involves an analysis of the way in which the two question and answer complexes are related to each other. Moreover, in 1928 he describes the context of the re-enacted thought as an 'element in a whole of thought' which checks and balances it. In his autobiography Collingwood describes the context of the re-enacted thought as 'real life' which he identifies with 'the superficial or obvious present'. This present makes up a 'primary series' of questions and answers which prevent the 'secondary series' of questions and answers, i.e. Nelson's, 'overflow' from 'encapsulating' them.[255] In this context, Collingwood stresses that the questions of 'real life' always arise from practical problems, from which it follows that all historical problems also arise from practical problems. 'Hence the plane on which, ultimately, all problems arise is the plane of "real" life: that which they are referred to for their solution is history.'

The difference between the formulation in the lectures of 1928 and reformulation in his autobiography suggests that Collingwood found the encapsulation theory by relating the logic of question and answer to practice; only because we can distinguish between the practical problems of real life, and the problems of the past, can we prevent historical questions and answers from overflowing present questions and answers. The historian re-enacting Nelson's thoughts knows that they are Nelson's because they can never function as answers to questions in 'real life', that is, as solutions to practical problems. Unfortunately, it is difficult to corroborate Collingwood's account of the development of his 'third principle'. Given its terminology, it probably went back to his meditations on the Albert Memorial which also centred around the question of the relationship between past and present questions.

When we turn to the papers that Collingwood published in the late 1920s, we find the problem of the identity and difference between questions appearing several times, but never in connection to practical problems. Collingwood discusses the identity and difference between questions in 'Oswald Spengler and the Theory of Historical Cycles' of 1927 and two years later in a 'Philosophy of

---

[254] R.G. Collingwood, *An Autobiography*, 113.
[255] Ibid.

Progress' of 1929, but the fullest account can be found in 'The Theory of Historical Cycles' of 1927. In this paper Collingwood points out that there is a sense in which, in any aspect of human life, there is only a single problem, which is constant throughout the ages. To say that there is a single problem is to commit oneself to the doctrine of progress.[256] Yet there is another 'equally important sense in which a problem is always different'.[257] To give Collingwood's example; at a given time in politics the problem may be how to impose on a centrifugal society of feudal barons a centralised government and at an other time it may be how to create, in too centralised a government, some kind of local political initiative.[258] From this view it follows that the historian's task is to discover what problems confronted men in the past, and how they solved them. Although all problems are always in one sense identical to each other, and in another sense always different from each other, the historian cannot deny a certain unity in history. There is always some unity running throughout history; it is held together in the unity of the historian's own thought even if all other bonds fail.

On this point, Collingwood distinguishes the subjective aspect from its objective aspect in terms of problems and solutions:

> The objective bond of history is continuity. This means that the solution of one problem is itself the rise of the next. Man is not confronted by changing circumstances outside himself; or if he is, that belongs to the mere externals of his life. The essential change is within himself; it is a change in his own habits, his own wants, his own laws, his own beliefs and feelings and valuations; and this change is brought about by the attempt to meet a need itself arising essentially from within.[259]

What Collingwood describes here is no less than his own interpretation of what the Italians would call 'ideal eternal history', that is, a theory of the universal and necessary characteristics of history as a process. For Collingwood, history is essentially a process of problems and solutions because human life always and everywhere consists of positing and solving problems. Moreover, man posits these problems for himself, and therefore it is a free and self-conscious process. Every problem is therefore both eternal and unique:

> In each phase men found themselves confronted by a unique situation, which gave rise to a unique problem, or the eternal problem in a unique form; in each phase, they did their best to solve this problem, for their whole life consisted simply in living, living under the peculiar circumstances which made life a problem of a peculiar kind. To live was to solve that problem, the condi-

---

[256] R.G. Collingwood, 'The Theory of Historical Cycles', in *Antiquity*, 1, 1927, 435–46, cited id., *Essays in the Philosophy of History*, 1966, 84.

[257] Ibid., 85.

[258] Ibid.

[259] Ibid., 86.

tion of surviving until the problem changed; to die was to bequeath a different problem to their successors.[260]

The beginning of this passage suggests that Collingwood thought of the relationship between eternal and unique problems in the same way as that of the relationship between the universal and empirical concepts; the universal or eternal
are 'embodied' in a unique form. Combining this with the passage discussed
above we reach the conclusion that man posits his own problems, concepts,
ideals, in a self-conscious reaction to his circumstances. This act 'embodies' the
eternal problems, universal concepts, or ideals. This embodiment is free in the
sense that the empirical level is not conditioned by the universal level and the
circumstances. From this distinction between the empirical and the universal
levels it follows that the objective bond of history as a continuous development
of problems and solutions must be seen as ideal for the historian:

> So far as we can see history as a whole, that is how we see it; as a continuous
> development in which every phase consists of the solution of human prob-
> lems set by the preceding phase. But that is only an ideal for the historian; that
> is what he knows history would look like if he could see it as a whole, which
> he never can.[261]

The implication of this passage is that there is always a clash between the subjective and the objective view of history. This view implies that all historical
questions arise from 'gaps' in our account of history.[262] According to Collingwood, it also implies that if the historian cannot understand the problems of
some period he must revise his own thought. In 'A Philosophy of Progress' of
1929 Collingwood says that the connoisseur of architecture is merely confessing
his own personal limitations if he says that he likes Gothic for its slenderness
and dislikes Norman for its fatness; he ought to like Gothic for its slenderness
and like Norman for its fatness.[263] History is therefore not only a critical activity
but also a self-critical activity.

'The Theory of Historical Cycles' shows how Collingwood solved his problem of the relationship between history *a parte subiecti* and history *a parte obiecti*.
He began by applying his view of the historian as an autonomous individual
who raises and solves his own problems on the basis of the evidence to history
as a whole, thus acknowledging that all human beings are historians of their
own. This view is in accordance with the first principle of the 'Libellus' according to which subject and object are two aspects of a single process. It is also an
application of Collingwood's view of history as a transcendental activity from
which it follows that history is a universal and necessary characteristic of mind.

---

[260] Ibid., 87.

[261] Ibid.

[262] Ibid.

[263] R.G. Collingwood, 'A Philosophy of Progress', in *The Realist*, 1, 1929, 64–77, cited from
id., *Essays in the Philosophy of History*, 111.

From this it follows that the object of the historian's question and answer activity is always also a question and answer activity; fundamentally, the historian deals with problems in the past in order to solve problems in the present.

This is also the theory that laid at the basis of Collingwood's article 'The Philosophy of History' of 1930. In the first part of this paper Collingwood largely repeats his 'Preliminary Discussion' of 1927, by pointing out that philosophy studies the universal and necessary characteristics of things and that history is a proper subject for philosophy because it is a universal and necessary human interest.[264] In the history of the idea Collingwood presents the most important philosophers of history and these are, unsurprisingly, Bacon, Vico, Hegel, and Croce, whose *Teoria e storia della storiografia* he describes as 'by far the most important work of our time on the subject'.[265] After this, Collingwood gives an outline of a philosophy of history which is obviously his own. He begins by repeating his view that history does not exist because one comes to know it by interpreting evidence. Collingwood's debt to absolute empiricism appears in his description of history as being based on data and evidence on the one hand, and principles on the other. Immediately after this he remarks that data and principles are not enough; only when the historian has a problem in his mind can he begin to search for data. The beginning of historical research is therefore always the asking of a question. Questions arise because they have a logical connection to previous thoughts. All history is therefore an interim report on the progress made in the study of its subject and every historian writes from his own point of view. According to Collingwood, it is futile to try to eliminate this subjective element from history. At the same time, he holds that history remains genuine knowledge even if different historians have different views of it. Then Collingwood gives an example that reminds us again of Gentile's *Sistema di logica*.

> If my thoughts about Julius Caesar differ from Mommsen's? Must not one of us be wrong? No, because the object differs. My historical thought is about my own past, not about Mommsen's past. Mommsen and I share in a great many things, and in many respects we share a common past; but in so far as we are different people and representatives of different cultures and different generations we have behind us different pasts, and everything in his past has to undergo a slight alteration before it can enter into mine.[266]

Dray interprets this passage as a clear example of Collingwood's constructivism.[267] But if we compare it closely to Gentile's example that we discussed at the end of chapter three, we find some interesting differences. Firstly, Gentile stresses that the new act of thought renders all previous acts of thought unactual, whereas Collingwood stresses that it is still possible to understand why

---

[264] R.G. Collingwood, *The Philosophy of History*, 121–3.

[265] Ibid., 135.

[266] Ibid., 139.

[267] Dray, *History as Re-enactment*, 259.

Mommsen was right. Secondly, Gentile says that Mommsen's history differs from Livy's because the subject has changed, whereas Collingwood says that it changes because the object has changed. Moreover, we have seen that Gentile always kept to the purity of the act of thought, whereas Collingwood stresses that all questions arise on the basis of previous thought. If we combine these differences we see that Gentile stresses that the historian's questioning activity is completely free thought, which produces itself and its own principles self-consciously, whereas Collingwood seems to hold that it is history as an object that somehow conditions the questioning activity. This is of course another way of saying that the past lives on in the present.

On this basis we may conjecture how Collingwood solved the problem of the relationship between the notion of the living past and the re-enactment doctrine. Regarding history as a process of questions and answers living on in the present, his most fundamental problem was to explain how past questions and answers relate to present questions and answers. Stressing the practical aspect of the question and answer activity, and observing that the past is 'encapsulated' in the present, the first step of the historian is to 'decapsulate' the past on the basis of the evidence. This decapsulation process begins by 'plunging' beneath the present to the past and proceeds by questions and answers. The aim of the decapsulation is to reconstruct past answers to past questions until a full identity is reached, which means that the historian can think the past thoughts for himself, or more precisely, that he is able to understand how the past answers relate to past questions. However, this identification between past and present is not the end of the process; the historian cannot dwell forever in the past, but must return to real life and solve his own practical problems from which he started. On this point the encapsulation starts; by comparing the past thought to his present situation, the historian constructs a new context for the past thought, thus giving it a new meaning, which it did not have in its own context.

Conclusion

At first glance, Collingwood's ideas on history in the 1920s seem only slightly different from the views of the Italians: many concepts, phrases, and examples remind us of Croce, Gentile, and de Ruggiero. But seen in the context of his development, some important differences lurk under the surface. In particular, Collingwood's idea of history as a process enabled him to reject all self-identical entities such as Croce's pure concepts and Gentile's transcendental ego. This is also the result of the identity of history *a parte subiecti* and history *a parte obiecti*; reality is seen as a process of positing and solving problems. In this view of reality neither pure concepts nor a transcendental ego needs to be presupposed; the only reality is that of ever newly arising problems and solutions. This process has both an objective and an ideal existence. Its objectivity is that reality, as it presents itself to us, must be seen as the outcome of the entire process; our reality is the last solution of this process which forms the starting point for our own problems. But the process as a continuous whole is an 'ideal', to be attained by historical thought. Guided by this ideal, the prime task of the historian, and therefore of all men, is to close the gaps between the past and the present. That is, the historian must show how his present problems are the outcome of a long process of positing problems and solving them. In order to understand his own problems, the historian must reconstruct this process to the best of his abilities. And since he recognises that all persons and communities posited their own problems, he must do his best to understand the principles upon which they are based. These principles are never given beforehand, because history is not an 'infinite given whole' but an ever-growing process of problems and solutions. From this it follows that the identity between the past and present can never be presupposed, but it must be found. When we study a past thought, we must not assume its identity with present thought; the only identity there is, is that all thought is an answer to a question. It is this metaphysics that lays at the basis of Collingwood's mature thought, as we will see in chapters nine and ten. However, in order to understand Collingwood's mature philosophy we must first turn to the development of the Italians in the 1930s.

Chapter Eight

The Later Development
of the Italians

Introduction

In Italy, the years 1929–36 are known as the 'period of consensus'.[1] During these years, Mussolini firmly established his dictatorship. Through both his Fascist Party and the corporations he controlled all means of communication, transport, and most of the economy. In the meantime, Mussolini tried to establish his position in international politics. In 1929, he placated the papacy by restoring the Pope's temporal power over Vatican City in the Lateran Treaties. In the 1930s Mussolini, after some futile attempts to turn the economic tide, responded to the recent recession by throwing his country into imperialist adventures. In the beginning of 1935, Italy occupied Ethiopia, ignoring the official disapproval of the League of Nations. A year later, Mussolini supported the insurgents in the civil war in Spain in close cooperation with the Nazis. In 1937, the Rome-Berlin axis was firmly established. Shortly afterwards, in 1938, Italy introduced a programme of discrimination against the Jews. At this time, Mussolini supported Hitler's claims in Czechoslovakia and Poland, but surprisingly enough, he maintained neutrality when Germany invaded Poland in September 1939.[2]

Croce, Gentile, and de Ruggiero were closely involved in these events. Gentile fiercely opposed to the Lateran Treaties, which undid large parts of his educational reforms by reintroducing religion in secondary schools.[3] Later in the 1930s, he viewed the racial discrimination with great discomfort because these were inimical to his philosophy.[4] Because of this criticism, Gentile lost respect within Fascist circles and over the years he became increasingly isolated. This gave Gentile some time to take up his philosophical studies. In 1931, he published *La filosofia dell'arte* (*The Philosophy of Art*), which contains a complete actualist aesthetics, and from 1934 onwards he worked on its sequel, *La filosofia della storia* (*The Philosophy of History*), which he left unfinished because of the

---

[1] Renzo de Felice, 'Fascism', 212.
[2] Ibid., 213.
[3] Romano, *Giovanni Gentile*, 223–32.
[4] Harris, *The Social Philosophy of Giovanni Gentile*, 244–5.

political difficulties at the end of the 1930s. Gentile published two chapters in his *Giornale critico*, which, together with some drafts in manuscript, give some impression of what was meant to be Gentile's final philosophy of history.[5] In 1943, in the middle of the crisis which broke out after Mussolini's fall in July, Gentile wrote *Genesì e struttura della società* (*Genesis and Structure of Society*), which he finished shortly before he was murdered by partisan commandos on 15 April 1944.

In the 1930s, Croce opposed the Fascists to the best of his abilities, gathering an active group of anti-Fascist intellectuals around him. In both Italy and abroad, Croce was acknowledged as the leader of the anti-Fascist movement, a role he courageously assumed despite the fact that he preferred the tranquility of his study room. The Fascist regime responded relentlessly. Although Croce could not be arrested without consent of the Senate, the authorities found enough other means to keep him under control. For years his house in Naples was under surveillance, and Croce himself was shadowed as soon as he left home.[6] However, this repression could not impede that Croce travelled through Europe to meet Italian exiles, to win support among intellectuals like Albert Einstein and Thomas Mann, and to give lectures like the famous 'Antistoricismo', read at the seventh international philosophical conference in Oxford in 1930.[7] Despite these time-consuming political activities, the restless Croce still managed to work on aesthetics and on the philosophy of history. In 1935, at the age of 69, he published a book with the ironic title *Ultimi Saggi* (*Last Essays*), and in the following year he published another work on aesthetics: *La Poesia*. However, by far the most important work of the 1930s was Croce's *La storia come pensiero e come azione* (*History as Thought and Action*) published in 1938. This was one of the two books that Collingwood read on his voyage to the Dutch Indies, where he wrote the first chapters of *The Principles of History*.[8]

As professor of the history of philosophy at the University of Rome, de Ruggiero took up his work on the multi-volume *Storia della filosofia*, publishing with Laterza *Rinascimento, Riforma e Controriforma* (*Renaissance, Reformation and Counter-Reformation*) in 1930, *L'età cartesiana* (*The Cartesian Epoch*) in 1933, *Da Vico a Kant* (*From Vico to Kant*) in 1937, and *L'età dell'Illuminismo* (*The Epoch of Enlightenment*) in 1938. De Ruggiero also regularly contributed to the British journal *Philosophy* and to some Italian periodicals. By the end of the decade, de Ruggiero had become increasingly active in the resistance against the Fascist

---

5   G. Gentile, *La filosofia della storia, Saggi e inediti*, Le Lettere, Florence, 1996, xxvii.

6   Fabio Fernando Rizi, *Benedetto Croce and Italian Fascism*, University of Toronto Press, Toronto, 2003, 173.

7   B. Croce, 'Antistoricismo' in *La Critica*, XXVIII, 1930, 401–9.

8   Vigorelli (ed.), 'Lettere di Robin George Collingwood a Benedetto Croce', 563, 29 January 1939.

regime.[9] In 1939 he was offered a Doctorate *honoris causa* by the University of Oxford, which could only be realised after the war because of the German invasion of Western Europe in May 1940.[10]

In this chapter I will follow the development of the three Italians, as a background to Collingwood's development in the same period to be discussed in chapters 9 and 10.

Gentile's Philosophy of Art

After taking a break from philosophical writing over nine turbulent years, Gentile returned to systematic philosophy with *La filosofia dell'arte* of 1931. Although outside Italy this book has never won the reputation of Croce's *Estetica*, it did not go completely unnoticed. E.F. Carritt, Collingwood's former tutor, recognised its importance and began to translate it in 1932 though without publishing the result.[11]

In the preface to the book, Gentile states that the work deepens and modifies his entire philosophy, and the footnotes reveal that he primarily had his *Sistema di logica* in mind.[12] In this work, Gentile had focused on the problem of the objectivity of thought; his main aim was to show how the act of thought develops itself on the basis of past thought, which it creates for itself. In this context, Gentile had paid special attention to the problem of the 'passage' from the past thought to the act of thought, thus neglecting the problem of the 'spontaneity' of thought, or the problem of the arising of the act of thought. To the question why the act of thought starts developing itself, Gentile did not have a good answer; by describing the beginning of thought as *causa sui* and the process of thought as *autoconcetto*, he offered a tautology instead of a real explanation. For the same reason, Gentile could not find a clear solution to the problem of the objectivity of knowledge, because as long as the spontaneity of thought was not accounted for, there could be no objective principles for interpreting it. Gentile was thus forced to rely on his notion of the *autoconcetto*, or the history of truth-norms that underlie all history, which he tended to hypostatise into an entity that transcends history. To the straightforward question: Why did this or that empirical ego think this thought as he did? Gentile could only answer: because the *autoconcetto* or the

9   Clementina Gily Reda and Angela Maria Graziano, *Il partito d'azione tra storia e metafora*, Grafic Way, Napels, 1995; De Felice, 'De Ruggiero, Guido', 253.

10   G. de Ruggiero, 'Letter to the University's Registrar', Oxford University Archive, UR6/HD/2C, dated 20 September 1940 concerning the Doctorate *honoris causa*; Id., 'Letter to the University's Registrar', Oxford University Archive, UR6/HD/2C, dated 11 December 1945. Without doubt Collingwood was involved in de Ruggiero's doctorate, because he was to translate the lecture.

11   In 1972 Gullace finished a new translation on the basis of Carritt's, but it seems that this translation has never attracted much attention; see G. Gentile, *The Philosophy of Art, Translated with an Introduction by Giovanni Gullace*, Cornell University Press, Ithaca and London, 1972.

12   G. Gentile, *La filosofia dell'arte*, Treves, Milan, 1931, vii–viii.

development of the transcendental ego arrived at that point. This hypostasis of the *autoctisi* eventually formed the basis of Gentile's Fascist 'philosophy'.[13] In *La filosofia dell'arte*, Gentile tries to solve both the problem of the spontaneity of the act of thought and the problem of the objectivity of thought with the notion of art. This double problem provides the outline of the book, which is divided into two parts. In the first one, with the title 'The actuality of art', Gentile describes art in terms of the pure act, that is, as a self-conscious act of thought. This view forms the basis of the second part, 'The attributes of art'. In this part Gentile deals with art criticism and the morality of art in terms of the pure act, in order to show that they play a vital role in society.

To describe art in terms of the pure act of thought, Gentile had to solve a difficult problem. Like Croce, Gentile holds that art begins with feeling. But feeling is immediate, whereas art as an act of thought is a mediate activity. The problem is therefore to show how feeling can be both immediate and the beginning of the act of thought. Gentile solves this problem by rejecting its presuppositions. In his view, there is not feeling on the one hand, and consciousness of it on the other; feeling is only actual in so far as we become aware of it; we become aware of our feelings by expressing them in language.[14] By expressing our feelings they become actual in the sense of being an act of thought. Art is therefore not an expression of emotions, as Croce held, but emotion in its actuality. By expressing emotions art does not supersede them, as Croce used to say, but it gives them a new form.[15] Moreover, consciousness of feeling is always a self-conscious activity; the artist is not only aware of his emotions, but also of his awareness itself. The expression of emotions in language is therefore a self-conscious act of thought; we express our emotions and know that we are expressing them.[16] From this it follows that there is no distinction between art and thought, as Croce held, but that all art is thought and all thought is art. On this basis Gentile states that since art is the expression of emotions, all thought contains emotions within itself. From this viewpoint, Ariosto's *Orlando furioso* is as much an expression of Ariosto's philosophy as the *Ethica* is an expression of Spinoza's feelings.

From the identity of art and thought it follows that art develops in the same way as thought, that is, as the self-conscious act of thought. Referring to 'Il torto e il diritto delle traduzioni' of 1920, Gentile calls this self-conscious expression of feeling in language *autotradursi* (self-translation).[17] The process of self-translation can be described as the self-conscious expression of feelings and emotion in language. Gentile calls the first moment of this process the 'subjective moment'

---

[13] See chapter 6, p. 192.
[14] G. Gentile, *La filosofia dell'arte*, 201–2, 233–6.
[15] Ibid., 152.
[16] Ibid., 229.
[17] Ibid., 278–82.

of 'indistinct feeling'.[18] This 'indistinct feeling' forms the object of the 'translation' by the self-conscious act of thought, and this translation forms the second moment of the process. The result of the process is a work of art which is the third or 'objective moment' of art.[19] With this theory of self-translation Gentile describes how we become aware of an indistinct feeling by naming it. This act of naming is always a self-conscious act: when we name a feeling we know that we give it a name and why we give it the name we give, because the act is always based on principles which it posits for itself.[20] From this it follows that the constructive activity of art must be viewed as a self-critical activity. Fundamental to Gentile's theory of self-translation is the view that the linguistic act does not cancel the feeling; the feeling remains immanent in language and thought. Every expression contains its feeling within itself and thus providing the object for a new translation by which the process is continued to infinity. Every new work of art is thus a translation of a previous work of art.[21]

On this basis, Gentile contends that art criticism is nothing but the perpetuation of the process of self-translation in the reverse order; it is 'going back the way that the artist went'.[22] Again, feeling is not superseded by art, but it remains immanent in language. From this it follows that all translation involves feeling; to substitute one language for another also means substituting one emotion for another. Likewise, the art critic, by continuing the self-translation of the artist, also continues the development of emotions begun by the artist.

Like art, the process of criticism has three moments. The first task of the critic is to reconstruct the 'abstract content' of the work of art. This amounts to rethinking the *pensiero pensato* of the poet, that is, his history. This rethinking involves, among other things, the reconstruction of the biography of the poet, the history of ideas with which he was acquainted, the customs of his times, considering the technical means of his art and of the language of his days and so forth. Yet, these historical studies are only 'preparatory' for the understanding of the creative moment of the poet in which he expresses his feeling, which constitutes the second moment in the critical process. In this moment the critic identifies himself completely with the feeling and the thought, or better, the feeling-thought, of the poet. The final phase of the critical process is the exposition of the work of art which is not a prosaic summary but a 'moved creation'.[23]

With this doctrine, Gentile comes nearer to a solution of the two major problems of *Sistema di logica*. In *La filosofia dell'arte* Gentile partly solves the problem of the 'spontaneity' of the act of thought by locating the impetus for thought in 'indistinct' feeling; thought arises when we try to express our feelings. Being

---

18 Ibid., 212.
19 Ibid., 281.
20 Ibid., 279.
21 Ibid.
22 Ibid., 283.
23 Ibid., 284–6.

immediate, feeling is indistinct, it is unknown, a *nescio quid*, which causes a problem for thought. Feeling thus becomes the 'pure subjective form' of all thought, the 'eternal principle that puts our soul in motion'.[24] All this takes place within the act of thought itself; there is not one process of feeling and emotion and another process of translating them, but there is only a single process which continuously expresses emotions. This process never stops because each new expression is emotional itself, thus serving as the first moment of a new act of thought. By thus identifying feeling with the first impetus for thought, Gentile solves the problem of the beginning of the dialectic; all thought begins as the expression of feeling. This thesis brings concrete experience back in the act of thought with the result that the beginning and development of the dialectic does not need to be explained by the very abstract notion of the *autoconcetto*. In short, by acknowledging the reality of feeling in the act of thought, Gentile gives actualism a human face again.

For this reason, *La filosofia dell'arte* has important implications for the interpretation of language and therefore also for the interpretation of historical texts. In this context, Gentile argues that the critic, or the historian of art, does not have some kind of object before him which he must try to understand in some way, but the poet and the critic are part of a single process. The poet begins by expressing his emotions in a self-conscious act of thought. This act of thought is constructive, because it 'produces' thought in the form of language. The act is also self-critical because it is based on principles of which it is conscious. Each product of the act of thought thus forms the beginning of a new act of thought; the artist 'listens' to his own expressions and self-consciously translates them into new expressions. The work of the critic is therefore not fundamentally different from that of the poet; by reading and listening he continues the self-translation of the poet. By translating the work of art, the critic tries to understand the artist's language by rethinking the act of thought which produced it. On the basis of the identity of feeling with language and thought this entails that the critic somehow has to take the feeling 'behind' a linguistic act into account; the interpretation of language involves not only thought but also feeling. According to Gentile, this kind of rethinking of the expression of feeling is intersubjectively valid because the translation from the poem to the feeling is a mediate activity and therefore rethinkable. From this viewpoint, every reader of Dante is able to understand what feelings are expressed in his poem, because feeling has an immediate and mediate aspect. In its immediacy, that is as pure feeling, the poem is not understandable. However, in its mediacy, that is as a linguistic act, the poem is understandable because we can rethink the feelings and thoughts that produced it. For this reason we must study Dante's biography in the context of the time in which he lived in order to understand the emotions he was expressing in *La Divina Commedia*. In the same way we must take the emotions of

---

[24] Ibid., 126, 166.

Spinoza into account if we want to understand his *Ethica,* and again this entails a study of his times.

On this point Gentile was severely criticised by de Ruggiero. In his review for *Philosophy* the latter remarked sharply that 'if we approach a little nearer to Gentile's long artistic equations (art = subjectivity = form = nature = sentiment = ...) we find that they are all lost in the same fog, which recalls the Hegelian maxim that "in the darkness all cows are black"'.[25] From this perspective, de Ruggiero completely rejected Gentile's identity of feeling and art, arguing that 'it will never succeed in convincing anyone, for example, that to fall in love and to sing of love are not two different things'.[26]

De Ruggiero's criticism was justified, because in *La filosofia dell'arte* Gentile removes the distinction between subject and object by resolving both into the act of thought with the result that immediate experience, art, and art criticism cannot clearly be distinguished. Yet, Gentile's 'identities' express the important truth that the expression of emotion is itself an emotional activity. Every musician, for example, knows from experience that it is impossible to sing a song of love without having felt love within oneself. Moreover, most musicians would agree with Gentile that emotion and thought are 'identical'; the expression of love in a song of love is a very difficult process which certainly involves thought.

But de Ruggiero's criticism implicitly also points to another difficulty of Gentile's philosophy of art. Gentile only recognises expressed feeling as actual and real; feelings that are not expressed are not actual feelings. Feeling only becomes actual when a self-conscious act of thought has shed its light on it. This view raises a difficulty concerning the status of indistinct feelings. Do these feelings simply remain in the dark? Gentile's answer to this question is clear; indistinct feelings are immediate and not actual and therefore not real. Consequently, Gentile rejects the importance of 'the unconscious' in art. Even dreams are not part of our actual experience, because our experience is always the 'construction' of our thought and dreams are not thought.[27] However, if dreams are not actual, in Gentile's sense of the words, are they then not real? Gentile himself does not deny the reality of dreams, because he evidently talks about them. In this context, he maintains that dreams are not real if we are not aware of them.

This position shows both the strengths and the weaknesses of Gentile's theory of art. His identification of the real with the act of thought compels him to recognise only those feelings that can be identified by thought. But it also forces him to draw a very sharp line between the immediate and the mediate; immediate feelings are not known, not actual, and not real, whereas the mediate is known, actual, and real. On this basis Gentile throws large parts of our experi-

---

[25] G. de Ruggiero, 'Philosophy in Italy', in *Philosophy,* VI, 1931, 494.

[26] Ibid.

[27] G. Gentile, *La filosofia dell'arte,* 109–17.

ence, such as 'vague feelings' and 'dreams', overboard unless we are conscious of them.[28] Only in conscious thought do they become fully actual and real aspects of our experience. However, this position raises a new difficulty; how are we to distinguish between poetry and history if both are seen as equally valid forms of thought? Once again we are back at one of the central problems of the philosophy of history, with which Gentile would deal in *La filosofia della storia*.[29]

Gentile's philosophy of art is often too bold, but it is not altogether wrong. On the contrary: with the identity of feeling, language, and thought, he is on an interesting track. Dante did not merely express his feelings, but he expressed them self-consciously; the language of the *Divina Commedia* was partly developed in order to express the emotions of a particular philosophy. And even in the case of a very 'unphilosophical' poet like Ariosto, we must have some idea of his general philosophy in the context of the whole history of philosophy in order to understand his language. Vice versa, Spinoza's *Ethica* is not quite understandable if we do not take the philosopher's emotions into account. We may think of his fear of persecution, his being banned by the Jewish society in Amsterdam, and so forth. The *Ethica* may even be read as solution to the problems which were raised by such emotions, and it may even be maintained that it is because of our understanding Spinoza's emotions that his *Ethica* appeals to us. It is this intimate relationship between language and philosophy that Gentile wants to clarify. But in order to make them clearer than he did, a much more detailed analysis of the relationship between language and philosophy is needed. More specifically, a detailed theory of the relationship between feeling, consciousness, and self-consciousness is required.

Gentile did not give us a more detailed analysis of consciousness. As more often in his works, he offers deep insight but little elaboration. Yet, even with its oversimplifications, *La filosofia dell'arte* is an advance on his *Sistema di logica* because it does relate feeling to the act of thought, and thus achieves an empirical and linguistic basis which was absent in his *Sistema di logica*. Not surprisingly, therefore, *La filosofia dell'arte* is the first work in which Gentile does not fall back on the transcendental ego in order to make the act of thought move; by acknowledging feeling as the impetus for thought, Gentile explains how empirical egos begin to think. However, this vindication of the empirical ego forced Gentile to defend himself against charges of subjectivism. This was the main problem of *La filosofia della storia*.

Gentile's Later Philosophy of History

In August 1934, Gentile wrote an outline for what he regarded as the crown of his philosophical work: *La filosofia della storia*. The outline, which was found in the *Fondazione Gentile* in the early 1990s, shows that *La filosofia della storia* was to

---

[28] Ibid., 109–12.
[29] Ibid., 112–7.

be a massive book containing three large parts each consisting of ten chapters in which he would have systematised almost all of his writings on philosophy, history, and action.

In the first part Gentile intended to deal with 'Pragmatic History, or Abstract Historical Logos', and to discuss concepts such as space, time, fact, historical determinism, periodisation, progress, and universal history.[30] In Part II, 'Storia *pensante*, or Concrete Historical Logos', he would have dealt with nature and history, with 'actual history as self-conscious historical subject', eternal history, and the meaning of history.[31] Part III would have dealt with the 'unity' of the diverse forms of history, such as the history of art, the history of religion and science, and the history of philosophy.[32] In the conclusion Gentile intended to introduce a new theme in his philosophy of history; the problem of the future and related subjects such as prediction, profetism, millenarism.[33]

In 1937, Gentile published the introduction and the first chapter of the work in his *Giornale Critico*. After that, political affairs forced him to postpone further work on the book. In 1943 he returned to it, using the published articles as a first version, but in August of that year he postponed its completion again in order to work on *Genesì e struttura della società*.[34] When he was murdered in April 1944 he left his magnum opus unfinished. Only the outline, the introduction, and the first chapter and some parts of the second chapter, all covered with Gentile's notes of 1943, have survived. Apart from this project, Gentile also published 'Il superamento del tempo nella storia' ('The Transcending of Time in History'), which played a role in Collingwood's later philosophy of history.[35]

In the introduction to *La filosofia della storia*, Gentile claims that his philosophy of history is 'new'. The old philosophy of history, as practised by Hegel, was rightly rejected by working historians for being a non-empirical construction based on preconceived concepts.[36] Though Gentile endorses the historians' rejection, he does not agree with the reason they give for it.[37] In his view, historians presuppose a dualism between subject and object for which it is possible to have *a priori* thought on the one hand, and an external world which is 'immediate' and therefore only thinkable *a posteriori*, on the other. According to Gentile, this position is wrong because history in its immediacy does not exist. At best, it can be seen as a point of departure for historical thought which, by

---

[30] G. Gentile, *La filosofia della storia*, 13–5.

[31] Ibid., 15–6.

[32] Ibid., 16–7.

[33] Ibid., 17–8.

[34] Ibid., xxxiii.

[35] Ibid., xxxii; Cf. chapter 9, pp. 341–342.

[36] G. Gentile, 'Introduzione a una nuova filosofia della storia', in *Giornale critico della filosofia italiana*, XVIII, 1937, cited from *Frammenti di Estetica e di teoria della storia*, II, OC XLVIII, Le Lettere, Florence, 1992, 21–2.

[37] Ibid., 23.

destroying immediacy, becomes identical with philosophy. Moreover, the categories which the philosophers abstract from empirical thought are not their own inventions but categories with which every historian works.[38]

In Gentile's view, the same false distinction between the empirical and the *a priori* aspect of history lay at the basis of the classic philosophy of history which never overcame the dualism between *storia eterna* and *storia in tempo*, or between *verum* and *certum*, because the unity of the *storia eterna* and *storia in tempo* was posited as a 'result' not as a 'principle'.[39] In other words, classic philosophers of history failed to recognise that history contains a philosophy of history within itself and that philosophy of history contains its own account of history within itself. According to Gentile, the new philosophy of history posits the unity of *storia eterna* and *storia in tempo* as a principle; it does not distinguish between philosophy of history and history proper. From this perspective history is always also a philosophy of history; even the simple chronicler expounds his philosophy in his chronicles, and all philosophy of history is always a history as well because fundamentally all philosophers deal with history.[40] There is no difference between the categories that underlie history and the philosophy of history; philosophers did not invent these categories for themselves but they share them with historians. The new philosophy of history is therefore the study of the categories that underlie historical experience. In Kantian terms it is: 'The Transcendental Analytic of historical thought, or the theory of the a priori categories of this thought which in its synthesis of category and intuition constitutes history.'[41]

According to Gentile, the new philosophy of history is closely related to history because it arises from the methodological problems in historiographic practice. However, it is not to be identified with history proper, just as the philosophy of art is not to be identified with art itself.[42] Nor is the new philosophy of history a kind of methodology distinct from historical thought; the object of the new philosophy of history is always historical thought in action, that is, it studies the principles which underlie the method of historians.[43] From this point of view, the new philosophy of history is identical with philosophy proper, because history is the philosophical self-consciousness of the spirit.[44]

With this position, Gentile takes up the doctrine of absolute immanentism which he had defended from his first book. But in *La filosofia della storia* he relates this doctrine to history in its immediacy. Just like feeling in art, history in its immediacy is the starting point of historical thought, which develops itself in a

---

38 Ibid., 23–7.
39 Ibid., 30.
40 Ibid., 30.
41 Ibid., 37.
42 Ibid., 39.
43 Ibid., 40–1.
44 Ibid., 42–6.

self-critical way on the basis of philosophical principles. As usual, here Gentile focuses on the development of historical thought. His major problem is therefore to explain how objectivity is constituted within the act of thought. This is the problem that he left unsolved in *Sistema di logica* and to which he returns in the first chapter of *La filosofia della storia* which carries the title 'L'oggetto della storia' ('The Object of History').

Gentile begins his analysis of the historical object from the familiar distinction between history and historiography, or *res gestae* and *historia rerum gestarum*. In his view, this distinction is important to understand the notion of the certain (*il certo*) which has been attributed to history. The certain is true, but truth is not obtained by argument, but on the basis of experience. The certain was the ideal of positivist philosophers who claimed that all knowledge is based on experience of the world as it presents itself to us. Objective knowledge could only be obtained by studying the facts as they were. With regard to history the positivists claimed that the facts had to be studied without any presuppositions.[45]

This positivism has been the basis of the 'ingenuous historian'. In Gentile's view, the ingenuous historian starts with an unknown 'x' to which the source refers. Then his thought proceeds in four phases: a) he studies the source which he b) criticises and c) interprets in order to d) reconstruct the unknown fact x. According to Gentile, the 'ingenuous historian' interprets the thought process differently from the empiricist and the 'sophistical philosopher', or the 'rationalist'. The ingenuous historian tries to make d) the reconstruction as faithful as possible to a) the sources in order to reconstruct the historical reality, or 'x', as truthfully as possible. The fixed point of this logic is the source from which the historian starts and to which he returns thus describing a circle: he thinks that d = c = b = a = x and therefore that d = x.[46]

According to Gentile, this circularity of the logic of the ingenuous historian explains the nature of historical fact. For the ingenuous historian 'fact' is not a Parmenidean being, but a Platonic idea, that is, concept or ideality. History in its ideality is what it is, and the historian tries to make historiography as perfect a representation of x as possible by refraining as much as possible from all kinds of subjective distortions.[47] But since there is always some subjective stain on the 'gold of historical reality', Gentile says, the work of the historian will never be finished.[48]

After this description of the philosophy of the 'ingenuous historian', Gentile reinterprets his position in terms of actualist logic. He describes historical fact as *pensato*, which is never immediate because thought is always mediation. The

---

[45] G. Gentile, 'L'oggetto della storia', in *Giornale critico della filosofia italiana*, XVIII, 1937, cited from *Frammenti di Estetica e di teoria della storia*, II, OC XLVIII, Le Lettere, Florence, 1992, 51–3.

[46] Ibid., 70–1.

[47] Ibid., 73.

[48] Ibid., 74–6.

pensato and the *pensare* are always found in a union; all concepts are the products of the act of thought. The act of thought is always conscious and self-conscious; it is conscious of its object, that is, the *pensato,* and of its own thinking. The concrete form of self-consciousness is therefore a double act; the subject posits itself as object of its own act of thought. The *pensato* comes into existence by the mediation of the act of thought which posits it as different from itself, that is, as an object. As a result of the act of thought, it is 'immediate', that is, it is now a known object. It thus becomes the presupposition for a new act of thought. Gentile concludes that the 'immediate' fact is always *pensiero pensato,* or the product of thought. As immediate, the *pensato* presents itself as being given to the act of thought; it is something that presents itself 'en bloc to *pensiero pensante*' which must take it or leave it.[49]

Gentile calls this 'giveness' of the past the 'positivity' of the history, which forms the basis of the distinction between poetry and history. Historical fact is a *pensato* and this means that it presupposes a *pensare.* The distinction between *pensato* and *pensare* is only possible as an abstraction from the whole process of self-consciousness. The immediacy of thought thus belongs to the *pensiero pensato* and, once thought, it remains thought forever:

> It is what is; and there is no place for opposition, reserve or resistance of any kind against the truth which is in that way assured, the truth which puts the mind in blocks and flattens every arbitrary velleity of it.[50]

According to Gentile, this relationship between *pensiero pensato* and *pensiero pensante* explains the difference between poetry and history. Both poetry and history are creative thought, and as such it is impossible to distinguish them completely. However, unlike poetry, history is inextricably bound to its own positivity:

> ...the poetical creation differs from history by the consciousness which accompanies its characteristic liberty, by which the subject frees itself from any link with the positivity of actual, natural or historical reality. This is the basis of the distinction between art as consciousness of the pure subject, and history, which is consciousness of an objective reality, in which the subject forms itself by its synthesis with the subject.[51]

Gentile points out that art does not lack positivity; its positivity is only 'provisional' and partial, whereas the historical positivity is 'definitive and total'.[52] Yet, it is impossible to distinguish art and history completely, because both are moments within the act of thought. The act of thought begins as art and ends as history; the 'history' of the poetic moment thus becomes 'legend' for the historical moment. In other words, we begin with a 'provisional' and partial positivity

---

[49] Ibid., 75–8.
[50] Ibid., 78.
[51] Ibid.
[52] Ibid., 79.

and end with a new, more complete and definitive form of positivity.[53] But this positivity is only the *terminus ad quem* of the whole process which continues to infinity. According to Gentile the relation between art and history entails that history is already immanent in art, but this can only be seen from the point of view of history, not from the point of view of art. In other words, the historian understands that the fable and legend are already attempts at history.[54]

On this basis, Gentile draws a conclusion that he considers of 'capital import-ance' for the understanding of history. The object of history, Gentile says, is reality as a whole. However, if we look closer at the distinction between the ideal and the real, we see that it is simply the difference between two points of view from which we try to understand reality. This entails that history is always immanent in the actuality of the spirit, that is, all acts of the spirit have some 'positive' reality before it.

> Because, when the difference between history and poetry deepens, this dis-tinction appears as that what it is, that is, as a simple difference between points of view, in which that what is no longer history, was once history: and having ceased to be history, it is no longer nothing (it was poetry, but not any-more); the consequence is that all is history in the actuality of the spirit; and always when the spirit actualises itself, it is in front of something that is really existing and positive.[55]

This difficult passage expresses the kernel of Gentile's new philosophy of his-tory, which can be paraphrased as follows: if history is immanent in art and art is immanent in all forms of the spirit, it follows that history is also immanent in all forms of spiritual activity. As 'the first presence of a given fact' it is 'the cer-tainty of all faith'.[56] History thus forms the basis of art, science, and philosophy. Every work of art or sience is rooted in history, because both are based on know-ledge of reality, or history. History forms the basis of all forms of experience presenting itself as 'an absolute *quid*', the 'concrete *hic et nunc*'. Even philosophy is based on history; when it studies the ideas of man and God, being and becom-ing, it always conceives these concepts based on the positivity of history.[57] Gentile concludes:

> Nothing is thought that is not moving from the historical position, in which the object is posed immediately as that which exists; and it exists for itself, as given to the thought which thinks it.[58]

With this thesis Gentile seems to identify history with perception, thus acknow-ledging that history is the basis of all thought. Moreover, since thought is iden-

---

[53] Ibid.
[54] Ibid., 80.
[55] Ibid., 81.
[56] Ibid., 83.
[57] Ibid., 82.
[58] Ibid., 83.

tical with reality, he concludes that history is reality, and vice versa that reality is history.

In order to understand Gentile's *La filosofia della storia* we must keep in mind that it starts with the same problem as *La filosofia dell'arte*; in both books Gentile tries to explain the empirical aspects of the act of thought without losing sight of the problem of its objectivity. In *La filosofia dell'arte* he tries to interpret the experience of the artist and the critic in terms of actualist logic, and in *La filosofia della storia* he does the same for the experience of the historian. At the same time, *La filosofia della storia* forms the counterpart to *La filosofia dell'arte* in the sense that *La filosofia dell'arte* deals with the subjective aspects of the act of thought, feeling, emotions, and language, whereas *La filosofia della storia* deals with the objective aspects, that is, historical facts as based on evidence.

This is an important complement to the *Sistema di logica*. In that work Gentile had only partly solved the problem of objectivity on the basis of the notion of the *autoconcetto*. But in *La filosofia della storia* Gentile tries to find an extra foothold for the objectivity of history by presenting it as the experience of the ingenuous historian; namely as facts which are obtained on the basis of evidence. For the historian, historical evidence refers to a given x, an historical fact, which he tries to represent as truthfully as possible on the basis of his interpretation of evidence. Following the lines of his actualist philosophy, Gentile contends that the x, the historical fact, is a product of a past act of thought, which the historian gives to himself in order to reflect on it. Up to this point, there is nothing new about Gentile's thesis, although he had never dealt at such length with the problem of evidence. The real novelty of *La filosofia della storia* is that the historian cannot go beyond the facts, that is, he cannot simply construct facts, but he must 'take or leave' the facts as they were produced by past thought. These facts therefore function as presuppositions of the act of thought. With this thesis Gentile limits the freedom of the act of thought; thought is still free, in the sense that it decides by itself about which object to think, but it is not free in the sense that it completely 'creates' this object. The starting point for the historian is always historical fact as interpreted by himself. But historical fact also provides the truth-criterion for itself. The historian can never pass over the positivity of history. Even the poet cannot completely neglect the 'positivity of history'; like every human being he has to face the reality of historical fact. Historical thought is therefore the fullest realisation of the act of thought, and history becomes the basis of art, science, and philosophy.

Herein lies the novelty of Gentile's position. In his systematical work, Gentile used to emphasise the creative aspects of thought at the cost of the objective positive aspects of it, but now he almost reverses the roles. In the *Sistema di logica* he had based his notion of objectivity on the *autoconcetto*, or the history of truth-norms, which he identified with the history of philosophy, but now he bases objectivity on the positivity of history, or plain historical fact, as constructed on the basis of evidence. With this Gentile shifts from the history of philosophy as the norm for all truth to history *tout court* as the basis of all thought. The kernel of this new thesis is the notion of the 'positivity' of history.

Seen in Gentile's development, the vindication of the positivity of history amounts to a re-evaluation of the *pensato*. The *pensato* now plays an active role in the *pensante*, it conditions the range of subject matters for the *pensante*. In other words, the historian's act of thought is conditioned by the history of thought itself. The historian's knowledge of the past has come from the past itself; the historian possesses knowledge of some basic facts, the basis of which he uses to build his new interpretation.

At the same time, Gentile remains within the limits of actualism; the *pensato* is still an abstraction, or construction of the *pensante*; the 'basic facts' or 'positivity' are still 'nature', 'mechanism', that presents itself as 'immediacy' to the *pensante*. As immediate the past is a dead past, which is what it is, namely, a solid block of facts until a new historian comes to think about it and thus relives them. As in *La filosofia dell'arte*, Gentile sharply distinguishes between immediacy and mediacy with the consequence that the positive facts are only actual for the historian's present self-conscious act of thought. In this way, Gentile overlooks the possibility that history may be actual outside the present thought of the historian even if the historian is not aware of it. This was the idea of the 'living past' that forms Collingwood's philosophy of history.

From the perspective of Gentile's own development, it is very difficult to see how the thesis of the 'positivity of history' can be made compatible with the rest of his system, and especially with *La filosofia dell'arte*, to which *La filosofia della storia* is so closely linked. In *La filosofia dell'arte*, Gentile tried to account for the subjective aspects of the mind, feelings, emotions, imagination; and the main result of *La filosofia dell'arte* is a vindication of emotion as a form of 'immediacy', as the first stage of the act of thought. In *La filosofia della storia*, he presents us with another objective form of immediacy; historical fact as the beginning of all thought. We seem therefore to be confronted with two kinds of immediacy; emotions and historical fact. Thought may begin by reflecting upon our emotions, or by reflecting upon historical facts. How these two forms of immediacy are related to each other is difficult to understand. In *La filosofia della storia* Gentile makes it clear that the latter is more fundamental because, despite its freedom or spontaneity, art presupposes history; the artist always lives and works in an historical world which he can never entirely neglect. Nonethelesss, it is clear that the two forms of immediacy need to be more closely connected. This was what Gentile would finally do in *Genesì e struttura della società* with his theory of the transcendental dialogue. But he first clarified his position in 'Il superamento del tempo nella storia'.

The Transcending of Time

As in *La filosofia della storia*, Gentile's intention in 'Il superamento del tempo nella storia', written in 1934–5 for *Philosophy and History*, is to account for the objectivity of history.[59] Gentile begins the paper by pointing out that reality is spirit and that spirit is a process which has three moments: a beginning, a development, and a result. A misunderstanding of these moments leads to a distinction between a non-historical and an historical reality.[60] The naturalist, for example, distinguishes between non-historical nature and thought and interprets the first as a 'condition' for understanding the latter.[61] Along the same lines, the 'historicist' distinguishes between history and historiography. In this way he reduces history to nature, that is, to an objective reality that forms the truth-condition of the historian's thought. History is thus seen as an 'antecedent' or 'presupposition' for historiography.[62] Gentile justifies the historicist's claim that history must be based on objective facts ordered in a strict chronology. Taking this as a starting point, Gentile's aim is to reinterpret the historicist's claim on the basis of the theory of the pure act of thought.[63] This brings him to the basic problem of reconciling the objectivity and the temporality of historical fact with the subjectivity and the eternity of the act of thought. Gentile had dealt with this problem in *Teoria generale dello spirito* and *Sistema di logica,* but now, after *La filosofia della storia,* he is much more inclined to take the historian's view of 'objective fact' seriously in order to show that it presupposes the pure act of thought.

Gentile begins by pointing out that historicism is based on a false distinction between *vérités de fait* and *vérités de raison*. According to Gentile, it is said that a *vérité de fait* presupposes something outside itself whereas a *vérité de raison* does not do so. In this context, he points out that by presupposing something as an antecedent to thought, a *vérité de fait* raises the idea of time. From this it follows that for a *vérité de fait* reality as whole is an antecedent, that is, a past which makes the *vérité de fait* true. In other words, the past is the truth-condition for the *verité de fait*.[64] How can the past be a truth-condition, Gentile asks, if it is not real, if it lies beyond the actual existent, that is, if it is dead? On this point, the historicist is caught in a dilemma: on the one hand, the past is everything, in the sense that it is the truth condition for all thought; on the other hand, the past is nothing because it is not actual.[65]

In order to solve this dilemma Gentile analyses the concept of the past. His first step is to show how the past can be known even if it is not actual:

---

59 G. Gentile, *La filosofia della storia*, xxxii; Klibansky, Raymond and H.J. Paton (eds.), *Philosophy and History: Essays Presented to Ernst Cassirir*, Clarendon Press, Oxford, 1936, 91–105.

60 G. Gentile, 'Il superamento del tempo nella storia', in *Rendiconti della Reale Accademia dei Lincei*, XI, 1936, cited from *Frammenti di Estetica e di teoria della storia*, II, OC XLVIII, Le Lettere, Florence, 1992, 3–4.

61 Ibid., 4.

62 Ibid., 6–7.

63 Ibid., 7–8.

64 Ibid., 9–10.

65 Ibid., 10–11.

> To know it, in the only way that is possible, is to make it live again, to actual-
> ise it; and that means to take it out of time and free it from its chronological
> character, in order to transfer it from the abstract world of facts to the concrete
> world of the act (the historian's act) of thought, to which all facts belong in the
> synthesis of self-consciousness.[66]

The crux of this passage is that the reliving or 'actualisation' of the past involves
its extemporalisation. When we 'transfer' abstract facts to the realm of self-
conscious thought, we strip them of their chronological character in order to
think them according to the logic of the self-conscious act of thought. According
to Gentile, this simply means that we can understand the *vérités de fait* only as
being based on the *vérités de raison*. But this leads to a new problem: how can the
eternal act of thought think history in time whereas it is itself out of time?[67]
Gentile solves this problem by presenting the act of thought as the only 'fixed
point' in the 'chain' of time from which we 'construct' by adding new 'links':

> The only link of the chain which, in fact, has a relative fixity is the one we
> hold in our hand, not the first but the last, starting from which we retrace the
> course of the past, and seek the yesterday of each today and the antecedent of
> every fact. And in this we are constrained by the same logic which, by hypo-
> stasation the object of self-consciousness, drives us, so to speak, to plunge
> form the eternity of thought into the past of time. The only fixed point from
> which we can start is not a present following a past, but eternity issuing in a
> temporal given: that is the link to which we bind one by one all the other links
> of a chain producible to infinity.[68]

This passage shows that it is not the past that constitutes the self-conscious act of
thought, but the latter that creates the past by positing a past for itself. In this
context, Gentile speaks about 'turning history up side down' and about 'trans-
ferring the temporal series'.[69] Because the present act of thought creates time, it
transcends time: that is, it is in time in so far as it is actual, and it is not in time in
so far it considers itself creating it.

With this position, Gentile advocates the view rejected by de Ruggiero and
Collingwood in 1920 as the 'neutralisation of time'; by which they mean the
view that all pasts lose their chronological character and become identical presents for the act of thought.[70] This is also Collingwood's underlying criticism in
his review of *Philosophy and History* in 1937. On the whole, Collingwood is
positive about Gentile's contribution. He agrees with Gentile that time is trans-
cended in history 'because the historian, in discovering the thought of a past

---

[66] Ibid., 14.
[67] Ibid., 15.
[68] Ibid., 15.
[69] Ibid., 15–6.
[70] See chapters 6, p. 178, and 7, p. 227.

again, re-thinks that thought for himself'.[71] According to Collingwood, this is 'an important idea and a true one', though he points out that the historian who tries to understand the past 'must be or make himself the right kind of man, a man capable of entering into the minds of the person whose history he is studying'.[72] It is interesting to note that Gentile himself does not draw this implication in 'Il superamento', so it may be seen as an admonition to the philosopher of Fascism. Even more interesting is the fact that Collingwood begins his comment with the remark that Gentile works out 'one implication of the truth, that what the historian seeks to do is to discover the thought of historical agents'.[73] This suggests that there is another implication as well and, as we will see in the next chapter, this other implication is the objective existence of the past which is not elaborated by Gentile.

History and Action: *Genesis and Structure of Society* (1944)

In 1943 Gentile continued his work on *La filosofia della storia* but postponed its completion again in order to write *Genesi e struttura della società*. The book was written in very difficult circumstances. On 24 June, Gentile delivered his *Discorso agli Italiani* (*Address to the Italians*), in which he made an emotional appeal to the Italians to hold together. On 10 July, the allies invaded Sicily, and two weeks later Mussolini was forced to resign. In September, however, Mussolini, helped by the Germans, established the Fascist Republic in the North of Italy which split the peninsula in two. In these circumstances, Gentile thought that it was his duty to expound his moral and political views. Apart from an analysis of the relationship between the individual and society which forms the kernel of the book, Gentile also discusses economics and philosophy of history. The book ends with a long chapter on death and immortality.

In the preface to the book Gentile indicates that the most important chapter deals with the 'transcendental society'. In this chapter Gentile starts from his original conception of *societas in interiore hominis*; or the view that society is immanent in the individual.[74] Gentile explains that there is no real individual who does not have within him an *alter* which is his *socius*. By the act of thought the subject assimilates this *alter* into itself. The *alter* thus takes on a spiritual quality; it is not a mere object but a subject like himself; it speaks, wills, and thinks like himself.[75] The poet talks to the moon which thus becomes his *alter*,

---

71 R.G. Collingwood, Review of 'Klibansky, Raymond, and H.J. Paton, eds., Philosophy and History: Essays Presented to Ernst Cassirer', in *English Historical Review*, 52, 1937, 144.
72 Ibid., 143–4. See chapter 9, pp. 341–342.
73 Ibid., 143.
74 G. Gentile, *Genesi e struttura della società, Saggio di filosofia pratica*, Sansoni, Florence, 1946, cited from *Genesi e struttura della società, Saggio di filosofia pratica*, OC IX, Le Lettere, Florence, 1987, 33.
75 Ibid., 33–5.

and to the naive imaginings of the man who lacks our ordinary experience, everything becomes alive and acquires human feelings.[76] The object that the subject finds present within itself must ultimately be another self, an *alter ego* capable of enjoying liberty. In order to be itself the subject must renounce its solitude, it must and it does have another self.[77] Gentile describes the relationship between the *ego* and the *alter ego* as 'a transcendental dialogue'. This dialogue does not necessarily take place between individuals, it can also be held within one individual. The latter is even more fundamental because it is only on the condition that we can talk to ourselves that we are able to talk to others; the first ears to hear us are not those of others but our own. Hearer and speaker are the same man and yet not the same; a single personality imitates itself from within and is actually present and active in the internal dialogue which constitutes the unique act of thought. The act of thought is expressed in language which can be communicated to others.[78]

According to Gentile, the 'transcendental dialogue' is of fundamental importance because it is the genesis of all society.[79] Society is constituted by free dialogue between men. This formation of society is historical; accordingly history is seen as an infinite dialogue between men of different places and different times. The aim of this process is 'culture', which was the ideal of classical humanism. In the Renaissance, 'culture' meant intellectual culture, especially art and literature.[80] But with the advance of industry in history the concept has to be widened so as to include the work of those who work at the foundations of culture, such as workers, peasants, craftsmen, and so forth.[81] At the foundation of culture, man is in contact with nature and labours within it. Labour is a self-conscious activity; man's work therefore reveals the activity of thought and this can be found in the work of artists and philosophers. The new, historical humanism must therefore be a humanism of labour which embraces every form of human activity.[82]

Genesi e struttura della società is one of Gentile's most controversial books. Some interpreters have seen it as an apology for Fascism. Others regard it as the expression of the true, dialogical aspect of actualism. Morra describes it as 'a myth of social action' and Harris interprets it as a metaphysics of democratic method.[83] But seen in the context of Gentile's development, the notion of the transcendental society must be seen as Gentile's solution to the problem which

---

[76] Ibid., 35–6.

[77] Ibid., 36.

[78] Ibid., 36–9.

[79] Ibid., 39.

[80] Ibid., 111.

[81] Ibid., 111–2.

[82] Ibid., 112.

[83] Gianfranco Morra, 'La storia nel pensiero di Giovanni Gentile', in *Giovanni Gentile, La Vita e il Pensiero*, X, 1962, 388; Harris, *The Social Philosophy of Giovanni Gentile*, 329.

he left open at the end of *La filosofia dell'arte* and *La filosofia della storia*.[84] The problem concerns the beginning of the dialectic. In *La filosofia dell'arte* Gentile found this in emotions, in *La filosofia della storia* in historical fact, and he regarded both as forms of immediacy that call for mediation by the act of thought. In *Genesì e struttura della società* Gentile synthesises these views in three steps. Firstly, he identifies the *pensato* with 'the other self' within us. Secondly, he argues that this other self gradually becomes actual, real by a process which comes very close to the 'self-translation' of emotions. Thirdly, and this is the crux of the argument, Gentile recognises that the *pensato* becomes a *pensante* within ourselves. By thinking about our other self, it begins to think and to speak to us. The same view may be applied to other individuals because the transcendental dialogue is not hampered by empirical boundaries; when we begin to think about other individuals, whether in the past or in the present, we make them part of our internal dialogue. The other individual is not a mere *pensato* anymore, a construction of our thought, but a real individual that becomes alive within us; it talks to us, it challenges us, it asks us questions and answers our questions. In short, the past thought is now regarded as a present thought; and the dead past becomes a living past. In this way Gentile recognises the 'otherness' of the *pensato* which is not a construction of our present act of thought, but something that exists independent of us within ourselves. Gentile stresses that the internal dialogue can only take place where the persons involved are really different. This difference itself is gradually overcome in the dialogue itself but not cancelled; the outcome is not absolute agreement but mutual comprehension.[85]

With this theory Gentile attempts to solve the problem of the beginning of the dialectic; all thought begins as a dialogue between the self and the non-self. This non-self may be an incomprehensible emotion, another individual, or a past fact. The aim of the dialogue is to resolve the difference between the non-self and the self in mutual comprehension. In Gentile's terms one might say that the act of thought is now seen as a *pensante un pensato come un pensante* (a present thought thinking a past thought as a present thought); the free self-conscious act of thought thinks the past thought in order to make it a present thought.

This view has important implications for Gentile's idea of history, even if he does not work this out in his last work. Contrary to his earlier views, the relationship between the present and the past is not that of a creative act and its product, but of two partners in a dialogue, in which the historian never removes the otherness of the past but tries to understand it. The aim of history would then be to establish mutual comprehension between all peoples of all places and all times and as a basis of society.

---

[84] This paragraph is based on Rik Peters, 'Talking to Others or Talking to Yourself, H.S Harris on Giovanni Gentile's Transcendental Dialogue', in *CLIO, A Journal of Literature, History and the Philosophy of History*, 27. 4, 1998, 501–15.

[85] G. Gentile, *Genesì e struttura della società*, 39–40.

All this may be dismissed as grandiloquent nonsense, but it is as far as we can get in an historical world as Gentile conceived it. To the question of whether there is anything that exists prior to this transcendental society that contains all civilisation and all of human history Gentile would answer: 'no!' If we want to 'imagine' a universe and a world of nature prior to the act of thought, he says, we can only see it as an 'amorphous potentiality', because everything that comes into existence is a creative self-conscious act of thought. Gentile thus remained loyal to his doctrine that reality is the pure act of thought, or that reality is history. He continued to see reality from a human point of view, because man can only understand what he has made himself. But on the basis of the theory of the transcendental society, Gentile also stressed that human beings always create their world in cooperation with their past selves and other human beings. This view of human cooperation lies at the basis of Gentile's ethics, which he called the 'humanism of labour'. In this way Gentile solved the problem that he could not solve in *Sistema di logica*. In that book he had tried to found an *etica del sapere* on the basis of the *autoconcetto,* but the very subjectivism to which this led prevented him from completing his ethics.

In *La filosofia della storia*, Gentile might have tried to complete his system by incorporating his theory of dialogue into his concept of history, but he was murdered on 15 April 1944. Therefore we can only guess the final synthesis between his notion of dialogue and history.

Croce's Final Position: *History as Thought and Action* (1938)

After finishing his famous historical tetralogy with *Storia d'Europa* in 1932, Croce turned back to aesthetics and philosophy of history. The products of these revisions are *La Poesia* published in 1936 and *La storia come pensiero e come azione*, published in 1938. The latter book is a new elaboration of the problem of the relationship between theory and practice. As we have seen, Croce had not solved this problem in his *Teoria e storia della storiografia* of 1917.[86] On the one hand, he claimed that all history is contemporary history, that is, it comes forth from our practical interests. On the other hand, he kept firm to the distinction between theory and practice; history is a form of thought and should be as neutral as possible. In his own tetralogy, Croce himself had crossed the boundaries between theory and practice as laid down in his *Filosofia dello spirito*. And in his 'Antistoricismo' he had called upon all intellectuals to take history into account in order to overcome the political crisis in Europe. Finally, in *La storia come pensiero e come azione* he laid down a philosophical basis for this conception of the relationship between history and action.

Croce begins his exposition with the notion of the unity-distinction of theory and practice in its 'circularity'; historical thought is necessary for practice and practice is necessary for historical thought in the sense that it always deals with

---

[86] See chapter 2, pp. 68–69.

human action. This had been Croce's theory since his *Filosofia della pratica,* but in *La storia come pensiero e come azione* he specifies the role of history in this circle more precisely than ever before. 'History', Croce says, 'is preparatory but not determining action':

> Action is preceded by an act of knowledge, the solution of a particular diffi- culty, removal of a veil form the face of reality, and yet, as action, it springs exclusively from an original and personal inspiration of purely practical qual- ity and genius. There is no way of deducing this theoretically by means of a concept of 'knowledge of what to do', because knowledge is always of things done, never of things to do. And that which is given that name (knowledge of what to do) is already a doing or nothing, empty babble.[87]

From this strong link with practice stems the essentially moral character of his- torical thought which is the essence of its contemporaneity. All history stems from practical problems in the present and this makes all history 'contemporary history'.[88] In several places Croce explains how practical problems are 'embod- ied' in history. In this context he often stresses that history is a question and answer activity. For example, when he discusses Droysen's thesis that all history consists of the asking of questions, Croce points out that a distinction should be made between the mere philological question and the historical question. According to Croce, there is a great difference between a question about the documents and chronology of the Lutheran reform and a question about the character of that reform; the former arises from a pure technical and erudite need, the latter from a moral need.[89]

The ultimate aim of history is 'historical catharsis', or the liberation of man from the burden of the past. Man carries the past within himself, Croce says, every man is a 'compendium' of history, an historical microcosmos. But in order to be free he must liberate himself from his own history by studying it. Croce summarises this view as follows:

> We are products of the past and live immersed in a past which envelops us on every side. How can we advance towards new life, how create new action, without getting out of the past, without getting over it? But how can we get over the past, if we are in the past, if the past is, in fact, ourselves? There is only one way out, that of thought, which does not break the link with the past, but raises above it ideally and converts it into knowledge. We must look the past in the face, or, discarding metaphors, we must reduce it to a mental problem and resolve it into a new proposition of truth which will form the ideal premiss for our new action and new life.[90]

---

87   B. Croce, *La storia come pensiero e come azione,* 170.
88   Ibid., 11.
89   Ibid., 122–3.
90   Ibid., 33–4.

In another passage, Croce identifies this 'overcoming' of history for practical needs with historical 'catharsis' on the basis of which he establishes a criterion for the historicity of a work of history:

> An historical book is to be judged only for its historical quality just as a book of poetry is judged for its poetical quality. Historical quality may be defined as an activity of comprehension and intelligence, stimulated by some need in the practical life, which cannot realize itself in action until first fantasies, doubts and obscurities stand in the way are chased aside by the positing and solving of a theoretical problem, that is, by an act of thought. It is the seriousness of a need of life that provides the necessary presupposition (of history).[91]

In this passage, Croce argues that the value of history is found in its 'comprehension' and 'intelligence' which are needed for rational action. Good history therefore always arises from practical problems, that is, economic or moral problems, whereas bad historical questions are not rooted in practice. Croce gives Ranke and Burckhardt as examples historians who did not ask questions which were relevant for action. In Croce's view both historians did not have any profound ethical and political interest and for this reason their histories do not contain any historical problems, at the most they contain some bogus problems.[92] Ranke (1795–1886) always tended towards to pacifism, quietism, and conservatism, Burckhardt to irrationalism and pessimism. According to Croce, the German historicists, notably by Meinecke (1862–1954), sanctioned this kind of history without an historical problem. Against his views, Croce posits his idea of ethico-political history which vindicates the idea of the practical relevance of history.

Seen from Croce's development, the most important novelty of *La storia come pensiero e come azione* is the idea of the practical relevance of historical questioning. In his *Teoria e storia della storiografia* Croce still held that we are never allowed to ask an historian to justify his questions; every historian is free to ask the questions he wishes to ask. Nevertheless, in *La storia come pensiero e come azione* Croce holds that we must judge the questions of an historian by their relevance for moral and political action. However, despite this close link between history and practice, Croce still makes a distinction between them. Although history arises from practical problems it is never to be identified with practice itself; history is the necessary condition for practice but not practice itself. Croce can therefore never agree to Gentile's complete identity of theory and practice, according to which all historical thought must be judged as a moral act and historical truth as a duty. Likewise, Croce's criterion of the historicity of a work of history still reveals his attitude of a critic who wants to judge a work of art without objective criterion.

We find the same difference reappearing in Croce's and Gentile's views on the role of history in society. Both Croce and Gentile hold that man is a product

---

[91] Ibid., 9.
[92] Ibid., 80–2.

of his past which continuously surrounds him. We are 'immersed in history', Croce says, and 'history is immanent in all activities of the spirit', says Gentile. However, Croce's notion of man as a 'microcosm of history' is different from Gentile's notion of the *societas in interiore homine*. Croce's view that history 'surrounds' us still suggests a distinction between history and the historian. Accordingly, the historical catharsis must be seen as 'lifting' oneself out of history. A concrete example of this thesis is Croce's distinction between the historiography written by political parties and historiography proper. Political parties are 'immersed' in the course of history, and their histories are always 'tendentious', whereas true history does not have a practical aim and lifts itself above the parties in order to obtain truth.[93] For Gentile, the practice of history is always immanent to life. Consequently, he thinks that we cannot lift ourselves out of it, though we can enter into a dialogue with it. This dialogue is already a moral act in which we are completely immersed. Accordingly, the historian cannot lift himself above the parties, because this would amount to establishing a party of his own.

In the years after *La storia come pensiero e come azione* Croce would gradually develop the contrast between politics, which falls under the category of utility and morality, into the contrast between the 'vitality' and 'morality'. Croce's concept of 'vitality' is difficult to grasp, but he usually identified it with the 'irrational' impetus of all human activity. On this basis he came to regard the function of history as the 'overcoming' of vitality. In *La storia come pensiero e come azione* we already find the first ingredients of this view, for example when Croce urges that 'vitality' has its own 'ratio' which must be understood.[94] In this context, he gives the examples of action guided by 'vanity', 'folly', and the effect of 'natural events' which break into history such as 'explosions', 'revolutions', and so forth. Obviously, Croce had a form of history in mind that could deal with the 'irrationalities' of his own days, and this suggests that he was not completely satisfied with his ethico-political history. Until his death in 1952, Croce would wrestle with the problem of 'vitality', without coming to a solution however.[95]

De Ruggiero's Return to Reason (1933–1940)

Apart from his series on the history of philosophy, Guido de Ruggiero continued his studies, begun in 1928, of contemporary British and German philosophy which he discussed in *Filosofi del novecento*. In the preface of this book, written in September 1933, de Ruggiero presents this work both as continuation and as a revision of *La filosofia contemporanea* of 1912. The latter work was written in the times of the 'idealist ressurrection', whereas the former is a reflection of 'a critical revision of idealism'. In 1933, de Ruggiero also published 'Revisioni

---

93　Ibid., 163.
94　Ibid., 151.
95　Roberts, *Benedetto Croce and the Uses of Historicism*, 98–101.

idealistiche' ('Idealist Revisions'), one of the very few papers in theoretical philosophy he produced in the 1930s. De Ruggiero begins this article with the startling question 'are we still idealists?', explaining that this question arose because he found that idealism had changed since its revival at the beginning of the century.[96] De Ruggiero recognises that idealism had triumphed over its adversaries and that it had permeated all levels of culture. But, de Ruggiero avers, 'dilagando s'è fatto stagnante' ('while spreading it stagnated'), and worse; idealism had betrayed its original mission.[97] Traditionally, de Ruggiero says, idealism stands for 'the cult of the ideal' and for a 'detachment from empirical and contingent things'.[98] In his view this 'cult' was based on a sharp contrast between the ideal and the real. If this contrast is neglected, idealism and 'reality suddenly flattens itself' and spirit takes on the forms of nature again.[99] In de Ruggiero's view this 'flattening' infects the victorious idealism of his day, which thinks of reality as being completely dematerialised and completely spiritualised and can be understood by simple formulas which dispense thought with any labour. It lacks a criterion of discrimination and confounds good and bad, wisdom and folly. All this leads to indifferentism and laziness because: 'if everything is thought why take the trouble of thinking, and if everything is good, why fight?'[100]

According to de Ruggiero, not all idealists are at fault. Croce, for example, still assigns the task of raising new questions for philosophy to the distinction between theory and practice.[101] Nevertheless, others have brought idealism to a *reductio ad adsurdum* and 'the complete emptying of all its content, to a state of a so perfect self-sufficiency, which borders on death'.[102] Ironically, de Ruggiero concludes that 'by skimming hegelism, nothing is left but the scum'. The extreme limit of this movement is of course Gentile's actualism. This philosophy oversimplifies the 'work of thought' by converting all problems of knowledge into metaphysical problems. In this context, the basic error of actualism is its overvaluation of the present act of thought at the cost of the content of thought. Actualists do not make the basic distinction between *pensare* and *pensato* so that the *pensato* is identified with the *pensare*, being with thought, the real with truth, existence with essence, and the that with the what. According to de Ruggiero, from this 'accentuation of actuality' follows a 'mental indifferentism'. Actualists do not see thinking as a laborious inferential activity in which each thought is connected to another, but as a process which jumps from act to act so that the essence of reality is identified with mere 'actualising' and the function of philos-

---

[96] G. de Ruggiero, 'Revisioni idealistiche', in *L'educazione nazionale*, 1933, 138–45, 138.
[97] Ibid.
[98] Ibid.
[99] Ibid.
[100] Ibid., 139.
[101] Ibid., 140.
[102] Ibid.

ophy is restricted to saying that there is something actual.[103] From this viewpoint, only two alternatives present themselves. The first is to 'pulverise' the
mental activity into an infinite series of acts of thought which leads to an
'extreme relativism'. The other is to recognise that each act of thought is the
object of the subsequent act of thought which leads to the view of 'progressive
encapsulation' of all acts of thought in a single act of thought that transcends
them all. The actor of this unique act is the absolute spirit. De Ruggiero is highly
critical of this notion. In his view, the absolute spirit 'oscillates' between the
individual thinker on the hand and God on the other, but at its heart it is only an
'empty concept'. Some anxious religious minds may recognise God in this concept, and some 'titanic minds' may recognise some superman in it.[104]

De Ruggiero himself does not deny that reflection on the activity of knowing
can have a decisive influence on the comprehension of reality.[105] But he keeps to
the distinction between *pensante* and *pensato*, between the subject and the object,
truth and reality, between essence and existence. According to de Ruggiero, a
known world is not 'inert matter', but it has a development and a definite meaning. Once this is recognised it is not necessary to reject the notion of the Absolute
Spirit completely; because all thought presupposes a unifying principle. However, this principle must not be seen as being an act but as an ideal, because only
as an ideal does the notion of unity allow for its opposite that is diversity. For
example, when we interpret the relationships between men we should not
impose some 'superior consciousness' on their minds but we should do justice to
the 'intimacy' and 'impenetrability' of each. Only on the condition that we take
idealism in this sense does de Ruggiero finally answer his initial question, 'are
we still idealists?' with a wholehearted 'yes'.

The highly critical 'Revisioni idealistiche' show that de Ruggiero had learned
from the British philosophers, discussed in *Filosofi del novecento*, that there was
more than the pure act of thought in the world, and that the riddle of the universe cannot be solved by a simple empty formula of subject, object, and synthesis. In comparison to his earlier development, de Ruggiero pays more attention to the importance of the object, for the world outside, for nature, for facts,
and on this basis he concluded that thinking needs a firm method. But his faith
in idealism itself remains unshaken. The fault of the actual idealists is that they
confounded *pensare* and *pensato*, the ideal and the real. Yet idealism can still be of
value as a 'cult of the ideal' if this distinction between the ideal and the real is
kept intact.

This vindication of the 'ideal' can be found in de Ruggiero's historical works
of the 1930s which show a development in the direction of a rehabilitation of
'metahistorical principles'. Instrumental in this development were his prepara-

---

[103] Ibid., 143.
[104] Ibid., 144.
[105] Ibid., 141.

tory studies for *L'eta dell' Illuminismo* of his *Storia della filosofia* published in 1938. As he later confessed, he began his studies with the usual idealist prejudices against the unhistorical character of the Enlightenment philosophy. Soon, however, he discovered that the philosophers of the Enlightenment were as unhistorical as he initially supposed them to be.[106]

The impact of his studies of the Enlightenment is reflected in 'Il ritorno alla ragione' ('Return to Reason'), a paper which he wrote in April 1940 for the occasion of his Doctorate *honoris causa* at the University of Oxford. 'Il ritorno alla ragione' is a wholehearted appeal to return to the ideals of the Enlightenment. According to de Ruggiero, the force of this movement was its firm belief in the universality of reason. Reason was not a privilege of the few, but belonged in the public domain. It bound individuals together; 'reason was the common denominator of judgments', it is 'the we that emerges from the relation between me and you'.[107] After the Enlightenment, reason took its first serious blow from Romanticism, which formed the basis of all kinds of irrationalist movements in the course of the nineteenth century. The fault of the intellectuals was that they were not alarmed by the rise of tendencies such as Sorel's syndicalism and others, because they longer believed in the effectiveness of culture.[108] This is, in de Ruggiero's view of the *trahison des clercs*, the betrayal by men of culture of the universal human values that had always been the essence of their mission. The final result of this betrayal is that all kinds of activist, nationalistic, and racist streams have not been stopped.[109]

From this point of view, de Ruggiero calls for a revival of the ideals of the Enlightenment which in his view amounts to a revival of reason. Here lies a task for the historians who already show a renewed interest in the Enlightenment. In this way the ideals of justice, liberty of the individual, peace between the peoples, and a cosmopolitical culture, which are still alive, can be reinforced. But de Ruggiero warns that all this does not mean that all ideals of the Enlightenment are to be taken literally, because, although the ideals of the Enlightenment are universal and transcend time, they have always been embodied differently in history. The polemic of the Enlightenment was directed against the irrationalism in the institutions, traditions, and thought.[110] The contemporary polemic is directed against the irrationalism that comes from below; racism, extreme nationalism, and so forth. But the two polemics do not destroy irrationalism; they do not consider irrationalism as something merely negative but as a ferm-

---

[106] G. de Ruggiero, 'Il ritorno alla ragione', in *Mercurio*, 1, 1944, 80–98, cited from Cicalese, M.L. (ed.), in *Nuova Antologia*, 1994–95, 37. This was de Ruggiero's lecture to be delivered in 1940 for his Doctorate *honoris causa* at the Univerity of Oxford.

[107] G. de Ruggiero, 'Il ritorno alla ragione', 39.

[108] Ibid., 43–4.

[109] Ibid., 44.

[110] Ibid., 47.

entation of new problems and experiences. Reason must not destruct these experiences but elevate them to a higher plane.[111]

As usual, de Ruggiero took a radical stance. Whereas Croce and Gentile remained true to their historicism, he embraced the transhistorical universal values of the Enlightenment. At the same time, de Ruggiero argued that every period calls for a different embodiment of these ideals. He thus tried to synthesise the historicism of his youth with his belief in 'meta-historical' principles of his maturity. It is difficult to see how he intended to elaborate this synthesis because during the war de Ruggiero was deeply involved in the resistance and after the war he became involved in politics. In 1945, he became the first Minister of Education of the new Government and a year later Ambassador to the United Nations in New York. In these functions de Ruggiero tried to realise the meta-historical principles of reason until 1948 when he died from a heart attack at the age of 60.

Conclusion

The central theme of the development of Croce, Gentile, and de Ruggiero in the 1930s was the 'revision of idealism'. Gentile revised his actualism by solving the problem of the spontaneity of the act of thought in his *La filosofia dell'arte* by recognising 'feeling' as the beginning of the act of thought. In *La filosofia della storia*, Gentile acknowledged history as the only basis of all spiritual activity. Along these lines, Gentile made his actualism both more concrete and historical. The crown of this development is his theory of the transcendental society by which he finally overcame the subjectivism of his *Sistema di logica*.

Croce also revised his earlier views by a further rapprochement between history and practice. This view culminates in his idea of 'historical catharsis' which expresses Croce's belief that historical thought is the only form of thought by which we can overcome our human finiteness.

In contrast to Croce and Gentile, de Ruggiero chose a new direction. Whereas Croce and Gentile tried to overcome their own belief in timeless principles and their development leaned towards an absolute historicism at the end of their lives, de Ruggiero ended his philosophical life by embracing the universal and transhistorical ideals of the Enlightenment.

Despite all of these developments none of the three philosophers abandoned the principles which helped their philosophies from their earliest development. Gentile remained faithful to his identity of reality with the pure act of thought. Likewise, his notion of history remained construction, although his notion of 'dialogue' opens very interesting perspectives for this constructivism. Croce never left the basic principles of his *Filosofia dello spirito* and despite his rapprochement between history and practice he kept on distinguishing between the two. Finally, de Ruggiero's plea for the revival of the Enlightenment ideals

---

[111] Ibid., 48–9.

fits well with his thesis that the ideal and the real should be kept in opposition in order to avoid a 'levelling' of the ideals which guide thought and action.

Chapter Nine

Collingwood's Later Development

Introduction

Collingwood's development in the 1930s began promisingly and ended dramatically. Around 1930 he had completed the foundations of his philosophy of history. On this basis, he further refined his philosophical method in his moral philosophy lectures of the early 1930s.[1] The first fruit of this rapprochement between philosophy and history was *An Essay on Philosophical Method*, written in 1932 and published in 1933. After this publication, Collingwood planned to write a series of philosophical books. Though it is not clear how Collingwood envisaged this series, he certainly first thought of writing a metaphysical treatise and a book on ethics.[2] Two years later, in his 'Report as University Lecturer in Philosophy and Roman History' of 18 January 1935, Collingwood mentions *An Essay on Philosophical Method* as a 'preface to a series of philosophical works' comprising 'certain large works not yet written: these should be completed in the next 3 years or so if I continue to have leisure for them'.[3] In this context, Collingwood mentions his studies on 'metaphysical problems connected with the idea of Nature, Matter, Life, Evolution' with which he hoped 'to advance a branch of philosophical thought which has lately been brought again into prominence by Alexander and Whitehead'.[4] As a 'by-product' of these studies Collingwood also mentions the lectures of 1934, in which he had dealt with the history of the idea of nature, and the 'co-operation with various psychologists, biologists, physicists etc. in and out of Oxford, with regard to the philosophical aspects of their own work'.[5]

---

[1]   James Connelly and Giuseppina d'Oro, 'Editors' Introduction' in R.G. Collingwood, *An Essay on Philosophical Method, Revised Edition,* Clarendon Press, Oxford, 2005, xxv.

[2]   Guido van Heeswijck, *Metafysica als een Historische Discipline, De Actualiteit van R.G. Collingwood's 'Hervormde Metafysica'*, Van Gorcum, Assen and Maastricht, 1993, 36-7; Boucher, *The Social and Political Philosophy of R.G. Collingwood*, 28.

[3]   Cited by van der Dussen, *History as a Science*, 439.

[4]   Ibid.

[5]   Ibid., 440.

In 1934, Collingwood was appointed to the prestigious Waynflete Chair of Metaphysical Philosophy at Magdalen College, succeeding the retiring J.A. Smith. The new function gave him the necessary leisure to work out his philosophical series. After his inaugural lecture, 'The Historical Imagination', held on 28 October 1935, he prepared a new course of lectures on the philosophy of history, which were later published as *The Idea of History*, and a course on 'The Central Problems in Metaphysics' which would form the basis of *An Essay on Metaphysics*. Meanwhile, Collingwood continued his lectures on 'Nature and Mind' begun in 1934 and his lectures on Roman Britain, and began an extensive study of folklore and magic.[6] Outside Oxford, Collingwood's star began to rise. In 1936, his contribution to *Roman Britain and The English Settlements* appeared, and he was invited to deliver a public lecture for the British Academy in May which was published as 'Human Nature and Human History'.

In 1937, Collingwood felt ready to complete his philosophical series and began to write *The Principles of Art*, which he almost finished in the same year. While working on the proofs of this book in January 1938, he suffered a stroke that put him out of work for some months. On the advice of his doctor, Collingwood asked for a leave in order to improve his health conditions. Faced with the threat of a sudden death, he decided to write his autobiography, hoping to leave at least an outline of his philosophy.[7] The remaining years of Collingwood's life were a race against the clock, in which he frantically tried to finish his series. During a voyage to the Dutch East Indies from October 1938 to April 1939 he wrote *An Essay on Metaphysics* and the beginning of *The Principles of History*, which he considered as his *magnum opus*. Back at home, he wrote another book during a sailing trip to Greece. Immediately after his return, on 1 September 1939, Collingwood decided to write *The New Leviathan* as a contribution to the war effort.[8] While working on these projects, Collingwood suffered another series of strokes, which eventually incapacitated him completely. In 1941, Collingwood stopped lecturing, and on 9 January 1943 he died at the age of 53, leaving his series unfinished.

In spite of this dramatic turn in his life, Collingwood kept contact with his Italian friends. Until his retirement, he continued to read their publications, and he wrote them long letters to keep them *au courant* of his personal affairs. In April 1938, Collingwood wrote to Croce to announce the publication of *The Principles of Art*.[9] In the letter, Collingwood did not mention his first stroke, but a few months later he informed the Italian about his illness in a letter written from

---

6   Boucher, *The Social and Political Philosophy of R.G. Collingwood*, 196–206.
7   R.G. Collingwood, *An Autobiography*, 118.
8   Van der Dussen, 'Collingwood's "Lost" Manuscript of The Principles of History', in *History and Theory*, 36, 1997, 32–62; Boucher, 'The Principles of History and the Cosmology Conclusion to *The Idea of Nature*', in *Collingwood Studies*, 2, 1995, 140–74.
9   Vigorelli, 'Lettere di Robin George Collingwood a Benedetto Croce (1912–1939)', 562, 20 April 1938.

the Dutch East Indies.[10] In the same letter, Collingwood wrote that he was reading Croce's *La storia come pensiero e come azione*.

Collingwood's direct contacts with Gentile, though never close, broke off altogether. However, Collingwood did not lose track of the Italian. He was probably involved in Carritt's translation of *La filosofia dell'arte*, finished in 1932, and three years later Collingwood wrote a positive review of Gentile's contribution to *Philosophy and History*, a collection of essays in honour of Cassirer edited by R. Klibansky and H.J. Paton.[11] Even in his autobiography, with its vehement rejection of Fascism and Nazism, Collingwood was not entirely negative about Gentile:

> There was once a very able and distinguished philosopher who was converted to Fascism. As a philosopher, that was the end of him. No one could embrace a creed so fundamentally muddle-headed and remain capable of clear thinking.[12]

This passage shows that Collingwood still valued the pre-Fascist Gentile, though he did not accept that he had become a Fascist. Probably, it was Gentile's quality as a philosopher that made his adherence to Fascism so indigestible for Collingwood. Seen from the viewpoint of the unity of theory and practice, Gentile's Fascism could mean only two things; the theory could be right, but then it had to be shown that it had nothing to do with Fascist practice, or both theory and practice were wrong, in which case both had to be revised. Given Collingwood's debt to actualism, this is one of the dilemmas which Collingwood had to face in the 1930s. His position was therefore not unlike de Ruggiero's in the same decade. Like his friend, Collingwood sought to overcome the difficulties of actualism by merging his own philosophy with the latest developments in Anglo-Saxon philosophy. Like de Ruggiero, Collingwood chose *la via più ardua*.

Collingwood's contact with de Ruggiero was only interrupted by the events which broke off all of Collingwood's activities. In January 1932, he made a trip to Italy meeting de Ruggiero before travelling to Greece.[13] After this, the two friends continued to exchange letters, books, and articles. In February 1934, Collingwood reacted to de Ruggiero's comments on *An Essay on Philosophical Method*, and in June 1937 he announced *The Principles of Art* and the lectures which would later become *The Idea of History*.[14] In July 1938, Collingwood informed his friend about his stroke in the beginning of that year.[15] In reaction to

---

10 Ibid., 562–3, 29 January 1939.
11 R.G. Collingwood, Review of 'Klibansky, Raymond, and H.J. Paton, eds., Philosophy and History: Essays Presented to Ernst Cassirer', 143–4.
12 R.G. Collingwood, *An Autobiography*, 158.
13 R.G. Collingwood, 'Letters to Guido de Ruggiero', letters of 4, 18, and 24 January 1932 and the 7 February 1932.
14 Ibid., 7 February 1934 and 12 June 1937.
15 Ibid., 24 July 1938.

this letter, de Ruggiero immediately invited Collingwood to his house in Naples, but Collingwood declined because he was about to leave for the Dutch Indies.[16]

After this letter, contact between the two friends did not break off. In 1939, Collingwood probably met de Ruggiero in Naples after his voyage to Greece and was certainly involved in the doctorate *honoris causa* granted to the Italian by the University of Oxford. Collingwood would never attend this doctorate because the war prevented de Ruggiero from travelling to Oxford. In 1946 he was still honoured with the doctorate, delivering 'Il ritorno alla ragione' in Collingwood's translation.[17]

In spite of the the contact with the Italian philosophers, there seem to be less Italian traces in Collingwood's later works than in the works of his middle period. Around 1930, Collingwood gave up translating Italian works in order to concentrate on his own. Except for the review of Klibansky's collection of essays, and some scattered remarks in his later works, he did not discuss Italian philosophy in his publications. In his manuscripts of the 1930s, however, Collingwood constantly referred to Italian philosophy, although more implicitly than explicitly. After more than twenty years of intensive study, the Italian philosophers belonged to Collingwood's most familiar internal conversation partners so that he no longer needed to mention them by name. Moreover, when Collingwood explicitly discussed the Italians, he often used their thought in order to develop his own position.

In this chapter, I will reconstruct Collingwood's development from 1933 until 1937. In these years he wrote some of his best known books and articles such as *An Essay on Philosophical Method, The Idea of Nature,* and *The Idea of History.* Seen from the perspective of Collingwood's life's work these writings were only preparations for the philosophical system he never finished. Special attention will be paid to Collingwood's 'Human Nature and Human History', because he regarded this lecture as a programme for his own philosophy. How he carried out this programme in his last works will be the subject of the next chapter.

The Preface to the Series: *An Essay on Philosophical Method* (1933)

An Essay on Philosophical Method is one of the most important works in Collingwood's development because it is the first published product of the rapprochement between philosophy and history. Moreover, it is also a specimen of the rapprochement between theory and practice, since Collingwood had developed his method in the course of his moral philosophy lectures. Most importantly, the book provided the starting point of Collingwood's investigations for his philosophical series.

Collingwood himself was very proud of his achievement in *An Essay on Philosophical Method.* In his autobiography he wrote:

---

[16] Ibid., 21 October 1938.
[17] See chapter 8, p. 283, n. 10.

It is my best book in matter; in style, I may call it my only book, for it is the only one I ever had the time to finish as well as I knew how, instead of leaving it in a more or less rough state.[18]

Collingwood's opinion was shared by Knox, who thought of it as a 'philosophical masterpiece'.[19] But most of the reviewers of the book, like C.J. Ducasse, F.C.S. Schiller, Gilbert Ryle, and W.G. de Burgh, were negative. Ducasse, for example, cynically remarked that 'not only Mr. Collingwood wholly fails to establish any of the principles of the premises upon which he bases his methodological conclusions, but that each of these premises is demonstrably false'.[20] Ryle attacked Collingwood's idea of philosophy in *Mind*, to which Collingwood replied in private correspondence.[21] After the war the negative criticism of the book continued. A.J. Ayer (1910–1989), for example, saw *An Essay on Philosophical Method* more as 'a contribution to Belles Lettres than to philosophy'.[22] Even Collingwood's first interpreters like Donagan, Mink, and Rubinoff did not discuss *An Essay on Philosophical Method* in depth. In 1974, Martin, one of the first interpreters who devoted more attention to *An Essay on Philosophical Method*, rightly remarked that the book had largely been ignored.[23] Since Martin's paper, however, attention for *An Essay on Philosophical Method* has been growing. Boucher showed how Collingwood applied his method in moral and political philosophy, and Connelly related the method to his metaphysics.[24] Finally, in 2005, Connelly and d'Oro published a new edition of *An Essay on Philosophical Method*, which they regard as 'one of the most sustained attempts within the philosophical tradition to articulate a conception of philosophy as first science and to defend the thesis of the autonomy of philosophy'.[25]

From the moment of its publication several critics and interpreters have related *An Essay on Philosophical Method* to Italian philosophy. According to Knox, Collingwood's idea of philosophy and its method differed considerably from Croce's historicism. Unlike the Italian, Knox says, Collingwood still drew

---

18 R.G. Collingwood, *An Autobiography*, 118.
19 T.M. Knox, 'Collingwood, Robin George (1889–1943)', in L.G. Wickham & E.T. Williams, *Dictionary of National Biography 1941–1950*, Oxford University Press, Oxford, 1959, 169.
20 C.J. Ducasse, 'Mr. Collingwood on Philosophical Method', in *Journal of Philosophy*, 33, 1936, 95.
21 G. Ryle, 'Mr. Collingwood and the Ontological Argument', in *Mind*, 44, 1935, 137–51.
22 A.J. Ayer, *Philosophy in the Twentieth Century*, Weidenfeld and Nicolson, London, 1982, 193.
23 Rex Martin, 'Collingwood's Essay on Philosophical Method', in *Idealistic Studies*, 4, 1974, 224.
24 Tariq Modood, 'Collingwood and the Idea of Philosophy', in Boucher (ed.), *Philosophy, History and Civilization*, 32–61; Boucher, *The Social and Political Philosophy of R.G. Collingwood*, 28–37.
25 Connelly and d'Oro, 'Editors' Introduction', xcvii.

distinctions 'between historical study and philosophical criticism, between historical thought as concerned with the individual and philosophical thought as concerned with the universal, and between the attitudes appropriate to the study of philosophy and the study of history'.[26] G.R.G. Mure (1893–1979) held that 'Collingwood's Philosophical Method, constitutes, incidentally, a criticism of Croce's separation (is it distinction or opposition?) of distincts and opposites within philosophy'.[27] Along the same lines, A. Russell held that Collingwood reversed Croce's analysis of the relationship between the distinct and opposite concept, though he avows that he cannot offer an explanation for this reversal.[28] Contrary to these views of Collingwood's achievement, M. Brown held that *An Essay on Philosophical Method* is an unsuccessful attempt to reconcile Croce's theory of distincts and Gentile's act of thought.[29] Finally, Connelly and d'Oro notice that in the 1920s Collingwood, influenced by both Croce and Gentile, had moved towards a dialectical manner of thinking and presentation, though he had not developed a fully philosophically adequate account of the dialectic. This was achieved in *An Essay on Philosophical Method* with the notion of the idea of the scale of forms, which they see as 'the culmination of an engagement with Hegel, Plato, Bradley, Croce and Gentile on the nature of a dialectical scale and on the nature of the philosophical concept'.[30] In this context, Connelly and d'Oro point out that notion of the scale of forms expresses Collingwood's view that philosophical concepts overlap not only in their extension, but also in their intension. In their view, this intensional view of philosophical concepts formed the basis of Collingwood's defence of the autonomy of philosophy and its method against early analytical philosophy, which tended to identify meaning with extension. In contrast to this position, Collingwood pointed out that the meaning of philosophical concepts is intensional because philosophical distinctions do not refer to reality. In a later essay, Connelly and d'Oro say that, for Collingwood, philosophical distinctions are purely semantic: 'philosophical concepts do not carve out a segment of reality, but rather provided a way of describing it.'[31] Accordingly, the task of the philosopher is not to classify but to distinguish concepts which coincide in their instances.

Connelly's and d'Oro's reading of Collingwood's *Essay on Philosophical Method* is highly instructive for understanding his development. Firstly, by stressing the importance of Collingwood's conceptual approach of language, the authors highlight the importance of language and meaning in Collingwood's philosophy without putting it in the same box with analytical philosophy. Sec-

---

26   T.M. Knox, 'Editor's Preface', viii–ix.
27   G.R.C. Mure, *Idealist Epilogue*, Clarendon Press, Oxford, 1978, 21.
28   Anthony F. Russell, *Logic, Philosophy and History*, 106n.
29   Brown, *Neo-Idealistic Aesthetics*, 200–6.
30   Connelly and d'Oro, 'Editors' Introduction', xxxi.
31   J. Connelly and G. d'Oro, 'Robin George Collingwood', in *Stanford Encyclopedia of Philosophy*, http://plato.stanford.edu/entries/collingwood/.

ondly, by taking philosophical distinctions as being purely semantic, Connelly and d'Oro are able to connect Collingwood's notion of philosophical concepts to his notion of absolute presuppositions, thus contradicting Knox's view that Collingwood converted to a kind of Crocean historicism. In spite of the merits of their interpretation, Connelly and d'Oro fail to do full justice to the relationship between *An Essay on Philosophical Method* and Collingwood's earlier development. Firstly, though Collingwood stressed the intensionality of philosophical concepts, he never said that philosophical distinctions should be taken as purely semantic for that reason. Instead, Collingwood always discussed the problem of meaning of concepts in the context of his logic of question and answer, which is not mentioned by Connelly and d'Oro. Secondly, although Connelly and d'Oro rightly point out the influence of Hegel and the Italians on Collingwood's development of the method, it is not entirely clear what role these thinkers played exactly. Connelly's and d'Oro's interpretation thus raises the question of how Collingwood's view of intensionality should be related to his logic of question and answer, and to the question of what role his predecessors played in this connection.

Fortunately, the answers to these questions can be provided by *An Essay on Philosophical Method* itself. As Collingwood himself avers, one of the most important implications of his method is that a philosopher must work out his own position by consolidating and criticising certain more or less definite philosophical positions.[32] Assuming that Collingwood applied this doctrine to his own philosophy when writing *An Essay on Philosophical Method*, it follows that the book can be read as an intellectual autobiography, though stated in highly abstract terms.

Seen from this point of view, references to Italian philosophy leap to the eye from the beginning of the book. '*E pur si muove*', Collingwood cites Galileo, stressing that philosophy is an activity going on in our minds from which it follows that 'it is possible to answer the question what philosophy is by giving an account of philosophical method'.[33] The quote in this passage may be read as a nod to the Italians who characterised philosophy as a never-ending quest having its own method.[34] In particular, Croce and de Ruggiero had formulated the identity between philosophy and history in terms of a dialectic of question and answer. Along the same lines Collingwood says: 'the entire history of thought is the history of a single sustained attempt to solve a single permanent problem, each phase advancing the problem by the extent of all the work done on it in the shape of a unique presentation of the problem.'[35]

---

[32] R.G. Collingwood, *An Essay on Philosophical Method*, 195–8.

[33] R.G. Collingwood, *An Essay on Philosophical Method*, 3.

[34] See for Croce, chapter 2, pp. 57–58, for Gentile, chapter 3, pp. 88–89, for de Ruggiero, chapter 4, pp. 100–114.

[35] R.G. Collingwood, *An Essay on Philosophical Method*, 194.

When we turn to the central notion of overlap, more references to the logic of question and answer can be retrieved. The most important example of overlap is one between the three kinds of goodness: *iucundum, utile, honestum.*[36] In his autobiography, Collingwood gives the same example to discuss the development of his rapprochement between theory and practice. In this context, Collingwood remarks that from 1919 the main idea of his moral philosophy lectures was that actions cannot be divided into three separate classes, the moral, the political, and the economic, but that every action is always moral, political, and economic at the same time.[37] This view of action, Collingwood says, was the application of the most striking principle of his logic of question and answer, according to which no two propositions can be in themselves mutually contradictory, since there are many cases in which one and the same pair of propositions are capable of being thought, either that or the opposite, according to how the questions they were meant to answer are reconstructed in one way or in another.[38] This passage in the autobiography shows that Collingwood's notion of intensional overlap, and its corollary of multiple descriptions, stems from his logic of question and answer; one single action can be described in different ways according to the questions one asks.

In Chapter 3 of *An Essay on Philosophical Method*, Collingwood further elaborates the notion of overlap by asking the following question:

> Of what kind, must the differences between the species of a philosophical concept be, that an overlap between them should be possible?

Seen in the light of Collingwood's development, the meaning of this question is perfectly clear. In the previous chapter of the essay, he had introduced the notion of overlap as a typical feature of philosophical concepts, and asked the reader to 'provisionally accept this notion as a matter of fact'.[39] This position strikingly corresponds to Collingwood's own views around 1919. By that time, he had accepted the notion of overlap as 'synthesis of opposites', but he had not yet proven how it was possible. This is the problem that Collingwood addressed in the 'Libellus de generatione', elaborated in *Speculum Mentis*, and applied in the lectures on moral philosophy and philosophy of history in the second half of the 1920s.

In *An Essay on Philosophical Method,* Collingwood reduces this decade of philosophical labour to three logical steps from which he deduces three consequences. Firstly, he sketches what he calls a 'preliminary idea of the scale of forms', which consists of differences of degree and kind only. Secondly, after stating this 'preliminary' account of the scale of forms, Collingwood raises an 'urgent difficulty':

---

[36] Ibid., 42.

[37] R.G. Collingwood, *An Autobiography,* 148.

[38] Ibid., 40.

[39] R.G. Collingwood, *An Essay on Philosophical Method,* 45.

This is the question whether the idea of a scale of forms, as hitherto stated, serves to explain the overlap between the species, of a philosophical genus. The answer is yes, if they are opposites: no, if they are distincts.[40]

Thirdly, Collingwood tests the claim that the overlap between philosophical species should be explained by opposites. At first, he seems to be positive about this explanation because it leads to a 'simple and straightforward rule of philosophical method':

> ...since philosophical specification is into opposites and non-philosophical into distincts, any distinctions found in a philosophical subject-matter must be either banished from it as alien to the sphere of philosophy or else interpreted so as to appear cases of opposition. It is not enough to show that these distinctions contain in themselves an element or aspect of opposition; that will not save them; the element of distinction must be completely eliminated and nothing except pure opposition allowed to remain.[41]

According to Collingwood, this rule leads to the first consequence that the 'embarrassing idea' of a scale of forms can be dispensed with. In this context, Collingwood frankly admits that this consequence 'cannot fail to seem attractive' because it amounts to the claim 'that philosophy has taken power to jettison all distinctions as merely empirical, and is free to simplify itself at discretion by relegating to a non-philosophical sphere, labelled as history, science, or what not, all the conceptions with which it has no wish to deal, and to concentrate afresh on its cardinal problems'.[42]

However, Collingwood warns, the same rule will necessarily lead to a second consequence. When it is applied to philosophical concepts, all distinctions between them will finally vanish. The result of this will be that 'there is no longer one philosophical problem or group of problems in logic, one in ethics, and so forth, for the characteristics that mark off each of these from the rest are examples of distinction and therefore extraneous to philosophy; and nothing is left except a single pair of opposites'.[43] But even this idea seems attractive to some minds, Collingwood dryly remarks. Only a third consequence of the same rule will cause 'alarm'. This happens when the oppositions which we find in empirical thought, such as the opposition between warm and cold, must be handed over to the philosopher.[44]

Again, Collingwood describes his own development in logical terms. He starts from the most important problem Croce and Gentile had left for posterity. This was the problem of the relationship between distinct and opposite concepts, which had formed the basis of their *concordia discors*. What Collingwood presents

---

[40] Ibid., 63.
[41] Ibid., 65.
[42] Ibid., 66.
[43] Ibid.
[44] Ibid., 66–8.

as the 'preliminary account of the scale of forms' therefore roughly corresponds to Croce's *teoria dei gradi*, which differentiates philosophical species only by degree and kind, but not by opposition. The 'more urgent question' of how the overlap can be explained was raised by Croce himself in *Ciò che è vivo e ciò che è morto della filosofia di Hegel*. In that book, Croce agreed with the German philosopher that philosophical concepts are internally related by opposition: good and bad, true and false, freedom and necessity, and so forth. In a letter to Ryle, Collingwood writes that he describes Croce's position in *An Essay on Philosophical Method* as 'the overlap' or 'coincidence of opposites' according to which opposite terms like, for example, good and bad will be at the end of the scale of forms, whereas all intermediate forms will be part of both opposites, each being good and bad to a certain degree.[45] But, unlike Croce, Collingwood remarks that the coincidence of opposites is not peculiar to philosophy; wherever there is a scale of degrees, there is a coexistence of opposites: water at any given temperature is hot in so far it attains that temperature, and cold in so far that it only attains that temperature. In contrast to Croce, Collingwood thus affirms a dialectical relationship between empirical concepts. But, Collingwood remarks, the view of overlap as mere opposition inevitably leads to 'a curious result':

> If overlapping is characteristic of philosophical species and if opposites overlap while distincts do not, philosophical species are always opposites and never distincts.[46]

In his correspondence with Ryle, Collingwood conveys that the above passage describes Gentile's position.[47] As we saw in chapter 3, Gentile literally said that he did not intend to wipe out distinctions, but that he wanted to explain them by the dialectic of the act of thought, which is a dialectic of opposites. On this point, it is important to notice that in *An Essay on Philosophical Method* Collingwood presents Gentile's position as a 'curious result' of Croce's distinction between empirical and philosophical concepts, leading to a 'straightforward rule of philosophical method', by which he probably refers to Gentile's 'method of immanence'. Collingwood avers that the straightforward rule at first seemed 'attractive'to him, because it clearly indicated the task of philosophy: 'any distinctions found in a philosophical subject-matter must be either banished from it as alien to the sphere of philosophy or else interpreted so as to appear cases of opposition.'[48] In this description, we recognise both Croce's expulsion of science and religion from the sphere of the spirit and Gentile's tendency to reduce all distinctions to the opposition of *pensiero pensante* and *pensiero pensato*. But the second consequence, Collingwood continues, the wiping out of all distinctions with the result that nothing is left but a 'single pair of opposites' resulting in 'the mere

---

[45] Ibid., 63, 273.
[46] Ibid., 64.
[47] Ibid., 273.
[48] Ibid., 65.

abstract idea of opposite terms, colliding eternally in a void', raised his doubt.[49] In this context it is interesting to notice that Collingwood almost literally repeats Croce's rejection of actualism as a form of mysticism, thus showing that he had taken Croce's criticism of Gentile very seriously. Collingwood's doubt became 'alarm' when he recognised the 'third consequence', or the view that 'if opposition is the principle of philosophical specification and distinction that of non-philosophical' amounts to 'restrict the work of philosophy to the exposition of a single clash of opposites, endlessly repeated in endless historical avatars'.[50]

In this verdict, which does not go back to Croce, we recognise Collingwood's own criticism of Italian idealism as a 'myth of process' in the 'Libellus de generatione'. But even this was not the end of Collingwood's development because he continues his logical autobiography with the phlegmatic remark that 'alarm is not the best motive for rejecting a philosophical argument'.[51] After this, Collingwood presents the fundamental dilemma to which his 'alarm' led:

> Is the relation between philosophical specification by opposites and non-philosophical specification by distincts itself a case of distinction or of opposition? If distinction, then specification in general is a non-philosophical concept, since it is specified on the non-philosophical principle; and thus the attempt to maintain a dualism of philosophical and non-philosophical thought has ended by absorbing the conception of philosophical thought into a system of non-philosophical thought in which its own characteristics are necessarily lost. But if it is a case of opposition, every concept is in some degree philosophical and in some degree non-philosophical; the assigning of this or that particular concept to one or other category is impossible; philosophical logic as the logic of opposites has triumphed over non-philosophical logic as the logic of distincts, and with this triumph is has destroyed the distinction between itself and its opponent.[52]

Here Collingwood restates the central problem of the 'Libellus' in the form of a dilemma. It was this dilemma that was of paramount importance for Collingwood's own development, because by solving it he could establish his own position with regard to his predecessors.

In the following pages, Collingwood describes the development of the solution of the fundamental dilemma in abstract logical terms by criticising the positions of his opponents. With regard to the differences of degree and differences of kind, he argues that they are always found in a combination of the two; when attempts are made to distinguish kinds of good it is constantly found that some kinds are more truly good than others.[53] This discovery enabled Collingwood to release philosophical thought from two groups of errors. The first is the 'fallacy

---

[49]　Ibid., 66.

[50]　Ibid., 67.

[51]　Ibid., 68.

[52]　Ibid., 68.

[53]　Ibid., 78.

of calculation', according to which philosophical differences are always suscep-tible to measurement and calculation.[54] The other is the 'fallacy of indifference', according to which the species of a philosophical genus differ only in kind, from which it would follow that all pleasures were equally pleasant, all good things or good acts equally good.[55] Collingwood does not mention the philosophers who committed these errors, but the first may apply to the utilitarian school of Bentham (1748–1832). The fallacy of indifference is more difficult to attribute to a specific philosophical movement, but it may well be a form of pantheism, which Collingwood had criticised in the 'Libellus'.

With regard to the notions of opposition and distinction, Collingwood saw that they are also found in a combination of the two. This view is based on the idea that the lower end of the scale lies not at zero, but at unity, or the minimum realisation of the generic essence.[56] As such it is distinct from other realisations, but as the limiting case it is an opposite relative to the rest of the scale.[57] For example, extreme wickedness is a form of action, which, however bad, is not completely devoid of goodness. When considered in itself, Collingwood says, a vice really achieves something good: relief from pain, good fellowship, or a sense of emancipation. Likewise, error really does enshrine some truth. But when vices and errors are considered in relation to higher cases all is changed; the lower forms will then be considered as positively bad and erroneous.[58]

According to Collingwood, the combination of distinction and opposition between the terms of a philosophical concept destroys two groups of errors. The first is the 'fallacy of the false positive', which consists in making a positive term from what is really a negative one. The second is the 'fallacy of null opposition', which places the opposite of any positive term at the zero end of the scale. Both are based on the false disjunction between opposition and distinction.[59]

Whether or not Collingwood had the Italians in mind here is not clear, but it is significant that the 'fallacy of the false positive' describes one of the major difficulties in Croce's philosophy strikingly well. As we saw in chapter 2, Croce firmly held that thought never errs. Accordingly he sought to explain error as a form of action which is distinct from thought. It was this difficulty that de Ruggiero pointed to in *La filosofia contemporanea*, calling for a revision of the rela-tionship between distinction and opposition. Collingwood dealt with this prob-lem in *Truth and Contradiction* of 1917, in which he sought to explain truth and error as being species of the genus thought. The 'fallacy of null opposition', on the other hand, describes Gentile's way of reducing all error, evil, and ugliness to the level of the *pensato* which is abstract and not actual. Against this view,

---

54 Ibid., 80.
55 Ibid.
56 Ibid., 81.
57 Ibid., 82.
58 Ibid., 84.
59 Ibid., 85–6.

Collingwood argued in the 'Libellus' that the past, which stands for Gentile's *pensato*, has a concreteness and actuality of its own, since it is not dead but lives on in the present.

In *An Essay on Philosophical Method* Collingwood states the same idea of the living past in logical terms. The relation of opposition only occurs between a higher and a lower form in the scale of forms, but considered in itself even the minimum case of the scale must be seen as actual: 'it does something', Collingwood says.[60] For example, even the lowest vice achieves something good, at least in the view of the person who commits it. Re-translated into actualist terms, this means that the *pensato* makes part of the *pensante*, from which it follows that their relationship is not one of pure opposition. In fact, to conceive opposition without a fusion with distinction is to commit the fallacy of null opposition. This description reflects Collingwood's main objection against Gentile; if the past is seen as a mere construction of present thought, present thought opposes itself against some void, or 'nullity'. Against this view Collingwood held that historical truth presupposes some idea of the reality of the past. Along the same lines, Collingwood shows in *An Essay on Philosophical Method* that the past is somehow real as 'distinct', that is, as an aspect of the present; evils and errors are actual and must be fought against.[61]

Collingwood states the logical upshot of these investigations in the notion that philosophical thought combines the difference of degree, kind, opposition, and distinction.[62] Only on the basis of this notion of difference Collingwood finally gives a full account of the notion of overlap:

> The higher of any two adjacent forms overlaps the lower because it includes the positive content of the lower as a constituent element within itself. It only fails to include the lower in its entirety because there is also a negative aspect of the lower, which is rejected by the higher: the lower, in addition to asserting its own content, denies that the generic essence contains anything more, and this denial constitutes its falsehood. Thus, utilitarianism is right to regard expediency as one form of goodness; its mistake is to think that there is nothing in even the highest forms of goodness that cannot be described in terms of expediency; and therefore a better moral philosophy would reaffirm utilitarianism while denying one part, this negative part, of its doctrine. The lower overlaps the higher in a different sense: it does not include the higher as part of itself, it adopts part of the positive content of the higher, while rejecting another part. Utilitarianism, for example, claims much of the contents of better moral theories as sound utilitarian doctrine, but dismisses the rest as so much error or superstition. What is true of utilitarianism as a specific kind of moral theory is true also of expediency as a specific kind of goodness.[63]

---

[60] Ibid., 83.

[61] Ibid., 85.

[62] Ibid., 88.

[63] Ibid., 90.

In this passage Collingwood condenses more than two decades of work in a few lines centring on the notion of intensional overlap. Interestingly, Collingwood gives an example from the history of philosophy, which reflects the fact that he developed the notion of 'overlap' in that context. Collingwood's logical formulation sounds familiar; it is a refined version of the language which he used in the 'Libellus' in order to describe the notion of the 'living past' as a synthesis of opposites.

Seen from the perspective of Collingwood's development, the crucial question to be addressed now is: how does the full notion of overlap resolve the great dilemma of the relationship between non-philosophical and philosophical specification? At first glance, Collingwood does not solve this problem, for he does not take it up again. Implicitly, however, he does solve it by denying it. On the basis of the fusion of distinction and opposition, the whole question of whether the relationship between distinction and opposition itself must be seen as one of opposition or distinction cannot be raised, for raising it means drawing a false disjunction between distinction and opposition. In short, as the product of an endless historical question and answer process, the relationship between distinction and opposition is *a priori* a fusion of distinction and opposition.

The most important implication of this view is that non-philosophical thought and philosophical thought are always fused. What does this mean? Collingwood says that if the distinction between the non-philosophical and philosophical thought is stressed too much, non-philosophical thought will reduce philosophical thought to itself. If, on the contrary, opposition is stressed too much, philosophical thought 'triumphs' over non-philosophical thought.[64] On this basis, we may conclude that if non-philosophical and philosophical thought 'overlap', the difference between them will be a synthesis of the differences in degree, kind, and of opposition and distinction. As a lower form of thought, non-philosophical thought adopts only a part of philosophical thought while rejecting another part. It is not difficult to guess that this part is the self-reflective aspect of philosophical thought. In other words, non-philosophical thought is lower in so far as it denies its own philosophy. Philosophical thought includes the positive content of the lower as a constituent element within itself and rejects its non-philosophical, or non-universal, aspect. This means that philosophy does not reject the results of non-philosophical thought, or 'experience', but rather builds on it. It transcends experience by adding something new, that is, a philosophical aspect.

In terms of Connelly and d'Oro, this 'adding' may be seen as drawing semantic distinctions in order to explain experience. Although Collingwood does not explicitly state this solution to the dilemma in these terms, we can find examples of it in all chapters of *An Essay on Philosophical Method*. In some of them we find Collingwood stating his own position with regard to the Italians. The

---

[64] Ibid., 68.

most important example is in the chapter on the idea of a system in which Collingwood deals with the problem of matter and form of philosophy. As we have seen, Croce only recognised the spirit in its fourfold distinction as the proper subject matter of philosophy and its method as the 'elaboration of concepts'. Gentile also saw the spirit as the proper subject matter, but he did not make any distinctions, the subject matter of philosophy being simply *pensiero pensato*, or history, which must be studied by the method of immanence. In *An Essay on Philosophical Method* Collingwood responds to both views, by employing the notion of the scale of forms:

> If the concept of philosophy is a philosophical concept, different groups of philosophical topics will not only overlap, they will be philosophical in different ways and also to varying degrees; and the methods appropriate to them will correspondingly conform in different ways and in varying degrees to the general idea of philosophical method. The various parts which together make up the body of a philosophy will thus form a scale in whose ascent the subject-matter becomes progressively philosophical in the sense of coming more and more to be the kind of subject-matter of which philosophy is in search, and the method becomes progressively philosophical in the sense that it comes to exhibit more and more adequately the proper nature of philosophical thought.[65]

On this point, Collingwood distances himself from the Italian idealists. He differs from both Croce and Gentile by making a semantic distinction between the different subject matters and different method. For the Italians this was inconceivable. Both Croce and Gentile held that there is only one subject matter and method for philosophy, although they differed in its specific content and form. Collingwood now allows for different subject matters which form a whole, and different methods, which are organically related to each other.

This difference makes clear to what extent Collingwood's system was going to differ from the Italians. Again 'overlap' is the key term. In the first place, the subject matter of Collingwood's system was to consist of various forms of experience which would 'overlap', not in the Crocean sense of differing in degree and kind, nor in the Gentilian sense of identities, but in the Collingwoodian sense of differing in degree, kind, opposition, and distinction. Through this logical form, Collingwood acknowledged the continuity between the various forms of experience. In this view art, history, and philosophy are not to be treated as distinct or identical realms of the spirit, but as forming a continuous whole of overlapping forms which can be semantically distinguished. Moreover, science, the Cinderella in Croce's and Gentile's systems, would find a place in Collingwood's. Unlike Croce, Collingwood would not 'jump' from art to philosophy, nor would he resolve all forms of experience into philosophy, as Gentile had done in *Teoria generale dello spirito come atto puro*. In contrast to these views,

---

[65] Ibid., 189.

Collingwood would gradually pass 'Dall'arte alla filosofia' as de Ruggiero had laid down in his paper of 1921 to be followed by Collingwood himself in *Speculum Mentis*.

In the second place, Collingwood's view of the continuity between the various forms of experience has important implications for philosophical method itself, which he elaborates under the heading of 'Philosophy as a Branch of Literature'. In this chapter, Collingwood argues that philosophy expresses itself in language which implies that 'comprehension or understanding what the writer means' always comes before criticism, or asking whether it is true.[66] Along these lines, Collingwood describes the task of the critic as follows:

> Criticism is always... the bringing to completeness of a theory which its author has left incomplete. So understood, the function of the critic is to develop and continue the thought of the writer criticized. Theoretically, the relation between the philosophy criticized and the philosophy that criticizes it is the relation between two adjacent terms in a scale of forms, the forms of a single philosophy in its historical development; and in practice, it is well known that a man's best critics are his pupils, and his best pupils the most critical.[67]

In this passage Collingwood not only describes how to proceed when studying the other philosophers, but also how he would apply the method to his own thought. In this section we have seen how Collingwood brought Croce's and Gentile's philosophy of philosophy to completeness, in the next sections we will see how he employed the method in order to bring his own philosophy to completeness.

Preparing the Series: Nature and Mind (1933–36)

After finishing *An Essay on Philosophical Method* Collingwood first applied his method to metaphysics and in particular to cosmology, which by this time he regarded as 'the main subject at present demanding attention from serious philosophers'.[68] Collingwood's interest in cosmology did not come out of the blue. In the 'Libellus', Collingwood had expressed his hopes for a new metaphysical movement in British philosophy. Over the course of the 1920s this hope went from dream to reality; Alexander published *Space, Time and Deity* in 1920, and Whitehead followed with *Process and Reality* in 1929. Both in his correspondence with Collingwood and his in his *Filosofi del novecento*, de Ruggiero had written positive accounts of these books.

During the 1920s Collingwood himself had concentrated on the philosophy of mind and in particular on the philosophy of history which formed the basis of his philosophical method. After the completion of this method Collingwood felt

---

66 Ibid., 217.
67 Ibid., 219–20.
68 Cited by van der Dussen, *History as a Science*, 192–3.

that his own metaphysics of mind needed to be reconciled with the recent developments in British philosophy. From 1933 until 1936 Collingwood wrote many preliminary studies which he saw as the 'groundwork of a future treatise'.[69] Due to ill health, however, he never wrote this book. Only its 'by-product', the lectures on the history of the idea of nature, was posthumously published as *The Idea of Nature* in 1945. In 1995, the original conclusion of this work, which contains the outlines of Collingwood's metaphysics, was found in the Archives of Oxford University Press and published together with *The Principles of History*.[70] Together with the manuscripts on cosmology, this original conclusion to *The Idea of Nature* throws new light on Collingwood's development because they show how Collingwood interpreted Italian philosophy after the completion of his study of philosophical method.[71]

In 1933, Collingwood began his cosmological investigation with 'Notes Towards a Metaphysic'. These notes begin with a comparison of Spinoza as the classic example of a metaphysics of nature, and with Croce and Gentile as the champions of the metaphysics of the mind. According to Collingwood, Spinoza rightly began with his concept of God as *causa sui* which he interprets as the 'totality of laws of nature or categories'. Spinoza thus made God's thought the 'logical *prius* of Mind'.[72] Against this view Collingwood points out that mind 'is very recalcitrant to being treated as a product', and he concurs with Kant in not following Spinoza's abandonment of the 'spontaneity of the mind'.[73] This leads Collingwood to the question: 'can Mind be at once a product of the evolutionary process, and also possessed of spontaneity and autonomy?'[74] Collingwood's answer to this question is affirmative, but he points out that 'the idea of production or cause can be reinterpreted so as to include, instead of excluding, the spontaneity of the effect'.[75] This means that mind must be seen as a 'self-producing product' which is 'in an eminent degree the latest product, that spontaneity and autonomy which primarily belong to the laws of forces that are the process's absolute ground'.[76]

After this conclusion Collingwood passes straight on to Gentile's metaphysics. This suggests that he saw a close connection between Gentile's notion of the

---

[69] Ibid., 439–40.

[70] Boucher, 'The Principles of History and the Cosmology Conclusion to *The Idea of Nature*', 140.

[71] On the first page of 'Notes towards a Metaphysic B', Dep. 18/4, Collingwood wrote: 'For convenience I copy into this book the following, which was written 19 Aug. 1933, before any notes in the preceding book: it was in fact the starting point from which that began.'

[72] Ibid., 1–2.

[73] Ibid., 3–4.

[74] Ibid., 4.

[75] Ibid., 5.

[76] Ibid., 7–8.

autoctisi, or self-creative thought, and Spinoza's notion of *causa sui*. This is not completely beside the mark. All his life Gentile admired Spinoza; he edited his *Ethica* in 1915, and in most of his own works he refers to him. Collingwood does not discuss this direct link between Spinoza and Gentile, but finds the origin of Gentile's metaphysics in Croce's rejection of Hegel's dialectic. This interpretation is not entirely correct, for it was Gentile who induced Croce to his reform of Hegelian dialectic. Collingwood certainly knew this, as his earliest criticisms of Croce's philosophy shows, but here, in the context of a metaphysical discussion, he seems to focus on the ideal relationship between the two Italians.

Collingwood begins the section on Croce and Gentile with a most revealing remark:

> The time has not yet come, when I, at any rate, can make a total judgement of Croce's philosophy, and therefore of Gentile's, which on the whole I regard as a fossilized or arthritic version—containing in general the same ideas, but working them out with blind disregard of all not in the immediate field of vision—of Croce's. But I am obliged here to comment on one aspect of their fertile and many-sided discussion of History.[77]

This passage clearly shows that as late as 1933 Collingwood's attitude to the Italians was still ambivalent! On the one hand he valued their philosophy of history, on the other hand he was highly critical of Gentile, and by implication also of Croce, because he regarded actualism as a bad imitation of the latter's philosophy. Collingwood accordingly begins with a criticism of Croce's reform of Hegelian dialectic:

> Croce, whose antagonism to Hegel has served in a highly instructive way to mark his own limitations (as he says himself, in beginning to read Hegel he came to 'grips with his own consciousness'), opposing the universal to the individual, contends that philosophy thinks the former, history the latter: that Hegel was utterly mistaken in supposing that there could be a philosophy of history, because historical reality (the individual) can be cognised only in one way (viz. by historical thinking) and simply escapes the philosophical point of view (Ciò che è vivo, VII). The individual contains the universal as its predicate, and hence history contains philosophy as a subordinate moment (the methodological moment: Storiografia, appendix III). And it easily follows that every historical fact, being concrete, has as predicates all the categories known to philosophy. Hence all the categories are present equally, en bloc as it were, in every historical fact, and the distinction between one and another fact cannot ever be expressed by referring one to one category and another to another.[78]

This passage shows Collingwood's total command of Croce's philosophy: in a few lines he summarises the essence of four of his most important works!

---

77 R.G. Collingwood, 'Notes towards a Metaphysic, B' cited from id., *The Principles of History*, 127–8.

78 Ibid., 128.

Collingwood's main target is *Ciò che è vivo e ciò che è morto della filosofia di Hegel*. In this book, Croce held against Hegel that pure concepts are not related by opposition to each other, but by distinction; opposition occurs only within each pure concept but not between them. Thus Croce expressed his view that the diverse activities of the spirit are related to each other by implication and not by opposition. In this way, Croce sought to secure the autonomy of the four activities of the spirit; art, philosophy, economic and moral action. The unity of the spirit was established in *Filosofia della pratica* by presenting the spirit as a 'circle' of activities. In the *Logica* of 1909, he made the final step by pointing out that the predication of existence to a representation implies the predication of all predicates.

It is this view that Collingwood attacks in the above passage. He points out that the predication of existence implies the predication of all other predicates with the result that all individual judgments will have the same logical form. According to Collingwood, this makes the distinction between one fact and another impossible because the categories cannot be referred to each other. What Collingwood means by this is not entirely clear, but he seems to have in mind that when all predicates are equally present in each individual judgment, all judgments will express the same thought. Seen from a logical point of view, each fact will then be an equal instantiation of beauty, truth, utility, and morality. This view of the judgment makes it impossible to say, for example, that one work of art is more beautiful than another, or that one philosophy is truer than another. When all predicates are equally present in the judgment one can only say that one work is different from another. If distinction between facts is logically impossible, all facts are abstractly identical, and this pushes the whole notion of process out of sight because all facts will have to be seen as equal instantiations of the universal spirit.

In terms of *An Essay on Philosophical Method*, Croce's rejection of the notion of opposition leads to a view of abstract distinction, that is, pure distinction without a fusion with opposition, and to abstract identity, that is, the identity of empirical thought, instead of identity in a scale of forms, which is the identity of the generic essence. Applied to history, this means that each fact of history is related to the class of which it is an instance but not to other facts. This view may rightly be called Spinozism for all facts are seen as equal embodiments of the same universal spirit which, like Spinoza's God, forms the logical *prius* of all facts.

In the lectures on the philosophy of history of 1936, we find an important complement to this criticism. According to Collingwood, Hegel's whole philosophy of history turns on the principle that every historical process is a dialectical process in which one form of life, for example Greece, generates its own opposite. In Collingwood's view, Croce accepted Hegel's view that concepts are related by opposition, but at the same time he pointed out that instances of concepts, or individual things, are related by distinction. According to Collingwood, Croce's criticism of Hegel's dialectic does not get to the heart of the problem, because it implies that we should never use words like opposition or synthesis in history, but only difference. In Collingwood's view this is only true when we talk of the 'outward events' of history, but not when we are talking of the inward thoughts that underlie these events. We can describe the 'outward events' of the colonisation of New England without any dialectical language, Collingwood says, but when we try to see these events from the inside, that is, as a deliberate attempt on the part of the Pilgrim Fathers to carry out a Protestant idea of life, then we have to use dialectical terms.[79]

Collingwood's two criticisms of Croce complement each other. In the 'Notes Towards a Metaphysic' it is Croce's notion of abstract identity that is under attack, in the lectures of 1936 it is abstract difference. Seen from the outside, historical events are related by distinction to each other, but seen from the inside, that is, seen as instantiations of concepts, events are related by opposition to each other because concepts are related to each other by opposition. Croce's stress on the empirical aspect of history turns all concepts into empirical concepts; Greek life and Roman life are only 'empirical' concepts, each being merely different from the other.

In *An Essay on Philosophical Method* Collingwood himself had overcome Croce's position with the notion of the scale of forms. In this scale, each concept differs from other concepts in degree, kind, opposition, and distinction. From this point of view, the Greek and Roman ideals of life also differ in a fourfold way. They differ in kind, for each tried to realise a different kind of ideal, and they differ in degree to the extent that these ideals overlap. But Greek and Roman life were not merely different but also opposed to each other, that is, the Romans tried to realise ideals that stood opposed to the Greek ideals. From Collingwood's point of view, Croce fails to recognise the fusion of the differences of degree with difference in kind and the fusion of distinction and opposition. Likewise, Croce's Spinozism is based on a false disjunction between distinction and opposition and this pushes the notion of development completely out of sight.

According to Collingwood, Gentile shares this Spinozism with Croce:

The past is, on this [Gentile's] view, an abstraction from the present, which alone is actual; history is a projection of thought backwards into time, like a jet of water thrown backwards by some marine animal to push it forwards. There is therefore no real development; only an eternal present, which does not enrich itself by taking up the past, but defecates a past out of itself. This seems to me to be subjective idealism. It follows from the indifference of logical structure between fact and fact; since in everything that matters every fact is identical with every other, all presents are the same present, differing 'merely empirically' i.e. not at all. The past being a mere abstraction from the

---

79   R.G. Collingwood, *The Idea of History*, 119.

present, past facts cannot be known in their concreteness, and there is no
series of facts; everything is in a timeless present.[80]

Again, Collingwood uses his philosophical method to explain the relationship
between Croce's and Gentile's positions. Like Croce, Gentile regards past facts as
'abstractions', that is, as embodiments of empirical concepts. Collingwood thus
attacks Gentile's notion of history as *pensato* as being related to the *pensante* by
opposition. Seen from the viewpoint of Collingwood's philosophical method,
Gentile, like Croce, makes a false disjunction between distinction and opposition, although, unlike Croce, he stresses the opposition above distinction. The
result is an absolute opposition between the past and the present, the past being
identical with 'nature', or a 'thing', the present being concrete, that is, self-
conscious and *ipso facto* rational, instead of a process. In 'Notes Towards a
Metaphysic, A', Collingwood specifies Gentile's denial of process, by pointing
out that he 'reduces history to a purely logical sequence'.[81]

In the sequel to the above passage, Collingwood gives an interesting analysis
of Gentile's development which led him to this view:

> Gentile seems to me to have concentrated his attention on the epistemological
> notion of the historian building up his history into the past and so forming his
> perspective of past time, but to have neglected the problem of the relation
> between perspectives; and each man's perspective is for him a subjective-
> idealistic world, in which the object is not spirit (*pensiero pensante*) but idea
> (*pensiero pensato*). The problem of development, which had been pushed out of
> sight by Croce's polemic against Hegel, has been wholly overlooked by
> Gentile, with the result that Fascist thought, egocentric and subjective, can
> rightly be called by Croce 'antistoricismo'.[82]

This passage is a clear indication that Collingwood saw Gentile's position as
something which we would today call constructivism. In Collingwood's view,
this position is based on the logical and ontological priority of the *pensiero pensante*, or the historian's present thought, as being constitutive of the past.
According to Collingwood, this position fails to understand spirit; it does not
understand man's perspectives of the past from within, but from the outside;
they are not living ideas, but brute facts, without relation to the other facts.
Referring to Croce's famous lecture of 1930, Collingwood concludes that this is
the 'antistorismo' that lies at the basis of Gentile's Fascism.

Collingwood's juxtaposition of Spinoza and the Italian idealists is highly
instructive for his own development. In his view, Spinoza took God or nature as
the logical *prius* for mind and thus denied the spontaneity of mind; he saw mind

---

[80] R.G. Collingwood, 'Notes towards a Metaphysic, B' cited from id., *The Principles of
History*, 128.

[81] R.G. Collingwood, 'Notes towards a Metaphysic, A', Dep. 18/3.

[82] R.G. Collingwood, 'Notes towards a Metaphysic, B' cited from id., *The Principles of
History*, 128–9.

primarily as a thing produced by the natural process and not as a self-producing process. Croce and Gentile took mind as the logical *prius* for nature and history and finally rejected the spontaneity of both. They both took nature and history as objects produced by the mind, and not as autonomous processes. Moreover, like Spinoza, who saw God as the totality of categories which underlie all phenomena, the Italians saw mind as the totality of categories which underlie all phenomena. The result of both approaches is that all categories are always embodied *en bloc* in all historical events. The past thus becomes an endless concatenation of identical facts, each fact being an embodiment of the same eternal spirit called God or *spirito*, or *pensiero pensante*.

This criticism of Spinoza and the Italians enables us to specify the terms of the central problem of Collingwood's manuscripts on metaphysics; we cannot start from nature and deduce mind from it, nor can we start from mind and deduce nature from it. Interpreting mind in terms of natural processes amounts to denying the spontaneity of the mind, whereas interpreting nature in terms of the mental amounts to viewing nature as an abstraction from mind.

How the relationship between nature and mind should be expressed in other terms is explained by Collingwood as follows:

> Nature is the realm of change, Spirit is the realm of becoming. The life of the spirit is a history: i.e. not a process in which everything comes to be and passes away, but a process in which the past is conserved as an element in the present. The past is not merely a precondition of the present but a condition of it. Whereas in nature the past was necessary in order that the present may now exist (e.g. there must have been an egg that there may now be a hen) the past being thus left behind when the present comes into being, in history, so far as this is real history and not mere time-sequence, the past conserves itself in the present, and the present could not be there unless it did. Thus, if there is a history of thought Newton's physics still stands as a necessary element in Einstein's if it does not, there is no history but only change.[83]

In this passage, which follows directly upon his criticism of the Italians, Collingwood takes up the notion of the living past just as he had done in the 'Libellus'. This suggests not only that the notion of the living past formed the basis of Collingwood's criticism of the Italians, but also that he developed it in confrontation with their views. The starting point of Collingwood's philosophy is that it is not the present that keeps the past alive, but the past keeps itself alive. The past can therefore not be reduced to a mere *pensato*, or an abstraction made by present thought. The past is an active force in the present in the sense that the present would not be what it is without the past. In the 'Libellus' Collingwood expressed this idea by saying that 'the object is process too', and in *An Essay on Philosophical Method* by saying that 'it does something'. In the above passage he goes beyond this position, by making the preservation of the past the *funda-*

---

[83] R.G. Collingwood, 'Notes towards a Metaphysic, B' cited from id., *The Principles of History*, 130.

mentum divisionis between nature and mind; though nature has a past, it has no 'living past' and therefore no true history, whereas the mind does have a history because its past lives on in the present.

Obviously, these theses still needed elaboration before their implications for historical thought could be clarified. Most importantly, the notion of the living past calls for a reinterpretation of Gentile's dialectic of *pensante* and *pensato*. But this was a difficult task; on the one hand Collingwood seems to have realised that he could not go beyond the fundamental doctrine that the real is *pensiero pensante*, or, as he used to express it, that 'reality is history'. On the other hand he could not regard the past as a mere construction of present thought. Somehow past thought had to be vindicated as a real force in the present without being dependent on present thought. These problems were crucial because the development of Collingwood's own philosophy depended on their solution.

As usual, Collingwood dealt with these problems by studying their history. In the manuscripts on metaphysics he follows the history of distinction between nature and mind from the Greeks to contemporary philosophers. The upshot of his investigations can be found in what Collingwood himself regarded as a 'by-product'; the lectures which were posthumously published as *The Idea of Nature*.

The Idea of Nature

In the lectures on the history of the idea of nature, Collingwood traces the special problem of the relationship between nature and mind to Descartes.[84] Spinoza tried to solve it on a materialistic basis, followed by Leibniz with his dual substance theory, but both left the problem unsolved.[85] Berkeley (1685–1753) started from a whole new metaphysical position. In his view, mind is the sole substance from which it follows that nature must be seen as a creation of mind, that is, it exists empirically for our everyday perception.[86] Kant developed Berkeley's position by showing that nature 'is an essentially rational and necessary product of the human way of looking at things'.[87] Kant's position was rejected by Hegel as 'subjective idealism' according to which mind is the 'presupposition or creator of nature'. According to Hegel, in Collingwood's paraphrasing, the basic fault of the subjective idealists is that they think that whatever is not material must be mental, with the consequence that they interpret the concept not as a presupposition for thought but as a way of thinking.[88] Against this view, Hegel posited his own 'objective ideas' by which he acknowledges the existence of the concept (as a presupposition) separate from the act of thought.[89]

---

[84] R.G. Collingwood, *The Idea of Nature*, 103–4.

[85] Ibid., 105–6, 110–1.

[86] R.G. Collingwood, *The Idea of Nature*, 114.

[87] Ibid., 116.

[88] Ibid., 123.

[89] Ibid.

By making these concepts, or the Idea, the source of nature and mind, Hegel founded his own objective idealism. According to Collingwood, thinkers such as Alexander and Whitehead take up this objective idealism, although they do not refer to Hegel. These thinkers see reality as a self-creative process, that is, as a process that continuously produces new patterns having new qualities. But whereas Alexander followed the empiricists by holding that these new qualities are immanent in the patterns, Whitehead followed Plato, and implicitly Hegel, when he thought of them as both immanent and transcendent; the qualities are not merely empirical qualities of the new occasion, but also 'eternal objects', which form the presupposition of the cosmic process.[90]

From an historical perspective it is not surprising that Collingwood's analysis of Berkeley's and Kant's subjective idealism bears much resemblance to his criticism of Croce and Gentile in the 'Notes Towards a Metaphysics'. Like Berkeley and Kant, Croce and Gentile recognised mind as the sole substance, regarding nature primarily as a product of mind whether in the form of 'pseudo-concepts' or in the form of *logo astratto*. Collingwood's sympathy for Hegel's rejection of this view indicates a possible solution of the problem. Like Hegel, Collingwood thought that the concept must not be seen as an act of thought, but as a presupposition for the act of thought. In itself, this interpretation of the concept does not differ from Croce's or Gentile's, but Collingwood stresses that the concept is not dependent for its existence on the act of thought. Concepts, Collingwood says, echoing Hegel, 'do not exist in our heads only'.[91]

In the original conclusion to the lectures on the idea of nature, he elaborated this idea into the outlines of a new cosmology. Its basis is in Hegel's terms the objective Idea, or, in Whitehead's terms, eternal objects, which are logically and ontologically prior to nature and mind. In this context, nature and mind are considered as self-creative processes that embody the eternal objects in various stages; space-time, matter, life, and mind. The concept of process implies that one and the same thing can be the product of a process as well as an eternal object. The eternal objects are thus not given once and for all, but they are created by the process itself. The difference between them is that nature does not create itself, whereas history does. A natural process is mere change, an historical process is 'becoming'. The substance of history, or 'becoming', is 'human activity'; its changes are therefore not 'in virtue of external causes', but 'in virtue of its own autonomous self-development'.[92] Along these lines, Collingwood describes history as a 'kind of process in which the thing undergoing the process forms itself, or comes into existence as the process goes on'.[93] He illustrates this

---

[90] Ibid., 162, 170.

[91] Ibid., 123.

[92] R.G. Collingwood, 'Conclusions to Lectures on Nature and Mind' cited from Id., *The Principles of History*, 263.

[93] Ibid.

concept with the help of an example from English constitutional history, which he describes as a 'more or less constant change in the manner in which England has governed itself'.[94] With this description of 'becoming' Collingwood seems to return to Gentile's notion of *autoctisi* with all its implications, but he also brings the notion of the eternal object into play:

> It is characteristic of becoming that it is creative or rather self-creative. What it has brought into existence passes out of existence again, but does not pass out of being. Thus, the revolution of 1688 was produced by the self-development of the English constitution in the 17th century, as an event in time, it happened, then stopped happening; since the existence of an event is its happening, that revolution does not now exist, it is an event which is not going on now. But the historian can still think about it: that is to say, it is still an object for historical thought. Its being, in this sense, is timeless: that is to say, it is in the strict sense of the words an eternal object. Thus all historical events become eternal objects.[95]

In this passage Collingwood strengthens the metaphysics of mind with the insights of British process metaphysics. By redefining the event as an eternal object he shifts the notion of eternity from the act of thought to the past itself.

From this important thesis Collingwood draws two very important conclusions. First, if historical events are eternal objects, their existence is not dependent on the act of thought, that is, it is not a mere construction by the historian as the Italians would have it:

> The eternal being of an historical event does not consist in or depend on its being known to historians. The revolution of 1688 enjoys its eternity, through being a permanent element in the politic experience of the English people: even if they forget the event itself, the fact that they have lived through it would continue to colour their political outlook and influence their political activity. It is only because historical events leave permanent traces in the subsequent course of history that the historian can find out anything about them: for the historian begins his work from documents and sources of various kinds, and all these must be things existing in the world contemporaneously with himself.[96]

This passage clearly reveals how Collingwood uses Whitehead's notion of the 'eternal object' to refine his own notion of the 'living past'. When past events are 'eternal objects', that is, self-identical elements in experience, then they cannot be regarded constructions of the act of thought. On the contrary, the past plays a role in present experience even if we are not aware of it. We can say, therefore, that the past still exists in the present; it is an actual force in present experience.

---

94   Ibid.
95   Ibid., 264.
96   Ibid., 264–5.

But Collingwood does not rule out the act of thought, because the past can only be known by interpreting evidence, which is the work of the act of thought. This is Collingwood's second corollary; history is not empirical knowledge, or perception as he himself had held in the 1920s, but it is 'strictly inferential':

> The historian argues to his conceptions: he argues that because the data are thus and not otherwise the past event must have been of such and such a kind. His object, therefore, the past event, is not only an eternal object, but also a necessary object, an object that must be what it is, and is known rationally in apprehending its necessity.[97]

In short, history exists as an element in our actual experience even if we are not aware of it. The existence of history is not dependent on the act of thought. But its being known is dependent on the act of thought; it is only by thinking rationally that we come to know what history is.

In the two passages above we see how Whitehead's metaphysics helped Collingwood strengthen his own position. By defining past events as eternal objects he could avoid Gentile's talk about history as a 'creation' of the present act of thought and further specify his own notion of the living past. At the same time, he used the concept of history, as developed by the Italians, in order to overcome some difficulties as he found them in Alexander's and Whitehead's cosmologies. This difficulty concerned the exact relationship between eternal objects and processes. Alexander had based his cosmology on the notion of space-time and subsequently he had only admitted 'transient objects' in reality. Whitehead had developed the notion of eternal objects, but in Collingwood's view he had not solved the problem of their realisation in process with the result that he came to see them as a transcendent presupposition of processes. Collingwood claimed to have solved both problems with the help of the notion of history in which each event is both a product of thought and an eternal object, in other words, the eternal objects are not given once and for all, but they are produced by the process itself, and once produced they join the other eternal objects.

This conclusion formed the basis of Collingwood's solution to the problem of the relationship between nature and mind. Around 1935, he wrote 'Realism and Idealism' in which he presented objective idealism as the ideal synthesis between materialism and subjective idealism. According to Collingwood, objective idealism agrees with subjective idealism that the world consists of ideas which are logically prior to nature. But unlike the subjective idealist he did not hold that these ideas can only exist in our heads, or that their existence depends on being thought. For the objective idealist, ideas have an independent existence; they are logically and ontologically prior to matter and to thought. The objective idealist can therefore agree with the materialist in saying that the material world was prior to mind. He can also agree with the subjective idealist in saying that the material world could not exist except as logically posterior to these ideas.

---

[97] Ibid., 265.

With regard to the relationship between realism and objective idealism Collingwood pointed out that there is no necessary antithesis. In his view realism is primarily a theory of knowledge, whereas objective idealism is not a theory of knowledge at all, but a metaphysics or a theory of reality.[98] Consequently, there need not be a quarrel between them; objective idealism agrees with realism that 'we know the object itself as it really is'.[99]

Seen in the light of his development, Collingwood had been expressing these views all throughout his life. Already in his first book, *Religion and Philosophy*, he had refused to make a choice between realism and idealism, and in the 'Libellus' he considered the antithesis between realism and idealism as illusory. The only novelty of 'Realism and Idealism' is Collingwood's leniency towards realism, although it should be stressed that he interpreted that doctrine as an epistemology, not as a metaphysics. Collingwood's resistance to subjective idealism is not new at all: the notion that ideas have an objective existence goes back to Collingwood's earliest musings about the living past.

Preparing the Series: History (1935–37)

In 1934, after more than twenty years of tutoring at Pembroke, Collingwood was appointed to the Waynflete Chair of Metaphysical Philosophy at Magdalen College. Collingwood immediately set himself to work. On 28 October 1935 he delivered his inaugural 'The Historical Imagination', and after this he prepared two new courses. The first of these were the lectures on the philosophy of history, which were later published as *The Idea of History*. The second course was 'Central Problems in Metaphysics', which contained a lot of the material he would later use in *An Essay on Metaphysics*. Apart from these lectures, Collingwood continued to lecture on 'Nature and Mind' and on 'Roman Britain'. Inspired by his new position Collingwood also began to plan and execute new publications. In 1936, he published *Roman Britain and the English Settlements*, and in the same year he began an extensive study of folklore and fairy tales on which he also hoped to publish a book. The most prestigious project, however, was Collingwood's lecture for the British Academy, delivered on 20 May 1936.

While working on these projects, the worsening political climate in Europe began to worry Collingwood. In 'The Present Need of a Philosophy' of 1935, he wrote that the twentieth century 'needs a reasoned conviction that human progress is possible and that the problems of moral and political life are in principle soluble'.[100] But in spite of this belief in progress Collingwood was not an easy optimist. In 'Man goes Mad' of 1936 he gives a gloomy picture of the world; the

---

[98] R.G. Collingwood, 'Central Problems in Metaphysics', 1935, Dep. 20/1, 107.
[99] Ibid., 103.
[100] R.G. Collingwood, 'The Present Need of a Philosophy', in *Philosophy*, 9, 1935, 262–5, cited from Id., *Essays in Political Philosophy*, Oxford University Press, Oxford, 1989, 169.

collapse of liberalism under attacks from the left and the right, the rise of dictatorship and militarism and the decline of the agricultural society convinced Collingwood that a new science of human affairs was most urgently needed.[101]

In what follows I will first discuss Collingwood's inaugural and 'Human Nature and Human History', because these were his first public statements of his new philosophy of history. Next, I will discuss how he elaborated this philosophy in his university lectures and manuscripts.

The Foundations of the Future

Collingwood's choice to read 'The Historical Imagination' at his inaugural to the Chair of Metaphysical Philosophy shows that he definitely wanted to present himself as a philosopher of history. History was important, because, as he tells his audience, its problems had largely been ignored in England. Taking this general ignorance into account, Collingwood carefully employs his philosophical method, beginning with the most ordinary notions of history, such as 'opinion', 'perception', 'memory', and 'authority', to proceed to his own position according to which history is a form of the imagination based on an 'innate idea' of the past which functions as a criterion for historical inference.

The latter thesis has been the subject of many controversies. Firstly, Collingwood's view of the relationship between *a priori* imagination and re-enactment is not clear. As Dray points out, many interpreters associate the two notions, whereas others, among them Dray himself, prefer to distinguish them.[102] Secondly, the *a priori* aspect of historical imagination has been contested. According to Donagan, the conception must not be confounded with Collingwood's later notion of an absolute presupposition, whereas Mink identifies the two.[103] Thirdly, Pompa has discussed Collingwood's notion of the criterion for the historical imagination and van der Dussen has indicated its importance for historical inference.[104]

Seen in the light of Collingwood's development, his theory of *a priori* imagination can best be seen as an elaboration of his notion of the ideality of history of the 1920s. As we have seen, Collingwood borrowed this from actualism and in particular from de Ruggiero's dialectic of question and answer, merging it with his own archaeological experience. The close parallels between 'ideality' and '*a priori* imagination' corroborate this interpretation. Firstly, both the ideality doc-

---

[101] R.G. Collingwood, 'Man Goes Mad', 1936, cited from Id., *Essays in Political Philosophy*, Oxford University Press, Oxford, 1989, 179-83.

[102] Dray, *History as Re-enactment*, 191-3.

[103] Donagan, *The Later Philosophy of R.G. Collingwood*, 211; Mink, *Mind, History, and Dialectic*, 85.

[104] Pompa, 'Collingwood's Theory of Historical Knowledge', 168-81; W.J. van der Dussen, 'The Historian and His Evidence', in W.J. van der Dussen and L. Rubinoff (eds.), *Objectivity, Method and Point of View, Essays in the Philosophy of History*, Brill, Leiden, 1991, 154-70.

trine and the doctrine of the historical imagination seek to explain how the historian gets an object before him, despite the fact that it is not actually present. This is shown by the terminological resemblances between the two doctrines. In the lectures of 1928 Collingwood describes 'ideality' as 'being an object of thought without having actuality' and an 'ideal event' is described as 'object of thought without actually occurring'.[105] In his inaugural address, Collingwood says that the special task of the historical imagination is to imagine the past; not as an object of possible perception, since it does not now exist, but able through the activity of imagination to become an object of our thought.[106] In other words, the historical imagination produces the object for historical thought.

Secondly, the range of ideality is unlimited; the Matterhorn ten years ago, a piece of music in the past, a battle, or entire historical periods are all ideal objects or events.[107] In 'The Historical Imagination', Collingwood gives more modest examples such as the 'interpolation' that Caesar travelled from Rome to Gaul, when we are told that he was in these different places, or the 'interpolation' on the basis of Tacitus that Suetonius's account of Nero's policy in Britain must be wrong.[108] Collingwood describes these 'webs of imaginative construction' as 'the historian's picture of his subject'.[109] But various interpreters have rightly shown that the historical imagination has an unlimited range. Not only can the historian imagine things that were imaginable for human beings in the past, but he can also imagine things that went beyond their experience. To give Collingwood's example quoted by Dray: 'The historian who sketches the economic history of the Roman Empire depicts a state of things which no contemporary saw as a whole.'[110] According to Dray, historical imagination is a synthetic activity that goes beyond 'colligation' as developed by Walsh or 'configuration' as developed by Mink; it is the activity by which the historian periodises history 'relating particular to particular to discern a larger whole of fact'.[111]

Thirdly, 'ideality' provides the basis for the questioning activity of the historian. This is also the case with the *a priori* imagination, as the following example shows:

> The hero of a detective novel is thinking exactly like an historian when, from indications of the most varied kinds, he constructs an imaginary picture of how a crime was committed, and by whom. At first, this is a mere theory, awaiting verification, which must come to it from without.[112]

---

[105] R.G. Collingwood, 'Outlines', 440.

[106] R.G. Collingwood, *The Idea of History*, 242.

[107] R.G. Collingwood, 'Outlines', 440–1.

[108] R.G. Collingwood, *The Idea of History*, 245.

[109] Ibid., 242.

[110] Dray, *History as Re-enactment*, 215.

[111] Ibid.

[112] R.G. Collingwood, *The Idea of History*, 243.

In this passage, Collingwood repeats his familiar identification of imagination with hypothesis. In *Speculum Mentis* he also identified this activity with the questioning activity and he would do so again in *The Principles of History*. As in *Speculum Mentis*, Collingwood makes it clear in this passage that the imagination forms only a first, but necessary, phase of any inquiry. The result of this phase is an 'imaginary picture' which he identifies with 'hypothesis', just as he had done in the 1920s. This hypothesis awaits verification and this is clearly another phase, or another aspect of the inquiry, for it 'must come to it from without'. For several reasons, which will become clear at the end of this chapter, I suggest that this 'second phase' must be seen as re-enactment which complements the historical imagination.

In spite of the resemblances between the ideality doctrine and the doctrine of the *a priori* imagination, there are also important differences. Firstly, in the 'Outlines' of 1928 'ideality' is simply posited; in 'The Historical Imagination' Collingwood stresses the act of imagining. This is completely in accordance with the actualist view that the 'product' of the mind can only be understood in terms of an activity.

Secondly, Collingwood presented the ideal object as a 'construction' by the historian based on evidence and historiography. In 'The Historical Imagination' he adds the innate idea of history as a basis.[113] The introduction of this 'innate idea of history' is the product of Collingwood's objective idealism since it functions as the logical *prius* of question and answer activity of the historian, even if the historian is aware of this.

Thirdly, the 'content' of this innate idea changes in time.[114] This view of the innate idea has led some interpreters to regard it as an immature version of Collingwood's later conception of an absolute presupposition. At first glance, this interpretation is not correct, because innate ideas are universal and necessary concepts, whereas absolute presuppositions are culturally dependent and vary in time. In order to bridge the gap between universality and historicity, Collingwood points out that the 'innate' idea may be filled with content provided by historical thought itself, which suggests that the formal aspect of historical thought is universal and necessary, but not its content. In other words, all human beings necessarily have a concept of history, but this does not imply that they all have the same concept of history. Seen in the light of Collingwood's development, the innate idea of the historical imagination can best be seen as a transition from the earlier notions of transcendental concepts of the 'Preliminary Discussion' of 1927 and that of the philosophical concepts of *An Essay on Philosophical Method* to the absolute presuppositions of *An Essay on Metaphysics*.

This interpretation is corroborated by the fact that Collingwood tries to connect the imagination to *The Idea of History* by means of the logic of question

---

[113] Ibid., 247.
[114] Ibid.

and answer. Firstly, he shows that imagination forms the basis of questioning, which implies that the historian's questions are logically based on *The Idea of History*. Secondly, *The Idea of History* also functions as a condition for historical truth. In Collingwood's view, this truth can never be attained by the imagination alone, for its result is always something imagined, not what really happened; it gives us hypotheses, not historical truth. In order to obtain historical truth, we cannot content ourselves with something that might have happened, but we must be certain that it actually happened. This certainty cannot be achieved by an act of imagination only but needs to be complemented by re-enactment, or the act of thought, which relates the products of imagination to a larger whole. Imagination is therefore the first phase of historical thought which needs to be complemented by re-enactment, which forms the second phase. Stated in the terms of *Speculum Mentis*: imagination and re-enactment are the systole and diastole of historical knowledge.

The Programme: 'Human Nature and Human History' (1936)

When Collingwood was asked to deliver a lecture for the British Academy is not clear, but he began preparing it a long time before its delivery, obviously intending to show the best of himself. Van der Dussen indicates that some of the themes of the lecture appear in 'Reality as History' of December 1935 and in 'Notes on History of Historiography and Philosophy of History', written in Spring 1936.[115] Collingwood describes 'Reality as History' as 'an experimental essay designed to test how far the thesis can be maintained that all reality is history and all knowledge historical knowledge'.[116] The essay seems to be inspired by Alexander's 'Historicity of Things', but we should not forget that Collingwood also identified the notion of 'reality as history' with Gentile's pure act as early as 1920. Not surprisingly, therefore, Collingwood mentions the Italian idealists at the beginning of the essay, which may therefore be seen as another study of the relationship between British and Italian philosophy.

    To the central question of whether reality may be seen as history, Collingwood replies with a wholehearted 'no'. Repeating the conclusion of his metaphysical investigations he concludes that nature cannot be resolved into history because nature does not preserve its own past as mind does.[117] This conclusion reveals that Collingwood stood still closer to Croce and Gentile, who had a stronger tendency to distinguish nature and mind, than to Alexander and Whitehead. This is also Collingwood's position in his review of 'The Historicity of Things', where he criticises Alexander for identifying nature and history too

---

[115] Van der Dussen, *History as a Science*, 174.
[116] R.G. Collingwood, 'Reality as History', 1935, Dep. 12/9, cited from Id., *The Principles of History*, 171.
[117] Ibid., 207–8.

much. He agrees with Alexander about the 'timefulness' of the natural world, but he is not satisfied with his assumption that timefulness constitutes the whole of history. The events historians study, Collingwood says, are not mere events, but actions, that is, outward expressions of thought.[118] The question of why things happen therefore has a different meaning for the scientist and the historian; for the scientist it refers to kinds of natural occasions, for the historian it refers to the thought of the actor.[119]

In Collingwood's view, this is the truth that Gentile works out in 'The Transcending of Time in History'. Like Alexander, the Italian holds that reality is historical, but for very different reasons. For Gentile, mind is the only reality and nature is only a construction of ideas, a product of human thought, existing and therefore developing with the development of the thought that constructs it. For the scientist, nature is not historical but his thought which has constructed it is certainly historical. Then Collingwood turns to Gentile's central thesis:

> Time is transcended in history because the historian, in discovering the thought of a past agent, re-thinks that thought for himself. It is known therefore, not as a past thought, contemplated as it were from a distance through the historian's time-telescope, but as a present thought living now in the historian's mind. Thus, by being historically known, it undergoes a resurrection out of the limbo of the dead past, triumphs over time, and survives in the present.[120]

Here, Collingwood takes sides with Gentile when it concerns history; for it is the Italian and not Alexander who realised that the historian deals with the thought of agents. In Collingwood's view this is an 'important idea and a true one' because it shows that 'history is not a story of successive events', but 'the actual possession by the historian'.[121] According to Collingwood, it entails that 'the historian must be, or make himself, the right kind of man; a man capable of entering into the minds of the persons whose history he is studying'.[122] Against the background of Collingwood's earlier criticisms of Gentile, it is hardly conceivable that he is completely uncritical of his position. However, Collingwood presents Gentile's position as 'one implication of the truth', remaining silent about the other implication. On the basis of the previous chapters we know that Collingwood criticised Gentile for blurring the distinction between nature and history by identifying the *pensato* with nature. From this it follows that history is as much a construction of the present thought as nature, and that history, or the truth about history, just represents the latest stage in the development of historical thought. The other implication of the truth is that thought as expressed in

---

[118] R.G. Collingwood, Review of 'Klibansky, Raymond, and H.J. Paton, eds., Philosophy and History: Essays Presented to Ernst Cassirer', 143.

[119] Ibid.

[120] Ibid.

[121] Ibid.

[122] Ibid., 144.

actions lives on in time independently from historical thought. Not surprisingly, this is indeed the line of thought which Collingwood would work out in the metaphysical epilegomena to his lectures on the philosophy of history of 1936.

The 'Prepatory Notes' for 'Human Nature and Human History', which he wrote on on 9 March 1936, show that Collingwood's starting point was actualism. After a brief historical introduction about Hume's theory of human nature and Kant's development of it, Collingwood firmly concludes that 'what is falsely called human nature is really human history' and continues that 'the fundamental theses of such a view would be something of this kind':

> 1) Human nature is mind. We are not talking about bodily nature: only of mental (with the proviso that mind always means embodied mind).
> 2) Mind is pure act. Mind is not anything apart from what it does. The so-called powers of faculties (δυναμεις) of mind are really activities (ἐνέργεια). Activity does not a) exhibit or reveal the nature of mind, or b) develop or explicate its unrealised potentialities: it is mind.
> 3) The pure act posits itself and its own presupposition at once. The past belongs to the present, not the present to the past. Whereas in nature the present is the caused effect of the past, in mind the past is the analysed content of the present. Thus what the mind is and what it does are its past and present respectively.
> 4) Past time therefore is the scheme of mind's self-knowledge. It can know itself only sub specie praeteritorum. To know oneself is simply to know one's past and vice versa. The philosophy or science of the human mind thus = history.[123]

These four theses expound the canon of actualism, no less and no more. This need not surprise us, because in 'Central Problems in Metaphysics' Collingwood had pointed out that 'subjective idealism' is to a certain extent compatible with objective idealism; the objective idealist agrees with the subjective idealist that the world consists of ideas which are logically prior to nature, but he denies that these ideas can only exist in our heads. Ideas, according to the objective idealist, are logically prior to both nature and mind. From this it follows that nature can not be seen as a mere product or construction by mind. This calls for a new elaboration of the relationship between nature and mind which Collingwood formulates immediately after stating the canon of actualism:

> My present difficulty is this. I think I can make good the above theses without difficulty in the case where human nature = rationality: it is easy, as Hegel showed, in the extreme case where what you are studying in history of philosophy. But how far down the scale can you go? Hegel thought you could go down as far as objective mind, but not as far down as subjective mind. If so, subjective mind is nonhistorical (though its *esse* is certainly *fieri*: but not historice *fieri*). Psychology (in the objective sense) has no history. In this part of

---

123 R.G. Collingwood, 'Human Nature and Human History', 1936, Dep. 12/11, cited from Id., *The Principles of History*, 220.

his being, man is simply an animal. His instincts, that is, are not historically conditioned. Is this so? I think it probably is. Subjective mind might be said to = unconscious mind. And historicity = consciousness = self-consciousness. This must be worked out.[124]

Here we find Collingwood opening a new line of research. In the manuscripts on metaphysics he had elaborated the difference between nature and mind, in the above passage Collingwood directs his attention to the point where nature and mind 'overlap', that is, in unconscious mind, the realm of feeling and emotion, the realm which is traditionally studied by psychology. Collingwood's intention is 'to go down the scale'; he starts from reason as it is embodied in 'objective mind', in order to go down to the realm of feeling and emotion. In short, Collingwood wants to investigate to what extent the four theses of actualism are valid in the lower realms of human mind. This involves no less than a complete philosophy of mind in which the relationship between feeling and thought is elaborated in the general context of human self-knowledge.

The programme for this project is expounded in the final version 'Human Nature and Human History', which Collingwood read for the British Academy in May 1936. This lecture shows how Collingwood presented his ideas to an English audience. Keeping its background in mind, he does not begin with the canon of actualism, but with Hume's notion of human nature with which it was more familiar. Collingwood attacks this notion gently though decisively; the science of human nature broke down because its method was distorted by the analogy of the natural sciences.[125] Then he introduces history as an alternative method for studying human affairs. But he immediately warns against the view that all reality is history, as Alexander held in 'The Historicity of Things', and he concludes that the task is to delimit the sphere of historical knowledge.[126] This is done in the second paragraph, called 'the field of historical thought', where Collingwood contrasts Alexander's notion of the historicity of all things with that of the ordinary historian who holds that only human affairs are historical. According to Collingwood, this contrast goes back to a different interpretation of the term 'event'. In this context, Collingwood makes his well-known distinction between the inside and the outside of an event. The outside of an event, Colling-wood says, is describable in terms of bodies, whereas the second can only be described in terms of thought.[127] From this it follows that the scientist cannot discover the thought of the events and he therefore remains outside of them. The historian can and must discover the thought within the events he is studying. There is a fundamental distinction between nature and history; a natural process is always a process of mere events, whereas the historical process is always a

---

[124] Ibid., 220.
[125] R.G. Collingwood, *The Idea of History*, 208.
[126] Ibid., 209.
[127] Ibid., 213.

process of thoughts.[128] Not all reality is history; only human reality is history. From this it follows that nature can only be studied by scientific methods and history only by historical methods.[129] On this basis Collingwood is able to show in the third section that history is the proper form of human self-knowledge. In this context, Collingwood applies the results of his metaphysical investigations to history. A past thought is an eternal object because time makes no difference to it; at any time the historian is able to think the same thought that created a situation in the past.[130] But thought is never a mere object, it is an activity of thought which can be understood only in so far as the historian re-enacts it in his own mind. The past thought is therefore always objective and subjective at once. From this it follows that historical inquiry reveals to the historian the powers of his own mind, that is, history gives him self-knowledge.[131]

Collingwood's British Academy Lecture has always been the subject of much controversy. In particular, Collingwood's distinction between the inside and the outside of events has been criticised as often as it has been defended.[132] Strangely enough, the concept of self-knowledge, which plays a central role in it, has been neglected by most interpreters, probably because they found it too vague.

In the light of Collingwood's development a few points can be made about 'Human Nature and Human History'. Firstly, Collingwood intended it as an answer to the most recent developments in the philosophy of history, especially to Alexander's 'Historicity of Things'. Secondly, Collingwood's doctrine of the inside and the outside of events, which makes up part of his answer to Alexander's thesis, is based on the theory of pure act. In this context, the resemblances between this paper and Gentile's 'La storia' of 1925 seem more than a coincidence. Both papers are meant as a vindication of history as a form of human self-knowledge against all positivistic and naturalistic claims. One of the bases of this vindication is the 'canon of actualism' as stated by Collingwood in the preparatory manuscript. Interestingly, Gentile and Collingwood elaborate these theses in almost the same way. For example, Collingwood's distinction between the inside and outside of events is similar to Gentile's distinction between *logo astratto* and *logo concreto* and both are elaborations of the central thesis; mind is pure act. However, despite these similarities, we find some doctrines in Collingwood's argument that are definitely not actualistic. The most conspicuous example is his description of historical fact as an eternal object and the application of this notion to the history of mathematics as 'living on' in contemporary mathematics.[133] On this point, Collingwood unveils the other implica-

---

128   Ibid., 215.
129   Ibid., 216.
130   Ibid., 218.
131   Ibid., 218.
132   Dray, *History as Re-enactment*, 38.
133   R.G. Collingwood, *The Idea of History*, 225–6.

tion of the thesis that all reality is historical, namely the view that the 'eternity' of thought does not depend on the ever-present act of thought, but on the past thought itself. But in 'Human Nature and Human History' Collingwood does not deal with the connections between the notion of the eternal object and the metaphysics of the pure act. For this reason Collingwood rightly calls the paper a 'programme' in his letter to de Ruggiero.

Before he could work out this programme, Collingwood had to do some further research on three topics, which he indicates in the conclusion to his lecture. Firstly, he aims at a further emendation of historical method and this implies a more precise distinction between nature and mind.[134] As we have seen above, Collingwood tried to find this distinction on the basis of the 'preservation' of the past, not in the Gentilian sense of the eternity of the *pensiero pensante* but in Whitehead's sense of 'eternal objects'. This point therefore indicates the elaboration of the notion of 'eternal objects' in history. Secondly, Collingwood notices that historical analysis of our intellectual possessions must show how they have been built up in the historical development of thought. This is the point which traditionally belonged to the Hegelian school, but this has now to be revised in the light of the first point.[135] Finally, with regard to the non-rational elements of mind, Collingwood intends to build up a philosophical psychology.[136] This is the point which Collingwood describes as the problem of 'going down the scale' in the preparatory manuscript to 'Human Nature and Human History'. This point has to be elaborated in connection with the first and the second point; that is, the realm of feeling and emotion has to be connected to mind and its history.

The History of the Idea of History (1936)

In the original preface to the lectures of 1936 Collingwood specifies the task of the philosophy of history in almost the same terms as in his autobiography:[137]

> Our task, in studying the philosophy of history, is to discover the chief characteristics of historical knowledge: how it goes to work, and what kind of objects it apprehends: that is to say, to think out an epistemology and a metaphysics of history.[138]

Didactally following the principles of his own philosophical method, Collingwood first offered his audience an historical overview of the epistemology and metaphysics of history before proceeding to his own views in the 'metaphysical epilegomena'. The *basso continuo* of the historical part of the lectures is the

---

[134] Ibid., 228-9.

[135] Ibid., 229-30.

[136] Ibid., 231.

[137] R.G. Collingwood, *An Autobiography*, 77.

[138] R.G. Collingwood, 'Introductory Lecture', 1936, Dep. 15/3, inserted page opposite to 12.

dissolution of the notion of substance. Since this was also the major theme of the 'Libellus', the historical part of the lectures may therefore be seen as a more sophisticated account of the transition from the 'world of being' to the 'world of becoming'. According to Collingwood, substance was the chief category of Graeco-Roman philosophy.[139] The first challenge to the doctrine of substance came from the Christian doctrine of creation.[140] This doctrine gradually dissolved the notion of substance in the sense that it began to understand all reality as activity. Collingwood mentions St.Thomas who rejected the conception of divine substance and defined God in terms of activity, or *actus purus*. Berkeley refuted the conception of material substance and Hume finished his work by rejecting the conception of spiritual substance and thus prepared the way for the third period in the history of historiography.[141]

Collingwood's account of the history of metaphysics forms the basis of the periodisation of the history of *The Idea of History* into three periods; Graeco-Roman, Christian, and Modern. This periodisation is not unique to *The Idea of History*, as it is also found in *The Idea of Nature* and in *An Essay on Metaphysics*. For each of these three periods, Collingwood discusses the relationship between the metaphysical level, the general epistemological level, or the philosophy of mind, and the specific epistemology of history as a form of experience. As Goldstein noticed, the whole composition is based on the idea of a scale of forms, each period in the history of *The Idea of History* exemplifying a higher stage with regard to its metaphysics, its philosophy of mind, and historical method.[142] Few scholars, however, have taken notice of the fact that Collingwood discusses Croce at the end of the historical part, which implies that he regarded the philosophy of the Italian as at the highest stage in the philosophy of history.

Collingwood presents Croce as the sole follower of the Vichian criticism of Descartes' metaphysics, which he regards as more promising than the more influential British empiricist anti-cartesianist tradition. For this reason, Collingwood begins his discussion of Croce with 'La storia ridotta' of 1893, where Croce identified history with art. Collingwood is very positive about Croce's first essay. This is not surprising because by identifying history with art Croce took up Vico's notion of imagination as the basis for knowledge and on this basis he was able to elaborate a view of historical method as both critical and constructive.[143] In Collingwood's view it was this idea of historical method as based on imagination which makes the Italian tradition more promising than the British.

---

[139] R.G. Collingwood, *The Idea of History*, 42.
[140] Ibid., 46.
[141] Ibid., 47.
[142] Goldstein, 'The Idea of History as a Scale of Forms', in *History and Theory*, 29.4, 1990, 42–50.
[143] R.G. Collingwood, *The Idea of History*, 203.

But Collingwood is also highly critical of Croce's attempt to resolve nature into mind, although he thinks that it does not affect Croce's philosophy of history.[144] This rejection follows of course from Collingwood's own distinction between nature and mind on the basis of his notion of the preservation of the past, or living past, as elaborated in his notes on metaphysics. Not surprisingly, therefore, the living past is the theme that Collingwood develops *à outrance* in the metaphysical epilegomena to the historical part of his lectures.

The Presuppositions of History: Three Epilegomena (1936)

Collingwood wrote the three epilegomena according to a very subtle didactic scheme. It roughly corresponds to that of the 'Outlines of a Philosophy of History' of 1928 reformulated on the basis of a scale of forms. The first epilegomenon deals with the possibility of historical thought and corresponds to the section 'quality' in the 'Outlines', the second broadens the notion of 'act of thought' and roughly corresponds to the section 'quantity' in the 'Outlines'. The third epilegomenon deals with progress, that is, with the relation between the acts of thought in time and corresponds with the section 'relation' in the 'Outlines'. This sequence indicates that the epilegomena of 1936 should be read as a whole; when bits and pieces are taken out, the unity of the lectures, and therefore their meaning, is destroyed. Furthermore, we must not lose sight of Collingwood's didactic intentions. Too often have the epilegomena been read as Collingwood's final word in the philosophy of history. But, like all of Collingwood's lectures, they should primarily be seen as 'finger exercises' for the real work that was yet to come. From this viewpoint, the epilegomena of 1936 should in the first place be read as a sequel to the historical introduction to *The Idea of History* which ended with Croce. Collingwood's main aim was to show his students how he intended to go beyond Croce and therefore beyond all philosophers of history, because the Italian had said the last word in the philosophy of history.

In the first epilegomenon Collingwood starts from the question 'How, or on what conditions, can the historian know the past?'[145] For the answer to this question he refers to the conclusion of his historical review of *The Idea of History*; namely, that the historian must re-enact the past in his own mind. The good listeners in the audience must have noticed the terminological change with regard to the last lecture, where Collingwood had dealt with Croce. In that context, he had presented the Italian's thought as the highest stage in the philosophy of history, but he had consequently used 're-living' and not 're-enactment' as the key term. In the first epilegemenon Collingwood only uses the notion of 're-enactment' which shows that he wants to make a difference with all previous philosophers, and in particular with Croce.

---

[144] Ibid., 200.
[145] Ibid., 282.

The central theme of the first epilegomenon is the preservation of the past in history. As we have seen above, Collingwood regarded this as the *fundamentum divisionis* between nature and mind. In the historical part of the lectures Colling-wood had shown that his predecessors, including Croce, had failed to recognise this distinction between nature and mind and this had drawn them into all kinds of attempts to resolve nature into mind or vice versa. In Croce's case this failure led to the resolution of nature into mind, that is, nature is seen as a product of thought from which it follows that the idea of nature is nothing but the history of that idea. Collingwood had his doubts about this resolution; in his view the distinction between nature and mind should be drawn on the basis of the way in which natural and historical processes preserve their own past.

The first epilegomenon must be read against this background; it is a study of 'the act of thought' with a particular stress on the way in which it 'lives on' in time. For didactic reasons, Collingwood presents his analysis as a defence against two objectors. The first objector rejects the possibility of re-enactment by pointing out that no two acts of thought can be identical. On this view my understanding of Euclid's statement that the angles at the base of an isosceles are equal implies that Euclid and I affirm the same truth. In Collingwood's view this does not entail that we perform exactly same act of thought, but only the same kind of thought. The relationship between the past and present act of thought must therefore be seen as a relationship of numerical difference and specific identity; the two acts of thought are different acts of the same kind.

Collingwood's reply to this objection is a perfect example of his philosophical method, starting from a primitive notion to be developed into more complex notions. Firstly, he shows that an act of thought can be sustained over a lapse of time, secondly, that an act of thought may be taken up after an interval of time, and thirdly, that an act of thought can be revived in different contexts.[146] Finally, and here is the key idea of the argument, he shows that the objector necessarily contradicts himself when he denies the three points:

> [The objector] maintains that although the object of two people's acts of thought may be the same, the acts themselves are different. But, in order that this should be said, it is necessary to know 'what someone else is thinking' not only in the sense of knowing the same object that he knows, but in the further sense of knowing the act by which he knows it: for the statement rests on a claim to know not only my own act of knowing but someone else's also, and compare them.[147]

Donagan qualifies the objector as a 'realist' and Collingwood's reply as 'muddled'.[148] I agree with the first qualification if we take 'realist' in the epis-

---

[146] Ibid., 285–6.

[147] Ibid., 288.

[148] Donagan, *The Later Philosophy of R.G. Collingwood*, 220.

temological sense of a philosopher who assumes a reality outside the act of thought. Seen in this light, Collingwood's reply is not muddled at all; it is essentially an application of the actualist thesis of the logical priority of the act of thought over the content of thought. From this thesis, Collingwood rightly draws the consequence that the identity of two contents of thought can only be asserted by re-enacting the act of which they are the product. For this reason Collingwood explicitly avers that not only the object of thought stands outside time but also the act of thought itself.[149] Saari finds this claim superfluous because it would have been sufficient to show the identity of the content of thought. In his view, Collingwood's mistaken belief that the acts of thought must be identical led him to some obscure thesis of the survival of the past.[150] But Shoemaker provides the perfect reply to Saari's objection. He rightly interprets Collingwood as holding that both content and act 'transcend time'. Shoemaker thus literally, but unknowingly, repeats Gentile's language! According to Shoemaker, Collingwood's thesis is only understandable when the distinction between the act of thought and its content is seen as 'metaphorical'. What Collingwood means then is that 'the act (the entire process) is co-extensive with the content'.[151] From this it follows that in order to understand a conclusion the entire process of thought must be taken into account. For example, in order to understand Plato, it is not enough to assent to or reiterate his conclusion, but we have to revive the activity by which he came to these conclusions, that is, Plato's argument.[152] Shoemaker agrees with Collingwood that thought can never be a mere object; it is always an 'act'; our understanding of thought is therefore not complete until we have re-enacted the whole act of thought itself. For this reason Collingwood rightly claims that the act of thought and not only the object or content of thought must transcend time.[153]

Here, Shoemaker in clear language repeats what Gentile stated since his first book; namely the logical priority of the act of thought *pensiero pensante* over the content of thought *pensiero pensato*. Shoemaker's discussion shows how Collingwood applies the most important corollary of this thesis against the realist; one can never deny the act of thought because the denial itself is always an act of thought. Another important corollary of this thesis is that when the historian studies the past it is absolutely necessary that he does not re-enact a part of the act or thought, but the whole act; he must rethink Plato's entire argument, and not parts of it. Collingwood stresses this point in several places. What he presents in the first half of the first epilegomenon may therefore be seen as the living

---

[149] R.G. Collingwood, *The Idea of History*, 287.

[150] Heikki Saari, *Re-Enactment, A Study in R.G. Collingwood's Philosophy of History*, Abo Akademi, Abo, 1984, 82.

[151] Robert G. Shoemaker, 'Inference and Intuition in Collingwood's Philosophy of History', in *Monist*, 53, 1969, 111.

[152] Ibid., 110–1.

[153] Ibid., 111.

part of actualism; it is the claim that history is only possible because two acts of thought can be identical. In order to understand what he regarded as the dead part of actualism we have to turn to the second objector.

The second objector admits the possibility of re-enactment but he denies that we ever obtain knowledge of the past by it. When we re-enact a thought, the objector holds in Collingwood's terms, it becomes our own, that is, it becomes subjective or present thought and ceases to be objective, or past thought. According to Collingwood, this is the essence of Oakeshott's doctrine that the historian only knows the past as his present experience, and of Croce's doctrine of the contemporaneity of the past.[154] To this Collingwood might have added the Gentilian thesis of the priority of the *historia rerum gestarum* over the *res gestae* which transforms all history into an *historia sui ipsius*.[155] According to Collingwood, the main drawback of these views is that they bridge the gap between the past and the present 'from one side only', that is, by the power of the present thought.[156] On the basis of these statements, Collingwood's problem may be seen as an attempt to show that the gap can be bridged from the other side as well, or, in other words, that thought is self-identical because it has a power to sustain and revive itself in different contexts.[157]

Collingwood's argument for this thesis consists of several steps. Firstly, he explains that to be aware of an act of thought means being self-conscious. Secondly, he rejects the view that thought cannot be objectified (a view sometimes held by Gentile). Combining the two theses, he states that an act of thought can be an object of thought not as a mere object, but only as an act. On this basis Collingwood reaches the important conclusion that the re-enactment is never immediate; when re-enacting Becket's (1118–1170) thought I do not simply become Becket, because all thought is reflective; that is, I know that it is Becket's thought that I am re-enacting.

Up to this point Collingwood repeats his position of the 'Outlines' of 1928, but after this point he expands it considerably. Collingwood first introduces the notions of thought in its immediacy and thought in its mediacy.[158] By thought in its immediacy Collingwood means thought as it occurs at a certain time and in a certain context of other acts of thought, emotions, sensations, and so forth. By thought in its mediacy Collingwood means thought that is lifted above the flow of experience.[159] Collingwood indicates that thought is lifted above immediate

---

154 R.G. Collingwood, *The Idea of History*, 289.
155 See chapter 3, pp. 82–83.
156 R.G. Collingwood, *The Idea of History*, 293.
157 Ibid.
158 Ibid., 297–9.
159 Ibid.

experience by argument; thought in its mediacy therefore refers to the logical structure of thought.[160]

Then Collingwood presents two rival doctrines. The first doctrine holds that anything torn from its context is mutilated and falsified; all things are thus internally related to each other. According to Collingwood, this view stresses thought in its immediacy. The rival doctrine regards all acts of thought as atomically distinct from one another; or in external relations. According to Collingwood, this doctrine overlooks the immediacy of thought. Both views make history impossible; the first ends in scepticism, the second turns history into a collection of unknowable facts.[161]

Collingwood's audience, which had followed the historical part of the lectures, knew well whom he was criticising. In the historical part of the lectures Collingwood had argued that Bradley saw reality as immediate experience, having the immediacy of feeling.[162] In Bradley's view, thought can never grasp reality because it divides, it distinguishes and mediates and thus destroys the immediacy of feeling. In Collingwood's view Bradley thus bequeathed to his successors the following dilemma:

> Either reality is the immediate flow of subjective life, in which case it is subjective but not objective, it is enjoyed but cannot be known, or else reality is that which we know, in which case it is objective and not subjective, it is a world of real things outside the subjective life of our mind and outside each other.[163]

In Collingwood's view, Bradley himself accepted the first horn of the dilemma by holding that all experience is the immediate flow of subjective life. The realists accepted the second horn of the dilemma, holding that 'what mind knows is something other than itself, and that mind itself, the activity of knowing, is immediate experience and therefore unknowable'.[164] The first doctrine which attacks the possibility of re-enactment is that of the British idealists and realists, for both agree that reality is immediate.

The second doctrine is more difficult to recognise. It is not the doctrine of the realists because Collingwood held that for them mind is immediate experience with which he had already dealt.[165] Is the second doctrine then Collingwood's interpretation of the Italian idealists? In order to answer this question it is of the highest importance that we take Collingwood's notion of thought in its immediacy and thought in its mediacy as a species of a scale of forms, that is, there is no disjunction between the two, but both forms of thought 'overlap'. From this it

---

[160] Ibid., 300–1.
[161] Ibid., 298–9.
[162] Ibid., 141.
[163] Ibid.
[164] Ibid., 141–2.
[165] Ibid., 142.

follows that no thinker represents one of the two extreme positions, but always some intermediary position. Collingwood presents the British idealists and realists as occupying one extreme end of the scale; both stress the immediacy of thought and reality. The other extreme of the scale is represented by those who stress the mediacy of thought by substituting logical analysis to experience, and convert reality in sheer objectivity outside the mind. As we have seen, already in 1933 Collingwood had criticised both Croce and Gentile for turning the past into an objective spectacle. Moreover, he had explicitly criticised Gentile for reducing history to a logical sequence. The question now arises; did the Italians make a false disjunction between immediate experience and thought or not?

The answer to this question is again affirmative. On the basis of chapter 2 we know that Collingwood had good reasons for regarding Croce's distinction between intuition and thought in this way. For, despite his doctrine of the unity of the spirit, Croce did not overcome the disjunction between intuition and thought and this led him to a monadistic view of history. Gentile had committed the opposite error of reducing all immediacy to thought in its mediacy; thought in its immediacy is only *pensato*, and therefore not actual thought and *norma sui*, thought in its mediacy is *pensante* and actual and *norma sui*. Therefore, Collingwood's criticism of the second doctrine seems to be directed more to Gentile's philosophy than to Croce's, because the latter at least recognised the realm of art as an autonomous form of experience. It is likely, therefore, that Collingwood had Gentile's doctrine in mind when he elaborated his re-enactment theory to the view that the gap between past and present can be bridged from both sides.

To sum up, all the doctrines that Collingwood criticises in his first epilegomenon make a false disjunction between thought in its immediacy and thought in its mediacy. The British idealists, from Bradley onwards, tended to reduce all thought to immediate experience, with the result that all reality is the immediate flow of subjective life. The realists also held that thought is an immediate experience, but they saw reality as a world of things outside our mind. In spite of their difference, both idealists and realists did not recognise the reality of thought in its mediacy. The Italians did recognise thought in its mediacy but they tended to identify all thought with it, that is, they did not recognise thought in its immediacy. Against this Collingwood developed his view that both forms of thought overlap and that only thought in its mediacy is identical with itself through the different contexts of time. It is on this basis that Collingwood shows how thought 'lives on' in time and how the gap between the present and the past can be bridged from both sides. This thesis is elaborated in the second epilegomenon where Collingwood explains what he means by thought in its mediacy.

After having shown that the gap between past and present can be bridged from two sides, Collingwood moves in the second epilegomenon to the question of the subject matter of historical knowledge. This involves a further deepening of the notion of the act of thought: 'how much or how little is meant to be included under the term thought?'[166] This question reminds us of the question Collingwood raised in the preparatory notes for 'Human Nature and Human History': how far down the scale can we go? In the second epilegomenon, Collingwood answers this question by giving an outline of his philosophy of mind. He begins by contrasting feeling and thought and then distinguishes three levels of consciousness. The first level is that of mere consciousness, or awareness. The second level is that of self-consciousness in which we become aware of our activity of feeling as making part of our self. For example, when I say 'I feel cold' I must be aware of the continuity of myself.[167] Self-consciousness forms the basis of memory and perception. But memory and perception are only 'unconscious thinking'; we remember and perceive without being conscious that we are thinking.[168] When we become conscious of our own thought, we reach the third and highest level of thought which Collingwood calls 'reflective thought' and which he describes roughly as 'thought about the act of thinking'.[169] In another passage he extends the meaning of reflective thought as follows:

> ...reflective thought, that is, one which is performed in the consciousness that it is being performed, and is constituted what it is by that consciousness. The effort to do it must be more than a merely conscious effort. It must not be the blind effort to do we know not what, like the effort to remember a forgotten name or to perceive a confused object; it must be a reflective effort, the effort to do something of which we have a conception before we do it.[170]

In other words, we never plan our perception, we just perceive, whereas in reflective thought we plan our thinking and later refer to that plan in order to judge its success or failure.

Reflective thought is only one kind of reflective activity, which Collingwood describes as follows:

> A reflective activity is one in which we know what it is that we are trying to do, so that when it is done we know that it is done by seeing that it has conformed to the standard or criterion which was our initial conception of it. It is therefore an act which we are enabled to perform by knowing in advance how to perform it.[171]

Interestingly, here Collingwood presents mental activity as an attempt to realise a conception of itself which is logically prior to it. In another passage, Collingwood describes this 'initial conception' as purpose, ideal, or as a plan which serves as a criterion or standard on which the activity can be judged after its

---

166 Ibid., 305.
167 Ibid., 306.
168 Ibid., 307.
169 Ibid.
170 Ibid., 308.
171 Ibid.

performance. In his view, it is this idea, or purpose, that makes the activity universal:

> An act is more than a mere unique individual; it is something having a universal character; and in the case of a reflective or deliberate act (an act which we not only do, but intend to do before doing it) this universal character is the plan or idea of the act which we conceive in our thought before doing the act itself, and the criterion by reference to which, when we have done it, we know that we have done what we meant to do.[172]

From the universal aspect of the activity it follows that there cannot only be history of reflective activities such as politics, warfare, economic and moral activity on the practical side, but also of art, religion, science, philosophy on the theoretical side, for these are all reflective activities, that is, purposeful activities.[173] Collingwood thus overcomes the distinction between theory and practice and he pays much attention to showing that the theoretical activities are done on purpose.

He gives the example of a scientist who is trying to discover the cause of malaria and concludes:

> ...every actual inquiry starts from a certain problem, and the purpose of the inquiry is to solve that problem; the plan of the discovery, therefore, is already known and formulated by saying that, whatever the discovery may be, it must be such as to satisfy the terms of the problem.[174]

In this passage Collingwood identifies reflective activity with the activity of positing and solving problems along the lines he had laid down in the 1920s. Along the same lines, he shows in the second epilegomenon that art and religion can be seen as the positing and solving of problems from which it follows that there can be a history of these activities.

As with all of Collingwood's epilegomena, the second to the lectures of 1936 has been the subject of much controversy between Collingwood's interpreters. In particular, Collingwood's notion of reflective activity has been criticised for its intellectualism. In this context, Dray summarises these criticisms and criticises Collingwood for having two meanings for reflective thought. In its technical sense reflective thought means 'thought about thought' and in its ordinary sense it means 'thought performed in the consciousness that it is being performed'.[175] According to Dray, Collingwood shifts from the technical sense to the ordinary sense and thus opens the door to all the intellectualistic dicta of the second half of the epilegomenon. When reflective thought is taken in the ordinary sense, the claim that history can only re-enact reflective thought amounts to saying that he

---

[172] Ibid., 309.
[173] Ibid., 309–15.
[174] Ibid., 312.
[175] Dray, *History as Re-enactment*, 113.

can re-enact all thought that has been consciously performed, that is, unreflective thought. But in the technical sense, the claim runs that the historian can only rethink reflective thought or thoughts about unreflective thought.[176] Dray finds the shift of meaning completely inexplicable and even ponders whether it is due to external factors.[177]

Dray's question can be answered satisfactorily when we place it in the context of Collingwood's development and his relationship to the Italians. As we saw in chapter 3, it was Gentile's notion of the pure act of thought that led him to the intellectualistic view that all history can be reduced to the history of philosophy. This is exactly the view that Collingwood criticises in the first epilegomenon. His main target is the view which confuses thought in its mediacy and thought in its immediacy, or in other terms, the view which identifies all experience with either immediate experience or reflective thought. But, as we have also seen in chapter 3, Gentile's position cannot simply be denied without self-contradiction; a true act of thought is always done in the consciousness of doing it. The only way left open to Collingwood was to specify the notion of self-consciousness further than Gentile had done. The goal of this specification was therefore to establish both a minimum and maximum range for self-consciousness. From this perspective, Bradley or Dilthey *cum suis* had claimed too little for self-consciousness, with the result that they identified the historian with the psychologist.[178] Gentile, however, had claimed too much for self-consciousness with the result that he identified all history with the history of philosophy. Between this minimum and maximum Collingwood tried to specify self-consciousness as a scale of forms. First of all, he describes the lowest form of self-consciousness as the 'most rudimentary form of thought'.[179] Next, he describes how this rudimentary form of self-consciousness develops into other forms like remembering and perceiving. In Collingwood's view these forms of thought are also forms of self-consciousness, but only to a small degree, for they depend on a different activity, namely thought, of which they are not aware. The highest form of self-consciousness is reflection proper. This is the highest stage because it does not depend on any other activity; it is self-conscious thought, or thought about thought. This description of reflective activity comes close to Gentile's sense of it, namely as thought without presuppositions, and it was by reducing all forms of self-consciousness to this sense that he came to identify all spiritual activity with philosophy. Collingwood himself also identified 'thought about the act of thinking' with 'reflection' or philosophy, as the second epilegomenon shows. Against this background, it is understandable that Collingwood shifts the meaning to the somewhat looser ordinary sense of the notion of self-consciousness;

---

[176] Ibid., 113–4.
[177] Ibid., 112.
[178] R.G. Collingwood, *The Idea of History*, 173.
[179] Ibid., 306.

only this enables him to describe art, politics, and so forth as reflective activities without identifying them with philosophy.

On this basis, Collingwood clarifies his position with regard to the first epilegomenon, and therefore his relationship to other philosophies. In the first epilegomenon Collingwood showed that the gap between the past and the present must be bridged from both sides, that is, from the side of the present act of thought and from the side of the past act of thought. The present act of thought bridges the gap, because being itself a self-conscious act of thought it can be a host for the past thought. The past thought bridges the gap because in its mediation it is lifted out of the flow of experience.

In the second epilegomenon Collingwood further describes this mediation as 'reflection'. In what sense does this reflective activity transcend time? In the first epilegomenon Collingwood shows that it is the logical aspect of thought, or the structure of the argument, that transcends time. In the second epilegomenon he identifies the logical aspect or the argument with reflection. Reflection transcends time in a double sense. By the act of forming a purpose, the mind lifts itself above the flow of immediate consciousness, because it is a pure act, that is, it is not conditioned by immediate consciousness. After the accomplishment of the act, mind transcends time by reflecting on what it has done. In positing itself, mind thus transcends past and present.

Because of this power to transcend the flow of immediate consciousness, reflective activity can be re-enacted. The plans, ideas, purposes of actors are dependent on, but not conditioned by, the experience from which they arise. That formation of purposes is a free or a pure act. Immediate experience compels us to make purposes, for even not acting is an act, but it can never condition the content of our purposes. Yet, purposes find themselves in a logical relationship with experience, and it is this relationship that stands outside time. It is for this reason that Collingwood says that reflective activity has a universal aspect.

This argument shifts the burden of re-enactment from the act of thought to a particular aspect of it; namely purpose, plans, and ideas, which are logically prior to the act, and which function as a criterion for it. This calls for a further development of the re-enactment doctrine. In the first epilegomenon we saw that it is not the content of the act that must be re-enacted, but the act itself as an act; that is, the entire process of thought must be re-enacted in order to establish its content. On the basis of Collingwood's description of reflective thought we may now add that re-enactment of the entire process of thought, that is, thought in its mediation, involves the re-enactment of the ideas or purposes that logically precede the act of thought. And when we identify reflective thought with the positing and solving of problems we may say that it is not the answer but the question and its presuppositions that matters in historical understanding. This was what Collingwood meant in the following example:

> In practice, the common difficulty for the historian is to identify the problem, for whereas the thinker is generally careful to expound the steps of his own thought, he is talking as a rule to contemporaries who already know what the problem is, and he may never state it at all. And unless the historian knows what the problem was at which he was working, he has no criterion by which to judge the success of his work.[180]

It is difficult to identify the problem of a thinker, because as a rule he does not formulate the purposes of his thought and for this reason his thought cannot be judged. Yet, the purpose, or initial conception, or presupposition of an activity must be known, for not only the whole activity or enactment logically depends on it, but also our activity as historians, or the re-enactment. The problem is therefore to discover the purpose, or the initial conception, or presupposition of a reflective activity. This involves a closer study of the ways in which purposes-presuppositions are linked to each other and this is the subject matter of the third epilegomenon on progress.

In the third epilegomenon, Collingwood starts from the notion of reflective thought as an activity of positing and solving problems in order to establish a minimum definition of progress:

> Every act whose history we may study, of whatever kind it is, has its place in a series of acts where one has created a situation with which the next has to deal. The accomplished act gives rise to a new problem; it is always this new problem, not the old problem over again, which the new act is obliged to solve.[181]

In this passage, Collingwood makes it clear that the new act, and this is clearly a reflective act, is always done in the context of the past; what gives rise to new problems are accomplished acts. In the second epilegomenon Collingwood had shown that problems come into existence with plans or initial conceptions. We can say therefore that new ideas, plans, or initial conceptions of the new activity are always established on the basis of the experience of the old activities. But in order to speak about progress the new acts must be of a new kind, they must belong to new specific types. That is, the new acts must be realisations of new purposes, new ideas. And even that is not enough, for these new types must also be considered as an improvement on the older types. According to Collingwood, it is not easy to say whether a change was an improvement or not, for it depends on the point of view from which it is regarded. Collingwood gives the example of a community of fish-eaters which develops a more efficient method of fishing. From the point of view of the older generation this change is a form of decadence, because it is not in accordance with their way of life, whereas the younger generation regards it as progress.[182] The historian cannot establish whether the

---

[180] R.G. Collingwood, *The Idea of History*, 313.
[181] Ibid., 324.
[182] Ibid., 325.

change was one of progress because he must take the conditions and the consequences of it into account and this implies that he enters with equal sympathy
into both forms of life. Collingwood then criticises most of the criteria for
progress that are based on sheer optical illusion and misunderstanding of the
past. According to Collingwood, there is only one true criterion for progress
which he formulates as follows:

> If thought in its first phase, after solving the initial problems of that phase, is
> then, through solving these, brought up against others which defeat it; and if
> the second solves these further problems without losing its hold on the solu-
> tion of the first, so that there is gain without any corresponding loss, then
> there is progress. And there can be progress on no other terms. If there is any
> loss, the problem of setting loss against gain is insoluble.[183]

In this passage Collingwood identifies reflective activities with the process of
positing and solving problems, as in the second epilegomenon. His point is that
only reflective activities can create progress on the basis of historical knowledge.
The solution to a problem is only a better solution when it also solves the problems of the past without loss. But this implies that in the formulation of my
problem, or of the purpose, I must take the history of the problem into account,
that is, I must see to what extent my predecessors succeeded or failed to solve
their own problems and this implies that I have to know their purposes or plans.
All progress is therefore based on reflective activity, thought about thought, or
history.

According to Collingwood, it is impossible to say that there is progress in
happiness, or in art, for the first is an unreflective experience and the second
arises from unreflective experience which has no history.[184] The history of
morality, economic life, and politics has a double aspect with regard to progress,
because on the one hand they arise from an unreflective experience and on the
other hand they are the product of reflective experience.[185] Only in science,
philosophy, and religion is it possible to speak unambiguously about progress
because these are all reflective activities.[186] At the end of the epilegomenon
Collingwood not only shows that history is the only possible way of establishing
whether progress has occurred but also that it is the only way to create progress.
The reason for this is that progress only happens when what was achieved in the
preceding phase is retained by mind. The two phases are related by a continuity
of a peculiar kind. Giving the example of Einstein and Newton, Collingwood
points out that 'if Einstein makes an advance on Newton, he does it by knowing
Newton's thought and retaining it within his own, in the sense that he knew

---

[183] Ibid., 329.
[184] Ibid., 330.
[185] Ibid., 330–1.
[186] Ibid., 331–3.

what Newton's problems were, and how he solved them'.[187] According to Collingwood, this mental retaining of the past is essential to all progress and he ends his lectures with a most eloquent plea for the use of history:

> If we want to abolish capitalism or war, and in doing so not only to destroy them but to bring into existence something better, we must begin by understanding them: seeing what the problems are which our economic or international system succeeds in solving, and how the solution of these is related to the other problems which it fails to solve. This understanding of the system we set out to supersede is a thing which we must retain throughout the work of superseding it, as a knowledge of the past conditioning our creation of the future.[188]

This passage enables us to relate the third epilegomenon to the previous two. As we have seen above, the main point of the first epilegomenon was to show that the act of thought must be re-enacted as an act, which yielded the notion of complete re-enactment in contradistinction to incomplete re-enactment. In the second epilegomenon Collingwood introduced his notion of reflective thought, which he identified with the positing and solving of problems. From this view of the act of thought it follows that 'complete re-enactment' means; the complete rethinking of the problems and solutions in relation with the presuppositions on which they are based. The question that remained open concerned the way in which these problem and solution complexes are related to each other. It is to this question that the third epilegomenon provides the answer. Problems and solutions and their presuppositions are related to each other by historical thought. The basic point of the third epilegomenon is that we can progressively solve our problems when we study the problems and solutions of the past. Most of the time we formulate our ideals quite unreflectively and the result is always mere destruction of old ways of life. But if we try to solve our problems without destroying the solutions of others, we have to think historically. The more we understand the past problems, the better we are able to formulate our own problems and the better we are able to solve them. This is not cheap optimism, because the understanding the past is a hard task. Collingwood was determined to continue on *la via più ardua*, as we will see in the next chapter.

---

[187] Ibid., 333.
[188] Ibid., 334.

Chapter Ten

Collingwood's System

Introduction

When Collingwood died on 9 January 1943, his 'New Science of Human Affairs' was far from complete. He had only published *An Essay on Philosophical Method* and *The Principles of Art* more or less as he had planned. Despite his heroic efforts to finish his philosophical series once he became ill, he only published *An Autobiography*, *An Essay on Metaphysics*, and *The New Leviathan*. The rest of Collingwood's life's work was scattered in dozens of articles and thousands of pages of manuscript, amongst which the first chapters of the book he considered as his magnum opus: *The Principles of History*.

After Collingwood's death, his literary executor Knox did not publish this enormous legacy as a philosophical system. Though he regarded *An Essay on Philosophical Method* as 'an introduction to a philosophy not yet written', he did not discuss this philosophy at length.[1] Moreover, despite Collingwood's explicit claim in *An Essay on Philosophical Method* that philosophy should be systematic, Knox concluded that Collingwood's 'philosophical writings make up not so much one system as a series of systems'.[2] Following Knox's indications, Collingwood's first interpreters mainly discussed parts of his legacy, without taking the larger philosophical context into account. Along these lines, many publications appeared on specialised topics like Collingwood's conception of art, his re-enactment doctrine, and his idea of metaphysics. Only twenty five years after Collingwood's death Rubinoff and Mink broke this trend by seriously attempting to reconstruct Collingwood's philosophical system on the basis of his published works. After 1978, when Collingwood's manuscripts became available in the Bodleian, their efforts were continued by many other interpreters, who tried to fit the fragments of Collingwood's system together. In close cooperation and often with great effort, these interpreters have succeeded not only in discerning the details in his system, but also its contours as a whole.

In this chapter, I will try to make a further step by reconstructing Collingwood's last works as a philosophical system. This aim is justified by the fact that Collingwood repeatedly expressed his intention to publish a philosophical series. Moreover, despite his deteriorating health and the outbreak of the war,

---

1   Knox, 'Editor's Preface', xxi.
2   Ibid., vii.

Collingwood never changed his plans. On the contrary, from the moment he knew that he had not much longer to live, Collingwood, both in his autobiography and in letters to the Delegates of Clarendon Press, most emphatically expressed his intention to finish his philosophical series.[3] Finally, at the end of his life, he authorised his wife to publish *The Principles of History* even though he had not finished the book. Facing death, Collingwood was determined to leave his new science of human affairs to posterity.

In order to reconstruct Collingwood's philosophical system, we will first have to know how he envisaged it. One of the first and most elaborate statements of the project can be found in a long letter of 12 June 1937 to his ideal interlocutor Guido de Ruggiero:

> Now for some chatter about my own concerns. The problem of a synthesis of philology and philosophy, which your own history solves in practice with such brilliance, still torments me as the fundamental problem of the modern world. A year ago I published a paper on the conception of 'human nature', arguing that what went by that name in the 18th century was really human history, falsely crystallized into a special case of 'nature', and implying that the so-called sciences of mind were faulty in so far as they treat mind as something given, to be analysed like a natural object, instead of something whose only reality is its historical process. This thesis involves a programme of recasting the science of mind (including the Crocian science of spirit) into the forms of history; not into the form of history wie sie steht und geht, but into a new form of history, not merely philological but philosophical. The philosophy in it is not, as Croce has said, simply its methodology. The absorption is mutual: the product is not philosophy based on history nor history based on philosophy, it is both these things at once. I think you will understand what I mean, and will very likely say you have heard it, and thought it, long ago.[4]

This letter reveals that Collingwood had a very clear conception of his project. Starting from 'Human Nature and Human History', his explicit aim is to recast the science of the mind into a form of history. These words might be interpreted as the liquidation of philosophy by history, as interpreters like Knox thought, but this was certainly not Collingwood's aim. Though he formulates his projects in Vichian terms as a synthesis of philology and philosophy, he did not aim to identify philosophy and history, as Croce and Gentile had done. Unlike Croce, Collingwood did not regard philosophy as the methodology of history, nor did he see history as the basis of philosophy, but he strove for a 'mutual absorption' of history and philosophy. The 'new form of history' is therefore philosophical and historical at the same time. The gist of the new history is that it does not regard mind as a given, natural object but as an historical process, which, not being given, must be reconstructed. In other words: Collingwood's programme

---

3 R.G. Collingwood, *An Autobiography*, 118; Peter Johnson, *The Correspondence of R.G. Collingwood. An Illustrated Guide*, Collingwood Society, Swansea, 1998, 25–34.

4 R.G. Collingwood, 'Letters to Guido de Ruggiero', 12 June 1937.

is to show that human nature is human history; mind is what mind does, from which it follows that the question of what mind is resolves the question of what mind has done.

De Ruggiero undoubtedly understood Collingwood's programme. The synthesis of philology and philosophy had laid at the basis of his own absolute empiricism which he further elaborated in his *Storia della filosofia*. In his letter, Collingwood refers to this work as a practical example of the synthesis of philology and philosophy. This suggests that he viewed his own programme as a theoretical elaboration of that synthesis. This interpretation of Collingwood's later development is corroborated by the fact that he saw absolute empiricism as the main source of inspiration for the 'Libellus'. As we have seen, this book was the starting point of his own development in the 1920s, culminating in 1933 in *An Essay on Philosophical Method*, which formed the basis of his philosophical system.

In his letter to de Ruggiero, Collingwood gives some details about the way in which he would carry out his programme. In this context, he mentions that he intends to publish a book on the philosophy of history based on the lectures he was currently giving. The goal of this book was a 'concrete methodology of present-day historiography'. Collingwood hopes to achieve this aim by integrating the problems of modern historiography in their historical context. In order to do this, he would take Croce's *Teoria e storia della storiografia* 'inside out'. Unlike Croce, he would not begin by expounding his own views and end with a historical appendix, but merge history and philosophy. People, Collingwood says citing Hegel, 'are annoyed by having the Absolute fired at them out of a pistol!'[5] Again, this reference to the absolute is a clear indication that Collingwood did not aim for a liquidation of philosophy, but at its integration with history.

The same ideas lay behind a second project in the programme: *The Principles of Art*, which he describes as follows:

> I am writing now a long book on Aesthetic, working on similar principles. I am arguing that it is a mistake to lump Greek art and medieval art and Renaissance art and modern art together under the name Art, and to search for a formula that covers them all: still worse, to construct a formula to fit modern art and then force it upon Greek art etc. These different arts have had a different function in society (medieval art a religious function, Renaissance art a luxury-function and so on) and therefore a different essence in themselves. The problem of 'the nature of Art' should become the problem of the nature of modern art; and the solution of this problem is the historical problem (but philosophical as much as historical) of the genesis of modern art.[6]

As in his book on the philosophy of history, he would not start from an abstract concept, but from an actual problem: *The Principles of Art* was meant as an

---

5 Ibid.
6 Ibid.

answer to the problem of modern art. Furthermore, like the problem of modern history, the problem of modern art was to be solved by exploring the genesis of modern art. According to Collingwood, this problem is an historical problem, because not being based on an abstract concept it assumes that different arts had different functions in society. From this it follows that they have a different essence in themselves. Finally, it is by exploring these different, historically conditioned essences that Collingwood hopes to contribute to the problem of modern art, thus contributing to a rapprochement between theory and practice.

The letter to de Ruggiero gives a very clear picture of the steps in Collingwood's programme of recasting the science of the mind into a form of history. Firstly, the recasting starts from contemporary, practical problems; its subject is the problem of modern art and the problem of modern history. Secondly, the recasting tries to solve these problems by reconstructing their genesis in both an historical and philosophical way. This reconstruction is historical because it takes the historically conditioned functions of the forms of the mind into account. It is philosophical because it tries to grasp the 'essences' of these functions. Therefore, recasting does not aim to elaborate a single essence for the forms of the mind, but points to a concept which takes the development of 'essences' into account.

Seen from the context of Collingwood's development, this is just another phrasing of his idea of the scale of forms in which the generic essence is embodied in a series of overlapping species as elaborated, which formed the kernel of his philosophical method. It is most likely therefore that Collingwood would carry out his programme along the lines of this method. Seen from this point of view, recasting the science of the mind means solving contemporary problems by reconstructing their genesis as a scale of forms. As we have seen, the main aim of Collingwood's method is to enhance our understanding of experience by bringing it to completion on the basis of philosophical distinctions. It is this more complete, both historical and philosophical, understanding that forms the basis for solving contemporary problems.

In his letter to de Ruggiero, Collingwood does not mention other projects, but given the fact that he wanted to recast the science of the mind, including Croce's *Filosofia dello spirito* and other contributions to it, among which, of course, his own, the entire project would at least also comprise the recasting of religion, science, philosophy, and their practical counterparts in ethics and politics. For each of these forms of experience, Collingwood would solve present-day problems by exploring their history. Along these lines, he would merge the history of art in *The Principles of Art,* and on the history of *The Idea of History* would prepare *The Principles of History.* The history of ethics and politics, which Collingwood had discussed at length in his lectures on moral philosophy, would form the basis of a treatise on this subject, which he had planned as early as 1933. Along the same lines, Collingwood's lectures on the idea of nature and his lectures on the problems of metaphysics might have resulted in a cosmology, which would probably also comprise a theology. In short, when Collingwood started to write his philosophy in 1937, he probably had about six to eight volumes, aside from *An Essay on Philosophical Method*, in mind.

After his first stroke, Collingwood did not change his mind on the series. On the contrary, he wrote his autobiography in order 'to put on record some brief account of the work I have not yet been able to publish, in case I am not able to publish it in full'.[7] Unsurprisingly, therefore, *An Autobiography* closely follows the outlines of the project as given in the letter to de Ruggiero. The recasting of the science of the mind into a new form of history now appears as 'The New Science of Human Affairs'. The synthesis of philosophy and philology is rendered as the rapprochement between philosophy and history, and Collingwood's aim to contribute to contemporary problems appears as the rapprochement between theory and practice. But above all, *An Autobiography* is the story of Collingwood's development of the notion of the living past. This is no coincidence, because it was on the basis of this notion that Collingwood elaborated his own philosophy since his early development. Moreover, it was on the basis of the notion of the living past that he had always hoped to raise action in human affairs to a higher potential.[8] Though Collingwood did not mention the living past in his letter to de Ruggiero, the Italian, who had followed his friend from his early development, would have understood that the living past would form the backbone of his programme.

After finishing *An Autobiography*, Collingwood began a race against the clock, often working on several projects at the same time. Despite this time pressure, however, he kept to his plan of recasting the science of mind. Following his original plan, he wrote a scheme for his *magnum opus*, *The Principles of History*, which he left unfinished. After this, Collingwood still followed the plan, but increasingly reduced the number and size of the volumes. Compared to the enormous amount of preparatory research, both *An Essay on Metaphysics* and *The New Leviathan* only give fragments of the entire 'New Science of Human Affairs'. All in all, Collingwood wrote probably less than half of what he had in mind.

The aim of this chapter is not to reconstruct the other half, but to show the outlines of his philosophical system. In order to realise this, I will start from the published books, which I will analyse as parts of the programme of recasting the science of the mind. Since large parts of this new science are not finished, I will try to fill some of the gaps by comparing the Italian models to Collingwood's achievements, drawing from his development as discussed in the previous chapters and his autobiography, which is, after all, a *livre de bonne foi*.

---

7   R.G. Collingwood, *An Autobiography*, 118.

8   Ibid., 106.

The Principles of Art (1938)

After *An Essay on Philosophical Method*, *The Principles of Art* was the only work of his series Collingwood finished as he intended. The book may therefore be seen as the only completely finished product of the programme of recasting the science of the mind. Firstly, in conformity with the three steps of his programme, Collingwood explicitly starts from contemporary problems in art. In the preface to the book he writes: 'everything written in this book, has been written in the belief that it has a practical bearing, direct or indirect, upon the condition of art in England in 1937.'[9] Secondly, in the first two books Collingwood tries to solve these problems by an historical reconstruction of their genesis from the Greeks to the present. Finally, in Book III Collingwood presents his own theory of art, focusing on its practical implications for the situation in England at the time of writing.[10]

Behind this three part organisation lies Collingwood's philosophical method, which he mentions in several places.[11] In conformity with his method, he starts Book I with some common ideas about art in order to trace them back to what he calls 'the technical theory of art'. The main thesis of this theory, whose origins are found in Ancient Greece, is its identification of art with craft.[12] Collingwood challenges the identification by discussing the distinctions on which it is based. The main distinction is the one between means and an end which he typically tests by comparing it with the artistic experience. In the end the technical theory of art breaks down because its main distinction does not hold.[13]

Along the same lines, Collingwood criticises the identification of art with representation, magic, and amusement in the subsequent chapters. Throughout the text Collingwood's strategy is the same: he breaks down identities by challenging the distinctions on which they are based. In conformity with his method, this breaking down is not based on a lack of correspondence between theory and experience, or coherence between parts of the theory, but on failing to give sufficient meaning to experience. The technical theory of art does not hold, Collingwood argues, because there is no way in which the distinction between means and end can meaningfully be employed in describing artistic experience.[14]

At the end of Book I, when he refuses to reject the technical theory of art, Collingwood's philosophical method comes to the fore again. Following the principle of concrete negation and affirmation of his method Collingwood says: 'To a person who knows his business as a scientist, historian, philosopher, or

---

9   R.G. Collingwood, *The Principles of Art*, vi.
10   Ibid., 332.
11   Ibid., 21, 22n,43, 73, 165, 183, 187n, 281.
12   Ibid., 9.
13   Ibid., 20–6.
14   Ibid., 108.

any kind of inquirer, the refutation of a false theory constitutes a positive advance in his inquiry.'[15] Collingwood himself advances his inquiry by formulating three new questions: what is the distinction in art which resembles the distinction between means and end but is not identical with it, what is the relationship between art and emotion, and what is the kind of making which is involved in art?[16]

After a long discussion, in which he carefully employs his philosophical method, Collingwood provisionally answers the last two questions by stating that art expresses emotions by creating an imagination.[17] On this basis he formulates three new questions: what is emotion?, what is imagination?, and what is the connection between them?, to be answered in Book II. Book I thus shows a meticulous application of *An Essay on Philosophical Method* in recasting the theory of art into a form of history. Throughout the book, Collingwood draws philosophical distinctions wherever they are lacking, as, for example, in the identification of art with craft, magic, and amusement. Along the same lines he challenges pure distinctions by showing that they do not meaningfully describe artistic experience. Typically, both the critical and the constructive parts of Collingwood's analysis proceed by asking and answering questions, which shows that his philosophical method is intrinsically related to the logic of question and answer.

In Book II, Collingwood again employs his method, focusing on the notion of the scale of forms. Starting from the two extremes in the scale of consciousness, feeling and thinking, he tries to establish imagination as an intermediary form. With this aim Collingwood enters the field on which the Italians had played a major role. Though he is well aware of this, he does not mention them or his other predecessors too often, not because he dismisses them, but because, as he says in the preface, he has something of his own to say.[18] Given this aim, it is not surprising that Collingwood brings the notion of overlap into play in order to establish his own theory of the relationship between feeling, imagination, and thought.

The distinction between feeling and imagination, to begin with, has much in common with both Croce's and Gentile's theories. In this context, Collingwood, like Croce in his essays on aesthetics from 1917 to 1920, distinguishes between feeling and imagination; feeling is the flux of immediate emotions, imagination is the expression of emotions. But for Croce emotions only exist in so far as we become conscious of them by expressing them; an unexpressed emotion is not a real emotion.[19] Along the same lines, Gentile only recognised emotions in their

---

[15] Ibid., 106.

[16] Ibid., 108.

[17] Ibid., 151.

[18] Ibid., vi.

[19] See chapter 6, pp. 169–170.

actuality, that is, emotions of which we are aware by expressing them.[20] Collingwood agrees with Croce and Gentile that we become conscious of our feelings
by expressing them. But, since we express emotions as a function of our 'selective attention', a part of our emotions always remains unexpressed. Crucially,
and in contrast to the Italians, Collingwood does not infer from this that
unexpressed emotions are not real. On the contrary: unexpressed feelings have a
life of their own and have a definite function in the mind, though the mind is not
always conscious of this. Most importantly, when unexpressed feelings distort
the expression of other feelings they may even drive someone to complete insan-
ity.[21] It is of the highest importance, therefore, that one becomes conscious of his
feelings by expressing them. Unlike Croce and Gentile, Collingwood thus recognises the overlap between the unconscious and the conscious activities of the
mind.

The principle of overlap also guides Collingwood's discussion of the relationship between imagination and thought. Upon first sight, Collingwood's distinction between imagination as producing ideas and thought as producing relations
between ideas seems to repeat the first pages of Croce's *Estetica*. But for Collingwood this distinction is only the starting point for a more extensive analysis of
the overlap between imagination and thought. In this context, Collingwood
explicitly describes imaginative consciousness as 'thought in its absolutely fundamental and original shape', because, without it 'we should have no terms
between which intellect in its primary form could detect or construct relations'.[22]
As a form of thought, Collingwood says, imaginative consciousness has the
bipolarity that belongs to thought as such: 'this is how I feel' has the opposite
'this is not how I feel'.[23] Moreover, like thought, imaginative consciousness can
'err' and eventually lead to 'corrupt consciousness'.[24] In spite of these similarities
between imagination and thought, Collingwood does not identify these forms of
consciousness as Gentile tended to do. Like de Ruggiero, Collingwood does not
overlook that imagination is a special kind of thought with its own properties.
Like thought, imagination expresses truth, but not about the relationship
between things, but about individual things. For this reason, it does not proceed
inferentially, but by a dialectic of expression.[25]

On this basis, Collingwood presents emotions, imagination, and thought as a
scale of three overlapping forms of consciousness. The first overlap occurs
between emotions and imagination. Imagination selectively attends to emotions
and expresses them. In this process, it does not 'annul' the emotions, but
expresses them in a new form which brings about new emotions. The second

---

20 See chapter 8, p. 297.
21 R.G. Collingwood, *The Principles of Art*, 285.
22 Ibid., 216.
23 Ibid.
24 Ibid., 217.
25 Ibid., 288.

overlap occurs between imagination and thought. Imagination and thought are 'identical' in the sense that both exhibit the generic essence of consciousness. At the same time, they differ in kind (imagination and thought express a different kind of truth), in degree (the truth of thought is more certain than that of imagination), in opposition (the truth of imagination and thought may contradict each other), and in distinction (the truth of imagination and thought may express different truths). Furthermore, thought does not replace imagination, but builds on it, or, in other words, imagination is a constitutive element of thought. Finally, imagination has its own emotions and these emotions are therefore also 'taken up' and transformed by thought into the emotions of the intellect. From this it follows that thought in its secondary form, or *a priori* thought, is affected by the lower levels, with the consequence that it does not exist in some 'pure' way.[26]

In Collingwood's theory of language we find a corresponding overlap between the various forms of expression. Like Croce, Collingwood distinguishes between imaginative language, or poetry, and intellectual language, or prose. With imaginative language we express what we feel by saying something, with intellectual language we express what we think or mean by our words. But for two reasons poetry and prose cannot be separated. Firstly, imaginative language is conditioned by selective attention, from which it follows that imaginative language is also dependent on thought. Secondly, intellectual language builds on imaginative language. From this it follows that intellectual language can never be seen as pure symbolism.[27] On the basis of the same principle of overlap we cannot distinguish between sentences that express emotions and sentences that make statements; all sentences express emotions and make statements at the same time, but always different emotions and different statements.[28] Philosophers who try to separate emotions and thought are therefore committing the 'fallacy of the propositional assumption', according to which sentences express emotions or make statements, but never both.[29] On the basis of this assumption many philosophers make a false distinction between language proper and 'symbolism', or between the emotive use of language and the scientific use, in order to submit language to logical analysis.[30]

Collingwood's Theory of Understanding

Collingwood's philosophy of language has important implications for his theory of understanding, which is based on it. This theory needs discussion because Collingwood explicitly builds on it in *The Principles of History*. Collingwood

---

26 Ibid., 167–8.
27 Ibid., 225–6.
28 Ibid., 266–7.
29 Ibid., 260.
30 Rik Peters, 'Collingwood on Hegel's Dialectic', in *Collingwood Studies*, 2, 1995, 107–25.

expounds his theory of understanding as an analysis of speaking and hearing. In his view speaking is a single experience made of two elements. Firstly, there is a sensuous experience having an emotional charge of which the person who has the sensuous charge becomes conscious by attending to it, thus converting it into an idea. Secondly, there is a controlled bodily action by which he expresses this idea. These two elements occur simultaneously in a single act, which is an act of imagination by which we become conscious of our emotions by expressing them in some kind of language.[31] As an example Collingwood gives the case of a child who expresses his satisfaction at throwing off his bonnet and exclaiming 'hattiaw'.[32] According to Collingwood, the expression 'hattiaw' is a form of speech because the speaker is his own first hearer; the child is conscious of his own expression and of himself expressing it. The speaker is in a 'double situation'; as speaking he knows what he feels by expressing it in words, as hearing his own words he comes to know his emotions. The person to whom the expression is addressed, in this case the child's mother, knows this double situation and therefore speaks to the child with the words that he hears addressed to him, and thus constructs in herself the idea which the words express. On this basis Collingwood concludes:

> Understanding what someone says to you is thus attributing to him the idea which his words arouse in yourself; and this implies treating them as words of your own.[33]

On the basis of this thesis, Collingwood draws some important implications for his theory of understanding. Firstly, he points out that understanding is an act of the imagination and not an act of thought.[34] Secondly, since understanding is an act it is not based on the community of language: one does not first acquire a language and then use it; to possess and to use it are the same because language only exists as an act.[35] Thirdly, since understanding is an act of the imagination and not of thought, understanding does not proceed by inference, that is, it does not proceed by arguing on the basis of certain logical principles. From this it follows, in the fourth place, that there is no assurance that speaker and hearer understand each other. According to Collingwood, there is only a 'relative assurance' based on the fact that both parties are not talking nonsense to each other.[36] Finally, understanding is dependent on the imaginative capabilities of both hearer and speaker. In Collingwood's view, this implies that the speaker should not have a 'corrupt consciousness'; one must not deliberately direct one's attention to some emotions at the cost of disowning some others, because that will

---

31 R.G. Collingwood, *The Principles of Art*, 249–50.
32 Ibid., 239.
33 Ibid., 250.
34 Ibid., 251.
35 Ibid., 250.
36 Ibid., 250-1.

infect one's expression. The hearer from his side must have an impression corresponding to the idea which the speaker intends to convey. And, like the speaker, he should not suffer from corruption of consciousness, that is, the deliberate disowning of some emotions which will lead him to attributing the wrong idea to the words he hears.[37]

Collingwood's theory of overlapping forms of consciousness, and its corollary, the theory of understanding, form the basis of his own theory of art, by which he completes the recasting of aesthetics. The main thesis of his theory is that art is a form of language, which he expounds in Book III with a focus on its practical implications. The first implication is that art is a form of self-knowledge; by expressing his emotions in imagination, the artist comes to knowing himself, which is at the same time a making of himself in relation to his world.[38] The second practical implication is that the audience must be viewed as understander.[39] From this it follows that artists always collaborate with their audiences. By combining the two practical implications, Collingwood portrays the artist as a spokesman for his community, whose aim is to tell his audience the secret of its heart.[40] Thus Collingwood concludes: 'Art is the community's medicine for the worst disease of the mind, the corruption of consciousness.'[41] With this conclusion, Collingwood completes his recasting of aesthetics into a form of history. The reconstruction of the genesis of *The Principles of Art* provides a new set of principles by which he hopes to contribute to a solution of the problem of modern art. Collingwood's own solution to this problem is clear: though craft, representation, amusement, magic, and thought may be involved in art, art itself is none of these, but rather imaginative self-knowledge of the mind.

With this thesis Collingwood firmly established his own position with regard to his predecessors in aesthetics, and to his own earlier positions. For Collingwood, as for Croce, understanding, and *ipso facto* self-understanding, is an act of the imagination and not an act of thought. But, unlike Croce, Collingwood allows for conceptual elements in imagination and for imaginative elements in thought. For example, Archimedes' outcry 'eureka!' expresses the emotion of having made a scientific discovery.[42] At the same time, Collingwood does not merge the understanding of language and re-enactment of thought, as Gentile does. Collingwood's theory of understanding fuses understanding and re-enactment into a single whole. By the act of imaginative understanding we reach the level of 'ideas' but not yet the level of thought. Since there is no formal difference between the ideas which I form by myself and the ideas which I form

---

[37]   Ibid., 251.
[38]   Ibid., 291–2.
[39]   Ibid., 311.
[40]   Ibid., 336.
[41]   Ibid.
[42]   Ibid., 267.

through communication, it follows that the latter can form the object of subsequent thought. 'Understanding' is therefore the first and necessary phase in all communication; it yields 'ideas' which can serve as the object for the intellect, that is, the ideas function as terms between which the intellect tries to establish relations. We have seen above how this is done; the intellect relates terms by asking and answering questions. Just as I can ask questions about the lady I admire, I can ask questions about the lady that my friend admires; I simply continue his self-understanding for myself.[43]

The difference between Croce's, Gentile's, and Collingwood's theories of language is illustrated by their interpretations of Dante. As we have seen in chapter six, Croce, following his distinction between imagination and thought, tended to concentrate on the purely poetic passages at the cost of the more philosophical passages in the *Divina Commedia*. In contrast, Gentile saw the poem, including the alleged poetic passages, as an expression of Dante's philosophy. In contrast to both Italians, Collingwood merged the two views by presenting the *Commedia* as an expression of intellectual emotions; Dante has fused the Thomistic philosophy into a poem expressing how it feels to be a Thomist.[44]

With *The Principles of Art* Collingwood also completed his earlier views on the relationship between imagination and thought. In his 1935 inaugural lecture and in his 1936 epilegomena in the lectures on *The Idea of History*, he had analysed both forms of consciousness separately, now he describes them as aspects of a single cognitive process. The kernel of this philosophy of the mind is that thought begins in the imagination, which produces ideas by selectively attending to emotions. Next, the intellect produces relations between the ideas. This work of the intellect is inferential and proceeds on the basis of certain principles, which are the object of second-order thought. The most important implication of this philosophy of the mind is that, since imagination and thought are continuous, 'understanding' and 're-enactment' are also continuous.

The basis of Collingwood's theory of overlapping forms of consciousness is the principle of the living past, expressed in the logical principle of the overlap of classes; every 'lower' form of consciousness is taken up and survives in a 'higher' form of consciousness. However, in *The Principles of Art* Collingwood elaborates the overlap between the forms of consciousness in only one direction. Concentrating on the ways in which the lower forms are present in the higher, and in particular on the way in which emotions are modified by each level of consciousness, Collingwood does not explicitly deal with the problem of how the higher forms are present in the lower, though the principle of overlap demands this. Fortunately, Collingwood gives two clues for the interpretation of this overlap. Firstly, he shows that selective attention always occurs concurrently with thought while being modified by it in such a way as that combination

---

[43] Ibid., 288–9.
[44] Ibid., 295.

requires.[45] In *The Principles of Art*, Collingwood does not go further into this but it is clear that thought somehow guides selective attention. He does not give examples of this but, expanding on one of his own, we may think of the very plausible difference between the ways by which a child and an adult direct their attention to a passing car. Secondly, Collingwood gives an important clue for the way in which he understood the overlap between the first and second level of thought in his discussion of the philosophies of Berkeley, Hume, and Kant. According to Collingwood, Berkeley held that the laws of nature are without exception learned from nature, or in Collingwood's own terms, that they are all 'empirical laws, or laws of the first order, discovered and verified by noting the relations between sensa'.[46] In contrast to Berkeley, Hume and Kant showed that these first-order laws implied second-order laws which Kant called the 'principles of understanding'. According to Collingwood, this doctrine entails that sensa may be 'wild' relatively to the first-order laws, 'in the sense that the laws, as not yet known, give no account of its place in any family'.[47] But, relative to the second order laws, events, or sense, can never be wild in this sense, because no event can escape the second-order laws. For example, no event can escape the 'principle of understanding' that every event must have a cause. From this viewpoint, Kant discovered that there are no wild sensa relative to the second-order laws, and this discovery enabled him to explain their existence in a new way, which Collingwood formulates as follows:

> We are saying that certain sensa, though in the light of the second-order laws we know that they must admit of interpretation, have not yet been actually interpreted, and perhaps cannot be interpreted except through the discovery of first-order laws as yet unknown to us.[48]

This passage, though seldom discussed, is important in order to understand the higher forms of consciousness, and in particular the logic of question and answer, because it explains how we discover what we do not yet know. This discovery involves at least two elements; a 'wild sensum' and 'second-order' thought. It is only on the basis of the latter that we can discern the former as being 'wild'. Discerning 'wild sensa', then, is the first step in any inquiry, it is the first impetus for asking questions, which characterises first-order thought. In order to uncover the principles of thought, Collingwood continued his recasting of the science of the mind in *The Principles of History* and *An Essay on Metaphysics*.

---

45 Ibid., 204.
46 Ibid., 186.
47 Ibid.
48 Ibid., 186–7.

The Principles of History (1939)

On 14 February 1939, Collingwood wrote to his son: 'I have just begun writing *The Principles of History* which will go down to posterity as my masterpiece.'[49] However, Collingwood's editor Knox deemed the first chapters of the work unworthy of publication because the project had become 'impossible' or 'unnecessary'.[50] In his view, '*The Principles of History* was either a philosophical work, an attempt to describe what history is, and to explain how historical knowledge is possible, or else it was no more than autobiography'.[51] In Knox's view the first possibility was not open to Collingwood because he had resolved philosophy to history, but Knox remains silent concerning the second possibility.[52] When the manuscript of *The Principles of History* was found in 1995 Knox's verdict could immediately be rejected. According to the editors Dray and van der Dussen, there were no serious philosophical difficulties that prevented Collingwood from finishing *The Principles of History*. In their view the book remained unfinished because Collingwood did not have the time to complete it after his decision to write *The New Leviathan* in September 1939.[53] This view has been challenged by David Boucher who argued that Collingwood had serious difficulties in the final elaboration of the re-enactment theory, which eventually caused him to stop the project.[54]

In my view, Collingwood's project had become neither impossible nor unnecessary, as Knox claims, though he may have come across some difficulties, as Boucher says. However, seen from the perspective of Collingwood's development, and from the perspective of recasting the science of mind, there were no insurmountable problems. This claim can be corroborated by three arguments. Firstly, in *An Autobiography* Collingwood says that he developed his philosophy of history by exploring two kinds of problems. On the one hand, he focused on 'epistemological problems' which he centred around the question 'how is historical knowledge possible?', on the other hand, he explored 'metaphysical problems' which were concerned with the historian's subject matter: 'the elucidation of terms like event, process, progress, civilization, and so forth.'[55] *The Principles of History* follows the same plan. The scheme for the book, written on 9 February 1939, comprises an exposition of history as a science in order to explore its metaphysical underpinnings in the subsequent chapters on 'action', 'process', and

---

49   Cited by van der Dussen, *History as a Science*, 34.
50   Knox, 'Editor's Preface', xvii.
51   Ibid.
52   Ibid.
53   Van der Dussen, 'Collingwood's "Lost" Manuscript of The Principles of History', 36–9.
54   Boucher, 'The Principles of History and the Cosmology Conclusion to *The Idea of Nature*', 170.
55   R.G. Collingwood, *An Autobiography*, 77.

'change', to conclude with the conception of re-enactment and history as self-knowledge.[56]

Secondly, seen from the perspective of recasting the science of the mind, *The Principles of History* would complement the philosophy of mind of *The Principles of Art*, just as Croce's *Logica* complements his *Estetica*. Collingwood explicitly underscores this complementary relationship between the two books by stating that the 'science of aesthetic is an indispensable pre-condition to any science of historical method'.[57] Moreover, *The Principles of History* would have the same composition as *The Principles of Art*, which also indicates that Collingwood saw the two books as complementary. Book I of *The Principles of Art* was meant as a 'preliminary account of art'. Similarly, Book I of *The Principles of History* is intended as 'a simple account of the most obvious characteristics of history as a special science'.[58] In Book II of *The Principles of Art*, art is given its place among the other forms of consciousness. Book II of *The Principles of History* 'would be in the main an account of the relation of history to natural science and "the human sciences"'.[59] In Book III of *The Principles of Art*, Collingwood dealt with the practical consequences of his theory of art. Likewise, Book III of *The Principles of History* would deal with the practical implications of the philosophy of history, thus completing the recasting of the philosophy of history begun in the 1936 lectures on the history of *The Idea of History*.[60]

Thirdly, and most importantly, in his autobiography Collingwood had stressed the importance of the idea of the living past in his philosophy of history. Not only was this the basis of his metaphysics of process since the early 1920s, but it was also the principle which would make history truly relevant to practice; history was to inform people about the ways in which the past was encapsulated in the present in order to raise their action to a higher potential.[61] Along the same lines, the notion of the living past would have played a key role in *The Principles of History*. According to the scheme for the book, it was to be introduced in third chapter of Book I. The title of this chapter was 'Conception of Re-enactment, and Contrast the Dead Past and Completeness'. This heading suggests that Collingwood somehow identified re-enactment with the living past and incompleteness. Seen in the light of the rapprochement between theory and practice, as expounded in *An Autobiography*, this section would then have provided the basis for the third part of *The Principles of History* in which Collingwood would have dealt with the practical implications of the philosophy of his-

---

[56] R.G. Collingwood, *The Principles of History*, 245–6.

[57] Ibid., 52.

[58] Ibid., 245–6.

[59] Ibid.

[60] Ibid.

[61] R.G. Collingwood, *An Autobiography*, 106.

tory. This third part would thus be the prelude to the book on ethics and politics that would be the next in the series.

According to the scheme for the book, the central point in the final part of *The Principles of History* would be the idea that history negates the distinction between theory and practice because, unlike science, which presupposes its object, history enacts it, entailing that it is not an object at all. On this basis, Collingwood would have worked out a distinction between a scientific society which turns on the idea of mastering or serving people, and an historical society which turns on the idea of understanding them.[62] In conformity with his programme of recasting the science of mind, Collingwood would thus have worked out the practical implications of his philosophy of history. Again this shows that Collingwood never gave up his project; on the contrary—facing death he redoubled his efforts.

Unfortunately, Collingwood never had an opportunity to finish *The Principles of History* as he intended. Significantly, the remaining manuscript breaks off at the point where he would expound the crux of his entire philosophy of history, in the chapter called 'The Past', where he lays down the first principle of the idea of the living past, the idea which had guided his life's work. How, then, would Collingwood have completed his *magnum opus*? I will answer this question by interpreting the completed chapters, by drawing from Collingwood's development, and focusing on his relationship with the Italians, whose philosophy of history he had always valued.

From this point of view, the first thing of note is that Collingwood intended *The Principles of History* to replace three epilegomena that followed the lectures on the history of *The Idea of History* of 1936. These lectures end with 'scientific history' culminating in Croce's philosophy of history. Part I of *The Principles of History* builds on this, by stating that history is a science *sui generis*. For Collingwood, as for de Ruggiero, 'science' meant a body of organised thought, proceeding as a systematic process of questions and answers. It is this sense of 'science' Collingwood employs in chapter 1 of *The Principles of History* to analyse the activities of historians. After a comparison of scientific and historical inference he illustrates his thesis on the basis of a mini-detective story with the title 'Who Killed John Doe?' Collingwood invents this story in order to illustrate his contention that 'the questioning activity is the predominant factor in history as it is in all scientific work'.[63]

Seen in the light of Collingwood's philosophy of mind, the first chapter of *The Principles of History* deals with first-order thought. This becomes clear in the second chapter, entitled 'Action', where Collingwood explicitly refers to his theory of understanding in *The Principles of Art*. Collingwood starts by pointing out that historians ask questions about '*Res gestae*, deeds, actions done in the

62 R.G. Collingwood, *The Principles of History*, 246.
63 Ibid., 29.

past'.[64] Restricting action to deeds expressing thought, and noticing that thought is always expressed in language, Collingwood concludes that 'evidence is in the nature of language or of a notation of language'.[65]

In the section 'Evidence as language', Collingwood further elaborates this idea by fusing the notion of understanding to the historian's questioning activity. In this context, he points out that the relationship between historical evidence and the conclusions drawn from it, historical knowledge, is the relationship between what such things 'say' and 'what it means'.[66] To find out what things say is an aesthetic process, Collingwood says.[67] This process is not history proper but an essential preliminary to history. The aesthetic act of 'reading' or 'finding out' what the evidence says is, in itself, not inferential but furnishes the premises for the historical inference.[68] Being an aesthetic act, finding out what the evidence says forms the basis of the historian's autonomy. The starting point of any genuinely historical argument is therefore not 'this person, or this printed book, or this set of foot prints, says so-and-so', but 'I, knowing the language, read this person, or this book, or these footprints, as saying so-and-so'.[69] Since this act is autonomous, it follows that the evidence is always an experience of the historian himself; 'an act which he has performed by his own powers and is conscious of having performed by his own powers; the aesthetic act of reading a certain text in a language he knows, and assigning to it a certain sense'.[70] On this basis Collingwood concludes that 'the historian does not find his evidence but makes it, and makes it inside his own head'.[71]

With this conclusion Collingwood stands the common sense view of history on its head. The ordinary view of history is that we discover the evidence and construct history. Contrary to this Collingwood holds that it is the other way around; we make the evidence and discover history. This view is in line with the objective idealism Collingwood had employed in his philosophy of history since 1933; only if historical facts are 'eternal objects' can the historian truly discover them. From this perspective, the Italian idealist view that facts are not discovered but constructed amounts to subjective idealism.

Collingwood's analysis of the relationship between reading the evidence and historical inference, that is, between finding out what the evidence says and what the evidence means, complements the theory of understanding of *The Principles of Art*. What we get by reading the evidence is 'ideas' or 'terms' which form

---

64   Ibid., 40.
65   Ibid., 49.
66   Ibid.
67   Ibid., 52.
68   Ibid., 53.
69   Ibid., 54.
70   Ibid., 54.
71   Ibid. 54; R.G. Collingwood, *The Idea of History*, 251.

the object of first-order thought, which relates them on the basis of second-order principles. From this it follows, that the way in which the historian questions his findings from reading the evidence is conditioned by the principles of second-order thought, that is, the principles of history. In other words, the way in which the historian relates his reading of the evidence in order to answer his questions is dependent on his idea of metaphysical notions such as 'action', 'event', 'process', and so forth. Vice versa, these notions also condition what the historian will see as a 'wild sensum', or in historical terms, as new and unexpected evidence or facts.

In Collingwood's view, the most important of these principles is the idea of freedom, which follows from the historian's discovery of his autonomy with regard to the evidence and eventually entails the discovery of free agency in the past. This discovery provides Collingwood with a basis for distinguishing nature and history, and to reject all forms of historical naturalism. In this context, he polemises with Alexander, who reduces nature to history, and with Marx who reduces history to nature.[72] To illustrate the difference between nature and history, Collingwood compares the work of an archaeologist to a geologist in order to show that the former is always concerned with thought processes and the latter only with natural processes.[73] At the end of these discussions Collingwood concludes as follows:

> All history is the history of thought. To know about events and names and dates, which for the scissors-and-paste historian is the end of historical inquiry, is for the scientific historian merely its means; merely the collection of what he hopes will prove capable of being read as language, and thus lead to the only thing that truly is historical knowledge: insight into the mind of the person or persons who at a certain time and in certain circumstances did the action which, merely as something that has happened, is called an event.[74]

In this passage, Collingwood repeats the first of the three fundamental propositions of his philosophy of history as expounded in *An Autobiography*, which clearly shows that Collingwood had not changed his mind on this issue. However, in contrast to the previous statements of the first principle of his philosophy of history, Collingwood now includes emotions in the realm of thought. In this context, he gives the example of an officer who builds a fort in the course of a campaign and argues that the historian should take the emotions of the officer into account in order to understand his action. Fortifications are a protection against dangers and providing protection against danger will be accompanied by certain emotions.[75] In this context, Collingwood warns that not all of the officer's emotions should be taken into account but only those for which we

---

[72] R.G. Collingwood, *The Principles of History*, 56-7, 103-7.
[73] Ibid., 61-2.
[74] Ibid., 67.
[75] Ibid., 63.

have evidence and which are related to his thought. Collingwood summarises this point as follows:

> All history is the history of thought. This includes the history of emotions so far as these emotions are essentially related to the thoughts in question: not of any emotions that may happen to accompany them; nor, for that matter, of other thoughts that may happen to accompany them.[76]

Dray and Boucher have wondered about this inclusion of emotions in the theory.[77] But seen from the perspective of Collingwood's development and the principle of the living past it follows straight from the philosophy of mind as expounded in *The Principles of Art*. There he had argued that the lower levels of consciousness are not superseded but taken up and absorbed into the higher levels of consciousness. From this it follows, firstly, that feelings and emotions do not disappear when thought begins but that they 'live on' in thought, conditioning and colouring it. Secondly, it follows that an historian, who tries to understand thoughts, must also take past emotions into account.

According to his scheme for the book, Collingwood would at this point have passed to a discussion of re-enactment. Instead, he extends the discussion on the relationship between nature and history in a long chapter on 'Nature and Action', which would have been the subject of Part II of *The Principles of History*. In this context he discusses the 'science of human nature' and 'psychology', and he dedicates a long section to the relationship between action and natural environment and another section to the dispute between Hegel and Marx on this matter.[78] The conclusion of this discussion runs as follows:

> The action which history studies is 'free', not determined by natural conditions but determined by itself. The discovery that this is so is a discovery intimately related to the discovery that historical thought is 'free' or autonomous, i.e. not dependent upon natural science for the solutions of the problems that arise out of its subject-matter, but able and obliged to solve all such problems for itself. The so-called problem of human freedom solves itself, the moment history becomes a science.[79]

With this statement Collingwood lays the basis for Part III of *The Principles of History* where he would have dealt with the practical implications of the distinction between science and history. In that context Collingwood would have explained that 'a scientific morality will start from the idea of human nature as a thing to be conquered or obeyed: a historical one will deny that there is such a

---

[76]   Ibid., 77.
[77]   W.H. Dray, 'Broadening the Subject-Matter in *The Principles of History*', in *Collingwood Studies*, 4, 1997, 2–33; Boucher, 'The Principles of History and the Cosmology Conclusion to *The Idea of Nature*', in *Collingwood Studies*, 2, 1995, 166–7.
[78]   R.G. Collingwood, *The Principles of History*, 103–7.
[79]   Ibid., 109.

thing, and will resolve what we are into what we do'.[80] Given this aim, it is not surprising that Collingwood continues his analysis with a long section on 'Freedom'. The kernel of Collingwood's argument is again that the idea of freedom is intimately related to *The Idea of History*:

> The discovery that the men whose actions he studies are in this sense free is a discovery which every historian makes as soon as he arrives at a scientific mastery of his own subject. When that happens, the historian discovers his own freedom: that is, he discovers the autonomous character of historical thought, its power to solve its own problems for itself by its own methods. He discovers how unnecessary it is and how impossible it is for him, as a historian, to hand these problems over for solution to natural science; he discovers that in his capacity as historian he both can and must solve them for himself. It is simultaneously with this discovery of his own freedom as historian, that he discovers the freedom of man as a historical agent. Historical thought, thought about rational activity, is free from the domination of natural science, and rational activity is free from the domination of nature.[81]

On this point, Collingwood is gathering more ammunition for Part III. By stipulating that the idea of freedom and the idea of history mutually presuppose each other, Collingwood, in conformity with his programme in 'Human Nature and Human History', chooses history and not the human sciences for the realisation of the rapprochement between theory and practice in a free society. Or, in the words of the scheme for the book, a society that turns on the idea of mutual understanding will be based on history and not on human science.

The distinction between science and history as a basis for action is also a central theme in *An Autobiography*. In that context, he points out that science can only provide us with 'ready-made' rules, whereas history can give us an 'insight' into the situation at hand.[82] Interestingly, it is exactly at this point that Collingwood introduces the idea of the living past in relation to action, arguing that 'high potential action' requires insight into the living past.[83] Seen from the perspective of his autobiography, it is not surprising that Collingwood continues the section on freedom with a chapter entitled 'The Past', which would have been the cornerstone of *The Principles of History*.

According to the scheme, the chapter would have contrasted re-enactment with the dead past or completeness, thus implying an identification of re-enactment with the living past.[84] We will never know how Collingwood viewed this identification because the chapter is not complete. The beginning, however, is most promising. Along the lines of his philosophical method, Collingwood starts with a distinction of two senses of 'the past'. In the first sense, we contrast the

---

80 Ibid., 246.

81 Ibid., 101.

82 R.G. Collingwood, *An Autobiography*, 101.

83 Ibid., 106.

84 R.G. Collingwood, *The Principles of History*, 245–6.

past with the present as something distant in time. But there is a second sense of the past where the past also belongs to the present. Collingwood illustrates the second sense of the past as follows:

> A man who takes refuge in medieval charters from his thoughts about a threatening letter from a solicitor or a notice printed in red from the collector of taxes, brought him by the morning's post, or from disquieting news in the daily paper, is not taking refuge from the present in the past. He is not taking refuge from actual life in history. For the letter or newspaper about which he refuses to think is an historical document. That is why he refuses to think about it. It is a matter of history that the solicitor has threatened him, that the tax-collector has demanded more money than he has in the bank, or that the affairs of his country have entered upon a dangerous crisis. What he is doing is to pick and choose among various trains of historical thought, repressing some which are unpleasant to him and concentrating upon others which involve him in no such discomfort. The disquieting letter or newspaper, it is true, belongs not only to the past, in the sense that the events it reports are yesterday's events, but also to the present, in the sense that it serves as a medium through which those events have an impact here and now on the reader's mind. But this does not remove it from the sphere of history. It only confirms its historical character. All historical evidence is a medium through which past events have an impact on the mind of the historian; medieval charters no less than solicitors' letters.[85]

The examples in the above passages have many similarities with the examples of the living past in Collingwood's autobiography. In that book, he had defined the living past as traces of a past process which are still 'active' in the present. The conclusion in the above passage stresses the same point: the past leaves traces in the present, thus forming a 'medium' through which past events have an impact on the present mind. Even more interesting is the fact that Collingwood identifies these traces with evidence in the above passage. When we combine this view with his thesis in his inaugural lecture that the whole perceptible world is in principle evidence to the historian, we may infer that the whole world may be seen as the living past. From this it follows that we are dealing with the living past every single moment of our lives; medieval charters, solicitor's letters, and tax bills are all 'media' through which the past effects our minds. And when we turn from the solicitor's letter or the tax bills to the medieval charters, we just exchange one train of historical thought for another. Reality is the living past.

In this context, it is important to note that the living past is not something occult but something very familiar. In his autobiography Collingwood stresses this familiarity of the living past with an example of a man who has given up smoking:

> He gives up smoking, but his desire to smoke does not thereupon disappear. In his subsequent life the desire is what I call encapsulated. It survives, and it

---

produces results; but these results are not what they were before he gave up smoking. They do not consist in smoking. The desire survives in the form of an unsatisfied desire. If, after a time, he is again found to be smoking, that need not prove that he never left off; it may very well be that he never left the desire, and when the reasons against satisfying the desire disappeared he began once more to satisfy it.[86]

The similarities of this example with the examples of the 'solicitor's letter' and the 'tax bill' in *The Principles of History* immediately grab one's attention. Firstly, the idea of the living past is closely related to emotions; the 'desire' to smoke and the 'fear' from the 'threatening letter' have an impact on the present mind. Secondly, both examples illustrate that people are able to refuse thinking about the 'living past'; one man may refuse to consider his desire to smoke, another may refuse to think about the disquieting letter. Thirdly, when this living past is not taken into account, we may come to the wrong conclusions. In the case of the smoker we will wrongly conclude that the man never gave up smoking. In the case of the solicitor's letters we will not be able to explain why the man, who was frightened by those letters in the morning, takes refuge in history in the afternoon. Finally, both cases show that Collingwood firmly believed that we are able to uncover the living past, even if it is hidden in the present. Historical inquiry will show that the smoker once gave up smoking, just as it may show that the man studying medieval charters is repressing his fear of the solicitor.

The examples of the living past in *An Autobiography* and in *The Principles of History* make the same point. Past and present are not outside one another but they are merged; hidden beneath the present lives a past which is alive and has an impact on us, both emotionally and cognitively. It takes a trained historical eye to discern this living past. Only by careful reconstruction of the historical background are we able to understand that someone is not just a smoker but also someone who once gave up smoking but could not resist the desire to smoke. Historical understanding involves understanding how the past lives on in the present.

True, it is still a long way from understanding the smoker and the reader of the solicitor's letter to understanding the complex social relationships in an historical society. But in this context we should not forget that Collingwood, true to his philosophical method, only expounded the most primitive instance of the concept of the living past. By 1939 Collingwood had already analysed much more complicated forms of the living past in his philosophy of mind, in his histories of the ideas, and in the problem of the survival of Celtic art, which he saw as the best example of the rapprochement between philosophy and history.[87]

Most importantly, in his autobiography Collingwood had already indicated the relationship between the living past and action by distinguishing two kinds

---

[86] R.G. Collingwood, *An Autobiography*, 141.
[87] R.G. Collingwood, *An Autobiography*, 137–45.

of situations where historical insight is needed. The first kind of situation occurs when there are no rules to deal with the situation, the second kind occurs when one decides not to follow the rules.[88] Collingwood illustrates the first situation with the example of dealing with one's tailor. Everybody, he says, has rules to deal with his tailor, but these rules only allow one to deal with him in his capacity as a tailor and not 'as John Robinson, aged sixty, with a weak heart and a consumptive daughter, a passion for gardening and an overdraft at the bank'.[89] Of course, one can take all these factors into account, but then one soon gets beyond the stage at which rules can guide action. Of the second kind of situation, when one decides not to follow the rules, Collingwood gives no examples, but one might think of the situations when one decides to act according to his conscience, thus fulfilling his own personal duty. In both cases, Collingwood says, insight in the situation is required, and this involves understanding how the past is encapsulated in the present and constitutes a part of it not initially clear to the untrained eye.[90] In the case of the tailor and the ex-smoker, it is clear what this means: if one wants to deal with them as individuals, one cannot rely on the rules, but must try to understand them. This understanding clearly involves the 'living past' of the tailor, comprising his weak heart, his relationship with his consumptive daughter, just as it comprises the smoking past of the ex-smoker. Along the same lines, if one decides to reject the rules because he wants to act in his own way, he must try to understand the living past in which he is acting. Collingwood gives no examples of this but his criticism in his autobiography of the Treaty of Versailles and the appeasement politics point in the direction of politicians who fail to control human situations because they do not take the living past into account.[91] Along the same lines, in *The New Leviathan* Collingwood settled his accounts with this kind of politician by exploring the living past of Western civilisation.

Finally, with *The Principles of History* Collingwood would also have completed the second part of his philosophy of the mind. In *The Principles of Art* Collingwood had shown that 'understanding' is an act of the imagination. On this basis, there is no guarantee that speaker and hearer understand each other in the sense that they know of each other and that they think the same thought. In *The Principles of History* Collingwood shows that this understanding forms the basis of the historian's autonomous questioning activity by which he determines what the evidence means. This higher form of understanding involves both the understanding of emotions and the understanding of the way in which the past conditions the present. With this theory, Collingwood would have stressed the importance of history for action, just as the Italians had always done. But at the

---

[88]   Ibid., 103–4.
[89]   Ibid., 104–5.
[90]   Ibid., 106.
[91]   Ibid., 90.

same time, he differs from them about the central function of history. Where the Italians stress that the historian must relive the past in the present, Collingwood stresses that the primary function of history is to discover how the past is hidden in the present. For Croce, reliving the past was a preparation for action, for Gentile it was identical to action; for Collingwood, the analysis of the living past is necessary for understanding how the present situation is conditioned by the past. With this theory, Collingwood paved the way for the rapprochement between theory and practice, but before he dealt with that subject, he first continued his project of recasting the science of mind in *An Essay on Metaphysics*.

An Essay on Metaphysics (1940)

Collingwood's interpreters have always wondered about the place of *An Essay on Metaphysics* in his work. According to Knox, this book signalled Collingwood's conversion to an extreme form of historicism and relativism, comparable to Croce's liquidation of philosophy by history.[92] Knox's views were challenged by Rubinoff and Mink who saw a continuity in Collingwood's development and in particular between *An Essay on Philosophical Method* and *An Essay on Metaphysics*. According to Rubinoff, there was no 'radical conversion' in Collingwood's later development because the idea of absolute presuppositions as expounded in *An Essay on Metaphysics* is found within a methodology that respects the notion of truth as a scale of forms in *An Essay on Philosophical Method*.[93] Along the same lines, Mink argued that Collingwood's development between 1933 and 1941 is 'a smoothly continuous and internally consistent fulfilment of the programme of the Essay on Philosophical Method'. In this context, he points out that *An Essay on Philosophical Method* expounds the nature and function of *a priori* concepts, whereas *An Essay on Metaphysics* deals with their development.[94] Rex Martin held that Collingwood's book does not identify absolute presuppositions with *a priori* concepts but contrasts 'objective patterns and structures in our way of knowing', which can be arranged in a modified scale of forms.[95] In his introduction to the new edition of *An Essay on Metaphysics*, Martin also states that there was no connection between Collingwood's notion of absolute presuppositions and his logic of question and answer.[96] Van Heeswijck suggests

---

[92] Knox, 'Editor's Preface', viii.

[93] Rubinoff, *Collingwood and the Reform of Metaphysics*, 235.

[94] Mink, *Mind, History and Dialectic*, 146.

[95] Rex Martin, 'Collingwood's Claim that Metaphysics is a Historical Discipline', in Boucher (ed.), *Philosophy, History and Civilization*, 224-7.

[96] Rex Martin, 'Editors Introduction' in R.G. Collingwood, *An Essay on Metaphysics, Revised Edition with an Introduction and additional material by Rex Martin*, Oxford, Clarendon Press, 1998, xxiii; Id., 'Collingwood's Logic of Question and Answer its Relations to Absolute Presuppositions: A Brief History', in *Collingwood Studies*, 5, 1998, 122-36; Rik Peters, 'Collingwood's Logic of Question and Answer, its Relation to Absolute Presuppositions: Another Brief History', in *Collingwood Studies*, 6, 2000, 1-28.

that *An Essay on Philosophical Method* expounds the material object of metaphysics, whereas *An Essay on Metaphysics* deals with its formal object; from which it follows that the traditional science of pure being is not incompatible with a study of absolute presuppositions.[97] Connelly and d'Oro have stressed the similarities between the notion of philosophical concepts in *An Essay on Philosophical Method* and the notion of absolute presuppositions in *An Essay on Metaphysics*.[98] These views have been challenged by M. Beaney, who claims that Collingwood's reform of metaphysics was a failure because, adapting his position to Ayer's logical positivism, he failed to distinguish between propositions and absolute presuppositions.[99] Finally, R.J. Festin holds that absolute presuppositions must primarily be seen as pre-reflective, pre-interpretive, and precognitive communal beliefs.[100]

We can cast some light on these issues by interpreting *An Essay on Metaphysics* as a continuation of Collingwood's project of recasting the science of the mind into a form of history. From this point of view, it becomes clear that, just like the previous books in the series, its primary aim is to solve a practical problem. From the beginning to the end, Collingwood presents the book as a defence of metaphysics against the ongoing onslaughts by psychology, and, above all, Ayer's neo-positivist attacks. Furthermore, the defence of metaphysics is explicitly based on an historical reconstruction of the genesis of the onslaught. Just as he had done in *The Principles of Art* and *The Principles of History*, Collingwood starts from common ideas about metaphysics as the science of being, which he traces to Aristotle. Finally, and most importantly, Collingwood solves the problem of metaphysics by truly recasting it into a form of history; metaphysics is not the science of pure being but rather an historical study of absolute presuppositions of experience.

It is this view of metaphysics as an historical science that has caused most trouble for Collingwood's interpreters because it seems to involve a liquidation of philosophy by history, resulting in a radical form of historicism. From the perspective of Collingwood's development, however, these worries are not justified. To begin with, Collingwood's reform of metaphysics into a form of history was not an invention of his later years. In fact, it went back to the 'Libellus' of 1920, where he replaced the metaphysics of being with his own metaphysics of

---

[97] Van Heeswijck, *Metafysica als een Historische Discipline*, 62–3. Id., 'Collingwood's Metaphysics: Not a Science of Pure Being, but Still a Science of Being', in *International Philosophical Quarterly*, XXXVIII.2, 1998, 162.

[98] Connelly and d'Oro, 'Editors' Introduction', lxx.

[99] Michael Beaney, 'Collingwood's Conception of Presuppositional Analysis', in *Collingwood and British Idealism Studies, Incorporating Bradley Studies*, 11, 2005, 41–114.

[100] Raymun J. Festin, 'Collingwood's Absolute Presuppositions and their Non-propositionality', in *Collingwood and British Idealism Studies, Incorporating Bradley Studies*, 14, 2008, 73.

becoming. As we have seen, this metaphysics enabled him to criticise both British and Italian philosophy as forms of 'realism' which he saw as a denial of reality as a process. But Collingwood's rejection of the metaphysics of being never entailed a liquidation philosophy by history. Throughout the 1920s Collingwood defended the universality of the forms of experience and of the philosophical concepts which describe them. In *An Essay on Philosophical Method* Collingwood elaborated this view into the logic of the overlap between empirical and philosophical concepts, which lay at the basis of all his philosophical investigations between 1933 and 1937. Completely in line with this development, Collingwood, when formulating his programme of recasting the science of the mind into a form of history, explicitly distanced himself from Croce's identity of philosophy and history; his programme did not employ philosophy as the method of history, but its aim was a 'mutual absorption' of philosophy of history. Accordingly, in his autobiography, Collingwood looked back on his life's work not as a service to the identity philosophy and history, but to the rapprochement between philosophy and history.

This rapprochement between philosophy and history accurately describes the view he had held since his musings on the Albert Memorial. From that defining moment in his life, Collingwood saw that philosophy is immanent in all forms of experience, though not explicitly, as the Italians held, but implicitly. From the distinction between the implicit and explicit it follows that philosophical understanding always follows experience, philosophy is always thought about thought, or second-order thought. For this reason, philosophical universality cannot be imposed on experience from without, but it is formed within experience. Furthermore, art has no aspects that are universal for all times and places, each time has its own form of art, based on its own principles. However, this view of the relationship between experience and principles does not exclude the universality of philosophical concepts but makes them dependent on history. For Collingwood this meant that philosophical concepts apply without exception to all times, but that each time has its own conception of universality. Collingwood most likely discovered this idea during his meditations on the Albert Memorial, to elaborate it in the 'Libellus', probably discussing it with de Ruggiero as 'the inversion of time'.[101] But again, for both Collingwood and de Ruggiero this 'inversion of time' never implied the rejection of universal principles. On the contrary, by showing the continuity between history and philosophy they sought to explain the universality of principles. From this perspective, Collingwood could both explore the history of art, showing which principles were necessarily presupposed in earlier periods, and subsequently describe *The Principles of Art* in his own times. Likewise, he could write a history of *The Idea of History*, expounding the principles upon which the idea history in

---

[101] See chapter 7, p. 178.

the past had rested, and expound *The Principles of History* of his own times. If Collingwood's philosophy was historicist, it was definitely not relativistic.

In the 1920s and early 1930s Collingwood had pursued philosophy in this historical way and, as we have seen, he could easily hold his position with regard to the British realists and Italian idealists. This changed, however, when Ayer published *Language, Truth and Logic* in 1936. Here was a most formidable opponent because, unlike the realists who based their theories of knowledge on simplified examples of thought, Ayer had a much more sophisticated view of science and its methods. Moreover, he intelligently employed this knowledge of science for rejecting metaphysics in a new way. Metaphysics was not true or untrue, Ayer held, but simply meaningless because metaphysical statements cannot be verified.[102] This criticism pierced the heart of Collingwood's entire project of writing a series on the philosophical principles of experience. This explains why, as Ayer reports, Collingwood said 'If I thought that Mr Ayer was right, I would give up philosophy'.[103]

Against Ayer's onslaught on metaphysics, Collingwood reacted as he had done all his life. Just as he had refuted the realist denial of becoming in the 'Libellus', by showing the priority of becoming over being, he refuted Ayer's attack on metaphysics by showing that it is historical science, and not a science of pure being. The crux of Collingwood's refutation lies in his distinction between propositions, which are verified, and absolute presuppositions, which cannot be verified. In this way, Collingwood saved absolute presuppositions from Ayer's attack but at the same time he took upon himself the burden of proving that absolute presuppositions are meaningful.

In this context, some interpreters have noted that Collingwood makes a second distinction between assumptions, which we make deliberately, and pre-suppositions, which we cannot make at will. Van Heeswijck rightly observes that this distinction is extremely important because if the patterns of thought are only assumptions without any reference to reality itself, Collingwood's reformed metaphysics would be impossible. If, however, our patterns of thought are presuppositions that somehow refer to reality, then metaphysics can answer questions of the meaning of reality.[104] In my view, this interpretation is correct, but it also raises the question of how exactly absolute presuppositions relate to reality.

So far, Collingwood's interpreters have not given a clear answer to this question because they have not been able to trace the origin of Collingwood's distinction between assumptions and presupposition. In my view, this distinc-tion can best be seen as a defence, not against Ayer's attack on metaphysics, but

102 A.J. Ayer, *Language, Truth and Logic*, Penguin Books, Harmondsworth, 1976, 56.

103 A.J. Ayer, *Part of My Life*, Oxford University Press, Oxford, 1978, 166.

104 Van Heeswijck, 'Collingwood's Metaphysics', 272.

against the Italian idealists' view of reality, in particular Gentile's. Two arguments corroborate this view. Firstly, it would make the argument in *An Essay on
Metaphysics* completely congruent to Collingwood's defence of the metaphysics
of becoming against the British and Italian forms of realism in the 'Libellus'.
Secondly, Collingwood's argument would be in line with Roger Holmes's *The
Idealism of Giovanni Gentile*, which was published in 1937 by Macmillan. Though
there is no direct evidence that Collingwood read this book, it is very plausible
that he was one of its anonymous referees.[105] But even if Collingwood did not
referee Holmes's defence of Gentile's metaphysics against the neo-positivists,
the book sheds an interesting light on *An Essay on Metaphysics*.

Like Collingwood, Holmes acknowledges the neo-positivist rejection of
metaphysics as the most formidable objection to metaphysics in general and to
Gentile's metaphysics of the pure act of thought in particular.[106] In this context,
Holmes remarks that from Gentile's perspective the metaphysics of the pure act
cannot be demonstrated because all demonstration entails a transcendent logos.
Transcendentism is the position which actualism explicitly rejects on the ground
that philosophy has no presuppositions. According to a neo-positivist, however,
this claim for a philosophy without presuppositions renders Gentile's metaphysics meaningless. In order to defend the metaphysics of the pure act against
this charge, Holmes demands that actualism makes a distinction between
assumptions and presuppositions in order to show that certain non-demonstrable propositions are meaningful. According to Holmes this distinction
enables actualism to acknowledge the necessity of 'initial assumptions' in philosophy without giving up its claim that philosophy has no presuppositions. At
the same time, the recognition that some non-demonstrable propositions are
meaningful will provide the proper perspective from which to view Gentile's
starting point that reality is identical to the pure act of thought. Despite the fact
that this identity cannot be demonstrated along neo-positivist lines, it is, in
Holmes's terms, 'important to living itself' because it is presupposed by all other
systems of thought.[107] In this context, Holmes points out that even the neo-
positivist identification of the meaningful with the verifiable presupposes a

---

[105] Collingwood was not the anonymous author of the very positive review of Holmes's
book in *The Times Literary Supplement* of 1937: a check of the archives of *The Times*
revealed that the author was a certain 'Wood'. But Holmes mentions that a reader of
his book's manuscript pointed out the need for further clarification of his use of the
term 'solipsism' in order to distinguish it from 'subjective idealism' and 'mentalism'
(1937, 112n2). This makes it plausible that Collingwood did read Holmes's book
because Collingwood used exactly the same terms in 'Central Problems in Metaphysics' on which he was working around 1935. Moreover, before becoming a Dele-
gate of the Clarendon Press, Collingwood used to read for Macmillan, and around
1935 he certainly counted as the only active British expert on Gentile, since J.A. Smith
retired in 1935.

[106] Holmes, *The Idealism of Giovanni Gentile*, 210.

[107] Ibid., 212–4.

system of value on the basis of which it proceeds.[108] This value is established by the act of thought, and from this it follows that even the neo-positivist presupposes the metaphysics of the act of thought, whereas the metaphysics of the pure act itself is without presuppositions.[109] Finally, after this rescue operation of the metaphysics of the pure act of thought, Holmes most radically demands that actualism should give up the unwarranted presupposition of the Transcendental Ego: 'when the full expression of reality comes to be the "act of thinking", the Ego must necessarily fall with the Noumenon and the Absolute into disuse.'[110]

To a large extent, Collingwood's defence of metaphysics against the neo-positivist charges takes the same line of argument. Like Holmes, Collingwood makes a distinction between assumptions and presuppositions and he acknowledges a realm for metaphysical statements which are not true or false, yet are meaningful. Moreover, Collingwood's position undermines the notion of a universal transcendental ego, which is in line with Holmes's rejection of this notion and with his own position in the 'Libellus'.

But the differences between Holmes's and Collingwood's defences of metaphysics are even more interesting. Firstly, Holmes demands a distinction between assumptions and presuppositions in order to defend Gentile's metaphysics against the neo-positivists, whereas Collingwood calls for a distinction between propositions and suppositions. In this context, Collingwood remarks that although all assumptions are suppositions, all suppositions are not assumptions because assumptions are a matter of free choice, whereas suppositions are made unawares.[111] Secondly, Holmes acknowledges only one kind of presupposition, whereas Collingwood distinguishes relative presuppositions from absolute presuppositions in order to defend metaphysics against the neo-positivist attack. Thirdly, and most importantly, Holmes defends Gentile's view that metaphysics has no presuppositions whereas Collingwood most emphatically rejects this view:

> This is the greatest nonsense. If metaphysics is a science at all it is an attempt to think systematically, that is, by answering questions intelligently disposed in order. The answer to any question presupposes whatever the question presupposes. And because all science begins with a question (for a question is logically prior to its own answer) all science begins with a presupposition. Metaphysics therefore, either has presuppositions or is no science. The attempt at a metaphysics devoid of presuppositions can only result in a metaphysics that is no science, a tangle of confused thoughts whose confusion is taken for a merit.[112]

---

108 Ibid., 215.
109 Ibid., 211, 142.
110 Ibid., 226.
111 R.G. Collingwood, *An Essay on Metaphysics*, 27.
112 Ibid., 63.

Though this passage does not explicitly refer to Gentile's metaphysics, it certainly applies to it, for the Italian had always defended the view that the metaphysics of the pure act of thought is without presuppositions. In Gentile's view, the metaphysics of the pure act of thought is 'absolute'; it cannot be founded, verified, and has no history, since founding, verifying, and corroborating postulate principles that transcend thought. From this perspective, Gentile deconstructed all previous metaphysics as *logo astratto*, that is, as thought presupposing realities transcending the act of thought. In my view, this is the position Collingwood attacks in the above passage. In his view, metaphysics, being an historical science, shares its presuppositions with history, that is, metaphysical concepts like 'action', 'event', 'process' mentioned in *An Autobiography* and *The Principles of History*. Moreover, its results can be verified, all statements about presuppositions made in the past can be tested by historical evidence. Finally, since the absolute presuppositions of history change in time, metaphysics as an historical science would also change in time; every metaphysician will interpret the history of metaphysics from his own point of view.

To many interpreters this view of metaphysics as an historical discipline amounts to a liquidation of philosophy by history, resulting in scepticism and relativism. Even to Gentile, though one of the most historically minded philosophers of all times, Collingwood's position would have appeared as a form of radical historicism. He would have replied to Collingwood that the latter's reformed metaphysics presupposes the metaphysics of the act of thought because the metaphysician cannot deny that he is thinking.

To all these charges Collingwood had replies, though he does not elaborate them explicitly in *An Essay on Metaphysics*. To the charge of relativism Collingwood would have responded that the development of absolute presuppositions is not arbitrary but follows the logic of question and answer; people raise and answer questions in order to live. Although the question and answer activity, being based on the imagination, has a certain spontaneity, it develops in reaction to specific historical circumstances. For this reason it does not proceed in a random way, which is why we can discern a logic in it, though only with the benefit of hindsight.

Collingwood also formulated a response in *The New Leviathan* to the charge that his metaphysics presupposes the pure act of thought. Discussing whether the historical study of modern mind presupposes the theory of the pure act, Collingwood dryly remarks: 'You can have your cake and eat it too by holding that mind is "pure act", so that the question what mind is resolves itself without residue into the question what mind does; but whether this is defensible I shall not ask.'[113] In spite of this humorous tone, Collingwood was not making a joke here. From his perspective, the thesis that mind is pure act is an absolute presupposition which cannot be defended by demonstration or verification. But this

---

[113] R.G. Collingwood, *The New Leviathan*, 61.

does not mean that absolute presuppositions cannot be defended at all. In *An Essay on Metaphysics* Collingwood gives an example of a pathologist whose presuppositions are questioned by an inquirer. In the end, when questioned about the presupposition that everything that happens has a cause, the pathologist will 'blow up right in your face, because you have put your finger on one of his absolute presuppositions, and people are apt to be ticklish in their absolute presuppositions'.[114] However, Collingwood remarks, the more 'civil and candid' answer is:

> That is a thing we take for granted in my job. We don't question it. We don't try to verify it. It isn't a thing anybody has discovered, like microbes or the circulation of the blood. It is a thing we just take for granted.[115]

This example shows how absolute presuppositions are defended: not by verification but by showing that they are presupposed in a science, that is, by showing that they enable scientists to do their work. In other words: absolute presuppositions are defensible as long as they enable us to continue our question and answer activity. When this activity is blocked, for example when we cannot find an answer to our questions, or when two answers contradict each other, we must revise our presuppositions, first our relative presuppositions and eventually our absolute presuppositions. This historical metaphysics not only applies to the sciences but also to philosophy. Like all other 'sciences of the mind' philosophy develops by raising and answering questions on the basis of historically determined presuppositions. *E pur si muove* is the motto of Collingwood's philosophy.

From this point of view we can finally answer the crucial question of how absolute presuppositions relate to reality. The first thing to notice here is that absolute presuppositions take various forms following the overlapping forms of consciousness. From this it follows that the status of absolute presuppositions is dependent on the point of view from which we observe them. When we observe absolute presuppositions in practice, they appear as the self-evident beliefs upon which we think and act, as the example of the pathologist shows. When we observe absolute presuppositions from the perspective of second-order thought, as most interpreters have done, absolute presuppositions appear as the *a priori* concepts of first-order thought, that is, as the necessary principles upon which our question and answer activity are based. But seen from the perspective of first-order thought, absolute presuppositions are not explicit; even in 'high grade thinking' like history and science, we raise and answer questions without always being aware of making presuppositions, let alone absolute presuppositions. In fact, as soon as we start asking ourselves why we think what we think as historians or scientists, we move to second-order thought, or 'thought about thought'.

---

[114] R.G. Collingwood, *An Essay on Metaphysics*, 31.
[115] Ibid.

On this point we can raise Collingwood's own question: how far down the scale can we go? What is the form of absolute presuppositions 'below' first-order thought? Seen in the context of Collingwood's own philosophy of mind, this question brings us to the level of 'imagination'. In my view there are at least four reasons why imagination must be seen as the origin of absolute presuppositions. Firstly, Collingwood identified the imagination with the consciousness, which he describes in *The Principles of Art* as 'thought in its absolutely fundamental and original shape'.[116] Secondly, consciousness is the 'activity of thought without which we should have no terms between which intellect in its primary form could detect or construct relations'. Given Collingwood's later identification of this activity with asking and answering questions, it follows, in terms of *An Essay on Metaphysics*, that the ideas of consciousness have 'logical efficacy' to raise questions. Thirdly, already in his inaugural, Collingwood noted a close relationship between what he then called 'innate ideas' and 'the imagination'. Finally, and most importantly, the imagination is the birthplace of all meaning. By imagining human beings give the first meaning to reality, and this is exactly what presuppositions do; underneath thought, they give meaning to reality by imagining it. Absolute presuppositions are the *fons et origo* of all meaning: they are the first semantic distinctions by which the human mind gives meaning to existence.

This reading of the origin of absolute presuppositions comes close to Mink's, who held that the imagination as 'the theoretical consciousness in its most embryonic form' produces 'concepts'.[117] Mink, however, did not make the link to absolute presuppositions because he understood the concepts of imagination as particular, and absolute presuppositions as general. In his view, the content of a 'concept' of the imagination is not redness, but 'this particular red'.[118] But in Collingwood's eyes, this reduction of the content of concepts to particular sense data fails to do justice to the richness of the imagination. As an heir to Vico and his Italian successors, he also viewed a poem, a myth, or a painting as a form of cognition. From this viewpoint, the primary form of absolute presuppositions is created when, for example, the imagination of prehistorical man gives meaning to the thunder by naming it Jove, or when a modern scientist imagines the existence of a new particle. Seen from this perspective, absolute presuppositions are not pre-cognitive beliefs, but the primary form of cognition. As such, they do not consist of general concepts, but of concrete imaginative ideas. The meaning of these ideas is not theoretical but poetical; they do not refer to this or that reality, but to their own imaginative world. As such, they form the basis of first-order thought which relates them in terms of propositions, that is, as answers to questions, thus implicitly taking them as categorical, universal, and necessary prin-

---

[116] R.G. Collingwood, *The Principles of Art*, 216.
[117] Mink, *Mind, History and Dialectic*, 94.
[118] Ibid., 95.

ciples. Prehistoric men build an entire 'constellation' of questions and answer on the idea of Jove, and so do modern scientists on the basis of the idea of a particle. Only at the stage of second-order thought do the implicit principles of first-order thought become explicit.

This interpretation of the nature and function of absolute presuppositions enables us to see how Collingwood could have completed his philosophy of mind. In *The Principles of Art* Collingwood had shown that the raising of questions involves a confrontation between a 'wild sensum' and 'second-order' thought; it is only on the basis of the latter that we can discern the former as being 'wild'. When facing a 'wild sensum', second-order thought compels first-order thought to find new answers to our questions.[119] Transposed to *An Essay on Metaphysics* this means that wild phenomena only exist in view of our presuppositions and compel us to raise new questions until we find the right answer. But if we do not find the right answer to our questions, we will have to revise our absolute presuppositions. This revision always involves an act of the imagination. Before a philosopher, scientist, or historian starts asking 'what if', he has already imagined a new world. Examples of this can be found in all of Collingwood's works. In Anaximenes the surprising fact that a man can blow hot and cold finally induced him to give up Anaximander's notion of indeterminate primary matter.[120] In his discussion of Vico's philosophy in *The Idea of History*, Collingwood points out that Descartes' sceptical questions had no meaning for Vico, which led him to formulate the *verum factum* principle for his own philosophy.[121] In the third epilegomenon to the lectures on *The Idea of History*, Collingwood discusses the dialectic of questions and answers, under the heading of 'progress' in a more general way, giving many examples of how unsolved problems give rise to a revision of presuppositions. But the example Collingwood himself was most proud of was his discovery that the problem of the revival of Celtic art could only be solved by adopting the principle of the living past.[122]

After completing his philosophy of mind along these lines, Collingwood could also have extended his theory of understanding. In *An Essay on Philosophical Method* Collingwood had indicated two central questions for the interpretation of thoughts: 'what does it mean?' and 'is it true?' In *The Principles of Art*, and in *The Principles of History*, Collingwood pointed out that these questions presuppose an answer to the question: 'what does it mean?' To this question we get an answer by using our imaginative understanding. By treating the words of another as our own and by imaginatively attributing the idea that the words of another arise in ourselves, we come to understand the other. This non-

---

119 See chapter 10, pp. 371–2.
120 R.G. Collingwood, *The Idea of Nature*, 38.
121 R.G. Collingwood, *The Idea of History*, 66.
122 R.G. Collingwood, *An Autobiography*, 145.

inferential process forms the basis for answering the second question: 'what does it mean?' In order to find out what words mean, we must re-enact the thought which is expressed in them. In practice, this amounts to inferentially reconstructing the questions to which the words or actions were meant as an answer. Finally comes the question 'is it true?' In this context, it is important to note that Collingwood always took 'true' in the sense of 'right'; the principle for discriminating 'true' from 'false' thoughts is not correspondence, or coherence, but continuity: if the answer enables us to continue our own question and answer activity it will be accepted as 'right'.[123] If the answer does not enable us to continue our question and answer activity, it will be confined to a different plane; though it can be accepted as an answer to past questions, it will not be accepted as an answer to our present questions. By thus putting the thoughts into an historical perspective of questions and answers, its presuppositions can be relegated to a specific place on a scale of forms. Along these lines, the notions of 'utility', 'right', 'duty' can be arranged in a scale of forms as historically specific answers to the question 'what is good?' Most importantly, the final criterion in this arrangement is not theoretical but practical. In the end, our judgment of whether an answer enables us to continue our questioning activity is dependent on how we view the situation. Ultimately, practice decides what we take as right and wrong. Collingwood himself expressed this insight by his rapprochement between theory and practice, to which he devoted his last book.

The New Leviathan (1942)

On the day Collingwood returned to England from a journey in the Mediterranean, the Second World War broke out. Collingwood immediately stopped working on *The Principles of History* and began to write *The New Leviathan* as a contribution to the war effort. Suffering from deteriorating health, and working under immense time pressure, Collingwood decided to state his views in the form of short numbered theses on index cards which eventually formed the basis of the book. Probably due to this particular form and the fact that it was published during the war, *The New Leviathan* never attracted much attention from Collingwood's interpreters. To Knox the book represented Collingwood's radical historicism. Knox could only appreciate Collingwood's application of his philosophical method to ethics, and his 'defence of our (sic!) civilised way of life'.[124] Interestingly, though accepting Knox's account of Collingwood's later development, Alan Donagan stressed that '*The New Leviathan* exemplifies philosophy as a form of thought distinct from history no less than the Essay on Philosophical Method'.[125] Rubinoff and Mink mainly interpreted Collingwood's last book as a further specification of the philosophy of mind expounded in *The*

---

[123] R.G. Collingwood, *An Autobiography*, 37.
[124] Knox, 'Editor's Preface', xxii.
[125] Donagan, *The Later Philosophy of R.G. Collingwood*, 12, 16.

Principles of Art. With the publication of the new edition of *The New Leviathan*, David Boucher completely changed the perspective, by his claim that the book is 'the outcome of his life-long attempt to bring about a rapprochement between theory and practice'.[126] Along the same lines, James Connelly states that '*The New Leviathan* exhibits "in action" the unity of the method and subject matter of philosophy as conceived respectively by the Philosophical Method and Metaphysics'.[127]

Seen from the viewpoint of Collingwood's development, *The New Leviathan* was his last and most radical attempt to recast the science of mind into a form of history. More clearly than in the previous books of his series, Collingwood intended to solve a practical problem. In the preface to the book, he explicitly presents the book as a contribution to the war effort. The method by which Collingwood proceeds in *The New Leviathan* is more outspokenly historical than in his previous books: in several places Collingwood declares himself to be a devotee of the 'historical plain method'. Finally, and most importantly, by writing a philosophical history of modern civilisation, Collingwood explicitly intends to make part of that history and to contribute to it, thus achieving a complete rapprochement between theory and practice.

From this perspective, *The New Leviathan* relates history to practice as described in his autobiography, and as intended in Book III of *The Principles of History.* Faced with the war, Collingwood specifies the diagnosis he had already made in 1919: the situation is a revolt against civilisation. In view of this revolt, Collingwood takes on the role of the 'trained woodsman' who guides his fellow citizens by unveiling the hidden past in the present. In this context, Collingwood is especially concerned that the barbarisation of Germany went on 'underground', almost like a 'landslide' so that no one could explain it thoroughly, even if one wished.[128] Collingwood wants to open the eyes of his readers, and given the fact that barbarism is something historical, this can only be done in an historical way, that is, by reminding of how the principles of modern civilisation came into being, and how they live on in the present.[129]

In *The New Leviathan* the trained woodsman takes the form of the scientific historian, who, like all scientists, limits his objective: 'Take time seriously... NOW, choose where to begin your attack. Select the problems that call for immediate attention.'[130] The problem that calls for immediate attention is the

---

[126] David Boucher, 'Editor's Introduction', in R.G. Collingwood, *The New Leviathan or Man, Society, Civilization and Barbarism, Revised Edition, Edited and Introduced by David Boucher*, Clarendon Press, Oxford, 1992, xxiii.

[127] James Connelly, *Metaphysics, Method and Politics, The Political Philosophy of R.G. Collingwood*, Imprint Academic, Exeter, 2003, 43.

[128] R.G. Collingwood, *The New Leviathan*, 377.

[129] Ibid.

[130] Ibid., 254.

war; Collingwood wanted to show modern Europeans what they are fighting for in Part V by contrasting the barbarism, and in particular 'German Barbarism' in Part IV, with 'Modern Civilisation' in Part III. But since the notion of civilisation presupposes the notion of 'society', which in turn presupposes the notion of 'man', Collingwood starts with the latter. Behind this scheme lies Collingwood's notion of society and mind as a scale of forms, which enables him to arrange his questions from the higher forms to the lower as a series of presuppositions: in order to understand what we are fighting for, we need to know what civilisation is, but since the notion 'civilisation' presupposes what 'society' is, and 'society' presupposes what 'man' is, we must begin with man.

In the first chapters of the book, Collingwood, along the lines of his philosophical method, draws an important distinction between man as body and man as mind. Leaving the study of man as body to the natural sciences, he chooses to study man as mind. Mind is made up of thought, but thought has many forms, which Collingwood explores as a scale of forms, detailing the account of the forms of consciousness in *The Principles of Art*. The backbone of the scale of forms of the mind is the 'law of primitive survivals' which Collingwood formulates as follows:

> When A is modified into B there survives in any example of B, side by side with the function B which is the modified form of A, an element of A in its primitive or unmodified state.[131]

Seen from the perspective of Collingwood's development, this is just a more radical formulation of the principle of the living past because it stresses that the earlier form lives on unmodified in a later form. But like the principle of the living past, the law of primitive survival makes it clear that in order to understand form B you have to first understand from what state it modified, in this case A, in order to understand how A lives on in B.

The law of primitive survivals permeates *The New Leviathan*. Firstly, since people think in order to act, a practical element is always present in a case of theoretical reason.[132] Secondly, the lower forms of the mind, like feeling, appetite, hunger, love, passion, live on in choice and reason.[133] Thirdly, in all forms of civilisation some barbarism survives and this explains why a revolt against civilisation is possible.[134] Finally, and this is one of the most startling applications of the notion of the living past, Collingwood takes all the history of the modern European mind, including his own mind, as evidence for his inquiry.[135] Though most historians would follow Collingwood in taking many different forms of evidence for a history of civilisation, very few would take their own minds as

---

131 Ibid., 65.
132 Ibid., 100.
133 Ibid., 65–6.
134 Ibid., 283–4.
135 Ibid., 62.

evidence as an instance of civilisation as a whole. Yet, Collingwood's claim is perfectly compatible with the principle of the living past, which entails that reality, including one's own mind, can be seen as a field of evidence left by the past. From this point of view, one can study how reason works by studying how other people make arguments, for example in books, or by studying one's own arguments: all are products of the living past.

In order to unveil the living past of modern civilisation, Collingwood follows the 'historical plain method', which is based on two principles. Firstly, it rejects all 'science of substance': 'It does not ask what mind is; it asks only what mind does.'[136] Secondly, 'it renounces all attempt to discover what mind always and everywhere does, and asks only what mind has done on certain definite occasions'.[137] In this context, Collingwood remarks that the historical plain method does not exclude generalisations. The first principle can also be stated in terms of the theory of the mind as pure act, and the second does not exclude the question of what mind always and everywhere does. But Collingwood, taking his principle of the limited objective seriously, does not ask whether these positions are defensible. Along the same lines, Collingwood does not explore 'the essence' of things but only their 'relative essence', which he defines as the essence from a particular point of view.[138]

In this context, it is important to note that Collingwood does not deny the defensibility of the theory of the mind as pure act and the universality and necessity of principles of the mind, or the notion of essence; given the situation at hand, he simply does not ask the question. But according to the principle of the inversion of time it is perfectly legitimate to ask what should be considered as the universal and necessary principles of mind or civilisation at a particular point in history. In fact, Collingwood himself had raised these questions in *The Principles of Art* and in *The Principles of History*. Moreover, in 'What Civilisation Means' Collingwood discusses the possibility of a 'third-order ideal' of civilisation, which is 'the logical source of all other ideals of civilized conduct' being 'absolutely unqualified' in itself.[139]

Since it is Collingwood's aim to contribute to the war effort, he does not discuss the idea of civility as such, but only qualifies the particular ideals of modern civilisation. In *The New Leviathan* this takes the form of an historical analysis of the principles which are 'peace and plenty', 'law and order', and above all 'dialectics'.[140] Since Plato, dialectical thinking has been recognised as the way in which the intellect could find its way about in a Heraclitean world, which is a world of becoming. It gave rise to the distinction between eristical and

---

136 Ibid., 61.
137 Ibid.
138 Ibid., 300.
139 Ibid., 494.
140 Ibid., 181–2, 207, 304–7, 326–42.

dialectical discussions, the former being discussions in which each party tries to prove that he was right and the other wrong, whereas dialectical discussions aim to show that both parties can be right. Dialectics is also the way by which non-social communities, or communities in the state of nature, turn into societies.[141] Finally, in modern civilisation dialectics is the way in which to settle disputes about war and peace and law and order.

On this basis Collingwood defines barbarism as 'hostility towards civilisation'. It is 'the effort, conscious or unconscious, to become less civilized than you are, either in general or in some special way, and, so far as in you lies, to promote a similar change in others'.[142] After a review of the most important forms of barbarism, from the Saracens to the Germans, Collingwood finishes his book by expressing his expectation that the current barbarism will end because all champions of barbarism have withered away in the very hour of their victory.[143]

With this last line Collingwood completed the rapprochement between theory and practice, thus realising the ideal of a new science of human affairs he had been dreaming of since the First World War. For Collingwood, this new science was history, and it was to this science that he had devoted his life. In this life, he had been inspired by many of the great thinkers from Plato to White-head. But above all, Collingwood was influenced by the great Italian philosophers, from Vico to de Ruggiero. Italian philosophy raised many of Collingwood's questions, but his answers were definitely his own.

---

[141] Ibid., 183.
[142] Ibid., 342.
[143] Ibid., 387.

Conclusion:
The Living Past

Croce, Gentile, de Ruggiero, and Collingwood bequeathed a great legacy to posterity. Their highest hope was that future generations would use their thought to solve their own problems. Croce explicitly ended his *Filosofia dello spirito* by offering it as a 'strumento di lavoro' ('instrument for work'), and Collingwood claimed that he had laid the foundations of the future with his new science of human affairs. However, posterity was not well disposed to the legacy of the four and left the tools almost unused. After the Second World War, Croce's philosophy was considered as old-fashioned idealism and Gentile's was easily pushed aside as the philosophy of Fascism. De Ruggiero's contributions to systematic philosophy were already forgotten during his life, and after his death most of his historical works underwent a similar fate. Before long, the idealist heritage was regarded as a field for specialists. Italian philosophy thus lost contact with its own history and therefore with its own identity.

The fate of Collingwood's legacy was not much different. In the 1950s and 1960s bits and pieces of his philosophy of history were employed in the discussion on the nature of explanation in the social sciences and history. With the rise of narrativism in the 1970s Collingwood's star began to dwindle. Narrativists still acknowledged the relevance of his ideas for historical research, but they no longer thought them important for historical writing. With this excuse, philosophers of history gladly left the rest of Collingwood's philosophy of history to specialists.

Though everyone is free to choose the tools one needs, it should not be forgotten that if all you have is a hammer, everything looks like a nail. From the time that philosophers of history turned to techniques of literary criticism in the 1970s, all history began to look like a narrative. By focusing on historical writing, they gradually lost other aspects of historical practice out of sight. As a result of this, philosophy of history gradually estranged from practising historians, historical method, and above all from the historical experience of the general public. It was only by sudden 'turns' that other aspects such as historical experience, memory, presence were brought to attention. After all these turns, however, the time has come to integrate the fields in the philosophy of history.

In this context, the philosophies of Croce, Gentile, de Ruggiero, and Collingwood have much to offer. In the first place, the four philosophers were all practising historians who had first-hand experience of historical method, and in Collingwood's case also of archaeological method. For this reason they did not develop their philosophy of history by reading books, but by reflecting on their on their own practice as historians. In this context, the insistence of the four that imagination and thought are continuous, with the implication that aesthetics and philosophy of history complement each other, may throw new light on the continuity of historical research and historical writing.

In the second place, the three Italians had first-hand experience with political practice which gave their thought on the relationship between history and action a very sharp edge; the Italian wrote and reflected about history in order to make it; historical thought and action were continuous. Since Collingwood shared this idea with the Italians, his philosophy of history should be interpreted in its light; 'all thought exists for the sake of actions' is the motto of his philosophy.

Finally, and most importantly, the four philosophers deeply believed in the historicity of reality. At the core of this belief lay their conviction that the past is not dead, but living. To a large extent the philosophies of Croce, Gentile, de Ruggiero, and Collingwood can be regarded as the elaboration of this single idea. If it is insisted that their philosophies should have a name, the most appropriate would be 'pragmatic historicism'. Central to this form of historicism is the idea of the living past in which thought and action are united. From the perspective of this idea, each of the four philosophers offers interesting starting points for a further integration of the philosophy of history.

Croce's philosophy may be seen as a vindication of the empirical sense of the notion of the living past. All his life he emphasised the importance of the tangible traces left by the past in the present. It is this past that Croce tried to capture in his work as an erudite historian and literary critic, regarding knowledge of this past as the indispensable basis for practice. In this context, he stressed the importance of the relation between the practical interests of daily life for history. On this basis, he showed that historical questions arise from practical problems, which can be solved by constructing their history on the basis of evidence. Along these lines, Croce regarded reality as a construction of historical thought; reality is a product of the historical way of looking at things. In this reality there is no place for a transcendent God, an extramundane will, or 'providence', but only for human action, which is completely transparant to historical thought. The highest aim of historical thought is therefore 'historical catharsis', which 'liberates' man from the burden of the past. With this theory Croce drew his idea of the living past to its ultimate practical consequence: mankind has to think historically in order to live.

Although Gentile agreed to a large extent with Croce's idea of the living past, his own ideas of history were dominated by his experience as an historian of philosophy. As a specialist in this field, Gentile saw philosophy as an act of thought that develops itself by criticising its own past. Here lies the origin of Gentile's actualism, which may be seen as a metaphysics of mind, and, in particular, as a metaphysics of the historical mind. For Gentile reality is a product of historical thought: present thought always thinks about past thought which it generates for itself by a free act. This is the basic idea of Gentile's *etica del sapere,* which identifies thought and action. From this point of view, historical thought is a creative contribution to the reality of which it is part. This idea had both a tolerant and an intolerant side. On the one hand, Gentile showed that two individuals can and must understand each other by rethinking each others thought. On the other hand, Gentile believed that individual thought presupposed some supra-individual philosophical foundation. It was this idea that led him to a narrow presentism in his philosophy of history, and eventually to a defence of Fascism in his political philosophy. Only at the end of his life Gentile rediscovered his true self with the idea that all thought is essentially a dialogue.

De Ruggiero's idea of the living past differed in one important respect from that of Croce and Gentile. From the beginning of his career de Ruggiero acknowledged that reality can be seen from different perspectives, and in his histories of philosophy he showed himself a master in understanding perspectives that differed from his own. Accordingly, the *etica dello storicismo* prescribes that we try to understand each other as individuals in the function of our own individuality. Applied to the past, this principle yielded the important idea of 'inversion of time', according to which the present does not merely constitute a past for itself, but puts both the past and itself in a perspective; the more we identify ourselves with the past, the more we distinguish it from ourselves. The same principle also lies at the basis of de Ruggiero's conception of liberal method in his *Storia del liberalismo europeo* in which he shows that liberty can only expand on the basis of historical understanding.

Collingwood always agreed with the Italians that the past lives on in the present, but whereas the Italians did not conceive of a past outside the act of thought, he clearly saw that the past can live on even if we are not aware of it. This view of the living past was rooted in his religious beliefs and in his experience as an archaeologist, and it formed the core of Collingwood's process metaphysics, his philosophy of mind, and his philosophical method. If he had lived longer, the idea of the living past would have formed the basis of Collingwood's philosophical system, as its remains show. In *The Principles of Art* Collingwood showed how the lower orders of consciousness live on in the higher orders; feeling, emotion, imagination, thought, and action form a continuous whole. In the *Principles of History* Collingwood would have showed how the historian can understand how the past is encapsulated in the present, but at the very point he began to write about this, he stopped working on the book. However, both in *An Essay on Metaphysics* and in *The New Leviathan* Collingwood showed how to employ the notion of the living past in practice. In the first book, he shows how to discover how past presuppositions live on in present constellations of questions and answers. In *The New Leviathan* he shows in practice how to uncover the 'primitive survivals' of modern civilisation in order to make political action more effective.

Taken together, the philosophies of the four are not dead, but still living. Not in the sense that we can read their books and discuss them but because the problems they had to cope with are still confronting our times. The four philosophers bequeathed a rich toolbox to deal with these problems. But before we use these tools, we first need to know what they made for. This book is meant as a first step in that direction.

Bibliography

Primary Sources

Annotations contain the full title, publisher, first year of publication, and the edition from which the work is cited in the text. For the sake of convenience, the year of first publication is repeated in the left column.

Works by Croce Cited in the Text

1891   *I teatri di Napoli*, Pierro, Napoli, 1891, cited from *I teatri di Napoli*, Adelphi Edizioni, Milan, 1992.

1893   'La storia ridotta sotto il concetto generale dell'arte', in *Atti della Accademia Pontaniana*, XXIII, 1893, cited from *Primi Saggi*, Laterza, Bari, 1919, 3–41.

1894   'Di alcuni obiezioni mosse a una mia memoria sul concetto della storia', in *Atti della Accademia Pontaniana*, XXIV, 1894, reprinted and revised as 'Noterelle polemiche', in *Il concetto della storia nelle sue relazioni col concetto dell'arte. Ricerche e discussioni*, Loescher, Roma, 1896, cited from *Primi Saggi*, Laterza, Bari, 1919, 46–59.

1895   'Intorno alla storia della cultura (Kulturgeschichte)', in *Atti della Accademia Pontaniana*, XXV, 1895, cited from *Conversazioni Critiche, serie prima*, Laterza, Bari, 1918.

1896   'Intorno all'organismo della filosofia della storia', in *Il concetto della storia nelle sue relazioni col concetto dell'arte. Ricerche e discussioni*, Loescher, Roma, 1896, cited as 'Intorno alla filosofia della storia', in *Primi Saggi*, Laterza, Bari, 1919, 67–72.

1896   'L'arte, la storia, e la classificazione generale dello scibile', in *Il concetto della storia nelle sue relazioni col concetto dell'arte. Ricerche e discussioni*, Loescher, Roma, 1896, cited as 'Sulla classificazione dello scibile', in *Primi Saggi*, Laterza, Bari, 1919, 60–67.

1896   'Sulla concezione materialistica della storia', in *Atti della Accademia Pontaniana*, XXVI, 1896, reprinted in *Materialismo storico ed economia marxista*, Sandron, Milan, 1900, cited from *Materialismo storico ed economia marxista*, terza edizione economica, Laterza, Bari, 1978, 1–19.

1897   'Per la interpretazione e la critica di alcuni concetti del marxismo', in *Atti della Accademia Pontaniana*, XXVII, 1897, reprinted in *Materialismo storico ed economia marxista*, Sandron, Milan, 1900, cited from *Materialismo storico ed economia marxista*, terza edizione economica, Laterza, Bari, 1978, 53–104.

1900 *Materialismo storico ed economia marxista*, Sandron, Milan, 1900, cited from *Materialismo storico ed economia marxista*, terza edizione economica, Laterza, Bari, 1978.

1902 *Estetica come scienza dell'espressione e linguistica generale*, Sandron, Milan, 1902, cited from 9th edn. Laterza, Bari, 1950, textual differences with the 1902 edn. have been checked.

1902 'Les études relatives à la théorie de l'histoire en Italie, durant les quinze dernières années', in *Revue de Synthèse historique*, 1902, cited from *Primi Saggi*, Laterza, Bari, 1919, 177–192.

1905 *Lineamenti di una logica come scienza del concetto puro, Memoria letta all'Accademia Pontaniana*, Giannini, Napoli, 1905.

1907 *Ciò che è vivo e ciò che è morto della filosofia di Hegel*, Laterza, Bari, 1907, cited from *Saggio sullo Hegel*, Laterza, Bari, 1927, 1-143.

1909 *Logica come scienza del concetto puro*, Laterza, Bari, 1909, cited from 5th edn. 1928.

1909 *Filosofia della Pratica, Economica ed Etica*, Laterza, Bari, 1909, cited from 6th edn. 1950.

1911 *La filosofia di Giambattista Vico*, Laterza, Bari, 1911, cited from quarta edizione economica, Laterza, Bari, 1980.

1913 'Intorno all'idealismo attuale', in *La Voce*, V, n.46, 1913, cited from *Conversazioni Critiche, serie seconda*, Laterza, Bari, 1918, 67–82.

1914 *Cultura e vita morale, Intermezzi polemici*, Laterza, Bari, 1914, cited from 2nd edn. 1926.

1917 *Teoria e storia della storiografia*, Laterza, Bari, 1917, cited from 6th edn. 1948.

1918 'Il carattere di totalità della espressione artistica', in *La Critica*, XVI, 1918, cited from *Nuovi Saggi di Estetica*, Laterza, Bari, 1926, 117–134.

1918 'L'arte come creazione, e la creazione come fare', in *Atti della Accademia Pontaniana*, XLVIII, cited from *Nuovi Saggi di Estetica*, Laterza, Bari, 1926, 147–156.

1918 *Contributo alla critica di me stesso, Edizione di 100 esemplari fuori commercio*, reprinted in *Etica e politica*, Laterza, Bari, 1931, cited from *Etica e politica*, Laterza, Bari, terza edizione economica, 1981, 309–355. This autobiography was written in 1915.

1918 *Conversazioni Critiche, serie prima*, Laterza, Bari, 1918.

1918 *Conversazioni Critiche, serie seconda*, Laterza, Bari, 1918.

1919 *Primi Saggi*, Laterza, Bari, 1919.

1919 'Sulla filosofia teologizzante e le sue sopravvivenze', in *Atti della Accademia Pontaniana*, XLIX, 1919, cited from *Nuovi Saggi di Estetica*, Laterza, Bari, 1926, 341–358.

1920 *Ariosto, Shakespeare, e Corneille*, Laterza, Bari, 1920.

1920 *Nuovi Saggi di Estetica*, Laterza Bari, 1920, cited from 2nd edn. 1926.

1920   *La poesia di Dante*, Laterza, Bari, 1920.

1922   'Arte e critica', in *La Critica*, XX, 1922, 55–64.

1922   *Aesthetic, As Science of Expression and General Linguistic,* translated by Douglas Ainslie, Macmillan, New York, revised edition 1922, 133–134. The translation was revised by Collingwood, see his letter to de Ruggiero of 22 November 1921, Dep. 27.

1924   'Politica in nuce', in *La Critica*, XXII, 1924, 129–154, cited from *Etica e politica*, Laterza, Bari, terza edizione economica, 1981, 171–203.

1924   'Storia economico-politica e storia etico-politica', in *La Critica*, XXII, 1924, cited from *Etica e politica,* Laterza, Bari, terza edizione economica, 1981, 225–234.

1925   *Storia del Regno di Napoli*, Laterza, Bari, 1925.

1925   'La protesta contro il "Manifesto degli intelletuali fascisti"', in *La Critica*, XXIII, 1925, cited from Valeri, Nino (ed.), *La lotta politica dall'unità al 1925. Idee e documenti*, Monnier, Florence, 1973.

1925   Review of 'R.G. Collingwood, *Speculum Mentis or the Map of Knowledge*', in *La Critica*, XXIII, 1925, 55–59.

1926   *Cultura e vita morale, Intermezzi polemici*, seconda edizione raddopiata, Laterza, Bari, 1926.

1927   'Il presupposto filosofico della concezione liberale', in *Atti dell'Accademia di Scienza morali e politiche della Società reale di Napoli*, L, 1927, cited from 'La concezione liberale come concezione della vita', in *Etica e politica*, Laterza, Bari, terza edizione economica, 1981, 235–243.

1928   *Storia d'Italia dal 1871 al 1915*, Bari, Laterza, 1928.

1929   *Storia del età barocca in Italia*, Laterza, Bari, 1929.

1930   'Antistoricismo', in *La Critica*, XXVIII, 1930, 401–409.

1931   *Etica e politica*, Laterza, Bari, 1931, cited from *Etica e politica*, Laterza, Bari, terza edizione economica, 1981.

1932   *Storia d'Europa nel secolo decimonono*, Laterza, Bari, 1932, cited from quarta edizione economica, Laterza, Bari, 1981.

1937   'Come nacque e come morì il marxismo teorico in Italia (1895–1900). Da lettere e ricordi personali', in *La Critica*, XXXVI, 1937, 35–52, 109–124, cited from *Materialismo storico ed economia marxista*, terza edizione economica, Laterza, Bari, 1978, 253–294.

1938   *La storia come pensiero e come azione*, Laterza, Bari, 1938, cited from the quarta edizione economica, Laterza, Bari, 1978.

1946   'In commemorazione di un amico inglese, compagno di pensiero e di fede, R.G. Collingwood', in *Quaderni della Critica*, 4, 1946, cited from *Nuove pagine sparse*, I, Laterza, Bari, 1948, 25–39.

1948   *Nuove pagine sparse*, Laterza, Bari, 1948.

1956   'Note autobiografiche', in *Etica e politica,* 4th edn. Laterza, Bari, 1956, cited from *Etica e politica,* Laterza, Bari, terza edizione economica, 1981, 357–373. These notes were written in 1934.

1981   *Lettere a Giovanni Gentile, (1896–1924),* Arnaldo Mondari Editore, Milan, 1981.

Manuscript by Croce

1912   'Letter to Collingwood' about 1912 in Collingwood's personal copy of *La filosofia di G.B. Vico,* 1911. In private possession of Ms. Smith.

Works by Gentile Cited in the Text

If not otherwise stated, all citations are from the *Opere Complete* (abbreviated as *OC*) published by Sansoni and Le Lettere, Florence.

1896   'Arte sociale', in *Helios,* 3, 1896, cited from *Frammenti di estetica e di teoria della storia,* I, *OC* XLVII, Le Lettere, Florence, 1992, 251–261.

1897   'B. Croce, il concetto della storia nelle sue relazioni col concetto dell'arte', in *Studi Storici,* 6, 1897, cited from *Frammenti di estetica e di teoria della storia,* II, *OC* XLVIII, Le Lettere, Florence, 1992, 121–135.

1897   'Una critica del materialismo storico', in *Studi Storici,* 6, 1897, cited from *La filosofia di Marx,* Sansoni, Florence, 1974, 11–58.

1899   'La filosofia della prassi', in *La filosofia di Marx,* Spoerri, Pisa, 1899, cited from *La filosofia di Marx,* Sansoni, Florence, 1974, 59–165.

1898   'Rosmini e Gioberti. Saggio sulla filosofia italiana del risorgimento', in *Annali della R. Scuola Normale Superiore di Pisa, Filosofia e Filologia,* 1898, cited from *Rosmini e Gioberti, OC* XXV, Sansoni, Florence, 1958.

1899   *La filosofia di Marx,* Spoerri, Pisa, 1899, cited from *La filosofia di Marx,* Sansoni, Florence, 1974.

1899   'Il concetto della storia', in *Studi Storici,* 8, 1899, cited from *Frammenti di estetica e di teoria della storia,* I, *OC* XLVII, Le Lettere, Florence, 1992, 1–52.

1900   *L'insegnamento della filsofia ne' licei, Saggio pedagogico,* Sandron, Milan, 1900.

1901   Review of 'B. Croce, Tesi fondamentali di un'estetica come scienza della espressione e linguistica generale', in *Giornale storico della letteratura italiana,* XXXVIII, 1901, cited from *Frammenti di estetica e di teoria della storia,* I, *OC* XLVII, Le Lettere, Florence, 1992, 56–59.

1903   Review of 'B. Croce, Estetica come scienza dell'espressione e linguistica generale', in *Giornale storico della letteratura italiana,* XLI, 1903, cited from *Frammenti di estetica e di teoria della storia,* I, *OC* XLVII, Le Lettere, Florence, 1992, 72–86.

1906   'Il problema della filosofia della storia', in *Atti del Congresso internazionale di scienze storiche, Roma 1-9 Aprile, 1903'* vol. III, Accademia dei Lincei,

Roma 1906, cited from *Frammenti di estetica e di teoria della storia*, II, *OC* XLVIII, Le Lettere, Florence, 1992, 141–146.

1906 'La teoria dell'errore come momento dialettico e il rapporto tra arte e filosofia', cited from *Frammenti di estetica e di teoria della storia*, I, *OC* XLVII, Le Lettere, Florence, 1992, 86–94. The exact date of this paper is not known; Gentile wrote it for private use after reading the proofs of Croce's *Ciò che è vivo e ciò che è morto della filosofia di Hegel*, 1907, and published it in 1921 (see Bellezza Vito A., *Bibliografia degli scritti di Giovanni Gentile*, Sansoni, Florence, 1950, 78). Gentile mentions it in a letter to Croce of 13 January 1907, see Gentile, G., *Lettere a Benedetto Croce, Volume terzo, dal 1907 al 1909*, Sansoni, Florence, 1976, 19n2.

1908 'Il concetto della storia della filosofia', in *Rivista filosofica*, XI, 1908, cited from *La riforma della dialettica hegeliana*, Sansoni, Florence, 1975. This is Gentile's Inaugural in Palermo delivered in 1907.

1909 'Le forme assolute dello spirito', in *Il modernismo e i rapporti tra religione e filosofia*, Laterza, Bari, 1909, cited from *Il Modernismo e i rapporti fra religione e filosofia*, *OC* XXXV, Sansoni, Florence, 1962.

1909 *Il modernismo e i rapporti tra religione e filosofia*, cited from *Il Modernismo e i rapporti fra religione e filosofia*, *OC* XXXV, Sansoni, Florence, 1962.

1909 'Il circolo della filosofia e della storia della filosofia', in *La Critica*, VII, 1909, cited from *La riforma della dialettica hegeliana*, Sansoni, Florence, 1975, 138–149.

1911 Review of 'J. Delvaille, *Essai sur l'histoire de l'idée de progrès jusqu'à la fin du XVIIIe siècle*', cited as 'Il concetto del progresso', cited from *La riforma della dialettica hegeliana*, Sansoni, Florence, 1975, 174–182.

1912 'L'atto del *pensare* come atto puro', 1912, in *Annuario della Biblioteca filosofica di Palermo*, I, 1912, cited from *La riforma della dialettica hegeliana*, Sansoni, Florence, 1975, 183–195.

1913 *La riforma della dialettica hegeliana*, Principato, Messina, 1913, cited from 4th edition, Sansoni, Florence, 1975.

1913 *Sommario di pedagogia come scienza filosofica. I: Pedagogia generale*, Laterza, Bari, 1913, cited from *Sommario di pedagogia come scienza filosofica, I: Pedagogia generale*, *OC* I, Sansoni, Florence, 1970.

1913 'Il metodo dell'immanenza', in *La riforma della dialettica hegeliana*, Principato, Messina, 1913, cited from *La riforma della dialettica hegeliana*, Sansoni, Florence, 1975, 196–232.

1913 'Intorno all'idealismo attuale', in *La Voce*, 50, 1913, cited from *Frammenti di filosofia*, *OC* LI, Le Lettere, Florence, 1994, 33–58.

1914 *Sommario di pedagogia come scienza filosofica, II: Didattica*, Laterza, Bari, 1914, cited from *Sommario di pedagogia come scienza filosofica. I: Pedagogia generale*, *OC* I, Sansoni, Florence, 1970.

1915 'L'esperienza pura e la realtà storica', in *Libreria della Voce*, Florence, 1915, cited from *La riforma della dialettica hegeliana*, Sansoni, Florence, 1975, 233–262. This is Gentile's Inaugural in Pisa delivered in 1914.

1916 *I fondamenti della filosofia del diritto, in Annali delle ùniversità toscane, nuova serie*, 1916, I.5, cited from *I fondamenti della filosofia del diritto*, OC IV, Le Lettere, Florence, 1987.

1916 *Teoria generale dello spirito come atto puro*, Mariotti, Pisa, 1916, cited from *Teoria generale dello spirito come atto puro*, OC III, Le Lettere, Florence, 1987.

1917 *Sistema di logica come teoria del conoscere*, Vol I, Spoerri, Pisa, cited from *Sistema di logica come teoria del conoscere*, OC V, Sansoni, Florence, 1964.

1918 'Nuove idee estetiche di B. Croce', in *Il resto del carlino*, 27 July 1918, cited from *Frammenti di estetica e di teoria della storia*, I, OC XLVII, Le Lettere, Florence, 1992, 103–108.

1919 *Guerra e fede*, Riccardo Ricciardi Editore, Napoli.

1919 *Il tramonto della cultura siciliana*, Zanichelli, Bologna, 1919.

1920 *Dopo la vittoria*, Società Editrice La Voce, Roma, 1920, cited from *Dopo la vittoria*, OC XLIV, Le Lettere, Florence, 1989.

1920 'B. Croce, "Sulla filosofia teologizzante e le sue sopravvivenze"', in *Giornale critico della filosofia italiana*, I, 1920, cited as 'La filosofia teologizzante e B. Croce', cited from *Frammenti di filosofia*, OC LI, Le Lettere, Florence, 1994, 140–142.

1920 'Il torto e il diritto delle traduzioni', in *Rivista di cultura*, I, 1920, cited from *Frammenti di estetica e di teoria della storia*, I, OC XLVII, Le Lettere, Florence, 1992, 108–114.

1922 *Sistema di logica come teoria del conoscere*, Vol II, Laterza, Bari, 1922, cited from *Sistema di logica come teoria del conoscere*, Vol II, OC VI, Le Lettere, Florence, 1987.

1923 *I profeti del risorgimento italiano*, Vallecchi, Florence, 1923, cited from 3rd edn., Sansoni, Florence, 1944.

1923 'Il mio liberalismo', in *Nuova politica liberale*, I, 1925, cited from *Politica e Cultura*, I, OC XLV, Le Lettere, Florence, 1990, 113–116.

1924 *Preliminari allo studio del fanciullo*, de Alberti, Roma, 1924, cited from *Preliminari allo studio del fanciullo*, OC XLII, Sansoni, Florence, 1969.

1925 *Che cosa è il fascismo?*, Vallecchi, Florence, 1925, cited from *Politica e Cultura*, I, OC XLV, Le Lettere, Florence, 1990, 7–37.

1925 'Caratteri religiosi della presente lotta politica', in *L'Educazione politica*, 3, 1925, cited from *Politica e Cultura*, I, OC XLV, Le Lettere, Florence, 1990, 135–143.

1925 'Il fascismo nella cultura, Discorso di chiusura tenuto il 30 marzo 1925 al Congresso di cultura fascista a Bologna', cited from *Politica e Cultura*, I, OC XLV, Le Lettere, Florence, 1990, 90–110.

1925   'La storia', in *Scritti filosofici, per le onoranze nazionali a B. Varisco, nel suo LXXV anno di età*, cited from *Introduzione alla filosofia*, OC XXXVI, Sansoni, Florence, 1958, 104–120.

1925   'Manifesto degli intelletuali italiani fascisti agli intelletuali di tutte le nazioni', in *L'Educazione politica*, 3, 1925, cited from *Politica e Cultura*, II, OC XLVI, Le Lettere, Florence, 1991, 5–13.

1925   'Cavour giornalista e pensatore politico', cited from *Politica e Cultura*, II, OC XLVI, Le Lettere, Florence, 1991, 95–110.

1925   *Studi Vichiani*, Le Monnier, Firenze, 1927.

1931   *La filosofia dell'arte*, Treves, Milan, 1931.

1936   'Il superamento del tempo nella storia', in *Rendiconti della Reale Accademia dei* Lincei, XI, 1936, cited from *Frammenti di estetica e di teoria della storia*, II, OC XLVIII, Le Lettere, Florence, 1992, 3–20.

1937   'Introduzione a una nuova filosofia della storia', in *Giornale critico della filosofia italiana*, XVIII, 1937, cited from *Frammenti di estetica e di teoria della storia*, II, OC XLVIII, Le Lettere, Florence, 1992, 21–50.

1937   'L'oggetto della storia', in *Giornale critico della filosofia italiana*, XVIII, 1937, cited from *Frammenti di estetica e di teoria della storia*, II, OC XLVIII, Le Lettere, Florence, 1992, 51–90.

1946   *Genesì e struttura della società, Saggio di filosofia pratica*, Sansoni, Florence, 1946, cited from *Genesì e struttura della società, Saggio di filosofia pratica*, OC IX, Le Lettere, Florence, 1987.

1972   *The Philosophy of Art, Translated with an Introduction by Giovanni Gullace*, Cornell University Press, Ithaca and London, 1972.

1974   *Lettere a Benedetto Croce, Volume secondo, dal 1901 al 1906*, Sansoni, Florence, 1974.

1976   *Lettere a Benedetto Croce, Volume terzo, dal 1907 al 1909*, Sansoni, Florence, 1976.

1980   *Lettere a Benedetto Croce, Volume quarto, dal 1910 al 1914*, Sansoni, Florence, 1980.

1990   *Lettere a Benedetto Croce, Volume V*, Le Lettere, Florence, 1990.

1996   *La filosofia della storia, Saggi e inediti*, Le Lettere, Florence, 1996.

Works by de Ruggiero Cited in the Text

1911   'Il problema della deduzione delle categorie', in *Atti del IV Congresso internazionale di filosofia, Bologna 1911*, Kraus, Nendeln, Lichtenstein, 1968, 331–336.

1911   'L'idealismo delle scienze naturali e l'idealismo dei valori', in *La Cultura*, 1911/6, 189–193.

1911   'La filosofia dei valori in Germania', in *La Critica*, IX, 1911, 368–384, 441–448.

1912 'La filosofia dei valori in Germania', in *La Critica*, X, 1912, 41–51, 126–132, 211–219.

1912 'La redenzione come svolgimento dello spirito, Saggio di una dialettica della coscienza morale', in *Rassegna di Pedagogia*, VI, Sandron, Palermo, 1912, 5–28.

1912 'La scienza come esperienza assoluta', in *Annuario della Biblioteca filosofica di Palermo*, I, 1912, 229–339.

1912 *La filosofia contemporanea*, Laterza, Bari, 1912, cited from 6th edn. Laterza, Bari, 1951.

1912 'Per una storia dell'idea di progresso', in *La Cultura*, 1, 1912, 6–13.

1913 'La storia vivente', in *Il resto del Carlino*, 14 February 1913, cited from *Scritti Politici, 1912–1926*, Capelli, Bologna, 1963, 85–92.

1914 'Storia di oggi e storia di domani', in *L'Idea Nazionale*, 5 December 1914, cited from id., *Scritti politici, 1912–1926*, Capelli, Bologna, 1963, 119–124.

1914 *Problemi della vita morale*, Battiato, Catania, 1914.

1914 *Critica del concetto di cultura*, Battiato, Catania, 1914.

1916 'La pensée italienne et la guerre', in *Revue de Métaphysique et de Morale*, 1916, cited from Italian translation by Renzo de Felice in de Ruggiero, G., *Scritti Politici, 1912–1926*, Capelli, Bologna, 1963, 125–165.

1918 *La filosofia greca*, Laterza, Bari, 1918, cited from quinta edizione, Laterza, Bari, 1943.

1920 *La filosofia del cristianesimo*, Laterza, Bari, 1920, cited from terza edizione, Laterza, Bari, 1941.

1921 *L'Impero brittanico dopo la guerra*, Valecchi, Florence, 1921.

1921 *Modern Philosophy*, English Translation of *La filosofia contemporanea*, 1912, by A.H. Hannay and R.G. Collingwood, Allen and Unwin, London New York, 1921.

1921 'Arte e critica', in *L'Arduo, Rivista di Scienza, Filosofia e Storia*, 2, 1921, 397–416.

1922 'Dall'arte alla filosofia', in *L'Arduo, Rivista di Scienza, Filosofia e Storia*, 3, 1922, 31–50.

1925 *Storia del liberalismo europeo*, Laterza, Bari, 1925.

1928 'Nota', in *La filosofia contemporanea*, terza edizione, Laterza, Bari, 1928, 521–523.

1930 *Rinascimento, Riforma e Controriforma*, Laterza, Bari, cited from ottava edizione Laterza, Bari, 1966.

1931 'Science, History and Philosophy', in *Philosophy*, 6, 1931, 166–179.

1931 'Philosophy in Italy', in *Philosophy*, 6, 1931, 491–494.

1933 *Filosofi del novecento*, Laterza, Bari, cited from quarta edizione, Laterza, Bari, 1950.

1933 'Revisioni idealistiche', in *L'educazione nazionale*, 1933, 138–145.

1937 *Da Vico a Kant*, Laterza, Bari, 1937, cited from quarta edizione, Laterza, Bari, 1952.

1944 'Il ritorno alla ragione', in *Mercurio*, 1, 1944, 80–98, cited from Cicalese, M.L. (ed.), *Nuova Antologia*, 1994–5. This was de Ruggiero's lecture to be delivered in 1940 for his Doctorate *honoris causa* at the Univerity of Oxford.

1946 *Il ritorno alla ragione*, Laterza, Bari, 1946.

1946 'Oration by the Public Orator', in *Oxford University Gazette*, LXXVI, 1946, 467.

1963 *Scritti Politici, 1912–1926*, Capelli, Bologna, 1963.

Manuscripts by de Ruggiero

1920 'Letter to R.G. Collingwood', 28 June 1920, in private collection of Ms. Smith.

1940 'Letter to the University's Registrar', Oxford University Archive, UR6/HD/2C, dated 20 September 1940 concerning the Doctorate *honoris causa*.

1945 'Letter to the University's Registrar', Oxford University Archive, UR6/HD/2C, dated 11 December 1945.

Works by Collingwood Cited in the Text

1916 *Religion and Philosophy*, Macmillan, London, 1916.

1916 'The Devil', in Streeter, B.H. and Dougall, Lily, *Concerning Prayer: Its Nature, its Difficulties and its Value*, Macmillan, London, 1916, cited from Rubinoff, L. (ed.), *Faith and Reason: Essays in the Philosophy of Religion by R.G. Collingwood*, Quadrangle Books, Chicago, 1968, 212–233.

1921 'Translators' Preface', in Guido de Ruggiero, *Modern Philosophy*, Allen and Unwin, London New York, 1921, 5–7.

1921 'Croce's Philosophy of History', in *The Hibbert Journal*, 19, 1921, 263–278, cited from Debbins, W. (ed.), *R.G. Collingwood: Essays in the Philosophy of History*, University of Texas Press, Austin, 1966, 5–22.

1922 *Ruskin's Philosophy, An Address delivered at the Ruskin Centenary Conference, Coniston, August 8th, 1919*, Titus Wilson, Kendal, 1922, cited from Donagan, A. (ed.), *Essays in the Philosophy of Art by R.G. Collingwood*, Indiana University Press, Bloomington, 1964, 3–41.

1922 'Are History and Science Different Kinds of Knowledge?', in *Mind*, 3, 1922, 443–451, cited from Debbins, W. (ed.), *R.G. Collingwood: Essays in the Philosophy of History*, University of Texas Press, Austin, 1966, 23–33.

1923 'Science and History', in *The Vasculum*, IX, 1922, 52–59.

1923 'Can the New Idealism Dispense with Mysticism?', in *Proceedings of the Aristotelian Society*, Supplement, III, 1923, 161–175, cited from Rubinoff, L. (ed.), *Faith and Reason: Essays in the Philosophy of Religion by R.G. Collingwood*, Quadrangle Books, Chicago, 1968, 270–282.

1924 *Speculum Mentis*, Clarendon Press, Oxford, 1924.

1925 *Outlines of a Philosophy of Art*, Oxford University Press, Oxford, 1925.

1924 'The Nature and Aims of a Philosophy of History', in *Proceedings of the Aristotelian Society*, 25, 1924-25, 151-174, cited from Debbins, W. (ed.), *R.G. Collingwood: Essays in the Philosophy of History*, University of Texas Press, Austin, 1966, 34-56.

1926 'Some Perplexities about Time: With and Attempted Solution', in *Proceedings of the Aristotelian Society*, 26, 1926, 135-150.

1927 'Oswald Spengler and the Theory of Historical Cycles', in *Antiquity*, 1, 311-325, cited from, Debbins, W. (ed.), *R.G. Collingwood: Essays in the Philosophy of History*, University of Texas Press, Austin, 1966, 57-75.

1927 'The Theory of Historical Cycles', in *Antiquity*, 1, 435-446, cited from Debbins, W. (ed.), *R. G. Collingwood: Essays in the Philosophy of History*, University of Texas Press, Austin, 1966, 76-89.

1928 *Faith and Reason*, Benn, London, 1928, cited from Rubinoff, L. (ed.), *Faith and Reason, Essays in the Philosophy of Religion by R.G. Collingwood*, Quadrangle Books, Chicago, 1968, 122-147.

1929 'A Philosophy of Progress', in *The Realist*, 1, 1929, 64-77, cited from Debbins, W. (ed.), *R.G. Collingwood: Essays in the Philosophy of History*, University of Texas Press, Austin, 1966, 104-120.

1930 *The Philosophy of History*, Historical Association Leaflet, 79, 1930, cited from Debbins, W. (ed.), *R.G. Collingwood: Essays in the Philosophy of History*, University of Texas Press, Austin, 1966, 121-139.

1933 *An Essay on Philosophical Method*, Clarendon Press, Oxford, 1933.

1935 'The Present Need of a Philosophy', in *Philosophy*, 9, 1935, 262-265, cited from Boucher, David (ed.), *R.G. Collingwood: Essays in Political Philosophy*, Oxford University Press, Oxford, 1989, 166-170.

1936 *Roman Britain and The English Settlements*, Clarendon Press, Oxford, 1936.

1935 'The Historical Imagination', cited from Collingwood, R.G., *The Idea of History, Revised Edition with Lectures 1926-28, Edited with an Introduction by Jan van der Dussen*, Clarendon Press, Oxford, 1993, 231-249.

1936 'Human Nature and Human History', in *Proceedings of the British Academy*, 22, 97-127, cited from Collingwood, R.G., *The Idea of History, Revised Edition with Lectures 1926-28, Edited with an Introduction by Jan van der Dussen*, Clarendon Press, Oxford, 1993, 205-231.

1937 Review of 'Klibansky, Raymond, and H.J. Paton, eds., Philosophy and History: Essays Presented to Ernst Cassirer', in *English Historical Review*, 52, 1937, 141-146.

1938 *The Principles of Art*, Clarendon Press, Oxford, 1938.

1939 *An Autobiography*, Clarendon Press, Oxford, 1939.

1939 *The Principles of History*, Oxford University Press, Oxford, 1999.

1940 *The First Mate's Log*, Clarendon Press, Oxford, 1940.

1940 *An Essay on Metaphysics*, Clarendon Press, Oxford, 1940.

1940 'Fascism and Nazism', in *Philosophy*, 15, 1940, 168–176, cited from Boucher, David (ed.), *R.G. Collingwood: Essays in Political Philosophy*, Oxford University Press, Oxford, 1989, 187–197.

1942 *The New Leviathan*, Clarendon Press, Oxford, cited from Collingwood, R.G., *The New Leviathan, Revised Edition, Edited and Introduced by David Boucher*, Clarendon Press, Oxford, 1992.

1945 *The Idea of Nature*, Clarendon Press, Oxford, 1945.

1946 *The Idea of History*, Clarendon Press, Oxford, 1946, cited from Collingwood, R.G., *The Idea of History, Revised Edition with Lectures 1926-28, Edited with an Introduction by Jan van der Dussen*, Clarendon Press, Oxford, 1993.

1964 *Essays in the Philosophy of Art by R.G. Collingwood*, Indiana University Press, Bloomington, 1964 (Ed. Alan Donagan).

1966 *Essays in the Philosophy of History*, University of Texas Press, Austin, 1966 (Ed. Debbins).

1968 *Faith and Reason: Essays in the Philosophy of Religion by R.G. Collingwood* (Ed. Lionel Rubinoff).

1989 *Essays in Political Philosophy*, Oxford University Press, Oxford, 1989 (Ed. David Boucher).

1991 Vigorelli, Amadeo (ed.), 'Lettere di Robin George Collingwood a Benedetto Croce (1912–1939)', in *Rivista di storia della filosofia*, 3, 1991, 545–563.

1992 'Goodness, Rightness, Utility, Lectures delivered in Hilary Term 1940 and written as delivered', cited from Collingwood, R.G., *The New Leviathan, Revised Edition, Edited and Introduced by David Boucher*, Clarendon Press, Oxford, 1992, 391–479.

1993 'Lectures on the Philosophy of History', written in 1926, cited from Collingwood, R.G., *The Idea of History, Revised Edition with Lectures 1926–28, Edited with an Introduction by Jan van der Dussen*, Clarendon Press, Oxford, 1993, 359–425.

1993 'Preliminary Discussion, The Idea of a Philosophy of Something, and, in Particular, A Philosophy of History', written in 1927, cited from Collingwood, R.G., *The Idea of History, Revised Edition with Lectures 1926–28, Edited with an Introduction by Jan van der Dussen*, Clarendon Press, Oxford, 1993, 335–358.

1993 'Outlines of a Philosophy of History', written 1928, cited from Collingwood, R.G., *The Idea of History, Revised Edition with Lectures 1926–28, Edited with an Introduction by Jan van der Dussen*, Clarendon Press, Oxford, 1993, 426–496.

Translations by Collingwood

1913 Croce, B., *The Philosophy of Giambattista Vico*, Macmillan, New York, 1913, translation of *La filosofia di Giambattista Vico*, Laterza, Bari, 1911.

1920 De Ruggiero, G., 'La scienza come esperienza assoluta', 1912. This translation, mentioned by Collingwood in a letter to de Ruggiero of 1 July 1920, Dep. 27, has not been found yet.

1921 De Ruggiero, G., *Modern Philosophy*, Macmillan, New York, 1921, translation of *La filosofia contemporanea*, Laterza, Bari, 1912.

1922 *Aesthetic, As Science of Expression and General Linguistic,* translated by Douglas Ainslie, Macmillan, New York, revised edition 1922, translation of *Estetica come scienza dell'espressione e linguistica generale*, 3rd edn., Laterza , Bari, 1908 was revised by Collingwood, see his letter to de Ruggiero of 22 November 1921, Dep. 27.

1927 Croce, B., *An Autobiography*, Clarendon Press, Oxford, 1927, translation of *Contributo alla critica di me stesso, Edizione di 100 esemplari fuori commercio*, 1918.

1928 Croce, B., 'Aesthetic', in *Encyclopedia Britannica*, 14th edn., 1928.

1927 De Ruggiero, G., *The History of European Liberalism*, Clarendon Press, Oxford, 1927, translation of *Storia del liberalismo europeo*, Laterza, Bari, 1925.

1931 De Ruggiero, G., 'Science, History and Philosophy', in *Philosophy*, 6, 1931, 166–179.

Manuscripts by Collingwood Cited in the Text

All manuscripts are indicated by their title and deposit number (abbreviated as Dep.) in the Bodleian Library Oxford.

1912 'Marginal Comments in Croce, *Estetica*', 1912, in private collection of Ms. Smith.

1912 'Marginal Comments in Croce, *Filosofia della pratica*', 1912, in private collection of Ms. Smith.

1913 'Aristoteles De Anima Libri Tres—Translation and Commentary', 1913–14, Dep. 11.

1917 'Marginal Comments in Croce, *Teoria e storia della storiografia*', 1917, in private collection of of Ms. Smith.

1917 'Truth and Contradiction, Chapter II', 1917, Dep. 16/1.

1920 'Notes on Croce's Philosophy', written in July 1920, Dep. 19/1.

1920 'Libellus de Generatione', written from 20 until 23 July 1920, Dep. 28.

1920 'Notes on Hegel's Logic', 19 September 1920, Dep. 16/2.

1920 'Sketch of A Logic of Becoming', 19 September 1920, Dep. 16/3.

1920 'Notes on Formal Logic', 1920, Dep. 16/4.

1920 'Draft of Openening Chapters of a "Prolegomena to Logic" or the like', 1920, p. 16/5.

1920 'An Illustration from Historical Thought', 1920, Dep. 16/6.

1920 'Lectures on the Ontological Proof of the Existence of God', 1920, Dep. 2.

1921 'Lectures on Moral Philosophy for MT 1921, written at various times, May–October 1921', Dep. 4.

1923 'Action. A Course of Lectures on Moral Philosophy', written in September 1923 and rewritten in M.T. 1926, Dep. 3/1.

1925 'Some Perplexities about Time', 1925, Dep. 18/1.

1929 'Lectures on the Philosophy of History – II Trinity Term 1929', Dep. 12/6.

1920-38 'Letters to Guido de Ruggiero', 1920–38, Dep. 27.

1933 'List of Work Done', 1933, Dep. 22/2.

1933 'Notes towards a Metaphysic, A', written in September 1933, Dep. 18/3.

1933-34 'Notes towards a Metaphysic, B', 1933 until March 1934, Dep. 18/4, cited from R.G. Collingwood, *The Principles of History*, 119–140.

1934 'The Nature of Metaphysical Study', 1934, Dep. 18/2.

1935 'Conclusions to Lectures on Nature and Mind' cited from R.G. Collingwood, *The Principles of History*, 251–271.

1935 'Central Problems in Metaphysics', 1935, Dep. 20/1.

1935 'Reality as History', written December 1935, Dep. 12/9, cited from R.G. Collingwood, *The Principles of History*, 170–209.

1936 'Man Goes Mad', Dep. 24, cited from Boucher, David (ed.), *R.G. Collingwood: Essays in Political Philosophy*, Oxford University Press, Oxford, 1989, 177–186.

1936 'Introductory Lecture', 1936, Dep. 15/3. This is the original introduction to the lectures on the philosophy of history published as *The Idea of History* in 1946.

1936 'Notes on the History of Historiography and Philosophy of History', Dep. 13/2.

1936 'Human Nature and Human History', 1936, Dep. 12/11, cited from R.G. Collingwood, *The Principles of History*, 219–220.

1939 'Scheme for The Principles of History', 1939, cited from van der Dussen, W.J., *History as a Science, The Philosophy of R.G. Collingwood*, 1981, 431–432.

Secondary Sources

Ankersmit, F.R., 'The Dilemma of Contemporary Anglo-Saxon Philosophy of History', in *History and Theory*, Beiheft 25, 1986, 1–27.

– 'Croce als spiegel van onze tijd', in *Theoretische Geschiedenis*, 16, 1989, 319–331.

– *Sublime Historical Experience*, Stanford University Press, Stanford, 2005.

– 'Danto's Philosophy in Retrospective', in Arthur C. Danto, *Narration and Knowledge*, Columbia University Press, 2007, 364–395.

Atkinson, R.F., *Knowledge and Explanation in History, An Introduction to the Philosophy of History*, Cornell University Press, Ithaca, 1978.

Ayer, A.J., *Language, Truth and Logic*, Penguin Books, Harmondsworth, 1976.

Ayer, A.J., *Philosophy in the Twentieth Century*, Weidenfeld and Nicolson, London, 1982.

— *Part of My Life*, Oxford University Press, Oxford, 1978, 166.

Badaloni, Nicola, *Introduzione a Vico*, Laterza, Bari, 1988.

Beaney, Michael, 'Collingwood's Conception of Presuppositional Analysis', in *Collingwood and British Idealism Studies*, 11, 2005, 41–114.

Bellamy, Richard, *Modern Italian Social Theory, Ideology and Politics from Pareto to the Present*, Polity Press, Cambridge, 1987.

Berlin, Isaiah, *Vico and Herder, Two Studies in the History of Ideas*, Chatto and Windus, London, 1980.

Blackburn, Simon (ed.), *Index to Mind, Vol. 1–100*, (1892–1991).

Boucher, David, *The Social and Political Philosophy of R.G. Collingwood*, Cambridge University Press, Cambridge, 1989.

— (ed.), *R.G. Collingwood: Essays in Political Philosophy*, Oxford University Press, Oxford, 1989.

— 'Editor's Introduction', in R.G. Collingwood, *The New Leviathan or Man, Society, Civilization and Barbarism, Revised Edition, Edited and Introduced by David Boucher*, Clarendon Press, Oxford, 1992, xiii–lvii.

— (ed.), *Philosophy, History and Civilization, Interdisciplinary Perspectives on R.G. Collingwood*, University of Wales Press, Cardiff, 1995.

— 'The Life, Times and Legacy of R.G. Collingwood', in Boucher, David (ed.), *Philosophy, History and Civilization, Interdisciplinary Perspectives on R.G. ,Collingwood*, University of Wales Press, Cardiff, 1995, 1–31.

— '*The Principles of History* and the Cosmology Conclusion to *The Idea of Nature*', in *Collingwood Studies*, 2, 1995, 140–174.

Bosanquet, Bernard, Review of 'Gentile, *Riforma della dialettica hegeliana* and *Sommario di pedagogia*', in *Mind*, XXIX, 1920, 367–369.

— *The Meeting of Extremes in Contemporary Philosophy*, Macmillan, London, 1921.

Brown, Merle E., *Neo-Idealistic Aesthetics, Croce, Gentile, Collingwood*, Wayne State University Press, Detroit, 1966.

Burns, C.D.B., Review of 'Collingwood, R.G., *Speculum Mentis*', in *International Journal of Ethics*, 35, 1925.

Connelly, James and d'Oro, Giuseppina, 'Editors' Introduction', in R.G. Collingwood, *An Essay on Philosophical Method, Revised Edition*, Clarendon Press, Oxford, 2005, xiii–cxxii.

Connelly, James and d'Oro, Giussepina, 'Robin George Collingwood', in *Stanford Encyclopedia of Philosophy*, http://plato.stanford.edu/entries/collingwood/.

Connelly, James, *Metaphysics, Method and Politics, The Political Philosophy of R.G. Collingwood*, Imprint Academic, Exeter, 2003, 43.

Cannistraro, Philip V., *Historical Dictionary of Fascist Italy*, Greenwood Press, Westport, London, 1982.

Carlini, Armando, *Studi gentiliani*, Sansoni, Florence, 1958.

Carritt, E.F., *The Theory of Beauty*, Methuen, London, 1914.

Cavallera, Hervé A., *Immagine e costruzione del reale nel pensiero di Giovanni Gentile*, Biblioteca scientifica, Fondazione Ugo Spirito, Roma, 1994.

Cicalese, M.L., 'Res gestae e historia rerum nel giovane de Ruggiero', in *Critica storica*, 1979, 246–299.

Coli, Daniela, 'Guido de Ruggiero: Cultura e politica, 1910–1922', in *Annali dell'istituto di filosofia*, I, 1979, 359–386.

Danto, Arthur C., *Analytical Philosophy of History*, Cambridge University Press, Cambridge, 1965.

—*Narration and Knowledge,* Columbia University Press, New York, 2007.

De Aloysio, Francesco, *Storia e dialogo*, Capelli, Bologna, 1962.

Debbins, W. (ed.), *R.G. Collingwood: Essays in the Philosophy of History*, University of Texas Press, Austin, 1966.

De Felice, Renzo, 'Fascism', in Cannistraro, Philip V. (ed.), *Historical Dictionary of Fascist Italy*, Greenwood, Westport, London, 1982, 205–217.

—'De Ruggiero, Guido', in *Dizionario Biografico degli Italiani*, Istituto della Enciclopedia Italiana, Roma, 1991.

De Gennaro, Angelo, 'Croce and Collingwood', in *The Personalist*, 46, 1965, 193–202.

Del Noce, Augusto, *Giovanni Gentile, Per una interpretazione filosofica della storia contemporanea*, Il Mulino, Bologna, 1990.

Di Lalla, Manlio, *Vita di Giovanni Gentile*, Sansoni, Florence, 1975.

Donagan, Alan, 'The Croce-Collingwood Theory of Art', in *Philosophy*, 33, 1958, 162–167.

—*The Later Philosophy of R.G. Collingwood*, Clarendon Press, Oxford, 1962.

Dondoli, Luciano, *Genesi e svillupi della teoria linguistica di Benedetto Croce*, I, Bulzoni, Roma, 1988.

Dray, William H., *Laws and Explanation in History*, Clarendon Press, Oxford, 1957.

—*History as Re-enactment, R.G. Collingwood's Idea of History*, Clarendon Press, Oxford, 1995.

—'Broadening the Subject-Matter in *The Principles of History*', in *Collingwood Studies*, 4, 1997, 2–33.

Ducasse, C.J., 'Mr. Collingwood on Philosophical Method', in *Journal of Philosophy*, 33, 1936, 95–106.

Elsenhans, T. (ed.), *Bericht Über den III. internationalen Kongress für Philosophie zu Heidelberg, 1–5 September 1908*, Kraus, Nendeln, Lichtenstein, 1974.

Faucci, Dario, *Storicismo e metafisica nel pensiero crociano ed altri scritti*, La Nuova Italia Editrice, Florence, 1981.

Festin, Raymun J., 'Collingwood's Absolute Presuppositions and their Non-propositionality', in *Collingwood and British Idealism Studies, Incorporating Bradley Studies*, 14, 2008.

Flanigan, Sister Thomas Marguerite, 'Metaphysics as a "Science of Absolute Presuppositions": Another Look at R.G. Collingwood', in *The Modern Schoolman*, LXIV, 1986-87, 161–185.

Franchini, Raffaello, *La teoria della storia di Benedetto Croce*, Morano, Naples, 1966.

Gadamer, Hans-Georg, *Wahrheit und Methode. Grundzüge einer philosophischen Hermeneutik*, Gesammelte Werke, Band 1, J.C.B.Mohr, Tübingen, 1990. English Translation, *Truth and Method*, Sheed and Ward, London, 1979.

Garin, Eugenio, *Chronache di filosofia italiana*, Bari, Laterza, 1959.

— (ed.), *Croce e Gentile un secolo dopo, Saggi, testi inediti e un'appendice bibliografica 1980-1993*, Le Lettere, Florence, 1994.

Galasso, Giuseppe, *Croce e lo spirito del suo tempo*, Mondadori, Milano, 1990.

Gallie, H.W.B., *Philosophy and the Historical Understanding*, Shocken Books, New York, 1968 (1st ed. 1964).

Gentile, Benedetto, *Giovanni Gentile, Dal discorso agli italiani alla morte, 24 giugno– 15 aprile 1944*, Sansoni, Firenze, 1954.

Gily Reda, Clementina, *Guido de Ruggiero, Un ritratto filosofico*, Società Editrice Napoletana, Napels, 1981.

— 'De Ruggiero e Collingwood', in *Criterio*, IX, 1991, 75–83.

— (ed.), *Robin George Collingwood e la formazione estetica. Atti del Covegno di Napoli*, Giugno 2006, Graus editore, Napoli, 2007.

— 'Considerations on Collingwood and Italian Thought', in *Collingwood Studies*, II, 1995, 213-232.

— 'Collingwood e de Ruggiero e la formazione estetica', in id., *Robin George Collingwood e la formazione estetica. Atti del Covegno di Napoli, Giugno 2006*, Graus editore, Napoli, 2007, 21-63.

— 'Specular Phenomenology: Art and Art Criticism', in *Collingwood and British Idealism Studies: Incorporating Bradley Studies*, 17.2, 2011, 247-261.

Gily Reda, Clementina and Angela Maria Graziano, *Il partito d'azione tra storia e metafora*, Grafic Way, Napoli, 1995.

Gramsci, Antonio, *Il materialismo storico*, Torino 1975, 91-144.

Goldstein, Leon J., *Historical Knowing*, University of Texas Press, Austin and London, 1976.

— 'The Idea of History as a Scale of Forms', in *History and Theory*, 29.4, 1990, 42 – 50.

Gregor, A. James, *Giovanni Gentile: Philosopher of Fascism*, Transaction Publishers, New Brunswick, 2001.

Greppi Olivetti, Alessandra, *Due saggi su R.G. Collingwood, con un'appendice di lettere di Collingwood a G. de Ruggiero*, Livania editrice, Padova, 1977.

Gumbrecht, Hans Ulrich, *Production of Presence: What Meaning Cannot Convey*, Standford University Press, 2004.

Haddock, Bruce A., 'Vico, Collingwood and the Character of a Historical Philosophy', in Boucher, David (ed.), *Philosophy, History and Civilization, Inter-*

disciplinary Perspectives on R.G. Collingwood, University of Wales Press, Cardiff, 1995, 130–152.

Harris, H.S., *The Social Philosophy of Giovanni Gentile*, University of Illinois Press, Illinois, 1960.

—'Introduction', in Giovanni Gentile, *Genesis and Structure of Society*, University of Illinois Press, Illinois, 1960.

—'Croce and Gentile in Collingwood's *New Leviathan'*, in David Boucher (ed.), *Philosophy, History and Civilization, Interdisciplinary Perspectives on R.G. Collingwood*, University of Wales Press, Cardiff, 1995, 115–130.

Helgeby, Stein, *Action as History: The Historical Thought of R.G. Collingwood*, Imprint Academic, Exeter, 2004.

Holmes, Roger W., *The Idealism of Giovanni Gentile*, Macmillan, New York, 1937.

Hospers, John, 'The Croce-Collingwood Theory of Art', in *Philosophy*, 31, 1956, 291–308.

Jacobelli, Jader, *Croce e Gentile, Dal sodalizio al dramma*, Rizzoli, Milano, 1989.

Jones, Peter, 'Collingwood's Debt to His Father', in *Mind*, LXVIII, 1969, 437–439.

Johnson, Douglas H., 'W.G. Collingwood and the Beginnings of the *Idea of History'*, in *Collingwood Studies*, 1, 1994, 1–26.

Johnson, Peter, *The Correspondence of R.G. Collingwood. An Illustrated Guide*, Collingwood Society, Swansea, 1998.

—'R.G. Collingwood and the Albert Memorial', in *Collingwood and British Idealism Studies incorporating Bradley Studies*, 15, 2009, 7–40.

Johnston, William M., *The Formative Years of R.G. Collingwood*, Nijhoff, The Hague, 1967.

Inglis, Fred, *History Man. The Life of R.G. Collingwood*, Princeton University Press, Princeton, 2009.

Iiritano, Massimo, 'Picture Thinking', in *Robin George Collingwood e la formazione estetica*, 11–141.

—*Picture Thinking. Estetica e filosofia della Religione nei primi scritti di Robin Collingwood*, Rubbetino, Soveria Mannelli, 2006.

Klibansky, Raymond and H.J. Paton (eds.), *Philosophy and History: Essays Presented to Ernst Cassirer*, Clarendon Press, Oxford, 1936.

Knox, T.M., 'Editor's Preface', in R.G. Collingwood, *The Idea of History*, Clarendon Press, Oxford, 1946.

—'Collingwood, Robin George (1889–1943)', in Wickham, L.G. and Williams, E.T., *Dictionary of National Biography 1941–1950*, Oxford University Press, Oxford, 1959, 168–170.

—Review of 'The Formative Years of R.G. Collingwood by William M. Johnston', in *The Philosophical Quarterly*, 19, 1969, 165–166.

Kobayashi, Chinatsu, and Mathieu Marion, 'Gadamer and Collingwood on Temporal Distance and Understanding', in *History and Theory*, 50.4, 2011, 81–104.

Krausz, Michael, 'Ideality and Ontology in the Practice of History', in W.J. van der Dussen and Lionel Rubinoff, *Objectivity, Method and Point of View, Essays in the Philosophy of History*, Brill, Leiden, 1991, 97–111.

Labriola, Antonio, *Scritti Filosofici e Politici*, Einaudi Editore, Torino, 1976.

Lenin, Vladimir I., *The Teachings of Karl Marx*, International Publishers, New York, 1930.

Levine, Joseph M., 'Collingwood, Vico, and *The Autobiography*', in *Clio*, 9, 1980, 379–392.

Lo Schiavo, Aldo, *La filosofia politica di Giovanni Gentile*, Armando, Rome, 1971.

Lyttelton, Adrian, *The Seizure of Power, Fascism in Italy 1919–1929*, Princeton University Press, Princeton, 1987.

Martin, Rex, 'Collingwood's *Essay on Philosophical Method*', in *Idealistic Studies*, 4, 1974, 224–250.

— *Historical Explanation, Re-enactment and Practical Inference*, Cornell University Press, Ithaca and London, 1977.

— 'Collingwood's Claim that Metaphysics is a Historical Discipline', in Boucher, David (ed.), *Philosophy, History and Civilization, Interdisciplinary Perspectives on R.G. Collingwood*, University of Wales Press, Cardiff, 1995, 203–245.

— 'Editor's Introduction', in R.G. Collingwood, *An Essay on Metaphysics, Revised Edition with an Introduction and additional material by Rex Martin*, Clarendon Press, Oxford, 1998.

— 'Collingwood's Logic of Question and Answer its Relations to Absolute Presuppositions: A Brief History', in *Collingwood Studies*, 5, 1998, 122–136.

Meiland, Jack W., *Scepticism and Historical Knowledge*, Random House, New York, 1965.

Miller, Cecilia, *Giambattista Vico, Imagination and Thought*, Macmillan, New York, 1993.

Mink, Louis O., *Mind, History, and Dialectic, The Philosophy of R.G. Collingwood*, Wesleyan University Press, Middletown, 1969.

Modood, Tariq, 'Collingwood and the Idea of Philosophy', in Boucher, David (ed.), *Philosophy, History and Civilization, Interdisciplinary Perspectives on R.G. Collingwood*, University of Wales Press, Cardiff, 1995, 32–61.

Morra, Gianfranco, 'La storia nel pensiero di Giovanni Gentile', in *Giovanni Gentile, La Vita e il Pensiero*, X, 1962, 259–416.

Moss, M.E., *Benedetto Croce Reconsidered, Truth and Error in Theories of Art, Literature, and History*, University Press of New England, Hanover and London, 1987.

— 'Robin George Collingwood', in Ian P. McGreal, *Great Thinkers of the Western World*, Harper Collins, New York, 1992, 507–510.

Mussolini, Benito, *Scritti e Discorsi di Benito Mussolini, Volume II, La Rivoluzione Fascista*, Edizioni Librarie Siciliane, S. Cristina Gela, s.d.

Mure, G.R.G., *Idealist Epilogue*, Clarendon Press, Oxford, 1978.

Negri, Antimo, 'Il concetto attualistico della storia e lo storicismo', in *Giovanni Gentile, La Vita e il Pensiero*, X, Sansoni, Florence, 1962, 5–219.

— *Giovanni Gentile, 1, Costruzione e senso dell'attualismo*, La Nuova Italia, Florence, 1975.

— *Giovanni Gentile, 2, Svillupi e incidenza dell'attualismo*, La Nuova Italia, Florence, 1975.

— *L'Inquietudine del divenire, Giovanni Gentile*, Le Lettere, Firenze, 1992.

Nielsen, Margrit Hurup, 'Re-enactment and Reconstruction in Collingwood's Philosophy of History', in *History and Theory*, 20, 1981, 1–31.

Passmore, John, *A Hundred Years of Philosophy*, Penguin Books, Harmondsworth, 1984, 1st edn. 1957.

Patrick, James, *The Magdalen Metaphysicals, Idealism and Orthodoxy at Oxford, 1901–1945*, Mercer Univerisity Press, 1985.

Paul, Herman, *White*, Polity Press, Cambridge, 2011.

Peters, Rik, 'Collingwood's Reform of Hegelian Dialectic', in *The Bulletin of the Hegel Society of Great Britain*, 31, 1995, 90–105.

— 'Collingwood on Hegel's Dialectic', in *Collingwood Studies*, 2, 1995, 107–125.

— 'Croce, Gentile and Collingwood on the Relation between History and Philosophy', in Boucher David (ed.), *Philosophy, History and Civilization, Interdisciplinary Perspectives on R.G. Collingwood*, Universtity of Wales Press, Cardiff, 1995, 152–168.

— 'De Opkomst en Ondergang van het Europese Idealisme, in *Geschiedenis van de Wijsbegeerte in Nederland*, 6, 1995, 123–137.

— 'Talking to Others or Talking to Yourself, H.S Harris on Giovanni Gentile's Transcendental Dialogue', in *CLIO, A Journal of Literature, History and the Philosophy of History*, 27.4, 1998, 501–515.

— 'Collingwood's Logic of Question and Answer, its Relation to Absolute Presuppositions: another Brief History', in *Collingwood Studies*, 6, 2000, 1–28.

— 'Actes de présence: Presence in Fascist Political Culture', in *History and Theory*, 45, 2006, 362–374.

— 'Nolite iudicare. Hayden White between Benedetto Croce and Giovanni Gentile,' in *Storia della storiografia*, 58, 2010, 19–35.

— 'Italian Legacies', in *History and Theory*, 49, 2010, 115–129.

Peters, Rik and Peter van der Geer, *In plaats van praten. Debat en dialoog bij veranderprocessen*, Utrecht, Het Spectrum, 2004.

Pompa, Leon, 'Collingwood's Theory of Historical Knowledge', in Boucher, David (ed.), *Philosophy, History and Civilization, Interdisciplinary Perspectives on R.G. Collingwood*, University of Wales Press, Cardiff, 1995, 168–181.

Post, John Frederic, 'Does knowing Make a Difference to What is Known?', in *Philosophical Quarterly*, 15, 1965, 220–228.

Prichard, H.A., *Kant's Theory of Knowledge*, Clarendon Press, Oxford, 1909.

Rickert, Heinrich, *Die Grenzen der Naturwissenschaftlichen Begriffsbildung, Eine logische Einleitung in die historischen Wissenschaften*, Mohr, Tübingen, 1921.

Rizi, Fabio Fernando, *Benedetto Croce and Italian Fascism*, University of Toronto Press, Toronto, 2003.

Roberts, David D., *Benedetto Croce and the Uses of Historicism*, University of California Press, Berkeley, 1987.

— 'La fortuna di Croce e Gentile negli Stati Uniti', in Garin, Eugenio (ed.), *Croce e Gentile un secolo dopo, Saggi, testi inediti e un'appendice bibliografica 1980–1993*, Le Lettere, Florence, 1994, 253–281.

— *Nothing but History, Reconstruction and Extremity after Metaphysics*, University of California Press, Berkeley, 1995.

— *Historicism and Fascism in Modern Italy*, University of Toronto Press, Toronto, 2007.

Romano, Sergio, *Giovanni Gentile, La filosofia al potere*, Bompiani, Milano, 1984.

Rossi, Pietro, *Storia e storicismo nella filosofia contemporanea*, Lerici editori, 1960, cited from Nuova edizione, Mondadori, Milano, 1991.

Rotenstreich, Nathan, 'History of Philosophy and Progress', in *Revue Internationale de Philosophie*, 29, 1975, 90–112.

— *Philosophy, History and Politics: Studies in Contemporary English Philosophy of History*, Martinus Nijhof, The Hague, 1976.

Rubinoff, Lionel (ed.), *Faith and Reason: Essays in the Philosophy of Religion*, Quadrangle, Chicago, 1968.

— *Collingwood and the Reform of Metaphyisics. A study in the Philosophy of Mind*, University of Toronto Press, Toronto, 1970.

Runia, Eelco, 'Presence', in *History and Theory*, 45, 1–29.

Russell, Anthony F., *Logic, Philosophy and History*, University of America Press, Lanham, London, 1984.

Russell, L.J., Review of 'Collingwood, R.G., *An Essay on Philosphical Method'*, in *Philosophy*, IX, 1934, 350.

Ryle, Gilbert, 'Mr. Collingwood and the Ontological Argument', in *Mind*, 44, 1935, 137–151.

Saari, Heikki, *Re-Enactment, A Study in R.G. Collingwood's Philosophy of History*, Abo Akademi, Abo, 1984.

Sasso, Gennaro, *Benedetto Croce, La ricerca della dialettica*, Morano, Napels, 1975.

Scaravelli, Luigi, *Critica del capire*, La Nuova Italia, Florence, 1968. First edn. Sansoni, Florence, 1942.

Sheppard, Anne, *Aesthetics, An Introduction to the Philosophy of Art*, Oxford University Press, Oxford, 1987.

Shoemaker, Robert G., 'Inference and Intuition in Collingwood's Philosophy of History', in *Monist*, 53, 1969, 100–115.

Simmel, Georg, 'Die Probleme der Geschichtsphilosophie', in *Aufsätze 1887–1890, Über sociale Differenzierung. Die Probleme der Geschichtsphilosophie*, in

Georg Simmel, Gesamtausgabe, Heraugegeben von Otthein Rammstedt, Band 2, Suhrkamp, Frankfurt, 1989.

Skagestad, Peter, *Making Sense of History, The Philosophies of Popper and Collingwood*, Universitetsforlaget, Oslo, 1975.

Smith, J.A., 'Lectures on Gentile', *Manuscript of about 1916 or 1917*, Magdalen Ms 1026/XI/13.

— 'The Philosophy of Giovanni Gentile', in *Proceedings of the Aristotelian Society*, XX, 1919-20, 63-78.

— 'Philosophy as the Development of the Notion and Reality of Self-Consciousness', in *Contemporary British Philsophy, Second Series*, Allen and Unwin, London, 1925.

Smith, Teresa, 'R.G. Collingwood: "This Ring of Thought": Notes on Early Influences', in *Collingwood Studies*, 1, 1994, 27-43.

Struever, Nancy, 'Rhetoric: Time, Memory, Memoir', Walter Jost (ed.), *A Companion to Rhetoric and Rhetorical Criticism*, Blackwell Publishing, Oxford, 2004, 425-442.

Taylor, Donald S., *R.G. Collingwood, A Bibliography*, Garland Publishing, New York & London, 1988.

Turi, Gabriele, *Giovanni Gentile. Una biografia*, Torino, UTET, 2006.

Valeri, Nino, *La lotta politica dall'unità al 1925. Idee e documenti*, Monnier, Firenze, 1973.

Van den Braembussche, *Denken over Kunst, Een Kennismaking met de Kunstfilosofie*, Coutinho, Bussum, 1994.

Van der Dussen, W.J., *History as a Science, The Philosophy of R.G. Collingwood*, Nijhoff, The Hague, 1981.

— 'Collingwood on the Ideas of Process, Progress and Civilization', in Boucher, David (ed.), *Philosophy, History and Civilization, Interdisciplinary Perspectives on R.G. Collingwood*, University of Wales Press, Cardiff, 1995, 246-268.

— 'The Historian and His Evidence', in van der Dussen W.J. and Rubinoff, Lionel (eds.), *Objectivity, Method and Point of View, Essays in the Philosophy of History*, Brill, Leiden, 1991, 154-170.

— 'The Philosophical Context of Collingwood's Re-enactment Theory', in *International Studies in Philosophy*, XXVII, 2, 1995, 81-99.

— 'Collingwood's "Lost" Manuscript of the *Principles of History*', in *History and Theory*, 36, 1997, 32-62.

Van Heeswijck, Guido, *Metafysica als een Historische Discipline. De Actualiteit van R..G. Collingwoods 'Hervormde Metafysica'*, Van Gorcum, Assen and Maastricht, 1993.

— 'Collingwood's Metaphysics: Not a Science of Pure Being, but Still a Science of Being', in *International Philosophical Quarterly*, XXXVIII.2, 1998, 153-174.

—'Collingwood's Metaphysics: Not a Science of Pure Being, but Still a Science of Being', in *International Philosophical Quarterly*, XXXVIII.2, 1998, 153–174.

Vigorelli, Amadeo (ed.), 'Lettere di Robin George Collingwood a Benedetto Croce (1912–1939)', in *Rivista di storia della filosofia*, 3, 1991, 545–563.

Walsh, W.H., *Philosophy of History: An Introduction*, Harper & Row, New York, 1967.

Weber, Max, 'Knies und das Irrationalitätsproblem', in *Gesammelte Aufsätze zur Wissenschaftslehre*, herausgegeben von Johannes Winckelmann, Mohr, Tübingen, 1988.

White, Hayden V., *Metahistory, The Historical Imagination in Nineteenth-Century Europe*, John Hopkins, Baltimore, London, 1973.

—'Collingwood and Toynbee. Transitions in English Historical Thought', in *English Miscellany*, 8, 1957.

—'The Politics of Historical Interpretation, Discipline and De-Sublimation', in *Critical Inquiry*, 9, 1982, cited from id., *The Content of the Form. Narrative Discourse and Historical Representation*, John Hopkins University Press, Baltimore and London, 58–83.

—*The Content of the Form*, John Hopkins University Press, Baltimore, London, 1987.

—*The Fiction of Narrative: Essays on History, Literature, and Theory, 1957–2007*, John Hopkins University Press, Baltimore, 2007.

Wildon Carr, H., *The Philosophy of Benedetto Croce: The Problem of Art and History*, MacMillan, London, 1917.

Windelband, Wilhelm, *Präludien, Aufsätze und Reden zur Philosophie und ihrer Geschichte*, Zweiter Band, Mohr, Tübingen, 1924.

Index